THE UNITED NATIONS

THE UNITED NATIONS

CONFRONTING THE CHALLENGES OF A GLOBAL SOCIETY

EDITED BY
JEAN E. KRASNO

LYNNE
RIENNER
PUBLISHERS

BOULDER
LONDON

Published in the United States of America in 2004 by
Lynne Rienner Publishers, Inc.
1800 30th Street, Boulder, Colorado 80301
www.rienner.com

and in the United Kingdom by
Lynne Rienner Publishers, Inc.
3 Henrietta Street, Covent Garden, London WC2E 8LU

Library of Congress Cataloging-in-Publication Data
The United Nations : confronting the challenges of a global society /
edited by Jean E. Krasno.
     p.   cm.
Includes bibliographical references and index.
   ISBN 978-1-58826-255-4 (hardcover : alk. paper)
   ISBN 978-1-58826-280-6 (pbk. : alk. paper)
   1. United Nations. I. Krasno, Jean E., 1943–
JZ4984.5.U536   2004
341.23—dc22

                                                                2003025708

British Cataloguing in Publication Data
A Cataloguing in Publication record for this book
is available from the British Library.

Printed and bound in the United States of America

The paper used in this publication meets the requirements
of the American National Standard for Permanence of
Paper for Printed Library Materials Z39.48-1992.

*To the founders and members of the
Academic Council on the United Nations System (ACUNS),
who have worked so hard over the years to develop
a greater understanding of the UN and
to build cooperation between scholars who study the UN
and practitioners who work daily inside the Organization
to fulfill its goals.*

Contents

List of Illustrations   ix
Preface   xi

Part 1
Out of the Ashes of War

1   The UN Landscape: An Overview   *Jean E. Krasno*   3

2   Founding the United Nations: An Evolutionary Process
    Jean E. Krasno   19

3   The United Nations and the Formation of Global Norms
    Joe Sills   47

Part 2
Engaging Human Needs on a Global Scale

4   Human Rights: A Global Common Interest   *Charles Norchi*   79

5   Free and Fair Elections: Letting the People Decide
    Robin Ludwig   115

6   Agent of Change? The United Nations and Development
    Jacques Fomerand   163

7   Disarmament: Successes and Failures   *Derek Boothby*   193

8   To End the Scourge of War: The Story of UN Peacekeeping
    Jean E. Krasno   225

Part 3
Processes of Global Burden Sharing

9   Financing the United Nations   *Jeffrey Laurenti*   271

10   Informal Groups of Member States   *Jochen Prantl and
     Jean E. Krasno*   311

11   Reforming the United Nations: Lessons from a History in
     Progress   *Edward C. Luck*   359

List of Acronyms   399
Selected Bibliography   405
The Contributors   409
Index   413
About the Book   443

Illustrations

Photographs

International Court of Justice   9
United Nations flag   20
Signing of the UN Charter   41
Secretary-General Kofi Annan receives the Nobel Peace Prize   56
Eleanor Roosevelt examines a UDHR poster   82
Woman casting her ballot in Angola's first multiparty election   118
Somali mother and her children wait for UNICEF medical treatment   165
UNTAC peacekeepers teach a Cambodian soldier to deactivate a landmine   214
First summit-level meeting of Security Council heads of state   247
UNPROFOR observation post in Croatia   254
Armored personnel carriers and peacekeepers of NECBAT   256
Richard Holbrooke and former senator Jesse Helms visit the United Nations   286
Signing of the El Salvador peace accord   338
Secretariat building at United Nations headquarters   360

Tables

9.1   UN Assessment Rates for Selected Countries, 1946–2003   294
9.2   UN Voluntary Contributions, 1999   300
9.3   Contributions to UN Specialized Agencies, 1999   302
10.1   Use of the Veto in the UN Security Council, 1946–2000   315

Figures

10.1   Formal Meetings and Informal Consultations of the
          UN Security Council, 1988–2000   333
10.2   Resolutions and Presidential Statements of the UN
          Security Council, 1988–1999   334
10.3   Costs of UN Peacekeeping Forces, 1991–2001   344

Preface

Jean E. Krasno

The United Nations plays an enormous role in the global arena today, particularly when the large number of UN agencies, programs, and funds are included in an understanding of the UN system in its entirety. Yet, this vast system goes largely unnoticed both in the media and in the curriculum of most colleges and universities. The purpose of this book is to address this vacuum and to contribute to the education of students and the broader public on the complex history, evolution, and workings of the United Nations. The UN has evolved and adapted to the changing world around it since its inception in 1945, and each of the chapters in this book captures that evolutionary process as viewed from various perspectives, including: the formation of global norms, human rights, and the electoral process as a part of democratization. It is hoped that the reader will come away with a better understanding of the breadth, depth, and history of the efforts of human beings to work globally to prevent conflict and invent ways to govern international activity and interaction.

The writing of this book was a collective effort by a number of scholars who contributed their expertise to shedding light on the complexity of the UN system. It was particularly important in searching for authors that they each have not only an understanding of his or her field as it operates today but also an understanding of the history involved. Because we are in a changing world, it is important to know the past in order to fully appreciate the present and be better able to shape the future. This was a challenge that each author eagerly embraced.

The individual chapters originated as part of a series of occasional papers published by the Academic Council on the United Nations System (ACUNS) within a larger project titled "Building a Constituency for the UN Through Education." The project was undertaken jointly with the United Nations Association of the United States of America (UNA-USA). ACUNS and UNA-USA formed an advisory council of academics and practitioners to offer ideas on what issues ought to be addressed and to oversee the quality and progress of the writing and activities. Each author was commissioned to write an original draft paper, which was reviewed by the executive director of ACUNS and then sent to several expert scholars for comment before being published as an occasional paper. It was felt that, taken as a whole, the collection of papers offered a rare and useful overview of the UN system that would fit nicely into a book to be made available to a larger audience. The papers were revised for the book project, as well as updated to keep them current with UN activities.

*   *   *

The book and the series of occasional papers that preceded it have been made possible by the generous support of the Better World Fund, Soka Gakkai International, and the Arthur Ross Foundation. I am grateful for their faith in me and in ACUNS.

PART 1

OUT OF THE ASHES OF WAR

1

The UN Landscape: An Overview

Jean E. Krasno

The purpose of this brief chapter is to paint a broad landscape of the United Nations. This nearly universal Organization, with 191 members in 2003, can be viewed from several perspectives: as a focal point for global security issues, a world forum for debate, a network for developing universal norms and standards, and a vehicle for administering humanitarian assistance around the world, to name a few. The six principal bodies of the United Nations make up the core of the Organization, but its outreach goes far beyond the core to include a myriad of loosely affiliated funds, programs, agencies, and other related bodies. Since its inception in 1945, the UN has continued to grow and adapt to the challenges of a complex and changing world environment. Some UN activities that in 1945 appeared to be focal points of the UN landscape have retreated today from the foreground and in some cases have completely disappeared over the horizon, replaced by more relevant activities. Still, the central purpose of the UN has remained the maintenance of international peace and security. The Security Council, which holds the primary responsibility for security, remains the most publicly visible body. The Secretary-General is the single most important individual and the symbolic representative of the UN to the global public.

One of the most important recent evolutions in the UN has been the changing focus of the Organization from a primary concern for national security to the inclusion of human security within the state. The notion of state sovereignty as a centerpiece of the intergovernmental body is beginning to evolve to include the *responsibility* of the state to protect its citizens, not just the immunity of the state from interference. The Millennium Declaration, which was adopted by the Member States in 2000 and calls for the eradication of poverty, access to clean water, sanitation, and access to clean energy sources, is an example of the new emphasis on human security.

With two devastating world wars fresh in their memories, the founders of the United Nations wanted to create an organization that would prevent the outbreak of a third global conflict. Also fresh in their minds was the Great Depression and the economic disequilibrium that had preceded World War II, which many felt had contributed to the outbreak of the war. Therefore, conflict prevention was envisioned as incorporating several different approaches, including military might but not limited to it. In laying the groundwork for the United Nations in the UN Charter, the founders hoped that the nations that had united to fight the Axis powers would remain united to prevent future aggression and preserve peace, hence the name "United Nations." The concept was that the five major powers that had the largest militaries and had fought together during the war—the United States, the United Kingdom, the Soviet Union, China, and France—would lend their military might to the UN to fight any would-be aggressors. These five nations were given permanent seats on the UN's fifteen-member Security Council. In addition to the use of military force, coercion was to also include pressure through the use of economic sanctions and diplomatic isolation.

The use of coercion or the *threat* of force or sanctions, as spelled out in Chapter VII of the Charter, is only part of the picture, however. The UN is also to be a forum for dialogue and an environment in which negotiation and diplomatic solutions might replace the resort to war to settle disputes. Chapter VI of the Charter, titled "Pacific Settlement of Disputes," also calls for rule of law and arbitration in the peaceful pursuit of order. Economic and social inequities that might contribute to conflict are also addressed, as well as the means to prepare non-self-governing territories and colonies for independence, in the hope of avoiding wars of independence or conflict over these territories. All these tools for preventing conflict, however encompassing, depend on the cooperation of the collectivity of the member nations.

Allocation of Tasks and the Six Principal UN Bodies

Each of the aforementioned functions is allocated to one of the six principal bodies of the United Nations: the Security Council, the General Assembly, the Secretariat (headed by the Secretary-General), the Economic and Social Council, the Trusteeship Council, and the International Court of Justice.

The Security Council
The function of international peace and security is primarily allocated to the Security Council. Because the United Nations does not have its own military or its own economic resources, the Organization is dependent on the voluntary contribution of these assets by Member States to implement its decisions. Therefore, the Security Council, with its authority to create resolutions binding on all members and with the influence of the permanent five (P-5),

is the center of power within the UN system. Yet the distribution of military and economic power since 1945 has changed significantly and the economies of Germany and Japan are now much greater than those of the other P-5 members with the exception of the United States. However, the combined military strength of the P-5 is still significant and the constitutions of both Germany and Japan limit their abilities to send troops abroad, thus constraining their capacity to contribute to collective security. Efforts to reform the Security Council since its last enlargement in the 1960s from the original eleven members to fifteen have failed in recent years. The Charter states that any amendments must have the concurrence of the P-5, and no permanent member is likely to vote itself off the Council. Efforts to enlarge the Council to include the bigger economies have also been met with resistance from competitors and lack of agreement. The members of the UN seem to be resigned to accepting the Council in its present form, at least for the time being.

The General Assembly

The General Assembly, comprising all the Member States (51 in 1945, 191 in 2003), fulfills the function of a central forum for global dialogue wherein pressing issues of concern from population to the environment can be discussed. Each fall, the General Assembly opens with a general debate, during which many foreign ministers and heads of state take the podium to add their governments' positions to the dialogue. While General Assembly resolutions are not binding and are considered recommendations only, the Assembly has the authority to determine the budget of the UN, or "power of the purse." Because of its nearly universal membership, its pronouncements can offer a kind of moral authority or collective conscience, as they did for many years in condemning the practice of apartheid in South Africa. That is not to say that all the work of the General Assembly and the interests of its members have moral overtones. As with all large bodies, much of its work is tedious and repetitive. Nevertheless, the UN is the only place where all Member States have permanent representatives as ambassadors throughout the year, so that when a crisis or issue arises, formal or informal conversations can take place conveniently and in a timely manner.

The General Assembly has six main committees, which deal separately with issues from disarmament to international law:

First Committee: political and security issues, including disarmament.
Second Committee: economic and financial issues.
Third Committee: social, humanitarian, and cultural issues.
Fourth Committee: trusteeship issues.
Fifth Committee: administrative and budgetary issues.
Sixth Committee: legal issues.

These committees can also create subsidiary bodies. For example, the Sixth Committee, which deals with legal issues, created the International Law Commission (ILC), a body of legal experts, to advise the committee and prepare draft documents. It has continued to function throughout the decades and, for example, developed drafts for the eventual statute that established the International Criminal Court, which went into effect in July 2002.

A very important role of the General Assembly over the years has been to oversee the decolonization of some eighty countries that were not brought into the trusteeship system but are now sovereign independent members of the UN. Chapter XI of the Charter, titled "Declaration Regarding Non-Self-Governing Territories," pronounced that it was the responsibility of the colonial powers "to develop self-government" in the territories under their control, "to take due account of the political aspirations of the peoples, and to assist them in the progressive development of their free political institutions." In 1946, eight Member States produced a list of their combined non-self-governing "colonial" territories, which came to a total of seventy-two. By 1959, eight of them had become independent. Because of the slow pace of decolonization, in December 1960 the General Assembly passed resolution 1514 (XV), titled the "Declaration on the Granting of Independence to Colonial Countries and Peoples," also known as the "Declaration on Decolonization." The declaration called for immediate steps to be taken to end colonial practices, and the UN gradually oversaw elections in many of these countries as they transitioned to independence. East Timor, which joined the UN in fall 2002, is one of the latest to become independent. Today only sixteen non-self-governing territories remain, including the Falkland/Malvinas Islands, Western Sahara, Bermuda, the U.S. Virgin Islands, and others.[1]

The Secretariat and Secretary-General

While the General Assembly offers the opportunity for open debate and consensus building, the Secretariat is most often the focal point for diplomacy in crisis situations, wherein the "good offices" of the Secretary-General and his or her representatives are put into play. The Office of the Secretary-General directs the Secretariat, a substantial bureaucracy whose main purpose is to serve the Member States in their work as members of the Security Council, the General Assembly, or other bodies. The Secretariat is divided into eleven departments and offices, such as the Department of Political Affairs (DPA), the Department of Peacekeeping Operations (DPKO), the Department of Public Information (DPI), and the Office of Legal Affairs (OLA). The founders of the UN originally conceived of the Secretary-General as primarily an administrator. However, the Charter, in Article 99, gives the Secretary-General the authority to bring an issue before the Security Council, thereby leaving open a door for the Secretary-General to also play a political role in leading the administration of the UN. While the position has become considerably more dynamic over the years, it must be remembered that the Secretary-General serves the Member States and has no assets of his or her own to implement policy decisions. While it often appears to the public that the Secretary-General is also the political leader of the Organization, this is a false impression.

The position can be used as a bully pulpit to promote multilateralism and put issues like poverty eradication and HIV/AIDS on the world agenda, but the Secretary-General must walk a very fine line to maintain the legitimacy and impartiality of the UN while not offending any of the major powers. The personality of the Secretary-General can determine the role of the office. Javier Pérez de Cuéllar preferred to keep a low profile and delegate mediation between disputing parties to talented staff members. Dag Hammarskjöld often inserted himself directly into negotiations and in so doing suffered the wrath of Member States like the Soviet Union, which called for his resignation. Kofi Annan, the current Secretary-General, seems to have found the delicate balancing point. He will at times become directly involved or carefully select others to take the lead. The following is a list of the Secretaries-General who have served the UN over the years:

Trygve Lie (Norway), 1946–1952
Dag Hammarskjöld (Sweden), 1953–1961
U Thant (Burma), 1961–1971
Kurt Waldheim (Austria), 1972–1981
Javier Pérez de Cuéllar (Peru), 1982–1991
Boutros Boutros-Ghali (Egypt), 1992–1996
Kofi Annan (Ghana), 1997–2006

The Economic and Social Council
The Economic and Social Council (ECOSOC) was established to serve as the central body for discussing international social and economic concerns and to initiate studies and reports and promote humanitarian issues. ECOSOC also has the authority, along with the General Assembly, to call international conferences and to consult with nongovernmental organizations (NGOs). The global conferences on human rights, the environment, population, and women's rights, to just name a few, have been some of the most important contributions made by ECOSOC. These global conferences provide an important forum for including the voices of civil society in the workings of the UN as represented by NGOs affiliated with ECOSOC and DPI that participate sometimes directly in the conferences or in parallel NGO forums in a way not possible in other UN bodies. There are now some 1,500 NGOs that have consultative status with ECOSOC and that may send observers to meetings of ECOSOC and its subsidiary bodies. NGOs are increasingly viewed as important partners not only in representing civil society in the formulation of policies but also in implementing policies and norm promotion in countries around the world.

ECOSOC, a fifty-four-member body, holds one five-week session each year, held alternately in New York and Geneva. Its year-round work is carried out by its subsidiary commissions and committees. Some of these bodies include the Commission on Human Rights, the Commission on the Status of Women, and the Regional Commissions for Africa, Europe, Latin America and the Caribbean, Western Asia, and Asia and the Pacific. ECOSOC originally had eighteen members, but with a growing number of countries joining the UN from the developing world, the body was expanded in 1965 by a Charter amendment to include twenty-seven members and was enlarged again to its current membership of fifty-four in 1973. The members are elected by the General Assembly to serve a three-year term. Although ECOSOC is given the status of one of the six main organs of the UN, it actually functions under the General Assembly and is often criticized for duplicating the work of the Assembly's six main committees. Some critics have called for ECOSOC's elimination, but the majority of its membership, which comprises developing countries, is unlikely to listen to these demands.

The Trusteeship Council

Having fulfilled its function, the work of the Trusteeship Council is one of the activities of the UN that has disappeared over the horizon. Considered one of the six main bodies of the UN in the Charter, the Trusteeship Council was established to administer the eleven original trust territories and prepare them for independence or self-government. That work has been accomplished, but the Council still exists in theory and the UN continues to maintain the elegant Trusteeship Council chamber at UN headquarters next to the ECOSOC chamber. The trusteeship territories were not to be confused with colonial holdings. They were (1) territories held under the League of Nations as mandates and inherited by the UN, (2) territories detached from enemy states after World War II, and (3) territories voluntarily placed under the system.

Membership on the Council had its own peculiar system. It included Member States that had been given administrative authority over a trust territory, all of the P-5, plus a number of members not administering a territory that were elected by the General Assembly for three-year terms, the total number of which was to equal the number of states on the Council that were administering a territory. In 1994, the last of the territories, Palau, a Pacific island territory, gained independence and became a member of the UN. The role of the Council was to supervise the governance of the territories by the administering state and to receive petitions and grievances by the inhabitants seeking redress. The Council would make an annual report to the General Assembly on its work, thereby delegating accountability to the administering state. In this way it was to the advantage of the administering state to rid itself of this responsibility, and the Council put itself out of business by its success. Formally, the Trusteeship Council still exists, but with only the P-5 as members.

The International Court of Justice

The International Court of Justice (ICJ), also known as the World Court, is one of the six principal organs of the United Nations and replaced the Permanent Court of International Justice, which had functioned during the incarnation of the League of Nations. All members of the UN are automatically members of the ICJ, and the Court's statute is a part of the UN Charter. The Court, which is located in The Hague, settles disputes *between states.* Individuals cannot be members of the Court and no individual can be tried under the Court. The ICJ can also offer advisory opinions, but only designated UN bod-

UN Photo 186850/A. Brizzi

International Court of Justice, The Hague, the Netherlands.

ies like the General Assembly and the Security Council, not states, can request an advisory opinion.

The fifteen judges sitting on the Court are elected by the General Assembly and the Security Council based on their qualifications and serve a term of nine years. Five judges are elected every three years and a judge can be reelected, though no two judges can come from the same country. The full fifteen judges can hear a case or they can create a smaller body among the judges, called a chamber, if the parties so request. In 1993 the Court established a seven-member chamber to deal with environmental cases falling within its jurisdiction. If a party to a dispute requests an additional judge, that request can be granted if none of the fifteen are of the party's nationality. Many cases deal with boundary or territorial disputes and most are brought voluntarily by the parties to the Court. Some examples of cases brought before the Court include the dispute between the United States and Canada regarding the Gulf of Maine, the dispute between Libya and Malta regarding the continental shelf, the bor der dispute between Burkina Faso and Mali, and the dispute between Finland and Denmark regarding passage through the Great Belt.[2] Since 1946 the Court has delivered seventy-six judgments on cases ranging from land frontiers and maritime boundaries to hostage taking, the right of asylum, nationality, rights of passage, and economic rights. Over the years the Court has also issued twenty-four advisory opinions on such issues as the territorial status of Namibia and Western Sahara, the responsibility of Member States to pay expenses of the United Nations, and the legality of the threat or use of nuclear weapons.

While the Court heard relatively few cases during the Cold War period, this is changing according to ICJ judge Rosalyn Higgins:

> It is no coincidence that by 1992 the Court had over twelve cases waiting for disposal. This is exactly because states from all over the world are coming to the Court, not reluctantly dragged there by reference to instruments they now wished they had never signed, but voluntarily. This undoubtedly reflects an increasing confidence in the Court, not only as an institution of great competence and impartiality but one perceived as capable of ensuring that its interpretation of international law is at once predictable and responsive to diverse legitimate needs.[3]

Higgins's prediction that the Court would begin to hear more and more cases has proven correct. In 2004 the ICJ has twenty-two cases on its docket.

Voting Procedures Within the UN System

The United Nations uses an amalgamation of voting mechanisms borrowed from both domestic and international practices and grafted onto the decision-making procedures in the different UN bodies. Voting is a paramount activity in the UN and subject to extensive lobbying and vote trading. To illustrate, decisions are taken by vote in the Security Council, General Assembly, ECOSOC, special committees of the Council and Assembly, UN-sponsored global conferences, treaty conferences, and the governing bodies of the UN funds, programs, and agencies that make up the UN system.

At least four voting mechanisms function simultaneously with variations among the different bodies:

- The egalitarian practice of one country, one vote, borrowed from international law and treaty conference practice.
- The elitist great power privilege tradition, which evolved in Europe.
- Majoritarian decisionmaking, borrowed from democratic theory and practice.
- Consensus, or unanimity, based on European conference procedures and treaty law.[4]

Consensus, as had been required by the League of Nations, was seen as a stumbling block and had to be replaced. Unanimity meant that one country, no matter what its intentions, could block any action emanating from the League. That practice was to be avoided. The United Nations abandoned consensus in favor of majority voting in its standing bodies. However, consensus has been retained for multilateral treaty agreements formulated under UN auspices. Conference and other declarations that intend to represent global norms generally strive for consensus but may resort to majority rule if outliers continue to hold positions that would undermine the intent of the document.

The Security Council has the most complex system of voting among the UN bodies because its operating procedures include a mixture of the four elements:

- Egalitarian practice of one country, one vote: each of the fifteen members of the Council has one vote.
- Great power elite privilege: the five powers—China, France, Russia, the United States, and the United Kingdom—while having one vote each, also have permanent seats on the Council; the remaining ten serve two-year terms, are elected by the General Assembly, and cannot serve consecutive terms.
- Majoritarianism: an affirmative vote of the Council must have a supermajority of nine votes in favor to pass.
- Unanimity: affirmative consensus of the five permanent members must be achieved for a resolution to pass; even one P-5 negative vote, or veto, blocks passage; an abstention is not considered a veto and does not block a resolution from passing if there are nine votes in favor, and the veto cannot be used on procedural matters.

To further complicate matters, if a permanent member is a party to a conflict and the Council takes up the issue, that member loses its vote if the resolution falls under Chapter VI of the Charter, which calls for the peaceful settlement of disputes. However, that permanent member's vote is restored if the resolution falls under Chapter VII, which deals with enforcement measures. In writing the Charter, the founders understood that the major powers would need to agree on authorizing the use of force; fighting among the major powers was to be avoided. In addition, these powers would not join the UN if force could be used without their consent. But it was considered that all nations should accept peaceful solutions to a dispute.

On a few occasions, the Security Council, under manipulation primarily by the United States, has been able to circumvent the major power veto. Under the "Uniting for Peace" resolution, created in 1950, if the Security Council is unable to act, by procedural vote in the Council, the issue can be moved to the General Assembly. In this capacity, to avoid vetoes by the Soviet Union, decisions regarding North Korea in the 1950s were exercised by the General Assembly. This procedure was enacted again in 1956, this time to avoid vetoes by France and the United Kingdom regarding the conflict during the Suez crisis. It is less likely that the "Uniting for Peace" resolution would be exercised today because the major powers on the Council cannot be confident that the General Assembly, with its current 191 members, would cooperate or make a decision quickly enough in a crisis. The United States has also lost its dominance in the General Assembly since the mid-1960s, and other permanent members are unlikely to relinquish their privileges on the Council to the Assembly, where they don't have the veto.

Voting in the General Assembly is dramatically simpler than in the Security Council. All decisions are taken by majority vote, no consensus is required,[5] and there are no vetoes. Each member has one vote. Decisions on important issues are made by a two-thirds majority of those present and voting. These important issues include the budget, peace and security, election of members to the Security Council and ECOSOC, the admission of new members to the United Nations, the expulsion of members, and other such questions that the Assembly decides are important. All other resolutions require a simple majority of those present and voting. Because resolutions emanating from the Assembly are not binding, it was not considered essential to have consensus. Members not agreeing with the outcome are not required to comply. Of course, organizational questions decided by the Assembly, as listed above, are put into effect and assessments on members to pay the regular budget and peacekeeping costs are considered an obligation of membership as stated in the Charter and confirmed by an advisory opinion of the ICJ.

The election of the Secretary-General is an interesting case in which both the Security Council and the General Assembly are involved. The Charter states in Article 97, "The Secretary-General shall be appointed by the General

Assembly upon the recommendation of the Security Council." In practice, this has meant that the Security Council, after deliberation and a voting procedure that includes the veto, has selected its choice of a single candidate and the Assembly has always approved that choice. However, in recent years the Assembly made clear that it would only approve a candidate whose nationality was African because before Boutros-Ghali no Secretary-General had represented the African continent. When Boutros-Ghali only served one term and not the expected two, the Assembly reaffirmed its demand. In this way the Assembly has begun to assert its decisionmaking powers.

Voting in the remaining principal bodies of the UN is by simple majority, including decisions by the ICJ, for which the president of the Court, also one of the fifteen serving judges, can break a tie if one should occur. Voting by the governing boards of the UN's programs, funds, and agencies is determined by each organization's own procedures, as is voting by treaty bodies.

UN Programs, Funds, and Specialized Agencies

There are a myriad of organizations within the UN system that focus on specific issues. While it is beyond the purview of this chapter to elaborate on each of these entities, it is important to discuss them to some degree in order to offer some appreciation for the enormous scale of activities undertaken by the UN. Other entities will be discussed in later chapters in the book. At times people question the relevance of the UN, but this attitude reveals a general ignorance of the tremendous work the UN carries out on a daily basis around the world on issues of humanitarian assistance and economic and technical development, as well as educational issues ranging from the environment to population, human rights, and the role of women. A handful of bodies in the UN system are discussed below.

The World Bank (which includes the International Bank for Reconstruction and Development [IBRD] and the International Development Association [IDA]) and the International Monetary Fund (IMF) were created in 1944, prior to the UN's inception, as a part of what is known as the Bretton Woods system, named after the location where the first organizational meetings took place. They are considered a part of the UN system as "specialized agencies," but the UN has no decisionmaking authority over the Bank or the Fund, which are governed by representatives of their Member States. The World Bank, headquartered in Washington, D.C., has 184 member countries, which are responsible for how the institution is financed and how the money is spent. The IBRD raises almost all its money ($23 billion in 2002) in the world's financial markets. It issues bonds to raise funds and passes on the interest rates to its borrowers. The policies of the two loaning institutions have often come under criticism as conflicting with the humanitarian goals of the broader UN system, particularly regarding debt payments by developing countries and structural adjustment requirements on the budgetary structures of developing countries in order to qualify for loans. However, both institutions have made important development loans sought after by the developing world and have recently tried to make policy changes in debt forgiveness and the way in which loans affect the poor.

The United Nations Children's Fund (UNICEF), created in 1946 by the UN General Assembly at first to meet the emergency needs of children in post-war Europe, now serves children all over the world. Considered a "fund" and not a specialized agency, it is supported by voluntary contributions from governmental and nongovernmental sources and its own fundraising activities. Awarded the Nobel Peace Prize in 1965, UNICEF provides healthcare and nutrition for children (and mothers) and funds water supply and sanitation projects that affect children. Emergency relief for children during crises caused by civil wars or natural disasters takes about 20 percent of the budget. UNICEF is governed by its thirty-six-member executive board, composed of government representatives elected in rotation for three years by ECOSOC.

The United Nations Development Programme (UNDP), established in 1965, has some 130 offices around the world in developing countries and coordinates the development activity of the UN. The thirty-six-nation executive board sets the policy for the programs, which are funded by voluntary contributions and other sources amounting to about $2 billion per year. Each year UNDP publishes the *Human Development Report,* which provides both a narrative and a statistical assessment of development around the world and ranks nations using UNDP's Human Development Index on their capacity to provide not only income for their citizens but also education, health, sanitation, and so forth. Nations like Norway tend to rank highest in providing the best conditions at home, with life expectancy in the eighties and low infant mortality rates, while countries like Sierra Leone tend to rank at the bottom, with life expectancy in the thirties and very high rates of infant mortality. The huge gap between rich and poor is a constant issue within the UN, but efforts to address the problem have not been adequate. Still, UNDP does what it can to close the development gap or keep it from getting worse.

The World Health Organization (WHO), established in 1948, is governed by a thirty-one-nation executive board. All members of the UN are also members of WHO, which is headquartered in Geneva, Switzerland. Its primary purpose is to promote global health and it has been very successful in working with UNICEF and national governments to eradicate smallpox and polio. It has also worked hard to control malaria and other diseases of the poorer countries such as river blindness in West Africa. WHO also coordinates the UN's program on HIV/AIDS. Its annual budget is supported through voluntary contributions. While WHO has undertaken some specific health issue campaigns, its central strategy is based on primary healthcare, including health education, food supply and nutrition, safe water, sanitation, immunization, disease prevention, and the provision of essential drugs. Because of overlapping goals, WHO works closely with other UN bodies such as UNICEF (as mentioned), the Refugee Agency, the Office for the Coordination of Humanitarian Affairs (OCHA), the World Food Programme (WFP), and others to coordinate their activities.

The United Nations High Commissioner for Refugees (UNHCR), also known as the Refugee Agency, was founded in 1950 by the General Assembly originally to help with the 1.2 million refugees left homeless after World War II as well as other refugee issues. The 1951 Refugee Convention acts as the key legal document defining who is a refugee, the rights of a refugee, and the legal obligations of states. The purpose is to safeguard the rights and well-being and care for the needs of refugees around the world, who currently amount to nearly 20 million people in 120 countries. UNHCR works to guarantee the right to seek asylum and find safe refuge with the option to return home voluntarily or resettle in another country. During its more than fifty years in operation, UNHCR has helped over 50 million people. Legally a refugee is defined as someone who has had to leave his or her own country to find refuge. This definition does not account for the many others who are displaced within their own countries but nevertheless left homeless. UNHCR, with no mandate to help internally displaced persons (IDPs), does assist several million, but not all of the 20–25 million estimated to be displaced. To be able to assist IDPs, UNHCR must be requested to do so by the UN and must have consent of the country involved. UNHCR is headquartered in Geneva and is governed by a forty-six-nation executive committee. It depends entirely on voluntary contributions from governments, nongovernmental organizations, and individuals.

The World Trade Organization (WTO), a relatively new entity in the UN family, was established in 1995 as a permanent body to oversee international trade, replacing the General Agreement on Tariffs and Trade (GATT), which was serviced only by an ad hoc secretariat. The WTO, headquartered in Geneva in a large new building constructed specifically for the organization, is not considered a UN agency but undertakes cooperative arrangements and practices with the UN. It administers the twenty-eight agreements on international trade and is considered the watchdog in this arena. Trade disputes among the members are adjudicated under its dispute settlement "court." Currently, the WTO has 146 members, with some additional countries having observer status. Members of the GATT in 1995 automatically became members of the WTO. Recent new members are China, which joined in 2001, and Chinese Taipei (Taiwan), which joined in 2002. Interestingly, while countries like Sierra Leone and Armenia are members, the Russian Federation has only observer status as of 2004. The Ministerial Conference, where policy decisions are made, meets every two years; the 2003 meeting took place in Cancún, Mexico. The 1999 WTO meeting in Seattle, Washington, was the scene of mass demonstrations that erupted into violence when protesters of WTO trade policies and the effects of globalization took to the streets.

These brief descriptions represent only a few of the many organizations affiliated with the UN family. The following list names the funds, programs, agencies, and other organizations of the UN system, most of which have websites or can be searched through the UN's home page at www.un.org.

Funds, Programs, and Other Bodies
  UN Children's Fund (UNICEF)
  UN Conference on Trade and Development (UNCTAD)
  UN Development Programme (UNDP)
  UN Environment Programme (UNEP)
  UN Population Fund (UNFPA)
  UN Relief and Works Agency for Palestine Refugees (UNRWA)
  UN University (UNU)
  World Food Programme (WFP)
  UN High Commissioner for Refugees (UNHCR)
  UN High Commissioner for Human Rights (UNHCHR)
  UN Drug Control Programme (UNDCP)
  UN Development Fund for Women (UNIFEM)
  UN Research and Training Institute for the Advancement of Women
      (UNSTRAW)
  UN Institute for Disarmament Research (UNIDIR)
  UN Institute for Training and Research (UNITAR)
  UN Research Institute for Social Development (UNRISD)
  International Atomic Energy Agency (IAEA)
  International Criminal Court (ICC)

Specialized Agencies and Organizations
  International Labour Organization (ILO)
  Food and Agriculture Organization (FAO)
  United Nations Educational, Scientific, and Cultural Organization
      (UNESCO)
  International Civil Aviation Organization (ICAO)
  World Health Organization (WHO)
  World Bank
  International Monetary Fund (IMF)
  Universal Postal Union (UPU)
  International Telecommunication Union (ITU)
  World Meteorological Organization (WMO)
  International Maritime Organization (IMO)
  World Intellectual Property Organization (WIPO)
  International Fund for Agricultural Development (IFAD)

United Nations Industrial Development Organization (UNIDO)
International Seabed Authority
International Criminal Tribunal for the Former Yugoslavia (ICTY)
International Criminal Tribunal for Rwanda (ICTR)

Conclusion

The picture painted here is of a vast system with six principal organs at its center and a myriad of other loosely coordinated entities at the periphery. There is a great deal of overlap and duplication, but this is not necessarily bad in a world where so much needs to be done and the tasks are so complex. In some ways, almost every activity is connected to and dependent on others. Greater coordination and efficiency would be welcome, but the larger issue is more a lack of resources to implement the huge tasks assigned to the UN system. The UN regular budget for one year is now about $1.25 billion. That sum appears meager when compared to the U.S. Defense Department's annual budget of some $365 billion. Yet the United Nations is expected to address most of the world's problems. Inevitably, there are expectations placed on the UN that it cannot fulfill. The tendency is to claim that the UN is not doing enough. However, the UN does not have any resources of its own and cannot raise taxes or take out loans. It is completely dependent on the support of Member States and in some cases donors to carry out its missions. The UN can only become what its Member States want it to become.

Nevertheless, the UN has continued to grow and adapt as the world environment changes. The globe has been gradually carved into independent states, each with responsibilities within its boundaries and interests in the global community. But states are becoming more and more interdependent and global problems like the spread of disease will continue to require global solutions by a collective state system willing to address these challenges and supply the resources needed.

Notes

1. *Basic Facts About the United Nations* (New York: United Nations Department of Public Information, 1998), pp. 276–278.

2. Rosalyn Higgins, *Problems and Process: International Law and How We Use It* (Oxford: Clarendon Press, 1996), pp. 187–188.

3. Ibid., p. 188.

4. Inis L. Claude Jr., *Swords Into Plowshares: The Problems and Progress of International Organization,* 4th ed. (New York: Random House, 1984); see chap. 7, "The Problem of Voting," pp. 118–140.

5. The one exception to the use of consensus in the General Assembly is in establishing the budget, which is discussed in greater length by Jeffrey Laurenti in Chapter 9.

2

Founding the United Nations:
An Evolutionary Process

Jean E. Krasno

This chapter is not intended to be a comprehensive analysis of the history of the United Nations but rather a glimpse at the debates over some of the major issues that were a part of its creation. Many of these same discussions are still ongoing today and a review of the original debate, it is hoped, may shed light on the future evolution of the Organization. Much of the information has been gathered from a series of interviews with those people who were present at the key conferences and who worked as members of the delegations and behind the scenes as witnesses to the history that was being made.

Rationale for a World Body

To most of the world, the United Nations symbolizes the hope for international peace and security through global cooperation, dialogue, and collective responses to security threats. The UN flag, as it flies over UN offices and peacekeeping missions around the world, is a constant reminder of this aspiration. The flag's blue field holds a lonely Planet Earth embraced by olive branches. This cloth was woven from the last remaining threads of hope that had survived two devastating world wars.

In 1945, when the UN was created, nations were emerging from a second world war. Millions had been killed and maimed and much of Europe lay in rubble. The truth of the horrific genocide perpetrated against the Jews and other groups in Europe by the Nazis was coming to light. Yet only two decades before the outbreak of this renewed violence, the world had witnessed the close of what was thought to be "the war to end all wars." Modern war-fighting technology had demonstrated in these two global conflicts its efficiency at killing and destruction. In World War II, the bombing of innocent civilians and the razing of cities became a doable strategy. The inhumanity of humankind made the front pages of the news on a daily basis. Waves of fear

UN Photo 145618/J. Isaac

United Nations flag at UN headquarters in New York.

and guilt, images of the very dark side of human nature, washed over the world as it witnessed accounts of each new atrocity. Even as the deaths mounted, many began to seek some hopeful solution out of this despair. Many began to hope that those nations that united to defeat the Axis powers might stay united to prevent another world war.

Historical Base

The founders of the United Nations had history to draw upon for their plan. Nations had come together at various times to respond to crises, but the concept of an ongoing global organization was still considered experimental. The United Nations, as an intergovernmental organization, is based on the unit of the state, which in itself had not evolved until well into the seventeenth century, as historically recorded by the Treaty of Westphalia, an agreement reached among several European nations that ended the Thirty Years War in 1648.

At the onset of statehood, bilateral diplomacy was the primary means of communication and conflict resolution between states, but in nineteenth-century Europe that process began to change, and the concept of large-scale, multilateral conferences emerged as a tentative first step toward developing a dialogue on cooperation. Four major conferences took place between 1815 and 1822 in response to the devastation created by the Napoleonic Wars. The first of these, the Congress of Vienna, marked the primary attempt to reach a broader peace through agreement among stronger and weaker powers, through a balance of power, to deter future aggression like that of France under Napoleon. Over the next 100 years, leaders of Europe's greatest nations, referred to as the Concert of Europe, assembled some thirty times to discuss urgent political matters of the day. These resplendent gatherings took place in Berlin, Paris, London, and other cities throughout Europe. The most powerful countries became known as the "great powers," which formed a kind of executive committee of European affairs. The Concert gradually admitted new members, accepting Greece and Belgium in 1830 and Turkey in 1856. As UN scholar Inis Claude explains, "Diplomacy by conference became an established fact of life in the nineteenth century."[1]

At the same time, in addition to the focus on security issues addressed by the Concert, Europe was also engaging in international efforts to organize across state territories on other issues. River commissions were created to manage navigation on the Danube and Rhine. The Universal Postal Union and the International Telegraphic Union, institutions that still exist today, were created to address the increasing demand for intercommunication. Increased trade and migration brought the spread of diseases like cholera, which motivated a total of six international conferences dealing with health issues between 1851 and 1903. At about the same time, two international "peace" conferences were held at The Hague in the Netherlands, the first in 1899, at which twenty-six countries attended, and the second in 1907, at which the number of nations was expanded to forty-four, including most of Latin America. The contribution of the Hague Conferences was not only the introduction of non-European states, but also the sense of equality given to all those participating, in contrast to the "great power" hegemony of the Concert. In addition, the Hague Conferences introduced the notion that international relations might be based on standard norms and the regular convening of members. These conferences did not create a permanent institution, but they laid the groundwork for an established multilateral consultation process that eventually led to the formation of an international court (the Permanent Court of International Justice, which was located in The Hague) and the League of Nations following World War I.

Creation of the League of Nations

World War I brought an end to the Concert of Europe and a scheduled third Hague peace conference. But following the war, the two concepts reappeared and were merged into the formation of the League of Nations, which retained the great power executive committee status of the Concert in combination with the egalitarian universality of the Hague idea. The League Council became the executive committee, granting permanent status to five major powers, which would serve with a number of rotating members but which enjoyed greater power and influence. The League Council and League Assembly, reflecting the egalitarian ideal of the Hague concept, granted equal voting rights to all League members. The League not only merged the two earlier ideas but added another layer by establishing a permanent secretariat and regular meetings to further institutionalize the cooperation that had been initiated by the conferences, river commissions, and public unions.

However, the League experiment encountered a number of serious setbacks before its ultimate collapse at the outbreak of World War II, which it had failed to prevent. First, the United States, whose president, Woodrow Wilson, is credited with being the "father" of the League, never joined. Wilson, a Democrat, did not succeed in convincing the Republican-led Senate to give its consent to ratify the treaty that was required for membership. The permanent seat reserved for the United States was left unoccupied throughout the League's short life-span. This comment about the absence of the United States was made by someone present at the first meeting of the League Council: "As the afternoon wore on, the sun which streamed across the Seine and through the windows cast the shadow of the empty chair across the table. The shadow lengthened that day and the days that followed until the League died."[2] State Department staff member Alger Hiss explains: "Now it is true that in the early days of the League and up until World War II broke out, the State Department was so afraid of being identified with the League since the Senate had rejected the League, that we did not have a regular observer. We had Prentiss Gilbert in Geneva report unofficially; the League was hush-hush, but only for that reason; no real hostility to it."[3]

The other problem was that two of the permanent members on the League Council were Italy and Japan, which emerged as aggressor nations and formed an unholy union with Nazi Germany to ignite yet another global conflict. The League's rules of consensus gave everyone on the Council a veto, which deadlocked the organization. The procedures were clearly a stumbling block, but the will to act was also weak, leaving the League unable to effectively react when permanent member Japan invaded Manchuria, and Italy invaded Ethiopia. While economic sanctions were imposed on Italy, in fact they were removed when Italy completed its occupation of Ethiopia. The League's creators believed that war could be prevented through peaceful settlement and hoped to thwart aggression through collective action by its members. But the League Covenant never condemned war and only asked its members to wait three months before resorting to war. The League had been built on the premise that war was a mistake and that dialogue and negotiation could resolve disputes that might arise among its members. Ultimately, League members lacked the will to deal with the purposeful aggression of the Axis powers.

The War Years

U.S. president Franklin Roosevelt and his secretary of state, Cordell Hull, still believed in the Wilsonian concept of the League even though it had been discredited for failing to deal effectively with the aggressive tactics that eventually led to another worldwide conflict. During the war years, Roosevelt instructed his State Department staff to reconstitute a framework based on the League idea that would not only provide the means for consultation and peaceful settlement but also give the Organization enforcement powers, or "teeth" to prevent aggression. It was assumed that the new institution would have a plenary assembly and an "executive" council much as with the League. However, because the new organization was to have enforcement powers, a new strategy had to be devised. Under the League, the Council and the Assembly had concurrent responsibilities. The Council had enforcement authority but neither the will nor the effective means to carry it through. Ruth Russell, in her excellent book on the drafting of the UN Charter, describes the thinking of the State Department and Roosevelt at the time: "Given the fundamental decision to clothe the new institution with some kind of enforcement power, it was natural to think of making the smaller organ more of an executive agent for the whole organization and of centering in it the control of the security function."[4]

Roosevelt had expressed enthusiasm for an enforcement mechanism based on the wartime alliance of the four major powers: Britain, China, the Soviet Union, and the United States. France, which had been occupied by Germany from the onset of the war, was not a part of these preliminary discussions. In the Moscow Declaration of October 1943, Roosevelt and Hull carefully orchestrated an agreement among the four foreign ministers to pledge their countries to continuing wartime cooperation through the establishment of an organization committed to the maintenance of international peace. The atmosphere at the 1943 Moscow conference was positive on the Soviet side as well. Alexei Roschin, who attended the meeting for the Soviets, agreed: "Yes, it was positive at the Moscow conference on foreign affairs in 1943 when Molotov, Hull, and Eden met.[5] In principle it was decided that a [founding] conference should take place and the organization was set up."[6] However, in Washington, a State Department committee created to study these proposals did not favor the idea of providing such predominance for the major powers and suggested that there be a larger body more like the League Council in order to better balance the might of the "big four." These powers would still make up an executive committee, but any decision emanating from the body would require majority support of the whole Council, including the votes of those holding nonpermanent seats.

It was felt that the consent of the major powers was necessary because they would be providing the military force required to give the Organization the teeth it needed. These nations would not be willing to have their militaries conscripted into an enforcement action against their will. They would withdraw from the Organization. On the other hand, unanimity of the whole Council as had been required under the League was to be avoided. To ensure the solidity of the enforcement threat, the decisions of the Council would have to be binding on all the members in the Organization.

When President Roosevelt addressed the United States over the radio on Christmas Eve 1943, he had laid the groundwork for his case to the American people:

> Britain, Russia, China, and the United States and their allies represent more than three-quarters of the total population of the earth. As long as these four Nations with great military power stick together in determination to keep the peace there will be no possibility of an aggressor Nation arising to start another world war.
> But those four powers must be united with and cooperate with all the freedom-loving peoples of Europe, and Asia, and Africa, and the Americas. The rights of every Nation, large and small, must be respected and guarded as jealously as are the rights of every individual within our own Republic.[7]

The United States was the pivotal power and took the lead on the creation of this new organization. The fact that the United States was also a democracy is key to the evolution of the conceptual development underlying the structure and wording of the UN Charter. Roosevelt knew that the United States could not become a member of the new institution without Senate approval. He had learned from Wilson's experience that this could be difficult. He therefore set about early in the process to bring leaders of the Senate into the dialogue through a special committee headed by Republican senator Arthur Vandenberg and Democratic senator Tom Connally. Roosevelt invited another leading Republican to the delegation, Governor Harold Stassen, someone who had spoken out in favor of a United Nations and who at that time was serving on the staff of Admiral William Frederick Halsey Jr.:

> Then that message from President Roosevelt showed that he had remembered my advocacy and he named me as the third [member] of our party, the Republican Party. Senator Arthur Vandenberg was the Chairman of the Sen-

ate Foreign Relations Committee and the leading Republican in the United States Senate. Congressman Eaton was the Chairman of the House Foreign Affairs Committee, the leading Republican in the House. I was then the third Republican that he appointed. . . . As far as I know, I was the first one in active public life in the United States to advocate that there should be a United Nations.[8]

Senator Vandenberg was deeply concerned that the new organization would undertake to keep a "just" peace. In addition, the Senate Foreign Relations Committee noted a concern expressed by a number of civic groups for the position of smaller states within the Organization. Secretary Hull and Roosevelt took very seriously the senators' concerns because in the U.S. democratic system they needed the concurrence of the Senate and the American people. Senate concerns prompted Roosevelt to make this statement on June 15, 1944:

We are not thinking of a superstate with its own police forces and other paraphernalia of coercive power. We are seeking effective agreement and arrangements through which the nations would maintain, according to their capacities, adequate forces to meet the needs of preventing war and of making impossible deliberate preparations for war, and to have such forces available for joint action when necessary.[9]

Thus Roosevelt worked out a strategy to sustain support for his proposal to create a multilateral permanent body. He carefully courted both political parties and the American people, while at the same time orchestrating his plan on a global level with the major powers.

The Meetings at Dumbarten Oaks and Yalta

When the preparations for a new international organization were ready for discussion by the major powers, Roosevelt called a meeting together at a large estate named Dumbarton Oaks in Washington, D.C. Secretary Hull was ill and Edward Stettinius was placed in charge. The U.S. team that had contributed to the preparations included, among others, Ralph Bunche, Alger Hiss, Grayson Kirk, and an American of White Russian origin named Leo Pasvolsky.[10] The creation of the United Nations was a U.S. endeavor:

What was done by that research group up until at least the Dumbarton Oaks talks makes it proper to say that the United States really was the architect of the UN. That phrase has been prated about. But it's accurate—the Russians had too many distractions, the British didn't have the manpower, and we did—we had an extraordinary group of academic talent to work on all manner of things; to indicate how much dedication was involved: when Ralph Bunche was invited to join, it was unusual at that time to have any black officer in a position of importance. Cordell Hull was then Secretary of State and

was as interested in the UN as any, although the real father of the UN—
almost an obsession—was Franklin Roosevelt. When those in charge of gathering staff, the research staff, wanted Ralph Bunche particularly because of
his knowledge of Africa, Hull said OK (remember he was from Tennessee).[11]

Hiss describes the attitude of the team toward the League experiment:

The League was regarded as definitely our forerunner. There was no hostility toward it. There was a feeling that it had to be improved upon, that it had
failed, and that we could learn from its failure. It was not universal enough;
it was too Euro-centered, and it didn't seem to us to have the necessary powers that an international organization should have. And also we knew we
would in a literal sense succeed the League and take over its properties and
its functions. But the UN in no sense was hostile. The League was considered a brave experiment and there was much we could learn from its few
successes and its failures.[12]

The team set about preparing for the Dumbarton Oaks meeting, which
took place in two sessions. The Soviets and the British met with the Americans first, starting the discussions on August 21, 1944. The Soviets left on
September 28 and the next day the Chinese arrived for a nine-day meeting
with the British and Americans. This procedure was a political necessity at the
request of the Soviets, who had not entered the war in the Pacific against
Japan and did not want to appear to the Japanese that they were in collusion
with the Chinese. The meeting with the Chinese was largely a formality and
Hiss claims that they were not major participants in the process.

A significant outline of the UN Charter was produced at Dumbarton Oaks.
It was agreed that there would be a Security Council, a General Assembly, a
Secretariat, and an International Court of Justice. Alger Hiss, who took the notes
for the State Department at the meeting, explains that the "Economic and Social
Council was only barely sketched" and "trusteeship was not taken up at all."[13]
The question of voting procedures within the Security Council, including the
veto, was discussed but not settled at Dumbarton Oaks and was taken up again
at Yalta. In Washington, the Soviet ambassador to the United States, Andrei
Gromyko, headed the Soviet delegation. Alexander Cadogan represented the
British and Edward Stettinius headed the U.S. delegation. The Chinese delegation was led by the Chinese ambassador to London, V. K. Wellington Koo. Certain politically sensitive issues like the veto and trusteeship had to wait until the
meeting at Yalta, where the heads of state would take up these matters.

At Dumbarton Oaks no agreement was reached on exactly what the membership of the new organization ought to be except that members should be
"peace-loving" nations. Under instruction from Moscow, Ambassador
Gromyko stated that the Soviet Union wanted a seat for each of the fifteen
Soviet republics plus a seat for the Soviet Union itself, for a total of sixteen

members. Hiss remembers Roosevelt telling the U.S. team to say to Gromyko that if the Soviets insisted on this membership, "Tell him the whole thing's off."[14] Roosevelt basically took Gromyko's statement as a bargaining position, but nevertheless this issue would go through various stages before it was finally settled. Both Stettinius and Cadogan found Gromyko quite "compatible" to work with and they felt that he understood the U.S. position on the fifteen republics. It was mentioned that if such membership were allowed, the United States could invite all of its forty-eight states to join.

Another point of contention between the Soviets and the Western powers that surfaced at Dumbarton Oaks was the issue of what the competence of the Organization should be. The British and the Americans both agreed that the Organization should address economic and social issues as well as strictly security considerations. The belief was that hostilities in Europe that had contributed to conflict had in part arisen from economic and social problems and that any organization dealing with the prevention of war would have to also address those issues that underlay the fundamental causes. The Soviets, on the contrary, felt strongly that the new structure should only deal with security. Alexei Roschin, adviser to the Soviets, explains that they were "strongly against" any other competency for the Organization. They were committed to the idea of collective enforcement even to the extent that they strongly supported the creation of the UN Military Staff Committee, which would be made up of the military chiefs of staff of the five major powers. The Soviets also wanted the veto to apply to all decisions emanating from the Security Council even on procedural matters. Interestingly, Alger Hiss recounts that initially the British and most particularly Churchill were not in favor of the veto and had to be convinced: "The initial attitude of Churchill, we understood to our surprise, was against the veto. . . . I think it's because he didn't fully understand the issue. We were told . . . that Marshal Smuts had persuaded Churchill to accept and to insist upon, to be in favor of the veto for the Great Powers."[15]

A number of things that had been left unfinished at the Dumbarton Oaks meeting were resolved at Yalta a few months later. In contrast to the Washington meeting, the Yalta meeting took place at the level of heads of state. Roosevelt, Churchill, and Stalin met at Yalta from February 4 to February 11, 1945. The issue of membership was essentially resolved even though some of the agreements unraveled by the time the delegates reached the San Francisco Conference in April. The term "peace-loving nations" was defined at Yalta to mean those countries that had declared war on the Axis powers by March 1, 1945. Argentina still had not declared war and had been supporting Nazi Germany, to the anger of the Soviets in particular. The Soviets at Yalta felt that the agreement meant that Argentina would not become an original member and would not be invited to the San Francisco Conference, where the UN Charter would be finalized.

On the issue of the fifteen republics, Stalin suggested at Yalta that the Soviet Union plus three republics—Lithuania, the Ukraine, and Byelorussia—should be original members. The U.S. position was absolutely negative. These republics were constituent parts of the Soviet Union and not sovereign states. But every time the issue came up, the Soviets would say to the British, "And what about India?" Churchill was adamant that India, which was still under British control, had to be a member, whatever one's view on its sovereign status. This was the stalemate until a diplomatic mistake was made that ironically cleared up the matter. Alger Hiss, who again was the secretary and note-taker at Yalta, describes what happened. The foreign ministers (for Britain, Anthony Eden, for the Soviet Union, Vyacheslav Molotov, and for the United States, Edward Stettinius—who had taken over as secretary of state for the failing Cordell Hull on December 1, 1944) met in the morning at their dacha and the heads of government met in the afternoon at another dacha:

> It was my duty to read the minutes as soon as they were completed, and to my surprise I saw that the minutes said that agreement had been reached, that votes would be given to White Russia [Byelorussia] and the Ukraine. So I rushed up to Eden and said, "Mr. Eden, it's a mistake, we didn't agree." And he, quite testily—which wasn't his usual manner—said, "You don't know what's happened, speak to Ed." I went to Stettinius and he threw up his hands and said that after the meeting on which there was substantial agreement on many matters, he had reported to Roosevelt as he usually did and had started by saying, "Mr. President, it was a marvelous meeting. We reached general agreement."
>
> At that moment Bohlen brought Stalin in for a personal call on Roosevelt. Not a negotiating call, really just a courtesy call. Roosevelt in his expansive way said, "Marshal Stalin, I have just been getting a report from my Secretary of State on the morning meeting and he told me there was agreement on everything." Stettinius started to grab at Roosevelt's sleeve, but Stalin came back quickly "and the two republics too?" And Roosevelt said, "Yes."[16]

Once the error was made, Roosevelt thought about later saying to Stalin that it was a mistake but decided against it. He understood that Stalin was seeking a balance in what was heavily a Western organization. He did at one point ask Stalin if Hawaii and Alaska could be admitted as members and Stalin consented, but that would have been impossible under the U.S. Constitution.[17] In the end, it was generally agreed that representatives from the Ukraine and Byelorussia could come to San Francisco and once there they would be accepted as voting members. The other agreement on representation that was reached at Yalta was that Poland would be represented by a joint delegation made up of government members in exile in both London and Moscow.

Trusteeship was another contentious issue at Yalta, but in this case Churchill was the one who bristled. At one of the plenary sessions, Stettinius read out the proposal for a Trusteeship Council. Churchill, who had apparently not been briefed beforehand, was caught completely off guard and literally "blew up." Eden had not had time to clear it with Churchill before Yalta, even though Eden and Stettinius with the UK and U.S. delegations had met first at Malta before going on to the Yalta Conference. Eden had said at Malta that he had not had time to clear it with the prime minister. Churchill shouted that he had not been elected the king's first minister "to preside over the liquidation of the British Empire." Roosevelt, who was presiding, had to call for a recess. Churchill was simply fuming. Hiss was asked to write down in plain language what "trusteeship" stood for. So in longhand he wrote that "the territories in trusteeship shall be territories mandated under the League, territories detached from the Axis powers and such other territories as any member nation may wish to place in trusteeship."[18] When Churchill read the statement, he said that, in this case, trusteeship was "all right." So the crisis passed. Of course, the Americans were well aware that after the war, with the weakened condition of both France and the United Kingdom, their colonies might in fact fall under UN decolonization. The Soviets were supportive of the trusteeship idea and held a very anticolonialist position, which to some seemed like pure hypocrisy.

The other issues that seemed to have been resolved at Yalta were the veto and the competency of the General Assembly. Stalin finally agreed to allow the General Assembly to deal with whatever issues that arose in the international arena, including economic and social subjects. The Soviets accepted that the Council would be reserved for security issues and would be the central mandatory body on security affairs. An important issue related to the veto was also met with general agreement. Gladwyn Jebb (UK) had served as Cadogan's assistant at Dumbarton Oaks and again at Yalta. Jebb and Cadogan had discussed at Dumbarton Oaks the idea that when deciding on peaceful means of settling disputes, which became Chapter VI of the UN Charter, the great powers would lose the right to veto, which was surprisingly accepted by Stalin at Yalta. As Jebb describes, "A permanent member would have a veto [on Chapter VII], but . . . they would not have a veto on the previous section, which dealt with the pacific settlement of disputes."[19] Stalin also agreed that the veto could be limited to substantive issues and was not to be exercised on administrative matters or peaceful settlements. That agreement was later challenged by his foreign minister, Vyacheslav Molotov, at San Francisco. But there was also general agreement at Yalta that there ought to be an Economic and Social Council.

Other ideas were floated during this period, some which were never taken up. Jebb describes a suggestion made by Churchill to create regional security councils:

> That was Churchill's idea, but I always thought that that was slightly dotty. He hadn't thought it out. The idea was that there was going to be a Council

of Asia. . . . He thought that because we wanted a Council of Europe there should be a Council of Asia, but he hadn't thought it out. It was nuts. Even his idea of a Council of Europe, nobody knew—and he was quite incapable of explaining—whether the Russians should be in or out, whether we should be in or out, what our influence should be.[20]

These ideas, which seemed so outlandish at the time, are sixty years later at the heart of current political debates. Nevertheless, ideas that were deemed unusable at the time were left for another day and the meeting at Yalta was generally congenial. It was felt by Alger Hiss that Churchill, Stalin, and Roosevelt believed that they had achieved a cooperative arrangement and genuine agreement on the principles of the new organization. This spirit had begun well before Yalta at Dumbarton Oaks, where Stettinius, Gromyko, and Cadogan had cultivated a cooperative atmosphere.

The Chapultepec Conference

Revisions were made in the Dumbarton Oaks proposal after the Yalta meeting, and the document was then distributed to the nations that were invited to meet in San Francisco to write the final UN Charter. However, the Latin Americans, who would make up twenty-one of the original fifty-one members, convened a preliminary meeting in Chapultepec, outside Mexico City, in February and March 1945, called the "Inter-American Conference on the Problems of Peace and War." Ambassador Perez Guerrero and Parra Perez of Venezuela, among others, attended the conference. Padillo Nervo and his assistant Alfonso Garcia Robles represented Mexico. Perez Guerrero explains that U.S. secretary of state Edward Stettinius came to Mexico directly from Yalta. The Latin Americans had several concerns: they called for a stronger General Assembly, universality of membership, and assured representation for Latin America on the Security Council. The role of regional organizations was of particular importance and this was discussed extensively in Mexico. As described by Perez Guerrero:

> The Pan-American Union was in existence, not the OAS [Organization of American States] as it became later on after the Conference of Bogota. But there it was the opinion of Parra Perez among other people—others as well, and in the end it was the opinion that prevailed—that that organization should be called upon to play a role in conflicts that would arise within the region, involving the whole hemisphere.[21]

The Latin American countries were prepared to press for the role of regional organizations, which was later taken up in San Francisco and became a part of the UN Charter. Also, in Chapultepec there was support for Argentina to join the original members of the United Nations as well as support for issues like decolonization. The Latin Americans would take these ideas with them when they arrived in San Francisco the next month.

The San Francisco Conference

The San Francisco Conference was to finalize the structure and language of the Charter for the new organization, now to be called the United Nations, named after the title given to those nations that had united as allies to defeat the Axis powers. While the atmosphere was enthusiastic, as the war in Europe was drawing to a close, there were still a number of unresolved issues to be debated and resolved. President Roosevelt, who had been the energy behind the creation of the UN, would not make it to San Francisco. He died of a massive cerebral hemorrhage on April 12, 1945, only days before the conference opened on April 25. He was succeeded by his vice president, Harry Truman.

Many of the delegates had arrived by train, crossing the vast plains and winding through the high mountains of the western United States before arriving in the "City by the Bay" in early spring 1945. They were impressed by the massive size of the United States, which in contrast to Europe had not been touched by the devastating destruction of the war. There was a sense of enthusiasm and many had never been to such an international gathering. As Perez Guerrero of Venezuela describes: "There was a genuine spirit of co-operation, I suggest. Some of the countries, like Saudi Arabia, were very new. My first conversation on oil with Saudi Arabia date from that time, from the train taking us to San Francisco with some of the younger chaps of the Saudi Arabian delegation."[22]

Spring in San Francisco was a welcome change from the bombing, fires, and rubble of the war. Plans were made to receive the international delegations with enthusiasm and touches of elegance. The main plenary sessions were to take place in the opera house at the civic center and the adjacent veterans' memorial building. Special chefs were brought in to prepare the food and hotels made room to house these important guests.

In Washington, other preparations were being made. Oliver Lundquist, who was on loan to the State Department from the U.S. Office of Strategic Services (OSS), was assigned to work on the graphic presentations for the San Francisco Conference. His team was in charge of designing an official delegate's badge as a credential to identify members of the conference. They did not really start out to design a logo for the UN:

> We were thinking in terms of getting a delegate button, badge and credentials made for San Francisco and it was not any long range plan on our part. We had several ideas on it and had a little contest among ourselves in the agency and came up with this one which was designed by a fellow named Donald McLaughlin—I have to give him primary credit for it—he was one

of my assistants at the San Francisco Conference and he was more in charge of the actual graphic work there.[23]

Lundquist explains that the color blue was purposefully selected, and that when the design was shown to Stettinius, the secretary of state responded: "'Oh that's fine and I like that color.' We had used the blue color as the opposite of red, the war color, and then peace. . . . So then we referred to it as Stettinius blue. It was a gray blue, a little different than the modern United Nations flag."[24] Lundquist explains that the symbol of the globe was slightly different in the original design:

> Well, actually, it looked superficially like the existing one except that the latest one has been changed slightly. We had originally based it on what's called an azimuthal north polar projection of the world, so that all the countries of the world were spun around this concentric circle and we had limited it in the southern sector to a parallel that cut off Argentina because Argentina was not to be a member of the United Nations. We centered the symbol on the United States as the host country. . . . Subsequently, in England our design was adapted as the official symbol of the United Nations, centered on Europe as more the epicenter I guess of the east-west world, and took into account the whole earth including Antarctica. By then, of course, Argentina had been made a member of the United Nations so that it was no longer necessary to cut them off.[25]

Major Themes and Debates at San Francisco

At San Francisco the founders had to come to agreement on the major themes and language to be used in the UN Charter. While they had agreed upon the major purpose of the Organization—to maintain international peace and security—they had to reach consensus on other points: membership in the Organization; competency of the General Assembly and Security Council; trusteeship; self-defense; the role of the Security Council and the power of its members, including the use of the veto; the role of the Secretary-General; the framework for the use of force by the United Nations; and human rights.

Membership

Immediately, the issue of membership exploded. The Latin American countries who had met in Mexico insisted at the San Francisco Conference that Argentina be accepted for original membership. Nelson Rockefeller, assistant secretary for Latin American affairs in the U.S. State Department, had attended the Mexico meeting and supported the Latin American position on Argentina. The Latin Americans wanted "universal membership," meaning that all countries would be eligible for membership. Taking most of the delegations by surprise, including the Americans, Argentina was proposed for membership in the opening sessions at San Francisco. Foreign Minister Molotov, leading the Soviet delegation, was furious that the Yalta agreement had been ignored. But the Latin Americans had twenty-one votes at the conference and refused to accept the membership of the Ukraine and Byelorussia. The U.S. position taken by Truman was that while the Americans had agreed to admit the two republics as members, this did not necessarily mean that they could become original members and participate in the conference.

The issue of the three candidates was sent to committee. Molotov tried unsuccessfully to have the Argentine issue removed from the agenda altogether. As a gesture of goodwill, the Latin Americans agreed to vote in favor of the two republics and the motion was passed unanimously. But Molotov still refused to equate this with an acceptance of Argentina, calling the Argentine government fascist and throwing himself into a tirade, which was captured by the press covering the conference. Senator Vandenberg thought that the entire episode had "done more in four days to solidify Pan America against Russia than anything else that happened."[26] Molotov, apparently in retaliation on the Argentine issue and because Poland was still not represented, began to object to limitations on the veto and the broad competence of the General Assembly that had been resolved at Yalta. President Truman had to resort to sending a special envoy to Moscow to seek an audience with Stalin to clear things up. Alexei Roschin, who was among the Soviet delegation in San Francisco, says that Stalin accepted the envoy's presentation of the matter and informed Molotov to adhere to the decisions taken at Yalta on the veto and the General Assembly. Argentina was accepted as a member and the conference proceeded. Molotov eventually left San Francisco and, to everyone's relief, Ambassador Gromyko took up the leadership of the Soviet delegation.

Competency of the General Assembly

Ambassador Garcia Robles of Mexico, who took part in the Chapultepec Conference, and was also part of the Mexican delegation at San Francisco, recalls that the Latin Americans also emphasized the importance of enhancing and making more specific the powers of the General Assembly. It was agreed that the General Assembly could take up any matter considered important to the members, but that when the Security Council was seized with an issue, the General Assembly would refrain from taking up the matter. The competency of regional organizations in relation to the UN as had been discussed in Mexico was also agreed upon and this language was entered into the Charter. This provision recognized the right to resolve a local issue regionally before handing it over to the international body.[27] Importantly, it was eventually agreed that the General Assembly would not only be able to address economic, social, and security issues, but that it would have power over the budget.[28]

Trusteeship

The issue of trusteeship was resolved at the conference, but again not without controversy. Majid Khadduri, a member of the Iraqi delegation, recalls that the Arab countries were concerned about the status of Syria and Lebanon, which had been invited to participate in San Francisco. Both countries had been League of Nations mandates of France before the war. But because France had been occupied by the Nazis, it was not able to function as a mandatory power during the war years and Syria and Lebanon had been left on their own. They therefore considered themselves independent.

The Arab delegations wanted to make sure that countries that had been invited to become members of the United Nations would not fall into the category of trusteeship, which would throw Syria and Lebanon back under French control. Because the League mandates were still in force,[29] technically France was still the mandatory power over Syria and Lebanon. In response to the Arab proposal, France tried to force Syria to sign a treaty delineating certain demands that would maintain some French control. Syria refused and in May 1945, during the San Francisco Conference, France began bombing Damascus. The United States and Britain protested the bombing and insisted that the French withdraw, highlighting that the world was trying to establish peaceful relations and ought not to resort to war tactics. When the French withdrew, the Syrians claimed their independence and refused to negotiate any further with the French.[30] Khadduri explains that the Arab countries wanted assurances that these countries would not fall under the Trusteeship Council:

> For this reason Arab countries proposed that there should be something mentioned in the Charter of the United Nations that these countries should never be considered under the Trusteeship system of the United Nations but should be treated as independent since they had already been participating in the San Francisco Conference. This matter was taken to the steering committee. It was suggested to add a special Article (Article 78), which states that "The trusteeship shall not apply to territories which have become members of the United Nations."[31]

Colonial issues, as such, were not to be discussed at the conference, so as not to alienate the colonial powers, but there was another reason. The United States itself had been internally split on the issue. Lawrence Finkelstein, as a young member of the staff, witnessed this debate from inside the State Department:

> The thing that I wanted to emphasize that I think is fascinating is that the reason that the colonial agenda was not as far advanced by the time the San Francisco Conference began as were most of the other issues of the Charter is that there had been a deep split in the US government on this issue going back for years. This emerged sharply in the late spring of 1944 as planning

for the Dumbarton Oaks conversations was moving into an advanced stage. There had been a lot of preparation in the State Department of drafts for a trusteeship plan and a declaration having to do with principles of colonial government. There had been some consultations with the British. Most thought that this plan was ready to proceed, but it was the military service which threw a monkey wrench into the works for two reasons. The first, they were very concerned that these questions would involve territorial issues which might open up disputes among the countries still conducting the war against the Axis. We are talking about 1944. Their main argument was that they didn't want to introduce any unnecessarily contentious issues that might cause splits particularly between us and the Russians. The second issue was the belief particularly in the navy that it had to have the islands which we were winning island by island from the Japanese, some of which had been under League of Nations mandate after WWI but others which had not. So, the navy was against any concept of trusteeship which might international-ize those islands and thus deprive the navy of US sovereignty over them. On this they were clearly opposed by the President himself, but somehow or another the navy managed to keep the issue alive. It persisted in the internal debates in Washington right up to the eve of the San Francisco Conference. Indeed they were settled only by a late hour decision, perhaps the last one President Roosevelt reached before he died in Warm Springs. The final shape of the US proposals did not appear until a working group on the train going from the East Coast to San Francisco on the way to the Conference reworked the proposals and came up with the draft that the United States introduced at the Conference.[32]

Still the issue was not completely settled and a debate arose on whether to use the word "independence" in the Charter when talking about the goal of the administration of colonies or trusteeship territories. According to Finkel-stein, Stassen did not want to use the word because he was worried about los-ing the approval of the colonial powers, mainly the British. His staff tried to dissuade him in his car on the way to making his speech, but, ignoring them, he gave a powerful address against using the term, which received very neg-ative headlines in the press. This was a massive embarrassment to the United States, itself a former colony. General Carlos Romulo, head of the Philippine delegation at San Francisco,[33] recalls the fight that ensued:

> And in the Trusteeship Committee, we were discussing a proposal of the superpowers or the colonial powers then, that the aspiration of non-self-gov-erning peoples should be self-government. I opposed that. I said, "That's not complete. Their aspiration should be self-government or independence. Because self-government is not independence." Well we had a real fight on that. . . . We discussed the point for 2 nights. Finally, we won. It's "self-gov-ernment or independence." And I don't remember the number of votes. But I think, in the committee, we won by 12 or 14 votes. So, I got a note from Stassen after my reply to the statement of Lord Cranborne [with Stassen say-ing]: "Congratulations. Well done."
>   So that's why I always say that the contribution of the Philippines to the Charter [was] two words: *or independence.* But that opened the door for the

non-self-governing peoples which were under trusteeship at that time, to enter the United Nations.[34]

Ultimately, a compromise was reached so that "independence" was included as a goal for the trust territories but was not included in the wording that dealt with all other colonies. The concept of self-determination also met with some confusion during the conference. It did not signify, as is interpreted today, democracy. It simply meant self-rule, as opposed to colonial rule, be it monarchy, oligarchy, dictatorship, or democracy. The term "independence" was seen as interchangeable with "self-government" or "self-determination." So, these ideas did not include the concept of democratic rule, just national self-rule by whatever authority might emerge. As Finkelstein says, "They put the word 'independence' in one part and not in the other. That's the compromise they consciously reached. Although self-determination was interpreted by Stassen and others as broad enough to incorporate independence."[35]

Self-Defense

Neither Dumbarton Oaks nor Yalta had addressed the issue of self-defense and it was not included in the Dumbarton Oaks provisions. The issue, however, launched a heated debate in the Mexico meeting that carried over to San Francisco. While Stassen had been against the use of the term "independence," he explains that he took a different stand on the issue of self-defense. Stassen recalls that he threatened to withdraw from the conference and let everyone know his reasons if the right to self-defense were not written into the Charter. Stassen explains why he took such a strong stand:

> I was concerned as to the matter of self-defense in a circumstance if the Security Council was not acting and what effect that might have. So I originated the suggestion that there would be some kind of a section about nothing in the Charter shall impair the inherent right of self-defense if an armed attack occurs. And that was at first pretty much rejected; of course there was a general sort of a mind-set of those who had worked on the original Dumbarton Oaks draft of objecting to any change in it, especially in the early stages, but it soon became apparent that it needed changing. . . . I circulated it to our United States delegation, then after they agreed it ought to be in there, then [they] brought it up in the five-power meetings and talked it over and it finally stayed in.[36]

The Veto Debate

The principle that there should be a veto was settled at Yalta, but the issue opened up again in San Francisco. In fact, the word "veto" never appears in the Charter and the San Francisco participants often referred to it as the "unanimity" clause. Nevertheless, the United States needed the veto in order to gain Senate ratification and also because it did not want to be put in the position of committing its resources and troops in enforcement action in all parts of the world against its will. The veto probably produced the most disagreement in San Francisco and according to U.S. participant Lawrence Finkelstein "came very close to wrecking the Conference." Finkelstein explains: "So, the question was not whether there should be a veto but how far down in the process of decision making the veto should apply. Here the United States wanted to avoid the application of the veto to decisions that an issue should be discussed. The Russians were arguing that the decision to discuss should be subject to the veto as well."[37]

Molotov was very outspoken on the veto and it became a serious issue that divided the big five. The U.S. delegation and the Republicans on the team were very concerned. Stassen describes the discussion:

> One of the crucial questions on the veto power was whether the veto could stop even a discussion and whether the veto could prevent any kind of action in the Assembly. There was a lot of earnest examination of just how that should work out. Really Senator Vandenberg and I, and I think the United States delegation, after a lot of discussion, concluded that if the veto could completely stop any kind of expression in the United Nations and any kind of inquiry, any kind of Assembly action, it would be better not to make a start under those circumstances. That led to President Truman sending Harry Hopkins over to see Marshal Stalin. . . . Then out of those further negotiations and the further conference of Hopkins with Marshal Stalin came the revisions down to the point where the actual practice has followed since that time.[38]

President Truman sent Harry Hopkins to Moscow in May 1945, during the conference, and Hopkins went to see Stalin with Averell Harriman, U.S. ambassador to the Soviet Union. Hopkins was able to get Stalin to overrule Molotov. At that point, then, there was agreement among the five on the extent of the veto, which was based on the "chain of events theory."[39] The theory contended that once an item was on the agenda, there could take place a "chain of events" that could lead to threats to the interests of the great powers, which the veto was established to protect. As Finkelstein explains:

> So, it came out that, although there can be no veto on discussion as such or on a decision to put an item on the agenda of the Security Council, beyond that the veto is pretty pervasive. That statement of the five powers that I referred to, that they imposed upon the rest of the Conference, also included the so called double veto. Namely that if there were dispute as to whether the veto should apply or not, that decision itself would be subject to a veto.[40]

On the issue of the veto, Khadduri states that the Arab countries were essentially pro-Western and therefore accepted the great powers' need for a veto in the Security Council.[41] The smaller countries were generally opposed to the veto, but the major powers, now joined by France, which had been liberated at the end of the war, presented a unified front. The Latin Americans were particularly resistant to the idea and along with General Carlos Romulo of the Philippines and Foreign Minister Herbert Evatt of Australia put up a fight but eventually had to retreat.[42] The smaller powers, according to Finkelstein, "resented the notion of the veto to begin with and knew that they were going to have to swallow it because there would be no Charter without it and they couldn't afford not to have the Charter."[43] In the final vote on the veto, thirty-three nations supported it, two (Cuba and Colombia) voted against it, and fifteen countries chose to abstain.[44] Finkelstein relates an anecdote from the conference regarding the veto:

> [Senator Tom] Connally was sent on behalf of the US delegation to read the law, the riot act, to the other smaller countries on the question of the veto. He was sent deliberately because everybody understood that he would control whether or not there could be Senate approval. He was a large imposing man, a very memorable character. He always wore a black string tie and he had a twenty gallon hat. He was a Texan. He wore a sort of preacher's black coat. He was marvelous and he played it up. He built up this persona. He was a fourth of July orator, a stump orator with orotund rhetoric. He was a lot of fun. There he was and he went down to this committee III, 3, to tell them that "if you don't lay off on this veto you're not going to have a Charter. You're going home without it."
>
> The place next to the US place was occupied by the British, the UK next to the US in alphabetical order around the table. The British on this occasion were represented by a mild mannered, very distinguished professor of history who later became Sir Charles Webster. There was old Connally waving his arms as he spoke as though he were addressing 50 thousand people down there in Austin, Texas on the fourth of July. I watched this poor old Charles Webster slump lower and lower and lower to avoid having his head knocked off by this waving arm and finally you could barely see the top of his head over the table.[45]

The Role of the Secretary-General

In San Francisco, the role of Secretary-General of the UN was considered primarily an administrative position. Ruth Russell's summary of the discussions on the election of the chief administrator demonstrates that a number of options were considered.[46] It was suggested that the General Assembly elect the Secretary-General on its own. Others proposed that the Security Council could nominate three candidates, from which the General Assembly could select one. It was also discussed whether or not the Deputy Secretaries-General ought to be elected by the Assembly as well. It was settled that the General Assembly would elect the Secretary-General upon the nomination of the Security Council. The Soviet delegate argued that the nomination of the Secretary-General was not a procedural matter and therefore was subject to the veto. The British and French supported this point and the United States highlighted that the major powers had to have confidence in the chief administrator and therefore had to have some control over the selection. The United States also pointed out that the General Assembly had the power to reject an unsatisfactory candidate. The position was generally considered as a bureaucratic function. Nevertheless, the Secretary-General was given the power under Article 99 of the Charter to bring an issue to the attention of the Security Council, thus adding a political competence to the office. Today the nature of the position as global leader has evolved well beyond the original intent.

The Use of Force

Clearly the founders of the UN intended for the Organization to be able to use force to deter aggression.[47] This was carefully delineated in Chapter VII of the Charter, specifically in Article 42. Alger Hiss, who was appointed secretary-general of the San Francisco Conference, recalls the attitude at the time:

> One reason why I feel confident that military force was foreseen from the beginning is that this was one of the strong reasons why the veto was insisted upon. Because otherwise, it would mean that American forces could be called out by non-American officials and this just wouldn't go down with the American Congress. So I think we oversimplified the idea of a military contingent that would be readily available. This is why the Military Staff Committee seemed so important and of course when the Cold War began it fell into complete disuse, as we were assuming a unanimity of the Permanent Members on enforcement.[48]

The Allied powers had worked well together during the war to defeat the Axis powers and it was felt that this cooperation could continue in peacetime. The United States particularly had worked closely with the British through the Combined Chiefs. It was a model that seemed immediately available. The Soviets initially also concurred. Alexei Roschin explains that at Dumbarton Oaks,

> we insisted that the Military Staff Committee should function as a regular body and we even proposed the creation of [an] international army in order to mix in the different parts of the world to establish a guarantee of security. Later we changed this position; we considered that our attitude concerning the presidency of Truman and his administration was rather complicated and here it was the beginning of the Cold War.[49]

Roschin asserts that the Soviets did not know about the U.S. atomic bomb during the conference, which ended in June 1945, and that they only found out at the time of the bombing of Hiroshima in August. Roschin says that the bomb, of course, changed everything.[50] But during the San Francisco Conference, not even the U.S. delegation knew about the bomb, which was top secret. As the Cold War became more evident and superpower cooperation less possible, no Member State ever signed an agreement with the UN to provide troops. In addition, tired of the war, the troops wanted to go home. Once that happened, it was difficult to remobilize.

Human Rights

The global community that gathered in San Francisco to work on the UN Charter and to observe and influence the proceedings had been deeply troubled by emerging evidence of the Holocaust and the contempt for human rights demonstrated by the Nazi regime. Human rights were considered important, but the Charter was primarily focused on collective action as a means of stopping aggression rather than dealing with individual suffering. Determining how to enforce respect for human rights was beyond the scope of the conference but most felt the need to pay moral homage to the concept. As Inis Claude observes, the founders were remarkable in their ability to both look back and look forward. They did not know exactly what they were creating, but they were determined to achieve a "just and lasting peace."[51]

Provisions on human rights brought up by the United States at Dumbarton Oaks had been opposed by the other leaders. But in Chapultepec, the issue came up again and was discussed with Stettinius. The Latin American delegations and some forty groups representing professional, labor, business, religious, and women's organizations strongly lobbied for the inclusion of human rights at San Francisco. Women delegates from several Latin American countries insisted that the phrase "to ensure respect for human rights without distinction as to race, sex, condition or creed" be incorporated.[52] Ultimately, provisions for a human rights commission were written into the Charter. It is clear the great powers never intended to enforce these moral considerations, particularly with respect to the equal sovereignty of the members and other provisions in the Charter that specifically state that the domestic issues of members are beyond the purview of the UN. However, those who lobbied for the inclusion of human rights were visionaries who knew, or at least hoped, that these words would take on greater impetus as the UN matured. At the first meeting of the UN General Assembly in 1946, Eleanor Roosevelt was asked to chair the human rights commission, which was charged with writing the Universal Declaration of Human Rights.

The United Nations Is Born

The Charter of the United Nations was signed by fifty members at San Francisco on June 26, 1945; Poland, which never arrived, was nevertheless allowed to sign as an original member in the months that followed, bringing the total of original members to fifty-one.[53] Alger Hiss describes the euphoria as the final draft was signed. He explains that Truman placed tremendous importance on it, so much so that the original document was given its own

Signing of the UN Charter in San Francisco, June 26, 1945. *From left to right:* Secretary of State Edward Stettinius, Senator Tom Connally, Senator Arthur Vandenberg, and seated, Sol Bloom, House of Representatives.

parachute on the flight back to Washington even though Hiss, who was carrying it, had to travel without one:

> It was decided that there was no proper—let's call it receptacle, place of safekeeping—for the Charter. The United Nations hadn't come into existence, and the conference Secretariat would be disbanded. And it was agreed that Truman would keep it in the safe in the White House. Since the US had been the host, this would be appropriate. I was therefore deputed to carry the Charter to the White House and deliver it to him for that kind of safekeeping. And the army put a plane at my disposal for that purpose. The humorous aspect of this was that since the Charter was so valuable it had a parachute attached to it—and I didn't.[54]

After signing, each nation undertook through its own process to ratify the Charter. On July 28, 1945, the U.S. Senate approved the Charter by a vote of eighty-nine to two. With the Senate's consent in hand, Truman signed the ratification act for the Charter. The bipartisan participation by the Senate throughout the process proved to be a very successful strategy. Never before had a treaty been so publicly debated. By October 24, 1945, twenty-nine countries had signed and ratified the Charter, constituting a majority of the original fifty-one signatories. October 24 continues to be celebrated as the birth date of the United Nations. On that day the United Nations was officially constituted, and by December 27 all the original members had ratified the Charter. While there had been inklings of the Cold War during the negotiating process, there was still a feeling of hope that this new international cooperation could be sustained. Delegates of the participating nations at San Francisco formed a preparatory commission and met in London to make arrangements for the first meeting of the United Nations and to plan for the transfer of certain activities from the League to the UN. Enthusiasm still filled the hall at the first opening session of the General Assembly in London on January 10, 1946.

The United Nations celebrated its fiftieth anniversary in 1995. In the course of its first half century, the UN has withstood the pressures of the Cold War, decolonization, and numerous regional crises. The UN Secretariat has matured into a competent international bureaucracy, much larger and more complex than anticipated in 1945; the Secretary-General, once primarily considered to be an administrator, has become a major world leader. With the end of the Cold War and the new era of globalization, the UN has been under pressure to reform. It has been suggested that the Security Council ought to reflect changes in the global power balance and should become more transparent. But the Charter has proven to be a flexible instrument; it has been amended only three times, once to enlarge the Security Council from its original eleven members to today's fifteen, and twice to enlarge the Economic and Social Council, which at present has fifty-four members. The UN has grown from its

fifty-one member-signatories in 1945 to 191 members in 2004. Decolonization, including the trust territories, so sensitive an issue at Yalta and San Francisco, was constructively and effectively overseen by the General Assembly
and the Trusteeship Council. All the former colonies and trust territories are
now independent members of the UN and the Trusteeship Council no longer
has any real function.

Any organization must adapt to the changing times and the UN has continued to find ways to creatively shape itself to its new environment. However, the UN will need to continue to evolve and change as the political and
security environment changes around it. If for some reason it fails to adapt, it
may be pushed aside by more relevant institutions or it may cease to exist, like
the Concert of Europe and the League of Nations before it. An examination of
the debates and issues of its birth facilitates an understanding of how it may
or may not need to change. Perhaps the concurrence of the major powers is
needed to solidify enforcement and maintain a credible deterrence. But by
what criteria do we measure which are the major powers of a given era? If we
give them this power, how can we be sure they will share the same sense of
global responsibility and act in concert? Through the pressures of a growing
democratic civil society, the UN is being forced to become more accountable
for its actions, as are the Member States, which drive its decisions and policies. The institution will have to adapt to this changing environment.

Carlos Romulo, one of the founders of the UN at the San Francisco Conference in 1945, says succinctly: "We have, in the United Nations, the only
world forum that we will ever have. You abolish the United Nations and we'll
have to create another one. Voltaire once said, the great French writer, 'if we
didn't have a god, we'd have to create a god.' The same thing is true."[55]

Today the United Nations occupies a political space at the center of the
global dialogue. One cannot pick up a newspaper without almost daily finding some article on the UN. As was stated in the Millennium Declaration in
2000, "Responsibility for managing worldwide economic and social development, as well as threats to international peace and security, must be shared
among the nations of the world and should be exercised multilaterally. As the
most universal and most representative organization in the world, the United
Nations must play the central role."

Notes

1. Inis L. Claude Jr., *Swords Into Plowshares: The Problems and Progress of
International Organization,* 4th ed. (New York: Random House, 1984), p. 25.

2. Ibid., p. 87. This comment, by Edwin L. James, was quoted in his obituary,
New York Times, December 4, 1951.

3. Yale-UN oral history interview with Alger Hiss, October 11, 1990, p. 5.

4. Ruth B. Russell, *A History of the United Nations Charter: The Role of the
United States, 1940–45* (Washington, D.C.: Brookings Institution, 1958), pp. 228–229.

5. The Chinese foreign minister was not in Moscow at the meeting but signed later.

6. Yale-UN oral history interview with Alexei Roschin, May 25, 1990, p. 3.

7. *Public Papers and Addresses of Franklin D. Roosevelt: The Tide Turns, 1943* (1950), p. 562 n.

8. UN oral history interview with Harold Stassen, April 29, 1983, p. 4.

9. *U.S. Department of State Bulletin* 10 (June 17, 1944): 552–553.

10. Leo Pasvolsky spoke Russian and worked with the Soviets on English-Russian language issues for the writing of the Charter in San Francisco. Ruth Russell dedicated her book *History of the United Nations Charter* to him.

11. Yale-UN oral history interview with Alger Hiss, February 13, 1990, pp. 1–2.

12. Ibid., p. 3.

13. Ibid.

14. Ibid., p. 6.

15. Ibid., p. 7.

16. Ibid., pp. 11–12.

17. Ibid., p. 13.

18. Ibid.

19. UN oral history interview with Gladwyn Jebb, June 21, 1983, p. 26.

20. Ibid., p. 35a.

21. UN oral history interview with Ambassador Perez Guerrero, April 22, 1983, p. 12.

22. Ibid., p. 19.

23. Yale-UN oral history interview with Oliver Lundquist, April 19, 1990, pp. 5–6.

24. Ibid., p. 6.

25. Ibid., pp. 6–7.

26. Quoted in Russell, *History of the United Nations Charter,* p. 639.

27. Oral history interview with Alfonso Garcia Robles, March 21, 1984, located in the UN Dag Hammarskjöld Library.

28. Ruth Russell describes that there had been general agreement even in earlier drafts that the General Assembly would decide the budget, but there continued to be discussion on what role the Council might also play in these decisions. Ultimately, it was agreed that the Assembly would have that authority. See Russell, *History of the United Nations Charter,* pp. 377–378.

29. The League was not officially terminated until early 1946, a few weeks after the UN General Assembly's first meeting.

30. Yale-UN oral history interview with Majid Khadduri, March 20, 1997, Washington, D.C., pp. 12–13.

31. Ibid., p. 8.

32. Yale-UN oral history interview with Lawrence Finkelstein, November 23, 1990, pp. 15–16.

33. The Philippines was not independent at that time.

34. UN oral history interview with General Carlos P. Romulo, October 30, 1982, p. 8.

35. Interview with Finkelstein, p. 19.

36. Interview with Stassen, p. 26.

37. Interview with Finkelstein, p. 23.

38. Interview with Stassen, p. 10.

39. The "chain of events" theory was written into the minutes of the U.S. delegation by Leo Pasvolsky, in a volume of *Foreign Relations of the United States* (1945), in an official document series of the conference.

40. Interview with Finkelstein, p. 26.

41. Interview with Khadduri, p. 22.

42. Interview with Romulo, p. 4.

43. Interview with Finkelstein, p. 23.

44. Russell, *History of the United Nations Charter,* p. 739.

45. Interview with Finkelstein, pp. 27–28. In another version of the Connally story, it was rumored that while he was warning the delegates that killing the veto provision would kill the entire Charter, he calmly tore the draft Charter into shreds and, at the climactic moment, scattered the shreds on the floor. Letter from Inis Claude to Jean Krasno, April 2001.

46. Russell, *History of the United Nations Charter,* pp. 854–859.

47. Any enforcement, of course, would be subject to the veto and so would be applied selectively. Using collective force selectively does not convey the same meaning as collective security when it is defined narrowly to mean the calling for a guarantee of action against any and every possible aggressor. By inserting the veto provision, the founders clearly meant that collective action should only occur if the big five agreed, and certainly not against one of them. That would have been considered very dangerous. Letter from Inis Claude to Jean Krasno, April 2001.

48. Yale-UN oral history interview with Alger Hiss, October 11, 1990, p. 1.

49. Interview with Roschin, p. 9.

50. Ibid., p. 10.

51. Claude, *Swords Into Plowshares,* p. 80.

52. Anne Winslow, ed., *Women, Politics, and the United Nations* (Westport, Conn.: Greenwood Press, 1995), pp. 6–7.

53. The Soviets had arrested the London Poles when they arrived in Moscow to meet with their counterparts, the Lublin faction. This was a clear violation of the Soviets' agreement to let them meet and select a joint delegation to go to San Francisco. This event took place during the conference and the news headlines created quite a stir, a warning that the Cold War was not far off. Toward the end of the conference an agreement was finally reached on a provisional government for Poland, but not in time to reach San Francisco. Russell, *History of the United Nations Charter,* p. 929.

54. Interview with Alger Hiss, October 11, 1990, pp. 8–9.

55. Interview with Romulo, p. 11.

3

The United Nations and the Formation of Global Norms

Joe Sills

There is one universal organization in the world today that can set globally accepted standards and norms of behavior. That is the United Nations. And its normative power resides not only in the Organization as a whole, but also in its individual agencies, programs, funds, and the international agreements that fall under its auspices. A case in point is the statement of Gro Harlem Bruntland, director-general of the World Health Organization (WHO) and former prime minister of Norway. When asked in an interview what the most important role of WHO might be, Bruntland replied simply: "To set standards and norms."[1] The intent of this chapter is to describe and evaluate the role of the UN system in establishing these global norms.[2] This will be done through a *tour d'horizon* of the principal organs, programs, and specialized agencies that compose the system.

A norm is an accepted behavior, or set of behaviors, which can differ from society to society. It is necessary to distinguish between "global" and "local" norms; the inherent difficulty lies in establishing global norms that can transcend the great diversity within the world's cultures. For example, while polygamy in some cultures is an established norm, it is unacceptable in others. Norms are legitimized to the extent that members of the group practice the behavior without question.[3] Norms set the standards for our daily activities. But norms can change. Some assert that there is an evolutionary tendency toward self-preservation and welfare of the whole, if not a moral sense of fairness. If this is true, then the evolution of norms *may* be toward developing a greater sense of stewardship toward the planet and its peoples. But there is much evidence to the contrary. In the more basic sense, global norms can bring order to what might be chaotic in the absence of standards. As we share information and become more broadly aware of a more universal sense of preservation, we may see the need to reorder our norms and abandon others

47

in the interest of the whole.[4] The United Nations is the forum where much of this debate is played out.

Treaty norms are the most concrete, understandable, and probably the most important international standards; however, the efforts and accomplishments of the United Nations go far beyond treaty norms. Indeed, these efforts might usefully be considered as a spectrum ranging from a treaty legally binding on those states that ratify it, to the assertion of broad, largely rhetorical, and clearly unobtainable goals, such as "a world free of drugs." In between, there is a sizable array of methods utilized by the organizations in the UN system to facilitate and, on occasion, regulate relations among states and to influence their behavior. Taken together, they make possible what has been termed "the superordinate function of the United Nations in setting, monitoring, and enforcing standards,"[5] which one close observer has called the UN's "biggest historical achievement."[6] Sets of rules and the bodies organized to enforce norms around a particular issue like arms control or environmental concerns are known as regimes. In the words of Thomas Franck:

> Love them or hate them, however, international regimes are likely only to increase their importance in the governance of humanity. International regimes are necessarily normative and administrative solutions to international problems. No amount of wishful thinking can justify a state "opting out" of regimes that regulate trade, the environment, communications, transportation, human rights, collective security, arms or disease control.[7]

At the Beginning

When representatives of fifty nations met in San Francisco in 1945 to establish a new world organization,[8] their primary motivation, as articulated in the preamble to the UN Charter, was "to save succeeding generations from the scourge of war." The outcome of their efforts, the Charter, is the continuing basis for the standards and norms created by the United Nations itself and, to a significant extent, by the organizations of the UN system. The Charter is an international treaty binding on all states that are parties to it, currently 191 members. In terms of U.S. jurisprudence, Nina Schou has described the Charter as "the most solemn and universal of the US treaties," which, as the supreme law of the land, "the President is required faithfully to execute." She continues: "By agreeing to respect a treaty norm, states consent to conform their practice to the treaty standard, notwithstanding domestic legal or constitutional provisions to the contrary."[9] And Christopher Joyner writes: "The UN Charter furnishes the fundamental constitutional law for operating the only general-purpose, near-universal organization operating in the world today."[10]

Certain specific norms regarding conflict were laid out in the Charter. While war and aggression by name were not specifically outlawed in the

Charter, it was stated that "armed forces shall not be used, save in the common interest." The UN Charter was thereby laying the groundwork for creating a norm of peaceful settlement of disputes rather than resorting to war. However, the use of force for self-defense is protected as an accepted norm in the international system. Other norms, such as self-determination and independence, are set forward in the Charter as goals for all states, important features anticipating decolonization.

Nevertheless, the attention of the San Francisco Conference was focused primarily on creating a structure for the UN, and deciding questions of membership and the functions and powers to be allocated to its various parts. With the notable exception of human rights, where pressure from nongovernmental organizations (NGOs) was a major factor, the conference did not devote significant attention to the role of the United Nations in articulating and encouraging the development of non-treaty-based norms.[11] However, it opened the door for the creation of norms in the years to come.

The United Nations and International Law

The International Court of Justice (ICJ), as explained in Chapter 1, is one of the six principal organs of the United Nations. Its statute, which is annexed to the UN Charter, forms an integral part of the Charter. All UN Member States are ipso facto parties to the ICJ statute (Charter, Articles 93 and 94). The statute is almost totally concerned with the operations of the Court: organization, competence, procedure, advisory opinions, and amendment. Article 59 states: "The decision of the Court has no binding force except between the parties and in respect of that particular case." Nevertheless, the Court tends to apply the legal principles contained in its decisions and advisory opinions in later cases, and its views are given substantial weight by other international tribunals. However, the few and comparatively unimportant issues with which the Court dealt over the years before the end of the Cold War, largely through no fault of its own, rendered it of marginal importance in the development of international law. Now that the ICJ has many more cases on its docket, some twenty-two in 2004, that role will inevitably change.

Nevertheless, the UN's considerable achievements in the development and codification of international law over the years have come primarily from directions other than the legal decisions of the ICJ. Since 1945, the United Nations has exercised the central role in the development and codification of a body of international law that has become the basis of law applicable to relations among nations. The UN achieved this through the initiation of over 500 multilateral agreements that address mutual concerns and are legally binding for the nations that ratify them.[12] This frequently pioneering work has tended to focus on problems that have become increasingly more international in scope: the environment, the oceans, crime, drugs, and terrorism are examples. In areas such as human rights, environmental law, and crime prevention, "soft law" resolutions of the General Assembly and of global conferences have contributed substantially to the growth of international customary law.

Charlotte Ku has described two sets of functions of international law. One is the operating system and the other is normative, but "the separations between the operating and normative may not always be clear."[13] The two functions are interactive and mutually reinforcing. If the norm development is weak, the functional operations also will be weak, because much of international law by its nature is self-enforcing through consent. Therefore, the UN's role in building consensus on norms is key to the observance of, and compliance with, international law. Ku also explains that the major powers need to be brought along with the process. Law cannot get ahead of the will of the key players or it simply will not be observed. Domestic civil society plays an important role in building the expectation of normative behavior on such issues as human rights and environmental protection. This is an ongoing process. When addressing the UN treaty process, it is important to heed Ku's observation: "In other words, the operating and normative systems of international law must remain in alignment, so that the normative needs of the community can be met through existing but adaptable legal frameworks."[14]

The International Law Commission (ILC), which was established in 1947 by the General Assembly's Sixth Committee, is significant in this process. It comprises thirty-four experts, representing the world's principal legal systems, who serve in their personal capacities. Charged with promoting the development and codification of international law, the ILC focuses on preparing draft treaties or agreements dealing with subjects either chosen by the ILC or referred by the General Assembly. When the ILC finishes a draft, the General Assembly normally convenes a conference of UN Member States, wherein the draft is converted into a treaty open to state signature.

The ILC's work has often been criticized for being tedious, and its drafting process may go on for a decade or more. But it has had some major successes, among them its draft instruments for the four 1958 Geneva Conventions on the Law of the Sea, which entered into force in the 1960s. Its most recent success has been its work in preparation for the statute creating the International Criminal Court (ICC), agreed to in Rome in June 1998. On April 11, 2002, ten new countries ratified the ICC statute, bringing the total to sixty-six ratifications, surpassing the sixty needed to activate the statute, and the ICC went into force on July 1, 2002. In addition, the UN Commission on International Trade Law (UNCITRAL), established by the General Assembly in 1966, is the primary UN legal body on this issue, with a mandate to develop conventions, model legislation and rules, and guidelines on elaborating and harmonizing international trade law.

The Security Council

The Security Council, established by the Charter as one of the six principal organs of the United Nations (Article 7[1]), is assigned "primary responsibility for the maintenance of international peace and security," and all UN Member States "agree that in carrying out its duties under this responsibility the Security Council acts on their behalf" (Article 23[1]). Further, they "agree to accept and carry out decisions of the Security Council" (Article 25).

These Charter provisions give the Council authority that goes far beyond making recommendations and setting standards or goals. The Council is empowered to make decisions that, given the status of the Charter as a binding international treaty, all members of the United Nations are obligated to honor, even though they may not have participated in making the decisions (if they were not one of the fifteen members of the Security Council), or even though they may have opposed the decisions. The five permanent members—China, France, Russia, the United Kingdom, and the United States—whose concurrence is necessary for decisions by the Council (Article 27[3]),[15] are also bound by a decision of the Council once it has been passed.

The Council's powers to maintain international peace and security are defined in Chapters VI and VII of the Charter. Chapter VI empowers the Council to act to encourage, assist, and recommend actions that call for peaceful solutions to a dispute. However, Chapter VII, titled "Action with Respect to Threats to the Peace, Breaches of the Peace, and Acts of Aggression," is a different matter. The Council can decide upon actions short of the use of armed force, including "complete or partial interruption of economic relations and of rail, sea, air, postal, telegraphic, radio and other means of communication, and the severance of diplomatic relations" (Article 41). If the Council deems these measures inadequate, "it may take such action by air, sea, or land forces as may be necessary to maintain or restore international peace or security" (Article 42). This includes the use of military force.

The reality of the deployment of UN forces, as it has evolved and become known worldwide as UN peacekeeping, is not explicitly covered in the Charter.[16] It is now accepted that participation of UN Member States in peacekeeping operations is totally voluntary. Indeed, a frequently recurring fact of UN life is the spectacle of the Secretary-General, following approval by the Security Council of a peacekeeping mandate, pleading with Member States to make available the forces required to implement it.

All Member States have an obligation to support a peacekeeping force once it is deployed based on a decision of the Security Council. However, members, especially those that have a direct interest in the dispute at question, sometimes disregard this obligation and may even work to thwart the UN's efforts. For example, the United States looked the other way in regard to the arms embargo on the former Yugoslavia, allowing weapons to cross the border into Bosnia and Croatia to help arm those fighting against the Serbs. In the case of East Timor, the Indonesian government was either unwilling or unable to control militias who were violating UN Security Council mandates, or was even instructing them to do so. Sanctions—especially economic ones—established by the Council against certain states are also frequently circumvented. For instance, Jordan continued to trade with Iraq after sanctions were imposed in 1990, and various West African leaders participated in illegal diamond and arms deals, which continued to finance brutal civil wars in the region. Consistently damaging to the authority and credibility of the United Nations as an institution are the frequent occasions where resolutions of the Security Council are simply ignored, such as early resolutions outlawing apartheid and numerous resolutions calling for an end to violence in the Middle East.

The effect of this is to convert what should be binding decisions of the Security Council into exhortations, thus rendering them little more than recommendations. Implicitly recognizing this, in recent years the Council has turned increasingly to statements rather than resolutions, agreed to in closed meetings (referred to as "consultations"), which are then read out by the president of the Council and issued afterward as UN press releases. Taken collectively, however, Security Council decisions, like case law, may on occasion set standards, or norms, for future decisions. For example, intervening in states for humanitarian purposes, once considered beyond the reach of the United Nations, has gradually become something acceptable for discussion, if not practice, by the Council. However, intervention has been carried out on a case-by-case basis, rather than being considered a generic norm. Unlike case law, precedent is not as decisive in decisions of the Council, which is a highly political body.

There is an additional area where the Security Council has taken actions that have led to the creation of new norms and standards. Chapter X, Article 29, empowers the Council to "establish such subsidiary organs as it deems necessary for the performance of its functions." Most notable among recent exercises of this authority under the Chapter VII mandate to maintain international peace and security has been the creation of the ad hoc tribunals: the International Criminal Tribunal for the Former Yugoslavia (ICTY) and the International Criminal Tribunal for Rwanda (ICTR). Member States are thus obliged to cooperate with the tribunals as "a universal legal obligation of the highest order. In addition to this general obligation to cooperate, the Statutes of the Tribunals impose specific obligations on Member States to surrender fugitives, gather evidence, conduct searches and seizures and locate persons at the request of the Tribunals."[17] These ad hoc tribunals have contributed to setting norms for international justice and provided the main experiential base for the International Criminal Court, whose statute establishes a new level of norm-setting on such concepts as genocide, crimes against humanity, and war crimes, which are punishable under the Court.

The UN Compensation Commission (UNCC) is a subsidiary body of the Security Council established to evaluate and pay claims resulting directly from Iraq's invasion and occupation of Kuwait in 1990–1991. Among other claims, the UNCC is engaged in a precedent-setting activity of processing claims for environmental losses, valued by claimants at some $50 billion. This represents the world community's first deliberate assessment and valuation of the environmental consequences of war. The procedures of the UNCC are establishing new standards for compensation tribunals. The nonadversarial nature of the proceedings and emphasis on swift results will provide a model for future tribunals, especially those dealing with environmental disasters.[18]

Sadly, the tribunals and Compensation Commission demonstrate that Security Council decisions are, to a large degree, case-by-case and enforceable only against relatively small and weak or defeated states, and only then when the permanent five choose to exert the necessary pressure. Thus the actual powers of the Council, debated at length in San Francisco and spelled out in the Charter, only sporadically come into play as envisaged, and even then often in a weakened and compromised fashion, a far cry from what was foreseen at the creation of the United Nations.

The General Assembly

The General Assembly, as discussed briefly in Chapter 1, was created as the primary deliberative organ of the United Nations, with each Member State having one vote, and with its decisions (other than on budgetary and administrative matters) only being recommendations to the Member States. Certainly intended if not explicitly stated by the Charter was that, given the moral authority and weight of the UN behind them, actions of the Assembly would be central to the establishment of new international guidelines in all their forms.

Although General Assembly resolutions are nonbinding, they have often been the beginning of conventions and treaties drafted under UN auspices. According to Joyner, "General Assembly 'declarations,' largely because of their bold assertive quality, have demonstrated the greatest likelihood of evolving into conventions adopted by the international community."[19] He goes on to say that "declarations by the General Assembly can function as instruments to distill and crystallize into tangible form the international community's consensus regarding a customary norm."[20] The landmark 1948 Universal Declaration of Human Rights, which was adopted by the Assembly, is the best example. What started as a General Assembly resolution (albeit one whose exceptional nature was recognized at the time) has become the foundation of future UN efforts in the field of human rights. Other examples of conventions that have evolved out of General Assembly declarations are the 1967 Outer Space Treaty, the 1968 Treaty on the Nonproliferation of Nuclear Weapons, and the 1971 Seabed Arms Control Treaty. All sought to limit the spread of weapons of mass destruction to new geographic areas.

An example of a series of actions by the Assembly relating to a specific issue is that concerning persons with disabilities. In 1975 the Assembly adopted the Declaration on the Rights of Disabled Persons, aimed at setting standards for equal treatment and access in order to facilitate integration into society. The International Year of Disabled Persons (1981) and the UN Decade of Disabled Persons (1983–1992) led to the adoption by the General Assembly in 1993 of the Standard Rules on the Equalization of Opportunities for Persons with Disabilities, which serve as guidelines for policy and a basis for technical assistance. These UN efforts, and those of NGOs, academics, and professional societies in various countries, created standards, as well as goals, and aided in building national capacities to assist citizens with disabilities.[21]

The Secretary-General

The Secretary-General, who heads the Secretariat, is not only the UN's chief administrative officer, but also the spokesman for, and symbol of, the Organization. The Secretary-General of the League of Nations had been almost totally an administrator, and that was the primary role envisaged by the San Francisco Conference for the UN Secretary-General.[22] Over the years, however, the office has developed in a number of ways that have expanded its scope and stature, especially as an articulator of the principles and goals of the United Nations.

The San Francisco Conference decided to give a limited political dimension to the office by enabling the Secretary-General to "bring to the attention of the Security Council any matter which in his opinion may threaten the maintenance of international peace and security" (Article 99). However, of far greater importance has been the provision in Article 98 that the Secretary-General "shall make an annual report to the General Assembly on the work of the Organization."[23] Successive Secretaries-General have increasingly utilized this report, issued at the opening of the regular session of the General Assembly each September, to identify what they feel are the major issues and concerns facing the Organization, thus seeking to define its future agenda and to influence the establishment by the United Nations of norms and goals.

Secretary-General Boutros Boutros-Ghali (1992–1996), in addition to his annual reports, issued *An Agenda for Peace,* which analyzed ways of strengthening the UN's capacity for peacemaking and peacekeeping.[24] This study was done at the request of the Security Council, meeting on January 31, 1992, at the level of heads of state and government. The Secretary-General subsequently added in 1994 a companion volume titled *An Agenda for Development,* which would "complement *An Agenda for Peace* by addressing the deeper foundations of global peace and security in the economic, social and environmental spheres."[25]

The current UN Secretary-General, Kofi Annan (1997–2006), in a clear effort to shape the United Nations of the future, issued what is surely the most comprehensive analysis and series of proposals emanating from that office: *We the Peoples: The Role of the United Nations in the Twenty-First Century,* which appeared on the occasion of the Millennium Summit of the General Assembly in 2000. In it, he characterized the United Nations as "the only body of its kind with universal membership and comprehensive scope, and encompassing so many areas of human endeavor. These features make it a uniquely useful forum for sharing information, conducting negotiations, elaborating norms and voicing expectations, coordinating the behavior of states and other actors, and pursuing common plans of action."[26] He then delineated a set of priorities for the United Nations (including many involving other bodies of the UN system) far more comprehensive in scope and detail than those emanating from any previous Secretary-General.

Another area in which the Secretaries-General have attempted to influence matters has been using the office as a bully pulpit. The second Secretary-General, Dag Hammarskjöld, was known for his analytical, cerebral speeches, which were broadly admired.[27] However, Secretary-General Annan discovered the perils of the bully pulpit when, in an address to the General Assembly, he referred to the "developing international norm in favour of intervention to protect civilians from wholesale slaughter."[28] This was broadly interpreted as asserting the right of the international community to intervene in such cases with or without the approval of the sovereign state involved, a proposition many do not accept.

Over the years, however, Secretaries-General have not been free from controversy. The Soviet Union was very displeased with the first Secretary-General, Trygve Lie, because of the UN's role in Korea in the early 1950s, and demanded the resignation of Secretary-General Hammarskjöld over UN involvement in the Congo, which appeared to serve Western interests. When Hammarskjöld died in a plane crash in Africa, the major powers agreed upon a far less controversial figure in the quiet diplomat who represented Burma, U Thant. Nevertheless, Hammarskjöld had ushered in the new concept of peacekeeping and established a set of norms for the deployment of troops from contributing countries to keep the peace in regions of the world emerging from conflict. It was the United States' turn to express disapproval when it blocked the reelection of Boutros Boutros-Ghali. The importance of the office reached a new level of international recognition with the announcement

UN Photo 210384 C/Sergey Bermeniev

UN Secretary-General Kofi Annan receives the Nobel Peace Prize, jointly shared with the United Nations, December 2001. Annan is responsible for writing and promoting the Millennium Declaration.

of the 2001 Nobel Peace Prize to both the United Nations and Kofi Annan as Secretary-General.

The Specialized Agencies

While a handful of UN agencies were mentioned in Chapter 1, this section elaborates on the major role these fourteen specialized agencies, along with the International Atomic Energy Agency (IAEA), have played in establishing norms and standards for the world community.[29] Broadly, they do this in four ways:

1. They are the focal points, and frequently the impetus, for the negotiation and execution of binding international instruments in their respective areas of competence.
2. Their research, statistical work, and monitoring functions provide the basis for intergovernmental agreements, understandings, and working agreements that, though falling short of binding treaty status, are widely accepted norms.
3. They provide extensive and valuable advice and assistance to Member States, especially developing countries, assisting them in planning and implementation, including adherence to treaty obligations.
4. They facilitate the creation of networks, both formal and informal, among practitioners, including NGOs and, increasingly, corporate sector representatives whose concerns parallel those of the agencies.

Six agencies are concerned with specific functional areas in which they are mandated to set international standards and regulations. They deal with ideas, issues, and day-to-day working arrangements that cross borders and are thus dependent on international regimes for their successful functioning.

- The International Civil Aviation Organization (ICAO), founded in 1944, sets international standards for the safe and efficient operation of air transport and facilitates cooperation among nations in civil aviation.
- The International Maritime Organization (IMO), established by a convention adopted in 1948, sets standards for shipping safety and the prevention of marine pollution from ships. Almost all the world's merchant fleets are bound by three key IMO conventions on safety at sea. About 40 conventions and protocols and 800 codes and recommendations have emanated from the IMO and have been widely implemented.
- The International Telecommunications Union (ITU), founded as the International Telegraph Union in 1865, has 191 Member States and nearly 600 members from nongovernment sectors: corporate entities, communications operators and broadcasters, and regional and international organizations. The ITU develops standards facilitating the interconnection of national communications infrastructures into global networks, and international regulations and treaties governing the sharing of the radio frequency spectrum and satellite orbital positioning. ITU recommendations have been the basis for electronic signatures in e-commerce.
- The Universal Postal Union (UPU) has created and monitors a system in which every member agrees to transmit the mail of other members by the best means used for domestic mail. The UPU sets indicative

rates, weight and size limits, and conditions of acceptance of various mailed items, including small packages.

- The World Meteorological Organization (WMO) monitors global weather conditions, provides scientific information about weather-related matters, and develops agreements on standards, codes, measurements, and communications.
- The World Intellectual Property Organization (WIPO) works to protect intellectual property, which comprises industrial property and copyrights. WIPO administers fifteen international treaties on industrial property and six on copyrights. A central part of WIPO's program is the development and application of international norms and standards, particularly to keep up with new technologies. Since 1999, WIPO's Arbitration and Mediation Center has helped resolve disputes in the generic top-level domains of the Internet (.com, .net, and .org).

Three UN agencies are lending institutions:

- The World Bank Group comprises five institutions whose mandate is to finance development in less-developed nations. The World Bank Group has been described as a de jure but not de facto part of the UN system. In fact, in recent years, the World Bank has been more closely involved in cooperative efforts with other bodies in the system through such programs as the Joint UN Programme on HIV/AIDS (UNAIDS) and in cooperative efforts to eliminate poverty.
- The International Monetary Fund (IMF), like the World Bank in years past, has only limited involvement with other parts of the UN system (other than the Bank, with which it works very closely). The Fund focuses on international monetary cooperation, promotes orderly exchange arrangements, and provides credits to members to alleviate balance-of-payments problems.
- The International Fund for Agricultural Development (IFAD) was established in 1977 as an outgrowth of the 1974 World Food Conference. It provides loans and grants to improve food production and nutrition; many other regional and financial institutions cofinance IFAD projects.

Five specialized agencies combine research, standard-setting, and assistance to developing countries:

- The UN Industrial Development Organization (UNIDO), the newest of specialized agencies (1985), works with governments and businesses to create sustainable industrial development in developing countries and countries in transition (former Soviet republics now independent).

- The UN Educational, Scientific, and Cultural Organization (UNESCO) was established in 1946 to address issues of education; the natural, social, and human sciences; culture; and communication. Much of UNESCO's work involves establishing norms and standards in these areas and providing technical assistance to developing countries to meet them. In recent years, UNESCO has been particularly active in promoting press freedom and the free flow of information.

The others in this group are known informally as the "big three" due to their size and worldwide influence in their areas of competence:

- The World Health Organization (WHO) is the major player in the global effort to improve health norms and standards around the world. An important part of this is carrying out research and field programs to control and eradicate disease. By working with governments, especially those in developing countries, to develop appropriate health policies and systems, WHO is central to efforts to improve health worldwide.
- The Food and Agriculture Organization (FAO) was established by the United Nations to promote agricultural development and food security, especially in rural areas of developing countries. Its research and data-collecting, and worldwide network, enable it to function as an international forum for food and agricultural issues.
- The International Labour Organization (ILO) was established in 1919 (its constitution was Part XIII of the Treaty of Versailles) and in 1946 became the first specialized agency of the United Nations. From its inception, the ILO has established and monitored standards for work-related issues that have been adopted into national legislation of almost all countries.

  By 2003 the ILO had adopted over 180 treaties, eight of which establish core norms for defining, protecting, and promoting human rights in the workplace.[30] The ILO Convention on the Worst Forms of Child Labour (1999) illustrates how norms can be established and implemented: the treaty codifies the norms; the process spreads the norms throughout legal systems around the world; signature and ratification of the treaty place these norms into national law; and treaty mechanisms, with ILO assistance and education programs, implement and monitor the standards. As of early 2004, 132 countries had ratified the convention. The International Programme on the Elimination of Child Labour (IPEC), founded in 1992, has recently received voluntary funding from twenty-five donors, has projects totaling more than $200 million under way in some seventy countries, and has created a statistical information and monitoring program.

The ILO has utilized "time-bound programs" to facilitate and evaluate progress in eradicating the worst forms of child labor. The treaty sets the standards. The ILO works with the government to build partnerships with civil society, business, and workers to meet specific goals over a set time, usually ten years, with measurable benchmarks along the way. This program began in June 2001 in El Salvador, Nepal, and Tanzania; as many as twenty countries are expected to develop such programs in the next few years.[31]

These and other agencies cooperate on such interagency projects as UNAIDS and the Codex Alimentarius:

- Founded in 1996, UNAIDS is perhaps the most visible example of a cooperative effort within the UN system, one that creates valuable guidelines and standards for the world's efforts to eradicate AIDS and operates as a catalyst and coordinator of action, rather than a direct funding or implementing agency. WHO has joined with the UN Children's Fund (UNICEF), the UN Development Programme (UNDP), the UN Population Fund (UNFPA), UNESCO, the UN Drug Control Programme (UNDCP), the ILO, and the World Bank to cosponsor UNAIDS. UNAIDS and WHO, working with medical institutions and specialists, have implemented a global, country-by-country, standardized surveillance system for tracking HIV/AIDS. World AIDS Day, December 1, is designated to raise AIDS awareness. Finally, by collecting and evaluating worldwide best practices, UNAIDS is able to inform countries of the best models available for HIV prevention.
- The Codex Alimentarius, or "food code," dates from 1961 and is a joint project of WHO and the FAO. The Codex Alimentarius Commission, while nonbinding on Member States, has played a significant role in formulating and harmonizing standards for consumers, food producers and processors, and both national food control agencies and international trade in food, including the development of codes governing hygienic processing, and makes recommendations on compliance with them. The codex standards have become a worldwide benchmark against which national food measures and regulations are evaluated.

Finally, there is one more organization to note:

- The International Atomic Agency (IAEA) is an autonomous agency that operates under the aegis of the United Nations. Its main areas of work are verification, safety, and technology. The agency develops guidelines and norms for its member countries in regard to the safety of civilian nuclear programs. It also establishes basic standards, regulations, and codes of practice for radiation protection, including in the transport of radioactive materials. The 1968 Treaty on the Nonproliferation of Nuclear Weapons, extended in 1995, calls for states party to the treaty to accept IAEA nuclear safeguards and for nonnuclear states to refrain from building nuclear weapons.

Norm-Setting on Human Rights

While Chapter 4 goes into greater detail on human rights, UN achievements in setting norms in the field of human rights have been substantial and need mention in any discussion of the UN and norms. The largest survey of public opinion ever conducted—a 1999 Gallup poll of 57,000 adults in sixty countries—showed that, worldwide, the protection of human rights was regarded as the most important task facing the United Nations. Further, the younger the respondent, the greater the importance assigned to this goal.[32]

The promotion of human rights norms in international behavior has been a primary goal of the United Nations from its inception. The major impetus for the creation of the Organization was the tragedy of World War II, which included the greatest systematic violation of human rights in recorded history: the Holocaust. The preamble to the Charter puts forth as a purpose of the United Nations "to reaffirm faith in fundamental human rights, in the dignity and worth of the human person, [and] in the equal rights of men and women," and Article 1 states that friendly relations among nations should be "based on respect for the equal rights and self-determination of peoples."

Today, virtually every organization in the UN system is involved in the protection of human rights. Indeed, when Secretary-General Kofi Annan reorganized the Secretariat into four key areas—peace and security, development, humanitarian assistance, and economic and social affairs—he designated human rights as a fifth, "crosscutting" theme that served to unify the UN's work in the four areas. However, including these human rights provisions in the Charter was not easily done, and only the active lobbying of about forty NGOs in San Francisco, strongly aided by support from Latin American delegations, persuaded the conference to include specific human rights language in the Charter.[33]

It was recognized in the early stages of the drafting of the Charter that a proposed international bill of human rights, patterned on the U.S. Bill of Rights, could not be binding on all states without effective sanctions, particularly if a state were charged with violating rights of its own citizens that were supposedly guaranteed. Historian Ruth Russell notes further:

The [drafting] subcommittee reported that it has also considered proposals that the Organization "assure" or "protect" fundamental human rights, rather than merely "promote" and "encourage respect for" them. It thought, however, that "assuring or protecting" such human rights should be primarily the concern of each state. But if such rights and freedoms were grievously outraged so as to create conditions that threaten peace or to obstruct the application of provisions of the Charter, then they cease to be the sole concern of each state.[34]

While this paragraph presages many of the issues regarding human rights that have concerned the United Nations over the years, it is significant to note that the drafting group's view was that to cease being the sole concern of the state, human rights violations had to threaten peace or obstruct the application of the Charter.

Although time alone would have made it impossible to draft an international bill of human rights at San Francisco, it was clear that the delegates were nowhere close to agreement on how to do so. It is likewise obvious that the nations assembled in San Francisco did not comprehend the potential of the language on human rights they had embedded in the Charter.

The cornerstone of contemporary human rights law was laid when the General Assembly on December 10, 1948—a day now observed worldwide as Human Rights Day—approved the Universal Declaration of Human Rights. In Articles 3 to 21 the declaration covers civil and political rights, such as the right to life, freedom from slavery and torture, the right to judicial remedy, freedom of religion, and the right to peaceful assembly and association. In Articles 22 to 27 it then enumerates economic, social, and cultural rights, including the rights to work, to form trade unions, to enjoy an adequate standard of living, and to participate in social security, education, and cultural life. The declaration was remarkable not only in its provisions, but also in its crafting of a common statement of mutual aspiration from countries with very different cultural and legal backgrounds, and at varying stages of development.

The impact over the years of the declaration has been considerable. It basically established and defined the norms the United Nations has subsequently embraced in realizing one of its great achievements: the creation of a comprehensive body of human rights law. However, as a resolution of the General Assembly, it constituted only recommendations to Member States. Much work remained to be done. As one scholar observed: "Even if human rights are thought to be inalienable, a moral attribute of persons that the state cannot contravene, rights still have to be identified—that is, constructed—by human beings and codified in legal systems."[35] The Universal Declaration of Human Rights has played this role of identifying rights; it has served as the inspiration for some eighty conventions and declarations.[36]

Since it was founded, the United Nations has devoted to the cause of human rights many of the tools at its disposal: world conferences, covenants, declarations, monitoring, technical assistance, and education. This effort has created a body of standards and norms, as well as a continuing agenda. However, the United Nations is devoid of the necessary power to enforce these standards of behavior. Many nations continue to ignore these norms, resulting in a world full of blatant violations of human rights. Thus, while there remain some lacunae in the legal structure for the protection of human rights, the overwhelming task faced by the world community is to ensure compliance with the extensive norms, treaty-based and otherwise, that are in place.

The World Conferences

For many centuries, intergovernmental conferences have taken place, frequently following wars and with a goal of defining the postwar milieu. The 1648 Peace of Westphalia, which ended the Thirty Years War, was one of the first such conferences. Other conferences in Europe focused on river navigation and health issues after international outbreaks of diseases like cholera. The Hague Conferences of 1899 and 1907 were the first to call for ongoing international legal agreements on a number of issues, including disarmament. "The Hague system introduced the concept of general long-term commitments by all states—not just important states—to restrict their behavior in order to ensure self-preservation."[37] Following World War I, the 1919 Treaty of Versailles created the League of Nations, which formally ceased to exist when the United Nations officially came into existence on October 24, 1945. The San Francisco Conference, in June 1945, established the United Nations. In the early days, these conferences were held to establish specific legal instruments. Little thought was given to utilizing the methodologies of conferences to define global problems and suggest global solutions. International leaders had not yet come to realize that, in addition to treaty-based norms, these gatherings could create other norms that were nonbinding but widely accepted. In addition, leaders could mobilize public opinion and civil society to influence states to honor the norms. Using conferences as a basis for establishing norms—identifying problems and suggesting solutions—was to become a regular practice of the United Nations.

UN Congresses on the Prevention of Crime and the Treatment of Offenders

Among the oldest and most far-ranging UN standards and norms are those in the crime prevention and criminal justice field, most of them emerging from the quinquennial UN congress on the prevention of crime and the treatment of offenders, begun in 1955. These include standards of minimum rules for the treatment of prisoners, as well as the noninstitutional treatment of offenders, treatment of juvenile delinquents, basic rights of victims of crime and abuse of power, and prevention of criminality. Basic principles have also been agreed upon for various professions, such as independence of the judiciary and the roles of prosecutors and lawyers, and model treaties have been adopted to facilitate mutual cooperation in criminal matters, the exchange of prisoners, and the transfer of criminal proceedings.

In December 2000 in Palermo, Italy, 124 of the UN's 189 Member States signed a new UN Convention Against Transnational Organized Crime, and close to 80 also endorsed two protocols on trafficking in women and children and smuggling of migrants. The rapidity with which this treaty text was completed— in less than two years—demonstrated the awareness of governments that they could not successfully combat global crime without strong new standards.

The norms and guidelines in the prevention and criminal justice field have provided a yardstick to facilitate harmonious action by states with different systems, promoted legislative reforms, and furthered regional and international cooperation against crime.[38]

The Stockholm Conference on the Human Environment

The series of global conferences that have affected so significantly the work of most parts of the UN system began with the 1972 Stockholm Conference. This conference is credited with bringing global environmental concerns "front and center" on the international agenda. It was clearly recognized by the leadership of the conference that this was the essential first step for the desired creation of new international norms for environmental issues. The foundation of the conference was the growing realization that "many of the causes and effects of environmental problems are global: this is beyond the jurisdiction and sovereignty of any nation-state. . . . Global frameworks and other institutions are necessary in order to help organize and coordinate international action."[39]

The UN Environment Programme (UNEP), which was created at Stockholm, has a central goal of focusing world attention on emerging environmental problems through research and synthesis of information leading to a number of international conventions, including: (1) the Vienna Convention for the Protection of the Ozone Layer (1985) and the Montreal Protocol (1987) and its amendments, which ban the production and sale of chlorofluorocarbons, which deplete the ozone layer; and (2) the 1992 Framework Convention on Global Climate Change, which deals with the emission of carbon dioxide and other greenhouse gases, which are largely responsible for global warming, and the 1997 Kyoto Protocol, which addresses global warming. The scientific basis of global warming has been firmly established by the work of the Intergovernmental Panel on Climate Change, which was organized by UNEP and the World Meteorological Organization in 1988 and which constitutes a worldwide network of 2,500 scientists and experts. The 1992 UN Convention on Biodiversity and the 2000 protocol dealing with the safe use of genetically modified organisms have established norms in this area of growing international concern.

Over the years, the international community has also increasingly recognized that environmental issues can have consequences for general global security and should be accorded a corresponding significance. For instance, local environmental problems such as urbanization, deforestation, and natural resource scarcity can exacerbate underlying ethnic and social tensions and produce refugee flows. Recognition has grown that environmental degradation can have a significant negative effect on political, economic, and social progress in developing countries. For example, desertification, the process of degrading usable land into unproductive desert (caused by overgrazing and clear-cutting forests), removes large areas of land each year from productive development.

The success at Stockholm set a process in motion that led to, among other things, conferences in the 1970s on population (1974), human settlements (1976), primary healthcare (1978), and science and technology for development (1979). UN-sponsored conferences in the 1980s focused on aging (1982), women (1980 and 1985), population (1984), and drug abuse and trafficking (1987).[40]

Increasingly, the developing countries, which numerically dominate the United Nations, have insisted that these conferences be firmly linked to development, and that the agendas and the plans of action emanating from them be organized around this linkage, including significant provisions for transfer of resources.

UN World Conferences in the 1990s
The major global conferences of the 1990s included:

World Summit for Children, New York, United States (1990)
World Conference on Education for All, Jomtien, Thailand (1990)
UN Conference on Environment and Development, Rio de Janeiro, Brazil (1992)
World Conference on Human Rights, Vienna, Austria (1993)
World Conference on Population and Development, Cairo, Egypt (1994)
World Summit for Social Development, Copenhagen, Denmark (1995)
Fourth World Conference on Women, Beijing, China (1995)
Second UN Conference on Human Settlements, Istanbul, Turkey (1996)
World Food Summit, Rome, Italy (1996)

A gathering at the 1997 Ottawa Convention under Canadian auspices produced a treaty on the use of landmines; in 1998 a UN-sponsored conference in Rome produced the ICC statute; and the conference in Kyoto produced the 1997 protocol. A global conference focused on racism took place in Durban, South Africa, in 2001,[41] and the United Nations conference on Financing for

Development was held in Mexico in March 2002. The World Summit on Sustainable Development took place in Johannesburg in September 2002.

The broadened definition of development, which emanated from the global conferences of the 1990s, has led to an emerging consensus "that economic development, social development, and environmental protection are interdependent and mutually reinforcing components of what is now commonly termed 'sustainable development.' . . . The themes of each conference . . . are all interrelated, integral pieces of the jigsaw that makes up sustainable development."[42]

UN world conferences serve the building of global norms in a number of ways:

1. They attract media attention to the issue, which allows the consciousness-raising message on new norms to spread to concerned individuals and groups and to the general public.
2. They provide a forum for reaching consensus on universal standards. The conference sessions and preparatory meetings bring together ideas that are continuously refined until, in most cases, agreement is reached.
3. Their declarations provide a moral authority that strengthens grassroots efforts to build support for normative behavior. Declarations set the new norms of behavior as standards.
4. They bring into the process the power of civil society, not only to shape norms but also to provide a constituency for consent and implementation. The involvement of NGOs throughout the process inserts normative ideas into the agreements, and with this sense of ownership NGO representatives take them home for promotion.
5. They offer language through the declarations that can be used in the eventual codification of international norms in the form of treaties and conventions, and in the codification of national laws adopted by parliaments.

UNICEF's Experience in Implementation

Perhaps no example better illustrates the value of setting goals and then rigorously measuring progress toward meeting those objectives than that of UNICEF following the World Summit for Children in 1990. Prior to the summit, UNICEF had launched a "Child Survival and Development Revolution," which addressed the major causes of child mortality. UNICEF built on the widespread success of this initiative by adopting at the summit additional goals for improving the lot of children in the 1990s.[43]

This process demonstrates a "best case scenario" of a successful UN effort. Research and field experience combine to define the problem and outline reachable solutions. When intergovernmental mechanisms come into play, leaders must avoid setting goals at the lowest common denominator if their decisions are to have any value. In the case of UNICEF, it was just the opposite: The goals were very ambitious and were also expressed in quantitative and measurable terms. These goals became the basis for national plans of action, with the relevant agencies and programs providing advice in drafting or revising the plans, technical assistance in implementing them, and where available, funding. Targets were set—Richard Jolly, former acting director of UNICEF, characterizes them as "baseline human goals"—and over subsequent years assessments were made of progress toward goals undertaken.[44]

General norms were set on health and education for children, and promoting equality for boys and girls. Specifically, the eradication of polio was a major goal, one toward which there has been significant progress. Preventive medicine is also promulgated through immunization, providing vitamin supplements and clean water, promoting breast-feeding, and training community health workers to provide prenatal care and hygienic delivery practices.

Nongovernmental Organizations: Civil Society

While NGOs have played a role in the UN's activities since the San Francisco Conference in 1945, it was, with some exceptions, a relatively marginal role—with most UN Member States happy to keep it that way—until the advent of UN global conferences. About 300 NGOs were present at the Stockholm Conference, whose subject was the environment, in 1972. By 1992 in Rio, at the Earth Summit, that number had grown to 1,400.[45] NGOs, particularly those oriented toward advocacy, have been essential parts of the preparations for and follow-up to the conferences, as well as being active participants in the hour-by-hour unfolding of events as they progress. As a result, NGOs are playing an increasing role in the permanent UN organs and bodies that focus on social and economic issues. They are also central to building support for and monitoring the implementation of UN decisions. At the Earth Summit, NGOs organized their own parallel conference, the "NGO Forum," a few miles away from the official intergovernmental gathering. Many NGO representatives moved back and forth between the two, carrying ideas and progress reports. NGO secretariats operated like think tanks on environmental issues, preparing data analyses and statistics on environmental problems under discussion.

After Rio, the tradition of holding an NGO forum parallel to the official meeting became the norm. NGOs like Parliamentarians for Global Action (PGA), an organization of members of parliament (MPs) from some 100 countries, have a leg in both the NGO forums and the intergovernmental meetings because the MPs are members of the PGA and also frequently official members of governmental delegations. At the Social Summit in Copenhagen (1995), the PGA carefully wrote language for the official declaration that was hand-carried by the MPs into the official discussions. Other NGOs were busy doing the same thing.

Indeed, it is hard to imagine the recommendations of the global conferences coming to fruition without the leadership, rather than just the participation, of civil society. This view is not always shared by diplomats, especially
as regards policymaking at world conferences. Most diplomats would prefer
NGOs to present their views quietly, let the diplomats decide on their fate, and
then aid governments in implementation with their direct constituencies. But
to embrace this attitude is, truly, to live in another world. Today's problems
are simply too large and complex for governments to solve by themselves.[46]

Spurred on by the global conferences has been the creation of what Secretary-General Kofi Annan has termed "global policy networks." He states:
"These networks—or coalitions for change—bring together international institutions, civil society, private sector organizations, and national governments in
pursuit of common goals." They "help set global policy agendas, frame debates
and raise public consciousness . . . they make it easier to reach consensus and
negotiate agreements on new global standards, as well as to create new kinds
of mechanisms for implementing and monitoring these agreements."[47]

An example of this kind of network is the Coalition for the International
Criminal Court, which established a clearinghouse for NGO advocacy work
on the Court. This pooling of effort and ideas keeps concerned NGOs
informed of one another's work through a real-time network utilizing the
Internet and e-mail.

Boutros Boutros-Ghali's Observation
The sixth Secretary-General of the United Nations has observed:

> The UN world summits of the 1990s emerged as a wholly new factor for
> achieving change on the world stage. A bitter critic of these conferences
> described them accurately: "UN meetings are not just talkathons. They are
> opportunities to seed international law with new norms and rights, many of
> them hidden in apparently routine language. Though not immediately bind-
> ing on any nation, after some time they may be cited as 'customary' inter-
> national law and acquire some legal force. . . . UN conferences now have a
> precise use in hardball international politics." Although some have criticized
> the conferences as a way of circumventing national parliamentary or con-
> gressional politics, they were in fact democratic in a larger sense and the
> beginning of a new form of people's control of their own destinies on issues
> too large or too suppressed by special interests to be handled by domestic
> national politics.[48]

Those who are fearful of having to support financially and politically the
emerging norms on such matters as human rights, population control, and sustainable development, foresee and often fear the consequences of these norms
taking hold. But as Boutros Boutros-Ghali states, these gatherings are the
closest we have come to global democracy.

The United Nations and Terrorism

The United Nations reacted quickly and decisively to the attacks on the United States on September 11, 2001, the opening day of the fifty-sixth General Assembly. The Secretary-General immediately condemned them in the strongest terms. The Security Council met within twenty-four hours of the collapse of New York City's Twin Towers to consider and approve unanimously a French-drafted resolution "that would define the framework for the international response to the terrorist attacks."[49] Resolution 1368 said that the attacks posed a "threat to international peace and security" and called on the world community "to combat by all means" this threat, thus raising the possibility of Chapter VII enforcement action and clearly sanctioning the use of military force. Jeffrey Laurenti observes: "Never before had the Council recognized military 'self-defense' as applicable against actions perpetrated by non-state actors."[50]

On September 28, a second resolution (1373) was adopted unanimously by the Council, one that Laurenti states "astonished international law experts with its boldness in requiring specific actions of Member States in their domestic legislation in order to combat the threat the Council identified to international peace and security."[51] Resolution 1373 created for states a new legal obligation to cooperate against terrorism, including in bringing the perpetrators, organizers, and sponsors of terrorism to justice. It stressed the accountability of those aiding, supporting, or harboring those responsible for acts of terrorism. The Council established its Counter-Terrorism Committee and required that all UN Member States submit national reports on their actions to ensure the full implementation of the resolution.

Prior to September 11, the main thrust of United Nations action against terrorism had been the drafting and adoption by the UN and its specialized agencies of a network of international legal instruments related to such topics as aircraft hijacking, hostage taking, the physical protection of nuclear material, actions threatening maritime safety, and plastic explosives.[52] In addition, UN efforts had already begun to formulate both a comprehensive convention against terrorism as well as a convention against nuclear terrorism.

An aspect of the Security Council resolutions that is especially interesting as regards treaty-based norms is raised by the fact that some binding provisions in resolution 1373 were taken from the 1997 Convention for the Suppression of Terrorist Bombing and the 1999 Convention for the Suppression of the Financing of Terrorism. The first is in force, but with only twenty-nine ratifications; the second has only four ratifications and is not in force. "The Council's action made these provisions effective immediately for all states, not just those that choose to ratify [the two conventions]."[53] Following the Security Council's actions, the General Assembly devoted a week to a previously scheduled debate on terrorism. One hundred sixty-eight representatives and observers spoke, the most ever to address an agenda item.

The Terrorism Prevention Branch of the UN Office for Drug Control and Crime Prevention was founded in April 1999 to carry out research and facilitate technical cooperation. To date, the branch has focused on analysis; it maintains an extensive database on terrorist incidents and related information. A global terrorism survey is under way, and the branch has been mandated by the Crime Commission to assist Member States in the promotion and implementation of UN conventions against terrorism.

The current and pending treaties and protocols are the basis for the UN's norms and standards in the battle against terrorism. The actions of the Security Council have provided both a framework for the international response to terrorist attacks and international legitimacy for that response. And the prompt and unanimous response by UN Member States has created a strong international consensus, which the former chairman of the Counter-Terrorism Committee, Sir Jeremy Greenstock (UK), stated must be nurtured and translated into global participation if the international effort against terrorism is to succeed.[54]

Globalization

The United Nations has been constantly evolving to meet the challenges of a world in perpetual flux. However, this ability to respond to a new situation is being challenged as never before by globalization, which is described as "an inevitable, technologically driven process that is increasing commercial and political relations among people of different countries."[55]

Through advances in technology and telecommunications and the fall of trade barriers, material goods, information, money, and ideas move around the world at an unprecedented speed and volume. For example, the transfer of "back office" information technology facilities to India in recent years has enriched a significant number of that country's citizens. In contrast, the globalization of financial markets severely exacerbated the Asian financial crisis of 1997–1998. The swift flight of capital away from countries in Southeast Asia thrust millions of people into poverty almost overnight. In Indonesia, for instance, following the financial crisis, poverty levels rocketed from 8.6 percent to 19.2 percent.[56]

An inextricable part of globalization has been the growing insistence from developed donor countries that a market-based economy is the sine qua non of economic development. Indeed, for many, insistence on market-based economies is inextricably linked to democratic systems of governance. The problem with this is clear: Globalization and market-based economics treat both countries and people quite unequally. As globalization takes hold, the gap between the wealthy and the poor, both among and within countries, is widening rather than narrowing. Globalization is most certainly *not* a tide that raises all ships. Rolf Bruer of the Deutsche Bank observed: "We have learned, however, that uncontrolled market forces left to build up or destroy in their own, almost instinctive manner, may not, in fact, be capable of making globalization work for everyone."[57] Nearly half the world's 6 billion people must live on less than $2 each day. Some 1.2 billion—500 million of whom live in South Asia and 300 million in Africa—struggle to survive on less than $1 daily.[58] Globalization may, in the future, contribute significantly to the livelihood of these desperate people, but to date it has done very little to help them.

Secretary-General Annan has addressed extensively the challenge of globalization and the role the United Nations can play in establishing norms that will ameliorate its negative impacts. He states, "The problem is this: The spread of markets outpaces the ability of societies and their political systems to adjust to them, let alone to guide the course they take. . . . Globalization operates on Internet time." He has argued that development should be placed at the heart of globalization, rather than globalization being allowed to determine the fate of development.[59]

To help close this gap, the Secretary-General proposed the Global Compact. Following a series of consultations, the compact was launched in July 2000 with senior executives from some fifty major companies, along with leaders of labor, human rights, the environment, and development organizations. The compact is not a regulatory instrument or code of conduct; it utilizes transparency and dialogue to identify and disseminate best practices. This has indeed been a source of criticism from some who argue that there should be a binding code on corporations. But until the UN is in a position to monitor and enforce such a code, guiding principles may be the best avenue for now.

The Global Compact encompasses nine principles, drawn from the Universal Declaration of Human Rights, the ILO's Fundamental Principles for Rights at Work, and the Rio Principles on Environment and Development:

- support and respect for the protection of internationally proclaimed human rights,
- noncomplicity in human rights abuses,
- freedom of association and the effective recognition of the right to collective bargaining,
- the elimination of all forms of forced and compulsory labor,
- the effective abolition of child labor,
- the elimination of discrimination in respect of employment and occupation,
- a precautionary approach to environmental challenges,
- greater environmental responsibility, and
- encouragement of the development and diffusion of environmentally friendly technologies.[60]

The Global Compact is but one part of what must be an intensive, continuing effort by the entire UN system to meet the challenge of globalization. Through its nine principles, and building on existing strategies and methods, the compact illustrates well how the UN system can develop norms and standards for today's world.

Conclusion

This chapter has clearly established the critical function of norms, standards, and goals in the UN system, in which they are pervasive throughout. In some areas, such as human rights, they are well publicized and known. In others, such as the standard-setting and monitoring done by the specialized agencies, they are largely unknown and unappreciated.

It is useful to visualize these norms as a spectrum, ranging from treaties legally binding on those states that ratify them, to broad, largely rhetorical goals. Within this spectrum, there is a broad array of methods available to the UN system to facilitate its work. Creating new norms, refining existing ones, and elaborating the regimes created to enforce and sustain them are continuing tasks. The goal is no less than to bring some order to what may be, in the absence of standards, a confusing, even chaotic, international landscape.

The continuing elaboration of norms does not, however, mean that more and more of them are being honored. One of the most striking and discouraging characteristics of today's world is the extent to which agreed-upon norms and standards are ignored and contravened. Why is this the case? Obviously, sovereign nations seek to maximize achievement of their policy goals. While many try to do so within the framework of treaty regimes, others do not. In the absence of treaty regimes, checks on state behavior are lessened. As Olara Otunnu, Special Representative of the Secretary-General for Children and Armed Conflict, noted: "The international community has done very well in terms of developing and elaborating norms, standards, and rules against the use of child soldiers. But where we have not been effective is their application on the ground. Words on paper do not save a child in war."[61]

The tools available to the UN system in its search for greater adherence to global norms are, as noted, numerous. The UN system establishes norms and standards and seeks to persuade and, on occasion, pressure states into honoring them. However, it cannot force them to do so. Rather, state behavior is monitored and evaluated, and other states and public opinion are enlisted to encourage adherence. The most promising mechanism available to UN agencies and programs is systematic monitoring of adherence to time-bound quantitative goals that states have agreed to, as shown in the UNICEF and ILO examples. A critical element in this process is the provision of assistance to states to aid them in living up to the norms and standards they have accepted. However, the shortage of human and financial resources severely limits the ability of the UN system to provide assistance to developing countries to help them meet their commitments.

Over the last three decades, the series of UN-sponsored global conferences has given a major impetus to the identification, analysis, and solution of global problems, including the formation of new global norms. These conferences have also significantly broadened the role of nongovernmental organizations, which have a critical role in helping to produce, interpret, and press for enforcement of norms arising from them. At the same time, the Secretaries-General of the United Nations have emerged as a significantly more important factor in developing and advocating norms and standards. Boutros-Ghali's *Agenda for Peace* and *Agenda for Development* and Kofi Annan's far-reaching proposals in *We the Peoples* are landmarks.

The UN system has faced no greater challenge in the economic and social arenas than that posed by globalization. To be successful in the years ahead, the United Nations must play a central role in establishing norms that will ameliorate the negative impact of globalization and, through such devices as the Global Compact, help make globalization work for all the world's people.

Notes

1. Gro Harlem Bruntland, interview with *Foreign Policy*, January–February 2002, p. 26.

2. The UN system is made up of the six principal organs—the General Assembly, the Security Council, the Economic and Social Council, the Trusteeship Council (which is inactive), the International Court of Justice, and the Secretariat—the various programs, funds, and offices (such as the UN Children's Fund and the UN Development Programme), and the specialized agencies.

3. See Hedley Bull, *The Anarchical Society: A Study of Order in World Politics* (New York: Columbia University Press, 1977), p. 56.

4. See Stephen Korner, *Kant* (New Haven, Conn.: Yale University Press, 1982).

5. Tobias Decibel, "Strengthening the UN as an Effective World Authority: Cooperative Security Versus Hegemonic Crisis Management," *Global Governance* 6, no. 1 (2000): 30–31.

6. Ambassador Vladlen Martynov, Russian academician and director of the Institute of World Economy and International Relations, in *United Nations Chronicle* 2002, no. 2 (a quarterly magazine), p. 18.

7. Thomas M. Franck, ed., *Delegating State Powers: The Effect of Treaty Regimes on Democracy and Sovereignty* (Ardsley, N.Y.: Transnational, 2000), p. 12.

8. See Jean Krasno, *The Founding of the United Nations: International Cooperation as an Evolutionary Process* (New Haven, Conn.: Academic Council on the United Nations System, 2001).

9. Nina Schou, "Instances of Human Rights Regimes," in Franck, *Delegating State Powers,* pp. 210–211.

10. Christopher C. Joyner, *The United Nations and International Law* (Cambridge: Cambridge University Press, 1997), pp. 435–436.

11. Ruth Russell, *A History of the United Nations Charter: The Role of the United States, 1940–45* (Washington, D.C.: Brookings Institution, 1958). This is the definitive work on the creation of the Charter and the San Francisco Conference.

12. *Basic Facts About the United Nations* (New York: United Nations Department of Public Information, 2000), p. 259. This publication is a valuable source of information about the structure and programs of the various parts of the UN system.

13. Charlotte Ku, *Global Governance and the Changing Face of International Law* (New Haven, Conn.: Academic Council on the United Nations System. 2001), p. 7.

14. Ibid., p. 35.

15. This is, of course, the well-known "veto." Over the years, there has been a de facto amendment of this provision; the Council now takes decisions when a permanent member abstains from the vote, thus replacing the requirement for concurrence with one of nonopposition.

16. There is a sizable literature on UN peacekeeping, much of it devoted to suggestions for improving it. See particularly the publications of the International Peace Academy. *Blue Helmets: A Review of United Nations Peace-Keeping,* 3rd ed. (New York: United Nations, 1996), is the most comprehensive record of the UN peacekeeping operations.

17. Kristan Boon, "Instances of International Criminal Courts," in Franck, *Delegating State Powers,* p. 174.

18. See www.uncc.org for detailed information about the UNCC and a comprehensive bibliography.

19. Joyner, *United Nations and International Law,* p. 443.

20. Ibid., p. 446.

21. *Basic Facts,* pp. 238–240.

22. Krasno, *Founding of the United Nations,* p. 31.

23. The annual report of the Secretary-General on the work of the Organization is published each September by the Department of Public Information, New York. It is also a General Assembly document, as consideration of the report is an agenda item at the Assembly session.

24. Boutros Boutros-Ghali, *An Agenda for Peace 1995,* 2nd ed. (New York: United Nations Department of Public Information, 1995). This edition contains the text of the report as well as relevant documents and statements.

25. Boutros Boutros-Ghali, *An Agenda for Development* (New York: United Nations Department of Public Information, 1995), p. 12.

26. *We the Peoples: The Role of the United Nations in the Twenty-First Century* (New York: United Nations Department of Public Information, 2000), p. 6.

27. See Wilder Foote, ed., *The Servants of Peace: A Selection of the Speeches and Statements of Dag Hammarskjöld* (London: Bodley Head, 1962).

28. Address by the Secretary-General to the General Assembly, September 20, 1999. A/54/PV.4, pp. 1–4.

29. *Basic Facts* has useful summaries of the specialized agencies and International Atomic Energy Agency, including contact points at each for additional information. Much of what follows is drawn from this publication.

30. See *Basic Facts,* p. 231. The eight are:

(i)   Treaty on Forced Labour (1930), which requires the suppression of forced or compulsory labor in all its forms.

(ii)   Treaty on Freedom of Association and Protection of the Right to Organize (1948), which establishes the right of workers and employers to form and join organizations of their own choosing without prior authorization and lays down guarantees for the free functioning of such organizations.

(iii) Treaty on the Right to Organize and Collective Bargaining (1949), which provides for protection against antiunion discrimination, for protection of workers' and employers' organizations, and for measures to promote collective bargaining.

(iv) Treaty on the Abolition of Forced Labour (1957), which prohibits the use of any form of forced or compulsory labor as a means of political coercion or education, and punishment for the expression of political or ideological views, or for participation in strikes.

(v) Treaty on Equal Remuneration (1951), which calls for equal pay and benefits for work of equal value.

(vi) Treaty on Discrimination (1958), which calls for national policies to promote equality of opportunity and treatment, and to eliminate discrimination in the workplace on the grounds of race, color, sex, religion, political opinion, national extraction, or social origin.

(vii) Treaty on Minimum Age (1973), which aims at the abolition of child labor, stipulating that the minimum age for employment shall not be less than the age of completion of compulsory schooling.

(viii) Treaty on Worst Forms of Child Labour (1999), which prohibits child slavery, debt bondage, prostitution, pornography, dangerous work, and forcible recruitment for armed conflict.

31. *Eliminating the Worst Forms of Child Labour: An Integrated, Time-Bound Approach* (Geneva: International Labour Organization, 1999).

32. *We the Peoples*, pp. 15–16.

33. See Clark M. Eichelberger, *UN: The First Twenty Years* (New York: Harper and Row, 1965), pp. 69–70.

34. Russell, *History of the United Nations Charter*, p. 780.

35. David P. Forsythe, *Human Rights in International Relations* (New York: Cambridge University Press, 2000), p. 3. Quoted in Mohammed Ayoob, "Humanitarian Intervention and International Society," *Global Governance* 7, no. 3 (July–September 2001): 226.

36. *Basic Facts*, p. 213. This publication's summary of the UN's efforts regarding human rights (pp. 215–241) is especially useful. See also www.unhcr.ch.

37. See Ku, *Global Governance*, p. 14.

38. See *Compendium of United Nations Standards and Norms in Crime Prevention* (New York: United Nations, 1992).

39. Diane Bui, "The Instance of Environmental Regimes," in Franck, *Delegating State Powers*, p. 33.

40. There is a list of selected UN conference dates from 1947 to 1996 in Michael Schechter, ed., *United Nations–Sponsored World Conferences* (Tokyo: United Nations University Press, 2001), p. 4.

41. The controversy surrounding the Durban conference—with the United States walking out in protest, largely over attacks against Israel—points up the downside of such conferences. John Manley, foreign minister of Canada, observed: "It hasn't been a good experience for the world community. It has not been a good experience for the United Nations and I hope we don't have to see this happen again." However, some felt the outcome was helpful. Reed Brody, director of advocacy for Human Rights Watch, stated: "If governments would really put into place what they agreed to here,

the world would be a much better place." Rachel L. Swarns, *New York Times*, September 10, 2001, p. A10.

42. Masumi Ono, "From Consensus-Building to Implementation: The Follow-Up to the UN Global Conferences of the 1990s," in Schechter, *United Nations–Sponsored World Conferences*, pp. 169–171.

43. Richard Jolly, "Implementing Global Goals for Children: Lessons from UNICEF Experience," in Schechter, *United Nations–Sponsored World Conferences*, pp. 10–28.

44. See Jolly's valuable list of eleven factors explaining the success of UNICEF's efforts, in ibid., pp. 21–27.

45. See Ku, *Global Governance*, p. 30.

46. For a detailed account of the role of NGOs before, during, and after one major global conference, the UN World Conference on Human Rights in 1993, see Clarence J. Dias, "The United Nations World Conference on Human Rights: Evaluation, Monitoring, and Review," in Schechter, *United Nations–Sponsored World Conferences*, pp. 29–62.

47. *We the Peoples*, pp. 70–71.

48. Boutros Boutros-Ghali, *Unvanquished: A U.S.-U.N. Saga* (New York: Random House, 1999), pp. 174–175.

49. Jeffrey Laurenti, "Terrorist Attacks Yield New United Nations Roles," *The Inter Dependent* (publication of the United Nations Association of the United States of America) 27, no. 3 (Fall 2001): 5.

50. Ibid.

51. Ibid.

52. See *Basic Facts*, pp. 270–271, for a complete list of these conventions and protocols.

53. Laurenti, "Terrorist Attacks," p. 6.

54. Press conference at UN headquarters, New York, January 10, 2002.

55. Mark Weisbrot, *Globalization: A Primer* (Washington, D.C.: Center for Economic and Policy Research, 1999) p. 1.

56. Ibid., p. 6.

57. Rolf E. Bruer, chief executive officer of the Deutsche Bank, speaking on October 23, 2001, at the American Institute for Contemporary German Studies, available at www.unglobalcompact.org.

58. *We the Peoples*, p. 19.

59. Excerpts from speeches given by Secretary-General Kofi Annan between January 1999 and July 2000, cited by *The Globalist*, available at www.theglobalist.com.

60. See www.unglobalcompact.org.

61. Quoted in Norimitsu Onishi, *New York Times*, May 9, 2000, p. A8.

PART 2

ENGAGING HUMAN
NEEDS ON A GLOBAL SCALE

4

Human Rights:
A Global Common Interest

Charles Norchi

In the wake of World War II and with the Holocaust fresh in their minds, delegates to the United Nations San Francisco Conference in 1945 took into consideration that the manner in which a government treated its own people on its own soil may no longer be its own business. The constitutive document of the new organization, the United Nations Charter, reaffirmed "faith in fundamental human rights, in the dignity and worth of the human person, in the equal rights of men and women and of nations large and small."[1] Its goal of saving "succeeding generations from the scourge of war" would require preventing broad assaults on human dignity. The Charter provided for a human rights commission and by virtue of activities in other Charter and treaty-based organs, the new United Nations would become the driving force in building an international human rights culture for the widest fulfillment of human dignity. As former UN High Commissioner for Human Rights Mary Robinson observed, "The human person is at the centre of everything the United Nations does. . . . We can all make a difference by becoming aware of how the different parts of the international human rights system seek to encourage the implementation of internationally agreed standards, where they matter, in the daily lives of people."[2]

Global discourse is gripped by the sounds of voices expressing diverse perspectives about the promotion, application, and evolution of human rights norms. These are genuine. They are not the haranguings of the fringes of society, but are pleas for full participation in the human rights system on respectful terms. To neglect these calls is to give sustenance to spoilers in the global human rights agenda. This chapter is intended as a contribution toward greater awareness of human rights goals.

Long before the San Francisco Conference, human beings were demanding respect for human dignity. Contemporary demands for human rights from across the globe derive from enduring features of humankind's great traditions, religions, and philosophies. They are markers in the historical trend of movements for human freedom spanning centuries.

Human rights are "rising common demands,"[3] among them the demand to be free from torture, the demand for the right to associate with other human beings, the demand to express what is on one's mind, the demand to freely believe or not believe, and the demand for freedom from despotic tyranny, both political and religious. These calls for human dignity were preludes to the founding of the United Nations.

The formulation of common demands as *claims* to human dignity and the authoritative protection of those claims is the essence of human rights in the UN system. Common demands for human dignity became authoritative claims under the UN, which became the formal arena where those claims were asserted and deprivations of dignity might be remedied. In 2002 the highest-ranking UN official tasked with working to protect human dignity explained, "Human rights have universal ownership; we must make this rhetoric a reality."[4]

The United Nations Charter

The framing of the UN Charter was a revolutionary moment in international law. Where previously international law provided little protection to citizens of a state against that state, the framers of the Charter recognized evolving demands for human rights, postulating and prescribing new protections of fundamental rights of the individual against his or her own state. At the San Francisco Conference, approximately forty nongovernmental organizations (NGOs) pressed the delegates to include human rights language in the draft.

The resulting UN Charter is remarkable for its expression of world community demands for the affirmation of human dignity. This constitutive document of the UN organization is animated by commitments to "reaffirm faith in fundamental human rights, in the dignity of and worth of the human person, in the equal rights of men and women and of nations large and small," and hence to "practice tolerance and live together in peace with one another as good neighbors" and "to employ international machinery for the promotion of the economic and social advancement of all peoples." Thus, among the primary goals of the United Nations are "to develop friendly relations among nations based on respect for the principle of equal rights and self-determination of people . . . and to achieve international cooperation in solving international problems of an economic, social, cultural or humanitarian character, and in promoting and encouraging respect for human rights and for fundamental freedoms for all without distinction as to race, sex, language or religion" (Article 1). Further, the Charter imposes duties upon Member States to promote "universal respect for, and observance of, human rights and fundamental freedoms for all without distinction as to race, sex, language or religion," toward the "creation of conditions of stability and well-being which are necessary for peaceful and friendly relations among nations based on respect for the principle of equal rights and self-determination of peoples" (Article 55).

The Charter authorizes certain UN organs to address human rights problems. Article 13 provides that the General Assembly "shall initiate studies and make recommendations for the purpose of promoting international cooperation in the economic, social, cultural, educational and health fields, and assisting in the realization of human rights and fundamental freedoms for all without distinction as to race, sex, language or religion." The Economic and Social Council, pursuant to Article 64, "may make arrangements with the members of the United Nations and with the specialized agencies to obtain reports on the steps taken to give effect to its own recommendations and to recommendations on matters falling within its competence made by the General Assembly," and further "may communicate its observations on these reports to the General Assembly." Also, Article 73 imposes special human rights obligations upon Member States, "which have or assume responsibilities for the administration of territories whose peoples have not yet attained a full measure of self-government"; these are obligations of trusteeship.[5]

The United Nations Charter, like any constitutive document, is organic. Beyond mandating the creation of a human rights commission, the Charter did not stipulate which actions would enable the UN to fulfill its primary purpose of "promoting and encouraging respect for human rights." This was left to UN practices and procedures as they evolved. But the Charter gave new voice to ongoing demands for human rights and thus made possible extensive promotional activity and new human rights prescriptions. Soon after the San Francisco Conference, those demands received new authoritative expression in a paramount global pronouncement, the Universal Declaration of Human Rights (UDHR).

An International Bill of Rights

The Universal Declaration of Human Rights reflects the claims of humanity in a community of states and is the centerpiece of the International Bill of Human Rights, which also consists of the International Covenant on Economic, Social, and Cultural Rights, and the International Covenant on Civil and Political Rights and its two optional protocols. The Commission on Human Rights became a principal human rights policymaking body in the UN system. The commission's first task was to draft an international bill of human rights in which basic rights and freedoms would be defined. The commission, comprising eighteen Member States, held its first plenary session in January 1947 with Eleanor Roosevelt, the widow of U.S. president Franklin Roosevelt, as its chair. Other important players who advanced the early human rights standard-setting of the commission were Rene Cassin of France, Charles Malik of Lebanon, Peng Chun Chang of China, Hernan Santa Cruz of

Chile, Alexandre Bogomolov and Alexei Pavlov of the Soviet Union, Lord Duekeston and Geoffrey Wilson of the United Kingdom, William Hodgson of Australia, and John Humphrey of Canada.

The challenge for the members of the commission was to translate demands for the fulfillment of values into an authoritative text that would recognize claims to human rights, many of which conflicted with the claims of states. They worked with the belief that an international bill of human rights could achieve the status of global prescription in a world of ideological and cultural variation. The drafting committee prepared two documents. One was in the form of a declaration that set forth general principles and standards of international human rights. The other document was in the form of a convention, or treaty, that defined specific rights and their limitations.

In 1948 the Cold War was heating up and decolonization was on the horizon. That year, in the newly built Palais de Chaillot in Paris, the UDHR was presented to the fifty-six Member States of the United Nations General Assembly. Every word and clause was scrutinized and parsed in 1,400 rounds of voting. Finally on December 10, 1948, forty-eight states voted in favor,

UN Photo 23783

Eleanor Roosevelt examines a Universal Declaration of Human Rights poster, November 1949.

eight abstained. It was a historic achievement and important moment in the development of international human rights.

The language of the UDHR specifies the centrality of human dignity as the fundamental goal of the international system, beginning with its preamble as adopted and proclaimed by the General Assembly: "Whereas, recognition of the inherent dignity and of the equal and inalienable rights of all members of the human family is the foundation of freedom, justice and peace in the world." The thirty articles of the UDHR (see this chapter's appendix) are an expression of the human pursuit of universal values. In a world of vast cultural distinctions, the UDHR is best approached initially using values as a map rather than concepts that may be bound and circumscribed by particular legal traditions.

The entire declaration is animated by the value of respect, beginning with Article 1, which holds that "All human beings are born free and equal in dignity and rights. They are endowed with reason and conscience and should act towards one another in a spirit of brotherhood." Many articles address the value of power as rightfully pursued by individuals and as exercised by states against people. Thus the UDHR guarantees the rights of life, liberty, and security of the person; recognition and equal protection before the law; recourse to national courts; fair and impartial criminal trials; presumption of innocence in a criminal trial; freedom of movement within and right of return to one's country; right of asylum; right to a nationality; and right to participate in the governance of one's country. Other articles address values and demands relating to the power of the state and the well-being of the person. Hence slavery and torture are declared unlawful, as is arbitrary arrest and detention. Arbitrary interference with a person's privacy and home is prohibited. Freedom of thought, conscience, and religion is guaranteed. The demands for affection are addressed in the right to marriage and the right to freely associate. Demands for enlightenment are addressed in guarantees of freedom to hold opinions and to receive and impart information and ideas through any media regardless of frontiers. The rights to an education, to participate in cultural life, to enjoy the arts, and to share in scientific advancements are all guaranteed in the declaration. Values of well-being, wealth, and skill are expressed in the guarantee to a right to work. Other demands for well-being are addressed in the right to social security and the right to rest and leisure. The values of wealth in association with well-being are addressed in the right to an adequate standard of living, and special protections for motherhood and childhood born in or out of wedlock. Wealth as a value is addressed in the right to own property alone as well as in association with others, and the arbitrary deprivation of property is prohibited.

The articles of the declaration became prescriptive as the international system evolved. In 1948, most of the language was merely aspirational, as acknowledged by the General Assembly in the preamble of the UDHR:

> This Universal Declaration of Human Rights as a common standard of achievement for all peoples and all nations, to the end that every individual and every organ of society, keeping this Declaration constantly in mind, shall strive by teaching and education to promote respect for these rights and freedoms and by progressive measures, national and international, to secure their universal and effective recognition and observance, both among the peoples of Member States themselves and among the peoples of territories under their jurisdiction.

The UDHR's gradual acceptance by states marked a transition in international relations "from Hobbes to Locke in the sense that states were to do more than merely use or threaten force to repress humanity's evil impulses: they were to follow positive standards that would permit the pursuit of other legitimate purposes."[6]

In the UDHR preamble the UN General Assembly proclaimed the declaration as "a common standard of achievement for all peoples and all nations . . . to promote respect for these rights and freedoms . . . to secure their universal and effective recognition and observance." Although a respected scholar has written that the Universal Declaration, "in formal terms, is not legally binding, but possesses only moral and political force,"[7] this is not the generally accepted view. The more general view is that the UDHR is an authoritative interpretation of the UN Charter, and that it is customary international law, or in general terms, an accepted standard of behavior.[8]

In support of the view that the Universal Declaration of Human Rights is customary international law, Oscar Schachter pointed to the following factors:

- incorporation of human rights provisions in many national constitutions and laws;
- frequent references in United Nations resolutions and declarations to the "duty" of all states to observe faithfully the Universal Declaration of Human Rights;
- resolutions of the United Nations and other international bodies condemning specific human rights violations as violations of international law;
- statements by national officials criticizing other states for serious human rights violations;
- a dictum of the International Court of Justice that obligations *erga omnes* in international law include those derived "from the principles and rules concerning the basic rights of the human person" (ICJ Barcelona Traction, 1970); and
- some decisions in various national courts that refer to the Universal Declaration as a source of standards for judicial decision.[9]

Thus there is clear evidence that the document, by virtue of the demands of individuals and intense promotion of the standards expressed in it, is widely accepted as authoritative and that the UDHR is the constitutive text of the global public order and a statement of the goals of the world community. It has been called a Magna Carta for all humanity.[10]

The Security Council

Nearly every UN body and agency performs a human rights function. The Security Council is particularly important as it is responsible for international peace and security, which have critical human rights components and implications. Among the central purposes of the United Nations as expressed in the Charter is the maintenance of international peace and security, primary responsibility for which is conferred upon the Security Council. Article 2(7) significantly provides that "nothing contained in the present Charter shall authorize the United Nations to intervene in matters which are essentially within the domestic jurisdiction of any State or shall require the Members to submit such matters to settlement under the present Charter," with the caveat that "this principle shall not prejudice the application of enforcement measures under Chapter VII."

The United Nations Charter in Article 2(4) provides that Member States "shall refrain in their international relations from the threat or use of force against the territorial integrity or political independence of any state." Article 51 provides that nothing in the Charter "shall impair the inherent right of individual or collective self-defense if an armed attack occurs" against a member. Article 11 authorizes the General Assembly to "discuss any questions relating to the maintenance of peace and security brought before it by any Member of the United Nations," and to make recommendations "with regard to any such questions to the State or States concerned or to the Security Council or both," and any member may "call the attention of the Security Council to situations which are likely to endanger peace and security."

The Security Council has the capacity to perform critical roles in the protection of international human rights, depending on the political will of its Member States. And although sovereignty and the territorial integrity of states are notions enshrined in the Charter, these notions have evolved with changes in international relations. A state could hide behind a veil of sovereignty as it abused its own people. But the International Bill of Human Rights lodges a not-so-subtle challenge to state sovereignty as indicated by Article 21(3) of the UDHR: "The will of the people shall be the basis of the authority of the government."

Indeed, the UN and new international organizations would become, as Stanley Hoffmann has described, halfway houses "between state sovereignty and world government."[11] And cracks in the sovereign monolith widened when, in a famous *obiter dicta*, the International Court of Justice said in a land-mark decision that "sovereignty is . . . essentially a relative notion; its content depends on the stage of development in international law."[12] As Michael Reis-man has observed, "International law still protects sovereignty but—not sur-prisingly—it is the people's sovereignty rather than the sovereign's sover-eignty. . . . [T]he international human rights program . . . [b]y shifting the fulcrum of the system from the protection of sovereigns to the protection of people, works qualitative changes in virtually every component."[13]

Human rights practitioners, and increasingly governmental elites, claim the veil of sovereignty should be pierced in cases of pervasive and extreme human rights violations. A government's sovereign claims can be lost if its treatment of its citizens falls below minimal standards set by the international human rights system. Where that human rights threshold lies is a key issue for twenty-first-century international relations.

Other UN Bodies and Agencies

The General Assembly supervises the human rights programs and is the final arbiter of standards adopted, issues addressed, and the proportion and nature of administrative and budgetary resources devoted to the UN's human rights machinery. The General Assembly approves decisions taken in subsidiary human rights bodies, but it can also instruct those bodies in addressing new problems, or resolving highly controversial issues: structural, political, or sub-stantive. The General Assembly is where political negotiations occur on many critical aspects of country proposals on resolutions that the Commission on Human Rights later adopts, although the commission is organizationally sub-sidiary to the Economic and Social Council (ECOSOC).

All six principal organs of the United Nations perform important functions in UN human rights efforts. Specialized UN agencies also contribute to the protection of human rights, including the International Labour Organization (ILO), the United Nations Educational, Scientific, and Cultural Organization (UNESCO), the World Health Organization (WHO), the Food and Agriculture Organization (FAO), the Office of the High Commissioner for Refugees, and the Office of the High Commissioner for Human Rights. The human rights–related activities of each agency are detailed in their respective websites (see the book's Bibliography).

UN World Conferences on Human Rights

With the UDHR in place and invoked continuously, demands for the invigor-ation and extension of existing standards and effective mechanisms for their application led the United Nations to convene global human rights conferences. Article 28 of the UDHR stipulates, "Everyone is entitled to a social and international order in which the rights and freedoms set forth in this Declaration can be fully realized." This provision recognizes demands for a world public order of human dignity that have yielded proposals and extensive promotional activity toward such an international architecture. In critical efforts to clarify the common interests of the world community, world conferences, as discussed by Joe Sills in Chapter 3 on global norm-setting, have become important techniques of the UN human rights program as well. The first global meeting on human rights took place in Teheran in 1968. Two decades later the General Assembly called for the convening of a world meeting that would review and assess progress made in human rights since the adoption of the UDHR, and identify obstacles and explore ways in which these obstacles might be overcome.

The UN World Conference on Human Rights was held in Vienna, Austria, from June 14 through June 25, 1993. The conference agenda was set by the forty-seventh session of the General Assembly in 1992. It included an examination of the link between development, democracy, and economic, social, cultural, civil, and political rights, and an evaluation of the effectiveness of United Nations methods and mechanisms with the aim of recommending ways to ensure adequate financial and other resources for UN human rights activities.

Prior to the World Conference on Human Rights, four preparatory committee meetings were held. From the first meeting in Geneva in September 1991, it was clear that these were tasks that raised difficult and divisive issues regarding state sovereignty, universality, the role of NGOs, and questions concerning the feasibility, viability, and impartiality of new or strengthened human rights instruments. The preparatory process included three key regional meetings, in Tunis, Costa Rica, and Bangkok. These meetings produced declarations identifying concerns and perspectives of the African, the Latin American and Caribbean, and the Asian and Pacific regions. In addition, informal meetings in Europe and North America and satellite meetings throughout the world involved broad spectrums of civil society. At the final preparatory meeting, in May 1993, the preparatory committee concluded a draft final document upon which the conference began its work.

The key outcomes of the World Conference on Human Rights are embodied in the Vienna Declaration and Program of Action, which were adopted on June 25, 1993, by a consensus of 171 states. The document was later endorsed by the UN General Assembly in resolution 48/121. The final document broke new human rights ground in a number of key areas. First, it promotes the interdependence of democracy, development, and human rights. Second, the document supports the creation of new mechanisms to promote and protect the rights of women, children, and indigenous peoples. It calls for a Special Rapporteur on Violence Against Women, for universal ratification of the Convention on the Rights of the Child, and for a General Assembly proclamation of an International Decade of the World's Indigenous Peoples. Third, the Vienna Declaration calls for rapid ratification of all international human rights instruments and for additional resources for the UN Center for Human Rights. Finally and most noteworthy, it calls for the establishment of a High Commissioner for Human Rights. Each of the foregoing goals has been achieved in whole or in part.

One unanticipated outcome of the conference was to underscore the position of NGOs as performing a range of critical functions in the international human rights system. Specialized human rights nongovernmental organizations have proliferated since the end of the Cold War. They perform a variety of functions including collecting and disseminating human rights intelligence, promoting norms and standards, calling attention to substandard state behavior, appraising the efficacy of the human rights system, and in certain circumstances, serving as initial movers of the application of human rights law. As Dinah Shelton has observed, "Civil society has insisted on the right to participate in the development of international human rights governance structures. Non-state actors, particularly human rights nongovernmental organizations, have played an essential role at every stage—from negotiating norms and standards to enforcing them—creating a global human rights movement."[14]

The World Conference on Human Rights opened the UN human rights system to wide participation spanning government delegates and the broad international human rights community. Some 7,000 participants, including academics, treaty body representatives, national institutions, and representatives of more than 800 NGOs—two-thirds of which were grassroots organizations—assembled in Vienna to appraise every dimension of the human rights system. Because of the conference, NGO participation and efficacy greatly expanded across the human rights system. Each NGO sought to convey some variation of the message presented by the executive director of one international NGO: "To be born human, to be thrust into the human condition, guarantees very little in this harsh life. Thus, it is left to the nations and peoples of the world to ensure that to be born human guarantees one thing: human dignity. If the World Conference on Human Rights achieves little else, it must achieve the universal affirmation of that guarantee."[15]

The Vienna Declaration and Program of Action were born of extensive scrutiny and debate over the status and efficacy of the global human rights machinery. They represented demands to strengthen the application functions of instruments at the center of the human rights system and built upon the Universal Declaration of Human Rights of 1948. United Nations Secretary-General Boutros Boutros-Ghali, in a message to the conference, told state delegates that by adopting the Vienna Declaration and Program of Action they had renewed the international community's commitment to the promotion and protection of human rights, with "a new vision for global action for human rights into the next century."

The Office of the High Commissioner for Human Rights

Rising common demands for human dignity resulted in a fundamental human rights codex. But how were standards to be applied? What was the effective UN implementing machinery? Among the most significant advances in the international human rights system and application of its norms was the establishment of the Office of the High Commissioner for Human Rights (OHCHR) and the related reforms of the UN Center for Human Rights. Following the recommendation of the Vienna Declaration and Program of Action, resolution A/48/141, adopted by the UN General Assembly on December 20, 1993, established the position of UN High Commissioner for Human Rights (UNHCHR). The resolution specifies, inter alia, that the High Commissioner be appointed by the Secretary-General of the United Nations and approved by the General Assembly "with due regard to geographical rotation, and have a fixed term of four years with a possibility of one renewal for another fixed term of four years, and be of the rank of Under-Secretary-General."

The High Commissioner is to function "within the framework of the UN Charter, the Universal Declaration of Human Rights, and other international instruments of human rights and international law, including the obligations, within this framework, to respect the sovereignty, territorial integrity and domestic jurisdiction of States and to promote the universal respect for and observance of all human rights, in the recognition that, in the framework of the purposes and principles of the United Nations Charter, the promotion and protection of all human rights is a legitimate concern of the international community." The implementing legislation also recognizes the importance of the promotion of sustainable development and the right to development. The tasks of the new office include promoting and protecting civil, cultural, economic, political, and social rights; coordinating all human rights activities throughout the UN system, including UN education and public information programs; improving the efficiency and effectiveness of UN human rights machinery; engaging in dialogue with all governments in the implementation of its mandate; and supervising the UN Center for Human Rights, now called the Office of the High Commissioner for Human Rights. The OHCHR is headquartered at the Palais Wilson in Geneva, with a liaison office in New York at UN headquarters.

The High Commissioner is now the principal UN official with responsibility for United Nations human rights activities under the direction and authority of the Secretary-General. The central task of the High Commissioner is to integrate human rights thinking and standards across all the concerns and

work of the United Nations, and thus the OHCHR participates in all UN programs—peace and security, economic and social affairs, development cooperation, and humanitarian affairs. In addition to its coordinating responsibilities,
the office services UN human rights treaty bodies and annually receives some
400,000 formal complaints of human rights violations. It maintains a human
rights database to respond to existing or unfolding situations requiring immediate attention and/or preventive action, and a twenty-four-hour fax hotline.

The OHCHR disseminates human rights information and promotes
related education worldwide. All official documents are published on a regularly updated website. A technical-cooperation program assists states lacking
adequate resources or recovering from conflict to implement their human
rights obligations. Needs assessment missions are conducted in consultation
with concerned governments. These cooperative human rights activities are
supported by a voluntary trust fund that donor countries maintain. The
OHCHR works with governments to establish national human rights institutions for the implementation of human rights standards, including guidance
and practical training. Field offices in specific countries enable the OHCHR
to monitor situations, investigate abuses, and provide advisory and technical
services. The office also works on a regional basis to encourage best practices
in securing human rights protection. Increasingly, the OHCHR participates in
United Nations peacekeeping and peacebuilding activities.

The OHCHR works with civil society components specialized to human
rights: the NGOs, academic institutions, and policy research centers. These
entities perform critical functions of intelligence, promotion of standards,
invocation for the defense of victims, and continuing appraisal of the system.
The OHCHR administers financial support to NGOs from trust funds supported by governments and other donors. These include:

Voluntary Fund for Victims of Torture
Voluntary Trust Fund on Contemporary Forms of Slavery
Voluntary Fund for Indigenous Populations
Voluntary Fund for the International Decade of the World's Indigenous
    People
OHCHR Indigenous Fellowship Program
Assisting Communities Together (ACT)

The High Commissioner is the Secretary-General of the United Nations
Decade for Human Rights Education, from 1995–2004. According to its
spokesperson, the OHCHR is working to promote human rights education by

• developing human rights education and training materials for specific
   audiences;

- supporting national efforts for human rights education in the context of its technical-cooperation program;
- facilitating information-sharing through the organization of international and regional seminars and workshops and the development of specific resources; and
- supporting local efforts for human rights education through the Assisting Communities Together project, which provides financial assistance to human rights grassroots initiatives.

The first High Commissioner was José Ayala Lasso of Ecuador, who assumed office on April 5, 1994. On September 12, 1997, he was succeeded by Mary Robinson, former president of Ireland. On September 11, 2002, High Commissioner Robinson was succeeded by Sergio Vieira de Mello of Brazil, who was tragically killed in a bomb blast at UN headquarters in Baghdad, Iraq, on August 19, 2003. Louise Arbour, a former war crimes prosecutor in Yugoslavia and Rwanda, has been nominated to become the new High Commissioner.

The High Commissioner is an international civil servant in the employ of the United Nations, that is, the Member States. The tenure of Mary Robinson was animated by the view that the High Commissioner was also the leader of the international human rights movement, comprising primarily NGOs, and a moral authority and voice for human rights victims. Thus there was a tension in the functions of the office and these were perhaps inevitable in the early life of the institution. That tension becomes especially apparent in trying to identify who the High Commissioner's clients are. Are they the victims who may live in states that pay the bills for the functioning of the office? Are they the NGOs that compose the human rights movement, each with its special interests? Are they the states that, in many instances, may be in the position to remedy human rights abuses? Are they the UN Secretariat and Secretary-General, to which and to whom the High Commissioner is accountable? These are fundamental questions that may take years and significant changes in the international system to resolve.

High Commissioner Vieira de Mello, early in his tenure, identified key challenges facing his office and those committed to human rights:

> First and foremost, we need to arrive at the universal ratification of human rights treaties. . . . We need to focus with equal emphasis on the legal and democratic framework of society as a condition for sustainable development. . . . We should seek ways and means of building democracy combining popular participation in decision-making and control with accountability of those who govern, and a clear concept of the rights and responsibilities of those who are governed. This triad—the rule of law, popular participation and responsibility, as well as accountable governance—will remain at the center of my Office's attention.[16]

The Commission on Human Rights

Article 68 of the Charter provides that ECOSOC "shall set up commissions in economic and social fields and for the promotion of human rights." Thus the Commission on Human Rights is referred to as a Charter-based organ. Its members drafted the UDHR beginning in 1946, and in those early years the commission was mostly occupied with drafting and promoting standards. In 1967 the commission began to identify specific human rights violations, and by 1972 human rights complaint petitions were on the rise. Most of these were the product of new participants in international relations: the NGOs.[17] The early commission had institutional growing pains. State members were not interested in creating a strong global adjudicative human rights arena. Instead, the commission evolved from a drafting body into a respectable reservoir of intelligence about human rights violations, and from there into a forum in which members could be mobilized to call attention to and characterize behavior falling below international human rights standards.

Today the Commission on Human Rights is the principal UN body concerned with the global human rights condition. As Mary Robinson observed, "The Commission on Human Rights has been the central architect of the work of the United Nations in the field of human rights. Though consisting of representatives of governments, it is meant to embody the conscience of humanity for a world of peace and development grounded in respect for human rights."[18] It comprises fifty-three states and meets annually for six weeks during March and April at the UN's Geneva office. The OHCHR supports the commission meetings and assists experts, whom it appoints. It also conducts research for the commission and prepares an annual report for its consideration. The commission is further assisted by working groups, experts, representatives, and rapporteurs who focus on specific human rights issues or situations. Typically, more than 3,000 delegates from member and observer states and NGOs participate. Governments, NGOs in consultative status with ECOSOC, UN officials, and invited dignitaries address the commission on a wide range of general and specific human rights concerns. It adopts about 100 resolutions and decisions annually.

The commission's work is further supported by the Subcommission on the Promotion and Protection of Human Rights, which is the commission's subsidiary body and think tank. It undertakes human rights studies and makes specific recommendations to the commission on a wide range of issues and situations. The subcommission comprises twenty-six experts, who are elected by the full Commission on Human Rights. It meets for three weeks in August in Geneva.

As a matter of international law, the work of the commission is based on specific mandates provided in ECOSOC resolutions. These mandates have provided the commission with procedures and mechanisms evolved and refined over many years to examine human rights violations worldwide. The commission can monitor, investigate, and issue public reports on human rights situations occurring in states, or on broad human rights phenomena not confined to any particular state.

Many human rights situations are considered confidentially under the "1503 Procedure," which is named for ECOSOC's resolution 1503, adopted in 1970. It authorizes the commission to examine complaints appearing to reveal a consistent pattern of gross human rights violations. This procedure was revised in 2000 to allow the subcommission to annually appoint a geographically representative five-member Working Group on Communications. The group receives complaints from individuals and groups who allege violations and considers any government responses. If the Working Group on Communications finds reasonable evidence of a consistent pattern of gross violations of human rights, it refers the matter to the Working Group on Situations.

The Working Group on Situations meets at least one month prior to the opening of the full Commission on Human Rights. It examines the confidential reports it has received from the Working Group on Communications and decides whether to refer the situations to the commission. If the working group brings a situation to the commission's attention, it does so in a confidential report that identifies the central issues of concern. The working group may also transmit a draft resolution or draft decision recommending action to be taken by the full commission.

During its annual meeting, the Commission on Human Rights considers situations referred to it in two separate closed sessions. In the first, concerned states are invited to make presentations. A discussion with commission members ensues based on the contents of confidential files and the report of the Working Group on Situations. Prior to the second closed session, commission members may submit an alternative or amendments to reports previously transmitted by the Working Group on Situations. Draft texts are circulated in confidence. In the second closed session, members of the commission discuss and may take action on draft resolutions or decisions, during which period the concerned state has the right to be present. Actions that may be taken by the commission in its second closed meeting are:

- Discontinue consideration of the matter.
- Retain the situation under review pending further information from the concerned government and ancillary information that the commission may receive under the 1503 Procedure.
- Keep the situation under review and appoint an independent expert.
- Discontinue the matter under the confidential 1503 Procedure and consider the same matter under the public 1235 Procedure.

Since 1978 it has been customary for the chairman of the Commission on Human Rights to announce the names of countries under 1503 Procedure examination. The 1235 Procedure, named for a 1967 ECOSOC resolution, affords public examination and debate. It allows wider participation in the process than does the 1503 Procedure. Notably, this participation includes international and national human rights NGOs, and ultimately the world media. Important options under the 1235 Procedure are the appointment of a Special Rapporteur of the commission, or a Special Representative of the Secretary-General, to investigate a situation, and public criticism of a government by a resolution adopted by the full commission.

The commission can designate a thematic rapporteur or working group to examine violations relating to a theme such as arbitrary detention, disappearance, or torture. For exigent circumstances there are "urgent action" procedures that can be used under extraconventional mechanisms. Anyone may address a communication to the Office of the High Commissioner for Human Rights about a serious human rights violation that is about to be committed— for example, concern that a detained individual is about to be tortured, or that an extrajudicial execution is imminent—or has been very recently committed, such as a disappearance. The "urgent action" communication is typically addressed to the Special Rapporteur concerned with extrajudicial, summary, or arbitrary executions, or to the Working Group on Arbitrary Detention. The Working Group chair or rapporteur may then communicate with authorities of the concerned state, requesting clarification of the case, and appeal to the government to undertake measures to guarantee the rights of the victim.

The Commission on Human Rights is more effective in certain of its functions than in others, largely because of the interests of Member States of the commission and the UN. As a reservoir of human rights intelligence, as an appraiser of standards and their implementation, as a point to expose substandard state behavior, the commission occupies an essential place in attempts to build a world public order of human dignity. Although the commission performs roles contributing to the formulation of prescriptions and their application, those roles remain the near exclusive domains of states and those functions are primarily engaged outside the commission. Sergio Vieira de Mello called for a balance in the work of the commission between protection and promotion. He said that "the importance and effectiveness of its protection work is evidenced by the ever-increasing size and sophistication of its system of special procedures. However, protection goes hand in hand with promotion and we must stand ready to respond to requests by Member States for the provision of advisory services, in particular as a consequence of deliberations of human rights organs, as long as they are not a substitute for tangible improvements to domestic situations. Equally, the Commission must live up to its responsibility and be prepared to call an abuse an abuse wheresoever these occur."[19]

The commission has thirty-seven special procedural mandates in regard to monitoring and publicly reporting on global human rights trends and on situations within specific states. As Vieira de Mello observed:

> The Commission on Human Rights is central to United Nations action to promote and protect human rights. As one of the oldest UN intergovernmental bodies, it has a history of solid achievement in both defining the content of international human rights norms and in their promotion and protection. . . . The Commission remains a vital international forum for discussion of human rights issues. In particular, it continues in its role as the pre-eminent drafter of international human rights instruments.[20]

Treaty Bodies

In addition to Charter-based organs such as the Commission on Human Rights, there are human rights treaty bodies that are key for the application of human rights norms and standards. Treaty-monitoring bodies of independent experts supervise the implementation of key human rights multilateral treaties. At this writing there are six committees, with a seventh soon to be established:

- The Committee on Human Rights monitors the implementation of the International Covenant on Civil and Political Rights.
- The Committee on Economic, Social, and Cultural Rights monitors the implementation of the International Covenant on Economic, Social, and Cultural Rights.
- The Committee Against Torture monitors the Convention Against Torture and Other Cruel, Inhuman, or Degrading Treatment or Punishment.
- The Committee on the Elimination of Racial Discrimination monitors the International Convention on the Elimination of All Forms of Racial Discrimination.
- The Committee on the Elimination of Discrimination Against Women monitors the implementation of the Convention on the Elimination of All Forms of Discrimination Against Women.
- The Committee on the Rights of the Child monitors the Convention on the Rights of the Child.

The seventh treaty body will be established when twenty states ratify or accede to the new convention concerning the rights of migrant workers. Each of the treaty bodies is serviced by the OHCHR, with the exception of the Committee on the Elimination of Discrimination Against Women, which is supported by the Division of the Advancement of Women of the United Nations Secretariat in New York.

Upon state ratification of any treaty, that state assumes an international legal obligation to apply the treaty at the national level. Each of the multilateral human rights treaties require periodic reporting as to the national achievement of their mandated standards. State party reports along with independent intelligence from nongovernmental organizations and other sources are examined by the treaty body experts. A delegation representing the reporting state is present in the committee meeting. The treaty body experts make recommendations to the state party for any expected future action. The Committee Against Torture and the Committee on the Elimination of Discrimination Against Women may undertake confidential inquiries, acting upon information received pertaining to incidents and situations occurring in the territory of a state party. Bodies related to four treaties—the International Covenant on Civil and Political Rights, the Convention on the Elimination of Discrimination Against Women, the Convention Against Torture, and the International Convention on the Elimination of All Forms of Racial Discrimination—have procedures under which individuals may submit complaints. Persons submitting complaints must be from within the jurisdiction of states that have formally accepted such procedures. The formal procedures are found in optional protocols and declarations, depending on the respective international instrument.

The International Court of Justice and the Criminal Tribunals

The International Court of Justice (ICJ) is the principal judicial organ of the United Nations with its seat at the Peace Palace in The Hague, the Netherlands. It began work in 1946, when it replaced the Permanent Court of International Justice. The Court operates under a statute that is an integral part of the Charter of the United Nations. The Court settles legal disputes submitted to it by states in accordance with international law, and can render advisory opinions on legal questions referred to it by authorized international organs and agencies. The Court is composed of fifteen judges elected to nine-year terms of office by the United Nations General Assembly and Security Council and may not include more than one judge of any nationality.

The ICJ is not a human rights court per se. However, as former judge Stephen M. Schwebel has observed, "questions of human rights have arisen in a number of cases before the World Court, and in some cases, the Court has rendered judgments or given advisory opinions that have significantly influenced international law bearing on human rights."[21] For example, the Court's 1970 advisory opinion in the South-West Africa case turned on the protection of human rights. The Court found the presence of South Africa in Namibia to be illegal, and that the policy of apartheid as applied by South Africa in Namibia constituted "a violation of the purpose of the Charter of the United Nations."[22]

The Court's judgment in the Barcelona Traction case was also very important for human rights. The Court addressed obligations owed by a state to the international community as a whole, obligations *erga omnes*. "Such obligations derive, for example, in contemporary international law, from the outlawing of acts of aggression, and of genocide, as also from the principles and rules concerning the basic rights of the human person, including protection from slavery and racial discrimination."[23] Thus obligations flowing from human rights principles are the concern of all, they are *erga omnes*. Today this principle is unassailable.

Other international tribunals that are more specific to human rights concerns and have jurisdiction over individuals have emerged. On December 9, 1948, the UN General Assembly adopted resolution 260, which became the Convention on the Prevention and Punishment of the Crime of Genocide. Article 1 of that convention characterizes genocide as "a crime under international law," and Article 6 provides that persons charged with genocide "shall be tried by a competent tribunal of the State in the territory of which the act was committed or by such international penal tribunal as may have jurisdiction." The General Assembly invited the International Law Commission "to study the desirability and possibility of establishing an international judicial organ for the trial of persons charged with genocide." A draft statute was prepared by 1951, with a revised statute in 1953. From the origin of the idea of an international criminal court to the present there have been conflicting claims "between those who favor retaining exclusive control by the nation-state over the sanctioning of individual acts characterized as 'criminal' offenses and committed on its territory, and those who view the international community as authorized, or even mandated, to characterize certain egregious violations of human dignity as 'international crimes' to be prosecuted potentially in any criminal court on the planet, and to apprehend, unilaterally if need be, alleged perpetrators."[24]

After years of political delays, in 1994 the International Law Commission submitted a draft statute for an International Criminal Court (ICC) to the United Nations General Assembly. The Rome Statute (agreed in 1998) of the International Criminal Court entered into force on July 1, 2002. Three principles underpin the structure of the statute as explained by Mahnoush Arsanjani, the UN senior legal officer who served as secretary to the Committee of the Whole of the Rome Conference: "The first, the principle of complementarity, establishes that the court may assume jurisdiction only when national legal systems are unable or unwilling to exercise jurisdiction. . . . The second principle is that the statute is designed to deal only with the most serious crimes of concern to the international community as a whole. . . . The third principle was that the statute should, to the extent possible, remain within the realm of customary international law."[25]

Article 1 reads, "An International Criminal Court (the Court) is hereby established. It shall be a permanent institution and shall have the power to exercise its jurisdiction over persons for the most serious crimes of international concern, as referred to in this Statute, and shall be complementary to national criminal jurisdictions." It has authority to try individuals and hold them accountable for the most egregious human rights offenses and crimes: genocide, war crimes, and crimes against humanity, and eventually the crime of aggression. The Court has jurisdiction over crimes committed after July 1, 2002, when the statute entered into force.

One of the unresolved issues is the notion of holding an individual accountable for the crime of aggression. While aggression is included as a crime in the statute within the Court's jurisdiction, there is little agreement in the international community as to how to define a crime of aggression. One view is that the Security Council must find that an act of aggression has occurred. Other views would leave a finding of aggression to the General Assembly or to the International Court of Justice. In September 2002 the Assembly of States Parties to the Court established a special working group to elaborate proposals for a provision on aggression.

The International Criminal Court is a separate entity from the United Nations, but by a special legal instrument it will have a relationship with the UN. Its work will relate to the activities of the UN High Commissioner for Human Rights. The OHCHR has highlighted five key aspects. The first is the principle of complementarity to national criminal jurisdictions. The operation of the ICC statute is interwoven with the capacity of states to conduct national prosecutions. The OHCHR provides technical cooperation to states to assist them in adapting laws and practices consonant with international human rights standards, including the abolition of impunity for international crimes, and to achieve complementarity between the ICC statute and national criminal jurisdictions. The second is the inclusion of crimes against humanity in the ICC statute. This category covers an array of human rights abuses at the center of the UN human rights program. Third, the Rome Statute represents advances in gender justice that directly relate to the human rights concerns of the Convention on the Elimination of Discrimination Against Women and its related committee. Fourth, fair trial, a centerpiece of the statute, will be supported by the OHCHR with technical advice to jurisdictions in need of advice pertaining to relevant standards and their implementation. Fifth, the High Commissioner has indicated the desire to cooperate with the ICC on issues of transitional justice.[26]

By 2003 there were 139 state signatories to the Rome Statute. The government of the United States affixed its signature to the instrument on December 31, 2000. However, on May 6, 2002, the U.S. government conveyed the following communication to the Secretary-General:

This is to inform you, in connection with the Rome Statute of the International Criminal Court adopted on July 17, 1998, that the United States does not intend to become a party to the treaty. Accordingly, the United States has no legal obligations arising from its signature on December 31, 2000. The United States requests that its intention not to become a party, as expressed in this letter, be reflected in the depository's status lists relating to this treaty.[27]

The International Criminal Tribunal for the Former Yugoslavia (ICTY) was established by Security Council resolution 827, which was adopted on May 25, 1993. The ICTY, located in The Hague, was established by the Security Council in response to, and based on the threat to international peace and security posed by, pervasive violations of human rights in armed conflict and violations of international humanitarian law committed in the territory of the former Yugoslavia since 1991. The ICTY's mission is to bring to justice persons responsible for violations of international humanitarian law, and thereby bring justice to the victims, deter further such crimes, and contribute to the restoration of peace by promoting reconciliation in the former Yugoslavia. The ICTY has authority to prosecute crimes committed on the territory of the former Yugoslavia since 1991 in the following categories: grave breaches of the 1949 Geneva Conventions, violations of the laws or customs of war, genocide, and crimes against humanity. The ICTY chambers consist of sixteen permanent judges and a maximum of nine ad litem judges. The permanent judges are elected by the General Assembly of the United Nations for a term of four years and can be reelected.

ICTY investigations are initiated by the tribunal's prosecutor, presently Carla del Ponte, at her own discretion or on the basis of information received from tribunal investigators, private individuals, governments, international organizations, or nongovernmental organizations. A trial commences once the accused is physically present before the tribunal. The conduct of the trial draws on both civil law and common law systems: elements of the adversarial and inquisitorial procedures are combined. The rules of procedure and evidence guarantee that ICTY proceedings adhere to internationally recognized principles of a fair trial.

Although ad hoc, the tribunal is a fully operational legal institution that can render judgments and set crucial precedents in international criminal and humanitarian law. Many legal issues adjudicated by the tribunal were either not previously adjudicated or have been dormant since the Nuremberg and Tokyo trials. Important decisions of the ICTY include clarifications of the application of the Geneva Conventions, the further development of the command responsibility doctrine, and the interpretation of rape as a form of torture and a crime against humanity.

There are other important criminal tribunals. The Security Council by resolution 955 (1994) established the International Criminal Tribunal for Rwanda (ICTR) to prosecute persons "responsible for genocide and other serious violations of international humanitarian law." Acting under Chapter VII of the Charter, the Council adopted the statute of the ICTR, whose Article 1 limits the power of the tribunal to prosecute persons for violations committed in "the territory of Rwanda and Rwandan citizens responsible for such violations committed in the territory of neighboring States between 1 January 1994 and 31 December 1994." Many of the provisions of the statute are similar to the ICTY statute. The tribunal has rendered important decisions addressing issues of genocide, crimes against humanity, rape, and violations of the Geneva Conventions.

Human Rights and Peacekeeping

The UN Departments of Peacekeeping Operations and Political Affairs (DPKO and DPA) are responsible for peacekeeping operations. United Nations peacekeeping missions increasingly include human rights mandates. Missions that have been undertaken in Cambodia, El Salvador, East Timor, Sierra Leone, Kosovo, and elsewhere have been multidimensional. Hence UN peacekeeping forces—the "blue helmets"—contributed by member governments are no longer limited to monitoring a truce, overseeing combatant withdrawal, or maintaining a buffer zone. They may provide humanitarian relief, monitor elections, oversee judicial reforms, and promote and verify the observance of human rights standards. Mandates now generally explicitly include a human rights component.

In the post–Cold War international system, human rights have become a regular component of peacekeeping, and hence the OHCHR now performs important functions in peacekeeping operations. In November 2002 the OHCHR concluded a memorandum of understanding with DPKO to clarify their respective roles. The memorandum recognizes that protection and promotion of human rights have become essential elements of conflict prevention, peace maintenance, and postconflict reconstruction. It provides for expanded cooperation and the institutionalization of shared expertise, advice, training, and support. Thus the OHCHR is to be involved in the early stages of the Integrated Missions Task Force (ITMF), which is established for countries in which operations are planned and later implemented.

Human rights components of peacekeeping operations are to be based upon international human rights standards. An innovation is that operations will be charged with promoting an integrated approach to human rights, including civil, cultural, economic, political, and social rights. Also included are the right to development, and particularly the needs of women, children, minorities, internally displaced persons, and other vulnerable groups. The memorandum introduces an important human rights mechanism into peace-keeping by institutionalizing timely information alerts and exchanges. Thus, pursuant to the memorandum, the OHCHR will convey to DPKO critical information from the human rights treaty bodies, the UN Commission on Human Rights, and OHCHR field offices that may alert the operation to human rights crises and emergencies. DPKO will provide confidential situation reports to the OHCHR. At the termination of a peacekeeping operation DPKO will undertake special arrangements to protect human rights files and transfer these to the OHCHR. Information contained in such files can be critical for a return to the rule of law and the building of a human rights culture in the wake of armed conflict. As stated in the memorandum, "Human rights components of peacekeeping operations should normally combine promotion and protection functions so as to ensure a comprehensive approach to human rights in accordance with international human rights standards."[28]

Human Rights and War-Torn Societies: The Case of Afghanistan

Countries emerging from war face immense human rights challenges. Consider the case of Afghanistan. The world community expressed increasing alarm following the Soviet invasion of the country in 1979 and its subsequent decade of occupation. An indigenous resistance movement known as the mujahidin emerged to oppose the Soviet and regular Afghan army troops. Aerial bombardment with combined Soviet-Afghan ground operations was used against the Afghan resistance. Heavy firepower was used indiscriminately while helicopter gunships ferreted out mountain-based guerrillas. Civilians became targets. Human rights organizations collected evidence suggesting patterns of situations in which groups of civilians found themselves the object of attack.[29] Their cumulative records demonstrated that the Afghan people became victims of the final hot war of the Cold War. Over the ensuing years, human rights organizations conducted fact-finding missions to examine the situation in Afghanistan and submitted reports to UN bodies, governments, and the media. The General Assembly annually passed resolutions condemning the occupation.

In 1984 the UN Commission on Human Rights took an important step by establishing an Afghanistan mandate. The first UN Special Rapporteur for Afghanistan was Felix Ermacora of Vienna, an Austrian jurist and law professor who presented his initial report in 1985. From that year until 2003, a succession of Special Rapporteurs and their hardworking Geneva-based staffs compiled information, received and scrutinized complaints, conducted fact-finding missions, and prepared annual reports to the commission. They kept

Afghanistan's human rights issues alive, even when the media and NGOs had limited or no access to the country.

The Soviet army left Afghanistan in 1989, but the country remained engulfed in war as mujahidin factions brutally competed for power. They committed massive human rights violations and Afghans continued to be victimized by indiscriminate bombing, torture, and mutilation. By 1994, Taliban forces were sweeping across the country, imposing order as a religious oligarchy. Afghanistan became a captive nation. Women were banned from the work force and girls schools were shut down. Over 25,000 families headed by war widows had no means of support. Listening to music, watching television, and flying kites were among the banned activities. The soccer stadium was used for weekly lashings and executions. Terrorist training camps flourished and the country became host to Osama bin Laden and his Al-Qaida organization.

Although the UN Security Council imposed sanctions on the Taliban regime, through the 1990s most of the world turned its attention elsewhere. Afghanistan became a closed conflict and a largely forgotten human rights tragedy. But the work of the Special Rapporteur and the staff at the UN human rights office in Geneva continued. During the dark days of the Taliban, the Special Rapporteur was the ongoing focal point for documenting specific acts and patterns of human rights violations. With the participation of brave Afghans and human rights NGOs, the world was kept informed and pointedly reminded of the situation when the Special Rapporteur presented his annual report to the Commission on Human Rights.

The situation for the Afghan people changed in 2001. Following the September 11, 2001, Al-Qaida attack on the United States using hijacked passenger airliners, a U.S.-led military coalition dislodged the Taliban regime. UN-brokered talks were conducted in Bonn, Germany, on December 5, 2001. The resulting "Agreement on Provisional Arrangements in Afghanistan Pending the Re-establishment of Permanent Government Institutions," or Bonn Agreement, acknowledged "the right of the people of Afghanistan to freely determine their political future in accordance with the principles of Islam, democracy, pluralism and social justice," set as a goal "the establishment of a broad-based, gender-sensitive, multi-ethnic and fully representative government," and confirmed international legal obligations to which Afghanistan had been a party. From a human rights perspective, this war-torn nation had a future.

However, war-torn societies face formidable challenges in becoming postconflict states where human dignity is broadly respected and protected. The essential conditioning factors in achieving that end are human rights mechanisms, standards, and norms that become widely internalized. These factors can be new constitutions, courts, human rights commissions, truth commissions, a functioning civil society, and the all-important security environment enabling civilians to participate in such activities. This is where the UN human rights machinery becomes essential. For Afghanistan, security, a central government, a new constitution and judiciary, and an independent human rights commission would be key.

The Bonn Agreement mandated: "The Interim Administration shall, with the assistance of the United Nations, establish an Independent Human Rights Commission, whose responsibilities will include human rights monitoring, investigation of violations of human rights, and development of domestic human rights institutions." While Afghanistan is formally a party to the major international human rights instruments and many of those rights might become enshrined in a new Afghan constitution, those rights must be translated into positive human rights policies. To that end, the Afghan Independent Human Rights Commission is potentially an indispensable agent and it has received support from the OHCHR and international NGOs as it begins a program of monitoring, processing complaints, and promoting human rights standards across the country.

Human rights are now at the center of a new Afghan process that produced a draft constitution submitted to a Constitutional Loya Jirgah in late 2003. The United Nations has supported the Afghans in their constitutional drafting and implementation activities through a joint support project of the UN Assistance Mission in Afghanistan (UNAMA) and UN Development Programme (UNDP). This includes coordinating international technical and financial support through a Constitutional Support Unit.

Produced amid an uncertain security environment, the first draft constitution of the Islamic Republic of Afghanistan reflected many lofty goals and common demands of individual Afghans who have suffered years of war and misery. The document tracked important values specified by the world community in the UDHR.[30] Chapter 1 of the draft proclaims: "The state respects the fundamentals of the Charter of the United Nations Organization, honors the Universal Declaration of Human Rights." The draft was a rare optimistic glimpse of a society emerging from war. After so many years of deprivations, it was understandable that the Afghan people would invoke human rights values and the United Nations human rights system. The question to be resolved was whether, once Afghanistan became an independent state, such values would survive as rights and be implemented as national policies.

After multiple drafts and at times acrimonious debate, the 502 delegates to the Loya Jirgah approved a new constitution for Afghanistan. Observers criticized the Jirgah as scripted, with the majority belonging to voting blocs controlled by powerful warlords. Still, the outcome was a document that, if applied, might provide the new beginning Afghans sorely need. The new constitution balances the goals of an Islamic state with a promise to abide by the United Nations Charter and the Universal Declaration of Human Rights. It provides for a presidential system with a directly elected president, a bicameral national assembly, and an independent judiciary. Notably, it names all of Afghanistan's ethnic groups as part of the nation, allowing all groups to use and teach their languages in areas where they are the majority. Certain freedoms, such as the right to publish and to form social organizations, are limited. Equal rights for women are affirmed and two parliament seats for each province are reserved for women. The document does not address the relationship between Islam and international human rights law, nor does it provide for muscular institutions to protect those rights, except through the currently weak Afghan Independent Human Rights Commission. As the Loya Jirgah drew to a close, its chairman, Sibghatullah Mojaddedi, reflected, "If this constitution is not put into practice and not implemented, then it would not be given the respect that we have all promised."[31] The true challenge is that every Afghan now own the new constitution.

Words on paper, including constitutions, cannot by themselves ensure human dignity. Implementation is key, and this requires that words and the norms they express be internalized and accepted as authoritative by the community. Only then can there be a human rights culture. Societies that have emerged from devastating conflict are the most fragile members of the world community. They share the common condition of real estate trying to become a nation-state. Their stability and human rights achievements depend on the assistance of the world community, including the UN human rights system and those who support it.

Twenty-First-Century Human Rights Challenges

One can identify many human rights challenges in this complex post–Cold War international system characterized by the use of state and nonstate violence, a questioning of the universal nature of human rights standards, and widespread deprivations of human dignity of every order. These include the challenges of promotion, the challenges of application, the challenges of the particular, and the challenges and risks of norm termination.

Challenges of Promotion

Much of the success of the contemporary human rights program is owed to the promotion of standards and policies. The promotion of human rights standards and policies has been globally uneven. Effective promotion requires financial and technical assistance in countries and, importantly, in communities within those countries where differentiated perspectives on universal human rights prevail. Many of these states are war-torn and postconflict societies, such as Afghanistan. A promotional goal should be to build a human rights culture in every state sufficiently vibrant for regional diffusion. Achieving this goal would entail a strategy of decentralization, including the extension and support of OHCHR field presences. Resources, already limited, would have to be redirected to a wider array of field offices in developing countries.

Challenges of Application

Standard-setting and institution building have been the hallmarks of the contemporary human rights system. In the twenty-first century, human rights achievements will turn on the application of norms and standards. Application is "the specification of law to a particular set of events and the determination of a sanction."[32] Successful application will depend on the determined will of UN Member States and their peoples. The determined use of diplomatic instruments does not always work. Sometimes, economic and military instruments must be used to achieve the application of human rights in the most drastic circumstances. Clear human rights articulations emanating from the United Nations must be accompanied by equally clear communications of intent to control behavior inconsistent with those articulations.

Challenges of the Particular

In the twenty-first century there are cleavages among and within cultures and polities marked by those who, not being subject to tests of reason, do not rely upon revealed truth, and those for whom revelation is paramount despite its inaccessibility to reason.[33] There is an apparent schism between those who believe that ideas and institutions are human-made, and those who believe they are imposed by nature or divine will. The former perspective engendered Western civilization from the Enlightenment to the present, and with it human rights. In its extreme form the latter perspective represents a critical challenge that was manifested in the September 11, 2001, attacks on the United States and the West. Its ascendancy could amount to one of the most profound value shifts since the Age of Reason.

Political scientist Samuel P. Huntington wrote that "the principal conflicts of global politics will occur between nations and groups of different civilizations. The clash of civilizations will dominate global politics. The fault lines between civilizations will be the battle lines of the future."[34] Some states most in need of human rights promotion and advisory services are on those fault lines. Others equally in need are marked by the furrows of several civilizations.

Thus it is important not to attempt to freeze the Universal Declaration of Human Rights in time, influenced by some notion of original intent or swayed by the myth of a constitutional moment. The very concept of human rights must be "dynamic, responsive and adaptable. . . . [W]e must be culturally sensitive in our interpretation and application of some of the norms, while being more inventive in devising measures for the promotion and implementation of human rights which are less Western, more diverse, and more closely tailored to meet local cultures and traditions."[35]

The purposeful interplay of promoting and applying human rights norms and standards in a respectful dialogue with nonuniversal particularistic views would go a long way toward alleviating culturally specific tensions, enabling the task of clarifying a shared common interest. Many challenges to universal human rights are really a plea for a place at the Western-arranged table and attention to distinctive voices. But a human rights strategy that is sensitive to cultural variation must also be prepared to act on serious human rights deprivations where and when they occur. This will be difficult so long as any state is relegated to marginal participation in the international human rights system. As three pioneers in international human rights law observed:

> There would appear, however, to be an overriding insistence, transcending all cultures and climes, upon the greater production and wider distribution of all basic values, accompanied by increasing recognition that a world public order of human dignity can tolerate wide differences in the specific practices by which values are shaped and shared, so long as all demands and practices are effectively appraised and accommodated in terms of the common interest. The important fact is that the peoples of the world are today increasingly demanding the enhanced protection of all those basic rights, commonly characterized in empirical reference as those of human dignity, by the processes of law in all the different communities of which they are members, including especially the international or world community.[36]

Challenges and Risks of Norm Termination

The international system has witnessed great human rights achievements, including standard-setting, states undertaking new legal obligations, mechanisms and arrangements for achieving remedies, and increased participation of NGOs. Because of intense promotion and sustained invocation of assaults upon human dignity, a key achievement has been the broad acceptance and internalization of human rights norms. This is the result of vigilant appraisal of, and attention to, human rights situations by all members of what has become the international human rights movement: UN workers, advocates, the media, and any person committed to human dignity who is determined to speak up when violations occur. But normative attention and scrutiny of state and nonstate-actor behavior must be sustained and vigilant. This is imperative in the complicated post–September 11 world of pressing security concerns. Human rights norms require continued nurturing, or they lapse, are regularly breached, and are ultimately terminated.

Toward a World Public Order of Human Dignity

The United Nations system for the establishment and enforcement of human rights includes Member States, the International Bill of Human Rights, an expanding web of other instruments and conventions binding on states that have ratified them, UN Charter-based and treaty-based human rights organs, specialized UN agencies, and a proliferation of nongovernmental organizations and associations with UN consultative status that monitor the fulfillment of human rights and that report on behavior that falls below accepted norms. At the center of this activity has been the UN in establishing the goal of human dignity in the global common interest.[37]

As former UN High Commissioner for Human Rights Sergio Vieira de Mello said:

> Human dignity is a concept that underpins the entire corpus of human rights. It places the individual, as the holder of rights and responsibilities, at the center of our concerns. As human dignity is an inherent quality, it is wrong to say that a person can be deprived of his or her dignity. On the other hand, we can—and all too often do—impose conditions on people that are incompatible with human dignity.[38]

The goal of the UN's systemwide human rights program is to remove conditions incompatible with human dignity in the common interest of all humanity, a shared interest that is truly global.

Appendix: The Universal Declaration of Human Rights

Adopted and proclaimed by General Assembly resolution 217 A (III) of December 10, 1948.

Preamble

Whereas recognition of the inherent dignity and of the equal and inalienable rights of all members of the human family is the foundation of freedom, justice and peace in the world,

Whereas disregard and contempt for human rights have resulted in barbarous acts which have outraged the conscience of mankind, and the advent of a world in which human beings shall enjoy freedom of speech and belief and freedom from fear and want has been proclaimed as the highest aspiration of the common people,

Whereas it is essential, if man is not to be compelled to have recourse, as a last resort, to rebellion against tyranny and oppression, that human rights should be protected by the rule of law,

Whereas it is essential to promote the development of friendly relations between nations,

Whereas the peoples of the United Nations have in the Charter reaffirmed their faith in fundamental human rights, in the dignity and worth of the human person and in the equal rights of men and women and have determined to promote social progress and better standards of life in larger freedom,

Whereas Member States have pledged themselves to achieve, in co-operation with the United Nations, the promotion of universal respect for and observance of human rights and fundamental freedoms,

Whereas a common understanding of these rights and freedoms is of the greatest importance for the full realization of this pledge,

Now, therefore the General Assembly proclaims this Universal Declaration of Human Rights as a common standard of achievement for all peoples and all nations, to the end that every individual and every organ of society, keeping this Declaration constantly in mind, shall strive by teaching and education to promote respect for these rights and freedoms and by progressive measures, national and international, to secure their universal and effective recognition and observance, both among the peoples of Member States themselves and among the peoples of territories under their jurisdiction.

Article 1
All human beings are born free and equal in dignity and rights. They are endowed with reason and conscience and should act towards one another in a spirit of brotherhood.

Article 2
Everyone is entitled to all the rights and freedoms set forth in this Declaration, without distinction of any kind, such as race, colour, sex, language, religion, political or other opinion, national or social origin, property, birth or other status. Furthermore, no distinction shall be made on the basis of the political, jurisdictional or international status of the country or territory to which a person belongs, whether it be independent, trust, non-self-governing or under any other limitation of sovereignty.

Article 3
Everyone has the right to life, liberty and security of person.

Article 4
No one shall be held in slavery or servitude; slavery and the slave trade shall be prohibited in all their forms.

Article 5
No one shall be subjected to torture or to cruel, inhuman or degrading treatment or punishment.

Article 6
Everyone has the right to recognition everywhere as a person before the law.

Article 7
All are equal before the law and are entitled without any discrimination to equal protection of the law. All are entitled to equal protection against any discrimination in violation of this Declaration and against any incitement to such discrimination.

Article 8
Everyone has the right to an effective remedy by the competent national tribunals for acts violating the fundamental rights granted him by the constitution or by law.

Article 9
No one shall be subjected to arbitrary arrest, detention or exile.

Article 10
Everyone is entitled in full equality to a fair and public hearing by an independent and impartial tribunal, in the determination of his rights and obligations and of any criminal charge against him.

Article 11
(1) Everyone charged with a penal offence has the right to be presumed innocent until proved guilty according to law in a public trial at which he has had all the guarantees necessary for his defence.

(2) No one shall be held guilty of any penal offence on account of any act or omission which did not constitute a penal offence, under national or international law, at the time when it was committed. Nor shall a heavier penalty be imposed than the one that was applicable at the time the penal offence was committed.

Article 12
No one shall be subjected to arbitrary interference with his privacy, family, home or correspondence, nor to attacks upon his honour and reputation. Everyone has the right to the protection of the law against such interference or attacks.

Article 13
(1) Everyone has the right to freedom of movement and residence within the borders of each state.

(2) Everyone has the right to leave any country, including his own, and to return to his country.

Article 14

(1) Everyone has the right to seek and to enjoy in other countries asylum from persecution.

(2) This right may not be invoked in the case of prosecutions genuinely arising from non-political crimes or from acts contrary to the purposes and principles of the United Nations.

Article 15

(1) Everyone has the right to a nationality.

(2) No one shall be arbitrarily deprived of his nationality nor denied the right to change his nationality.

Article 16

(1) Men and women of full age, without any limitation due to race, nationality or religion, have the right to marry and to found a family. They are entitled to equal rights as to marriage, during marriage and at its dissolution.

(2) Marriage shall be entered into only with the free and full consent of the intending spouses.

(3) The family is the natural and fundamental group unit of society and is entitled to protection by society and the State.

Article 17

(1) Everyone has the right to own property alone as well as in association with others.

(2) No one shall be arbitrarily deprived of his property.

Article 18

Everyone has the right to freedom of thought, conscience and religion; this right includes freedom to change his religion or belief, and freedom, either alone or in community with others and in public or private, to manifest his religion or belief in teaching, practice, worship and observance.

Article 19

Everyone has the right to freedom of opinion and expression; this right includes freedom to hold opinions without interference and to seek, receive and impart information and ideas through any media and regardless of frontiers.

Article 20

(1) Everyone has the right to freedom of peaceful assembly and association.

(2) No one may be compelled to belong to an association.

Article 21

(1) Everyone has the right to take part in the government of his country, directly or through freely chosen representatives.

(2) Everyone has the right of equal access to public service in his country.

(3) The will of the people shall be the basis of the authority of government; this will shall be expressed in periodic and genuine elections which shall be by universal and equal suffrage and shall be held by secret vote or by equivalent free voting procedures.

Article 22

Everyone, as a member of society, has the right to social security and is entitled to realization, through national effort and international co-operation and in accordance with the Organization and resources of each State, of the economic, social and cultural rights indispensable for his dignity and the free development of his personality.

Article 23

(1) Everyone has the right to work, to free choice of employment, to just and favourable conditions of work and to protection against unemployment.

(2) Everyone, without any discrimination, has the right to equal pay for equal work.

(3) Everyone who works has the right to just and favourable remuneration ensuring for himself and his family an existence worthy of human dignity, and supplemented, if necessary, by other means of social protection.

(4) Everyone has the right to form and to join trade unions for the protection of his interests.

Article 24

Everyone has the right to rest and leisure, including reasonable limitation of working hours and periodic holidays with pay.

Article 25

(1) Everyone has the right to a standard of living adequate for the health and well-being of himself and of his family, including food, clothing, housing and medical care and necessary social services, and the right to security in the event of unemployment, sickness, disability, widowhood, old age or other lack of livelihood in circumstances beyond his control.

(2) Motherhood and childhood are entitled to special care and assistance. All children, whether born in or out of wedlock, shall enjoy the same social protection.

Article 26

(1) Everyone has the right to education. Education shall be free, at least in the elementary and fundamental stages. Elementary education shall be compulsory. Technical and professional education shall be made generally available and higher education shall be equally accessible to all on the basis of merit.

(2) Education shall be directed to the full development of the human personality and to the strengthening of respect for human rights and fundamental freedoms. It shall promote understanding, tolerance and friendship among all nations, racial or religious groups, and shall further the activities of the United Nations for the maintenance of peace.

(3) Parents have a prior right to choose the kind of education that shall be given to their children.

Article 27

(1) Everyone has the right freely to participate in the cultural life of the community, to enjoy the arts and to share in scientific advancement and its benefits.

(2) Everyone has the right to the protection of the moral and material interests resulting from any scientific, literary or artistic production of which he is the author.

Article 28

Everyone is entitled to a social and international order in which the rights and freedoms set forth in this Declaration can be fully realized.

Article 29

(1) Everyone has duties to the community in which alone the free and full development of his personality is possible.

(2) In the exercise of his rights and freedoms, everyone shall be subject only to such limitations as are determined by law solely for the purpose of securing due recognition and respect for the rights and freedoms of others and of meeting the just requirements of morality, public order and the general welfare in a democratic society.

(3) These rights and freedoms may in no case be exercised contrary to the purposes and principles of the United Nations.

Article 30

Nothing in this Declaration may be interpreted as implying for any State, group or person any right to engage in any activity or to perform any act aimed at the destruction of any of the rights and freedoms set forth herein.

Notes

1. Office of the United Nations High Commission for Human Rights 2001 Annual Report, 2001 (UNOHCHR, Geneva, Switzerland), p. 5.

2. Preamble to the UN Charter, June 26, 1945, 59 Stat. 1031, T.S. 993, entered into force October 24, 1945.

3. Myres S. McDougal, Harold D. Lasswell, and Lung-Chu Chen, *Human Rights and World Public Order: The Basic Policies of an International Law of Human Dignity* (New Haven, Conn.: Yale University Press, 1980).

4. Sergio Vieira de Mello, UN High Commissioner for Human Rights, "Their Dignity Will Be Mine, As It Is Yours," *United Nations Chronicle*, no. 4 (2002): 25–27.

5. See also Articles 75 and 87.

6. John D. Montgomery, "Fifty Years of Human Rights: An Emergent Global Regime," *Policy Sciences* 32 (1999): 80–81.

7. Antonio Cassese, *International Law in a Divided World* (New York: Oxford University Press, 1986).

8. See Philip Alston, "The Fortieth Anniversary of the Universal Declaration of Human Rights: A Time More for Reflection Than for Celebration," in Jan Berting et al., *Human Rights in a Pluralistic World* (London: Meckler, 1990), p. 4.

9. Oscar Schachter, *International Law in Theory and Practice*, 178 Recueil des Cours 21 (1991), pp. 334–335.

10. See Robert F. Drinann, *The Mobilization of Shame: A World View of Human Rights* (New Haven, Conn.: Yale University Press, 2001).

11. Stanley Hoffmann, *The State of War* (New York: Praeger, 1965), p. 70.

12. *The Nottebohm Judgment*, 54 A.J.I.L. 536, 1960, p. 545.

13. W. Michael Reisman, "Sovereignty and Human Rights in Contemporary International Law," *American Journal of International Law* 84 (1990): 869.

14. Dinah L. Shelton, "Human Rights," in P. J. Simmons and Chantal de Jonge Oudraat, eds., *Managing Global Issues* (Washington, D.C.: Brookings Institution Press, 2001), p. 424.

15. Charles Norchi, "The Universality Issue," NGO address at the World Conference on Human Rights, Vienna, 1993.

16. Sergio Vieira de Mello, UN High Commissioner for Human Rights, address to the OSCE Permanent Council, Vienna, November 21, 2002.

17. See Howard Tolley Jr., *The United Nations Commission on Human Rights* (Boulder: Westview Press, 1987).

18. Quoted at Commisson on Human Rights, www.eda.admin.ch/geneva_miss/e/home/confonu/cdh.html.

19. Vieira de Mello, "Their Dignity Will Be Mine," p. 26.

20. Ibid.

21. Stephen M. Schwebel, "Human Rights in the World Court," *Vanderbilt Journal of International Law* 24 (1991): 948.

22. *Legal Consequences for States of the Continued Presence of South Africa in Namibia (South-West Africa) Notwithstanding Security Council Resolution 276 (1970)*, 1971 I.C.J. 4.

23. *Barcelona Traction, Light and Power Company, Limited (Belg. v. Spain)*, 1970 I.C.J. 4, 32 (February 5).

24. Siegfried Wiessner and Andrew R. Willard, "Policy-Oriented Jurisprudence and Human Rights Abuses in Internal Conflict: Toward a World Public Order of Human Dignity," *American Journal of International Law* 93 (1999): 326.

25. Mahnoush H. Arsanjani, "The Rome Statute of the International Criminal Court," *American Journal of International Law* 93, no. 1 (January 1999): 22–23.

26. Sergio Vieira de Mello, UN High Commissioner for Human Rights, address to the International Criminal Law Network Conference, "Establishing the International Criminal Court," The Hague, December 18, 2002.

27. Unpublished letter dated May 6, 2002, from the U.S. government on file with the UN Office of Legal Affairs.

28. *Memorandum of Understanding Between the Office of the High Commissioner for Human Rights and the Department of Peacekeeping Operations*, concluded at Geneva, November 22, 2002.

29. Human rights organizations reported extensive and repeated violations. The victims were mostly civilians, and often children. See *Report of the Independent Counsel on International Human Rights Concerning Violations of the Laws of War in Afghanistan*, UN Doc. A/42/667 (1987).

30. For an analysis of how values are implicitly recognized in the Universal Declaration of Human Rights, see John D. Montgomery, "Human Rights as Universal Values," in John D. Montgomery, ed., *Human Rights: Positive Policies in Asia and the Pacific Rim* (Hollis, N.H.: Hollis, 1998).

31. Oral statement by the Chairman, Constitutional Loya Jirgah, Kabul, Afghanistan, December 29, 2003.

32. W. Michael Reisman and Aaron M. Schreiber, *Jurisprudence: Understanding and Shaping Law* (New Haven, Conn.: New Haven Press, 1987), p. 15.

33. See Charles Norchi, "A Pivotal States Human Rights Strategy," in Robert Chase, Emily Hill, and Paul Kennedy, eds., *The Pivotal States: A New Framework for U.S. Policy in the Developing World* (New York: W. W. Norton, 1999).

34. Samuel P. Huntington, "The Clash of Civilizations?" *Foreign Affairs* 72 (Summer 1993): 22.

35. Alston, "Fortieth Anniversary of the Universal Declaration of Human Rights," p. 7.

36. Myres S. McDougal, Harold D. Lasswell, and Lung-Chu Chen, "Human Rights and World Public Order: Human Rights in Comprehensive Context," *Northwestern University Law Review* (May–June 1977): 230.

37. "The essential meaning of human dignity as we understand it can be succinctly stated: it refers to a social process in which values are widely and not narrowly shared, and in which private choice, rather than coercion, is emphasized as the primary modality of power." Myres S. McDougal and Harold D. Lasswell, "The Identification and Appraisal of Diverse Systems of Public Order," in Myres S. McDougal et al., *Studies in World Public Order* (New Haven, Conn.: Yale University Press, 1960), p. 16.

38. Vieira de Mello, address to the OSCE Permanent Council, Vienna, November 21, 2002.

5

Free and Fair Elections: Letting the People Decide

Robin Ludwig

Since 1991, electoral assistance has become an important and well-known UN activity as countries around the world have begun to take steps toward more democratic government. The formal program of UN electoral assistance began with a mandate from the UN General Assembly in 1991, and a small Electoral Assistance Unit (EAU) was created within the Department of Political Affairs in 1992. Several major events during the 1980s led to the General Assembly's decision to provide a mandate for electoral assistance activities.

A critical factor was the end of the Cold War. One result was that peace agreements were concluded for a number of long-standing conflicts that had been fueled by tensions between East and West. Peace accords were reached on Angola, Cambodia, El Salvador, Nicaragua, and Mozambique. Included in the terms of the agreements were provisions for the conduct of elections under international auspices. In each of these cases, the United Nations was designated to provide assistance for elections. International agreement was also reached on Namibia's transition to independent statehood; the United Nations was called upon to supervise each phase of that process.

The end of the Cold War also brought about the disintegration of the Soviet Union into separate independent republics. These new states, as well as the former Eastern bloc, which included Bulgaria, Poland, Czechoslovakia, the German Democratic Republic, and Romania, moved quickly toward the holding of elections and the establishment of more democratic forms of government. In many of these cases, new and interim governments sought international advice and assistance in organizing and conducting elections, as well as in making the larger conversion from centralized systems to more democratic and mixed systems.

Another consequence of the Cold War's end was the disappearance of the primary alternative to Western liberal-democratic modes of governance. The collapse of the socialist command economy model left many developing countries without a viable source of guidance and support. Many African states were particularly affected by the withdrawal of Soviet financial assistance and other development aid. After years of seeking to replicate the Soviet model, these countries now confronted the reality that the Soviet system was literally bankrupt. Many states quickly recognized the need to change course; the most obvious route for them to take was toward the more democratic, market-oriented systems of the West and the resources those countries had to offer.

The United Nations was considered as a neutral actor in the midst of so many new and contradictory pressures. As a result, many countries sought UN assistance in undertaking the political transitions they required. The universal membership of the Organization helped to ensure that no one system for elections would be advocated. UN assistance, as compared to regional or bilateral assistance, was also viewed by many as having potentially fewer political motivations and, in certifying election results, as more likely to provide assessments based on established international standards.

A subtler factor in the demand for democratic change and electoral assistance was the emergence of human rights as an important foreign policy consideration. Many Western donors began to make financial assistance to developing countries conditional upon efforts by recipient governments to demonstrate "good governance." Good governance typically involves development of democratic institutions and processes, transparency, anticorruption measures, and encouragement of respect for human rights, particularly with regard to law enforcement and the judicial system.

The United Nations and Elections

The Decolonization Experience

Until the end of the Cold War, the United Nations had not been formally involved with elections in a sovereign state, but it did perform relevant work in the context of decolonization (as discussed briefly in Chapter 1), which took place largely in the 1960s and 1970s. In 1945, when the UN Charter was signed, almost a quarter of the world's population lived in dependent territories.[1] The original membership of the Organization totaled fifty-one countries. Africa, for example, had only four independent states: Egypt, Ethiopia, Liberia, and South Africa. Today, Africa is composed of some fifty-three sovereign states and the United Nations has 191 members. Decolonization effectively redrew the map of the world.

In keeping with its trusteeship and decolonization responsibilities under the Charter, the United Nations was requested to supervise the holding of referenda on the question of independent statehood in colonies and trust territories. Referenda were often organized by the colonial administrator in order to ascertain the wishes of the indigenous community regarding independent statehood. The UN's role was to ensure that such referenda were conducted fairly and that their results were legitimate.

General Assembly Debate on Electoral Assistance

The decision to provide electoral assistance to sovereign states was a controversial change in the activities of the United Nations. Two major concerns were raised in the General Assembly debates on this new role for the Organization. The first was that UN electoral assistance might constitute interference in the internal affairs of its Member States. The Charter states that "nothing contained in the present Charter shall authorize the United Nations to intervene in matters which are essentially within the domestic jurisdiction of any state" (Article 2). A second concern at this time, raised by India and China among others, was that the United Nations might promote a particular form of elections and governance. Their view was that such choices should be left to the discretion of each Member State. In addition, questions were raised about the basis upon which the Organization would choose the electoral system or procedures to be recommended.

As requests for electoral assistance began to increase, it was recognized that an ad hoc approach by the United Nations would not be sufficient. Although the UN role in the conduct of elections mandated by peace agreements was relatively clear and uncontroversial, the provision of assistance for any election required substantial planning and implementation, often within a very short time frame. Elections in Namibia took place in 1989, followed by elections in Nicaragua (1990), Angola (1992), Cambodia (1993), El Salvador (1993–1994), and Mozambique (1994). As international needs for electoral assistance began to grow in volume and complexity, the need for a systematic approach to the provision of electoral assistance was recognized within the Secretariat and supported by many Member States.

General Assembly Resolutions Related to Electoral Assistance

On December 17, 1991, the General Assembly adopted a resolution on enhancing the effectiveness of the principle of periodic and genuine elections (A/46/137). This resolution, sponsored by the United States, provided for the institutionalization of UN electoral assistance activities and requested the Secretary-General to designate a Focal Point for UN electoral assistance activities. The Focal Point is a person responsible for receiving all requests for assistance and determining the appropriate UN response. The Secretary-General designated the Under-Secretary-General for Political Affairs as the Focal Point and established a small unit within the Department of Political Affairs to assist him in evaluating each request for assistance and providing an appropriate response. The resolution also called for the establishment of a roster of election experts, creation of a voluntary trust fund for election observation activities, and the preparation of a clear set of guidelines for the provision of electoral assistance.

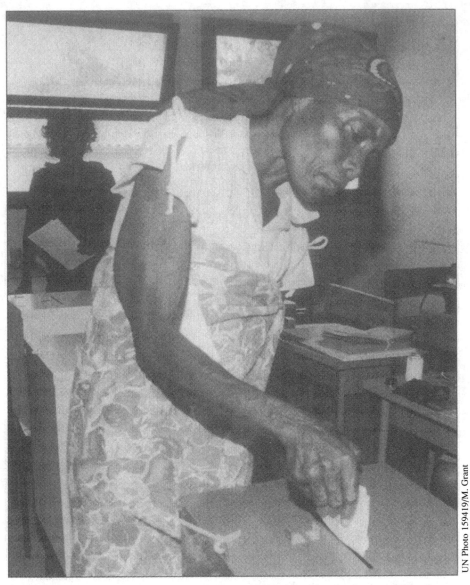

UN Photo 159419/M. Grant

A woman casting her ballot, participating in Angola's first multiparty election, September 1992.

In response to the concerns raised by Member States regarding potential interference in the internal affairs of states, a procedural requirement was established that the United Nations would provide electoral assistance only if a written request were received from an official representative of the particular Member State. This representative is normally the head of state, head of the election commission, or the prime minister. Although requests are occasionally received from political parties or nongovernmental organizations, such requests cannot be fulfilled.

An additional controversy arose in the debates regarding the physical location of the Electoral Assistance Unit. Some Member States and Secretariat staff believed that the office should be established within the Center for Human Rights, based in Geneva. Other Member States and UN officials believed that the office would be more appropriately placed in the Department of Political Affairs, based in New York. One of the reasons the latter view gained support was due to the type of assistance that was a priority at the time—elections held on the basis of peace agreements. In this context, elections were considered a tool in conflict resolution and an adjunct to peacekeeping operations. The office was ultimately established within the Department of Political Affairs and remains there today.

Even though the Electoral Assistance Unit was established in the Department of Political Affairs, regular reports on its work are always considered by the Third Committee of the General Assembly, which is responsible for human rights issues. Every two years the Secretary-General submits a report on the electoral assistance activities of the United Nations for consideration by this committee. The report and its accompanying resolution are titled "Strengthening the Role of the United Nations in Enhancing the Effectiveness of the Principle of Periodic and Genuine Elections and the Promotion of Democratization." Only after approval by the Third Committee is the report forwarded to the General Assembly for final approval and adoption of the resolution.

A second, related resolution (A/46/130), sponsored by Cuba, was adopted by the General Assembly in 1991. This resolution, titled "Respect for the Principles of National Sovereignty and Noninterference in the Internal Affairs of States in Their Electoral Processes," affirms among various considerations that "it is the concern solely of peoples to determine methods and to establish institutions regarding the electoral process, as well as to determine the ways for its implementation according to their constitution and national legislation." This item is also considered by the General Assembly on a regular basis. Cosponsors have included China, the Democratic People's Republic of Korea, the Lao People's Democratic Republic, Namibia, the United Republic of Tanzania, Vietnam, and Zimbabwe.

Procedures for UN Electoral Assistance
As indicated above, UN electoral assistance begins with the receipt of a written request for assistance by the Focal Point from the government or election commission. The request must normally be received with a minimum lead time of four months. Based on the timely receipt of a written request, the Electoral Assistance Division (EAD) usually organizes a needs assessment mis-

sion (NAM) to the country. A list of Member States that have requested electoral assistance is provided in the appendix to this chapter.

The purpose of the NAM is to determine whether the United Nations should provide electoral assistance and, if so, what type of assistance it should be. The NAM is normally composed of an EAD staff member and one elections consultant. They visit the requesting country for seven to ten days. During their visit they speak with government officials, the electoral commission, representatives of various political parties, the international donor community, the media, and representatives of civil society (such as the national bar association, women's groups, and human rights and religious organizations). Throughout their discussions, the NAM members seek to ascertain strengths and weaknesses in the existing electoral system and status of election planning, the political/security context in the country for the holding of elections, and whether support exists within the country for a UN role. If possible, the NAM members also travel outside the capital in order to obtain preliminary information on existing infrastructure such as roads, communications, utilities, and so forth.

Immediately following the mission, a report is prepared for submission to the Focal Point containing recommendations for UN action. The report also contains a preliminary budget for the recommended assistance. Prior to submitting its report, the NAM members often consult with other organizations that are potential providers of assistance in order to coordinate activities and avoid duplication of effort. The United Nations frequently consults with the Commonwealth,[2] the European Union, the Francophonie, and various regional organizations such as the Organization of American States (OAS), the Organization for Security and Cooperation in Europe (OSCE), and the African Union (AU, formerly the Organization of African Unity [OAU]). Other frequent partners include the International Institute for Democracy and Electoral Assistance (IDEA), the Carter Center, the International Foundation for Election Systems (IFES), and the National Democratic Institute (NDI).

Depending on the assessed needs and the time available before the election, a typical recommendation may focus on one type of assistance, such as coordination of observers, or may be more comprehensive, including one or more types of assistance. Only after final consideration and approval by the Focal Point will steps toward project implementation begin. In most cases this will involve preparation of a final project budget, discussions with donors to obtain the necessary funding, and recruitment of appropriate experts.

In the Field

Electoral Assistance Operations
By the mid-1990s, seven basic types of UN electoral assistance activities could be delineated: supervision; verification; organization and conduct;

coordination and support; support for domestic observers; technical assistance; and follow and report. Since that time, these models have been adapted and supplemented in accordance with the particular needs of requesting states.

In some cases, more than one type of assistance may be provided (for example, technical assistance with voter registration and international observation of the election) or assistance may be provided to the same country over several cycles of elections. The follow and report form of assistance, in which one or two officers are sent to observe an election and prepare an internal report for the Secretary-General, has been largely discontinued; it was found to be time-consuming and costly while having little positive effect on the electoral process.

The evolution in the types of assistance offered by the United Nations reflects not only the growing diversity of the requests received but also the positive change in national capabilities over the past decade as countries have strengthened their own electoral expertise. Most now have established independent national election commissions, many have provided them with permanent budgets and administrative staff, and many countries have established standards for political party and media activity. In Africa, Asia, the Caribbean, and other regions, associations of national election administrators have been created to encourage regional discussion of electoral issues and the sharing of expert services within the region. The creation of such networks is an important step in fostering and supporting sustainable electoral systems, a long-term goal of UN election assistance.

Supervision

Election (or referendum) supervision is close to becoming obsolete because it is only provided in nonsovereign states or territories. Namibia was the last major example of such assistance and, with its independence, there are few places where these procedures could apply. Supervisory assistance must be mandated by the Security Council or the General Assembly, and the relevant resolution must provide for the funding of such missions. A Special Representative of the Secretary-General is designated to oversee the mission. The role of the United Nations is to certify the legitimacy of each step in the election or referendum process.

The UN operation in Namibia, known as the UN Transition Assistance Group (UNTAG), was the culmination of over thirty years of UN involvement on behalf of the people of the territory. Although the Security Council had declared in 1969 that the continued presence of South Africa in the territory was illegal, nothing changed regarding Namibia's status as a de facto colony of South Africa. In 1978 the Security Council adopted resolution 435, which contained a plan for implementation of a settlement proposal that would lead to the establishment of Namibia's independence. Despite continued diplomatic efforts, little further progress was made until some ten years later.

In 1988, as the dynamics of the Cold War began to change, the governments of Angola, Cuba, and South Africa reached agreements for the withdrawal of Cuban and South African troops from Angola. The withdrawal of Cuban troops from Angola, which borders Namibia, had been politically linked to Namibian independence and was a condition set by South Africa. South Africa agreed to commit to a seven-month timetable for the implementation of resolution 435. This resolution called for the appointment of a South African Administrator-General to oversee elections for a Constituent Assembly in Namibia. This process would be conducted under the supervision and control of UNTAG, headed by the Special Representative of the Secretary-General, Martti Ahtisaari of Finland.

The basic goal of UNTAG was the holding of free and fair elections in Namibia. This required a change in existing political conditions so that an electoral campaign could be conducted in a democratic environment. Among the steps to be taken were a cease-fire between South Africa and Namibian rebel fighters, the South West Africa People's Organization (SWAPO); the dismantling and demilitarization of local paramilitary forces; release of all political prisoners and detainees before the start of the election campaign; repeal of all discriminatory and restrictive laws that might affect or impinge upon free and fair elections; and the return of refugees and former SWAPO forces under UN supervision. In addition to police and military components, the mission consisted of a large civilian component that was stationed throughout the country.

In carrying out his responsibilities for the political and electoral process, the Special Representative of the Secretary-General worked closely with the Administrator-General. He was required to assess the fairness and appropriateness of all measures taken by the authorities at each stage of the political process. Each stage of the electoral process, beginning with the registration of voters, continuing through the election campaign, to the counting of votes and publication of the results, was subject to his approval and certification.

At the time of the elections in November 1989, the mission had close to 8,000 staff members, including approximately 2,000 civilians, 1,500 civilian police (CIVPOL) monitors, and some 4,500 military officials. For Namibia's 23 electoral districts, some 358 polling stations were established, of which 215 were at fixed locations and 143 were mobile. At the fixed polling stations, 1,753 UNTAG electoral personnel supervised approximately 2,500 electoral officials appointed by the Administrator-General. In terms of UN electoral assistance, this remains the highest ratio of international staff to polling stations; such coverage is unlikely to be replicated.

Verification

Verification missions were the most common and well-recognized forms of electoral assistance operations in the early 1990s. They were relatively large, long-term, and typically organized in the context of peacekeeping missions and peace agreements. The concept of international election observation was developed and refined in the context of these missions, as hundreds of international observers were trained and deployed in order to report on the ongoing conduct of election processes up to, and through, the counting of the votes. A crucial aspect of verification missions is the provision of both geographic and chronological coverage of the entire process.

Verification missions are conducted in sovereign states and require a mandate from the Security Council or the General Assembly; this mandate also provides for the necessary extrabudgetary funding. Among the best known of these missions are Nicaragua (1990), Angola (1992), El Salvador (1993–1994), and Mozambique (1994). In each of these cases, a Special Representative of the Secretary-General was appointed to lead the mission. In contrast to supervisory missions, the government retains the responsibility for organizing and conducting the elections; the United Nations is responsible for verifying the legitimacy of the process.

The United Nations began formal preparations for the 1994 elections in Mozambique following the signing of a peace agreement in 1992 between the government of Mozambique and the Resistencia Nacional Mocambicana (Renamo) opposition. In December of that year, the Security Council established the UN mission in Mozambique (ONUMOZ), providing it with a complex and challenging mandate. Among its tasks were the verification and monitoring of the cease-fire, demobilization of former combatants, demining, and the return of refugees. Only after these tasks had been achieved could the scheduling and organization of elections begin.

Organizing elections in the context of larger peacekeeping operations led over several years to further refinements in terms of election timing and the need for flexibility and coordination of the various mission components. An important consideration for ONUMOZ and all other verification missions was the need to ensure that the conditions necessary for a legitimate electoral process were in place prior to the holding of elections. If an important peacekeeping element, such as the demobilization of soldiers, was to fall behind in implementation, plans for elections could be affected. Delays, however, could not always be avoided and were not totally within UN control.

The United Nations can sometimes face a serious dilemma as it works to create the necessary preconditions for a credible election. For example, delays may occur in activities such as the demobilization of troops, and the UN cannot control the speed with which former soldiers turn in their arms. As the mission timetable is delayed, however, the efficacy of the mission may be questioned by its Member States and the expense of the operation will grow. If elections are conducted without the necessary preconditions, however, the credibility of the results may be challenged and the entire exercise might ultimately prove futile. The work of the second UN Verification Mission in

Angola (UNAVEM II), and the unfortunate elections of September 29–30, 1992, should be reviewed and assessed in this context. Aldo Ajello, the Special Representative of the Secretary-General and head of the UN mission in Mozambique, was very aware of the UNAVEM II experience throughout the planning and implementation phases of ONUMOZ.

Although ONUMOZ was a multiphased, complex peacekeeping operation, its various phases and timing went generally according to plan. The electoral process formally began on December 9, 1993, with the designation of the twenty-one members of the Electoral Commission and the adoption of the Electoral Law by the Mozambican National Assembly. Both the UN Secretariat and the UN Development Programme (UNDP) played important roles in assisting with the preparations for elections. UNDP provided technical assistance to the Electoral Commission and its Technical Secretariat for Elections Administration in carrying out the provisions of the Electoral Law. The United Nations also assisted with the creation and functioning of the Electoral Tribunal, which included three international judges designated by the United Nations. The tribunal assisted in the training of 1,600 voter registration teams, civic education agents, and some 60,000 election day poll workers.

The UN observation of the electoral process formally began with the deployment of 126 long-term observers in June 1994. They were deployed throughout various provinces and districts of Mozambique, including the capital, Maputo. Their functions included the monitoring of voter registration, civic education campaigns, the press, and the activities of political parties and their leaders before and during the electoral campaign. They were also responsible for receiving complaints from individuals or political parties and forwarding such complaints to the National Electoral Commission.

The numbers of observers gradually increased until the final phase of the elections. At that time, some 2,300 international observers were deployed throughout the country. On November 19, 1994, the chairman of the National Electoral Commission formally announced the election results. The Special Representative of the Secretary-General declared that, based on reports from the international observers, the elections could be considered free and fair.

Organization and Conduct

The United Nations is rarely called upon to organize and conduct an election in a Member State. The first and most extensive mission of this kind took place with the Cambodian elections of 1993, which were conducted in the context of the largest and most complex peacekeeping operation in UN history. The UN role in the 1993 Cambodian elections was determined by the 1991 Agreements on a Comprehensive Political Settlement of the Cambodia Conflict (Paris Agreements). The agreements, which were signed by Cambodia and eighteen other nations in the presence of the Secretary-General, invited the United Nations to establish the UN Transitional Authority in Cambodia (UNTAC). Article 12, in the second part of the agreements, provided that the people of Cambodia would determine their own political future through a process of free and fair elections. This would be achieved by electing a constituent assembly, which would draft and approve a new Cambodian constitution and transform itself into a legislative assembly; this assembly would then create the Cambodian government. The elections were to be held under UN auspices.

The first UN needs assessment mission visited Cambodia in late 1991, and a detailed implementation plan for UNTAC was submitted by the Secretary-General to the Security Council in February 1992. In resolution 745, the Security Council established UNTAC, approved the implementation plan, and decided that elections should be held in Cambodia by May 1993 at the latest. Yasushi Akashi was designated by the Secretary-General as his Special Representative for Cambodia. Resolution 745 established a precedent in UN electoral assistance by providing a mandate for the Organization to conduct an election in a Member State. In its previous electoral assistance operations, the United Nations had verified or supervised the organization and conduct of elections by national authorities. In this case, however, the United Nations was mandated to assume the functions of a national authority.

The electoral component of UNTAC was responsible for five basic electoral activities: preparation of a legal framework, civic education and training, voter registration, political parties and candidates, and polling. The electoral calendar and system were also subject to UNTAC elaboration. As one component in the larger peacekeeping operation, the electoral activities and their timing were closely coordinated with the activities of the other civil and military components of UNTAC.

In the absence of an accepted Cambodian governing authority, the United Nations served as a quasi-government. Although planning for the Cambodian elections began in 1991, the first steps toward the 1993 elections included the repatriation of refugees from Thailand and other neighboring countries, initiation of a demining program, and establishment of a UN radio station. Each of these activities contributed to the creation of conditions for legitimate elections. Despite problems with political negotiations, voter registration began as scheduled in the original implementation timetable on October 5, 1992. By the close of voter registration on January 31, 1993, 4.7 million voters (some 96 percent of the estimated eligible population) were on the voter list.

By early May, the technical preparations for the elections were largely complete. Twenty political parties had been formally registered and an intensive voter education campaign had been conducted. All the necessary equipment, such as ballot boxes and ballot papers, had arrived in Cambodia. Some 50,000 Cambodian electoral officials had been identified and trained, and some 1,000 international polling station officers had been recruited. Although there were concerns that the election days might be affected by violence,

UNTAC continued its preparations and later conduct of the elections in accordance with its specified schedule.

The election campaign period closed on May 19, and the polls opened on May 23 following a four-day "cooling off" period. Polling took place from May 23 to May 28 with almost no incidents, despite threats of disruption by the Party of Democratic Kampuchea (PDK). Voter turnout was 4,267,192 voters, or 85.96 percent of registered voters. On May 29, Special Representative Akashi declared that the conduct of the elections had been free and fair. The final vote count proceeded slowly, however, due to the need for accuracy. On June 10 the Special Representative declared that the results fairly and accurately reflected the will of the Cambodian people and must be respected.

The United Nations also conducted the 1999 referendum to determine whether East Timor would remain a part of Indonesia or move toward independence, but the experience was significantly different from Cambodia's. The referendum was planned and implemented in months, rather than years. The lack of lead time reflected the rapid evolution of political conditions (primarily the scheduling of Indonesia's first multiparty elections in May 1999), which provided a single window of opportunity for holding the referendum. Given the chance to resolve this long-standing problem of decolonization, the Security Council agreed on May 7 that the United Nations should proceed despite a number of serious obstacles.

The East Timorese voting population was significantly smaller than the Cambodian population; some 446,953 East Timorese ultimately cast ballots in the referendum. An additional important contrast with Cambodia was the lack of a UN peacekeeping presence. No peacekeeping operation was mandated until the postreferendum period, and security in East Timor remained the responsibility of the Indonesian government. This provision of the May 5 Agreements, signed by the Republic of Indonesia and the Republic of Portugal, was to have serious consequences throughout and particularly after the conduct of the referendum.

In a massive and concerted effort, the United Nations organized and conducted the referendum in East Timor and at thirteen external polling centers between May 1 and August 30, 1999. The political transition occurring in Indonesia at that time made it imperative that the referendum be completed before the first meeting of the Indonesian People's Assembly (MPR), following national elections in June 1999. The still-acting government of President B. J. Habibie would then recommend to the newly constituted MPR that it should rescind the 1976 law integrating East Timor into Indonesia if the referendum proved this to be the preference of the East Timorese voters. A future Indonesian government might not be willing to make that recommendation.

The first needs assessment mission visited East Timor in early May 1999, shortly after the signing of the New York agreements. The organizational and logistic challenges were immense. The mission required some 1,000 international staff to work with approximately 4,000 locally hired personnel throughout East Timor to conduct registration and the subsequent voting at 400 polling stations. Transportation and communications infrastructures were extremely limited in East Timor and the Field Administration and Logistics Division (FALD) of the Department of Peacekeeping Operations assumed responsibility for organizing the necessary supply arrangements. Many involved with the implementation process believed that the referendum timetable set out in the May 5 Agreements was unrealistic from the very beginning.

Despite these challenges and serious security concerns, registration began on July 16 and continued for twenty-two days. The turnout was massive, and many registration centers required supplementary resources in order to handle the crowds of people waiting to register. Registration teams in many areas worked from dawn until dusk each day of the registration period to ensure inclusion on the lists of everyone entitled to register. Following the posting of registration lists and a fifteen-day campaign period, the referendum took place on August 30, 1999, only slightly delayed from the original target date of August 8. Some 98.6 percent of all East Timorese who had registered cast their ballots inside and outside the territory. The vote count was conducted centrally in Dili, similar to the procedure used in Cambodia, in order to ensure the secrecy of local voting patterns. The results of the referendum (78.5 percent for independence) were announced on September 4 by the Special Representative of the Secretary-General, Ian Martin, and certified shortly thereafter by the Independent Electoral Commission.

In order to assist East Timor in its transition toward independence, the Security Council adopted resolution 1272 on October 25, 1999, and established the United Nations Transitional Administration in East Timor (UNTAET). UNTAET, under the leadership of the Special Representative of the Secretary-General, Sergio Vieira de Mello, was given overall responsibility for the administration of East Timor. Among those responsibilities was ensuring the organization and conduct of credible elections in collaboration with the East Timorese people. Two critical elections were needed: elections for eighty-eight members of the new Constituent Assembly, and presidential elections.

The Constituent Assembly elections, held on August 30, 2001, were an important step toward independence. Although serious concerns existed, based on past experience, regarding the potential for violence and disruption of the process, the elections were conducted in the most peaceful environment encountered in United Nations electoral history. The members of the assembly were sworn in on September 13, 2001. Although they faced many new tasks and challenges, a priority was the drafting of the first constitution for an independent East Timor. Based on their work, the constitution was adopted in early 2002. The Constituent Assembly also decided that presidential elections should be held in the first two weeks of April 2002.

In beginning its preparations for the presidential elections, UNTAET placed increased emphasis on encouraging the involvement and participation of the East Timorese in its work. The operational plan for the elections included a strong focus on including East Timorese electoral officers in all aspects of electoral planning and implementation at headquarters, district, and local levels; conducting various types of training programs; and promoting greater district autonomy with support from headquarters. The Independent Electoral Commission also emphasized special measures to promote the participation of East Timorese women in the electoral process, whether as voters, election administrators, or candidates.

Presidential elections were held on April 14, 2002, following approximately four weeks of campaigning. Although only two candidates ran for president, several political parties had been established, providing an important basis for future electoral contests. Some seventy-two East Timorese and thirty-five international observer groups were accredited by the Independent Electoral Commission to observe the process. The first president of an independent East Timor became Jose Alexandre Xanana Gusmão, based on his receiving 83 percent of the vote.

The final step in East Timor's transition to independence came at midnight on May 19, 2002. At that time, the United Nations flag was lowered in Dili, the capital, and the new flag of the Democratic Republic of Timor-Leste was raised. On September 27, 2002, Timor-Leste became the 191st member of the United Nations, the first new independent state of the twenty-first century.

Coordination and Support

In the early 1990s, the growing number of requests for international observers led to several innovations. Due to the time required to obtain Security Council or General Assembly approval and the financial resources required for the large-scale missions described above, a new form of assistance was developed that could be implemented with a far shorter lead time and at significantly lower cost. By the end of the decade, this type of assistance was provided more frequently than any other observation-related assistance.

The coordination and support model was first effectively used in 1993 following a 1992 request by the government of Malawi for assistance in organizing and conducting a referendum on the question of single or multiparty government. Following two needs assessment missions, the Electoral Assistance Unit recommended that a small Electoral Assistance Secretariat (EAS) should be established in Malawi to coordinate the activities of international observers invited to follow registration, the campaign, polling, and the vote count. The EAS would communicate periodically with the Referendum Commission on the reports of the observers and would provide advice as to international standards and practice throughout the electoral process. The International Foundation for Election Systems (IFES) provided poll-worker training and civic education in the context of the broader EAS assistance project.

This mission varied significantly from large-scale verification and organization missions and conduct missions. In this case, the United Nations provided assistance based on the request of the Malawi government and without resort to the Security Council or General Assembly for approval. Financing of the observation was organized on a voluntary basis by inviting interested Member States to provide observers and pay for their costs, as well as a small additional fee to cover their coordination by the EAS. The rationale was that costs for each country sending observers would be lower by contributing to a pool of common expenses (such as briefing materials, briefings, deployment plans, and vehicles and drivers) than by organizing and paying for such resources independently. By working together, observers would also obtain broader coverage of the electoral process throughout the country, rather than relying on reports from a limited number of observers who visited perhaps five to eight polling stations.

The observers, once brought together, constituted a Joint International Observer Group (JIOG) composed of many nationalities. They were required to prepare a common statement after the referendum, but following its release they were free to issue additional statements on behalf of their delegations. Since the JIOG was not composed of UN employees, no statements made could be attributed to the United Nations. An advantage of this form of electoral assistance was that it safeguarded the integrity of the observer statement, since all observers left the country following the vote count and no participant remained in the country to suffer possible reprisals or enjoy potential benefits.

In the case of Malawi, the EAS deployed 210 international observers for the June 14, 1993, referendum. A number of observers also participated in observing registration and the campaign period. On June 17 the international observers gathered in Lilongwe for a debriefing and then issued a short statement regarding their observations on voting and the vote count. They found that the referendum process had provided a legitimate reflection of the wishes of the Malawi people.

The coordination and support model of election assistance was used in Malawi again in 1994 for its first multiparty elections. This model is the most frequently applied and adapted of all assistance models related to observation. It has been used in Armenia (1995), Cambodia (1997), Lesotho (1998), Nepal (1999), Niger (1999), Nigeria (1998–1999), Mali (1997), South Africa (1999), Tanzania (1995, 2000), and many other countries. Largely as a result of the effectiveness of the coordination and support model, the United Nations today rarely recruits individuals to serve as international observers. Individuals interested in participating in election observation are advised to contact their governments in order to be included on their national observer rosters.

One cautionary note regarding coordination and support missions is appropriate. As election observation has become more routine, it is tempting for sponsoring organizations and governments to send observers for very short periods of time—primarily for voting day and the vote count. Although this is clearly economical and easier to organize for sponsors than longer-term observation, observer statements made on this basis have very limited value. The observation may serve the purpose of confidence building among the voting population, but it does not provide a comprehensive electoral assessment. Common sense suggests election fraud and rigging will not occur on election day—when international observers and the media are watching—but much earlier, during boundary delimitation, registration, and/or the election campaign. It is therefore important to avoid "shortcuts" that undermine the validity of the observation and to ensure that international observers abide by established international standards for election observation; "observer tourists" should stay at home.

Support for Domestic Observers

In late May 1994 the United Nations received a request for electoral assistance from the government of Mexico. Its request was for two specific types of assistance: the preparation of an analytical report on the Mexican electoral system, and technical and financial assistance for national observers who would follow the electoral process leading to elections on August 21. In June the United Nations established the Technical Assistance Team in Mexico (ETONU-MEX) in order to assist with the national observation. ETONU-MEX ultimately provided assistance to fourteen national nongovernmental organizations that successfully mobilized 30,000 observers. ETONU-MEX contributed to their training, deployment, and the preparation of observer manuals and technical quick counts. During the election period, ETONU-MEX advised and evaluated the performance of Mexico's first domestic observation exercise. Domestic observation has been conducted in Mexico for national and some state elections since 1994.

The organization of domestic observation and monitoring groups has also occurred in Indonesia, Kenya, and several other countries. Although this is a very positive development, as it allows nationals to observe and comment on their own national process, it also requires resources that are not available in every country. Such operations require an effective network of civil society organizations whose members can be trained to take on this sensitive task and whose credibility is accepted. Financial resources must also be available. Finally, the observation methodology must be sufficiently comprehensive to ensure that the results justify the time and cost involved in the observation preparations and implementation.

Technical Assistance

Despite the international attention devoted to election observation, the type of assistance that is most frequently requested and provided is technical. Technical assistance may involve advisory services on a particular issue for several days, or it may require hands-on assistance for several months. As more national election administrators acquire experience and expertise, their needs for assistance have become increasingly specific and diverse. Technical assistance is the most flexible form of assistance, often the least intrusive, and generally aimed at national capacity building.

The Electoral Assistance Division maintains a roster of international election experts who may be called upon depending on their particular expertise and a requesting country's needs at any given time. Among the types of technical assistance that are frequently provided are electoral boundary delimitation, voter registration, computerization of registration rolls, preparation of election budgets and calendars, election administration, poll-worker training, civic education, and judicial review of election laws, constitutions, and other legal texts. Recent interest in external voting procedures and information technology applications has added new areas for expert advisory services.

Technical assistance is often combined with other forms of assistance. The United Nations may assist with computerization of voter registration rolls and provide coordination for international observers during the electoral process. Assistance may be given in sequence or simultaneously, depending on the need. The only true caveat in the combining of assistance models is that the United Nations does not participate in observing elections it is organizing and conducting.

In East Timor, for example, United Nations Mission in East Timor (UNAMET) was responsible for organizing and conducting the 1999 referendum but had no mandate to coordinate observers or to observe the electoral process. To undertake both tasks would have been a clear conflict of interest, since no organization should be placed in the position of evaluating its own conduct of an electoral process. In its role as referendum administrator, UNAMET ultimately accredited over 2,000 observers. They were provided general briefings and a code of conduct; all other arrangements for international observers were outside UNAMET's responsibility.

Future Trends in Electoral Assistance

Fundamental changes have occurred in the provision of UN electoral assistance during the past decade. Although some elections are still related to peace agreements and large-scale peacekeeping operations, the vast majority occur on a regular basis and without serious security constraints. It has also been learned that a successful election does not signal the end of a political process and international disengagement; an election is only one step in the longer-term and challenging process of democratization. Although the types of assistance requested are changing and diversifying, the overall demand for UN assistance remains high.

Among the most positive developments is the increase in national election administration expertise. In many countries the election commission and administrative staff now have permanent status, with regular funding from the national budget. This is in sharp contrast to the past practice in many countries of creating a new commission and administration for each election and obtaining funding on an ad hoc basis. This continuity is saving scarce resources in many countries, as new staffers do not have to be identified and trained, and elections can be scheduled with sufficient lead time to ensure early, economical purchasing of election materials. Instead of conducting an entirely new registration process for each election, the rolls can be maintained and updated on an ongoing basis.

As election administrators have become more capable, the need for international election observation has declined. Although observation will continue to be important, particularly in peacekeeping contexts, voters in many countries have now experienced two or more cycles of elections that were considered orderly, peaceful, and legitimate. The confidence-building elements of international observation are no longer as important when voters trust that elections in their countries will be conducted properly.

Regional associations of election administrators now exist in Africa, Central Asia, Eastern Europe, North America, and the Asian/Pacific and Latin American/Caribbean areas. A first global meeting of representatives from these and all other such associations took place in Ottawa, Canada, in April 1999. The meeting, sponsored by the United Nations, Elections Canada, International IDEA, and IFES, was designed to encourage networking and an exchange of experience among the various associations.

Taking advantage of new technologies, the United Nations, in partnership with UNDP, International IDEA, and IFES, is providing ongoing technical assistance to election administrators by means of a website and a CD-ROM titled "The Administration and Cost of Elections" (ACE). The ACE project provides comprehensive information and analysis on technical alternatives in election administration, functions, processes, and costs. Its advantages for election administrators are its comprehensive information base, easy computer access at any time, and no-cost availability.

Despite the progress that has been made in creating greater national and regional capacity to conduct elections without outside assistance, the path toward periodic and legitimate elections is not necessarily linear. History has demonstrated that young democracies do not always stay on that path, although they may return at some later stage. Elections are only one component in broader efforts at democratization; their significance is diminished if other important components, such as the rule of law, a free and diverse media, or an informed citizenry, are lacking.

Today, the greatest demand for UN support lies in technical assistance and advisory services. These will be further adapted as appropriate, targeting specific priorities such as civic education or boundary delimitation. In some cases the United Nations may conduct technical audits of specific components of an electoral process, such as registration or the vote count. In other cases, the UN may place conditions on its assistance in order to ensure that its support in one area cannot later be used to suggest the legitimacy of a larger process that is flawed.

Despite the changes in electoral assistance activities, several basic goals of UN assistance have remained constant: to provide the best possible assistance to the requesting state, tailored to meet its particular needs; to provide the least intrusive assistance possible and work closely with national counterparts; and to contribute to national capacity building. The ultimate goal for UN electoral assistance is for its membership no longer to need its services. Until that time, the United Nations will continue to respond to requests from its members in a timely and creative manner.

Appendix: Member State Requests to the UN System for Electoral Assistance, 1989–August 2003

Member State	Date of Request	Period of Assistance	United Nations Response[a]
Afghanistan	Feb. 2003	Ongoing	Providing assistance for the registration process in connection with the preparation of the elections scheduled for 2004.
Albania	Feb. 1992	Mar. 1992	Provided technical assistance. Elections held in Mar. 1992.
	June 1996	—	Unable to fulfill request for observers for the rerun elections on June 16, 1996, due to insufficient lead time.
	Aug. 1999	Sept. 1999–July 2001	Provided technical assistance related to the voter registration lists. Elections held in Oct. 2000 and June 2001.
Algeria	Aug. 1995	Sept. 1995–Nov. 1995	Provided follow and report for presidential elections held on Nov. 16, 1995.
	Feb. 1997	March 3–June 6, 1997	Provided coordination and support. Parliamentary elections held on June 5, 1997.

Member State	Date of Request	Period of Assistance	United Nations Response[a]
Angola	May 1991[b]	Apr. 1992–Dec. 1992	Provided verification and technical assistance. Presidential and legislative elections held in Sept. 1992.
	Aug. 2002	Under preparation	Under Security Council resolution 1433, the UN was mandated to provide technical assistance to the government of Angola for the preparation of elections. Assistance currently in abeyance.
Argentina	Sept. 1992	Nov. 1992–June 1994	Provided technical assistance. Elections held in Oct. 1993.
	Mar. 2003	Mar. 2003–current	Provided technical assistance in connection with the elections in Mar. 2003. Postelectoral assistance under preparation.
Armenia	Jan. 1995	Aug. 1995	Provided coordination and support (jointly with the OSCE). Legislative elections held on July 5 and July 19, 1995.
	July 1996	—	Unable to fulfill request for observers for presidential elections held on Sept. 22, 1996, due to insufficient lead time.
	Feb. 1998	Feb. 1998–Mar. 1998	Unable to fulfill request for UN observers. Provided technical assistance for the first round of presidential elections held on Mar. 16, 1998, and second round on Mar. 30, 1998.
	Mar. 1999	Apr. 1999–June 1999	Unable to fulfill request for observers to monitor the elections of the National Assembly of the Republic of Armenia held on May 30, 1999. Technical assistance provided.
	Aug. 2002	Sept. 2002–June 2003	Provided technical assistance. Local elections on Oct. 20, 2002, presidential elections on Feb. 19, 2003, and parliamentary elections on May 25, 2003.

Member State	Date of Request	Period of Assistance	United Nations Response[a]
Azerbaijan	May 1992	—	Unable to fulfill request for observers for the presidential elections to be held on June 7, 1992, due to insufficient lead time.
	Aug. 1993	—	Unable to fulfill request for observers for the referendum on Aug. 29, 1993, due to insufficient lead time and absence of enabling environment.
	June 1995	June 1995–Dec. 1995	Provided coordination and support (jointly with the OSCE). Parliamentary elections held on Nov. 12, 1995.
	July 1998	—	Unable to fulfill request for observers to the presidential elections held on Oct. 11, 1998.
	Aug. 2000	—	Unable to fulfill request to send UN observers for the Milli Majlis elections of Nov. 6, 2000, as observation activities are deferred to the OSCE, the regional lead organization.
	July 2002	—	Unable to fulfill request for observers for the referendum on the constitution on Aug. 24, 2002, due to lack of lead time.
Bangladesh	Feb. 1995	Mar. 1995	Conducted needs assessment mission and provided a technical report.
	May 1996	July 1996	Provided technical assistance. Elections held on June 12, 1996.
	Mar. 2001	Aug. 2001–Oct. 2001	Provided coordination and support of international observers. General elections held on Oct. 1, 2001.
Belarus	May 1994	—	Unable to fulfill request for observers for the presidential elections on June 23, 1994, due to insufficient lead time.
	Aug. 2000	—	Unable to fulfill request to send UN observers for the parliamentary elections in Oct. 2000.

Member State	Date of Request	Period of Assistance	United Nations Response[a]
Benin	Mar. 1995	Mar. 1995	Provided coordination and support (through UNDP). Legislative elections held in Mar. 1995.
	Feb. 1996	—	Unable to fulfill request for observers for the presidential elections on Mar. 3, 1996, due to insufficient lead time.
	Aug. 2002	Aug. 2002–Apr. 2003	Provided technical assistance for the preparation of local elections on Dec. 15, 2002, and legislative elections in Mar. 2003.
Bolivia	Oct. 2001	Dec. 2001–July 2002	Provided technical assistance for the general elections on June 30, 2002.
Brazil	Nov. 1993	Dec. 1993–Dec. 1995	Provided technical assistance. General elections held in Oct. 1994. Assisted in improving computerized electoral system.
Burkina Faso	Aug. 1996	Feb. 1997	Request for assistance to organize the electoral process. Needs assessment mission conducted in Feb. 1997 and technical report submitted. Legislative elections held on May 11, 1997.
	Apr. 1997	—	Unable to fulfill request for observers received through UNHCR due to insufficient lead time.
	Sept. 1998	—	Unable to fulfill request for observers for the presidential elections on Nov. 15, 1998, due to insufficient lead time.
Burundi	Dec. 1992	June 1993	Provided technical assistance and coordination and support. Presidential and legislative elections held in June 1993.
Cambodia	Oct. 1991[c]	Nov. 1991–June 1993	Provided organization and conduct. Elections held in May 1993.
	June 1996	Sept. 1997–May 1998	Provided technical assistance. National Assembly elections held on July 26, 1998.

Member State	Date of Request	Period of Assistance	United Nations Response[a]
	Oct. 1997	Apr. 1998–Aug. 1998	Provided coordination and support. National Assembly elections held on July 26, 1998.
	Feb. 2001	Mar. 2001–Aug. 2003	Provided technical assistance for the municipal elections in February 2002, followed by the parliamentary elections in July 2003.
Cameroon	Feb. 1992	Mar. 1992	Provided follow and report. Legislative elections held in Mar. 1992.
	Oct. 1997	—	Unable to fulfill request for observers for presidential elections on Oct. 12, 1997, due to insufficient lead time.
	May 2003	Under consideration	Request for assistance for the presidential elections in 2004. Needs assessment mission conducted in July 2003.
Cape Verde	Nov. 1995	—	Unable to fulfill request for financial assistance for the organization of the municipal elections on Jan. 21, 1996, due to lack of funds.
Central African Republic	June 1992[d]	Oct. 1992	Provided coordination and support. General elections held in Oct. 1992.
	July 1993	Sept. 1993	Provided follow and report. General elections held in Aug. and Sept. 1993.
	Jan. 1998	May 1998–Jan. 1999	Under MINURCA's mandate, provided technical assistance in the preparation of legislative elections held on Nov. 22, 1998 (1st round), and Dec. 13, 1998. Limited observation was also provided.
	Feb. 1999	Mar. 1999–Dec. 1999	Provided observation and technical assistance for the preparation of the presidential elections held on Sept. 19, 1999, through MINURCA and UNDP. Observation of the electoral process by MINURCA.

Member State	Date of Request	Period of Assistance	United Nations Response[a]
	June 2002	—	Request for assistance for the local elections scheduled for 2002. Due to political situation in the country, no activities were undertaken.
	July 2002	Under consideration	Request for technical and financial assistance to the electoral process.
Chad	Dec. 1992	Apr. 1993	Provided technical assistance in connection with the national conference held from Jan. to Apr. 1993.
	Jan. 1995	Mar. 1995–July 1996	Provided technical assistance. Presidential elections held on June 2 and July 3, 1996.
	Feb. 1996	Mar. 1996–July 1996	Provided coordination and support, in addition to technical assistance. Presidential elections held on June 2 and July 3, 1996.
	Apr. 2000	Nov. 2000–June 2001	Provided technical assistance in the preparation of the legislative, local, and presidential elections in Feb. and June 2001.
	Jan. 2002	—	Unable to fulfill request for financial assistance for the legislative elections in Mar. 2002.
Colombia	Feb. 1993	June 1993–Dec. 1994	Provided technical assistance in improving the electoral system.
	May 1999	—	Unable to fulfill request for technical assistance to reform electoral system.
	Nov. 2002	Dec. 2002–current	Request for technical assistance to reform the electoral system. Needs assessment mission conducted in Dec. 2002.
Comoros	Oct. 1995	Nov. 1995–Mar. 1996	Provided technical assistance and coordination and support. Presidential elections held on Mar. 6 and Mar. 10, 1996.
	May 1996	Dec. 1996	Provided technical assistance. Constitutional referendum held on Oct. 20, 1996, and legislative elections on Dec. 1, 1996.

Member State	Date of Request	Period of Assistance	United Nations Response[a]
	Nov. 1996	—	Unable to fulfill request for observers for the legislative elections held on Dec. 1, 1996.
	Aug. 2000	—	Request for technical and financial assistance to the electoral process.
	Nov. 2000	—	Second request for assistance in the preparation of the upcoming elections.
	May 2001	July 2001– May 2002	Provided technical assistance and coordination and support for the presidential elections on Apr. 14, 2002.
Congo	July 1992	Aug. 1992	Provided follow and report. Presidential elections held in Aug. 1992.
	Nov. 1992	May 1993	Provided coordination and support. Legislative elections held in May 1993.
	Mar. 1995	—	Unable to fulfill request for observers for the last phase of the legislative elections on Apr. 9, 1995, due to insufficient lead time.
	Mar. 1997	—	Unable to fulfill request for technical and material assistance. Presidential elections scheduled for July 27, 1997. Needs assessment mission conducted in early May 1997.
	May 1997	—	Unable to fulfill request for observers for the presidential elections on July 27, 1997.
	Feb. 1999	—	Request for assistance for upcoming elections. More detailed information requested. No further action taken.
	Mar. 2001	—	Request for assistance in connection with the upcoming referendum on the constitution and general elections received. Needs assessment proposed, pending adoption of the electoral calendar. No further action taken.

Member State	Date of Request	Period of Assistance	United Nations Response[a]
Côte d'Ivoire	Apr. 1995	July 1995–Nov. 1995	Provided coordination and support. Presidential elections held on Oct. 22, 1995, and legislative elections held on Nov. 26, 1995.
	Feb. 2000	Mar. 2000–Jan. 2001	Provided technical assistance in the preparation of the presidential elections on Oct. 22, 2000, and legislative elections on Dec. 10, 2000. Coordination and support to international observers discontinued.
	Nov. 2000	Nov. 2000–Dec. 2000	Continuation of technical assistance for the legislative elections on Dec. 10, 2000.
	Mar. 2002	May 2002–July 2002	Provided technical assistance and coordination and support. Local elections held on July 7, 2002.
	Sept. 2003	Under consideration	Request for assistance in connection with the upcoming elections in 2005.
Democratic Republic of Congo (the former Zaire)	Oct. 1998	—	Unable to fulfill request for funding the electoral census in preparation for a referendum and general elections in 1999.
Djibouti	Aug. 1992	Sept. 1992	Provided follow and report. Referendum held in Sept. 1992.
	Nov. 1992	Dec. 1992	Provided coordination and support. Legislative elections held in Dec. 1992.
	Mar. 1993	May 1993	Provided coordination and support. Presidential elections held in May 1993.
	July 1998	Sept. 1998	Provided technical assistance for presidential elections scheduled for Apr. 1999.
	Feb. 1999	Mar. 1999–Apr. 1999	Unable to fulfill request for observers for the presidential elections on Apr. 9, 1999. Limited technical assistance provided by UNDP.

Member State	Date of Request	Period of Assistance	United Nations Response[a]
	Dec. 2002	—	Unable to fulfill request for observers for the legislative elections on Jan. 10, 2003, due to lack of lead time.
Dominican Republic	Apr. 1996	—	Unable to fulfill request for observers for the presidential elections on May 16, 1996, due to insufficient lead time.
	Mar. 2002	—	Unable to fulfill request for observers for the elections on May 16, 2002, due to lack of lead time.
	Oct. 2002	—	Request for technical assistance to the electoral authorities on the registration system, external voting, electronic voting, and capacity building.
East Timor	May 1, 1999[c]	May 1999– Sept. 1999	Organization and conduct of popular consultation held on Aug. 30, 1999.
	Oct. 1999	Oct. 2000– June 2002	Under Security Council resolution 1272 (1999), UNTAET organized and conducted the elections for the Constituent Assembly held on Aug. 30, 2001, followed by presidential elections on Apr. 14, 2002.
	Apr. 2002	Nov. 2002– current	Providing technical assistance for the establishment of an electoral body.
Eastern Slavonia (Croatia)	Jan. 1996[f]	May 1996– June 1997	Provided organization and conduct. Elections held on Apr. 13, 1997.
Ecuador	Apr. 2002	—	Received request for technical assistance for the general elections on Oct. 2, 2002. Needs assessment conducted in June 2002 and agreement reached that OAS would provide assistance needed.
	Apr. 2003	May 2003– current	Request for technical assistance for the local elections of Oct. 2004. Needs assessment mission conducted in May 2003. Recommendations under consideration.

Member State	Date of Request	Period of Assistance	United Nations Response[a]
El Salvador	June 1992	Aug. 1992	Provided technical assistance in the preparation of a report on changes in the registration and identification procedures.
	Jan. 1993	Apr. 1993–Mar. 1995	Provided verification and technical assistance. General elections held in Mar. and Apr. 1994.
	Jan. 1997	—	Unable to fulfill request for observers for the legislative and municipal elections on Mar. 16, 1997, due to insufficient lead time.
	Mar. 1997	—	Unable to fulfill (second) request for observers for the legislative and municipal elections on Mar. 16, 1997.
	Sept. 1997	Oct. 1997–1999	Provided technical assistance to improve the electoral system. Elections held Mar. 1999.
Equatorial Guinea	Mar. 1993	Apr. 1993–Sept. 1995	Provided technical assistance. Municipal elections held on Sept. 17, 1995.
	July 1993	—	Unable to fulfill request to send observers for the elections scheduled to take place in Sept. 1993 due to absence of enabling environment. The elections were subsequently postponed to Nov. 1993.
	Aug. 1995	Sept. 1995	Provided coordination and support. Municipal elections held on Sept. 17, 1995. (Technical assistance also provided.)
	Jan. 1996	—	Unable to fulfill request for observers due to insufficient lead time. Presidential elections held on Feb. 25, 1996.
	May 1998	—	Request for coordination of international observers and for assistance in mobilizing resources in connection with the legislative elections scheduled for Nov. 1998. Elections were later postponed and no further action was taken.

Member State	Date of Request	Period of Assistance	United Nations Response[a]
	Jan. 1999	—	Unable to fulfill request to send observers for the legislative elections on Mar. 7, 1999, due to insufficient lead time.
	Apr. 2000	—	Unable to fulfill request to send UN observers for the municipal elections of May 28, 2000.
Eritrea	May 1992	Jan. 1993– May 1993	Provided verification and technical assistance. Referendum on independence held on Apr. 23–25, 1993.
Estonia	June 1992	—	Unable to fulfill request for observers for the referendum on June 28, 1992, due to insufficient lead time.
Ethiopia	Apr. 1992	May 1992– Mar. 1994	Provided coordination and support and technical assistance. Regional elections held in June 1992 and national elections held in June 1994.
	Apr. 1999	July 1999– May 2000	Request for assistance for the preparation of the national elections in 2000. The UNDP provided technical assistance.
Fiji	July 1995	July 1995– Dec. 1995	Provided technical assistance for the preparation of papers on power sharing in multiethnic societies.
	June 2001	July 2001– Sept. 2001	Observation provided. Under General Assembly resolution A/55/280, UNFEOM was created to observe the elections held from Aug. 25 to Sept. 1, 2001.
Gabon	Oct. 1993	Nov. 1993– Dec. 1993	Provided follow and report and technical assistance. Presidential elections held in Dec. 1993.
	May 1995	Apr. 1996– June 1996	Provided technical assistance. Legislative elections held on Dec. 15 and Dec. 29, 1996.
	July 1998	—	Unable to fulfill request for observers for the presidential elections on Dec. 6, 1998.

Member State	Date of Request	Period of Assistance	United Nations Response[a]
Gambia	Apr. 1995	May 1995– Feb. 1997	Provided technical assistance. Presidential elections held on Sept. 26, 1996, and parliamentary elections on Jan. 2, 1997.
	Sept. 1996	—	Unable to fulfill request for observers for the presidential elections on Sept. 26, 1996, due to insufficient lead time and absence of enabling environment.
	Mar. 2001	July 2001– Jan. 2002	Provided limited financial assistance through UNDP, and followed the electoral process. Presidential elections held on Oct. 18, 2001, and legislative elections on Jan. 17, 2002.
Georgia	Nov. 2002	Dec. 2002– Nov. 2003	Provided technical assistance for the parliamentary elections in Oct. and Nov. 2003.
Ghana	Apr. 1992	—	Offered to coordinate international observers instead of sending observers for the presidential and parliamentary elections to be held in Nov. and Dec. 1992. Government declined the UN's offer.
	Sept. 1996	Oct. 1996– Dec. 1996	Provided technical assistance and follow and report. Parliamentary elections held on Dec. 7. 1996.
	May 2000	July 2000– Dec. 2000	The UNDP provided donor assistance coordination. Presidential and parliamentary elections on Dec. 7, 2000.
Guatemala	May 1999	June 1999– Dec. 1999	Provided technical assistance for presidential and parliamentary elections of Nov. 7, 1999.
	June 2003	Under consideration	Request for assistance in connection with the general elections in Nov. 2003. Needs assessment mission conducted in July 2003. Recommendations under consideration.
Guinea	Mar. 1992	May 1992– Dec. 1993	Provided technical assistance and follow and report. Presidential elections held in Dec. 1993.

Member State	Date of Request	Period of Assistance	United Nations Response[a]
	Apr. 1995	June 1995	Provided follow and report. Legislative elections held in June 1995.
	Mar. 1998	Sept. 1998– Dec. 1998	Provided technical assistance. Presidential elections held on Dec. 14, 1998.
	Nov. 1998	—	Unable to fulfill request for observers to the presidential elections held on Dec. 14, 1998, due to insufficient lead time.
	May 2000	—	Request for assistance received. Needs assessment mission conducted in July 2000. Due to political and military developments, UN assistance was put on hold.
	Dec. 2001	May 2002– July 2002	Provided technical assistance. Legislative elections held on June 30, 2002.
Guinea-Bissau	Dec. 1992	Jan. 1993– Aug. 1994	Provided technical assistance and coordination and support. General elections held in July 1994.
	Mar. 1999	Mar. 1999– Feb. 2000	Provided technical assistance for the preparation of the presidential and legislative elections held on Nov. 28, 1999, and in Jan. 2000, as well as coordination and support of international observers.
	May 2000	Nov. 2000– Jan. 2001	Provided technical assistance in the preparation for the upcoming municipal elections, date to be announced.
	Dec. 2002	Jan. 2003– Oct. 2003	Provided technical assistance for the elections to be held in Oct. 2003 (postponed to Mar. 2004).
Guyana	June 1992	June 1992– Oct. 1992	Provided technical assistance. Elections held in Oct. 1992.
	Feb. 1996	Mar. 1996– Dec. 1997	Provided technical assistance. Parliamentary and regional Democratic Council elections held on Dec. 15, 1997.

Member State	Date of Request	Period of Assistance	United Nations Response[a]
	Sept. 1997	Oct. 1997–Dec. 1997	Provided additional technical assistance in the coordination of international observers for the same elections (see above).
	May 2000	May 2000–Apr. 2001	Provided technical assistance for the preparation of general elections in Mar. 2001, and coordination and support of international observers.
Haiti	July 1990	Nov. 1990–Jan. 1991	Provided verification and technical assistance. General elections held in Dec. 1990 and Jan. 1991.
	Sept. 1994	Oct. 1994–June 1997	Provided technical assistance. Legislative elections held in June and Sept. 1995, and presidential elections on Dec. 17, 1995. Elections for one-third of the Senate, the members of the communal section assemblies, and two members of the National Assembly held on Apr. 6, 1997.
	May 1999	May 1999–Sept. 2000	Provided technical assistance for the preparation of legislative and municipal elections held on May 21 and June 25, 2000.
	Sept. 2000	—	Unable to fulfill request for technical assistance for the presidential elections on Nov. 26, 2000, due to the political situation in the country.
Honduras	Mar. 1994	June 1994–Mar. 1995	Provided technical assistance in improving the electoral system.
	Sept. 1997	Oct. 1997–Dec. 1997	Provided technical assistance. Presidential, legislative, and mayoral elections held on Nov. 30, 1997.
	June 2001	—	Unable to provide technical assistance for the general elections scheduled for Nov. 25, 2001.
Hungary	Apr. 1994	—	Declined request for observers for the parliamentary elections to be held on May 8, 1994 due to insufficient lead time.

Member State	Date of Request	Period of Assistance	United Nations Response[a]
Indonesia	Feb. 1999[g]	Feb. 1999– July 1999	Provided technical assistance. General elections held on June 7, 1999.
	Sept. 2002	Nov. 2002– current	Providing technical assistance for the preparation of the 2004 general elections.
Jamaica	May 2002	June 2002– Nov. 2002	Provided technical assistance. General elections held on Oct. 16, 2002.
Jordan	May 2003	June 2003– current	Request for technical assistance. Needs assessment mission conducted in June 2003. Recommendations under consideration.
Kenya	Nov. 1992	Dec. 1992– Jan. 1993	Provided coordination and support. Legislative elections held in Dec. 1992.
	Oct. 2002	—	Unable to fulfill request for observers for the general elections in December 2002 due to lack of lead time.
Kosovo[h]	June 1999	Oct. 1999– current	Mandated by Security Council resolution 1244 (1999) to assist in the holding of elections. Several advisory missions conducted thereafter.
Kyrgyzstan	Dec. 1994	Jan. 1995– Mar. 1995	Provided follow and report and assessment of postelectoral support. Parliamentary elections held in Feb. 1995.
	Oct. 1995	Oct. 1995– Dec. 1995	Provided technical assistance and coordination and support. Presidential elections held on Dec. 24, 1995.
	Oct. 1998	—	Unable to fulfill request for observers for the referendum held on Oct. 17, 1998, due to insufficient lead time.
	Mar. 1999	—	Request to support the elections in 2000. Needs assessment mission conducted in Aug. 1999 and report submitted.
	Nov. 2002	Under consideration	Request for needs assessment mission for possible electoral assistance.

Member State	Date of Request	Period of Assistance	United Nations Response[a]
Latvia	May 1993	—	Unable to fulfill request for a UN delegation to observe the elections for the Fifth Saeima (parliament) in June 1993 because of insufficient lead time.
	Apr. 1994	—	Unable to fulfill request for observers for the local authorities elections in May 1994 because of insufficient lead time.
Lesotho	Aug. 1991	Nov. 1991–Dec. 1991	Provided technical assistance (Center for Human Rights assistance in drafting the electoral law).
	Oct. 1992	Dec. 1992–Mar. 1993	Provided coordination and support. General elections held in Mar. 1993.
	June 1997	Jan. 1998–May 1998	Provided technical assistance and coordination and support. Parliamentary elections held on May 23, 1998.
	Apr. 2001	May 2001–June 2002	Provided coordination and support. Parliamentary elections held on May 25, 2002.
	Mar. 2002	Apr. 2002–May 2002	Provided coordination and support of international observers for the elections on May 25, 2002.
Liberia	Feb. 1992	May 1992	Provided technical assistance regarding population data and preparation of constituency maps.
	July 1993	Aug. 1993–Aug. 1997	Provided verification and technical assistance. General elections held on July 19, 1997.
	Dec. 2002	—	Request for technical assistance in connection with the presidential and legislative elections in Oct. 2003.

Member State	Date of Request	Period of Assistance	United Nations Response[a]
Madagascar	Mar. 1992	Apr. 1992– Dec. 1992	Provided technical assistance and follow and report. Constitutional referendum held in Aug. 1992, presidential elections in Nov. 1992 and Feb. 1993, and legislative elections in June 1993.
	Apr. 1994	—	After requesting observers for the municipal and local elections to be held in July 1994, the government did not answer UN's offer to coordinate and support observers. Elections did not take place.
	Oct. 1996	Oct. 1996– Nov. 1996	Provided follow and report. Presidential elections held on Nov. 3, 1996.
	Sept. 2002	Oct. 2002– Dec. 2002	Provided technical assistance for the preparation of the legislative elections on Dec. 15, 2002.
Malawi	Oct. 1992	Nov. 1992– June 1993	Provided technical assistance and coordination and support. Referendum held in June 1993.
	Oct. 1993	Nov. 1993– Dec. 1994	Provided technical assistance and coordination and support. Presidential and parliamentary elections held in May 1994.
	Aug. 1998	Nov. 1998– June 1999	Provided technical assistance in preparation for the local presidential and legislative elections on May 19, 1999.
	Jan. 2003	Mar. 2003– current	Providing technical assistance in connection with general elections to be held in May 2004.
Mali	Sept. 1991	Dec. 1991– Apr. 1993	Provided technical assistance and follow and report. Presidential and legislative elections held in Apr. 1992.

Member State	Date of Request	Period of Assistance	United Nations Response[a]
	Jan. 1997	Feb. 1997–Aug. 1997	Provided technical assistance and coordination and support to the legislative elections held on Apr. 13, 1997 (subsequently annulled), and presidential elections held on May 11, 1997. Provided limited technical assistance to the legislative elections on July 20 and Aug. 3, 1997.
	Mar. 2002	Apr. 2002–current	Provided technical assistance in connection with the elections held in May 2002. Currently providing postelectoral assistance.
Mauritania	Apr. 2001	—	Request for assistance in connection with the parliamentary and municipal elections scheduled for Oct. 19, 2001, received. Request withdrawn in June 2001.
Mauritius	Nov. 1997	Feb. 1998–Apr. 1998	Provided technical assistance for the improvement of the electoral system.
Mexico	Apr. 1994	June 1994–current	Provided technical assistance to the Federal Electorate Institute (FEI). Provided support to national observers for the elections held in Aug. 1994. Continuing to provide technical assistance to the FEI.
	Nov. 1999	Nov. 1999–Aug. 2000	Provided support to domestic and international observers during the presidential and legislative elections held on July 2, 2000.
(Chiapas)	June 2000	July 2000–Sept. 2000	Provided technical assistance to national observers and coordination of international observers for the Aug. 20, 2000, elections in Chiapas.
	Apr. 2003	May 2003–Aug. 2003	Provided support to national observers for the legislative elections on July 6, 2003.

Member State	Date of Request	Period of Assistance	United Nations Response[a]
Mozambique	Oct. 1992[i]	Oct. 1992–Dec. 1995	Provided verification and technical assistance. Presidential and parliamentary elections held in Oct. 1994.
	Feb. 1999	Apr. 1999–Dec. 1999	Provided technical assistance in preparation for the general elections held on Dec. 3–5, 1999.
	Apr. 2003	May 2003–Oct. 2003	Provided technical assistance in connection with the local elections held in Oct. 2003.
Namibia	1978[j]	1989	Supervision of elections held on Nov. 7–11, 1989.
	July 1994	Sept. 1994–Dec. 1994	Provided coordination and support. General elections held in Dec. 1994.
	Oct. 1999	Oct. 1999–Dec. 1999	Provided limited assistance to the international observers for the general elections held on Nov. 30 and Dec. 1, 1999 (through UNDP).
Nepal	Feb. 1999	Feb. 1999–May 1999	Provided coordination and support to international observers. Parliamentary elections held on May 3, 1999.
	July 2002	June 2002–Oct. 2002	Coordination and support of international observers initiated in Sept. 2002. Assistance discontinued in Oct. 2002 due to cancellation of elections.
Netherlands (Antilles)	June 1993	Aug. 1993–Nov. 1993	Provided UN representation at the Referendum Commission of Curacao.
	June 1994	Oct. 1994	Provided UN representation at the Referendum Commission of St. Maarten, St. Estacious, and Saba.
	Nov. 1999	Nov. 1999–July 2000	Provided technical assistance to the St. Maarten Referendum Commission for the preparation of the referendum held on June 23, 2000.
Nicaragua	Mar. 1989	Aug. 1989–Mar. 1990	Provided verification and technical assistance. Elections held in Feb. 1990.

Member State	Date of Request	Period of Assistance	United Nations Response[a]
	Nov. 1993	Dec. 1993–Mar. 1994	Provided coordination and support. Elections (Atlantic Coast) held in Feb. 1994.
	Sept. 1995	—	Request for UN involvement in the elections scheduled for Nov. 1996. Needs assessment missions conducted in Mar. and Apr. 1996. No further action taken. Further request through UNDP (in Sept. 1996) for assistance in training and quick-count exercise declined due to insufficient lead time.
	Feb. 1998	—	Unable to fulfill request for observers for the Atlantic Coast elections on Mar. 1, 1998, due to insufficient lead time.
	June 1998	July 1998–1999	Provided technical assistance for the preparation of a study on the vote of Nicaraguans residing abroad.
	May 2000	—	Request to send UN observers for the municipal election of Nov. 5, 2000, not fulfilled, as observation activities were deferred to the OAS, the lead organization in the region. Technical monitoring provided instead on key electoral legal issues through the preelection period.
	Apr. 2001	June 2001–Nov. 2001	Provided technical assistance for the elections held on Nov. 4, 2001.
Niger	June 1992	Dec. 1992–Mar. 1993	Provided coordination and support. Referendum held in Dec. 1992, legislative elections in Feb. 1993, and presidential elections in Feb. and Mar. 1993.
	Dec. 1994	Dec. 1994–Jan. 1995	Provided technical assistance. Parliamentary elections held in Jan. 1995.
	Mar. 1996	Mar. 1996–July 1996	Provided technical assistance. Presidential elections held on July 7 and July 28, 1996.

Member State	Date of Request	Period of Assistance	United Nations Response[a]
	June 1996	—	Unable to fulfill request to coordinate international observers due to insufficient lead time. Limited logistical assistance provided by UNDP. Presidential elections held on July 7, 1996.
	Aug. 1998	—	Request for technical assistance for the local elections scheduled for Nov. 1998. Elections later postponed and no further action taken.
	June 1999	Aug. 1999–Dec. 1999	Provided technical assistance and coordination and support for the presidential and legislative elections. Elections held on Oct. 17 and Nov. 24, 1999.
	Apr. 2002	May 2002–current	Providing technical assistance for the local elections scheduled for the end of 2002 but later postponed.
Nigeria	Sept. 1998	Sept. 1998–Apr. 2002	Provided technical assistance and coordination and support of international observers. Local elections held on Dec. 5, 1998, elections for governors and state assemblies on Jan. 9, 1999, elections to the National Assembly on Feb. 20, 1999, and presidential elections on Feb. 27, 1999. Provided postelectoral assistance.
	Mar. 2002	June 2002–current	Provided technical assistance in connection with the general elections in April 2003. Currently providing post-electoral assistance.
Pakistan	Jan. 1997	1997–current	Unable to fulfill request for observers for the general elections held on Feb. 3, 1997, due to insufficient lead time. Currently providing technical assistance for the improvement of the electoral system.

Member State	Date of Request	Period of Assistance	United Nations Response[a]
Palestine[k]	Dec. 1995	—	Unable to fulfill request for observers because observation was to be coordinated by the European Union. Some logistical support provided by UNRWA. Elections held on Jan. 20, 1996.
	Dec. 2002	Dec. 2002– current	Providing technical assistance to the Central Elections Commission of the Palestinian Authority.
Panama	Nov. 1993	Dec. 1993– Feb. 1996	Provided technical assistance in improving the electoral system.
	Nov. 2002	—	Request for assistance in connection with the general elections scheduled for May 2, 2004.
Paraguay	Apr. 1993	June 5, 1993	Provided technical assistance and follow and report. General elections held in May 1993.
	Dec. 2002	Jan. 2003– May 2003	Provided technical assistance in connection with the general elections on Apr. 27, 2003.
Peru	1992[d]	July 1992– Dec. 1995	Provided technical assistance in improving the electoral system.
	Dec. 2000	Dec. 2000– Aug. 2001	Provided technical assistance for the preparation of the general elections held in May and June 2001.
	Aug. 2003	Under consideration	Request for a needs assessment mission for possible technical assistance.
Philippines	Nov. 1992[d]	May 1993	Provided technical assistance in the computerization of the electoral system.
Republic of Moldova	Jan. 1994	Mar. 1994	Provided follow and report. Parliamentary elections held in Feb. 1994.
	Feb. 1995	—	Unable to fulfill request for observers for the referendum on Mar. 5, 1995, due to insufficient lead time.

Member State	Date of Request	Period of Assistance	United Nations Response[a]
	Oct. 1996	—	Unable to fulfill request for observers for the presidential elections held on Nov. 17, 1996, due to insufficient lead time.
Romania	1990[d]	May 1990	Provided technical assistance. Elections held on May 20, 1990.
	Sept. 1992	Oct. 1992	Provided follow and report. Parliamentary and presidential elections held in Sept. and Oct. 1992.
	May 1996	—	Unable to fulfill request for observers for the local elections held on June 2, 1996, due to insufficient lead time.
	Sept. 1996	—	Unable to fulfill request for observers for the parliamentary and presidential elections on Nov. 3, 1996, due to insufficient lead time.
	May 2000	—	Unable to fulfill request to send UN observers for the local elections of June 4, 2000.
Russian Federation	Oct. 1993	Dec. 1993	Provided follow and report. National Assembly elections held in Dec. 1993.
Rwanda	May 1992	June 1992	Provided technical assistance (preparation of draft project document).
	Feb. 2001	Feb. 2001– Mar. 2001	Provided coordination and support and limited technical assistance for the municipal elections held on Mar. 6, 2001.
	Dec. 2002	—	Request for assistance in the preparation of the referendum on the new constitution scheduled for Mar. 2003 and presidential and parliamentary elections in July 2003.
	Apr. 2003	May 2003– Oct. 2003	Provided technical assistance for the presidential elections on Aug. 25, 2003, and parliamentary elections on Sept. 29, 2003.

Member State	Date of Request	Period of Assistance	United Nations Response[a]
São Tomé and Principe	Aug. 1994	Oct. 1994	Provided follow and report. Legislative elections held in Oct. 1994.
	Nov. 1995	—	Unable to fulfill request for material and financial assistance due to lack of funds.
	June 1996	—	Unable to fulfill request for observers to the presidential elections on June 30, 1996, due to lack of time and financial resources.
	Oct. 1998	—	Unable to fulfill request for observers to the legislative elections on Nov. 8, 1998, due to insufficient lead time.
	Oct. 2000	Feb. 2001– Aug. 2001	Provided technical assistance for the preparation of the presidential elections held in July 2001.
	Jan. 2002	July 2002– Dec. 2002	Provided technical assistance to strengthen the Electoral Commission.
Senegal	Feb. 1993	Mar. 1993– May 1993	Provided follow and report. Presidential and legislative elections held in Feb. and May 1993.
	Dec. 1999	Jan. 2000– Mar. 2000	Unable to fulfill request to send observers for the presidential elections held on Feb. 27, 2000. Follow and report provided by the UN resident coordinator.
	Mar. 2001	Apr. 2001	Unable to fulfill request to send UN observers for the legislative elections of Apr. 29, 2001, due to lack of lead time. The UNDP resident representative requested to follow the electoral process and report on its conduct and outcome.
Seychelles	June 1992	July 1992	Provided follow and report. Elections for the Constitutional Commission held in July 1992.
	July 1993	July 1993	Provided follow and report. Presidential and legislative elections held in July 1993.

Member State	Date of Request	Period of Assistance	United Nations Response[a]
Sierra Leone	Sept. 1993	Oct. 1993	Provided technical assistance (survey mission jointly with UNDP).
	Mar. 1994	June 1994–Mar. 1996	Provided technical assistance and coordination and support. Presidential and parliamentary elections held on Feb. 26 and Mar. 15, 1996.
	Oct. 1999	2000–June 2002	Mandated by Security Council resolution 1270 (1999) to provide requested support to the elections. Presidential and legislative elections held on May 14, 2002. Further assistance currently under consideration.
Solomon Islands	Oct. 2001	Oct. 2001–Dec. 2001	Expert election monitoring mission conducted during the parliamentary elections held on Dec. 5, 2001.
South Africa	Dec. 1993	Dec. 1993–May 1994	Provided verification. General elections held in Apr. 1994.
	Aug. 1998	Aug. 1998–June 1999	Provided technical assistance and coordination and support to international observers. General elections held on June 2, 1999.
	Aug. 2003	Under consideration	Request for technical and financial assistance for the upcoming elections in mid-2004.
Sri Lanka	Oct. 2001	—	Unable to fulfill request for observers for the parliamentary elections to be held on Dec. 5, 2001.
Sudan	Jan. 1996	—	Needs assessment mission conducted. Unable to fulfill request to send UN observers. Presidential and parliamentary elections held on Mar. 6 and Mar. 17, 1996.
	Oct. 2000	—	Unable to fulfill request to send observers for the presidential and parliamentary elections and referendum on constitutional amendments scheduled to take place between Dec. 11 and Dec. 20, 2000.

Member State	Date of Request	Period of Assistance	United Nations Response[a]
Swaziland	May 1993	—	Unable to fulfill request for financial assistance for the parliamentary elections to be held in 1993 due to unavailability of funds.
Tajikistan[l]	Jan. 1999	Mar. 1999–Mar. 2000	Several assessment missions conducted in 1999. Joint UN/OSCE observation mission for the legislative elections undertaken on Feb. 27, 2000.
	July 2003	Under consideration	Request for assistance for the preparation of the 2005 general election.
Togo	Apr. 1992	May 1992–Dec. 1992	Provided technical assistance. Referendum held in Sept. 1992.
	July 1993	Aug. 1993	Provided follow and report. Presidential elections held in Aug. 1993.
	Mar. 1998	May 1998–June 1998	Unable to fulfill request for observers. Provided technical assistance for the presidential elections held on June 21, 1998.
	Mar. 1999	—	Unable to fulfill request for observers for the legislative elections to be held on Mar. 21 (first round) and April 4 (second round) of 1999 due to insufficient lead time.
	June 2001	Dec. 2001–Feb. 2002	Provided technical assistance. Elections postponed.
	Oct. 2002	—	Unable to fulfill request for observers for the legislative elections on Oct. 27, 2002, due to lack of lead time.
Uganda	Oct. 1992	Nov. 1992–Dec. 1994	Provided coordination and support and technical assistance. Elections for the Constituent Assembly held in Mar. 1994.
	May 1995	Feb. 1996–July 1996	Provided technical assistance. Presidential elections held on May 9, 1996, and parliamentary elections on June 27, 1996.

Member State	Date of Request	Period of Assistance	United Nations Response[a]
	Apr. 1996	May 1996	Provided follow and report and assistance to the coordination of the activities of international observers, in addition to technical assistance. Presidential elections held on May 9, 1996, and parliamentary elections on June 27, 1996.
	June 1999	June 1999–July 2000	Provided limited technical assistance to the referendum on the system of governance in 2000 (through UNDP).
	May 2000	—	Unable to fulfill request to send UN observers for the referendum on the political system on June 29, 2000, due to lack of lead time.
	Feb. 2001	—	Unable to fulfill request to send UN observers for the presidential elections of Mar. 7, 2001, due to lack of lead time.
Ukraine	Jan. 1994	Mar. 1994	Provided follow and report. Parliamentary elections held in Mar. 1994.
	June 1994	June 1994	Provided follow and report. Presidential and local elections held in June 1994.
	Sept. 1999	—	Unable to fulfill request for observers for the presidential elections of Oct. 31, 1999, due to insufficient lead time.
	Nov. 2001	Feb. 2002–Apr. 2003	Unable to fulfill the request for international observers for the parliamentary elections on Mar. 31, 2002. Instead, the United Nations sent an officer to follow the electoral process and report to the Secretary-General on its conduct.
United Republic of Tanzania	June 1995	Apr. 1995–Nov. 1995	Provided coordination and support. General elections in Zanzibar held on Oct. 22, 1995, and in Tanzania on Oct. 29, 1995. Elections in Dar-es-Salaam were repeated on Nov. 19, 1995.

Member State	Date of Request	Period of Assistance	United Nations Response[a]
	May 1999	Aug. 1999	Request for assistance received and needs assessment mission conducted in Aug. 1999.
	Apr. 2000	June 2000–Nov. 2000	Provided coordination and support of international observers. General elections held on Oct. 29, 2000.
Uzbekistan	Oct. 1994	Nov. 1994–Dec. 1994	Provided follow and report. Parliamentary elections held on Dec. 25, 1994.
	Oct. 1994	—	Unable to fulfill request to send observers for the parliamentary elections scheduled for Dec. 15, 1999.
Venezuela	Oct. 1998	—	Unable to fulfill request to send observers for the presidential elections held on Dec. 6, 1998, due to insufficient lead time.
	Apr. 2000	—	Unable to fulfill request to send UN observers for the national elections scheduled for May 28, 2000.
	July 2000	—	Unable to fulfill request to send observers for the general elections on July 30, 2000, due to insufficient lead time.
	Nov. 2000	—	Unable to fulfill request to send an observer for the local elections on Dec. 3, 2000, due to insufficient lead time.
Western Sahara[m]	Apr. 1991[n]	1991–current	Mandated to provide organization and conduct. Mission currently in abeyance.
Yemen	June 1996	Dec. 1996–Apr. 1997	Provided technical assistance. Parliamentary elections held on Apr. 27, 1997.
	Mar. 1997	Apr. 1997	Provided follow and report. Parliamentary elections held on Apr. 27, 1997.
	Apr. 2000	Aug. 2000–June 2003	Provided technical assistance to the Electoral Commission. Local elections held on Mar. 15, 2001. Parliamentary elections held in June 2003.

Member State	Date of Request	Period of Assistance	United Nations Response[a]
Former Yugoslav Republic of Macedonia	Sept. 1994	Oct. 1994	Provided follow and report. Presidential and parliamentary elections held in Oct. 1994.
	Jan. 1998	Feb. 1998–Mar. 1998	Provided technical assistance in drafting the electoral law.
Zaire (now Democratic Republic of Congo)	May 1996	June 1996–Mar. 1997	Provided technical assistance. UN electoral assistance unit established in Sept. 1996 and closed in May 1997 due to political developments.
Zambia	July 1996	Nov. 1996	Provided follow and report. Parliamentary elections held on Nov. 18, 1996.
	June 1999	—	Request for assistance for the preparation of the 2001 presidential and parliamentary elections. Needs assessment mission conducted in Aug. 1999.
	Sept. 2000	—	Request for technical assistance and coordination and support for the 2001 presidential and parliamentary elections.
	Oct. 2001	—	Provided limited financial assistance through UNDP. Presidential, parliamentary, and local elections held on Dec. 27, 2001.
Zimbabwe	Nov. 1999	Dec. 1999–May 2000	Request for technical assistance in connection with the legislative elections on June 24–25, 2000. Missions conducted in Dec. 1999, Feb. 2000, and June 2000, but no UN involvement in the elections.
	June 2000	—	Unable to fulfill request to send UN observers for the parliamentary elections on June 24–25, 2000, due to lack of lead time.

Notes: a. Please refer to A/49/675, Annex III, for definitions of the seven different types of possible UN responses to requests for electoral assistance.

b. Date of signing of the Estoril Agreements.

c. Date of signing of the Paris Agreements.

d. Approximate date.

e. On May 5, 1999, the governments of Indonesia and Portugal signed an agreement under which the UN was responsible for the organization of popular consultation on the autonomy of East Timor.

f. Based on Security Council resolution 1037 (1996), the United Nations Transitional Administration for Eastern Slavonia, Baranja, and Western Sirmium (UNTAES) was established on Jan. 15, 1996, with a mandate "to organize Elections, assist in their conduct, and to certify the results."

g. Date of signing of the technical assistance project by the government and UNDP.

h. Kosovo is not a Member State.

i. Date of the signing of the General Peace Agreement.

j. Under the independence plan for Namibia, approved by Security Council resolution 435 (1978), the United Nations was mandated to supervise the elections for a Constituent Assembly.

k. Palestine is not a Member State.

l. Under the provisions of UNMOT's mandate.

m. Western Sahara is not a Member State.

n. Based on Security Council resolution 690 (1991), the United Nations Mission for the Referendum in Western Sahara (MINURSO) was established.

Notes

1. Harold K. Jacobson, *Networks of Interdependence* (New York: McGraw-Hill, 1984), p. 349.

2. The Commonwealth includes the United Kingdom plus the former British colonies and other specified English-speaking countries. The Francophonie includes French-speaking countries.

6

Agent of Change? The United Nations and Development

Jacques Fomerand

The maintenance of peace and security is the first purpose assigned to the United Nations in Chapter I of the UN Charter. In fact, no less than five of its eighteen chapters deal with peace and security issues. In contrast, only one article, Article 9, explicitly makes mention of "development" as an objective that the United Nations should "promote." Moreover, the term appears only in the context of a list of other objectives, reflecting the then prevailing orthodoxy in economic thinking—the achievement of "higher standards of living," "full employment," and "conditions of economic and social progress."

In spite of this thin constitutional basis, for the last three decades the United Nations has expanded by leaps and bounds in an uncoordinated process of growth, spawning a large network of agencies and programs concerned with humanitarian, economic, and social development questions. The creation of the United Nations International Children's Emergency Fund (UNICEF, now known as the United Nations Children's Fund), the Expanded Technical Assistance Programme, the Special Fund, the United Nations Development Programme (UNDP), the World Food Programme (WFP), the United Nations Conference on Trade and Development (UNCTAD), as well as such institutions as the International Development Agency (IDA), the International Finance Corporation (IFC), and the International Fund for Agricultural Development (IFAD), were some of the milestones of this pattern of institutional growth.

With the onset of the 1970s, and more markedly in the 1980s, United Nations growth and expansion in the economic and social fields slowly came to a halt. Increasingly frequent and pointed criticisms of excessive decentralization and redundancies led to a greater emphasis on "streamlining," "rationalizing," and "consolidating" an organization perceived by some of its key stakeholders as having grown out of control. In sharp contrast with the buoyant experience of the previous decades, only a handful of new institutions came into existence in the 1990s, including the Global Environmental Facility (GEF) and the Commission for Sustainable Development (CSD). The system now seems to have entered a cycle of controlled institutional inertia.

Although it is difficult to "prove" conclusively specific outcomes resulting from specific efforts, the United Nations development system can boast a number of substantial accomplishments in the field of development and human welfare. The health of millions has been improved and life expectancy has increased throughout the world as a result of immunization campaigns by UNICEF and the World Health Organization (WHO) against smallpox, malaria, and other parasitic diseases. Efforts supported by the United Nations have helped raise adult as well as female literacy in developing countries. The international human rights space has been broadened beyond all expectations after the formulation of more than eighty human rights treaties since the 1948 adoption of the Universal Declaration of Human Rights.

The UN mobilizes more than $1 billion a year for emergency assistance to people affected by war and natural disaster. According to UNDP estimates, since 1980 the UN system has delivered a total of $67.63 billion to promote development and human progress. Development has evolved into one of the fundamental tasks of the United Nations today. This chapter presents a broad-stroked description and assessment of the role of the United Nations in the promotion of development against the background of its evolving geopolitical environment (from the Cold War, to the rise and demise of the Third World coalition, to the current wave of globalization). Particular emphasis is placed on issues of legitimacy, governance, and effectiveness. The focus is primarily on the United Nations proper, including the UN Secretariat and the funds and programs set up for specific functional or political needs identified by Member States that report to the General Assembly. When appropriate, references are made to the UN specialized agencies, the World Bank, the International Monetary Fund (IMF), and the World Trade Organization (WTO), which make up the "United Nations system." These institutions by themselves warrant separate treatment extending beyond the deliberately limited scope of this chapter.

Structures

The UN development system is an outgrowth as well as a vast expansion of the little-known work of its predecessor organization, the League of Nations. The rise of totalitarianism and the failure of Western democracies to rise up to the challenge dealt a mortal blow to the political and security work of the League. Yet the League was able to promote international cooperation over a wide area of humanitarian and scientific activities, pioneering the combat of infectious diseases, slavery, and drug trafficking as well as drafting codes of conduct on the employment of labor. In fact, so successful were the League's activities that, at the prodding of Australia and other "willing" states, a committee was constituted in 1939 to strengthen the League's functional activities

A Somali mother and her children wait for medical treatment in the doorway of a clinic run by UNICEF, October 1992.

with a view to ensuring its political survival. The so-called Bruce Committee, named after its Australian chair, produced a report advocating a wide expansion of the League's economic and social functions. Many of the Bruce Committee's recommendations were incorporated into the UN Charter, including the creation of the Economic and Social Council (ECOSOC).

The work of the "other United Nations"[1] now spans a vast range of activities, including the compiling and standardizing of statistical data, setting technical and legal standards in functional areas of global interaction, and conducting policy-oriented research and analysis. On the humanitarian side it includes promoting child survival, human rights, and women's equality; improving the livelihood and security of the poor; ensuring sustainable environmental management; supporting refugees and vulnerable social groups; preventing AIDS; fighting illicit drug trafficking; and providing emergency relief to victims of war, flood, drought, and crop failure. This list is by no means exhaustive. The developmental work of the United Nations can be grouped essentially into four broad categories: (1) policy and analytical undertakings that provide the underpinning for intergovernmental deliberations; (2) facilitation of the efforts of Member States to set norms and standards and build consensus on a range of international issues; (3) global advocacy on development issues; and (4) support of national development efforts through technical cooperation activities in developing countries and countries with economies in transition.

These multifaceted tasks are carried out through a complex maze of institutions that emerged over time without a preestablished blueprint and largely as a result of political pressures. The General Assembly along with its Second Committee (which deals with economic and social issues) and its Third Committee (humanitarian issues) stands at the apex of the system as the UN's supreme policymaking organ on development. To add to the complexity, fourteen funds and programs report to the General Assembly, the most important ones being:

UN Development Programme (UNDP)
UN Fund for Population Activities (UNFPA)
UN Children's Fund (UNICEF)
World Food Programme (WFP)
UN Conference on Trade and Development (UNCTAD)
UN Environment Programme (UNEP)
UN Center for Human Settlements (Habitat)
UN High Commissioner for Refugees (UNHCR)

Another cluster of subsidiary institutions, all concerned with research, policy analysis and training, have their own governing bodies, and while enjoying varying degrees of autonomy, they also report to the General Assembly. They are:

UN Institute for Training and Research (UNITAR)
UN University (UNU)
International Research and Training Institute for the Advancement of
    Women (INSTRAW)
UN Institute for Disarmament Research (UNIDIR)
UN system Staff College

Under the authority of the General Assembly, as mentioned in Chapter 3, the Economic and Social Council also acts as a central forum for the discussion of economic and social issues, as well as coordination of UN activities in the economic and social fields and in regard to humanitarian questions and the governance of the UN's operational activities. ECOSOC has eight "functional commissions" (social development, human rights, narcotic drugs, crime prevention and criminal justice, women, population, statistics, and sustainable development) that report to it. In addition to the theme-oriented commissions, there are the five geographic regional commissions, listed in Chapter 1, that also report to ECOSOC, embodying a vague prescription for decentralization that has never disappeared from the development agenda, but for some critics adds to the burden of the system. A large number of session-specific standing committees and expert ad hoc bodies also report to ECOSOC. To further add to the list, over 1,500 nongovernmental organizations (NGOs) have consultative status with ECOSOC.

Finally, the UN development system also comprises twelve specialized agencies, including:

UN Educational, Scientific, and Cultural Organization (UNESCO)
World Health Organization (WHO)
International Labour Organization (ILO)
Food and Agriculture Organization (FAO)
UN Industrial Development Organization (UNIDO)
International Fund for Agricultural Development (IFAD)

Formally, these bodies report to ECOSOC. In practice, ECOSOC exerts only a loose degree of coordination, as the agencies have their own governing bodies and separate budgets. The Bretton Woods institutions—the World Bank, the International Monetary Fund and its affiliates, the International Development Association, the International Finance Corporation, and the World Trade Organization—do play an important role in development, but their relationship to ECOSOC is even more tenuous.

In terms of staffing and finances, the UN development enterprise is also impressive. Over $5 billion flows each year through the United Nations to promote development and eradicate poverty in poorer countries and provide humanitarian assistance. If one includes the World Bank and the IMF, the figure rises to over $30 billion. The UN itself devotes 30 percent of its regular budget resources to development, three times as much as for peace and security (excluding peacekeeping operations, which are funded separately). Of the 9,070 posts that compose the Secretariat, more than 3,500 are earmarked for international and regional cooperation for development, human rights, and humanitarian affairs.

An Uncertain Mandate

The UN development enterprise is no minor operation. Yet it rests on shaky political foundations because neither its raison d'être nor its legitimacy have been durably agreed upon by its main stakeholders. The most critical factor in this regard has been and remains the widely differing views of Member States about the very concept of development and the role of the United Nations therein. From the very inception of the Organization, two competing visions have vied over the ways and means to achieve "conditions of economic and social progress." One view is largely espoused by industrial powers, often referred to as the North, and in particular the United States, while the other is shaped by the demands and concerns of the South.

The first view assigns only limited functions to the United Nations in economic and social affairs. From this vantage point, the United Nations is a voluntary association of sovereign states with no discretionary, regulatory, or legislative functions. It may act "as a town meeting of the world where public opinion is focused as an effective force."[2] However, it is no more than a "center for the harmonization of national policies," a "catalyst," a "facilitator," and a "conveyor." The effective governance of cooperation for economic and social development and the management of the world economy are the province of the Bretton Woods institutions and other non-UN institutions such as the Group of Eight (G8) and the Organization for Economic Cooperation and Development (OECD).

Countries in the South prioritize the resolution of what they consider the structural problems of development, both domestic and international, that hamper their drive toward modernization, industrialization, and in today's parlance, "sustainable development." For the South, development cannot be left to the vagaries of international financial, monetary, and commercial markets. The state has an essential role in the definition of the development agenda and in the allocation of scarce resources required for development. Regulatory mechanisms and agencies must be put in place at the international and national levels to ensure that markets operate in such ways as to promote rather than hinder the resolution of developmental issues. For developing countries, the UN as the embodiment of a compact among sovereign and equal states should be the keystone of the governance architecture of the world economy and development cooperation. It should have authoritative decisionmaking powers especially in relation to the Bretton Woods institutions.

In this polarized setting in which the North uses the language of "effectiveness" and the South the normative rhetoric of "equity" and "democracy," any agreement on governance has proved elusive. Victories by one side have been matched by determined efforts by the other to undo the agreements reached on paper or to nibble at the margins of the prevailing "consensus." The result has been a seesaw process of legitimization of competing and largely mutually exclusive development concepts and policy practices.

Latin American countries took an early lead in instigating this debate. At Bretton Woods in 1944, when these institutions were created, Mexico succeeded in having the term "development" included in the official title of the World Bank, which is actually the International Bank for Reconstruction and Development (IBRD). At the first sessions of the General Assembly, proposals were made to enlarge the membership of ECOSOC, originally composed of eighteen states, and to place the "equitable adjustment of prices in international markets" on the list of ECOSOC conferences. In 1948, ECOSOC created the Economic Commission for Latin America, assigning it the task of "raising the level of economic activity in Latin America" and mandating it "to direct its activities especially towards the study and seeking of solutions of problems arising in Latin America from world economic activity in Latin America, from world economic maladjustments and towards other problems connected with the world economy."[3]

The mass entry into the UN of Third World countries arising from the process of decolonization in the 1960s emboldened the developing countries to press for a "New Deal" through the UN. One striking instance of their voting power was the creation in 1964 of UNCTAD, with the sweeping mandate to "formulate principles and policies on international trade and related problems of economic development."[4] Ten years later, developing countries again defied U.S. and European opposition and mobilized numerical majorities in the General Assembly in support of resolutions calling for a new international economic order (NIEO) and the adoption of a charter of economic rights and duties of states, two fundamentally illiberal normative statements asserting a right to nationalization without compensation, advocating producer associations and market arrangements for primary commodity products, and calling for the regulation of transnational corporations.[5]

At the same time, the structural growth of the United Nations throughout the 1950s and 1960s in the economic field owed as much to Third World pressures as to the political dynamics of East-West tensions. Early on, the Cold War turned the relatively benign "town meetings of the world" into engines of war in the arsenals of the superpowers. Bitter confrontations in the UN became the rule as the United States and the Soviet Union sought to sway international public opinion and enlist the support of Third World countries in their global struggle. President Harry Truman's Point Four proposals, which led to the launching of the Expanded Program of Technical Assistance, were designed to "encourage the development of democratic institutions and respect for human rights in a world menaced by totalitarianism."[6] The establishment of the International Finance Corporation in 1956 to promote private investment in developing countries, the creation of the International Development Association in 1960 with the power to make preferential loans to developing countries (both affiliates of the World Bank), and the creation of the UN Special Fund in 1957 were all Northern responses designed to placate the Soviet-supported Southern drive for a capital fund. Key Western nations resisted the notion of a capital fund because, placed under the authority of the United Nations, they would have no control over it.

But the more Third World leaders dreamed of turning the UN into a world development authority, the more inclined developed countries were to shun the Organization and to limit the scope of its activities to those originally envisaged in San Francisco in 1945. The United States led the counterattack against the "tyranny of the majority" through selective disengagement and the use of its financial weapon, the withholding of U.S. dues. Within the span of a few years, this objective was by and large achieved. Crushed by the weight of its debt crisis and locked in a debilitating "lost decade of development" in the 1980s, the Third World coalition collapsed as an organized political force. At the same time, the demise of the Soviet Union discredited the intellectual foundations of hitherto prevailing development strategies, allowing some to proclaim the triumph of liberalism as heralding an "end of history."[7]

The "politicization" of the UN and its advocacy of "statist theories" slowly faded into memory. UN administrative and budgetary growth came to a virtual standstill. Governments in the South restructured their public sector, opened their economies, and shifted to macroeconomic stabilization policies. A new development paradigm thus took hold of the UN agenda. Almost thirty years ago in the mid-1970s, Secretariat officials drew up inventories of development goals and objectives that had been "adopted" in various UN intergovernmental fora in implementation of the NIEO. Now the UN bills itself as the keystone of coalitions of change as it seeks new "partnerships" and "new structures of cooperation" in support of a development process deemed to be governed primarily by market forces.

Yet the current conventional wisdom of the "Washington Consensus," which prevails in particular in the World Bank and the IMF and which places a premium on the freeing of international markets, the deregulation and opening of national economies, and the pursuit of macroeconomic stability, still remains a matter of controversy, especially in the context of the global conferences sponsored by the UN. These meetings called to address specific global development issues and challenges have been held in a subdued though tense atmosphere sharpened by the social and economic inequalities between North and South and exacerbated by the unrelenting pace of globalization. Their underlying problematic still revolves around the two fundamental and politically unsettled questions: Exactly what is the proper mix of policies to promote the development process? and What should the legitimate role of the UN be?

UN Global Conferences

As discussed in Chapter 3, global conferences are a long-standing feature of multilateral diplomacy and many have focused on development. Initially, UN-sponsored conferences were framed primarily in a "functional" mold. The creation of the UN specialized agencies owes much to this functional credo and, from early on, countless numbers of meetings involving experts and responsible officials of national governments. These technical experts were called upon, under the aegis of the United Nations and its special agencies, to focus on fact-finding, information exchange, and policy-oriented research on technical subjects. With the onset of the 1980s and particularly in the decade of the 1990s, functionalism was overshadowed by a more populist approach with widely publicized, large-scale gatherings attended by high-level political representatives and drawing extensive participation of civil society groups.

UN global conferences have focused on a number of issues either directly or indirectly related to development, such as:

crime (every five years since 1947)
trade and employment (1947–1948)
the Law of the Sea (1973–1982)
new sources of energy (Rome, 1961; Nairobi, 1981)
employment (Geneva, 1976)
water (Mar del Plata, 1977; Dublin, 1992)
technical cooperation among developing countries (Buenos Aires, 1978)
primary healthcare (Alma Ata, 1978)
agrarian reform (Rome, 1979)
science and technology for development (Vienna, 1979)
desertification (Nairobi, 1979)
the least-developed countries (Paris, 1981, 1990; Brussels, 2001)
aging (Vienna, 1982)
women and gender issues (Mexico City, 1975; Copenhagen, 1980;
    Nairobi, 1985; Beijing, 1995; New York, 2000)
human rights (Teheran, 1968; Vienna, 1993)
population (Bucharest, 1974; Mexico City, 1984; Cairo, 1994)

food (Rome, 1974, 1996)
human settlement (Vancouver, 1976; Istanbul, 1996)
environment and sustainable development (Stockholm, 1972; Rio, 1992;
    Johannesburg, 2002)
drug abuse and trafficking (Vienna, 1987)
social welfare and development (Vienna, 1987; Copenhagen, 1995)
small island developing countries (Barbados, 1995)
disarmament and development (New York, 1987)
education (Jomtien, Thailand, 1990)
natural disaster prevention (Yokohama, 1994)
racism and racial discrimination (Johannesburg, 2001)
finance for development (Monterrey, 2002)
sustainable development (Johannesburg, 2002)

Occasionally, the General Assembly has stepped in to provide the setting for the functional equivalent of a global conference. Thus the Assembly held special sessions on human settlements (June 2001), HIV/AIDS (June 2001), and children (May 2002).

Grand meetings like these have generated considerable unease. Western governments and conservative think tanks portray them as lavish, costly talk shows too large to achieve meaningful results. The South complains that most of the policy objectives and developmental targets endorsed by the international community in the declarations and action plans of global conferences have been rarely, if ever, matched by adequate policy responses and commensurate financial commitments. Numerous NGOs and environmental groups have expressed the view that Western governments and large multinationals in effect conspire to ensure that UN global conferences are not effective policymaking instruments.

Like the General Assembly, which can only make recommendations, UN global conferences are not instruments of authoritative decisionmaking. In a globalizing, shrinking, and interdependent world, they approximate, at best, a global version of the "general will" of the international community. Taking into account the persistent lack of consensus over development policies, it is not surprising that UN global conferences have been used by different constituencies to legitimize their conflicting policy views and claims. Both North and South have pressed their own agendas over such key issues as globalization, energy, finance, debt, and trade, and their clashes have colored the proceedings. For instance, at the 2002 meeting on environment and development in Johannesburg, the developing countries' demand for the adoption of specific policy targets was a particularly contentious issue. The setting of environmental standards was labeled as a major barrier to market access and trade by the developing countries, but these same standards were considered sound sustainable development policies by the industrialized nations. The trade-distorting subsidies that developed countries grant to key sectors of their economies, notably agricultural subsidies, were a major target of developing countries. The countries of the South also seized the opportunity to clamor for relief from their debt burden. In response, developed countries focused on the need to end corruption and pressed developing countries to get their economies on a sound macroeconomic basis. Two major principles seemingly agreed upon ten years earlier at the Rio "Earth" Summit also resurfaced as divisive issues. The principle of common but differentiated responsibilities, for example, the notion that the industrialized countries should assume heavier burdens of responsibilities than the developing world in environmental policies, was questioned by Northern governments because they felt that developing countries were getting a free ride. The precautionary principle whereby lack of scientific certainty about environmental issues should not preclude collective policy action also became controversial as a result of lobbying by corporations engaged in genetic engineering of agricultural and farm products.[8]

Earlier definitions of development simply focused on the growth of gross national product. It is now recognized that development means increasing the availability and widening the distribution of basic life-sustaining goods and services such as food, shelter, healthcare, and human rights protection, raising levels of living (higher incomes, more jobs, better education), and expanding the range of economic and social choice available to individuals. A major step in this normative process was the 1976 ILO World Employment Conference, which examined the links among employment, poverty, and income distribution and resulted in the formulation of a strategy focused on employment creation and the satisfaction of basic needs. The importance now given to gender equality, social development, the environment, the need to secure the broadest participation of local communities in the process of development, the notion that development is a holistic process to be tackled in an integrated manner, and the concept of sustainability are ideas that germinated, crystallized, and won acceptance in UN global conferences.

In a similar vein, UN global conferences have drawn attention to emerging issues that transcend national boundaries, thus serving as early warning mechanisms for the international community. The acceleration of world demographic growth in the second half of the twentieth century, the aging of the population in the North, the depletion of the ozone layer, and global warming are examples that come to mind here. In this context, UN global conferences have contributed to changing and mobilizing public opinion by triggering the emergence of informal transnational "networks of concern" linked to one another through the Internet that nurture public support for solutions to global issues. Global conferences have in particular brought civil society organizations into the process of policy deliberation and formulation, through the concurrent participation of NGOs in national delegations or in parallel side events and "forums." "Track-two" (nongovernmental) diplomacy has certainly not superseded "track-one" traditional diplomacy by government leaders. But UN global conferences have provided new space for the participation of civil society in multilateral diplomacy. They have further enhanced NGO legitimacy and paved the way toward changes in national policies. One of the outcomes of the Copenhagen "Social" Summit was the so-called 20/20 Initiative of UNDP—a scheme whereby countries receiving aid should earmark at least 20 percent of their budgets and donor nations at least 20 percent of their aid budgets for investment in basic social services essential to human development priority concerns, such as health, education, and housing. Similarly, the conference on HIV/AIDS brought greater government awareness and knowledge of the scale and devastating implications of the deadly epidemic of HIV/AIDS and prompted national officials to take preventive action.

Finally, the proliferation of apparently disparate targets and policy prescriptions adopted in UN global conferences has compelled the United Nations to engage in a process of priority-setting and better coordination among its constituent units. The Secretary-General has taken the lead in mobilizing the UN system in the definition of a coherent framework of action embedded in the goals and policies agreed on at the Millennium Summit (2000) and the conferences in Monterrey and Johannesburg (2002) in particular. The three conferences integrated their focus on this ongoing effort to enhance coordination and collaboration among the UN system and to avoid duplication and establish a clearer division of labor within the system. All three reiterated a similar set of goals and targets, including progress toward poverty eradication, the elimination of hunger, the provision of access to energy and safe drinking water, and the provision of universal health services as an integral part of sustainable development.[9] Launching a new approach, the United Nations also seeks to identify civil society and private sector partners in support of measurable and accountable outcomes.

Days, Weeks, Years, and Decades

In conjunction with global conferences, the United Nations designates special days, weeks, years, and decades to promote causes that it stands for and advocates. Their basic objectives, broadly speaking, are identical: to raise the level of knowledge and concern for emerging or current issues through public information campaigns and statements by UN senior officials, to mobilize and nurture grassroots support through a variety of activities at the local, regional, and international levels, and to promote policy solutions. Days, weeks, and years cover a broad range of subjects and are frequent occurrences. In 2002, UN International Day for Disaster Reduction, for instance, highlighted the perils facing mountain communities. Its theme, "disaster reduction for sustainable mountain development," is linked to the International Year of the Mountain, observed in 2002. Thus, on numerous occasions, the Secretary-

General has warned that poor land use planning, environmental mismanagement, the lack of regulatory mechanisms, and other human activities increase the risk of natural disasters. And in his messages and public statements, he has urged the international community to adopt early warning and risk reduction measures and to develop new planning and forecasting tools to help reduce significantly the number of people losing their lives in mountain disasters.

Decades are rarer occurrences, but they are far more ambitious undertakings to the extent that they often define specific timetable goals, targets, and policies, and provide for their periodic review and evaluation of progress achieved in meeting them. For example, the first International Year for the Eradication of Poverty and the proclamation of the first United Nations Decade for the Eradication of Poverty were designed to "support a longer-term sustained effort to implement fully and effectively the commitments, recommendations, and measures undertaken, and the basic provisions already agreed upon at major UN conferences in the 1990s."[10]

The impact of this flurry of activities is difficult to assess, as they have drawn only limited academic interest. Perhaps the most extensively scrutinized was the first UN Development Decade, which was launched in 1961. Originally a U.S. initiative, the development decade and in particular the second development decade for the period 1971–1980 were progressively seized by the majority of developing countries in control of the General Assembly to press their development agenda and to legitimize their call for a new international economic order. The first development decade had been merely an exhortatory statement. At their urging, the second decade became an executive policy statement laced with quantified targets and specified corresponding policy measures bolstered by "commitments" at national and international levels and an ongoing system of oversight and policy correction. The changing political winds buffeting the Assembly in the 1980s and 1990s predictably weakened the appeal of the development decades. The UN is now involved in a fifth development decade, which in spite of bureaucratic persistence elicits so little interest as not even to be mentioned in UN official promotional material.

Policy Analysis and Studies

One of the major functions of the United Nations in development is to collect and disseminate economic and social information, monitor economic and social progress, and identify emerging issues of global concern. The unique global character of the UN system has made it a natural focal point for collecting data in the economic and social fields. Most of the agencies and bodies that make up the UN development system require their Member States to submit statistical data on economic and social issues, which the UN, in turn, uses to produce compilations of statistics. The *Statistical Yearbook,* the

Demographic Yearbook, and the *International Trade Statistics Yearbook* are all examples of the outstanding work of the Department of Economic and Social Affairs in this field. Closely related are the activities carried out primarily by the United Nations specialized agencies in the definition of international rules governing international commerce, telecommunications, transportation, and the like, through the standardization of technologies and procedures, international laws governing commercial transactions, and intellectual property rights, to cite only a few instances.[11] This soft infrastructure of the United Nations has steadily expanded and become an indispensable underpinning of the functioning of the global economy.

Concurrently, the UN produces a plethora of reports on an endless string of subjects, including national accounts, tax and accounting, finance and investment, natural resources, agriculture, industry, labor markets, the environment, human settlement, transnational corporations, transportation, refugees, displaced persons, public health, social statistics, gender issues, and children. Norm articulation and norm-setting, as discussed in Chapter 3, along with trend monitoring and early warning, are important functions provided for by these reports, which are often produced by expert consultants. To cite recent examples, a new study weaves around the idea that the role of the state in development should not be overlooked, especially in light of the increasing interest in government accountability arising from the transition toward an information-based economy. Its authors draw attention to the need to obtain a more comprehensive picture of government revenues and expenditures and of their utilization by developing indicators of the quality of government activities and policies.[12]

Another study of the use (and abuse) of natural resources maintains that the real security issue that the world needs to address now is the insidious global spread of poverty and environmental stress.[13] Published on the occasion of the first anniversary of the 2001 special session of the General Assembly on HIV-AIDS, yet another study highlights findings from a series of national demographic and health surveys directly relevant to the AIDS epidemic, which dramatically impacts on production by reducing the work force, especially in countries where a significant portion of the population is infected. It also provides a picture of HIV/AIDS-related awareness and behaviors across countries and population groups, data categorized by age and gender, as well as information about risk-related behaviors. The determinants of these behaviors and the context within which they occur have direct relevance to the effective targeting of AIDS prevention efforts.[14]

WHO has recently issued a world report on violence and health, the first comprehensive study of its kind, that seeks to address death and disability caused by violent acts. Focusing on the scale of the problem, it also covers issues related to the causes of violence and the methods for preventing the problem and reducing its adverse health and social consequences.[15]

The United Nations has always relied on outside expertise to produce special studies in support of intergovernmental processes. In recent years, however, this practice has gained further momentum. For example, at the request of the Economic and Social Council, the Secretary-General established the Information and Communications Technologies Task Force in 2001 to map out strategies for the development of information and communication technologies at the service of development in a strategic partnership with private industry, financing trusts and foundations, UN entities, and donor and recipient countries. The task force, billed to "harmonize economic and profit motives of the private sector with the human development goals," featured an innovative mechanism, as it was the first body in which representatives of governments, civil society, the private sector, nonprofit foundations, NGOs, educational institutions, and organizations of the UN had equal decisionmaking power.[16] In February 2002 the ILO set up the World Commission on the Social Dimension of Globalization, an independent body composed of former high-ranking government officials, think tanks and academics, labor and business leaders, and NGOs. The commission will present recommendations seeking a broad consensus on innovating ways to identify policies for globalization that reduce poverty and foster growth, employment, and development in open economies, and to identify policies that can make globalization more inclusive.[17]

Flagship Reports

Producing information for monitoring and early warning purposes is one thing; assigning meaning to it with a view to providing guidance to intergovernmental bodies quite another. The issue relates primarily to the so-called flagship reports of the UN—that is, those empirical and normative recurrent reports that lay down the foundations and the agenda for intergovernmental deliberations. The flagship reports have received little attention from academia. Yet they have made important contributions to international discussions on international economy, trade, and finance and their interactions with both long-term development and short-term microeconomic issues.

When it was first introduced in the postwar years, the *World Economic and Social Survey* was the only publication providing an overview of the global economy. More generally, flagship reports have endeavored to provide alternative policy, going beyond prevailing economic orthodoxy and broadening intergovernmental policy debates by adding important social and political dimensions to issues that would have been otherwise dominated by narrow economic and financial considerations. For example, UNDP's annual *Human Development Report* has challenged the focus on economic growth that has prevailed in the conventional wisdom since the end of World War II by arguing that people as agents of change and beneficiaries of change are the central aim of development rather than the accumulation of various forms of capital. This novel approach, foreshadowed in the important UNICEF publication *Adjustment with a Human Face* in 1987,[18] not only underlined the need for a greater variety and quality of statistical data but also contributed to important policy initiatives such as the 20/20 proposal referred to earlier.

These achievements notwithstanding, the extent to which UN flagship reports contribute to a better appreciation of the challenges arising from globalization and the liberalization of the world economy and offer credible alternatives to existing national and international policies remains uncertain. The proliferation of these reports projects the image of an organization lacking in coherence and unified purpose.

Economic Leadership Within the UN

The problem of lack of coherence was raised in the latest reform proposals of the Secretary-General, but it is by no means new and may be viewed as a symptom of the relative decline of UN intellectual leadership. In the late 1940s and early 1950s, development economists of exceptional talent held appointments in the UN Secretariat. Researchers such as Gerasimos Arsenis, Celso Furtado, Lal Jayawardina, Nicolas Kaldor, Michal Kalecki, W. R. Malinoswski, Jacob Mosak, Raul Prebisch, Hans Singer, Manmihan Singh, Victor Urquidi, and two Nobel Prize winners, Arthur Lewis and Gunnar Myrdal, developed influential ideas that shaped the development debate for at least two decades. Among these ideas were the critical importance of structural factors in the development process, notably the dynamic role of industry, and the constraints imposed by agriculture. The analysis of the dynamics of inflation and the secular tendency for the terms of trade of primary commodities to deteriorate were also ideas from this period. The concept of a trade constraint and of a trade gap, and the cumulative process whereby intercountry polarization of income takes place, were also created by UN thinkers.[19] This generation is gone and has not been replaced by staff of comparable quality. This has resulted in a loss of intellectual leadership by the United Nations Secretariat and a corresponding shift in gravitas toward the World Bank and UNDP.

The changing fortunes of the UN Department of Economic and Social Affairs provide an illustration of this evolution. In the 1950s the department (together with the Economic Commission for Latin America and the Caribbean [ECLAC]) provided fertile ground for innovative and ebullient development thinking. Today it is very much in search of a role. As a result of Third World political pressures, many constituent parts of the department were pulled away and turned into autonomous agencies, as was the case for UNCTAD, UNEP, and Habitat. The department has succeeded in maintaining the integrity and quality of its statistical and demographic work, but its original core function of assessing global economic and social trends has been weakened. Its flagship report, the *World Economic and Social Survey,* is a pale reflection of its former glory and has become proverbial for its sibylline balance.

Capacity Development and the Creation of UNDP

One of the most prominent and concrete manifestations of the UN's work in development is its large presence in the field and the countless technical assistance activities that it carries out in developing countries. Total UN technical cooperation assistance delivered in 2001 amounted to roughly $7 billion widely spread out over 150 countries.[20] Such voluntarily funded large-scale activities were certainly not envisaged by the drafters of the UN Charter. Nonetheless, the involvement of the UN's role in technical cooperation can be traced back to the very beginnings of the Organization. The first such mission (in Haiti) was authorized in a little-noted 1947 resolution of the Economic and Social Council.[21] In 1948 the General Assembly followed suit by appropriating $288,000 for technical assistance activities, a sum that it increased to $676,000 at its fourth session.[22]

The fieldwork of the UN received further impetus in 1949 with the creation of "an expanded programme of technical assistance for economic development for under-developed countries" through the United Nations and its specialized agencies.[23] As noted earlier, this program was an outgrowth of a U.S. proposal. The operational activities of the UN were expanded further yet by the creation in 1958 of the Special Fund, with preinvestment functions "to provide systematic and sustained assistance in fields essential to the integrated technical, economic, and social development of the less developed countries." Problems of coordination and competition among implementing agencies in the field and at headquarters and hopes that preinvestment would encourage lending by the World Bank led in 1965 to the merging of the Special Fund with the technical assistance program into a single agency, the United Nations Development Programme.

At the outset, technical assistance was operationally understood simply as the provision of expert advice, training, and demonstration. That included the pooling of particular know-how developed in individual countries and the application of that know-how to the problems of underdeveloped countries.[24] The program was funded by governments on an entirely voluntary basis. Services to be rendered were supposed to be decided by the governments concerned. With the establishment of UNDP, the United Nations expanded its operational work in preinvestment activities. Changing concepts of development have since led to novel definitions of the purposes and modalities of technical assistance.

In the early 1990s a UNDP-sponsored study emphasized the need for development to be "locally owned,"[25] and recent development policies stress capacity building and its sustainability.[26] The focus has turned to human resource development and institution building, with particular reference to the public sector. Growing attention to private enterprise and civil society organizations as partners in development and to the loose notion of governance have further broadened the concept of organizational engineering beyond the formal functions of public sector organizations. A recent UNDP study has proposed that the notion of "capacity development" should be grounded on a third dimension involving "capacities in the society as a whole."[27] Efforts are currently being made to develop a more consistent and coherent approach to capacity development within the UN system as well as benchmarks of progress made toward the achievement of the targets set by the Millennium Declaration and other UN global conferences.

Meanwhile, UNDP has drastically altered its capacity development activities with a focus on aspects of poverty eradication, gender, the environment, and good governance in postconflict rehabilitation and reconstruction situations. Under good governance, UNDP works to strengthen political institutions and government policy, train legislators and law enforcement officials, and reconstruct public services. Assisting in development strategies to combat poverty and organizing consultative fora for community-based organizations have become the mainstay of UNDP fieldwork. For example, UNDP has been supporting country efforts to start and maintain viable microfinance institutions that serve the poor, especially poor women. Relying on community participation, other projects seek to restore infrastructure and improve the local environment through such activities as reforestation, road repair, garbage removal, and rehabilitation of power lines and water supply.

Asking how these activities are planned, programmed, and implemented raises the thorny question of the coordination of UN operational activities, a long-standing issue that has not yet received any satisfactory answer. The creation of UNDP itself in 1965 was an effort to put an end to the scrambling for technical assistance funds among UN agencies both at headquarters and in the field and to ensure more unified and coherent programming. This did not deter a group of evaluators in the late 1960s from calling for drastic changes in the planning and administration of UN technical cooperation activities.[28]

UNDP's coordination of UN operational activities takes place at the country level and is the responsibility of the UN resident coordinator, who is also the UNDP representative. The UN resident coordinator is also expected to coordinate aid. One of his or her main tasks is to assess the development needs of the country in consultation with UN agencies reported in a "Common Country Assessment." In many emergency situations, the UNDP representative also acts as humanitarian coordinator for the UN system.

While this sounds good, the system has many built-in weaknesses. The programs often reflect the interests of donor governments, and UN agencies are reluctant to yield to the authority of a single UN official. They prefer to give priority to their own specialized activities by initiating and developing projects directly with governmental authorities. In this competitive environment, the dual functions of UNDP country head as representing both UNDP and the UN system creates another layer of operational difficulties. In emergency situations, the growing presence of NGOs with their own agendas and priorities adds another layer of complexity in the management and coordination of aid. These issues are compounded by the contradictory pushing and pulling of the General Assembly. In addition, ECOSOC presses for a broadening of UNDP mandates while UNDP's governing body wishes to simplify UNDP activities along functional lines. The political stalemate arising from the pursuit of diverging interests by donor countries and the unwillingness of developing countries to reform weakens the coordinating role of UNDP, particularly in the face of shrinking donor contributions.

The launching of the UNDP Assistance Framework (UNDAF), a coordination mechanism designed to promote an integrated approach and cooperation among UN agencies in cooperation with aid-recipient governments, has led to a degree of progress in the harmonization of the work of UN agencies. But by and large, and in the absence of a genuine culture of cooperation, joint programming and the streamlining of a proliferation of projects running on separate tracks remain more an aspiration than a reality. Under these circumstances, it is not surprising that UNDP has been most successful in its capacity development work in postconflict situations, where aid donors, international financial institutions, and UN agencies prefer to remain on the sidelines and are inclined to rely on UNDP expertise and networks. In many ways, this is consistent with the catalytic preinvestment function originally assigned to UNDP. In more competitive and politically stable conditions, the success of UNDP as a coordinating agency hinges on such contingent factors as the diplomatic and professional skills of the resident coordinator, the donor situation in a given country, and the policies and practices of the host government.

Disaster Relief and Humanitarianism

The modern era of disaster relief was triggered by the ravages of World War II, when there was an immediate need to address the resulting mass social disruptions, famine, devastation, and refugee flows. Yet the important UN role in providing, and especially in coordinating, worldwide disaster relief was never mentioned in the Charter. A large majority of World War II refugees were resettled first with the aid of the United Nations Relief and Rehabilitation Administration (UNRRA) and of its successor agency, the International Refugee Organization (IRO). Upon termination of its mandate in 1951, the IRO was superseded by the UN High Commissioner for Refugees (UNHCR), which today remains the UN agency concerned with refugee protection. In addition to the Red Cross, scores of NGOs sprung up to alleviate the misery of refugees. A second phase of the postwar era began in the early 1950s, brought on by the very success of the postwar reconstruction effort and the growing presence of developing countries in the United Nations. With the organizational imperative for their existence declining, many of the erstwhile relief organizations retooled themselves and shifted their attention to the issues of economic development in the Third World. Traditionally, disaster relief and development aid were only loosely tied, mostly in the sense that both were predominantly destined for developing countries. Disaster relief was considered short-term, a onetime response to a catastrophic event such as a cyclone or earthquake, while development aid was long-term, focused on basic infrastructural projects such as dams and roads, taking years, if not decades, to complete.

Unlike the model for the postwar disaster relief that was provided to Europe, however, it was soon recognized that Third World states did not have the institutional capacity to direct their own recovery efforts in the aftermath of disasters. In response to a series of natural disasters in Central America in 1965, the UN General Assembly for the first time passed a resolution calling for greater coordination among UN agencies, Member States, and the Red Cross in providing humanitarian assistance.[29] Neither the UN specialized agencies nor the Red Cross, however, were keen to lose any influence or responsibility to the UN itself, and Member States preferred the visibility provided by bilateral aid. The symbolic role of the UN in coordinating disaster relief was reflected in the Working Capital Fund, dedicated to disaster relief, which the Assembly set up in the same resolution. Its resources did not exceed $100,000 per annum for disaster assistance, with a cap of $20,000 per country, which was usually just a drop in the bucket of what was needed.

The impetus for the most dramatic changes to the humanitarian assistance regime has been the end of the Cold War, which led to a new convergence between U.S. and Russian interests and thereby afforded the UN a newfound authority to intervene in crisis situations. A direct outcome of this was UN Security Council resolution 688 of April 1991, which called for the creation of safe havens for Kurdish refugees stranded in the highlands of the Iraqi-Turk border. This landmark resolution established the very radical precedent that under certain conditions, military force could be sanctioned in support of humanitarian relief operations, and that such relief operations could occur without, and indeed contrary to, host country consent.

UN intervention in civil wars for the sake of humanitarian causes was soon witnessed in practice again in Bosnia (January 1991) and Somalia (July 1992). The disastrous outcome of the Somalia operation, however, led to a new *dis*inclination of the international community to intervene in nonstrategic civil wars, which in turn laid the groundwork for the next global humanitarian tragedy. Despite repeated early warnings, the UN reduced its presence in Rwanda just as the genocidal murder of some 800,000 Tutsis commenced in April 1994. The failure of the international community to prevent the genocide, as well as to adequately care for and protect the hundreds of thousands of refugees left languishing in camps in Zaire (now the Democratic Republic of Congo), had profound impacts on the humanitarian assistance regime. In particular, the clash between the norms of sovereignty and humanitarian intervention remains unresolved and has been further underlined by the UN's mixed record in other war-torn societies like Haiti and Chechnya, and the North Atlantic Treaty Organization's military intervention in Kosovo, initiated without UN Security Council authorization.[30]

The far-ranging General Assembly resolution 46/182 (1991) established the Department of Humanitarian Affairs, the precursor of today's Office of the Coordinator of Humanitarian Affairs (OCHA), which has now become the focal point of the UN's humanitarian relief efforts. In its first year of existence, OCHA responded to six international humanitarian crises, coordinating a total of $2.1 billion in multilateral aid through its appeal process. By 2002 the number of crises had risen dramatically to twenty-seven, although the amount of funding channeled through OCHA did not increase commensurately ($2.4 billion), in part for two reasons. First, the ratio of the amount of resources channeled through the consolidated appeals process relative to the funding requested by OCHA has steadily declined. In 1992, these appeals processes received 76 percent of funding requested, whereas by 2002 that number had declined to 57 percent.[31] Second, humanitarian assistance provided through bilateral channels has become much more important relative to multilateral aid, such that by 2000 total humanitarian aid flows from states were estimated to be close to $6 billion, roughly five times the amount passed through the consolidated appeals processes that year. One controversial effect of the increase in humanitarian aid has been that it appears to have happened at the expense of traditional development funding. As such, humanitarian aid accounted for roughly 10.5 percent of all official development assistance in 2000, up steeply from the 5.8 percent seen between 1989 and 1993.[32] Countries may be simply transferring funds from development aid to humanitarian assistance rather than increasing the total package.

Developing countries like India, Mexico, and China have expressed increasing unease about these trends. From their vantage point, humanitarian intervention under UN auspices remains controversial due to a lack of specificity in determining when the need for intervention should outweigh the principle of sovereignty. Donor states are now talking of sovereignty as less a right than a responsibility. This language has triggered suspicions by the developing countries that human-made or natural disasters can be used as a pretext for intrusions in what they consider to be internal affairs. Not surprisingly, every UN resolution on humanitarian assistance since 1988 includes language stressing that it is the primary responsibility of the state to take care of victims of natural disasters occurring on its territory and that the principles of humanity, neutrality, and impartiality should be given utmost importance in providing humanitarian assistance. As shall be seen below, developing countries' concerns of impartiality and neutrality also extend to the aid providers themselves. The politically tarnished image of some humanitarian actors, including NGOs and UN agencies, has proved damaging and has hindered their ability to provide effective relief.

A contributing factor to these changing perceptions is the aforementioned shift of humanitarian assistance through bilateral instead of multilateral channels. Bilateral provision of assistance is often preferred by donor countries, especially the United States, because aid recipients are more accountable and prestige is more directly conferred to the donor. However, these same qualities serve to increase the bias and perceived political motivation of aid. Bilateral aid is also often conditional, thus making it less effective. At the same time, increasing bilateral aid brings about a corresponding decrease in multilateral aid, thus hampering international coordination.

Still another concern of developing countries is that humanitarian aid is doled out haphazardly and targeted to a few high-profile cases and favored countries. For example, the largest recipient of humanitarian aid in 2003 was Afghanistan, in large part a consequence of U.S. interest in the region. This has led to a new class of forgotten tragedies, such as Eritrea, the Democratic Republic of Congo, and Sierra Leone, countries that have no perceived strategic value and that receive little to none of the funds requested during the process of annual donor appeals.

Last, although developing countries are careful not to call for a reduction in the level of funding for humanitarian assistance, they point out that funding does come out of countries' official development assistance packages and that emergency monies are often taken directly out of development accounts instead of being budgeted separately. Findings from a UN panel convened in 2001 to look at financing for development, often cited by developing countries, stress that current levels of funding are only covering roughly half of requirements. As such, any increases in funding for humanitarian assistance to make up for this shortfall must come from *new funding,* and more important must come from a specific line item in the contingency budget rather than from funds redirected from other development projects.[33]

Independent research shows that developing countries are largely correct in their observations regarding bilateral aid and the strategic targeting of aid.[34] However, the question of whether humanitarian assistance dramatically reduces funding for development budgets is considerably more nuanced than the numbers make it appear. First, the politicization of humanitarian intervention has vastly increased the scope of situations that call for humanitarian assistance. The response to human-made disasters, at $1.85 billion for 2001, now greatly outweighs responses to natural disasters, a $311 million cost for the same year. Second, this politicization has also meant that funding once earmarked for peacekeeping activities now often falls under the humanitarian rubric. Last, terminology and accounting also play a role. Beginning in 1999, some countries began to count aid given to refugees within their own borders as official humanitarian assistance, which had the effect of greatly increasing the amount of aid that was classified as humanitarian.[35] While there is no doubt that the total amount of official development assistance going to humanitarian aid has increased, within the UN itself humanitarian aid is still minuscule as compared to development spending. The 2003 regular budget for OCHA is a mere $9.5 million, and even with all of its extrabudgetary funding requests for headquarters and field operations combined, the total budget is still under $70 million. This compares with the $2.5 billion the United Nations appropriated for development work in 2001.

The dichotomy between development and humanitarian aid has today come full circle. That humanitarian assistance and development are two sides of the same coin is increasingly clear: indeed, every year now the Secretary-General presents a report titled *Humanitarian Assistance: From Relief to Development*. It is understood that it is often conditions of underdevelopment that allow disasters to occur or worsen their impact, and it is in responding to disasters that the seeds of development need to be planted. On the other hand, it is increasingly *less* clear as to what the word "humanitarian" means in terms of assistance. Over the next few years, it is probable that the humanitarian assistance regime will change anew as different notions of norms of sovereignty, impartiality, and humanitarianism vie for dominance in the UN.

The United Nations, Civil Society, and Business in Development

Academic organizations, think tanks, trade unions, and other private organizations and professional associations have been the focus of considerable attention in the past two decades or so, but they have been in the corridors of power for quite a long time. In 1910 a World Congress of International Associations, lobbying in support of the creation of the League of Nations, was held in Brussels with the support of the Belgian government and the Carnegie Endowment for Peace. Soon after, a Federation of International Institutions came into existence and focused on winning access for nongovernmental organizations to the League institutions. Articles 24 and 25 of the League Covenant granted a modicum of recognition to the activities of nongovernmental organizations, notably national Red Cross organizations. At an informal level, NGOs were allowed to participate in meetings of the League of Nations and given special facilities. Throughout World War II, nongovernmental organizations actively campaigned for the establishment of a successor organization. As stated in Chapter 2, they were conspicuously present at the UN's San Francisco Conference, and the United States invited numerous NGOs as consultants or observers. The provisions of the Charter dealing with education, health, human rights, and NGOs can all be traced back to demands articulated by NGOs themselves.

Article 73 of the Charter stipulates that the Economic and Social Council could make "suitable arrangements for consultation with nongovernmental organizations which are concerned with matters within its competence." These consultative arrangements were first set in 1950 by ECOSOC in its resolution 288B (X). They were subsequently amended in 1968 in resolution 1296 (XLIV). The formal arrangements thus set provide for a screening of an NGO's application for "consultative status" by a standing committee of ECOSOC, which grants it one of three different types of status based on the degree of "interest" and "competence" that it may bring to the deliberations of the Council. The modalities of NGO participation in ECOSOC have since been reviewed several times but have not led to significant changes in the system, owing primarily to the opposition of Member States. In this regard, it should be noted that the Charter does not grant any role to NGOs in meetings of the Security Council. NGOs have occasionally been allowed to address special sessions of the General Assembly. But with the exception of the Red Cross, and in spite of their repeated demands, they are not authorized to participate in the regular sessions of the Assembly. Even in UN global conferences, they meet in their own fora, at a safe distance from governmental conclaves.

The Charter thus legitimized a limited degree of participation to NGOs in UN proceedings. The system of NGO participation, however, has never been fully consensual, and its creation as well as its subsequent changes have provoked contentious and divisive debates. Governments and, to a lesser extent, UN officials have resisted a further institutionalization of NGO involvement in UN work, although consultative relations have been more extensive with the specialized agencies. This is especially true in the ILO, where NGOs have full voting rights together with the government and employer representatives composing each national delegation. In practice and behind these formal arrangements, civil society institutions have in fact progressively enlarged the scope of their activities in UN processes.

Two major factors have contributed to this trend, the first of which is changing concepts of development and governance and, in particular, the emphasis increasingly being placed on grassroots ownership of the development agenda. The recognition that alliances and partnerships between public and private actors produce more effective and sustainable solutions to development problems has given a center-stage role to nongovernmental organizations. Second, roughly speaking since the Stockholm Conference, NGOs have been deeply involved in UN-sponsored global conferences. Their numbers have grown exponentially since Stockholm and their presence has been felt far beyond the constrained formalism of ECOSOC arrangements. For instance, the 1992 Rio Conference had no less that 1,400 accredited NGOs, and 9,000 attended its unofficial Global Forum. Ten years later, the Johannesburg Summit accredited 925 NGOs and included 8,000 NGO participants.

The existence of transnational NGO networks is a reality that can no longer be ignored. They reflect the emergence of more pluralistic forms of governance and decisionmaking. Either formally or informally, they help influence the process of multilateral diplomacy through varying forms of lobbying with the media, governmental delegations, and international civil servants. They participate in the drafting of UN resolutions and in the preparation of the programs for UN global conferences. They also are indispensable partners in the implementation of UN projects, especially in the field. The United Nations has responded to this challenge, albeit still in an imperfect and inconclusive manner and essentially in noninstitutional terms.

The same observation applies to the UN's embrace of the private sector as illustrated by the Secretary-General's initiative to launch a Global Compact with large corporations. The Secretary General first aired the idea in January 1999 at the World Economic Forum in Davos. It has since evolved into a global network of several hundred private companies, international trade unions, two dozen international NGOs, and business schools.

Concretely, the operation of the Global Compact includes the convening of "policy dialogues" with the participation of business, labor, NGOs, the UN, and governments focused on the search for solutions to current problems. Discussions have thus been held on the role of the private sector in zones of conflict and in business and sustainable development. Private corporations are also invited to share instances of their practices on the Global Compact's website. Policy analysis and research are also encouraged for use in the corporate and academic worlds. Local networks for information exchange, the convening of similar policy dialogues, and the recruiting of new participants are being established. Ultimately, these multilayer activities are translated into multistakeholder projects in the field.[36]

Not surprisingly, the Global Compact has received mixed reviews. Northern governments laud it as a sound effort to mobilize the private sector in flexible and effective ways in the process of development. Southern governments are at best circumspect, considering it is only a second and imperfect best alternative to mandatory codes of conduct. Private corporations are still cautious and guarded. NGOs are most critical. They are especially skeptical of the compact's assumption that "the power of transparency, dialogue, and accountability" can lead to any significant changes in corporate policies and practices and that it can "generate positive impulses that . . . contribute towards governance and public policy [conducive] to a more beneficial relationship between business and society." From their perspective, the UN has all but lost its integrity in sanctioning a process that, in the final analysis, merely provides private corporations with a convenient public relations tool and a smokescreen for the continuation of policies inimical to human rights, labor standards, and protection of the environment. Be that as it may, the Global Compact is a clear illustration of the difficulties involved in devising international regime rules for development.

Conclusion: The Issue of Leadership

The United Nations is an interstate organization. This is why Inis Claude could write long ago that the UN had no purpose of its own and that it was above all a "tool" with "possibilities and limitations." Its Member States, however, had purposes that they sought to achieve through the Organization. And it was these purposes that the United Nations served. The changing purposes of the Organization, in turn, are a reflection of the changing balance of power among Member States or groups of Member States that vie for its control.[37] The United Nations has certainly not lost its statist birthmarks. This chapter has noted its gyrations in legitimizing first the developing countries' call for a new international economic order and, more recently, the Washington Consensus. It has also drawn attention to the fact that the initiation of its work in the field of technical assistance was a byproduct of the Cold War. The state-oriented base of the United Nations cannot be overlooked and still sets the broad parameters of not only its functioning, but also, and very importantly, its legitimacy.

But neither should the capacity of the United Nations to shape the political process be underestimated. Through the policy research that it undertook in the late 1940s and early 1950s, the Organization not only redefined the prevailing wisdom over the meaning of the concept of development, but it also placed development at the heart of the agenda of the international community and has since kept it in the forefront of its concerns, notably through the global conferences that it sponsored in the 1990s, and through 2002 at Monterrey and Johannesburg. Likewise, the United Nations vastly expanded the scope and meaning of its technical assistance and humanitarian work. The legitimacy that the United Nations derives from its universal membership lent credence to its Keynesian and ethical critiques of the Washington Consensus and has contributed to its reappraisal. States may not be ready to abdicate any power to the United Nations, but as Inis Claude acknowledges himself, Member States take seriously its verbal function even if it is inversely correlated to its executive function.[38] This does give to the Organization a modicum of influence in the political process. Moreover, the vagueness of the Charter provisions on development, the lack of consensus among Member States over its meaning and operationalization, not to mention their widespread tendency to lean on the United Nations whenever their major interests are not at stake, did create a political vacuum that paved the way toward an active and continuing involvement of the United Nations in development.

The concept of a United Nations merely responding to and acting on behalf of its stakeholders is only partially correct. In today's parlance, pundits would refer to the normative (rather than verbal) role of the United Nations stressed throughout this book. A critical variable in this process is the leadership roles of the Secretary-General and the Secretariat. The Global Compact, the Millennium Assembly, and the development goals and targets of the Millennium Declaration, around which the Secretary-General has mobilized the entire UN system,[39] as well as the current dialogue between the Economic and Social Council and the Bretton Woods institutions, were all initiatives of the Secretary-General. His leadership role may be fraught with political dangers and uncertainties, but he does have a considerable degree of latitude in shaping the political process and the development dialogue. This is especially true in the context of an increasingly pluralized international society and emerging system of governance in which the UN may be the linchpin, or agent, of coalitions for change involving a multiplicity of actors, civil society, business, and the epistemic community. The significance of this new emerging world order on the role of the United Nations and the Secretary-General in development is one of the biggest challenges confronting the Organization in the coming years.

Notes

1. To use the term of Robert Gregg, to contrast the lack of visibility of the UN economic and social work relative to the glare of public coverage of UN peace operations. Robert W. Gregg, "UN Economic, Social, and Technical Activities," in James Barros, ed., *The United Nations: Past, Present, and Future* (New York: Free Press, 1972).

2. John Foster Dulles, "The General Assembly," *Foreign Affairs* 24 (Spring 1947): 173.

3. UN Economic and Social Council, resolution 106 (VI), February 25 and March 5, 1948.

4. UN General Assembly, resolution 1995 (XIX), December 30, 1964.

5. UN General Assembly, *Declaration and Programme of Action on the Establishment of a New International Economic Order,* A/Res/3201 and 3202 (S-VI); and UN General Assembly, *Charter of Economic Rights and Duties of States,* resolution 3281 (XXIX), December 12, 1974.

6. U.S. Department of State, *Patterns of Cooperation,* International Organization and Conference Series, Publication no. 3735, I.9, p. 7.

7. Francis Fukuyama, *The End of History and the Last Man* (New York: Free Press, 1992).

8. For an excellent overview of these and other issues in the North-South negotiating process, see Pamela Chasek, *Earth Negotiations: Analyzing Thirty Years of Environmental Diplomacy* (Tokyo: United Nations University Press, 2001).

9. For an overall assessment of the significance and impact of UN global conferences, see Michael G. Schechter, ed., *United Nations–Sponsored World Conferences: Focus on Impact and Follow Up* (Tokyo: United Nations University Press, 2001).

10. UN General Assembly, resolution A/50/107, December 20, 1995.

11. On this point, see Marc Zacher, *The United Nations and Global Commerce* (New York: United Nations, 1999).

12. UN Department of Economic and Social Affairs, *World Public Sector Report: Globalization and the State 2000* (New York: United Nations, 2002).

13. "UN Report Paints Gloomy Picture of Planet," *New York Times,* August 14, 2002.

14. UN Department of Economic and Social Affairs, *HIV/AIDS: Awareness and Behavior* (New York: United Nations, 2002).

15. See www.who.int/violence_injury_prevention/violence/world_report/wrvh1/en.

16. See www.unicttaskforce.org/about/principal.asp.

17. See www.ilo.org/public/english/wcsdg/index.htm.

18. Giovanni A. Cornia, Richard Jolly, and Frances Stewart, eds., *Adjustment with a Human Face* (Oxford: Clarendon Press, 1987).

19. Sidney Dell, "Contributions of the United Nations to Economic Thinking and Action," *Journal of Development Planning* 17 (1987): 113–123.

20. UN Development Programme, *Information on United Nations Systems Regular and Extra-Regular Technical Cooperation Expenditures,* DP/2002/26/Add1, 2001, Addendum, Statistical Annexes, August 15, 2002, p. 12.

21. UN Economic and Social Council, resolution 51 (IV), March 28, 1947.

22. UN General Assembly, resolution 200 (III), December 4, 1948, and resolution 304 (IV), November 16, 1949.

23. UN Economic and Social Council, resolution 222 (IX), August 14–15, 1949.

24. P. S. Narasimhan, "Technical Assistance for Economic Development of Underdeveloped Countries," *India Quarterly* 8 (April–June 1952): 142–155.

25. Elliot J. Berg, *Rethinking Technical Cooperation: Reforms for Capacity Building in Africa* (New York: United Nations Development Programme, 1993).

26. UN General Assembly resolution 53/192, December 15, 1998.

27. Sakiko Fukuda-Parr, Carlos Loes, and Khalil Malik, eds., *Developing Capacity Through Technical Cooperation: New Solutions to Old Problems* (London: Earthscan in cooperation with United Nations Development Programme, 2002).

28. Sir Robert Jackson, ed., *A Study of the Capacity of the United Nations Development System,* 2 vols. (Geneva: United Nations, 1969).

29. UN General Assembly, resolution 2034 (XX), December 7, 1965.

30. See John Barton, *The State of the International Humanitarian System,* Overseas Development Institute Briefing Paper no. 1, March 1998.

31. Figures are from the OCHA 2002 annual report.

32. Margie Buchanan-Smith and Judith Randel, *Financing International Humanitarian Action: A Review of Key Trends,* Humanitarian Policy Group Briefing Paper no. 4, Overseas Development Institute, November 2002.

33. UN General Assembly, *Letter Dated 25 June 2001 from the Secretary-General to the President of the General Assembly,* UN Doc. A/55/1000.

34. Joanna Macrae, ed., *The New Humanitarianisms: A Review of Trends in Global Humanitarian Action,* Humanitarian Policy Group Report no. 11, Overseas Development Institute, 2002.

35. Buchanan-Smith and Randel, *Financing International Humanitarian Action.*

36. For a factual discussion of the Global Compact, see the UN-commissioned report by Jane Nelson, *Building Partnerships: Cooperation Between the United Nations System and the Private Sector* (New York: United Nations, 2002). A broader and more analytical study of the subject can be found in Sandrine Tessner with the col-

laboration of Georg Kell, *The United Nations and Business: A Partnership Recovered* (New York: St. Martin's Press, 2000).

37. Inis Claude, *The Changing United Nations* (New York: Random House, 1968), pp. xvii–xviiii.

38. Ibid., pp. 88–89.

39. On this point, see Jacques Fomerand, *The UN Secretary-General as an Actor in International Politics: The Need for Leadership in the United Nations Secretariat as a Global Actor,* United Nations Studies Series no. 3 (Tokyo: Japan Association for United Nations Studies, 2002), pp. 87–113.

7

Disarmament:
Successes and Failures

Derek Boothby

The Early Years: 1945 to 1982

When the United Nations began its work in 1946, there were those who antic-ipated that disarmament and armament regulation would probably be achieved comparatively quickly, whereas decolonization and independence of states would take considerably longer. Matters evolved rather differently. Decolonization proceeded quickly through the 1960s and 1970s, and the membership of the United Nations increased from 51 states in 1945 to 191 by 2003, while in the same period real progress in disarmament and arms regu-lation was disappointingly arduous and slow.

As the founders of the United Nations met in San Francisco from April 25 through June 26, 1945, to finish writing the UN Charter, the end of World War II was already within sight. Little did they know, however, when they signed the Charter on June 26, that less than three weeks later the age of nuclear weapons would be born. The first nuclear explosive test took place on July 16 in New Mexico, and three weeks later nuclear bombs were dropped on Hiroshima and Nagasaki: on August 6 and 9 respectively. The first blast of some 15 kilotons (equivalent to 15,000 tons of TNT) destroyed 90 percent of Hiroshima, whereas, due to the local geography, the 22-kiloton explosion over Nagasaki destroyed about one-third of that city. The two explosions killed or injured approximately a quarter of a million people and by 1950 a further 230,000 had died of injuries or radiation.

Since those days of summer 1945, the world has had to live with a dichotomy. On one hand, the authors of the Charter sought to establish a global mechanism for peace and collective security and the betterment of humanity through social progress, justice, faith in fundamental human rights, and respect for international law; and on the other hand, virtually at the same moment in history, human ingenuity had invented weapons with a destructive

193

capacity to annihilate the human race. The founders of the United Nations opened the Charter with this commitment: "We the peoples of the United Nations, determined to save succeeding generations from the scourge of war, which twice in our lifetimes has brought untold sorrow to mankind . . . have resolved to combine our efforts to accomplish these aims."

The primary purpose of the United Nations, as clearly stated in Article 1 of the Charter, is the maintenance of international peace and security, and, to that end, to take collective measures for the prevention and removal of threats to the peace. The Charter commits all Member States to refrain in their international relations from the threat or use of force against the territorial integrity or political independence of any state (Article 2). It accords to the Security Council primary responsibility for the maintenance of international peace and security (Chapter V) and provides a mechanism for the pacific settlement of disputes (Chapter VI). The Charter sets out action to be taken through decisions in the Security Council with regard to threats to the peace, breaches of the peace, and acts of aggression (Chapter VII).

The Security Council is charged with formulating a plan for a system of regulation of armaments "in order to promote the establishment and maintenance of international peace and security with the least diversion for armaments of the world's human and economic resources" (Article 26). The Council was to have the assistance of the Military Staff Committee, referred to in Article 47, and was to submit the plan to UN Member States. In addition, the General Assembly was specifically given the right to take up issues of disarmament. The General Assembly "may consider . . . principles governing disarmament and the regulation of armaments, and may make recommendations with regard to such principles to the Members or to the Security Council or to both" (Article 11).

With the emergence in the late 1940s of confrontation between the two principal military alliances, the North Atlantic Treaty Organization (NATO) and the Warsaw Treaty Organization, and the ensuing Cold War, which lasted until the collapse of the Soviet Union in 1991, the Security Council was unable to take any action on contentious issues such as a plan for the regulation of armaments. The Military Staff Committee, which was supposed to meet at the level of military chiefs of the five permanent members of the Security Council, and which also had the five most powerful military forces, was stillborn and has remained so to this day. Even agreement on the committee's rules of procedure was precluded by the general climate of mistrust and suspicion between the Soviet Union and the Western powers, and within two or three years their relations deteriorated further with the onset of the Cold War. The proponents of multilateral arms limitation and disarmament had to find other ways of making progress through the General Assembly and by the establishment of other bodies.

With the horrific devastation of Hiroshima and Nagasaki fresh in mind, in 1946 the General Assembly established the Atomic Energy Commission and gave it the task of ensuring that atomic energy would be used only for peaceful purposes. The United States proposed the creation of an atomic energy development authority for all phases of the manufacture and use of atomic energy. The goal was that once the authority was operating effectively, atomic weapon production would cease and stocks would be destroyed (the Baruch Plan). The Soviet Union, however, called for a convention prohibiting atomic weapons and their production to be achieved first, together with the destruction of all atomic weapons within three months of the convention entering into force (the Gromyko Plan). Moscow saw the former as preserving the U.S. advantage of military nuclear knowledge and capability, whereas Washington perceived the latter as eliminating the U.S. edge without first ensuring that atomic energy development would be under effective international control, and thus there was no agreement. This fundamental lack of trust between the two military giants would lead to a historic arms race that would continue for the ensuing four decades.

In 1947 the Security Council established another body, the Commission for Conventional Armaments, to make proposals for the general reduction of armaments and armed forces other than nuclear weapons. Again, however, there were major differences between the Western powers and the Soviet Union, and these clashes, together with a general deterioration in the international climate, resulted in the commission being unable to make progress.

In 1952 the General Assembly combined these two commissions into a single body, the Disarmament Commission, with the objective of making proposals for a coordinated, comprehensive program of arms limitations and reductions of armed forces and measures to eliminate all major weapons adaptable to mass destruction. With the Western powers seeking to give priority to the limitation and control of conventional weapons, and the Soviet Union preferring to focus on curbs on nuclear weapons, this effort did not find success either. In an inclusive effort to bring in the views of other states, in 1958 the membership was extended to all Member States of the United Nations. Frustrated by procedural difficulties, it was able to meet for only two sessions: in 1960 and 1965.

Recognizing that efforts to date had been futile, in 1959 the General Assembly began to look in other directions. It included in its agenda an item titled "General and Complete Disarmament Under Effective International Control" and sought partial measures that would attract broad support and contribute toward achieving the overall goal. Separately, in 1959 the major powers of Europe and the United States established the Ten-Nation Committee on Disarmament with equal Eastern and Western membership. Designated as a negotiating body, it was expanded in 1962 into the Eighteen-Nation Committee on Disarmament (ENDC) and endorsed by the General Assembly, with eight members added from nonaligned states. This became the Conference of the Committee on Disarmament (CCD) in 1969, with a membership of twenty-six states, and it was expanded yet again in 1975 to thirty-one states.

Faced with the continued buildup of arms across the board, the General Assembly turned to limiting the introduction of arms into specified geographical areas. By the late 1960s, a number of collateral agreements had been reached, with the principal aim of curbing the expansion of the arms race into areas in which it had not yet extended. These included:

- The 1959 Antarctic Treaty, which provided for the demilitarization of Antarctica.
- The 1963 Treaty Banning Nuclear Weapon Tests in the Atmosphere, in Outer Space, and Under Water, known as the Partial Test Ban Treaty.
- The 1967 Treaty on Principles Governing the Activities of States in the Exploration and Use of Outer Space, Including the Moon and Other Celestial Bodies, known as the Outer Space Treaty.
- The 1967 Treaty for the Prohibition of Nuclear Weapons in Latin America, known as the Treaty of Tlatelolco.
- The 1968 Treaty on the Nonproliferation of Nuclear Weapons, often called simply the Nonproliferation Treaty.

These treaties were dramatic undertakings in comparison to the years of failure and were visionary in the limitations they placed on the expansion of nuclear weapons deployment. Notwithstanding these achievements, none of these treaties produced actual reductions in levels of weapons, and global military expenditures continued to rise.

Again, it was through the General Assembly that an effort was initiated to slow and reverse the arms race. In 1969 the General Assembly declared the 1970s as the First Disarmament Decade and called upon states to intensify their efforts to achieve effective measures relating to the cessation of the nuclear arms race. The General Assembly called for nuclear disarmament as well as the elimination of nonnuclear weapons of mass destruction. The United Nations urged Member States to conclude a treaty on general and complete disarmament under effective international control. The General Assembly also drew attention to the importance of channeling a substantial part of the resources freed by disarmament measures toward the promotion of the economic development of developing countries: "disarmament and development."

It was hoped that declaring a "disarmament decade" would be an effective device for focusing attention on the issue, but it was essentially unsuccessful in that, in the first years of the 1970s, UN members achieved agreement on only two further important multilateral treaties:

- The 1971 Treaty on the Prohibition of the Emplacement of Nuclear Weapons and Other Weapons of Mass Destruction on the Sea-Bed and the Ocean Floor and in the Subsoil Thereof, known as the Sea-Bed Treaty.
- The 1972 Convention on the Prohibition of the Development and Stockpiling of Bacteriological (Biological) and Toxin Weapons and on Their Destruction, popularly called the Biological Weapons Treaty.

The latter was notable for being the first international agreement providing for real disarmament by the elimination of a category of existing weapons. However, it was to become the subject of much contention in later years in that it contained no verification provisions.

Thus, by the mid-1970s, thirty years after the foundation of the United Nations, there had been both progress and disappointment. On the positive side, the multilateral treaties that had been agreed upon were serving as the beginning of a framework of constraints on the deployment and expansion of weapons of mass destruction. The United Nations had been successful in carving out spaces for prohibiting the introduction of categories of weapons, but had not been able to eliminate or reduce arms. On the negative side, the Security Council had been unable to contribute anything to the regulation of armaments and disarmament. Hence the multilateral disarmament machinery that had been established had failed to make real progress on reducing arms. Annual global military expenditures were some $400 billion and rising, and the world continued to lie under the shadow of a potentially catastrophic nuclear exchange. Nuclear policy proclaimed by the superpowers had reached the alarming level of "mutual assured destruction" (MAD). Nuclear deterrence rested on the chilling understanding between the United States and the Soviet Union that each had sufficient nuclear weapons to destroy the other and the political will to use them if necessary.

First Special Session of the General Assembly Devoted to Disarmament, 1978

Once more, the General Assembly became the instrument of choice for a number of governments that wished to see the arms race halted and reversed. In 1976, on the initiative of nonaligned countries (those that refrained from identifying themselves with one side or the other in the East-West competition) and with support from East and West, the General Assembly decided to hold a special session devoted entirely to disarmament. By giving the issue more focused attention, the primary objectives were to establish by consensus a new global strategy for disarmament and to obtain fresh commitment at the highest levels of government to make progress.

The session took place at UN headquarters in New York from May 23 to June 30, 1978. Nineteen heads of state or government, fifty-one foreign ministers, and many other high-ranking officials took part, and the debate covered the entire spectrum of disarmament issues. The outcome was a consensus agreement embodied in the final document of the session and intended as the guideline for all future multilateral disarmament efforts within and outside the United Nations.

The final document recognized that the United Nations has a central role and primary responsibility in the field of disarmament. In four sections, the document identified goals, principles, priorities, and some specific measures that states should pursue on an urgent basis. Although a consensus document, some of the language was the result of hard bargaining and in the end meant different things to different people. For example, on priorities the wording was as follows: "Priorities in disarmament negotiations shall be: nuclear weapons; other weapons of mass destruction, including chemical weapons; conventional weapons, including any which may be deemed to be excessively injurious or to have indiscriminate effects; and reduction of armed forces." To the active nonaligned states, this clearly meant that the first priority should be nuclear weapons and therefore a major responsibility was laid on the nuclear weapon states to take action to pursue and achieve nuclear disarmament. But to the United States and its Western allies, there was nothing in the wording that identified an order in which the priorities should be taken, and as nuclear deterrence was a fundamental defense strategy of the time, they did not accept that nuclear disarmament should have first-priority status. To support the attainment of objectives of the final document of the session, the General Assembly in 1979 declared the 1980s as the Second Disarmament Decade, with goals consistent with the ultimate objective of the disarmament process: general and complete disarmament under effective international control.

During the years immediately following the special session, the international climate worsened. The hostility between the United States and the Soviet Union sharpened, military expenditures increased, and nuclear arsenals continued to grow. These and other factors, such as Soviet military action in Afghanistan, the occupation of the U.S. embassy in Teheran, and the holding hostage by Iran of U.S. embassy staff, all had negative effects on disarmament efforts. Negotiations ground to a halt on almost all the important issues. In this tense atmosphere, the lofty goals of the final document of the session moved even further out of reach.

Second Special Session of the General Assembly Devoted to Disarmament, 1982

The second special session of the General Assembly devoted to disarmament took place in New York from June 7 to July 10, 1982. More than 140 states took part in the debate, many expressing their deep concern at the lack of progress. Also present to give voice were more than 3,000 representatives from some 450 nongovernmental organizations (NGOs), and the streets of

New York witnessed the largest popular demonstration in U.S. history when an estimated three-quarters of a million people took part in an antinuclear rally. Streams of orderly protesters filled the streets, crowding past the United Nations hour after hour as they snaked their way back and forth through the streets and avenues, ending miles away in Central Park. Thousands of communications, petitions, and appeals with many millions of signatures were received by the United Nations from organizations, groups, and individuals all over the world.

Despite these expressions of public concern, and various efforts to find diplomatic language that would attract consensus agreement, in the end the political gaps between the West, the East, and the nonaligned proved too large to be bridged. To add to the difficulties, there were ongoing conflicts and international tensions in various parts of the world, and the atmosphere was not at all conducive to making concessions and compromises on matters that were related to the perceived national security interests of Member States, in particular those that were members of NATO or the Warsaw Pact. The concluding document of the session was weak and insubstantial.

Weapons of Mass Destruction

Nuclear Weapons

With China's first nuclear test in 1964, there were five declared nuclear weapon powers, the other four being the United States in 1945, the Soviet Union in 1949, the United Kingdom in 1952, and France in 1960. Year after year, non–nuclear weapon states pressed for a halt to the nuclear arms race. Their concerns mounted as the numbers of strategic and tactical nuclear weapons grew. During the Cold War, the Soviet Union and the United States made it clear that negotiations to limit nuclear weapons would be strictly a bilateral matter and a number of according agreements were made.[1] These, however, made little impact on actually reducing the overall numbers of nuclear weapons and delivery systems. Indeed, to some critics, the levels set by these agreements simply provided ceilings for the continuation of strategic weapons and their delivery systems: It was often averred that arms control was not part of the solution—it was part of the problem.

With the end of the Cold War in the late 1980s and early 1990s, the threat of a major nuclear exchange receded and the two major nuclear powers, Russia and the United States, themselves took steps to reduce their nuclear stockpiles, which represented some 98 percent of the world's nuclear weapons. By the end of the century, it was estimated that the nuclear stockpiles had been reduced by approximately half, to less than 30,000 warheads.

But although the threat of nuclear war has lessened and stockpiles have been reduced, large numbers of warheads and delivery systems remain. The consequences if a nuclear exchange were to take place would still be catastrophic. In 2001 the United States and Russia had a combined total of some 13,000 strategic nuclear weapons, and another 6,000 tactical nuclear weapons. Strategic weapons are those that have an intercontinental range and a magnitude far greater than those dropped on Japan. Strategic nuclear weapons vary from approximately 150 kilotons, or ten times the yield of the bomb dropped on Hiroshima, to 1–5 megatons (1,000 to 5,000 kilotons), primarily hydrogen bombs. Tactical nuclear weapons are those used in-theater with a magnitude more of the Hiroshima type (15 kilotons) or less.[2] The explosive yield of nuclear weapons depends on the type of target, whether intended for use against a large urban or industrial complex, against a hardened underground military control center, or more locally, against submarines (as with nuclear depth charges).

China, France, and the United Kingdom are believed to have a combined total of about 1,000 nuclear warheads. With the nuclear tests carried out by India and Pakistan in 1998, there are now seven countries with nuclear weapons, and for many years there have been reliable assessments that Israel has an undeclared nuclear weapon capability. Some potential nuclear countries have reversed their policies. South Africa announced in the early 1990s that it had ended its undisclosed nuclear program by destroying its half dozen or so nuclear devices. Argentina and Brazil signed an agreement in 1991 to end their rival nuclear weapon research programs and agreed to have the International Atomic Energy Agency (IAEA) participate in overseeing the agreement.

The 1978 final document of the first special session of the General Assembly devoted to disarmament had declared that effective measures of nuclear disarmament and the prevention of nuclear war had the highest priority. At its annual sessions the General Assembly has repeatedly adopted resolutions calling for action by the nuclear weapon states, especially the United States and the former Soviet Union, to pursue nuclear arms reductions and the cessation of the nuclear arms race. The responses to these calls have been varied. The United States, usually supported by the United Kingdom and France and their Western allies, has argued that the policy of nuclear deterrence during the Cold War actually preserved peace. However, with the end of the Cold War, nuclear weapons can be reduced, and it is important that they should not further proliferate through other countries developing or acquiring their own nuclear arms and threatening their neighbors. Certainly a better system to maintain world peace is needed, but it would be a perilous pretense to suggest that such a system is at present available. In the meantime, the Western nuclear powers maintain that nuclear weapons and nuclear deterrence continue to be essential components of a defensive military doctrine.

China has made a long-standing pledge never to be the first to use nuclear weapons during a military conflict, but has stressed that the two major nuclear powers should take the lead in significant arms reductions. Only then would

China be willing to join all other nuclear weapon states in reducing nuclear arsenals according to an agreed scale, as a step toward their elimination.

The Russian Federation and its predecessor, the Soviet Union, also declared a no-first-use policy, but have consistently maintained the view that nuclear arms reductions must be achieved primarily by bilateral negotiations with the United States. The West has never adopted a no-first-use policy, partly because the NATO alliance considered itself conventionally outgunned by the Soviet bloc and partly, as a deliberate aspect of deterrence policy, to always keep Moscow guessing at what might trigger a nuclear release by the United States and its allies.

For many years, India argued vehemently for a nuclear-free world, but at the same time had carried out in 1974 what the Indian government described as a "peaceful nuclear explosion" and thereby demonstrated a capability to develop nuclear weapons. All doubts about India's nuclear capabilities ended with its five consecutive nuclear weapon tests in 1998, which Pakistan repeated shortly afterward.

Nuclear Nonproliferation Treaty. The issue of nuclear nonproliferation has received major attention over the years. The Treaty on the Nonproliferation of Nuclear Weapons was adopted in 1968, came into force in 1970, and was extended indefinitely in 1995. The treaty has 188 parties, including the original five nuclear weapon states, but Cuba, India, Israel, and Pakistan are not members.

According to the treaty, all parties, including the nuclear weapon states, commit themselves "to pursue negotiations in good faith on effective measures relating to cessation of the nuclear arms race at an early date and to nuclear disarmament, and on a treaty on general and complete disarmament under strict and effective international control" (Article 6). The non–nuclear weapon states, for their part, undertake not to receive or control any nuclear weapons or other nuclear explosive devices and not to seek or receive any assistance in manufacturing such weapons or devices (Article 2). In return for this undertaking, the treaty provides for all parties to "facilitate, and have the right to participate in, the fullest possible exchange of equipment, materials and scientific and technological information for the peaceful uses of nuclear energy" (Article 4). The latter clause is implemented through the International Atomic Energy Agency, situated in Vienna. The IAEA is charged with two tasks under the treaty: to assist countries in developing nuclear power and technology for peaceful uses, and to operate a safeguards system with a view to preventing a diversion of nuclear energy from peaceful uses to weaponized or other explosive uses (Article 3).

The importance of the Nonproliferation Treaty cannot be overemphasized. It serves as the anchor of all the efforts to constrain the development and spread of nuclear weapons. At the same time, however, it has aroused significant criticism among some of the non–nuclear weapon states, which have pointed out that, while they have kept their side of the bargain, the nuclear weapon states have not carried out their Article 6 commitment, and that there are still more nuclear weapons now than there were when the treaty was signed in 1968.

The implementation of the treaty is reviewed every five years at a major conference held at United Nations headquarters in New York. The sixth review conference took place in 2000, at a time when progress on disarmament negotiations had been very slow, both bilaterally between the United States and the Russian Federation, and multilaterally in the Conference on Disarmament. Moreover, the U.S. Senate had rejected the Comprehensive Test Ban Treaty, and the declared intention to proceed with a U.S. national missile defense system threatened abrogation of the bilateral Anti-Ballistic Missile Treaty with Russia.

A breakdown in the conference would have seriously undermined the credibility of the Nonproliferation Treaty only five years after it had been indefinitely extended, largely at the wish of the nuclear weapon states. The nonaligned countries continued to press for a convention on nuclear weapons that would contain a specific timetable for their eradication, a demand that the nuclear weapon states have always stoutly resisted. However, a more central view was taken by the "New Agenda Coalition," consisting of Brazil, Egypt, Ireland, Mexico, New Zealand, South Africa, and Sweden, and eventually compromises were reached on meaningful forward action that were acceptable to the nuclear weapon states. An important element was the acceptance by the conference as a whole of a call for "an unequivocal undertaking by the nuclear-weapon states to accomplish the total elimination of their nuclear arsenals, leading to nuclear disarmament." By this, the nuclear weapon states reaffirmed their political commitment to the goal of the elimination of nuclear weapons without giving any dates by which that goal might be achieved. The next review is expected to take place in 2005.

Security assurances. In order to encourage non–nuclear weapon states to refrain from acquiring nuclear weapons, over the years certain assurances have been given by nuclear weapon states. Statements by the latter that they will come to the assistance of any non–nuclear weapon state threatened by the use of nuclear weapons are known as "positive assurances." Guarantees that nuclear weapon states will not use their nuclear weapons against non–nuclear weapon states are referred to as "negative assurances." There is no wording in the Nonproliferation Treaty that covers either form of assurance; thus they remain simply policy statements.

When the Nonproliferation Treaty was concluded, three states—the Soviet Union, the United Kingdom, and the United States—gave identical formal declarations of positive assurance that they would act, as permanent members of the Security Council, through the Council, to take the measures necessary to counter aggression with nuclear weapons or the threat of such aggression against a non–nuclear weapon state. Subsequently, on June 19, 1968, the Council adopted resolution 255 on the subject.

Between 1978 and 1993, negative assurances were given unilaterally by all five nuclear weapon parties to the Nonproliferation Treaty, although the wording was not uniform. The differences led to unease among the non–nuclear weapon states, many of which considered the negative assurances to be insufficient, and prolonged discussion at the Conference on Disarmament over many years in efforts to find a formula on effective international arrangements to which all could agree.

Nuclear free zones. Recognizing that large areas of the world are free of nuclear weapons, there have been a number of initiatives by non–nuclear weapon states to preserve that condition as a way of strengthening the security of the states involved. Adding to the 1959 Antarctic Treaty and the 1968 Treaty for the Prohibition of Nuclear Weapons in Latin America and the Caribbean (Treaty of Tlatelolco), the United Nations created:

- The 1972 Treaty on the Prohibition of the Emplacement of Nuclear Weapons and Other Weapons of Mass Destruction on the Seabed and Ocean Floor and in the Subsoil Thereof (the Seabed Treaty).
- The 1986 South Pacific Nuclear Free Zone Treaty (the Treaty of Rarotonga).
- The 1997 Treaty on the Southeast Asia Nuclear-Weapon-Free Zone (the Bangkok Treaty).
- The African Nuclear-Weapon-Free Zone Treaty (the Pelindaba Treaty), which was signed in 1996 but as of January 2004 had not yet received the necessary twenty-eight instruments of ratification for entry into force.[3]

Even though some of these treaties include significant sea areas, all respect the principle of freedom of movement on the high seas and thus do not constrain the carriage of nuclear weapons aboard ships of the nuclear weapon states. Their terms do, however, have the effect of precluding port visits by ships known to be carrying such weapons and this has led to a policy by nuclear weapon states of "neither confirming nor denying" the presence of such weapons aboard. In instances where such declarations have been insufficient for acceptance by the host government, such as New Zealand, the result has been the complete absence of visits by any ship of the foreign navy concerned.

The establishment of these nuclear free zones has underscored the important role that can be played by regional organizations and arrangements stemming from discussions and initiatives on placing limits on nuclear weapons that have taken place within the United Nations.

Efforts to ban nuclear tests. The banning of nuclear testing has been pursued for many years. Although nuclear weapon technology is now such that warheads can be designed, developed, and manufactured without the need for testing, as time passes the warheads age and doubts arise about their reliability. In some cases, there may also be a need to test trigger mechanisms and other refinements, although much can be achieved in sophisticated laboratory testing. Bans on testing strictly limit qualitative development of nuclear weapons, particularly for countries at the early stages of nuclear weapon acquisition. There is therefore considerable interest on the part of both established nuclear weapon states and non–nuclear weapon states in banning tests as a means to curb proliferation.

The first such treaty was a multilateral convention that prohibited certain types of tests and entered into force in 1963, the Treaty Banning Nuclear Weapon Tests in the Atmosphere, in Outer Space, and Under Water. This was followed by two bilateral treaties between the United States and the Soviet Union: the Treaty on the Limitation of Underground Nuclear Weapon Tests in 1974, which placed a 150-kiloton limit on the yield of an underground explosion (the Threshold Test Ban Treaty), and the Treaty on Underground Nuclear Explosions for Peaceful Purposes in 1976 (the Peaceful Nuclear Explosions Treaty).

But these were not enough. In Article 1 of the Partial Test Ban Treaty, the parties undertook to conclude "a treaty resulting in the permanent banning of all nuclear test explosions." The achievement of such a treaty, with universal membership and of unlimited duration, would be a major contribution to the maintenance of international peace and security. However, despite considerable efforts since 1963 to negotiate a treaty acceptable to all, the goal has so far proved elusive. The principal stumbling block for many years was that of reliable verification, but eventually a worldwide system of on-site inspections and seismic, infrasound, radionuclide, and hydroacoustic stations and laboratories was devised.[4]

One of the major achievements of the United Nations in the nuclear field is the Comprehensive Nuclear Test Ban Treaty (CTBT),[5] which was overwhelmingly adopted by the General Assembly after years of planning, hard work, and lobbying by many NGOs that advocate arms control. It was an achievement not only for curbing nuclear weapons, but also for halting nuclear contamination of the environment, even by underground testing. In 1996 the CTBT was opened for signature in New York. By Article 1 of the treaty, each party would undertake not to carry out any nuclear weapon test or any other nuclear explosion, and would prohibit and prevent any such nuclear explosion at any place under its jurisdiction or control. Article 2 provided for the establishment of the Comprehensive Nuclear Test Ban Treaty Organization, based in Vienna, to ensure the implementation of its provisions, including international verification of compliance. Article 14 declared that the treaty would enter into force 180 days after ratification by all the forty-four states named in Annex 2 to the treaty, which included all known nuclear weapon–capable countries. The need to obtain ratification by all forty-four states is a major bar to the achievement of agreement on the CTBT being translated into a successful treaty. Both India and Pakistan declined to sign the CTBT in 1996, and in 1998, following a change of party in government in New Delhi, India conducted nuclear weapon tests. Within weeks, India's tests were followed by those of Pakistan, and so both countries openly acknowledged that they had developed a nuclear weapon capability.

As of the beginning of 2004, 170 states had signed the treaty and 108 had ratified it. France, Russia, and the United Kingdom had ratified, but China and the United States had not. Israel had signed but not ratified, and neither India nor Pakistan were signatories.[6] On October 13, 1999, the U.S. Senate voted 51–48 to reject the CTBT. President Bill Clinton declared, "By this vote, the Senate majority has turned its back on 50 years of American leadership against the spread of weapons of mass destruction." Opponents explained their negative vote by saying that the treaty was not verifiable, that other countries could not be trusted to implement the treaty faithfully, and that it was fatally flawed.[7] Although not yet in force, the fact that so many of the Member States of the United Nations have signed the CTBT and more than half the membership have ratified it is in itself a powerful statement of world opinion. While every sovereign state has a right to decide what is in its own security interests, the wide and overt expression of support for the CTBT among the members of the United Nations illustrates the role of the world body in providing a source of political pressure and moral suasion. The United States adopted legislation in 1992 by which it declared a moratorium on nuclear testing. Despite not ratifying the CTBT, the United States has observed its provisions by continuing its moratorium. The principal reason underlying the moratorium is that the United States has not needed to conduct any nuclear explosive tests, although by 2003 there was a growing discussion in Washington that tests may be required in the next few years for scientific and technological reasons.

Chemical Weapons

Chemical weapons have been in existence for centuries. In 431 B.C., Spartan armies used burning sulfur in their sieges of cities, with the objective of disabling the defenders. During World War I in Europe, both sides used gases such as chlorine, phosgene, and "mustard gas," blistering the lungs, eyes, and skin of soldiers and resulting in 1,300,000 casualties, of which about 100,000 were fatal. The horrifying effects led to widespread revulsion and, in 1925, to an international agreement signed in Geneva, the Protocol for the Prohibition of the Use in War of Asphyxiating, Poisonous, or Other Gases, and of Bacteriological Methods of Warfare.

Although this protocol was generally observed during World War II, there were reports of use by Japan against China, and by Egypt against Yemen, in the early 1960s. Subsequently the United States used chemical defoliants in the Vietnam War to destroy the forest cover of Viet Cong forces. In the Iran-Iraq War of the 1980s, Iraq used chemical weapons against Iranian troops and against Kurdish insurgents, and following the defeat of Iraq in the Gulf War of 1991, very large quantities of Iraqi chemical weapons were found and destroyed by the UN Special Commission established by the Security Council to eliminate Iraq's arsenal of weapons of mass destruction. A further dimension was added in 1995 when a Japanese terrorist group, Aum Shinrikyo, used sharpened umbrella tips to puncture plastic pouches of the nerve agent sarin in the Tokyo subway, causing twelve deaths and injuring 5,000.

Chemical weapon agents are not particularly difficult to manufacture and virtually any country with a reasonably modern chemical industry could produce ingredients that, if used together, could constitute such weapons or serve as precursors to them. For example, triethanolamine is a precursor chemical for nitrogen mustard gas and can be found in a variety of lotions, ointments, and detergents (including shampoos, bubble baths, and household cleaners), as well as in industrial lubricants and surfactants.

During the 1970s and 1980s, recognizing the dangers of existing stocks and the growing risks of proliferation, the international community sought through the Conference on Disarmament in Geneva to build on the 1925 protocol to negotiate an agreement to ban the production of chemical weapons and eradicate existing stocks. Progress was slow, partly because of an impasse between the United States and the Soviet Union, and partly because of the search for a reliable system of inspections and verification. Multilateral negotiations proceeded more or less in parallel with bilateral negotiations between the two major chemical weapon states and resulted in an agreement signed by the Soviet Union and the United States in June 1990. Further multilateral work led to agreement on a convention within the Conference on Disarmament in September 1992, which the UN General Assembly adopted by consensus on January 13, 1993, as the Convention on the Prohibition of Development, Production, Stockpiling and Use of Chemical Weapons and on Their Destruction, more usually known as the Chemical Weapons Convention (CWC).[8] It was opened for signature in Paris on January 13, 1993, and came into force on April 29, 1997. As of February 14, 2004, 160 countries have become states parties to the CWC, including the United States.

The CWC is regarded as the first globally verifiable multilateral disarmament treaty. It prohibits the development, production, acquisition, retention, stockpiling, transfer, and use of all chemical weapons, which are defined in the convention as all toxic chemicals and their precursors, unless they are intended to be used for purposes not prohibited by the convention. The definition also includes munitions and devices specially designed to release toxic chemicals, as well as any equipment specially designed for delivering chemical munitions or devices.

An important part of the convention is the provision of extensive verification mechanisms by which all declared chemical weapons and their production facilities are subject to systematic inspections. These include provisions for a high level of intrusiveness; those in charge of verification can carry out immediate inspections if there is a suspicion that some violation of the agreement is taking place. For the Member States to agree to such an aggressive oversight mechanism indicates the seriousness of their determination to eliminate these weapons. The verification regime also extends to commercial chemical industry operations with the purpose of deterring, preventing, and if necessary, detecting attempts to bypass the ban by using so-called dual-use technologies and chemicals.

Another major task is the destruction of existing stocks, which is carried out under rigid control. Various deadlines have been set for the completion of destruction, but the amounts of chemical weapons to be destroyed in the Russian Federation and in the United States are such that there may have to be extensions. It has been estimated that the costs of destroying U.S. and Russian stocks may amount to some $20 billion.

To implement the convention, a special organization was established, the Organization for the Prohibition of Chemical Weapons (OPCW), with headquarters in The Hague, the Netherlands, and a staff of some 500 persons.[9] The CWC is a good example of multilateral cooperation, carefully and painstakingly negotiated, designed to establish and promote confidence among its parties in the interests of maintaining international peace and security. It illustrates vividly the positive product that members of the international community can achieve by working together for the benefit of all.

Biological Weapons

The main difference between biological weapons and chemical weapons is that the former are derived from living organisms in order to convey lethal diseases to humans. Because of the dangers to the originator, they are difficult to handle and store and their use can carry high risks for the attacker. Both sides experimented with biological weapons during World War II, with long-lasting effects—British experiments with anthrax spores on an island off the west coast of Scotland rendered the island uninhabitable for some fifty years due to the capacity of anthrax spores to lie dormant in the topsoil for a considerable time.

For forty years following the 1925 Geneva Protocol, chemical and bacteriological (biological) weapons were considered jointly in arms control efforts. In 1968 the General Assembly requested the Secretary-General to prepare, with the assistance of experts, a detailed report on these weapons types. Stemming from that report, the two types of weapons were dealt with separately. Gradually the views and political positions of the Western and socialist countries were brought together, and in 1971 a single draft convention was presented to the General Assembly. Building consensus on such a difficult issue after so many years of friction was a significant step forward for the United Nations.

The Convention on the Prohibition of the Development, Production, and Stockpiling of Bacteriological (Biological) and Toxin Weapons (more widely known as the Biological Weapons Convention [BWC]) was opened for signature on April 10, 1972, and entered into force on March 26, 1975, thereby becoming the first multilateral disarmament treaty banning the production and use of a complete category of weapons.[10] The parties to the convention undertake never to develop, produce, stockpile, or otherwise acquire or retain microbial or other biological agents or toxins for other than peaceful purposes, and to destroy or divert to peaceful purposes all agents, toxins, weapons, equipment, and means of delivery. Any party that finds another party not to be in compliance may lodge a complaint with the UN Security Council. The convention has always had a major flaw, however, in that, unlike the CWC, it contains no provisions for a verification mechanism. Without such provisions there can be no reliable way of ensuring the effectiveness of the treaty.

In light of rapid scientific progress and a disturbing discovery by UN inspectors in 1991 that Iraq (a party to the BWC) had a vigorous biological weapons program, considerable efforts were made in the 1990s by BWC parties to negotiate and develop a legally binding verification regime. By 2001 the text of a draft protocol was at an advanced stage, but also by the end of that year the attitude of the United States had hardened. On November 19, 2001, in Geneva, John R. Bolton, UN Undersecretary for Arms Control and International Security, declared that the United States had "rejected the flawed mechanisms of the draft Protocol" and that "countries that joined the BWC and then ignore their commitments and certain non-state actors would never have been hampered by the Protocol."[11] Bolton then went on to name Iraq, North Korea, Iran, Syria, and Sudan as countries possibly having biological weapon research programs, as well as the Al-Qaida terrorist network, which had shown interest in acquiring such weapons. "The BWC has not succeeded in dissuading these states from pursuing BW programs," stated Bolton, "and we believe that the draft BWC protocol would have likewise failed to do so."[12] In the face of such a flat rejection by the United States of the draft protocol, further work on it has now been suspended. The need for international action to tighten the BWC, however, is becoming increasingly vital as the risks of proliferation grow and therefore the dangers of a biological weapon capability falling into the hands of terrorists increase.

Amendments to the BWC and the agreements on satisfactory verification mechanisms are for the parties to decide, but in addition to meetings of the BWC membership, it is in the global forum of the United Nations that governments are able to voice their concerns and press for action to move this difficult issue forward to satisfactory resolution.

Conventional Weapons

In many respects, the term "conventional weapons" used in UN parlance is anachronistic. It originated with the establishment in 1947 of the Commission for Conventional Armaments in order to make a differentiation between weapons of mass destruction and all other weapons. As science and technology have progressed considerably since 1947, the term "conventional" now embraces weapons that the man or woman in the street may well regard as distinctly unconventional, such as excimer and chemical lasers, or fuel-air explosives.[13] UN disarmament language also includes the term "conventional disarmament" and it should be borne in mind that this refers to efforts to achieve reductions and limitations of conventional weapons. It is not the opposite of "unconventional disarmament." For many years, there was a large measure of resistance among nonaligned countries in the United Nations to progress in conventional disarmament. To a great extent this was because they saw such initiatives, which tended to come from the Western countries, as being primarily attempts to divert attention from efforts to achieve nuclear disarmament. There was also a concern among some of the more newly independent states that lurking beneath the surface there was perhaps a desire by the developed countries, which already had all the weapons they needed, to keep developing countries inadequately armed and thereby unable to defend themselves should external intervention become necessary.

Nevertheless, it was unarguable that year-in and year-out it was conventional weapons that were actually being used to kill people in violent conflict. In 1980, at the initiative of Denmark, the General Assembly approved in principle the undertaking of a study on all aspects of the conventional arms race, which was completed in 1984. For the first time at the United Nations, the nature, causes, and effects of the conventional arms race were explored in depth. Principles, approaches, and measures for conventional arms limitation and disarmament were also addressed.

At the time of the study, the Cold War was at its height. Annual global military expenditure had climbed to over $800 billion, with four-fifths of that amount being spent on conventional arms and armed forces by major military states. According to the study, conservative calculations indicated a total conventional weapons inventory of over 140,000 main battle tanks, over 35,000 combat aircraft, over 21,000 helicopters, over 1,100 major surface warships, and over 700 attack submarines. The study noted that, since the end of World War II, millions of people had been killed by conventional weapons in some 150 conflicts fought in the territories of over 71 states, mostly in the developing areas of the world. Among the conclusions of the study was a recognition that the problem of the conventional arms race was urgent and required concrete steps to be taken in the field of conventional disarmament.

Although not widely recognized at the time, the study broke valuable new ground. It contributed to focusing more attention on an aspect of disarmament on which no progress had been possible. Politically, the study attributed some 70 percent of global military expenditures to six main military spenders: China, France, the Federal Republic of Germany, the Soviet Union, the United Kingdom, and the United States. It also indicated that almost one-third of the expenditures were those of other countries, many of which could ill afford such defense budgets. Other UN studies in the early 1980s explored such topics as conventional disarmament, regional disarmament, and the relationship between disarmament and development. These reports, as well as external developments in the mid-1980s, such as accelerated efforts in Europe on confidence- and security-building measures and political changes in Eastern Europe, helped to shift the international community toward more proactive thinking regarding constraints on conventional weapons.

Reporting Military Expenditures

In 1980 the General Assembly adopted resolution 35/142 B, on the reduction of military budgets, which introduced into the United Nations a system for the standardized reporting of military expenditures. As with all General Assembly resolutions it imposed on Member States no compulsory requirement to report, but called upon them to report voluntarily, in a standardized format, expenditure on personnel, operations and maintenance, procurement and construction, and research and development.

Since 1981, annual reports publishing the information provided by Member States have been issued by the UN Secretariat. The report of the Secretary-General on objective information on military matters, including transparency of military expenditures, was contained in A/56/267 of August 3, 2001, to which fifty-five countries contributed information.

UN Register of Conventional Arms

In December 1991 the General Assembly adopted resolution 46/36 L, on transparency in armaments. Requesting the Secretary-General to establish a register of conventional arms, the resolution called upon all Member States to provide annually relevant data on imports and exports of conventional arms, together with available background information regarding their military holdings, procurement through national production, and relevant policies.

The register was established in January 1992 and technical procedures were developed later that year by a panel of experts. Over the years, various improvements to the definitions and reporting procedures have been made. Member States are now asked to report by May 31 each year information on seven categories of weapons: battle tanks, armored combat vehicles, large-caliber artillery systems, combat aircraft, attack helicopters, warships of 750 metric tons or above, and missiles and missile launchers with a range of at least 25 kilometers. The UN Department for Disarmament Affairs receives and compiles the information and stores it in a computerized database.

A recent report was issued as A/56/257 of July 31, 2001, to which ninety-four governments had submitted returns. According to the Department for Disarmament Affairs (Conventional Arms Branch), it has been estimated that the register captures over 95 percent of the global trade in the seven categories of armaments. The U.S. Congressional Research Service assessed the global arms trade to be worth more than $30 billion in 1999, of which 68 percent was absorbed by the developing world. The main producers and exporters are countries in the industrialized world. This imbalance is magnified by the budgetary portion these arms purchases command in many countries already struggling with extreme poverty. The Department for Disarmament Affairs has also issued a 2001 information booklet on the register to help disseminate this information.[14]

Small Arms and Light Weapons

On the occasion of the UN's fiftieth anniversary in 1995, Secretary-General Boutros Boutros-Ghali issued a supplement to his seminal 1992 report *An Agenda for Peace*.[15] In Section D of that document, he introduced the term "micro-disarmament" and stated, "By this I mean practical disarmament in the context of the conflicts the United Nations is actually dealing with and of the weapons, most of them light weapons, that are actually killing people in the hundreds of thousands."[16]

He went on to identify two categories of light weapons that merited special attention. First, small arms: "[These] are probably responsible for most of the deaths in current conflicts. The world is awash with them and traffic in them is very difficult to monitor, let alone intercept."[17] Second, antipersonnel landmines: "Work continues to try to deal with the approximately 110 million landmines that have already been laid. This is an issue that must continue to receive priority attention."[18]

The upsurge of interest in small arms and light weapons occurred in parallel with the increase in the number of violent conflicts that erupted following the end of the Cold War. The end of superpower confrontation, welcome as it was for lifting the risk of a nuclear exchange, did not lead to the expected peace dividend. At the same time that defense budgets of the members of NATO and the former Warsaw Pact were being reduced and their armed forces downsized, ethnic disputes and militant nationalist movements that had lain dormant now sprang into action. Wars became intrastate affairs with complex regional spillovers rather than interstate affairs. Factional leaders and warlords sought small arms and light weapons, and there was no shortage of suppliers.

The illicit trade in small arms grew rapidly and became a source of deep concern to governments, particularly those in poor and developing countries. In 1994, arising from an appeal of the president of Mali for assistance in the collection of light weapons circulating in his country, the Secretary-General sent a mission to Mali and other countries of the Sahara-Sahel region. The mission concluded that the overall security situation needed improvement before any weapons collection could be implemented, and that the situation was severely affecting socioeconomic development and creating a cycle leading to more illicit light weapons. The situation had to be addressed in the context of the whole region.

In 1995 the General Assembly requested the Secretary-General to prepare a study on small arms, with the help of a panel of governmental experts. In the ensuing report, the panel identified small arms as those designed for personal use, including rifles, machine guns, hand-held grenade launchers, and light weapons like those designed for use by several persons serving as a crew, such as portable antitank guns and portable launchers of antiaircraft missile systems.[19] The report noted, "Among the worst affected victims of recent conflicts fought primarily with small arms and light weapons are the inhabitants of some of the poorest countries in the world."[20]

The panel of experts drew particular attention to the major role of illicit small arms trafficking in fostering terrorism, drug trafficking, mercenary activities, and the violation of human rights. Among other suggestions for action, the panel recommended that the "United Nations should consider the possibility of convening an international conference on the illicit arms trade in all its aspects."[21] Accepting this recommendation, the UN Conference on the Illicit Trade in Small Arms and Light Weapons in All Its Aspects took place in New York from July 9 to 20, 2001. The outcome was the adoption of a wide range of political undertakings at the national, regional, and global levels. The initiatives embraced measures to introduce national laws to exercise effective control over production, export, import, transit, and transfer of such weapons. The UN conference encouraged regional negotiations with the aim of concluding relevant, legally binding instruments aimed at preventing, combating, and eradicating the illicit trade. The United Nations also encouraged countries to cooperate with the UN system to ensure effective implementation of arms embargoes decided by the Security Council and to encourage disarmament and demobilization of combatants and their reintegration into civilian life.[22]

Antipersonnel Landmines and the Ottawa Convention

The extensive use of antipersonnel landmines became an issue of increasing concern to a number of countries from the early 1970s. With the conflicts that erupted in Cambodia, Iran and Iraq, many places in Africa, and Europe, the scourge of landmines became even more evident. By the late 1990s the International Committee of the Red Cross (ICRC) and the United Nations estimated that there may have been 100–120 million mines already laid, and a further 100 million stockpiled for use. The ICRC has estimated that 2,000 people are involved in landmine accidents every month—one every twenty minutes—of whom about 800 die and the rest are maimed.

A UN review conference in 1996 failed to find consensus among the international community to improve on the provisions of the 1980 convention on conventional weapons discussed above. This prompted Canada, with a highly active nongovernmental involvement, to call for other like-minded countries to support a treaty to ban the use of antipersonnel landmines.[23] The "Ottawa Process," as it came to be known, quickly produced results, and when the Convention on the Prohibition of the Use, Stockpiling, Production, and Transfer of Anti-Personnel Mines and on Their Destruction (the Ottawa Convention) was opened for signature in December 1997, 123 countries signed it. As of February 2004, there are 141 states parties to the Ottawa Convention. The convention commits signatory countries to clear out minefields within ten years, destroy stockpiles of mines within four years, assist in the economic and social rehabilitation of mine survivors and victims, and report each year on the progress made in fulfilling these commitments.

Among the countries that have not yet signed the convention is the United States, on the grounds that for the time being the deployment of antipersonnel landmines in certain places will continue to be needed for the protection of U.S. troops and allies. However, U.S. production of antipersonnel landmines ceased in 1993, and under the Clinton administration the declared policy was to end the use of all antipersonnel landmines outside Korea by 2003 and to be in a position to sign the Ottawa Convention by 2006 if suitable options could be found that would allow the United States to maintain the war-fighting capability and safety of its men and women in uniform.[24] At the time of this writing, the current administration of President George W. Bush has made no policy statement on the issue.

Practical Disarmament Measures

In December 1997 the General Assembly adopted resolution 52/38 G, on consolidation of peace through practical disarmament measures. Interested governments met on a number of occasions and agreed on two main purposes: the examination of and, wherever possible, joint support of concrete projects of practical disarmament, particularly as designed and initiated by affected coun-

UN Photo 159491/J. Bleibtreu

United Nations Transitional Authority in Cambodia (UNTAC) peacekeepers teach a Cambodian soldier to deactivate a landmine, 1992.

tries; and the exchange of information about relevant lessons learned in the field of practical disarmament and its dissemination to interested countries.

Furthering the pragmatic approach, the group agreed that it should concentrate on hands-on proposals and avoid discussion of concepts, and that its key emphasis would be threefold: practical and attainable objectives, voluntary financial commitments as a means to achieve objectives, and focus on Africa and Central America as areas for immediate action. Subsequent activities supported by the group included a subregional seminar in Yaoundé in Cameroon on the training of trainers in practical disarmament measures, a workshop on weapons collection and integration of former combatants into civil society, held in Guatemala City, and a weapons-for-development exchange program in the Gramsh District in Albania.

Weapons Having Excessively Inhumane or Indiscriminate Effects

Long before the United Nations was established, there were international efforts to constrain the use of certain weapons that were thought to be too inhumane or indiscriminate. The St. Petersburg Declaration of 1868 banned the use of weapons that aggravated the suffering of the disabled. The Hague Conferences of 1899 and 1907 banned the use of poison or poisoned weapons and projectiles for the diffusion of asphyxiating or deleterious gases, and the 1925 Geneva Protocol prohibited the use of poison gas.

In 1972 a UN expert report on the use of napalm and other incendiary weapons described the horrendous effects of incendiaries on the human body and appealed for the prohibition of the development, production, stockpiling, and use of such weapons. In 1973 the General Assembly decided to broaden the question to include all other conventional weapons deemed to cause unnecessary suffering or to have indiscriminate effects, and to seek agreement on rules prohibiting or restricting their use. These steps eventually led to the calling of an international conference, which was convened in Geneva in 1979.

The conference focused its attention on drafting three protocols. The first protocol prohibited the use of any weapon whose primary effect was to injure by fragments that in the human body escape detection by x-rays. The second protocol related to the use of landmines, booby traps, and other devices, such as those activated by remote control or automatically after a lapse of time. The third protocol prohibited in all circumstances making the civilian population the object of attack by incendiary weapons. To cover these three protocols, there would be a general framework treaty. The outcome, in 1980, was the unanimous adoption of the Convention on Prohibitions or Restrictions on the Use of Certain Conventional Weapons Which May Be Deemed to Be Excessively Injurious or to Have Indiscriminate Effects (generally known as the Convention on Certain Conventional Weapons).

The rules agreed upon were not as strong as some countries wished, but at least they protected civilians to some extent and represented a useful development of humanitarian law.

Disarmament, Demobilization, and Reintegration

In recent years, UN peacekeeping operations have become much more complex than they were in the early 1990s. With societies and economies torn apart by savage internal conflicts, peace operations have widened to embrace conflict prevention and peacemaking, peacekeeping, and postconflict peacebuilding. In many of the intrastate conflicts, the combatants are often young men, and occasionally young women, who have been recruited or forced into combat service by warlords and factional leaders. Some may be as young as ten or eleven years old, and many have little or no education. A large number of combatants have no concept of security except that from the end of a gun, and they do not necessarily view the end of war bringing any benefits if they have no job, no education, and no future.

The Secretary-General has identified three key objectives for successful, comprehensive peacebuilding: consolidating internal and external security, strengthening political institutions and good governance, and promoting economic and social rehabilitation and transformation. The disarmament of former combatants, their demobilization from war service, and their successful reintegration into civilian life are major parts of achieving the peacebuilding objectives.

The disarmament process involves procedures for collecting and disposing of the small arms and other weapons that have been used by the combatants. Arrangements also often have to be made to recover weapons from the local population, to preclude the risk that weapons will be hidden for use in some future recurrence of the conflict. In times of uncertainty and tenuous security following a prolonged internal conflict, it is often not easy to persuade former combatants to surrender their weapons in return for an unknown future. Demobilization involves the disbandment of armed groups, and sometimes government forces as well, by gathering them together at preidentified collection points for administrative processing and discharge orientation.

UN peacekeeping operations have undertaken the disarming of combatants by directly collecting arms, destroying them, and making efforts to reintegrate former fighters into productive endeavors. This has taken place in El Salvador, Mozambique, Sierra Leone, and other UN operations. Within the United Nations, much attention is currently being paid to developing and implementing successful projects of disarmament, demobilization, and reintegration as effective contributions to the achievement of sustainable peace in place of the recurrence of violent conflict. The 2003 report on Sierra Leone by the UN Department of Peacekeeping Operations indicates that the UN

Mission in Sierra Leone (UNAMSIL) has been particularly successful in carrying out disarmament and demobilization, with some 40,000 weapons and 5 million pieces of ammunition destroyed.[25]

The most important ingredient is reintegration. Without careful planning and adequate resources, including programs for cash or in-kind compensation, as well as training and prospects for some kind of remunerative employment that will provide income for themselves and their families, former combatants will be very reluctant to commit themselves to the process. With young men, they may have never known any life other than violent conflict, and therefore the process may be one of original integration into society, rather than reintegration. With girls and young women, who often may have been abducted as sexual companions, they may face additional hazards of rejection in their home villages and even by their own families. For all former combatants, societal reconciliation and return to normalcy present major personal challenges that cannot be overcome without thoughtful and careful external assistance.

NGOs and Public Interest

In the consideration of disarmament at the United Nations, a vital part is played by nongovernmental organizations and the public. The active interest and support of the NGOs has often been instrumental in pressing certain issues, as was the case in the genesis and adoption of the Ottawa Convention on antipersonnel landmines. Many aspects of disarmament demand detailed knowledge and persistent attention, and the existence of NGOs, research and academic institutes, and well-informed members of the public has often served to encourage or discourage certain governmental initiatives, or spur government representatives to action.

The NGO Committee on Disarmament at UN headquarters in New York and the NGO Special Committee on Disarmament at the United Nations office in Geneva cooperate on a wide range of international disarmament issues. In his closing remarks, Ambassador Jayantha Dhanapala, president of the 1995 Review and Extension Conference of the Parties to the Treaty on the Non-Proliferation of Nuclear Weapons, said of the NGO community: "Over the past twenty-five years, non-governmental organizations have performed valuable services for the Non-Proliferation Treaty (NPT)—in encouragement, ideas, public support and advocacy of further progress toward the goals of the Treaty. I should like to pay them a sincere tribute for their dedication."[26]

For more than twenty-five years, the two NGO disarmament committees have networked with peace and disarmament NGOs around the world to provide civil society, UN Member States, and the Secretariat with a number of services:

- offering resources of expertise and information on disarmament,
- soliciting various viewpoints,

- supporting campaigns such as the banning of landmines and promotion of the Chemical Weapons Convention,
- encouraging activity of NGOs and civil society within the United Nations,
- informing NGOs of UN and international progress on disarmament through publications and conferences, and
- supporting coalitions around specific disarmament topics, such as the Comprehensive Test Ban Treaty, the extension of the Nonproliferation Treaty, and ideas such as Abolition 2000.

These committees are viewed as primary allies of the international movements for arms control, peace, and disarmament, and of UN bodies designated to serve these worldwide constituencies. Their functions are to inform NGOs of the status of negotiations, country positions on disarmament issues, and major obstacles and opportunities, and they assist NGOs in transmitting their expertise and proposals to the appropriate decisionmaking forums. The New York committee also publishes four regular issues of *Disarmament Times* each year and additional issues when events merit special coverage. *Disarmament Times* is the only independent, professionally produced newspaper devoted to accurate, objective reporting on arms control and disarmament activities in the UN context. As information-gathering is vital to their participation and the majority of NGOs on disarmament are never able to visit UN headquarters, the UN NGO committees on disarmament maintain websites and participate in electronic networks and online correspondence with hundreds of groups worldwide. In 2001 the New York committee initiated the Disarmament Journalists Network, which is an interactive global network of journalists informed about arms issues from a multilateral perspective.

In the 1950s and 1960s, individual scientists, experts, research institutions, and various NGOs were active in campaigns to stop radioactive fallout from nuclear testing and to prevent nuclear proliferation. By disseminating information and warnings about the dangers of nuclear testing and the spread of nuclear weapons, they stimulated public interest. This helped generate political pressure for governments to ban testing in the atmosphere in 1963, and to agree on the Nonproliferation Treaty in 1968. Two NGOs with consultative status with the Economic and Social Council were awarded the Nobel Peace Prize for their efforts to promote a world free of weapons: the International Physicians for the Prevention of Nuclear War (1985) and the International Campaign to Ban Landmines (1997).

UN Disarmament Machinery

The term "disarmament machinery" refers to the collection of organs, bodies, commissions, and committees in which multilateral arms limitation and disarmament are discussed and negotiated. Changes in the composition, names, and responsibilities have been made over the years to reflect the changing international situation. The primary bodies are briefly described below.[27]

General Assembly. Even though, according to the Charter, the Security Council has specific responsibilities for arms regulation, the main deliberative initiatives and actions on disarmament have consistently been taken by the General Assembly and its subsidiary organs. The General Assembly itself, composed of all the Member States of the United Nations, is the primary deliberative body. Although its resolutions have no binding power on Member States, when adopted by consensus or with large majorities they constitute expressions of global political attitude and opinion on major issues. Therefore the General Assembly serves as a source of powerful moral and political suasion that governments cannot easily ignore. By 1984, at perhaps the height of the Cold War, a quarter of all the resolutions adopted by the General Assembly concerned disarmament.

First Committee. With the same membership as the General Assembly, the First Committee is one of the Assembly's six main committees. Meeting from October to December each year, the First Committee deals exclusively with disarmament and related international security issues, weighing various proposals and positions and adopting draft resolutions for forwarding to the General Assembly for formal adoption.

Disarmament Commission. Stemming from the commission established in 1952, which did not meet after 1965, the Disarmament Commission was resuscitated by the final document of the 1978 first special session of the General Assembly devoted to disarmament to serve as a subsidiary forum for deliberation on disarmament issues when the Assembly is not in session. Unlike the Conference on Disarmament, the membership of the Disarmament Commission embraces all Member States of the United Nations. Meeting in one annual session of several weeks, it provides an opportunity for a more in-depth consideration of a small number of items, usually over a three-year cycle, and reports to the General Assembly.

Conference on Disarmament. Described in the final document of the 1978 first special session of the General Assembly devoted to disarmament as the "single multilateral disarmament negotiating forum," the Conference on Disarmament first met in 1979 and assumed the negotiating mantle of its forebears, the Eighteen-Nation Committee on Disarmament and the Conference of the Committee on Disarmament. At that time, the Conference on Disarmament comprised forty states, including all five nuclear weapon states. It meets at the Palais des Nations in Geneva, usually from January to September each year, has its own rules of procedure, develops its own agenda, and works by consensus. It is not a subsidiary of the General Assembly, but it takes into account the recommendations of the Assembly and reports to it annually or more frequently, as appropriate.

The terms of reference of the Conference on Disarmament include practically all multilateral arms control and disarmament problems. Currently the conference primarily focuses its attention on the following issues: cessation of the nuclear arms race and nuclear disarmament; prevention of nuclear war, including all related matters; prevention of an arms race in outer space; effective international arrangements to assure non–nuclear weapon states against the use or threat of use of nuclear weapons; new types of weapons of mass destruction and new systems of such weapons, including radiological weapons; and a comprehensive program of disarmament and transparency in armaments.

The Conference on Disarmament now has a membership of sixty-six states. The consensus requirement makes its work frustratingly slow and subject to blockage by a small number of members, or at times even only one. On the other hand, as a negotiating body, decisions affecting the national security of states cannot be decided by majority and against the wishes of a minority; to do so would quickly result in the collapse of the conference itself.

During the late 1990s the Conference on Disarmament began to find itself at an impasse. The United States, together with France and the United Kingdom, declined to accept the proposal by nonaligned members of the conference to begin negotiations on the elimination of nuclear weapons. Instead they urged negotiations to ban the production of fissile material for use in nuclear weapons, but the majority of other members of the conference would accept this only as part of a larger effort to achieve nuclear disarmament. Separately, China and Russia, concerned at the steps the United States was taking toward the establishment of a national missile defense system, have called for the conference to start discussions on the issue of preventing an arms race in outer space. The United States has opposed this proposal. The result of these political differences has been that by late 2003 the conference had achieved no substantive work for six years.

Department for Disarmament Affairs. Within the UN Secretariat, disarmament matters are serviced by the Department for Disarmament Affairs (DDA) under an Under-Secretary-General who answers directly to the Secretary-General. Originally a center for disarmament within another Secretariat department, the DDA was established in 1982 by the concluding document of the second special session of the General Assembly devoted to disarmament. In 1992 it was subsumed into the newly formed Department of Political Affairs, but Member States made it clear that disarmament was of such importance that it should be a department of its own. The DDA was reestablished in January 1998 by General Assembly resolution 52/12. The department advises the Secretary-General on disarmament-related security matters; monitors and analyzes developments and trends in the field of disarmament; supports the review and implementation of existing disarmament agreements; assists Member States in multilateral disarmament negotiation and deliberation activities toward the development of disarmament norms and the creation of agreements; and promotes openness and transparency in military matters, verification, confidence-building measures, and regional approaches to disarmament. It also interacts with nongovernmental organizations, academic institutions, research institutes, and individuals active in the field of disarmament; cooperates with organizations of the UN system and other intergovernmental organizations on matters related to disarmament; and provides to Member States and the international community objective information on disarmament and international security matters.

Conclusion

Secretary-General Dag Hammarskjöld once remarked: "The UN reflects both aspiration and a falling short of aspiration, but the constant struggle to close the gap between aspiration and performance now, as always, makes the difference between civilization and chaos."[28] And so it is with disarmament at the United Nations. The lofty goal of general and complete disarmament is far from being attained, and probably never will be. The contentious and competitive nature of humankind and the security dilemma are such that in all reality disarmament is unlikely to be either general or complete. But this does not deny the validity of the aspiration. In a world too often beset with death and destruction, where societies are fractured, economies destroyed, lives needlessly wasted, and the stability and security of civilization replaced by the savagery and chaos of war, the international community comes together at the United Nations to seek progress toward a sustainable peace that is more than just the absence of war.

Progress is often slow. In some directions, such as nuclear disarmament or constraints on conventional weapons, it may be perceived by the public at large as virtually nonexistent. And yet, as the treaties and conventions listed above illustrate, one by one states find it in their interest to use the forums and processes of the United Nations. In doing so, they seek agreement on highly sensitive issues through discussion, exchange of ideas, and compromise. To achieve this agreement, they are willing to surrender slivers of their national sovereignty and commit themselves to internationally agreed upon action to limit, reduce, or otherwise control certain weapons and their uses.

Perhaps, above all, the pattern of treaties, conventions, and resolutions at the United Nations has set a series of norms over the years, and it is these norms that become the guiding lights for international action. The wider the membership of a certain treaty or convention, the more it represents majority view and moral suasion. There is nothing that forces a Member State of the United Nations to sign and ratify a formal and binding agreement unless it so wishes, but for many states their commitment is an investment in their security by the commitments of others. The larger and more powerful the state, the more options it can afford, but even at that level there is value in mutually agreed upon and trustworthy agreements. Moreover, in democracies, which regularly see changes in leadership and policies, unilateral declarations of intent that can be denied by subsequent administrations are no substitute for legally binding, mutually agreed upon commitments. The pursuit of disarmament at the United Nations is often a cautious and intricate business, but so it should be, for nothing less than national and international security are at stake.

Notes

1. The Strategic Arms Limitation Treaty (SALT) I, 1972; SALT II, 1979; and the Strategic Arms Reduction Treaty (START), 1991.

2. Sheila Tobias, Peter Goudinoff, Stefan Leader, and Shelah Leader, *The People's Guide to National Defense* (New York: William Morrow, 1982), pp. 15–16.

3. The current status of these and other disarmament-related treaties can be found at http://disarmament.un.org/treatystatus.nsf.

4. A radionuclide is a type of atom that exhibits radioactivity and can be monitored. Hydroacoustics is the use of quasi-continuous acoustical and optical measurements to monitor physical and biological entities underwater.

5. For more information on the treaty and its signature, ratification, and status, as well as the commission that prepared it, see www.ctbto.org.

6. Ibid.

7. See *New York Times,* October 15, 1999, p. A1.

8. For more information about the CWC and the Organization for the Prohibition of Chemical Weapons (OPCW), see www.opcw.org.

9. The OPCW has a website (www.opcw.org) containing a wealth of information from which this section has been drawn.

10. As of the start of 2004, there were 150 parties to the treaty. See http://disarmament.un.org/treatystatus.nsf.

11. www.state.gov/t/us/rm/2001/index.cfm?docid=6231.

12. Ibid.

13. An excimer is a kind of molecule that exists in aboveground energy. An excimer laser is a weapon that uses a precisely directed beam of high energy to destroy or immobilize the target.

14. Both the latest report and the booklet are available at www.un.org/depts/dda/cab.

15. A/50/60, January 25, 1995.

16. Ibid., para. 60.

17. Ibid., para. 63.

18. Ibid., para. 64.

19. A/52/298, August 27, 1997.

20. Ibid., para. 19.

21. Ibid., para. 80 (k).

22. The full report of the conference (A/CONF.192/15) and other information are available at www.un.org/depts/dda/cab/smallarms.

23. Jodie Williams of Putney, Vt., won the Nobel Peace Prize for her efforts in organizing NGOs to mobilize support for the landmine agreement.

24. Statement by President Clinton on January 19, 2001, available at http://usinfo.state.gov/topical/pol/arms/stories/01011920.htm.

25. S/2002/267, March 14, 2002.

26. Jayantha Dhanapala was the Under-Secretary-General of Disarmament Affairs at the United Nations until he was replaced on July 1, 2003, by Nobuyasu Abe.

27. More details and other elements of the disarmament machinery, together with information on current activities, are available at www.un.org/depts/dda/index.html.

28. SG/420, March 28, 1955, quoted by Brian Urquhart in *Hammarskjöld* (New York: Alfred A. Knopf, 1972), p. 46.

8

To End the Scourge of War: The Story of UN Peacekeeping

Jean E. Krasno

The Early Years: The League of Nations to the End of the Cold War

Hundreds of young soldiers descend the metal stairs hastily anchored in place at the side of a transport plane, ship, or helicopter. They wear the blue cloth berets or caps, some with blue painted helmets, symbolizing the United Nations as they step onto uncertain soil. On their sleeves are the insignias of the nations, their homelands, from which they embarked days before. They represent their countries' contributions to a larger cause brought together by the United Nations to promote global peace. Step by step they come, step by step they land in Lebanon, El Salvador, Sierra Leone, East Timor, Congo: one person at a time, one crisis at a time.

Who are these peacekeeping soldiers and what is peacekeeping? Peacekeeping is never mentioned in the UN Charter, which lays down the goals and guidelines of the United Nations. The Charter in Article 43, in fact, spells out a plan for each member nation to enter into agreement with the UN to provide permanent national contingents to the UN for use when needed, a kind of UN army for collective security. But no nation ever followed through in establishing such an agreement. The UN never had the anticipated Allied forces that were supposed to unite for peace as they had done to fight the Axis powers during World War II. The UN was left with no teeth to fight aggression, preserve peace, or end the scourge of war as the Charter had promised. Born out of crisis and the need to find a solution, peacekeeping was conceived as an improvisation to fill the void. Countries would lend trained units of soldiers to the UN for short periods of time on a case-by-case basis, always reserving the right to say no.

A far cry from the force envisioned by the founders, countries have continued to volunteer peacekeepers to assist in monitoring cease-fire arrange-

225

ments, guarding buffer zones, observing compliance with human rights accords or border agreements, and more. When troop rotation is taken into account, over 1 million military and civilian personnel have taken part; and by 2003, over 1,800 had given their lives. By the end of September 2003, there had been since 1948, fifty-seven different peacekeeping missions sent into the field at a total cost of about $27 billion for the fifty-five-year period, a sum that is dwarfed by the U.S. annual Defense Department budget of over $300 billion. In 2003 there were fifteen current missions, deploying some 44,000 personnel from ninety countries, a figure that includes civilian police (CIVPOL), UN monitors and observers, and UN troops.

Early History During the League of Nations Period

Like most innovative ideas, the concept of peacekeeping, sending multilateral troops to secure a peace arrangement, did not emerge in a vacuum. In fact, before the term "peacekeeping" was created in 1956, the United Nations had already sent unarmed observers to stabilize tense situations. The theory was that observers would provide a kind of transparency to deter provocative acts of violence that could induce conflict.

A little-known fact, however, is that the League of Nations had also employed this practice well before the UN was created.[1] The League was developed after World War I as an initial attempt to form a permanent multilateral body to preserve peace. Created as a part of the Treaty of Versailles, which set the terms for the end of the war, the League was tasked with ongoing issues of international dispute. It was the first international body to set the precedent of deploying military personnel drawn from its member nations for the purpose of peaceful settlement of disputes. League missions consisted of numbers anywhere from a few military officers to a few hundred or a few thousand soldiers. These personnel were engaged in investigating activities, reporting, and monitoring the separation of conflicting forces. They oversaw adherence to boundary agreements or neutral zones and administered territories that found themselves with no governance structures after the war.[2]

The following examples illustrate the League precursors to later UN peacekeeping activities. For fifteen years, from 1920 to 1935, the League Council established a five-member commission to administer the Saar Basin, a province of ethnic Germans located on the border with France. At the end of World War I, France had been granted the coal rights to the region, but the League was given the responsibility of governing the region for the fifteen-year period, at the end of which the League was to administer a referendum for the Saar citizens to decide whether to become a part of Germany or join France. During the period, the commission consulted occasionally with the Saar people and reported regularly to the League. In 1934 the League Council organized a plebiscite with 1,000 League officials to carry out voter registration and the final balloting. The League also established a military force to ensure order during the registration and voting process, calling on 3,300 troops from Italy, the United Kingdom, Sweden, and the Netherlands. This marked the first multinational military operation under the auspices of an international organization. The citizens of Saar voted to reunite with Germany.[3]

Another example of the League's work took place in Danzig, now called Gdansk. Danzig was a German enclave on Poland's Baltic coast that had been a part of West Prussia before World War I. The Treaty of Versailles had removed it from German control, and created Danzig as a "Free City," under the protection of the League. The League did not govern Danzig as it had Saar, but had two key responsibilities: to draw up and guarantee Danzig's constitution, and to deal with disputes between Danzig and Poland. The League also appointed a High Commissioner for Danzig to mediate the frequent issues that emerged with Poland. The first ten years of the "Free City" worked well. But by 1938, Germany had reasserted its influence and Danzig was annexed by the Nazis on the first day of World War II.[4]

Other cases in Europe involving the League were Upper Silesia, a border area between Poland and Germany, Vilna (Vilnius), and Memel, the latter two in Lithuania. In Upper Silesia, League personnel administered a plebiscite to determine its status, decided the boundary between Germany and Poland, and heard complaints by minorities to reduce tensions. In Lithuania, the League helped to administer the area called Memel until Germany occupied it in 1939. The League was less successful in Vilna, where the Organization tried to establish a plebiscite and mediate a solution but failed due to power politics. Russia took over Vilna when the Nazis occupied Poland in World War II.

Outside the European theater, the League was also asked to settle other disputes. In the Middle East, through a commission of inquiry into the area around the city of Mosul, the League established the boundary between Iraq and Turkey, granting Mosul to Iraq. In Alexandretta, a small territory that had been a part of Syria, the League established a peace plan to carry out elections. But France, the colonial power in Syria, and Turkey did not cooperate with the plan, and the area fell to Turkey.

In Latin America, the League assisted in settling a dispute between Peru and Colombia that had erupted during the interwar period. In 1933, Peru seized Leticia, a territory on the Amazon River between the two countries. The League demanded the withdrawal of Peru and later took control of the region. Three League commissioners and a seventy-five-man military contingent of the League governed Leticia for one year, after which time the League returned Leticia to Colombia.

The Early Days of the UN
Many of the ambassadors to the League also served in the early delegations to the United Nations beginning in 1946, after the UN Charter was ratified.

Henri Vigier served as a member of the League's staff as well as a political officer on the staff of the UN in its early years. These diplomats were able to utilize their experiences with the League and the deployment of peace missions during the interwar years. Therefore, when complaints were received that trouble was brewing in the northern part of Greece, the UN delegates had history to draw upon. In 1947 the UN created the United Nations Special Committee on the Balkans (UNSCOB), which was the first UN deployment of an observer mission. UN observers were sent to northern Greece to investigate and monitor allegations of outside support from Albania, Yugoslavia, and Bulgaria (then all part of the Communist bloc) for Greek Communist guerrillas in their insurgency attempts to oust the Greek government endorsed by the West. Along with the investigations, UNSCOB was asked to assist the four countries in restoring normal relations after the war. To avoid continued Soviet vetoes that had thwarted the creation of the mission, the United States maneuvered the issue to the agenda of the General Assembly through a procedural vote in the Security Council. A General Assembly resolution established UNSCOB on October 21, 1947, and called upon Albania, Yugoslavia, and Bulgaria not to furnish aid to the guerrillas and to find a peaceful solution to the problem. Reports of the commission were submitted to the General Assembly, not the Security Council. Nevertheless, the commission included nine of the eleven countries serving on the Security Council at the time. The Soviet Union and Poland declined to serve on the commission. UNSCOB, which was terminated in 1951, was funded at a cost of $3 million under the UN regular budget.[5] The crisis dissolved, which marked the first UN observer mission a relative success.

While the term "peacekeeping" was not to appear until the 1956 Suez crisis, the year 1948 is often cited as the first official date for the deployment of a UN peacekeeping operation even though unarmed UN observers had already been sent to northern Greece in 1947 and would also be sent to the India and Pakistan–disputed area of Kashmir in 1949. But because this is an evolutionary process built on a number of previous experiences, like other inventions, it is hard to determine the exact beginning. The first recognized precursor of peacekeeping is the UN Truce Supervision Organization (UNTSO), created by the Security Council in June 1948.[6] Unarmed UNTSO observers were sent to the Middle East to monitor the truce agreements established at the end of fighting in 1948 between Arabs and the state of Israel, newly created on May 15, 1948. UNTSO, which reports to the Security Council, has continued to adapt to changes on the ground and operates today to observe and report violations of peace agreements. Headquartered in Jerusalem, UNTSO maintains observers in the Golan Heights, Lebanon, Egypt, and Jordan. Unarmed, their only protection is the symbolic legitimacy of the blue UN berets and insignias they wear on their uniforms.[7]

The Creation of UN Peacekeeping

When the Suez crisis erupted in 1956, the United Nations could draw on past experience and the building momentum that laid the groundwork for the next innovative step: UN peacekeeping, as it is thought of today. In July 1956, Egyptian leader Gamal Abdul Nasser had nationalized the Suez Canal, taking the lucrative revenues out of the hands of the former colonial powers, in order to pay for the Aswan Dam. England and France, in order to regain the canal, met secretly with the Israelis to formulate what in retrospect appears to have been a bizarre plan to regain the canal. Israel, which had been denied access to the canal and the Straits of Tiran by Egypt, was to attack Egypt from the east through the Sinai and move toward the Suez. France and England would then heroically announce that they would attack from the north at Port Said to save the canal from Israeli capture. They would then move in to retake control. The covert operation was put into action on October 29, 1956, as Israel launched its attack as planned, followed two days later by British/French bombing in the north. The U.S. Eisenhower administration immediately condemned the action by its former European allies, who were both permanent members of the UN Security Council. Brian Urquhart, political adviser to UN Secretary-General Dag Hammarskjöld, explained the event this way:

> The scenario was that the Israelis would invade the Sinai and get down to the Canal and the British and French would then give an ultimatum to Israel and Egypt, saying that unless they both withdrew their forces 10 miles back from the Canal the British and French would intervene to separate them and thereby keep the peace. It was one of the most self-serving pieces of bullshit ever created by anyone and no one believed it.[8]

Repeated attempts by the UN Security Council to pass resolutions demanding a halt to the attacks were vetoed by France and the UK. "In fact, it was at that point that Macmillan, the British Chancellor of the Exchequer, was told that financial assistance from the United States would cease, thereby threatening the British pound."[9] The United States then orchestrated the use of the mechanism first tentatively utilized for UNSCOB and more formally introduced for the Korean conflict to move the issue out of the Security Council and onto the agenda of the UN General Assembly through a special session of the Assembly convened on November 1, 1956. The mechanism had been formalized in 1950 during the Korean crisis the Assembly's resolution 377 (V), termed the "Uniting for Peace" resolution. According to "Uniting for Peace" the General Assembly can take up an issue if the Security Council is unable to act. The Soviets, who were preoccupied in 1956 by the Hungarian uprising, were delighted to see France and the UK humiliated before the international body by this maneuver. In 1947 and again in 1950, it had been the Soviets who had been denied their veto privileges by the shift to the General Assembly.

Secretary-General Dag Hammarskjöld was called upon to mediate a cease-fire. But the condition for the cease-fire put forward by the British and French was that "an international force would take the place of the British and the French. Actually, the British and French had suggested that they would be part of it, but that was ruled out."[10] The original idea put forward by Canada's foreign minister and delegate to the UN, Lester Bowles Pearson, was to subsume the British and French into a UN-authorized international force, but Hammarskjöld knew that this was a nonstarter; "you could never get the Security Council, not even the United States, to vote for the British and French staying on under the UN flag after what had happened."[11] The UN had to come up with something completely different, but had to do it before the British and French naval ships were to land on Egypt's Mediterranean coast on November 5, 1956. Then Lester Pearson, who had served as president of the UN General Assembly in 1952 and was well respected in the international forum, devised the idea of an armed UN peacekeeping force made up of soldiers drawn from Member States through voluntary contributions to secure a buffer zone between the parties. Urquhart explains:

> It was really all in Pearson's speech to the Assembly. Pearson said that it is not enough this time to ask for a cease-fire and to put in observers. You need something much larger than that. That will not do it because that will not secure the withdrawal of the Israeli, British or French forces. You need a peace and police force that will really police the border and have the physical power to do it. And the concept that was new was having actual troops. We had had individual officer observers—in the Middle East, in Kashmir, in Greece—at one point before then, but nothing approaching a force. And that was the difference.[12]

According to Urquhart, Hammarskjöld at first was not enthusiastic about the idea and had to be convinced. Once he saw how it could be orchestrated successfully, Hammarskjöld worked to solidify the concept.[13] Pearson's Canadian proposal was adopted by the General Assembly on November 4, 1956. Urquhart, Ralph Bunche, and other UN staff members met around the clock to try to implement the concept. The Egyptians were against the Canadians being a part of the force. The regiment the Canadians had earmarked for deployment was the "Queen's Own Canadian Dragoons," whose uniforms were identical to those of the British. Something had to be done to identify the multinational troops, who would be wearing their own uniforms, as UN troops. It was decided that the only clear way to do that was by their hats, "because it's the only thing you can see in a battle, and they have to be fairly bright and something completely different."[14] The team decided that the hats should be blue; according to Urquhart:

> It would emphasize the peaceful nature of the Force. . . . The only trouble with that was that the manufacturer could only do it in sufficient numbers in

seven weeks. So that was out. So then I, I think, finally said: you know the United States helmet liner, which is made of plastic, is a wonderfully light, perfectly comfortable hat once you take the metal part of it off, and surely it must be possible to dip it into a bucket of blue paint. And everybody said, yes. There was something like 3 million of these things in stores in Europe; and this is what we finally did: it was simple to spray paint them in Pisa, and that is where the blue helmet started, the reason being that we couldn't get anything else in time.[15]

After consultation with Egypt, Hammarskjöld accepted contingents from ten countries, including finally the Canadians, and the assistance of three additional nations. The Canadians covered transport and medical and dental units. UNTSO provided the first set of observers, who arrived on November 12, followed by the first UN Emergency Force (UNEF) units on November 15 and 16. The target strength of about 6,000 troops was reached by February 1957.[16] Hammarskjöld established several principles by which UNEF would operate to ensure the safety of the multinational force and to provide assurances to Egypt. Israel refused to allow UN troops on its soil and so the negotiations were primarily with Nasser. Hammarskjöld's principles included: (1) peacekeeping forces could only be deployed after a cease-fire had been reached; (2) the consent of the host country had to be granted before deployment; (3) UN troops could only fire in self-defense; and 4) the UN had to remain impartial. Hammarskjöld wanted to be sure that the UN troops would not become embroiled in the dispute and place themselves in danger. Troop-contributing countries would withdraw their troops if they became a part of the conflict. Urquhart explains that the Secretary-General knew that they were setting a precedent and wanted to be careful to get it right: "Now Hammarskjöld always had a great sense of establishing a precedent in everything he did, no matter how much of an emergency it was. He was always looking at what it would mean in historical terms and what it would mean for the future, which I think is one of the reasons that he was such a remarkable person."[17]

In 1958, Hammarskjöld was asked to write a report on the lessons learned from UNEF. The report demonstrates a careful analysis of the meaning of peacekeeping. Urquhart describes the report: "And he then wrote his own analysis, which was a masterpiece, dealing with all aspects of the UN and peacekeeping which have since come out: the question of sovereignty, the question of changing the nature and balance of the UN system, the question of the rights of the Security Council, the rights of the host country, the susceptibilities of those providing troops. It was a brilliant performance."[18]

UNEF is important not only for its contribution to peace but also because of the precedent established by the deployment of multinational armed troops to preserve the peace, the introduction of Hammarskjöld's principles, and the creation of the UNEF Advisory Committee, which was constituted of the troop-contributing countries to advise Hammarskjöld from time to time.

Lester Pearson won the Nobel Peace Prize in 1957 for his innovative concept. Pearson, Hammarskjöld, Urquhart, Bunche, and the troop-contributing countries are to be congratulated for their innovative spirit in creating what has been termed chapter "six and a half" of the UN Charter, somewhere between Chapter VI (peaceful dialogue and mediation) and Chapter VII (the use of force). UNEF not only established a precedent for peacekeeping, but is the reference point for what later was to be called "classic peacekeeping," meaning the type that provided security for a buffer zone between warring states and adhered to Hammarskjöld's principles.

UNEF I lasted about eleven years until the 1967 Six Day War. On May 16, 1967, Nasser had his chief of staff, General Mohammed Fawzi, send a letter to UN Force Commander Indar Rikhye stating that Egypt was withdrawing its consent to host the UN peacekeepers, and UNEF began leaving on May 29 under orders by Secretary-General U Thant. Some have criticized U Thant for removing the UN troops without first calling for debate of the issue in the Security Council or the General Assembly, where the peacekeeping operation was first authorized. U Thant traveled to Cairo to discuss the matter with Nasser but failed to convince him to reverse his decision. U Thant had consulted with the UNEF Advisory Committee, which was split on the issue,[19] and troop-contributing countries were already withdrawing their forces, fearing the worst if they overstayed their welcome.

Nasser was under political pressure at home to retake the territory occupied by the Israelis. Soviet reports on May 13 of an Israeli troop concentration along the Syrian border, later proven to be false, may have contributed to Egypt's response, which appeared to be a preparation for war. On May 22, Egypt closed the Straits of Tiran at Sharm el Sheikh to Israeli passage, which the Israelis considered an act of war, as they had already warned Nasser would happen. When war erupted on June 5, some UNEF troops were caught in the cross fire and fifteen UN personnel were killed. Thus began the Six Day War, in which Israel expanded its territory. UNEF II did not return to the Middle East until October 1973, after the October War, called the Yom Kippur War by the Israelis since Egypt launched its surprise attack on the Jewish holy day. UNEF II was removed in 1979 after the signing of the U.S.-mediated Camp David Accords, ending the conflict between Egypt and Israel and returning the Sinai to Egypt.[20]

The Belgian Congo: A Glimpse of the Future
In January 1960, Dag Hammarskjöld toured Africa as decolonization was beginning to take root. Belgium had agreed in January to give independence in six months to its colony, the Belgian Congo, with its capital in Leopoldville (now Kinshasa). The Secretary-General feared the precipitous handover would not go smoothly and asked Ralph Bunche to go to Leopoldville in May

1960, about a month before independence.[21] A few weeks after his arrival in the Congo, Bunche wrote this confidential note to Hammarskjöld:

> The attitude of sincere striving to pull this situation out of the fire which seems to characterize the high echelon of Belgian officialdom here appears to me to be in marked contrast of something close to derisive contempt, most thinly veiled, for all Congolese leaders, which I encountered on Friday in Brussels in my contacts with Belgian officials, even including Scheyven (Raymond), who took de Schryver's place as host at a lunch for me. The banter back and forth across the table between the Belgian officials in the presence of several Congolese, in the outmoded paternalistic and condescending tones, was downright embarrassing.[22]

Only days before independence ceremonies were to take place, a compromise was reached whereby rival dominant Congolese leaders from two of the larger tribal groups would share power: Joseph Kasavubu as president and Patrice Lumumba as prime minister. While this compromise lifted some of the internal unease, other tensions emerged during the independence ceremonies on June 30, when the new prime minister, Patrice Lumumba, denounced Belgium for its racist colonial rule. After independence, law and order was to be kept by the Force Publique, a Congolese army that still maintained its white Belgian officers. When it became clear to the low-paid Congolese soldiers that they would continue to be subjected to the harsh authority of the white officers, the central garrison at Thysville mutinied on July 5. The chaos, looting, and violence that followed quickly spread like wildfire to other cities and towns. The Congolese threw out all the Belgian officers, which meant that no officers were left: "At the port of Matadi the Congolese soldiers were convinced of rumours that their Belgian officers intended to disarm them as a preliminary to the landing of Belgian metropolitan troops who were to attack the nearby Thysville garrison. The European officers were locked up, European civilians were attacked, and several European women were raped."[23]

On July 9, some Europeans were killed in the attacks, and by the next day Brussels ordered the return of Belgian troops to protect the white population. Belgian troops landed in Leopoldville, Elizabethville, Matadi, and Luluabourg. In some cases, heavy fighting broke out between the Belgians and the Congolese forces. Panic led to the exodus of most of the Belgian population— roughly 100,000 Belgians had stayed on after independence—which included government administrators, technicians, and medical personnel, all of whom had agreed to stay initially for the transition. This left the country in a security crisis with a breakdown of essential services.[24] "There was nobody in the power station to do the switching; there wasn't anybody in the telephone exchange; there was nobody in the police station; there wasn't anybody in the whole transport system on which the country depended."[25] The lack of preparation for independence astounded the international community. Only about seventeen Congolese had university degrees. Practically no black person had ever been in the white-run hospitals, or even had a medical degree.

For the first time invoking Article 99 of the UN Charter, which gives the Secretary-General the authority to bring a matter before the Security Council, Hammarskjöld requested on July 13 an urgent meeting of the Council on the Congo crisis. "Hammarskjöld had taken the precaution of talking beforehand to all the members of the Council privately."[26] In its resolution 143, the Council called upon Belgium to withdraw its troops and authorized the Secretary-General to establish a peacekeeping force to meet the needed tasks.[27] This marked the second deployment of armed UN peacekeepers.

The UN Operation in the Congo (ONUC) was beset with complications from the onset. This time, peacekeepers were not going to be monitoring a buffer zone between two states, a relatively clear-cut task, but rather were going to be interposed in a situation of civil strife with no obvious boundaries. They had the consent of the Leopoldville government. The Congolese cabinet, with the assistance of Ralph Bunche, had sent a letter to the UN requesting assistance of a "technical nature." However, that consent was compromised when Katanga province declared secession on July 11, 1960, only six days after the mutiny. The Congo not only faced a state of anarchy, but now became embroiled in a civil war. Lumumba wanted the UN to take the side of the government to end the secession, but the UN was reluctant to abandon the principle of impartiality. Thus the UN embarked on a very messy task of trying to balance mediation and impartiality, with the deployment of UN troops in Katanga without full consent. These imponderables were to appear again in later years in Somalia and the former Yugoslavia.

While the risks for getting involved were great, the UN members also realized that the risks for not getting involved could be even greater. With each day that went by, the country was sinking into a worsening crisis. One of the largest and richest countries in Africa, with gold, diamonds, uranium, and other mineral deposits, the Congo was also strategically located in the center of the African continent, with two strategic airfields in Kamina and Kitona occupied through agreement by Belgium, a member of the North Atlantic Treaty Organization (NATO). If the international body did not intervene, the United States or the Soviet Union would naturally jump in to fill the void and the Congo would become enmeshed in the Cold War conflict.

Brian Urquhart offers his firsthand description of what happened immediately after the Security Council met to pass resolution 143 on July 13 and into the early hours of July 14:

> The moment the Council meeting ended we all went up to the Secretary-General's conference room on the thirty-eighth floor and sat down for another three hours to figure out the rudiments of that operation. Ham-

marskjöld ran the meeting, occasionally taking the telephone to call up various countries to get the first troops, and by 6:30 that morning we had, I think, four countries with the troops actually standing by; we had the United States Military Air Transport Command getting ready to go and pick them up and, incidentally, the Russians who flew in Ghanaian contingents from Accra. We had a name for the operation [ONUC]; we had the beginnings of a logistical system; we had a commander. . . . Bunche, who was in Leopoldville anyway having quite a difficult time in one way or another, was made the temporary Commander of the Operation until Von Horn could arrive from Jerusalem where he was the Chief of Staff of UNTSO.[28]

Urquhart was immediately sent to Leopoldville and found the airport under the control of Belgian soldiers flown in to deal with the emergency. They were nervous and trigger-happy. "The result was that the Congolese thought anyone who was obviously not Congolese was a Belgian. . . . The Congolese had never heard of the UN either. They believed it to be some exotic tribe, so that the UN flag meant absolutely nothing."[29] Bunche, who was the acting commander, told Urquhart to lead a UN military unit down to Thysville, where the main headquarters of the Congolese army were located and where the mutiny had started. What follows illustrates the ad hoc nature of peacekeeping at that time and how things were handled to get the UN troops, who began arriving on July 15, into the field quickly. Both Urquhart, who had also just arrived, and Bunche were standing in the control tower of the airport when the UN units, from different countries, began arriving. Urquhart recalls:

At that point we were in the control tower and noticed the Moroccans deplaning. I said to Ralph, "They are very good-looking soldiers; they are excellent. That's just what we want." So, sure enough, we got hold of the Moroccan Colonel—who became very famous later—by the name of Driss Ben Omar, a magnificent soldier, and explained the thing to him and said the lot had fallen on his unit. He was delighted; he said that would be fine if we could just have time to give them a meal, because they had not eaten for two days; that would be excellent.[30]

They found a train to take them to Thysville but couldn't at first find a driver. They managed to coax a Belgian engineer to drive the train, which arrived at the airport on a spur track. The regiment plus a black goat as a mascot boarded the train, which had to make several stops before arriving at Congolese headquarters. They stopped at every station to make a show of the UN's arrival, to a sometimes mixed reception.

Finally we got to Thysville where the real trouble was. There he did something that I had never seen done before. First of all, every mutineer we saw was ordered to report to barracks and the Colonel then personally drilled an honour guard for the raising of the UN flag in the barracks. It took two hours before it was good enough, in his view, to pass muster. That had a tremendous effect. People came from miles to see this amazing spectacle. He was remarkable and the Moroccans were wonderful troops.[31]

Ultimately, not only did the UN deploy troops to provide security, retrain the Congolese army, and carry out police duties, but the whole UN system became involved as well. Air controllers were supplied by the International Civil Aviation Organization (ICAO); the World Health Organization (WHO) provided doctors; the UN International Children's Emergency Fund (UNICEF, now the UN Children's Fund) delivered emergency food supplies.

While the UN had not wanted to become embroiled in the civil war, it became impossible to remain impartial. Lumumba believed that the UN should support unification of the country against the Katangan secession, and when that was not forthcoming he turned to the Soviets for assistance. In an attempt to deter all-out civil war, the UN shut down the airports so that Lumumba's army could not take off in the Soviet-supplied transport planes. The Soviets then began to cry foul and accused the UN of aligning with U.S. interests. By September 1960 the country faced an added crisis when President Kasavubu dismissed Prime Minister Lumumba, and Lumumba in turn dismissed the president. The UN acted to prevent further violence between the tribal supporters of each leader by shutting down the Leopoldville airport and temporarily closing down the radio station, now de facto run by the UN, in order to stop the effects of inflammatory speeches. The Security Council debated the matter from September 14 to September 17, but failed to reach any conclusion due to East-West differences. Using the "Uniting for Peace" resolution yet another time, the General Assembly took up the issue in an emergency special session from September 17 to September 20.

Violence continued that fall and UN peacekeepers came under attack; Irish, Tunisian, and Ghanaian units suffered casualties, with nine deaths. In November, Patrice Lumumba was kidnapped and on January 17, 1961, was taken to Katanga and assassinated under mysterious circumstances. Several troop contributors withdrew their forces and troop levels were reduced from their height at 20,000 to 15,000.[32] In April 1961 there were further setbacks. A Ghanaian detachment of ONUC was attacked and forty-four of its soldiers were brutally massacred. Other casualties continued throughout the rest of the year. The secession of Katanga under the leadership of its president, Moise Tshombe, with the help of Belgian mercenaries, was continuing to vex the UN. Over the summer there seemed to be promise that a cease-fire might be achieved and in September Secretary-General Hammarskjöld flew to Leopoldville in hopes of drawing that chapter to a close. When he arrived, he found quite the opposite. Hostilities had continued and UN troops were under severe attack. Only able to fire in self-defense, UN troops were in a very compromised position, unable to go on the offensive. Hammarskjöld decided to try to meet with Tshombe outside the Congo at Ndola, Northern Rhodesia, to try to arrange a cease-fire. Hammarskjöld, who had given so much of himself for peace, was tragically killed along with seven other UN staff members and the Swedish crew when his plane crashed on the night of September 17, 1961, shortly before arriving at Ndola.[33]

U Thant of Burma, who had been president of the General Assembly and ambassador of Burma to the UN, was named Secretary-General to replace Hammarskjöld. Several cease-fire arrangements were made and then immediately broken by Tshombe and his forces, the bulk of which were made up of mercenaries, primarily Belgian. The Security Council convened again in November 1961 to take up the matter. Security Council resolution 169 authorized the Secretary-General and ONUC to use force to remove the mercenaries.

This was a landmark decision for peacekeeping. Hammarskjöld's principles of having a cease-fire in place, consent of the parties, impartiality, and a policy of firing only in self-defense were now all out the window. Becoming embroiled in a civil conflict had meant that the UN (1) did not have a cease-fire in place, (2) did not have consent from the Katangese—and in some cases even consent from the Congolese government was elusive, (3) had not achieved impartiality in the face of secession, and (4) had discovered that a policy of firing only in self-defense only encouraged Tshombe and his mercenary army to run circles around ONUC. Nevertheless, the UN was still reluctant to go on the offensive and it took over a year before ONUC took the first steps. In December 1962, when Tshombe's forces began firing at UN positions, ONUC force commander General Prem Chand of India, who had reorganized and strengthened the UN forces, took advantage of the attack to respond in "self-defense." The UN finally went on the offensive and by January 4, 1963, ONUC had secured the Katangese capital, Elizabethville, and other key points at Jadotville, Kipushi, and Kamina. On January 14 the UN received a message from Tshombe announcing his readiness to end the secession, in which he asked the UN to implement a previous plan of action that had granted amnesty to the Katangese. President Kasavubu and Prime Minister Adoula of the Congo immediately confirmed the amnesty proclamation.[34] With the civil war ended, the UN was able to draw down its troops and authorized a reduced force of 3,000 to stay on through the first half of 1964 to complete the transition.

The crisis in the Congo had thrown the UN into its own parallel crisis. Two hundred fifty UN soldiers had been killed (more than any other UN operation before or since), a brilliant Secretary-General had died tragically trying to solve the conflict, and some $500 million had been poured into the operation. The operation was costing about $120 million a year at a time when the entire UN regular budget was only about $75 million annually. The Soviets accused the UN of siding with Western interests in the Congo and once again circumventing the Soviet veto by moving decisions to the General Assembly, where the West still had a majority. Soviet leader Nikita Khrushchev in an address to the UN General Assembly in New York on September 23, 1960, had demanded Hammarskjöld's resignation and his replacement by a troika that would represent Western, nonaligned, and Soviet interests. William Durch aptly describes the Soviet frustration:

> In early 1961, after Lumumba's murder, the USSR introduced resolutions calling for Hammarskjöld's dismissal and withdrawal of UN forces, which failed to garner majority support. Moscow then abstained on Security Council actions that gave ONUC authority to use force, but supported an April 1961 GA resolution condemning the continued Belgian military presence in Katanga—in part because it made no reference to the Secretary-General. The following November, two months after Hammarskjöld's death . . . the USSR supported a Security Council resolution that condemned the Katanga secession and authorized the new Secretary-General, U Thant, to use force to expel non-UN military personnel.[35]

There were tensions other than those between the Soviets and the Americans. The French, tending to side with the Belgians, allowed recruitment of mercenaries in areas under French control. The British also had business interests in the lucrative mining industries in Katanga province. The British paid their UN assessments, but both the French and the Soviets continued the practice of withholding payments for peacekeeping. Arrears were mounting to over $100 million; many other countries were also in default. The Congo operation had been sent into the field quickly by the Security Council without prior funding approval by the General Assembly.[36] The Assembly was suddenly faced with unexpected mounting bills and the inability to pay them because the funds were simply not there. The parallel crises placed the UN very nearly at the edge of collapse. The Soviets were two years in arrears on their payment of dues, which meant, according to provisions in the Charter, that they would lose their vote in the General Assembly. The Assembly got around that crisis by avoiding roll call votes in the interim. The Soviets challenged, saying that peacekeeping costs were not a part of regular dues. The Assembly requested an advisory opinion of the International Court of Justice, which declared in its report that peacekeeping costs were an obligatory part of UN membership.

In its attempts to provide security, law and order, and a unified Congo, the UN became engulfed in a storm of competing interests between East and West, economic interests of the colonial powers, and the pressure for decolonization, plus intertribal conflicts that continue today. The UN was criticized from all sides. In the end the civil war was brought to a close, the administration of the country was handed over to the Congolese after a period of UN apprenticeship, and UN agencies provided needed food and support during the period. These accomplishments went unnoticed by a critical international community. Severely burned, the UN did not fund another armed peacekeeping operation for ten years and kept peacekeeping at the level of observers. Furthermore, it did not send a peacekeeping mission to sub-Saharan Africa until the late 1980s, when the first UN Angola Verification Mission (UNAVEM I) was deployed in 1988 and the UN Transition Assistance Group (UNTAG) was deployed to Namibia in 1989.

From the Congo Crisis to the End of the Cold War

Still licking its wounds following the Congo-invoked institutional crisis, the UN took on a more cautious profile. UN observer missions in West New Guinea (1962–1963), Yemen (1963–1964), the Dominican Republic (1965–1966), and India-Pakistan (1965–1966) were kept to a minimum. UNEF II, introduced in 1973 after the October War of that year, was essentially undertaken to reestablish a buffer zone and followed the original Hammarskjöld principles. The UN Disengagement Observer Force (UNDOF, 1974–present) followed UNEF II after the 1973 war to observe the peace on the Golan Heights between Syria and Israel.

There were two exceptions to this overall cautious retrenchment approach: Cyprus and Lebanon. The major powers on the Security Council, especially the United States, considered these two situations too important to let them fester and threaten further to destabilize the bipolar status quo. In Cyprus (1964–present), the mission was initially (1964–1974) to patrol and observe tensions between Greek and Turkish Cypriots throughout the island. During the first ten years, the UN was able to mediate the temporary hostilities that erupted from time to time; however, with the coup d'etat in July 1974 and the resulting Turkish invasion in the north, the mission changed. UN troops endeavored to arrange local cease-fires to deter escalation of the killing and helped to provide humanitarian aid. Throughout the fighting, the UN continued to observe and report events. A cease-fire was achieved on August 16, 1974, and since that date UN troops have patrolled the cease-fire buffer zone, which stretches across the island and ranges from a few feet in width in some places to several miles in others. The UN has continued to offer its good offices to mediate the dispute, but has not entered into the fighting or taken sides, preserving its impartiality and reducing risks to peacekeepers. After the Congo-induced financial crisis, the only way the Security Council would approve a large-scale peacekeeping operation in Cyprus was to make the financing voluntary, a system that remains in place today. A main criticism of this mission and others like it that continue today, for example the one in Kashmir, is that the deployment of peacekeepers to monitor a buffer zone without resolving the underlying issues may, in fact, prolong the conflict by allowing the parties to leave the dispute unsettled without fearing a resumption of violence.

UN missions to Lebanon took place in two phases. The first, the UN Observation Group in Lebanon (UNOGIL), a small observer mission undertaken in 1958, was launched shortly after the Suez crisis. In May of that year, armed conflict broke out in the coastal city of Tripoli and soon spread to the rest of the country, threatening a civil war. The Lebanese government requested a meeting of the UN Security Council, charging that the United Arab Republic, primarily Syria, was encouraging the rebellion by supplying arms to rebels and by inciting violence through a radio and press campaign. In June, a high-level observer group was sent to Beirut under Security Council resolution 128 and the first military observers, drawn from UNTSO, arrived the next day. "The Secretary-General stressed that the Group would not be an armed police force like UNEF deployed in Sinai and the Gaza Strip."[37] However, tensions mounted when within a month the Iraqi government was overthrown and Jordan was under threat. Lebanese president Camille Chamoun requested intervention from the United States, which dispatched forces (later joined by the UK) to stabilize the government. UN observers were finally able to achieve freedom of movement throughout the country and were able to deter illegal arms from coming across the border. A peaceful election of a new president took place in Lebanon and tensions were reduced in Iraq and Jordan. By October 1958 a withdrawal plan had been completed, and by November the U.S. and UK forces began withdrawal along with the UN observers, who completed their withdrawal by December 9.

The second UN operation in Lebanon, the UN Interim Force in Lebanon (UNIFIL), began in 1978. Lebanon had received the largest flow of Palestinian refugees after the war with Israel in 1948. Then a new wave of refugees washed into Lebanon after the Palestine Liberation Organization (PLO) was thrown out of Jordan in 1970 following Black September, when the PLO had hijacked several passenger airliners and held them at the airport in Amman. By 1978, PLO forces had control over most of southern Lebanon and were heavily armed. Ghassan Tueni, who was ambassador to the UN for Lebanon from 1977 to 1982, recalls the situation:

> The Arab countries were all too happy that the Palestinians were operating from Lebanon and not from their own country, and they were sending arms, particularly Syria—and I am not sending an accusation here—I am only repeating what Syria itself acknowledged, with a certain sense of pride, that they were arming the camps. The Palestinians didn't have the means of buying all the hardware or armaments that they had. These were given to them by Syria, Libya, Iraq, Egypt, everybody—wittingly, knowing that they probably would be used against Lebanese, but so what? Nobody was concerned that this was weakening the Lebanese state, because the Lebanese state was not very popular with other Arabs at the time.[38]

The PLO used its bases in Lebanon to attack Israel along its northern border. In 1978 the PLO attacked an area near Tel Aviv and the Israelis retaliated by sending troops into Lebanon and occupying the country south of the Litani River. The Israeli retaliation, called Operation Litani, was very costly for Lebanon. Tueni describes the consequences for the Lebanese:

> It was destroying Lebanese villages, Lebanese homes, Lebanese houses. And there was a new wave of refugees; the Palestinians had already been refugees from Palestine, and they were now getting into Beirut because they didn't want to stay in the camps and be receiving this retaliation. But the Lebanese as well were migrating, and the whole Lebanese society was disrupted and there were tremendous economic problems. Lebanon was really falling apart.[39]

On March 15, 1978, Ambassador Tueni protested to the Security Council, saying that Lebanon was not responsible for the PLO bases and had no connection with the commando operations. By March 19 the Security Council had quickly passed resolution 425, calling for the withdrawal of Israeli forces and the establishment of a UN interim force for the purpose of confirming the withdrawal of Israeli troops. The United States, with President Jimmy Carter personally in the lead, was deeply embroiled in peace negotiations between the Egyptians and the Israelis at this time and did not want the embarrassment of an Israeli invasion on another border to threaten the Camp David process. The United States wanted the issue off the international agenda as soon as possible and others on the Council were willing to go along. Tueni got his resolution, which called for restoring peace and security in Lebanon and "assisting the government of Lebanon in ensuring the return of its effective authority in the area."

Israel completed its withdrawal from Lebanon by June 1978. However, UNIFIL was denied entry into the area immediately north of the Israeli border by an Israeli-supported Christian militia, thereby thwarting UNIFIL's freedom of movement into the most sensitive area of patrol. Armed PLO Fatah guerrillas easily infiltrated the area, making it impossible for the UN to stop the attacks that had perpetuated the crisis initially. Therefore, UNIFIL's mission was doomed from the start and the untenable situation worsened. UNIFIL spokesman Timur Goksel stated that there were some forty guerrilla groups in Lebanon.[40] Israel invaded again in 1982 to stop the attacks and this time went all the way to Beirut to hit the PLO camps there. Eventually, the PLO was forced out of Lebanon and moved its headquarters to Tunisia. Israel withdrew but maintained its own controlled "security zone" inside Lebanon's southern border for some twenty years until mid-2000, when it withdrew unilaterally. While UNIFIL has now moved to the border area, Hezbollah and other guerrilla groups have replaced the PLO and the border is still not fully secure.

Like many of the peacekeeping operations of the Cold War years, UNIFIL was seen by the superpowers as a way to remove a crisis from the international agenda, thereby ensuring it would not escalate into an East-West conflict over spheres of influence. Once that was accomplished there was little interest in taking the risks of using force to settle a conflict or using international resources to resolve the underlying disputes in other ways. The use of force to end the secession of Katanga in the Congo was seen as a pariah and no one wanted to revisit the institutional crisis that had resulted from what was considered the Congo morass.

The Watershed Years: The Thawing of the Cold War

Toward the end of World War II and during the first several months of 1945, when the founders of the UN were finalizing the Charter, tensions were building between the Western democracies and the Soviet Union. Each side worked to carve out its sphere of influence in the closing months of the war, with the Soviet Union taking Eastern and much of Central Europe while the United States and its European allies solidified Western Europe. Germany, which found itself split between the two spheres, was weakened and deterred from threatening Europe yet again. Berlin was cut off from the rest of Western Europe and surrounded by territory occupied by the Soviets, who also controlled the eastern sector of the city, leaving West Berlin under control by the Western allies. Attempts by Moscow to cut off Berlin were thwarted by a U.S.-led airlift campaign to preserve the city, but eventually, to stop East Germans from escaping into the West, the Soviet-dominated East German regime built what became known as the Berlin Wall, which was heavily guarded, functionally dividing Berlin into two sectors under different spheres of control.

Containment of Communism, as conceived by U.S. foreign policymaker George Kennan, became the focus for the United States. Even while the West turned a blind eye to Soviet infiltration and control of Poland and other European countries in proximity to Soviet territory, the Allies concentrated on curbing Communist influence in Greece and other parts of Western Europe, carefully drawing a "no go" line around the Soviet bloc. Europe was locked in a stalemate with an "iron curtain" closing off East from West. Elsewhere in Asia, Africa, and Latin America, tension between the two superpowers erupted in hot spots around the globe as each jockeyed for power in the region. A blow to many in the West came when Communists took control of mainland China in 1949, pushing Chiang Kai-shek, a friend of the United States, to the island of Taiwan. When Communist forces in North Korea attacked the South, U.S.-led troops, authorized by the UN, rushed in to contain Communism. In Vietnam, without going through the UN, the United States fought to hold onto Western influence in South Vietnam. With weapons and other support flowing into the North from the Communist world, over

50,000 Americans and hundreds of thousands of Vietnamese were killed in the years of fighting. The war spread to Cambodia and Laos, destabilizing the region. In the mid-1970s the United States pulled out after rising protests at home and Vietnam fell into the Communist sphere.

In Africa, the battle over spheres of influence played out through proxy wars, with the superpowers sending weapons and advisers to their client countries. The Soviets sent weapons to Egypt and welcomed Marxist Ethiopia into its sphere. In turn, the West heavily supported the dictator Major-General Mohamed Siad Barre in Somalia in containing his Ethiopian neighbor. As discussed, the Congo got caught in the tension and was wrestled away from the East-West battleground by the UN, although the Soviet interpretation would be that the UN leveraged the Congo into the Western sphere. In 1975, when Portugal overthrew its fascist regime, the new leadership established socialist governments in Portugal's former colonies Angola and Mozambique. In an attempt to overthrow these governments and wrest them away from the Communist sphere, the West and Western-friendly African states enlisted the help of rebel groups like the Union for the Total Independence of Angola (UNITA) and the Mozambique National Resistance (Renamo), assisted by South Africa. Angola responded by inviting Cuban troops under Soviet support to supplement its army. Civil wars decimated the countryside, destroyed infrastructure, and killed thousands of civilians in both Angola and Mozambique. In the name of containment, the United States and the West often found themselves on the dark side of moral issues like apartheid in South Africa and Namibia or at least looking the other way, thus allowing South African resources to fight these proxy wars.

Latin America suffered some of the same influences. The Sandinistas, under the leadership of Daniel and Humberto Ortega, overthrew the Nicaraguan dictator Anastasio Somoza Debayle and established a Communist-influenced government with Soviet and Cuban support. In order to thwart Communist influence in Nicaragua, the United States established and supported a rebel movement, the Contras, in addition to mining the port of Managua, Nicaragua's capital. In a reverse scenario in El Salvador, the United States supported the government while the Soviet Union and its ally Cuba supported the rebels of the Farabundo Martí National Liberation Front (FMLN). Chile was also caught up in the Cold War battleground. When elected president Salvador Allende, a socialist, began to nationalize certain key industries, the United States felt it had to step in to curb the spread of Communist influence in the Southern Hemisphere and supported a military coup orchestrated by Augusto Pinochet. Other countries in Latin America and elsewhere suffered from these tensions as well.

The Cold War Ends
In the mid-1980s conditions began to change. Although still not visibly apparent, the Soviet system was gradually crumbling from the inside.

Demographers like Murray Feshbach in Washington, D.C., began to report statistics on the Soviet Union. Infant mortality rates were rising, life expectancy was falling, and death by alcoholism was increasing at an alarming rate. The interpretation was that the system was deteriorating; there were long lines for food and shortages were everywhere. Yet the West failed to read the signals. The collapse of the Soviet Union has been attributed to many things. Some say that the West outspent Moscow on weapons and forced it to divert too much of its resources to the military. Others say that central economic planning and Soviet secrecy thwarted economic growth and innovation, causing the economy to fall further and further behind while the West was flourishing economically and technologically. So absorbed by the containment policy, the United States did not anticipate the Soviet demise and the world was shocked when in November 1989 the Berlin Wall was brought down by ordinary citizens using hammers and anything they could find to knock it to pieces. Overcome with tears and joy, East Berliners walked through the gates to see family members they had not seen for years or whom they had only heard about. Soviet leader Mikhail Gorbachev knew he could not stop the rushing flow of people, and that day changed everything. The fall of the Berlin Wall marked the beginning of the end of the Soviet empire, and that end marked a whole new beginning, a paradigm shift of major proportions.

The latter part of 1988 and the year 1989 were marked by other events that would have a profound influence on world security. Weakened economically, the Soviet Union could no longer support its international endeavors and Gorbachev was reaching out to the West to initiate economic ties. Candlelight revolutions moved across Central and Eastern Europe after the fall of the Berlin Wall as the people began to realize the Soviet dragon had lost its fiery threat. In the Southern Hemisphere, South Africa was weary of wars it could not win in Angola and Mozambique and the Soviets no longer wanted to pour resources into the region and support thousands of Cuban troops in Angola. The time was ripe to find a negotiated settlement and U.S. State Department diplomat Chester Crocker, in the last days of the Reagan administration, intermediated an agreement for the removal of Cuban troops from Angola, which meant that Namibia, no longer needed as a buffer to contain Communism on its northern border, could finally be given its independence from South Africa. In Asia, the Cambodian conflict was also ripe for a mediated solution. The cards were suddenly falling into place.

A number of presidential elections in different parts of the world would also determine events. In 1989, in El Salvador, President Alfredo Cristiani was elected on a peace platform; in South Africa, F. W. de Klerk took office on August 15, 1989, replacing President P. W. Botha; and in the United States, George Herbert Walker Bush took office on January 20, 1989, moving into the

Oval Office as his predecessor, Ronald Reagan, stepped into retirement. The thawing of the Cold War, the economic withdrawal of the Soviet Union, and the election of these men reshaped the political map.

The importance of the Bush election had a particular effect on Latin America. Immediately after his election in November 1988, Bush put his foreign policy team into place with James Baker as secretary of state and Bernard Aronson as assistant secretary of state for Latin America. In complete contrast to the Reagan administration, which supported the Contras and the Salvadoran government as major planks in the containment regime, Aronson was told to go to Central America and explore the possibilities of a nonmilitary solution to the conflicts.[41] The Contadora countries had for years been pressing for a nonmilitary solution in El Salvador; now Cristiani and the Bush administration were on board. What remained was the rebel forces, the FMLN.

A New Role for the UN

The UN, which had been to a great extent frozen out of playing an intermediary role by Cold War vetoes in the Security Council, was now about to enter center stage. President Bush had been ambassador to the UN in the Nixon administration and now took advantage of the thaw to act multilaterally, seeking both the legitimacy and the burden-sharing advantages of the UN while keeping the Soviets in a cooperative mood. Peace was now in both superpowers' best interests. However, there is an African saying that goes: "When the elephants make war, the grass suffers; when the elephants make love, the grass suffers." Now the parties on the ground in these poor developing countries worried that their interests could be trampled by these giants in the rush to discard the leftovers of the Cold War. In this case, the UN, with a watchful Third World membership, also served to advance and buffer the needs of the parties. The good offices of the Secretary-General played a positive role along with support from groups of Member States. UN peacekeepers were called in to provide security for transition processes that included voter registration, elections, new constitutions, humanitarian assistance, and police and judicial reform. What were once ad hoc missions run from the Department of Political Affairs now demanded several hundred staff members, leading to the creation in 1992 of the Department of Peacekeeping Operations. In these initial post–Cold War operations, although challenged from time to time, the UN was able to maintain consent of the parties, remain impartial, uphold a cease-fire, and retain a policy of firing only in self-defense. As Hammarskjöld had envisioned, upholding these principles would ensure greater success. However, other crisis events would prove to be more vexing and would throw the UN into a renewed turmoil, mirroring the Congo crisis of the 1960s.

Peacekeeping After the Cold War: Modern Complexities

During the forty-year period from 1948, when UNTSO was dispatched to the Middle East, to January 1988, as the Cold War was winding down, the UN had deployed thirteen UN peacekeeping operations. By contrast, during the next sixteen years, to the end of 2003, the UN launched forty-four additional peace operations. Several things led to the sudden increase, but the primary difference was the end to the East-West competition in the Security Council and the constant threat of the veto by members of the permanent five. While there were some 300 vetoes by Security Council members during the Cold War period, since 1991, when the Soviet Union ceased to exist, there have been fewer than ten. Not only has the Council overcome its deadlock, but its ability to agree on any number of issues has proliferated. By August 1990, at the outset of Iraq's occupation of Kuwait, there had been 660 Security Council resolutions in the UN's first forty-five years. Just some thirteen years later, in February 2004, the total had reached more than double that number with passage of Council's 1,527th resolution, on the situation in Côte d'Ivoire.

Many of the recent peacekeeping operations have been undertaken in situations of internal conflict and failed states. These scenarios would have been off-limits during the Cold War, not only because of territorial spheres of influence but also because the Council would not have been able to reach a consensus on a model for rebuilding a society emerging from instability. The UN would not have been able to support either a Communist ideology with a centrally planned economy or a democratic ideology based on private enterprise and capitalism. Hence the UN could not intervene. It is not that there weren't civil wars in progress during those years; they just weren't on the radar screen of the Security Council.

The end of the Cold War meant that a number of long-term civil wars, like those in Cambodia, El Salvador, and Mozambique, and wars of independence, like the struggle in Namibia, were suddenly ripe for mediated solutions. With Security Council consensus on Iraq in 1990 and 1991, it appeared that the UN was finally going to become the kind of collective security organization the founders had hoped for. In January 1992 the Security Council met in New York at the level of heads of state for the first time in its existence. A new-world-order euphoria filled the Council chamber. Peacekeeping successes in Namibia in 1989, El Salvador beginning in 1991, Cambodia in 1992–1993, and Mozambique in 1994 led many supporters of the UN to believe that peacekeeping was the answer to resolving international conflicts. These early successes involved old conflicts that were ripe for solution and were such that the major powers still had leverage over their former clients. But other conflicts were just as suddenly released by the end of repressive regimes buttressed during the Cold War. Siad Barre in Somalia, no longer needed by the West to contain Ethiopia, fled in defeat, leaving a power vacuum as the country fell into clan wars and anarchy. In Europe, with Tito dead and no Communist bloc on the horizon, Yugoslavia began to fall apart as its republics reverted to old nationalist rivalries. Instead of forming a loose federation of autonomous units, which could have avoided war and encouraged economic ties, power-hungry leaders preferred to incite hatred and grab territory, forcing people from their property through grotesque methods of ethnic cleansing.

Visions of starvation and genocide viewed around the world through globalized media coverage, referred to as the CNN factor, brought leaders to the United Nations to seek solutions. But these conflicts were not ripe for resolution and were not controlled by superpower resources. They were fueled from the inside and by regional nonstate actors, many with resources of their own from drugs, diamonds, and other contraband. These parties were either desperate to win or desperate to defend themselves. Like the Congo in the 1960s, these battles would drag the UN into an institutional crisis once again. Pressed by moral imperatives, the UN entered conflicts in Somalia and Bosnia

UN Photo 179194/UNSO-139

First summit-level meeting of Security Council heads of state, January 1992.

without universal consent from the parties to the conflict. There were no cease-fires in place, and it became immoral to remain impartial in the face of genocide in the former Yugoslavia and brutal disregard for human life in Somalia. In attempts to preserve impartiality and avoid risks to peacekeeping personnel, the UN only emboldened aggressive tactics by parties who had no real desire for a peaceful solution. Not going on the offensive to protect the safe areas in Bosnia enabled horrendous acts of brutal murder, yet going on the offensive to go after clan leader General Aidid in Somalia embroiled the UN and the United States in the conflict and set them up as targets. The UN was caught between a rock and a hard place.

The period that followed the end of the Cold War can best be divided into three stages, at times overlapping: early successes; followed by a period of failures; and acceptance of the difficulties of peacekeeping, with all the complex needs it entails, as a core program of the UN. It is of course impossible to cover in detail all forty-four peacekeeping operations since the end of the Cold War (see this chapter's appendix). Therefore, the following sections focus on a few examples from each of the three stages.

Early Successes

Namibia, El Salvador, Cambodia, and Mozambique are all considered UN successes and all resulted in the end to years of internal struggle that had been aided by outside support for each of the warring parties. Resources were no longer flowing in and the people were exhausted from years of hardship. Nevertheless, the parties needed an impartial and legitimate third party, the United Nations, to keep the process on track and provide resources that the universal UN membership could offer as incentives. Without this support each conflict would most likely have continued to fester. Each case is unique in its own way. The UN was closely involved in the peace process leading up to the deployment of peacekeeping in both Namibia and El Salvador. However, in Cambodia the Paris peace talks, which concluded the peace agreement, did not involve the UN until the agreement was already signed. Only at that point was the implementation handed off to the UN. For Mozambique, the peace agreement was mediated by a Catholic lay organization called Sant'Egidio and the UN was brought into the process only near the end.

The UN Observer Mission in El Salvador (ONUSAL) offers a very useful example because of the complex role the UN played and because of the many precedents that were set by the operation. The UN was heavily involved in both mediating the peace agreement, a process that went on for over two years, and implementing the final accord. After some twelve years of civil war and several attempts to end the conflict, in which over 75,000 people had died and 1 million had been displaced, the parties finally turned to the UN to conduct mediation. The government in its efforts to suppress the rebels had depended heavily on U.S. military support, which was soon to be curtailed because the

United States was no longer concerned about containing Communism. The rebel group, the FMLN, drew support from Nicaragua, Cuba, and the Soviet Union. In an effort to demonstrate that its movement was not weakened by the waning resources of the Communist bloc, the FMLN launched the largest attack of its twelve-year campaign in November 1989, almost at the same time as the fall of the Berlin Wall. The FMLN succeeded in taking much of San Salvador, the capital, forcing the government to accept that it could not end the conflict through military success. It would have to negotiate a settlement or the war could go on indefinitely. It was a sobering moment for the rebels as well as the government when the FMLN's November campaign failed to arouse the anticipated spontaneous uprising by the people. With a clear military stalemate and support diminishing, both sides decided independently to ask the UN to intervene.

Alvaro de Soto, political adviser to Secretary-General Javier Pérez de Cuéllar, became the principal mediator between the parties. He and his team began the peace process in late 1989, completing most of the negotiations by midnight December 31, 1991, when Pérez de Cuéllar left office and was replaced by Boutros Boutros-Ghali. The formal signing took place in Mexico in January 1992. The negotiation process was based on achieving agreement over several issues: a cease-fire, human rights, reducing and reforming the military, reforming the judicial and electoral systems, changing the constitution, and achieving greater economic distribution, including land distribution. It was hoped that a cease-fire would be one of the first issues to be agreed upon, but the FMLN knew that the threat of a return to hostilities was its central leverage over the government to make the changes the rebels had been fighting for all these years. The purpose was to subordinate the military under civilian control and create "a more participatory system of governance."[42] The FMLN wanted the government to first reduce and reform the military and to eliminate the "death squads" organized by the extreme right and protected by the government. This stalemate threatened to end the talks taking place in San José, Costa Rica, in July 1990 with no results.

De Soto's team introduced the idea of addressing a different issue on the agenda, one that might receive agreement, human rights. It appeared to be out of order to focus on human rights before achieving a cease-fire, but the strategy worked. Neither side wanted to return home empty-handed. At first it was envisioned that the UN human rights verification mission would follow the cease-fire, but as negotiations dragged on well into 1991, the parties with the support of the UN Security Council decided to launch the human rights aspect of the mission ahead of the final agreement. This was the first time the UN would conduct human rights verification, which was clearly interfering with the domestic affairs of a sovereign state, something protected in the UN Charter. Nevertheless, with the consent and encouragement of the parties, the urgency to achieve some level of progress, and the apparent enabling environment on the ground, the UN Security Council approved resolution 693 in May 1991, establishing ONUSAL.

The tasks of the mission were to verify compliance with the San José Agreement by monitoring the human rights situation, investigating specific cases, promoting human rights throughout the country, making recommendations for the elimination of human rights violations, and reporting to the Secretary-General.[43] ONUSAL's human rights mission was launched in July 1991 and its presence over the next several months enhanced the confidence building that was needed to allay fears that the peace process was faltering. For the first time, human rights became the cornerstone of a peacekeeping operation.

In addition, ONUSAL made a number of other creative contributions to the peace effort. Agreements were reached to reduce the military, put it under civilian control, and create a separate civilian police force, so that it would no longer be an arm of repression used by the military and the government for political purposes. A new police training academy was established whereby 20 percent of the trainees would be recruited from the military, 20 percent from the FMLN, and the remaining 60 percent from those who had never served in either force. The UN supplied the police trainers and civilian police monitors. While the UN had deployed CIVPOL observers prior to El Salvador both in Cyprus for the first time (1964) and in Namibia (1989), this was the first time the UN had overseen a process of police "reform." The constitution was altered to allow greater participation in the electoral process and a National Commission for the Consolidation of Peace (COPAZ) was created to oversee the implementation of the agreements. COPAZ was made up of members from the FMLN, the government, and the UN. This mechanism would become a standard practice in future peacekeeping operations to give the parties an oversight mechanism with UN guidance on a continuing basis.

Another important contribution was the establishment of a truth commission, which was agreed to by the parties in their negotiations in April 1991 in Mexico. At the time, it was agreed that the commissioners would all be foreigners, something the FMLN wanted, and that there would be no prosecutions, something the government wanted. Many people were surprised when the National Assembly voted to grant amnesty five days following the release of the commission's report on March 15, 1993, but this was part of the original conditions under which the commission operated. The three commissioners were Thomas Buergenthal, a U.S. law professor, Reinaldo Figueredo, former foreign minister of Venezuela, and Belisario Betancur, former president of Colombia. The jurisdiction of the commission included all serious acts of violence that had occurred during the period January 1980 through July 1991. It received over 22,000 complaints, including those involving executions, disappearances, and torture. Although the report did not offer much new information on human rights violations during the period, it did end the disputes over who had been responsible for what acts and it gave the people satisfaction that blame had been squarely placed on the guilty parties. "The most important new finding of the truth commission report was the attribution of responsibility for the murder of a group of Jesuit priests to Colonel Réne Emilio Ponce (who had become minister of defense), Colonels Zepeda and Montano (who had become vice ministers of defense), General Bustillo, and Commander of the Army First Brigade Colonel Elena Fuentes."[44]

The UN was also given the task of demobilizing the rebel fighters and a portion of the government military. While the UN had undertaken to retrain the Congolese military in the 1960s and had set up demobilization camps in cooperation with the Organization of American States (OAS) in Nicaragua (through the UN Observer Group in Central America [ONUCA]) in 1991, ONUSAL was the first UN peacekeeping operation to make demobilization and disarmament a central part of the mission. A number of problems were encountered in the process, but guns were collected from the former combatants in designated camps around the country and soldiers were reintroduced to civilian life. El Salvador was the first truly complex peacekeeping operation dedicated to attacking the root causes of the conflict: economic, social, and political inequality. ONUSAL was a learning process for the UN, and a number of the innovations that emerged were later improved upon and expanded in other peacekeeping operations. For example, in Mozambique, demobilized former combatants were given pay to allow them time to find a new source of livelihood and military officers who were willing to retire were given retirement benefits as incentives.

Peacekeeping Failures

After congratulating itself on a number of successes, the UN suddenly faced a series of catastrophic failures, and the international media did not hesitate to heap criticism on the Organization. Somalia, Rwanda, and Bosnia are examples of the inability of the UN to cope with new and festering internal conflicts where the parties had no interest in finding a peaceful solution. It is useful to begin with Somalia. A vacuum of power left over from the end of the Cold War led to clan warfare and general anarchy through most of the country. Many Somalis had been forced from their small subsistence farming communities into camps because of the fighting and looting of clan guerrillas, often referred to as "technicals," symbolized by heavily armed combatants riding in open pickup trucks. Serious drought compounded the crisis and massive starvation set in. An estimated 300,000 people died, 2 million were displaced, and approximately one-third of all Somali children under the age of five died from starvation.[45] International media coverage brought pictures of starving and dying Somalis to television sets around the globe. The "CNN factor" brought pressure to bear on the UN and its Member States to respond. In spring 1992, the UN Operation in Somalia (UNOSOM) was established initially as a small observer mission but was later authorized to deploy up to 4,219 troops in addition to 50 observers. But the peacekeeping mission very quickly ran into difficulties, particularly when the heavily armed faction under General Aidid refused to cooperate. Both the Aidid and Mahdi clans began attacking UN troops. "On 13 November, after being shot at with machine guns, rifles and mortars, the Pakistani troops in control of the airport returned fire. Although they remained in control of their position, the overall situation was bad. In the absence of a government or governing authority capable of maintaining law and order, Somali authorities at all levels were competing for anything of value. International aid had become a major (and is some areas the only) source of income."[46] The protection of the delivery of humanitarian aid became an increasing problem and the crisis deepened. The United States responded at the end of the Bush administration in January 1993 by sending in heavily armed troops, the Unified Task Force (UNITAF) (a non-UN operation led by the United States), to provide security for the delivery of aid. UNITAF was to be a short operation and was to be handed over to the UN once the crisis passed; however, the handover to UNOSOM II went badly as well-armed troops pulled out, leaving a vacuum of strength in the hands of the much weaker UN contingents. With no real consent, Aidid's forces again attacked the Pakistanis who had been attempting to disarm the clan. Many Pakistani soldiers were killed and their bodies dismembered and left in the road.

At this point, the operation in Somalia lost its way. U.S. forces, deployed independently of the UN, began to go after Aidid to hold him accountable. Without informing the UN for fear of leaks in information, a U.S. Ranger Delta Force carried out a secret raid on Aidid in October 1993. While executing the mission the U.S. force was ambushed by Somali clan members who deeply resented U.S. interference in their search for power and control. Eighteen U.S. soldiers were killed in the next several hours and one was dragged through streets of Mogadishu before television cameras, which showed the image over and over in the following days. The American public was outraged at the specter of the U.S. soldier's body desecrated in such a manner in a city and country few knew anything about. The public demanded to know why the United States was involved in Somalia and many feared another Vietnam. President Bill Clinton decided to withdraw troops over several months and a more cautious policy for peacekeeping engagement was put into place.

Pressured by the catastrophic humanitarian crisis in Somalia, the UN (and the United States) entered a situation in which there was no cease-fire and no reliable consent from the parties. The international force became caught up in the conflict by going on the offensive against one of the parties, removing its legitimacy as an impartial facilitator. This is exactly what Hammarskjöld had cautioned against when he established his principles of peacekeeping, which included a cease-fire, consent, impartiality, and a policy of firing only in self-defense. Despite the fact that the UN had helped to end the starvation, had enabled people to return to their homes and farms, and had worked to rebuild health and agricultural sectors, these successes were lost in a cacophony of derision toward the Organization.

The debacle in Somalia contributed to the humiliating failure of the UN to respond some six months later to the genocide in Rwanda in spring 1994. Earlier the UN had sent a light observer mission to monitor the border between Rwanda and Uganda, following an agreement to end attacks across the border from Uganda. After years of exile, Tutsi guerrilla fighters living in camps in Uganda had launched several attacks in an attempt to regain power in their homeland. However, the Rwandan internal situation was still not resolved. The moderate Hutu president had attended a peace conference held outside the country to find a solution and establish a power-sharing mechanism between the Hutu and Tutsi tribes. However, he was assassinated by an attack on his plane at the airport in Kigali upon his return. Hutu extremists who wanted to stop a power-sharing arrangement from taking place then launched a carefully orchestrated genocide campaign, using radio and other means to incite fear and revenge against all Tutsis. General Romeo Dallaire, UN Force Commander, immediately requested assistance, but instead the Belgian troops within the UN force were withdrawn after coming under attack from Hutus. Pleas to the UN Security Council went unheeded as the United States, fearing another Somalia, refused to acknowledge that genocide was taking place. Risk-averse U.S. officials continued to claim that nothing could be done to intervene in the civil dispute and called on the parties to find a peaceful solution. Reports of the slaughter in the daily press failed to garner support for an intervention.

The French finally obtained Security Council authorization for Operation Turquoise to establish a safe area in a sector of the country, but only after the worst of the attacks had taken place. Tutsi fighters were making their way across Rwanda to end the killing by pushing the extremist Hutus out of one town after another. In the end, the Tutsi army under the leadership of General Kagami took control and ended the genocide with no help from the outside. Tutsis and Hutus alike fled to neighboring Burundi, Tanzania, and eastern Zaire. Ad hoc refugee camps sprang up only to be hit by epidemic levels of cholera and other diseases. The World Health Organization and UN Member States finally responded by sending assistance to the camps, but only after some 800,000 Tutsis and moderate Hutus had been shot and hacked to death with machetes. General Dallaire insisted that if he had had a 5,000-troop, well-trained brigade deployed under his command when he had asked for help, he could have stopped most of the killing, but no one responded.

The United Nations is only capable of implementing what the Member States are willing to do. The UN does not have an army or resources of its own and is completely dependent on the will of its members. Lack of will and consensus of purpose were illustrated clearly in the case of Rwanda and soon thereafter again in Bosnia with the United Nations Protection Force (UNPRO-FOR). Mats Berdal explains: "The confused, hesitant, and reactive nature of the 'international community's' response to the disintegration of Yugoslavia provides the essential backdrop against which the history of United Nations

UN Photo 193541C/Jihad El Hassan

A UNPROFOR observation post in Croatia, January 1994.

operations in the Balkans during the first half of the 1990s must be viewed."[47] The crisis in Bosnia and Herzegovina is more complex than can be covered here, but the failure to protect the safe areas is clearly the greatest failure of the operation. Like Somalia, in Bosnia there was no peace to keep, and consent, particularly on the part of the Serb faction, was weak if not absent. Even the title "UNPROFOR" was misleading, because the force was never meant to protect civilians but only to protect the peacekeepers.

The delivery of humanitarian aid in the midst of war had been inconsistent, and countries with troops on the ground were reluctant to take risks that might put their troops in danger. There were continual capitulations to the aggressors, in most cases the Serbs. When conditions worsened in 1993 and 1994 in an attempt to respond to calls for action, the UN Security Council decided to create seven "safe areas." The UN Secretariat, in a report to the Council, recommended a force of some 34,000 troops to protect the areas. But the Council only authorized 7,600 and then only delivered about 3,000 soldiers. Underequipped and underforced, the UN troops were easily overrun in summer 1995 by Serb fighters who called their bluff. In Srebenica alone in July some 7,000 Muslims were murdered within a few days and in the same month the Bosnian Serb Army took control of the Zepa safe area and attacked Goradze and Sarajevo. UN peacekeepers were also taken hostage during the conflict. The Dutch battalion responsible for protecting Srebenica was too small and too weak to resist the Serb attack and could only stand by and watch as innocent civilians were raped, tortured, and murdered. A later investigation by a Dutch parliamentary inquiry was so scathing that the entire government was forced to resign. The signing of the Dayton Accords in November 1995 brought an end to the fighting, but only after thousands had lost their lives, including 211 peacekeepers, the worst loss of UN personnel since the 1960s Congo operation.

Recent Successes: Acceptance as a Core Activity

With lessons learned from both its successes and failures, the United Nations now recognizes that peacekeeping is a core activity of the Organization. The Brahimi Report, requested by the UN and released in summer 2000, laid out a plan for strengthening peacekeeping, calling on the UN to equip itself for Chapter VII operations when needed and to increase the Secretariat staff of the Department of Peacekeeping Operations (DPKO) to handle the workload more effectively and efficiently. The UN has undertaken to carry out many of those recommendations. What was once an ad hoc activity handled by a small group of staff members "able to fit into one car going to the airport,"[48] as Brian Urquhart describes, is now becoming a fully differentiated department. It must be remembered that DPKO, created in 1992, is barely more than ten years old. In the first years of the department the whole staff of 30 to 40 persons could sit around a table in a conference room. Now there are some 600 staff members, with political desk officers, logistics officers, and procurement, military, and support staff, a far cry from the early days. It is accepted that the UN will have to face the challenges of many different kinds of complex situations.

Accepting this reality along with the willingness of Member States to learn from past mistakes has enabled the UN to achieve a new series of successes in recent years: the successful transition of Eastern Slavonia in 1996–1998 (through the UN Transitional Administration for Eastern Slavonia, Baranja, and Western Sirmium [UNTAES]), after the Dayton Accords; the independence of East Timor in 1999–2002 after years of turmoil (through the UN Transitional Administration in East Timor [UNTAET]); the administration of Kosovo and preparation for self-governance, from 1999 to the present (through the UN Mission in Kosovo [UNMIK]); the monitoring of a buffer zone to keep the peace between Ethiopia and Eritrea while the border is demarcated, from 2000 to the present (through the UN Mission in Ethiopia and Eritrea [UNMEE]); and the end to civil war and rebuilding the country in Sierra Leone from 1999 to the present (through the Mission in Sierra Leone [UNAMSIL]).

The experience in Sierra Leone is worth some discussion here because of its complexity and because of the willingness of key Member States to rescue the mission when it fell into crisis in May 2000, threatening to repeat some of

Armored personnel carriers and peackeepers of the Netherlands and Canadian Battalion (NECBAT) serving with UNMEE, June 2001.

the failures of the worst cases in the early 1990s. The civil war in Sierra Leone erupted in 1991 when fighters of the Revolutionary United Front (RUF) launched attacks against the government. During a decade of fighting refugees fled to the capital, Freetown, and to neighboring states, throwing the country into chaos and threatening the stability of the region. The RUF supported itself by looting villages and by selling illegal diamonds from the mining-rich areas of Sierra Leone for guns and other supplies. The rebels were also aided by Charles Taylor in neighboring Liberia. Both Taylor and RUF leader Foday Sankoh met while undergoing training in Libya to carry out their guerrilla tactics. Some of the worst human atrocities on record were carried out by all sides of the conflict, including the kidnapping of children for service as soldiers and slave labor and the amputation of limbs, even of small babies, as terrorist tactics.

The UN became involved in 1999 with Security Council resolution 1270, which established UNAMSIL. UN troops were deployed slowly in 2000 and by May the RUF had taken advantage of the weak position of the UN to launch a last attempt to gain control. UN personnel were taken hostage, some of whom were killed, and 500 UN troops were surrounded and cut off from support while the rebels took their weaponry, trucks, and armored personnel carriers. It took a well-armed unit of British troops to free the hostages and rescue the operation. After the crisis, UNAMSIL was reorganized and the Security Council took measures to strengthen the number and offensive strength of the troops. A new force commander and deputy were put into place and the authorized troop strength was increased to 17,500, the largest troop deployment at the time.

UNAMSIL has built on previous peacekeeping operations in a number of ways and has added innovations of its own. Demobilization, begun in Nicaragua and El Salvador, has been taken well beyond the original concept. Sierra Leone has been able to benefit from the new policy of demobilization, disarmament, and reintegration (DDR). In this process, former combatants from both sides of the conflict were gathered in camp areas, where they lived together for several weeks and handed over their weapons, which in many cases they personally disabled before submitting them for destruction. They then went through a registration process during which they received an identification card and were asked to state what profession they wanted to enter. They were next given transportation and pay and taken to a camp near their village of origin, where they went through an education program. Vocational training centers in carpentry, mechanics, sewing, and other skills were set up with the help of nongovernmental organizations (NGOs). The program has been very successful and over 70,000 former combatants have been demobilized and disarmed and some 40,000 weapons and 5 million pieces of artillery have been destroyed. Some have finished the vocational training and have begun reintegrating into civilian life. Others have found trades on their own and so far none have returned to violence. The program has been so success-ful that noncombatants have been complaining of the lack of an equal pro-gram for them. The World Bank and other NGOs have now begun community development programs in order to benefit everyone and help to rebuild the country, which was decimated during the war.

Other innovations have been the Truth and Reconciliation Commission (TRC) and the Special Court for Sierra Leone, established because of the hor-rendous nature of the atrocities committed during the war. The Lomé Accords, which brought agreement to end the war, included amnesty for all the perpe-trators of human rights violations. This was considered necessary in order to gain the cooperation of the RUF. However, the UN added a "reservation" to the amnesty clause, saying that it reserved an exemption from granting amnesty if it should decide to prosecute on its own. Therefore, while the TRC takes testimonies from victims and witnesses, it is obliged to honor the amnesty provisions and cannot prosecute or pass evidence for prosecution. One of the innovations of the TRC, which builds on the truth commissions in El Salvador and later in South Africa, is the introduction of not only open hearings regarding specific atrocities, but also "thematic hearings" in which community leaders discuss the structural deficiencies of the governance sys-tem that allowed such atrocities to perpetuate. By May 2003 the TRC had taken some 7,000 private testimonies and was holding public hearings in each of the fourteen districts around the country.

In contrast to the TRC, the Special Court, which is operated by the UN in agreement with the Sierra Leonean government, can prosecute and convict those found guilty of major human rights crimes committed between 1996 and 2000. Several leaders have already been indicted and imprisoned, including RUF leader Foday Sankoh (who died of natural causes in 2003 while being held) and Sam Hingha Norman, internal affairs minister and former head of the Civil Defense Force, also known as the Kamajors. The Special Court pros-ecutor, David Crane (of the United States), also issued an indictment for the arrest of Charles Taylor, who stepped down as president of neighboring Liberia in 2003. The maximum sentence the court can impose is life in prison, in keeping with general UN policy.

While other peacekeeping operations have been completed and with-drawn after the first free and fair elections have taken place, UNAMSIL has stayed on past the first elections of May 2002, carefully monitoring certain benchmarks of development and stability before drawing down its forces gradually. By February 2003, there were still 15,255 troops and 256 military observers in the country. Military observers made daily rounds of camps, communities, and general hot spots and reported back to headquarters on con-ditions and potential troubles that might be brewing. Both UNAMSIL and government officials meet daily to discuss reports. In this way, the UN or the government not only can step in before things get out of control, but also can assess the stabilization process. By 2003, training of both police and military was also under way. In addition, efforts were being made to stabilize the region so that the ongoing civil war in neighboring Liberia would not threaten stability in Sierra Leone. UN peacekeepers, with support from the United States, were sent to Liberia in August 2003 as Charles Taylor was pressured to leave office.

Conclusion

UN peacekeeping has now matured into a core activity of the United Nations, a change from its ad hoc nature in the early years. But there is something about peacekeeping that will remain ad hoc, because much of the time the UN must respond quickly as a crisis erupts. The UN does not have its own army nor a rapid response mechanism and therefore is still dependent on the willingness and capacity of its Member States to deploy in crisis situations. This will continue to present problems for quick response or deployment into hostile environments because Member States will often refuse to send their soldiers under risky conditions. Nevertheless, there seems to be a greater acceptance of the complex nature of peace operations and that the UN needs to maintain an ongoing, in-depth capacity to meet these challenges more effectively than in the past. Also, there is a greater effort to build cooperative relationships with regional security organizations to share the burden. This has been the case in Africa with the Economic Organization of West African States (ECOWAS), which has played a major role in Sierra Leone and in Liberia, and now that NATO has deployed out of Europe for the first time into Afghanistan. However, most regions of the world do not have security organizations that can respond to conflict situations the way in which a universal, collective system like the UN can, and some parties to a conflict would prefer an impartial organization like the UN to intervene rather than a regional hegemon.

The challenges the UN faces, however, can be daunting. Conflicts today are exacerbated by the fact that many of the parties involved have no allegiance to a state; as subgroups proliferate, it becomes difficult or even impossible to find someone to talk to, let alone negotiate a peace settlement. Many groups are funded through drug trafficking or the smuggling of commodities like diamonds, which can be very lucrative, can be very difficult to stop in anarchic situations with unguarded borders, and can offer an incentive to keep the conflict going. This was the situation in the eastern part of the Congo in 2003, where the UN had once again been held hostage by violent attacks. It is encouraging that the UN is responding robustly, authorizing some 10,000 troops for the Congo (through the UN Organization Mission in the Democratic Republic of Congo [MONUC]) and 15,000 for Liberia (through the UN Mission in Liberia [UNMIL]), which was authorized in October 2003. But the expectations are enormous and may be beyond what Member States are willing to address. The UN has also come to realize that it must communicate and build a positive relationship with the local population in ways that have not been necessary in interstate conflicts, in which only the compliance of government leaders is needed. Now the UN needs the local population and many numbers of subgroups to cooperate and comply with peace operations. In the Congo, the UN is experimenting with the establishment of a countrywide radio network that broadcasts regular music and news programs intermixed with UN messages. The UN has used radio in the past—UNAMSIL has its own radio station—but often the UN has had to broadcast over government-run stations, which has been problematic. Local goodwill within communities has been enhanced by the peacekeepers themselves. Many UN peacekeeping contingents, at their own country's expense, run local programs to build schools, offer medical and dental care, and undertake any number of community development projects.

One of the biggest challenges for the UN is to combat the negative image created by the media, which much prefer to cover crises and failures. When peacekeeping operations are going smoothly, they are not considered newsworthy and successes go unnoticed. Morale among the UN staff and peacekeeping troops can be very low when the public does not appreciate their hard work and dedication, and the risks they encounter. The UN itself needs to do a better job of promoting its work. But expectations will often outstrip information and the capacity or willingness of Member States to respond. Reaction to the Brahimi Report to strengthen peacekeeping has been positive, but much rests on the continued support of Member States and the majors powers, particularly the United States.

Appendix: Past and Present UN Peacekeeping

Past Peacekeeping Operations

> UNSCOB: UN Special Committee on the Balkans, 1947–1951; headquarters: Salonica, Greece; purpose: set up prior to "peacekeeping" as such to observe and monitor the agreement not to assist guerrilla movement in Greece; strength: some 50 military observers and civilian staff; cost: $3 million.
>
> UNEF I: First UN Emergency Force, 1956–1967; headquarters: Gaza; purpose: establish a buffer zone between Egypt and Israel after Suez crisis; strength: 6,000; cost: $214 million.
>
> UNOGIL: UN Observation Group in Lebanon, June–December 1958; headquarters: Beirut; purpose: observe Syrian-Lebanese border and infiltration of arms and personnel into Lebanon; strength: 600 military observers; cost: $3.7 million.

ONUC: UN Operation in the Congo, 1960–1964; headquarters: Leopoldville (Kinshasa); purpose: restore order in the Congo and later end secession of Katanga province; strength: 20,000; cost: $500 million.

UNSF: UN Security Force in West New Guinea, 1962–1963; headquarters: Jayaphra; purpose: monitor cease-fire and oversee transition from Netherlands to Indonesia; strength: 1,600; cost: paid by Netherlands and Indonesia, total not available.

UNYOM: UN Yemen Observation Mission, 1963–1964; headquarters: Sana'a; purpose: observe disengagement of Saudi Arabia and United Arab Republic; strength: 200 military observers; cost: $1.8 million.

DOMREP: UN Mission in the Dominican Republic, 1965–1966; headquarters: Santo Domingo; purpose: observe cease-fire between conflicting factions; strength: 4 observers; cost: $280,000.

UNIPOM: UN India-Pakistan Observation Mission, 1965–1966; headquarters: Lahore and Amristar; purpose: supervise cease-fire along India-Pakistan border; strength: 100 military observers; cost: $1.7 million.

UNEF II: Second UN Emergency Force, 1973–1979; headquarters: Ismailia; purpose: supervise buffer zone between Israeli and Egyptian forces; strength: 7,000 military personnel; cost: $450 million.

UNGOMAP: UN Good Offices Mission in Afghanistan and Pakistan, 1988–1990; headquarters: Kabul and Islamabad; purpose: ensure implementation of agreements on situation in Afghanistan; strength: 50 military observers; cost: $14 million.

UNIIMOG: UN Iran-Iraq Military Observer Group, 1988–1991; headquarters: Tehran and Baghdad; purpose: verify and supervise cease-fire between Iran and Iraq; strength: 400 military observers; cost: $180 million.

UNAVEM I: First UN Angola Verification Mission, 1989–1991; headquarters: Luanda; purpose: verify withdrawal of Cuban troops from Angola; strength: 70 military observers; cost: $16.4 million.

UNTAG: UN Transition Assistance Group, 1989–1990; headquarters: Windhoek, Namibia; purpose: ensure the independence of Namibia and verify elections; strength: 9,000 military, police, and civilian staff; cost: $370 million.

ONUCA: UN Observer Group in Central America, 1989–1992; headquarters: Tegucigalpa, Honduras; purpose: verify cessation of aid to irregular fighters in Central America and monitor cease-fire between Nicaraguan parties; strength: 1,100 military observers and personnel; cost: $89 million.

UNIKOM: UN Iraq-Kuwait Observation Mission, 1991–2003; headquarters: Umm Qasr, Iraq; purpose: observe cease-fire line between
Iraq and Kuwait after Gulf War; strength: 50 observers and civilian
staff; cost: $12 million.

UNAVEM II: Second UN Angola Verification Mission, 1991–1995;
headquarters: Luanda; purpose: monitor cease-fire between government and UNITA rebel forces and observe elections; strength: at
height, 700 military, police, and civilian personnel; cost: $176 mil-
lion.

ONUSAL: UN Observer Mission in El Salvador, 1991–1995; headquarters: San Salvador; purpose: verify implementation of all agreements between government and FMLN rebel group, including
cease-fire; strength: 1,000 military and police observers, 140 civilian staff; cost: $107 million.

UNAMIC: UN Advance Mission in Cambodia, 1991–1992; headquarters: Phnom Penh; purpose: assist Cambodian parties to maintain
cease-fire and landmine clearance; strength: 1,500 military and
civilian personnel; cost: budgeted under UNTAC.

UNTAC: UN Transitional Authority in Cambodia, 1992–1993; headquarters: Phnom Penh; purpose: implement Paris peace agreement;
prepare Cambodia for elections, and monitor cease-fire; strength:
22,000 military and civilian personnel; cost: $1.6 billion.

UNPROFOR: UN Protection Force, 1992–1995; headquarters: Sarajevo; purpose: initially in Croatia for demilitarization of designated
areas, later extended to Bosnia to support delivery of humanitarian
aid and monitor "safe areas"; strength: 39,000 troops, observers,
police, and civilian staff; cost: $4.6 billion.

UNOSOM I: First UN Operation in Somalia, 1992–1993; headquarters:
Mogadishu; purpose: monitor cease-fire and escort delivery of
humanitarian aid, later worked with Unified Task Force (led by the
United States); strength: 4,500 military observers, security personnel, and civilian staff; cost: $43 million.

ONUMOZ: UN Operation in Mozambique, 1992–1994; headquarters:
Maputo; purpose: monitor cease-fire between government and Renamo rebel forces and oversee elections; strength: 8,500 troops, military observers, police, and civilian staff; cost: $490 million.

UNOSOM II: Second UN Operation in Somalia, 1993–1995; headquarters: Mogadishu; purpose: establish throughout Somalia a secure
environment for humanitarian assistance; strength: 28,000 military
and police personnel; cost: $1.6 billion.

UNOMUR: UN Observer Mission in Uganda-Rwanda, 1993–1994;
headquarters: Kabale, Uganda; purpose: monitor border between
Uganda and Rwanda and verify that no weapons were being taken

into Rwanda; strength: 81 military observers plus staff; cost: $2.3 million.

UNOMIL: UN Observer Mission in Liberia, 1993–1997; headquarters: Monrovia; purpose: monitor and assist ECOWAS West African peacekeeping force to end civil war; strength: 380 military observers, civilian staff, and UN volunteers; cost: $100 million.

UNMIH: UN Mission in Haiti, 1993–1996; headquarters: Port-au-Prince; purpose: implement Governors Island Agreement and create a stable environment for elections; strength: 1,700 military, police, and civilian personnel; cost: $316 million.

UNAMIR: UN Assistance Mission in Rwanda, 1993–1996; headquarters: Kigali; purpose: originally to monitor Arusha peace agreement between Rwandese parties but, caught in genocide, had to readjust several times; strength: originally 2,500 military personnel, then dropped to 270 in April–May 1994, then raised to 5,500; cost: $454 million.

UNASOG: UN Aouzou Strip Observer Group, May–June 1994; headquarters: Aouzou; purpose: verify withdrawal of Libya from Aouzou Strip in Chad according to decision of the International Court of Justice; strength: 15 military observers and staff; cost: $64,000.

UNMOT: UN Mission of Observers in Tajikistan, 1994–2000; headquarters: Dushanbe; purpose: monitor cease-fire between government and United Tajik Opposition and monitor 1997 peace agreement; strength: at height, 120 military observers; cost: $64 million.

UNAVEM III: Third UN Verification Mission, 1995–1997; headquarters: Luanda; purpose: assist government and UNITA rebel forces to restore peace; strength: 4,220 military troops, observers, and police; cost: $820 million.

UNCRO: UN Confidence Restoration Operation in Croatia, 1995–1996; headquarters: Zagreb; purpose: replace UNPROFOR, monitor crossing of military supplies over specified borders, facilitate humanitarian assistance to Bosnia, and assist a secure environment in Croatia; strength: 7,000 military troops, observers, and police; cost: budgeted under UNPROFOR.

UNPREDEP: UN Preventive Deployment Force (Macedonia), 1995–1999; headquarters: Skopje; purpose: preventive deployment along border, a first for UN, to deter conflict in rest of former Yugoslavia from spilling over into Macedonia, last extension vetoed by China; strength: 1,110 military troops, observers, and police; cost: $200 million.

UNMIBH: UN Mission in Bosnia and Herzegovina, 1995–2002; headquarters: Sarajevo; purpose: oversee police and police reform and coordinate humanitarian assistance following Dayton Agreements; strength: 2,050 police and military personnel; cost: not available.

UNTAES: UN Transitional Administration for Eastern Slavonia, Baranja, and Western Sirmium, 1996–1998; headquarters: Vukovar: purpose: administer the territory during interim period to provide stability and prepare for elections before area was returned to Croatia; strength: at height, 5,000 troops, 600 police, 470 civilian personnel; cost: not available.

UNMOP: UN Mission of Observers in Prevlaka, 1996–2002; headquarters: Cavtat; purpose: take over from UNCRO the task of monitoring demilitarization of Prevlaka peninsula, an area disputed by Croatia and the Federal Republic of Yugoslavia; strength: 30 military observers and staff; cost: budgeted under UNMIBH.

UNSMIH: UN Support Mission in Haiti, 1996–1997; headquarters: Port-au-Prince; purpose: monitor and train a national police force and promote capacity building in the country; strength: at height, 1,500 troops and police; cost: $56 million.

MINUGUA: UN Verification Mission in Guatemala, January–May 1997; headquarters: Guatemala City; purpose: verify cease-fire between government and Guatemalan National Revolutionary Unity rebel forces and verify demobilization; strength: 188 military observers and police; cost: $4.6 million.

MONUA: UN Observer Mission in Angola, June 1997–1999; headquarters: Luanda; purpose: consolidate peace and reconciliation; strength: at height, 3,550 troops, military observers, and police; cost: $300 million.

UNTMIH: UN Transition Mission in Haiti, August–November 1997; headquarters: Port-au-Prince; purpose: further professionalization of police; strength: 250 police, 50 military personnel; cost: $7 million.

MIPONUH: UN Civilian Police Mission in Haiti, December 1997–2000; headquarters: Port-au-Prince; purpose: train specialized police units and mentor police performance; strength: 330 police, 90 staff; cost: $60 million.

MINURCA: UN Mission in the Central African Republic, 1998–2000; headquarters: Bangui; purpose: enhance security, monitor disarmament and destroy weapons, and support elections; strength: 1,350 military, 24 police, 114 civilian staff, plus UN volunteers; cost: $100 million.

UNOMSIL: UN Observer Mission in Sierra Leone, 1998–1999; headquarters: Freetown; purpose: monitor situation in Sierra Leone and disarmament and demobilization; strength: 200 military observers and staff; cost: $60 million.

UNTAET: UN Transitional Administration in East Timor, October 1999–May 2002; headquarters: Dili; purpose: after August 1999 ballot, in which people chose independence, administer territory and prepare for elections and independence; strength: 6,300 troops, 1,300 police, 120 military observers, 740 civilian staff; cost: $1.2 billion.

Current Peacekeeping Operations

UNTSO: UN Truce Supervision Organization, 1948–present; headquarters: Jerusalem; purpose: monitor cease-fires, report to UN headquarters, assist other peacekeeping operations in the region; strength: 153 military observers, 100 civilian staff; cost: $26 million for 2003, total not available.

UNMOGIP: UN Military Observer Group in India and Pakistan, 1949–present; headquarters: Rawalpindi and Srinigar; purpose: supervise cease-fire line between India and Pakistan regarding disputed area of Jammu and Kashmir; strength: 44 military observers, 22 civilian staff; cost: $9.2 million for 2003, total not available.

UNFICYP: UN Peacekeeping Force in Cyprus, 1964–present; headquarters: Nicosia; purpose: supervise cease-fire and buffer zone between Greek and Turkish Cypriots and provide humanitarian assistance; strength: 1,225 troops, 35 police, 44 civilian staff; cost: $46 million for 2003, total not available, paid by voluntary contributions.

UNDOF: UN Disengagement Observer Force, 1974–present; headquarters: Camp Faouar; purpose: maintain cease-fire between Syria and Israel; strength: 1,043 troops, 80 military observers, 37 civilian staff; cost: $42 million for 2003, total not available.

UNIFIL: UN Interim Force in Lebanon, 1978–present; headquarters: Naqoura; purpose: confirm Israeli withdrawal from Lebanon, restore peace, and restore government authority; strength: 2,000 troops, 50 military observers, 118 civilian personnel; cost: $94 million for 2003, total not available.

MINURSO: UN Mission for the Referendum in Western Sahara, 1991–present; headquarters: Laayoune; purpose: monitor cease-fire between Morroco and Polisario in Western Sahara and organize and conduct referendum to decide status of territory; strength: 400 troops, military observers, police, and civilian staff; cost: $43 million for 2003, total not available.

UNOMIG: UN Observer Mission in Georgia, 1993–present; headquarters: Sukhumi: purpose: verify cease-fire and separation of forces of the government and Abkhaz authorities; strength: 115 military personnel, 100 civilian personnel; cost: $32 million for 2003, total not available.

UNMIK: UN Mission in Kosovo, June 1999–present: headquarters: Pristina; purpose: provide an interim administration of province after genocide attacks and NATO bombing in spring 1999, restore order, provide police and justice system, train new police, and monitor elections; strength: for 2003, 4,718 international police, 1,112 civilian staff; cost: $330 million for 2003, total not available.

UNAMSIL: UN Mission in Sierra Leone, October 1999–present; headquarters: Freetown; purpose: implement Lomé peace agreement to end ten-year civil war, disarmament, demobilization, and reintegration of former combatants, and rebuild and stabilize country; strength: at height, 17,500 troops, 260 military observers, 125 police, 320 civilian staff; cost: $543 million for 2003, total not available.

MONUC: UN Organization Mission in the Democratic Republic of Congo, November 1999–present; headquarters: Kinshasa; purpose: monitor cease-fire agreement, facilitate humanitarian assistance, and support landmine removal; strength: 7,500 troops, 550 military observers, 60 police, 600 civilian personnel; cost: $600 million for 2003, total not available.

UNMEE: UN Mission in Ethiopia and Eritrea, June 2000–present; headquarters: Asmara and Addis Ababa; purpose: monitor cease-fire over border dispute, ensure observance of security measures, and provide good offices; strength: 3,900 troops, 220 military observers, 240 civilian staff; cost: $197 million for 2003, total not available.

UNAMA: UN Assistance Mission in Afghanistan, March 2002–present; headquarters: Kabul; purpose: coordinate all UN activities, support transition process, fulfill Bonn Agreement, and manage humanitarian relief; strength: 443 civilian staff; cost: $38 million for 2003, total not available.

UNMISET: UN Mission of Support in East Timor, May 2002–present; headquarters: Dili; purpose: assist development of country and hand over operational responsibilities to government; strength: 3,370 troops, 95 military observers, 390 police, 440 civilian staff; cost: $193 million for 2003, total not available.

MINUCI: UN Mission in Côte d'Ivoire, May 2003–present; headquarters: Abidjan; purpose: facilitate implementation of agreement signed by Ivorian parties and assist ECOWAS and French troops; strength: 30 military observers, 40 civilian staff; cost: budget not available.

UNMIL: UN Mission in Liberia, October 2003–present; headquarters: Monrovia; purpose: monitor cease-fire at end of civil war in

Liberia, replace ECOWAS troops, and monitor human rights and elections; strength: authorized 15,000 troops, 1,115 police, plus staff; cost: budget is in planning stages.

Notes

1. For an examination of peace operations conducted by the League of Nations and the early days of the United Nations, see Alan James, *The Politics of Peacekeeping* (New York: Praeger, 1969).

2. Steven R. Ratner, *The New UN Peacekeeping: Building Peace in Lands of Conflict After the Cold War* (New York: St. Martin's Press, 1996); see chap. 4, "Fits and Starts: The League's and UN's Early Efforts at the New Peacekeeping," pp. 89–116.

3. Ibid.

4. Ibid., p. 95.

5. Karl Birgisson, "United Nations Special Committee on the Balkans," in William Durch, ed., *The Evolution of UN Peacekeeping* (New York: St. Martin's Press, 1993), pp. 77–83.

6. For a complete list of UN peacekeeping operations with start and end dates, see www.un.org/depts/dpko/dpko/home.shtml.

7. Mona Ghali, "United Nations Truce Supervision Organization: 1948–Present," in Durch, *Evolution of UN Peacekeeping*, pp. 84–85.

8. UN oral history interview with Brian Urquhart, July 20, 1984, located in the UN Dag Hammarskjöld Library, p. 6.

9. UN oral history interview with Brian Urquhart, October 15, 1984, p. 17.

10. Ibid.

11. Interview with Urquhart, July 20, 1984, p. 8.

12. Ibid., p. 9.

13. Interview videotaped with Brian Urquhart, New York, January 21, 2003, at UN headquarters.

14. Interview with Urquhart, July 20, 1984, p. 10.

15. Ibid.

16. *The Blue Helmets: A Review of United Nations Peace-Keeping*, 3rd ed. (New York: United Nations, 1996), pp. 42–43.

17. Interview with Urquhart, July 20, 1984, p. 13.

18. Ibid., p. 16.

19. UN oral history interview with Brian Urquhart, June 27, 1984, p. 9.

20. Mona Ghali, "United Nations Emergency Force I" and "United Nations Emergency Force II," in Durch, *Evolution of UN Peacekeeping*, pp. 104–151.

21. Brian Urquhart, *Hammarskjöld* (New York: Harper and Row, 1972), p. 389.

22. Confidential letter written by Ralph Bunche to Dag Hammarskjöld, June 27, 1960, UN Archives Library, S-216-1-2, RJB-trip to Congo, Bunche's letter/report to S-G, June 27–July 4, 1960.

23. Rosalyn Higgins, *United Nations Peacekeeping, 1946–67: Documents and Commentary*, vol. 3, *Africa* (Oxford: Oxford University Press, 1980), p. 12.

24. Ibid., p. 395.

25. Interview with Urquhart, October 19, 1984, p. 3.

26. Ibid., p. 2.

27. *Blue Helmets*, p. 177.

28. Interview with Urquhart, October 19, 1984, p. 5.

29. Ibid., pp. 6–7.

30. Ibid., p. 7.

31. Ibid., pp. 8–9.

32. *Blue Helmets,* p. 184.

33. Ibid., p. 192.

34. Ibid., pp. 194–195.

35. William Durch, "The UN Operation in the Congo: 1960–1964," in Durch, *Evolution of UN Peacekeeping,* pp. 323–324.

36. Ibid., pp. 331–332.

37. *Blue Helmets,* p. 115.

38. Yale-UN oral history interview with Ghassan Tueni, Beirut, Lebanon, March 17–18, 1998.

39. Ibid.

40. Yale-UN oral history interview with Timur Goksel, March 16, 1998.

41. Yale-UN oral history interview with Bernard Aronson, October 9, 1997.

42. Ian Johnstone, *Rights and Reconciliation: UN Strategies in El Salvador,* International Peace Academy Occasional Paper (Boulder: Lynne Rienner, 1995), p. 15.

43. *Blue Helmets,* p. 427.

44. Johnstone, *Rights and Reconciliation,* p. 46.

45. *Blue Helmets,* p. 287.

46. Ibid, p. 293.

47. Mats Berdal, "The United Nations in Bosnia, 1992–1995: Faithful Scapegoat to the World?" in Jean Krasno, Don Daniel, and Bradd Hayes, eds., *Leveraging for Success in United Nations Peace Operations* (Westport, Conn.: Praeger, 2003), chap. 1, p. 3.

48. Videotaped interview with Urquhart, January 21, 2003.

PART 3

Processes of Global Burden Sharing

9

Financing the United Nations

Jeffrey Laurenti

Far from being a dry, specialized subject of little interest outside the institution, the finances of the United Nations are the subject of high political drama, marked by conflicts among competing claims of global idealism, state sovereignty, international law, crass self-interest, and national power. The lifeblood of any political entity is cash flow: the financial resources it is able to devote to the priorities decided by its decisionmakers. States enjoy broad authority to extract those resources by taxation, restrained only by occasional constitutional limits, adverse consequences to their economic competitiveness, and the potential rebellion of irate taxpayers. States may delegate limited or broad taxing authority to inferior jurisdictions; thus, many U.S. states allow local governments and school districts to finance their activities through property taxes. At the international level, governments have been chary of delegating taxing authority to international agencies, and instead have elected to allocate funds for common international purposes from taxes they collect themselves. But the political battles over funding can be as contentious in global fora as in town meetings.

The United Nations, together with its specialized agencies, related institutions like the World Bank and International Monetary Fund (IMF), and other global and regional organizations, rely upon their Member States to contribute the funds needed to finance their activities. The United Nations requires approximately $1.58 billion a year (2004) for its regular budget to defray the costs of its core operations. Its political bodies—the General Assembly, the Security Council, and the Economic and Social Council—cost $12.7 million a year. The Secretariat, which carries out the mandates of these bodies, requires $1.57 billion a year in assessments. Programs that operate in the field, including those like the UN Children's Fund (UNICEF) and the UN High Commissioner for Refugees (UNHCR), spend $5 billion a year, raised primarily through voluntary contributions. A separate budget is formulated for peacekeeping. The UN regular budget and peacekeeping costs are financially supported through mandatory contributions of Member States.

A dozen specialized agencies, from the Food and Agriculture Organization to the World Meteorological Organization, all have their own assemblies of Member States, and most have smaller executive boards that provide policy guidance during the one or two years between meetings of the plenary assemblies; they have their own technically specialized secretariats. They also have their own programs in the field and their own budgets, which totaled $3 billion in 2000.

The one common thread for all of the UN-related organizations is that their funding comes almost entirely from the governments of their Member States. Those governments may collectively decide on a budget and raise the agreed amount by an assessment that all are bound to pay, or they may individually decide to contribute funds on a voluntary basis to specific programs. Either way, those funds are collected from citizens by their national tax systems and are allocated to the UN system by states. Even UNICEF, which has built the best grassroots, independent fundraising apparatus of any international agency, receives just 19 percent of its funds from nongovernmental sources.

There is little apparent interest, among either governments or citizens, in allowing international agencies a broad, autonomous funding stream of their own. The notion of yet another layer of political organization extracting taxes, at an international level of "community" to which relatively few people feel emotional allegiance, might dismay tax-weary citizens in any number of countries. Such possibilities also stir intense concern among nationalists fearful of creeping "world government." For the foreseeable future, financing for the UN system will come overwhelmingly from national treasuries.

This means, of course, that funding for UN organizations depends on the continued commitment of national politicians to the common purposes they share with leaders in other member nations. This commitment may waiver, especially when a government has political objectives strongly opposed by most other members of the world body. Although Member States have bound themselves to honor the process established in the UN Charter for approving and apportioning UN expenses, at times they have chosen to spurn those obligations. When the disaffected state is a large contributor, the affected international organization may swiftly feel the impact.

United Nations financing has thus become a political battleground between those who see the Organization's work as essential and effective, complementing countries' various national interests, and those who are skeptical of its global agenda and efficiency and suspicious that it may constrain national agendas. At stake in these conflicts is not only the financial solvency of the United Nations, but also the matter of which states and decisionmaking bodies shape the goals of international agencies and institutions. At all levels, decisions on budget priorities reflect the fundamental political values and interests of constituencies and political leaders alike.

Budget Making in the United Nations

From the start, the presumption of the states constituting the United Nations was that member governments would jointly decide its spending priorities through its political bodies, with delegates hammering out any differences among their respective governments' views on the activities the United Nations should undertake. The agreed core expenses would be paid by assessment on its entire membership. In acceding to the UN Charter, sovereign states assigned certain financial powers to the General Assembly, and obligated themselves to honor its collective decisions. In short, the Charter was to create a framework that would be legally binding on the Member States that ratified it; the United Nations was not to be financed through an annual pledging conference in which each member would announce how much it chose to donate that year.

The financing provisions of the Charter are succinct. The General Assembly shall "approve the budget of the Organization," and the expenses "shall be borne by the Members as apportioned by the General Assembly" (Article 17). The Assembly's decisions on budgetary questions—whether spending or raising money—are defined as "important questions [that] shall be made by a two-thirds majority of the Members present and voting" (Article 18). In fact, this "power of the purse" is one of the very few areas in which nations have conferred authority upon the General Assembly to make decisions binding on governments outside UN headquarters.

Initially, the agreed expenses were quite modest. These included a small Secretariat, which was to service meetings of the intergovernmental bodies with translations, documents, and administrative support; the handful of mediation missions the fledgling United Nations was handed in its earliest days, such as the effort to mediate an amicable political solution to the competing claims of Arabs and Jews as the British mandate over Palestine drew near its end; and the creation of a UN statistical office to compile reliable and comparable data from and about all nations. In its first year, the UN General Assembly approved a budget of $24 million. However, new responsibilities emerged, such as the creation of truce supervisory missions in Kashmir and Palestine, commissions on human rights, narcotic drugs, the status of women, and economic commissions for each region. There were also the costs of constructing a headquarters and the eventual establishment of information centers around the world, as well as core staffing for new assistance programs for children and refugees. These tasks represented the priorities the international community could agree upon, even as political hostilities deepened between

East and West. These priorities led to long-term budget growth, commensurate with the economic expansion that followed post–World War II reconstruction.

The system that evolved for budgetary decisionmaking is in some ways similar to that of states. Budgets are adopted on a biennial basis. Departments of the Secretariat and the agencies, programs, and commissions that receive at least some support from the regular budget—that is, the budget that Member States collectively approve and pay by assessment—submit proposed activity and spending plans for the coming biennium. The UN Department of Management assembles these into an integrated budget plan within the fiscal guidelines set by the Secretary-General and, so far as they are consistent with one another, by the General Assembly. Department heads, and government representatives in New York, may intercede directly with the Secretary-General to secure his recommendation on a budget line for particular "posts" (staff positions) or program priorities before he submits his budget proposal to the General Assembly; it is usually easier to win political approval of a new item if it has been accommodated within the Secretariat's spending plan than if it has not. That document also informs the Assembly of planned "extrabudgetary" spending—the programs and staff positions that the United Nations will undertake during the biennium with supplementary resources, usually voluntary donations dedicated by individual governments for specific activities, assuming those resources are realized.

From the moment the Secretariat's budget request goes to the General Assembly, it becomes subject to intense intergovernmental politics. The first chokepoint is the Advisory Committee on Administrative and Budgetary Questions (ACABQ), a panel of eighteen individuals elected for a three-year term by the General Assembly for their supposed expertise in fiscal policy and public administration, with a fixed number of seats allocated to each of the world's regions. "Expertise" often consists of being attached to one's national mission at the United Nations, and thus having become acquainted with a number of UN activities—and more important, with fellow delegates, whose votes determine who is elected to the committee. Because members of the ACABQ, which is a standing committee of the General Assembly, technically serve the whole United Nations as experts, rather than their own government, the United Nations provides for their living expenses in New York for each day the committee is in session. In a UN world where diplomats are shuffled in and out of New York every few years, ACABQ members have a remarkable longevity; throughout the last quarter of the twentieth century, its chairmanship was held continuously by a single individual: Tanzania's Conrad Mselle. Long tenure gives the panel members the institutional knowledge to stand up to the UN bureaucracy. Panel members are pleased to be seen as the scourge of the Secretariat, which often reviles the committee as a highly political group of micromanagers.

The ACABQ technically does not represent governments and is only advisory to the intergovernmental decisionmaking bodies, the General Assembly and its Fifth Committee, which deals with budgetary and administrative matters. But the ACABQ effectively is the primary budgetary decisionmaking organ in the UN political process. ACABQ budgetary recommendations are generally accepted as baselines by the Fifth Committee.

Representatives to the Fifth Committee—a "committee of the whole," meaning that all Member States belong—are typically mid-level diplomats whose duty during their few years in New York is to master the basics of the UN budget and strike the political deals needed to forge agreement on budgetary matters. Only a handful of delegates frame the debate, because within each regional group a few diligent diplomats emerge as the most knowledgeable or influential, and therefore as spokespersons for the group. The major dividing line at the start of the twenty-first century, as it had been for three decades, is between the industrialized countries and the developing countries, known in UN parlance as the Group of 77 (G-77, so called because 77 states originally formed the group). Both blocs have regional subgroups as well as hard-liners and moderates. At least since the 1980s, the fifteen Member States of the European Union (EU), becoming twenty-five members in 2004, have seen themselves as the moderates in the industrialized group, trying to broker deals between the G-77 and the most adamant opponents of UN spending, such as the United States. In the G-77, most Latin American countries are thought to be moderate on budgetary controversies—with the notable exception of Cuba, which is consistently one of the most strenuous advocates of increased spending for programs to benefit, at least symbolically, developing-country interests. With very distinct subgroups in the Arab world, South Asia, and newly industrializing East Asia, Asia is less cohesive than sub-Saharan Africa. Developing countries with skeletal staffing in their missions (and even less support from their capitals) often follow the lead of the few delegates from their region who have forceful personalities and a seeming knowledge of the budget. Once a budget is approved in the Fifth Committee, its adoption by the General Assembly—which is, after all, composed of the same Member States—is generally a foregone conclusion.

During the 1970s, different regional group priorities could be accommodated through budgetary growth, and in that decade UN regular budgets— even accounting for the oil-shock inflation of that period—grew at their fastest rate in the UN's history. By the 1980s, under pressure particularly from the conservative-minded leadership in the United States, real budget growth was cut sharply—indeed, the priority goal across all UN organizations in that period was budgetary restraint under a cap of "zero real growth." In the 1990s, the United States successfully pressed for an even tighter cap of "zero nominal growth." In an atmosphere of budgetary shrinkage, resource battles became particularly bitter. Western calls for increased staff for activities like human rights monitoring were parried by G-77 demands for more staffing for their development priorities and its members' regional projects, like expansion of the UN offices in Nairobi.

The Charter provision for a two-thirds majority to approve budget resolutions ensured that the Organization's growth for its first decades reflected the priorities of the Western countries that, with the Latin Americans, enjoyed a comfortable majority in the General Assembly until the early 1960s. By the 1970s, poorer countries had gained their freedom from colonial rule and had become a large majority of the membership. They reshaped UN budgetary priorities to their needs, which included development and a "fairer" economic order. Some Western governments wavered in their commitment to majoritarian democratic principles when they were no longer in the majority, and eliminating majority budgetary voting became a priority of U.S. policymakers in particular. By the late 1980s, a new system of "consensus" budget making was put in place, as we shall see below, that effectively ensured a single-power veto on budget levels. The United States deployed its financial dominance to ensure zero-growth and even shrinking real budgets for a decade.

By the start of the twenty-first century, most European Union countries were no longer willing to support adherence to zero-growth budgets. The United States, however, was still committed by congressional mandate to such a cap on UN-assessed budgets, and Japan was sympathetic. With the split between the fifteen EU members and the U.S.-Japan partnership, these seventeen countries, which have been assessed about four-fifths of the UN regular budget, no longer presented a united front in support of freezing the budget.

Assessments as Obligations:
The Cornerstone of UN Finances

The political process surrounding allocation decisions in the regular budget rests on a fundamental assumption: that after the budget is approved, the funds to implement it will materialize. The amount required to finance the agreed expenses is apportioned among Member States by a vote of the General Assembly. The Secretariat notifies each Member State at the start of each year of the amount of its assessed contribution, and its payment for the year is due in February. The system depends, of course, on each member paying its assessed share; hence the Charter makes the payment of assessments a treaty obligation of membership.

Anticipating that some governments might fail to provide their share of the funds for the common enterprise, the Charter's ·drafters included an enforcement mechanism in Article 19:

> A Member of the United Nations which is in arrears in the payment of its
> financial contributions to the Organization shall have no vote in the General

> Assembly if the amount of its arrears equals or exceeds the amount of the contributions due from it for the preceding two full years. The General Assembly may, nevertheless, permit such a Member to vote if it is satisfied that the failure to pay is due to conditions beyond the control of the Member.

Such an enforcement mechanism was farsighted, because not all political forces in major states were easily reconciled to the notion that the full membership of the United Nations should set budget priorities and levy assessments that national governments would be legally bound to pay. Opponents of entangling international organizations, especially in the United States, have seen such authority as an infringement on unfettered national sovereignty. In 1919, critics of the League of Nations, led by then–chairman of the Senate Foreign Relations Committee Henry Cabot Lodge, demanded a reservation to U.S. ratification of the League that would have declared, "The United States shall not be obligated to contribute to any expenses of the League of Nations, or of the Secretariat, or of any commission, or committee, or conference, or other agency organized under the League of Nations," leaving explicitly to the U.S. Congress full discretion to decide how much it would choose to appropriate.[1] Neither the United States nor any other state ever attached such a reservation to its ratification of the Charter of the United Nations, but at times this spirit has stirred in the political debate.

The Charter's financing framework functioned adequately in the UN's first fifteen years. The General Assembly approved and apportioned UN expenses, and Member States paid their assessments. The UN's first peace and security missions, in Palestine and Kashmir, were established as part of the Organization's regular budget—from which these truce supervisory commissions are still financed to this day. While the United Nations became a major sparring ground in the great ideological and political confrontation between East and West, most of its work program and budget were sufficiently insulated from those pressures. No major member sought to withdraw financial support during these early years. However, the UN intervention in the disintegrating Congo in 1960 ultimately shattered this tacit consensus among the major powers.

A Constitutional Crisis

Having successfully pioneered the concept of UN "peacekeeping" forces to guarantee the Israeli-Egyptian border after the 1956 Suez crisis, Secretary-General Dag Hammarskjöld sought to utilize peacekeeping once again in the Congo as the sprawling, newly independent territory descended into chaos. But international peacekeeping in a civil conflict proved problematic, foreshadowing the problems of nation building in failed states with which the United Nations would later be asked to deal after the end of the Cold War.

Moreover, various local antagonists moved quickly to line up patrons among outside powers, despite Hammarskjöld's painstaking efforts to quarantine the Congolese conflict from Cold War contamination.

At one point or another, Hammarskjöld's Congo policy displeased every major power or bloc, but none more than the Soviet Union. Moscow quickly soured on the operation, seeing its real purpose as an adroit process to preserve Western influence after formal decolonization. The Soviets were soon vetoing Security Council resolutions that authorized assertive UN actions. They became enraged when Hammarskjöld obtained authority from the General Assembly under the much-contested "Uniting for Peace" resolution, which asserted the Assembly's right to take decisions on peace and security policy when the Council was hamstrung by vetoes. Insisting that the Charter had conferred authority for peace and security policy exclusively on the Security Council, the Soviet Union branded the Congo operation illegal and re fused to recognize any assessment voted by the Assembly to pay for the mission. In this position Moscow enjoyed support, predictably, from its dependent Communist allies, but also from France. The French government wanted to keep security matters away from the unpredictable Assembly and in the hands of the Council, where it had a veto. The General Assembly sought an advisory opinion from the International Court of Justice, which ruled that Member States were indeed legally bound to pay all peacekeeping assessments adopted by the Assembly. Moscow was unmoved.

The Soviets did not succeed in scuttling the Congo operation. But Moscow's experiment in massive withholding wreaked havoc on UN finances. By 1964 it and other recalcitrant Member States had failed to pay fully a quarter of the Congo operation's $332 million cumulative cost, forcing the United Nations to raid its reserve and working capital accounts to pay the most pressing bills. Troop-contributing countries and suppliers went unpaid.

Moreover, the delinquencies precipitated a political crisis that threatened the Organization's very survival. In 1964, when cumulative Soviet arrears reached the two-year threshold specified in Article 19, the United Nations was faced with the choice of either depriving the Soviet Union and its allies of their votes, which would have provoked their withdrawal, or of nullifying the UN's sole sanction for fulfillment of members' financial obligations. The United States submitted a legal memorandum that warned:

> Failure to apply the Article would tempt Members to pick and choose, with impunity, from among their obligations to the United Nations, refusing to pay for items they dislike even though those items were authorized by the overwhelming vote of the Members. Indeed, the Soviet Union has already said that it will not pay for certain items in the regular budgets. How could any organization function on such a fiscal quicksand?
> Failure to apply the Article to a great power simply because it is a great power would undermine the constitutional integrity of the United Nations,

and could sharply affect the attitude toward the Organization of those who have always been its strongest supporters. . . .

[I]f it cannot get from its Members the funds to support its acts, all would be the losers. . . . Loyalty to the Organization, respect for the International Court of Justice and the rule of law, and consideration for the overwhelming views of Members, should be overriding.[2]

Diplomats that year earned their pay with a crafty dodge. Putting survival of the Organization above all else, they slogged through the General Assembly session without taking a recorded vote on anything. The only resolutions brought to the Assembly floor were those that all members agreed to adopt by consensus. With no votes, there was no occasion to invoke Article 19, and the United Nations survived as a universal organization.

The United Nations limped through the year with emergency voluntary contributions, largely from the West. In order to obtain agreement on a new peacekeeping mission—a UN force in Cyprus to keep warring Greeks and Turks apart—the West had to agree it would be financed strictly by voluntary contributions from the countries that wished to pay for it, an anomalous arrangement that lasted three decades. Happily, the Congo operation itself ended in 1964, after secessionist provinces were reintegrated into the Congo and central government authority was finally established. The UN's political crisis was resolved by a 1965 General Assembly decision to exclude unpaid assessments for the Congo operation from the calculation of the status of contributions and arrearages that would trigger the suspension of voting rights pursuant to Article 19. In exchange, the Soviets agreed to recognize that peacekeeping assessments were indeed a legally binding obligation of Member States.[3]

The opponents of the Congo operation appear in practice to have won the peacekeeping debate on constitutional principle, as in the nearly four decades that have followed, the General Assembly has not authorized a single one of the UN's dozens of peace operations in circumvention of the Council. Indeed, the United States at the start of the twenty-first century would almost certainly oppose any such circumvention as contrary to the Charter. But advocates of international law appeared to have won the constitutional debate on the legal obligation to pay UN assessments. By the late 1970s, virtually all UN Member States had accepted the principle that assessments collectively voted, including special assessments for peacekeeping, are binding on all.

Disaffection of an Outsized Contributor

In the 1970s, however, the United States began to deploy nonpayment as a political weapon, reflecting Washington's deepening estrangement from the United Nations as its influence there ebbed. By the UN's quarter-century anniversary in 1970, the liberation from European colonial rule and admission to the United Nations of scores of poor countries in Africa, Asia, and the Caribbean, together with an intensifying backlash against the U.S. war in Vietnam, deprived the United States of its traditional dominance in the General Assembly. Washington suffered its first major political defeat in the United Nations in 1971, losing its bid to preserve a seat for China's exiled Kuomintang government in Taipei when the Assembly recognized the Communist regime in Beijing as the representative of "China." The U.S. Congress reacted angrily by unilaterally slashing the U.S. UN contribution in retaliation. The General Assembly accepted the lower U.S. assessment level a year later—reaching a target originally agreed upon in 1946—when it admitted the two German states to membership. Their additional contributions made a reduction in the U.S. payment possible without having to raise assessments on the other members in order to cover costs.

As the 1970s wore on, the many developing countries showed group solidarity in pressing a common agenda on the reluctant few rich and powerful states. The glue that held together the different regional groups of the poverty-ridden South was a shared interest in a redistribution of economic power from the privileged North. Political logrolling resulted in the Third World uniting behind regional special causes as well, such as the Arabs' crusade against Israel and the Africans' campaign against continued white rule in southern Africa. Some of these issues—and the fact that the Soviets were in enthusiastic support of the Third World agenda—touched political lightning rods in the West. While European governments often sought to blur the confrontation lines, the United States was more prone to resist the challenges and pretenses of the Assembly majority, whose members, critics said, were effectively powerless in the "real" world.

One means by which Washington could remind other UN members of power realities was financial. In the late 1970s, as resentment against Third World domination of the agenda at the UN smoldered in Washington, the United States chose to resist the new majority by withholding some of its assessed contributions. An early drawing of the line occurred in 1978, when, at the initiative of freshman senator Jesse Helms of North Carolina, Congress targeted the spreading inclusion of "technical assistance" funds—monies for development assistance—in the assessed budgets of UN agencies. While Western countries, including the United States, had long contributed funds to UN agencies on a voluntary basis for development aid, the appearance of technical assistance grants in assessed budgets raised the specter that Third World majorities might begin to vote ever-larger assistance programs into agency budgets that Western governments would have a treaty obligation to pay. The U.S. Congress stipulated that the funds it appropriated for agency dues could not be paid if the assessed budgets included technical assistance programs. UN agencies refused to conform to that condition for U.S. contributions, and the Carter administration finally persuaded Congress to rescind it. But an unwritten understanding had been reached. The expansion of technical assistance programs in regular UN agency budgets ground to a halt.

Several controversies pitted the United States against developing-country majorities on an issue on which feelings traditionally ran strong in the United States: the Arab-Israeli conflict. In one such case, the United States followed its Israeli allies in bitter resistance to a proposal to establish an office in the UN Secretariat to help protect "the rights of the Palestinian people" and prepare for their self-rule in concert with the Palestine Liberation Organization, which Israeli and U.S. officials denounced at that time as terrorist. When the General Assembly voted to establish the office anyway, Washington branded the expense illegitimate and, by congressional decree in 1980, began deducting 25 percent of the amount budgeted for the office—arguably the proportionate share of the cost for the United States—from the U.S.-assessed contribution. The amount withheld was tiny, and did not intimidate the general membership into dropping its advocacy of Palestinians' rights—nor did Washington ever expect it would. Rather, the act was a symbolic protest intended to demonstrate to concerned domestic constituents Washington's fervent opposition to the Palestinian assertion of national rights. At the same time, this underscored the U.S. refusal to accept a UN program it opposed, despite the fact that an overwhelming majority of Member States supported the program.

Invoking a similar argument against "terrorist groups," congressional supporters of apartheid South Africa's rule in Namibia engineered a similar deduction in 1984. The United States withheld funds against the costs of a UN office in support of the South West Africa People's Organization, the liberation movement that would eventually sweep Namibia's elections at independence. In the same vein, the United States began deducting what it calculated to be its share of the costs of the UN office on the Law of the Sea, a landmark convention the Reagan administration decided to oppose in 1982. Neither of these actions deterred the UN from continuing these programs. In 1985 the U.S. Congress voted to withhold an amount it calculated as the U.S. share of cost-of-living adjustments for UN employees on the ground that these exceeded inflation adjustments for federal employees. Two years later, it mandated a withholding in response to allegations that UN employees from the Soviet Union and China were made to "kick back" much of their salaries to their home governments. Others saw this simply as exorbitant Communist taxes, but Washington conservatives called it a back-door subsidy for Communist enemies. That same year, the United States began holding back part of its contribution in a dispute with the United Nations over the tax treatment of U.S. citizens working for the United Nations.

Washington also began a campaign to halt the traditional growth in UN agency budgets, a move that was consonant with its efforts to halt the expansion of nonmilitary spending domestically. Through the late 1970s, the Western group as a whole had become increasingly resistant to Third World efforts to expand assessed budgets, which often grew faster than the rate of inflation. Now, Washington spelled out a concrete goal: "zero real growth." In this cause, it teamed up with the states of the Soviet bloc, which had always resisted the growth of UN budgets as well as of UN capabilities. For reasons of political prestige, the Soviet Union had traditionally overvalued its economic performance and thus paid artificially high UN assessments; but because of the drain of these assessments on its scarce hard currency reserves, the Soviet Union was consistently the most vociferous foe of UN budget increases.

At the same time, the United States began to raise a fundamental structural question on budgetary decisionmaking: the voting process. It argued that two-thirds majority voting in a one-state/one-vote system was inherently skewed against the small number of wealthy states. If members expect sovereign states to be bound by budgetary decisions of international bodies, said U.S. officials, voting in those bodies should be weighted to reflect each state's assessment—just as it has been in international financial institutions, such as the World Bank and IMF. Predictably, however, voting weighted by wealth and assessments drew a sharply unfavorable response from many states, including virtually all of the poor ones.

To lend muscle to its demands for reform, in 1985 the United States began to deploy the weapon of massive withholding of its assessed contribution, with Congress attaching a stringent condition on the payment of the coming year's assessment to the United Nations: unless the UN General Assembly adopted a system of voting weighted in proportion to each voting member's budgetary contribution, the United States would hold back a fifth of its contribution. Instead of registering a protest at a particular spending item deemed politically obnoxious in Washington, the United States was now using its large financial contribution as leverage for structural changes to tame the UN. Congress then compounded its withholding with a deep reduction in its appropriation for assessments to international organizations; in 1986 the United States paid only $100 million of its $210 million assessment.[4]

While other Member States insisted that the United States had an obligation under international law to pay its assessment, Washington officials dismissed arguments about the sanctity of international law as mere carping about legalisms that would forfeit the unique disruptive power that the large U.S. share of UN expenses gave them to cut through the inertia that often paralyzes multilateral politics. As for any distinction between assessed and voluntary contributions, congressional decisionmakers acknowledged that the former are politically easier to withhold than voluntary contributions. The latter go to specific causes, like children and the environment, to whose defense concerned constituencies are apt to rally, while nobody marches in support of regular budgets that largely support a "bureaucracy" that is faceless, friend-less, and therefore vulnerable. Payment of assessments, in this view, was a political issue, not a legal one.

Washington's withholdings soon brought the United Nations to the brink of insolvency. Reserve and capital accounts were raided to pay current expenses, prepayments were extracted from loyal Member States to get past cash-flow crises, and peacekeeping operations limped along as the regular budget borrowed from peacekeeping budgets, postponing reimbursements to troop-contributing countries until the long-promised U.S. payments came through. By 1987, Member States had reached agreement on a budgetary package that reduced UN staffing, had cut and frozen overall spending, and had established a new process for budgetary decisions that required general consensus—effectively setting aside the Charter rule of two-thirds majority voting. The new process gave Washington far more leverage, but not quite the level of control, and certainly not the wealth-weighted voting, it had sought.

The 1985–1988 withholding crisis starkly demonstrated the latent weak-ness of a financing system dependent on the willingness of major states to ful-fill dues obligations as a matter of international law. The United States had effectively wielded withholding of its large share of dues expenses as an instrument of power over the Organization to achieve the structural reforms it desired, breaking through the immobilization of a UN political system orga-nized around regional voting blocs. Many of the reforms were, to be sure, sup-ported in principle by other wealthy countries, and so represented an interest broader than just Washington's. On the other hand, the other Member States had refused simply to submit to Washington's demands, and a hard-fought negotiation produced a political compromise on reform of the budget process that accommodated the core interests of all major groups.

Late in 1988, with U.S. arrears having reached $308 million, President Ronald Reagan announced that the United States was satisfied with the progress on budgetary reform, and acknowledged that the unpaid assessments were indeed a legal obligation of the United States. This was the first such official U.S. acknowledgment of this obligation during his presidency. On behalf of his successors, he committed the United States to paying those arrears over five years. But support in Washington for fulfilling the commit-ment to repay those arrears fizzled in less than two years; ironically, this was at just the time the United Nations took center stage in resisting Iraq's con-quest of Kuwait. Six years after Reagan's commitment, the United States was still carrying forward past-due obligations of $221 million. Indeed, as post–Cold War peacekeeping missions grew in number, complexity, and cost, Congress legislated a unilateral cap on the U.S. share of peacekeeping costs. New conditions had to be met before U.S. dues would be paid. Among them were: an independent inspector-general's office would have to be created; a coalition of gay and lesbian groups would have to be suspended from UN-recognized nongovernmental status unless it ousted a member organization "promoting pedophilia" (through opposition to age-of-consent laws); and the United States would not allow the Security Council to approve a peacekeeping mission until congressional leaders had had two weeks' notice to scrutinize the proposal. When a party shift in Congress brought UN foes into the chairmanships of key committees in early 1995, Congress refused to appropriate funds for major peacekeeping operations, and U.S. arrears quintupled in just two years.

Dilemmas of a Solution

As the United States approached the two-year delinquency level set by Article 19 of the Charter for automatic suspension of a member's vote in the General Assembly, the Clinton administration agreed to accept dozens of conditions demanded by congressional opponents as the price for partial payment of arrears.[5] A number dealt with administrative reforms and budgetary restrictions sought by U.S. legislators in the name of efficiency; others entailed broad policy restrictions on UN actions, including a bar to creation of a "UN standing army" and prohibition of any discussion by UN bodies of international "taxes." The most bitterly contested conditions, however, were those that demanded a reduction in the U.S. share of assessed UN expenses, from 25 percent to 22 percent of regular budget expenses and from 30.4 percent to 25 percent of assessed peacekeeping expenses, and another that required the UN to write off the large U.S. arrears that would remain unpaid.[6]

Plainly this represented a major challenge to the autonomy and independence of the United Nations. To accept these conditions, warned many countries' representatives, would place the UN perennially under the whip of U.S. congressional overseers; legally binding obligations would have no meaning if powerful Member States could flout them at will. For their part, the UN's congressional opponents dismissed out of hand the notion that assessments duly voted under the Charter constituted a legal obligation, and some openly questioned whether, in the absence of authorities with the hard power to enforce it, international law is law at all. The fundamental dispute over legal obligation was reflected in the assertion of the United States that its arrears were in the range of $1 billion, rather than the $1.3 billion in unpaid assessments carried on UN books. Since U.S. law unilaterally deducted from UN dues payments the prorated amounts for such things as the offices of Palestinian rights and Law of the Sea and the UN's method of "equalizing" tax treatment of its staffers, and unilaterally set 25 percent as the ceiling on the U.S. share of peacekeeping expenses, Washington failed to recognize these as arrears. The U.S. administration allowed that these amounts were "in dispute." By contrast, congressional committee chairmen simply rejected these assessments out of hand, and insisted that all unpaid arrears claimed by the United Nations should be consigned to a dormant UN "special account," like the one created for the unpaid Soviet and French assessments for the Congo operation in 1965. Thus these assessments would be removed from calculation of the country's delinquencies for purposes of Article 19.

This, of course, only heightened the suspicion by other Member States that the plan to "end" the arrears controversy might just open the door to new waves of withholding, once the goad of Article 19 vote forfeiture was removed from Washington. Strikingly, the architects of the congressional conditions did not deign even to hint that satisfaction of current demands would lead them to abandon withholding in the future. Rather, they professed confidence that the rest of the Member States would caterwaul and then cave in, out of their craving for U.S. money and fear of U.S. withdrawal. Indeed, the possibility of U.S. disengagement from the United Nations—a specter first raised during the Reagan administration by its withdrawal from the UN Educational, Scientific, and Cultural Organization (UNESCO) and explicitly threatened in 1996 by the chairman of the Senate Foreign Relations Committee—weighed heavily in the calculus of international policymakers.

In a shrewd commingling of executive and legislative functions, the U.S. representative at the United Nations, Richard Holbrooke, brought a procession of congressional representatives to sell to a skeptical UN community the plan they had adopted unilaterally, with the implication that U.S. participation in the United Nations was at risk. The chairman of the Senate Foreign Relations Committee, Jesse Helms, made an unprecedented speech to a public meeting of the UN Security Council in January 2000 outlining his far-reaching critique of the United Nations. Other members of Congress also went to New York to meet with UN delegates to exhort them to accept the deal on offer, presenting an argument of realpolitik to counter other countries' invocation of the binding obligations of international law and the supposedly fundamental principle of assessments based on capacity to pay.

The central focus of contention was the U.S. rate of assessment, which became the main battleground in the Fifth Committee debate on the overall scale of assessments for the 2001–2003 triennium. Not till the last days of the General Assembly session in late December 2000 was a deal struck: The new scale of assessments would lower the ceiling on the U.S. contribution for regular expenses from 25 to 22 percent, as demanded by the U.S. Congress, and the U.S. rate for peacekeeping expenses from approximately 30 to 27 percent, which did not quite meet the 25 percent level stipulated by the U.S. legislation. This small deviation from the congressionally mandated checklist of conditions for payment on arrears thus formally satisfied the insistence of some of Washington's European allies that the U.S. demands had to be the object of negotiation, and not simply *diktat*. But on virtually every other substantive issue the membership yielded to U.S. demands. A French counter-

UN Photo 202832

Richard Holbrooke (U.S. ambassador to the UN) and Senator Jesse Helms standing outside the UN Security Council chamber, January 20, 2000.

proposal, automatically to restore the 25 percent ceiling if the United States had not paid off all arrears after three years, was watered down to a statement that the persistence of arrears at that time would trigger a General Assembly review of the ceiling. This threat of revocation was dismissed by Washington as hollow. Efforts to secure from Washington an explicit reaffirmation that dues are a legally binding obligation and a pledge not to withhold in the future were unavailing. The Europeans did insist on language that the new UN scale should not bind the specialized agencies, but the chances that any one agency could withstand the pressure to adopt the new scale seemed limited.

Moreover, the very fact that Washington had to make even a slight concession from its legislated demands meant that the Congress had to amend its checklist before the funds it promised could be released. This entailed the risk that some new flashpoint of disagreement between Washington and New York might arise before final passage of the amendments conforming to the UN deal and derail the promised payment yet again. Indeed, UN opponents in the House of Representatives succeeded in thwarting the payment until September 11, 2001, when the need to rally international support after the World Trade Center's destruction forced them to back down. Still, the fact that even firm UN opponents in the Senate had declared themselves satisfied with the assessment agreement raised hopes that the U.S.-UN relationship might be at least temporarily on a better track.

The battles over funding as the United Nations entered its second half century raised profound questions about the reliability of the assessment system and the autonomy of the United Nations in the face of financial pressure from its largest financial contributor. The reasons for nonpayment ranged from pique at particular programs that were politically disagreeable to the United States, to detailed complaints about administrative procedures, to demands for rewriting budget-making procedures and the bases for apportioning expenses. Although some of the reforms were widely acknowledged as improving UN efficiency, the withholding underscored the institution's political vulnerability and undercut claims that Member States have legal obligations to each other and international institutions based on the Charter and other instruments of international law.

The Scale of Assessments

The Capacity to Pay

At all levels of political organization, the apportionment of the revenue burden is one of the more painful duties of public service. In local governments that rely on property taxes to cover their expenses, the apportionment of those taxes sets off bitter battles. Among matters that can spark controversy: when and whether to conduct a revaluation of all real property; whether and how to discount value of residential property relative to industrial or commercial property; and whether to grant a community's largest corporate taxpayers a reduced assessment. The standards by which the "value" of real property is assessed vary widely.

Among international organizations, the bases for apportionment of expenses also vary considerably. Usually, each member's share of all members' economic product is an element of the apportionment, but assessment scales are frequently weighted to account for political considerations. In the Organization for Security and Cooperation in Europe (OSCE), a regional organization that was created only in 1994 (institutionalizing the periodic conferences reviewing implementation of the détente-era Helsinki Final Act), there is no specific formula for fixing assessments. Instead, these are determined by an informally constituted financial committee of experts with an eye to each member's relative status in both economic and political terms, subject to an arbitrary contribution ceiling of 9 percent. Accordingly, each of Europe's four major powers—Germany, France, Italy, and the United Kingdom—pays the same 9 percent assessment as the far wealthier United States and the immense but impoverished Russian Federation. By contrast, in the Organization of American States—a collection of developing countries with one mid-sized and one giant industrialized country—the United States alone pays 59 percent of the budget.

The International Monetary Fund sets the apportionment scale for Bretton Woods institutions by formulas that take into account a number of economic and trade indicators, including members' national income, gold and foreign exchange reserves, exports, imports, and variability in export income. However, the factors have historically been weighted to yield politically desired results.[7] Even so, the most artfully calibrated weightings in the multiple formulas now in use may still not produce the politically preferred outcomes, so the quotas calculated by formula are further refined in an overtly political process. Because voting power in the IMF and related agencies reflects a member's financial assessment, underassessed states are often eager to pay more—and overassessed states resist updating the quotas to avoid reductions that would weaken their voting power.[8]

Ad hoc adjustments increased France's IMF quota in 1947, and West Germany's and Japan's in 1959; in 1965, the quotas for Canada and Japan were not increased because that would have put them ahead of India, depriving New Delhi of its privilege (which ultimately proved unsustainable) of appointing its own Fund director. Even today, Japan is held to exactly the same quota as Germany, only a fraction higher than Britain's and France's (which are also anomalously equal). Other members deny Tokyo a quota proportionate to its share of the world economy, since its growth in voting power would have to come at the expense of other members whose economic share has been slipping.

Since its founding, the United Nations has based its assessment scales on the principle of "capacity to pay." Despite a number of deviations from strict capacity to pay, defined by reference to national income, the assessment scale fixed by the UN General Assembly and applied by all UN specialized agencies more closely reflects states' relative means than the apportionments of most regional organizations and even the financial institutions themselves. However, in contrast to the IMF and World Bank, at the United Nations there is little political incentive for states to want to pay higher assessments, and the periodic recalculations of the scale often inspire proposals for formula adjustments aimed at reducing assessments on particular groups of states.

As a result, a seemingly objective standard for assessing taxpayers—national income as a share of global income—is fraught with exceptions, weightings, and modifications: a maximum ceiling, a minimum rate, a write-off for low per capita incomes, a factor for debt relief, and a hedge against abrupt revaluations because of spurts of income growth (an exception now phased out). After all that, there is even a "process of mitigation" to accommodate appeals from individual Member States to lower the number derived from the assessment formula, for which the applicant member either supplies additional relevant information or pleads special circumstances.

Having quickly agreed on the principle that UN expenses "should be apportioned broadly according to capacity to pay," the first General Assembly finally concluded that "comparative estimates of national income would appear *prima facie* to be the fairest guide" to measure that capacity. The UN

Statistical Office would obtain data on national income from all Member States, prepare estimates to fill in whatever data individual members could not provide (based on any other sources of economic data available to it), and calculate each member's national income as a percentage share of the total income of all members. The formula devised by the United Nations would also guide the apportionment scales of each of the specialized agencies created as part of the UN system after World War II.

The difficulty, right from the start, lay in accurately assessing national income, since relatively few members had good statistical data. The first assessment scale was based on available national income data for 1938 to 1940; two years later, the UN Statistical Office had current data—but from only twelve of the fifty-eight Member States. Reporting rates improved dramatically over the next forty years; by 1988, 88 percent of Member States were supplying timely data. The quality of the data also improved, and the Statistical Office earned a reputation for reliable work as it cross-checks the data submitted by governments with other economic data from external sources. The national data are not, however, always comparable, and the Statistical Office has often struggled to find ways of comparing income data from radically divergent systems of economic accounting.[9]

Since 1958 the General Assembly has adopted the scales of assessment for three-year periods. The UN Committee on Contributions—a panel of experts elected by the Assembly and tasked with periodically reviewing the methodology, data, and alternatives for apportioning the expense burden among Member States—evaluates current data and reexamines the assessment scale every three years. It offers a range of options to the General Assembly for ways to modify the scale to address perceived inequities or disproportionate impacts. Those recommendations go to the Fifth Committee of the General Assembly for debate and decision at the political level.

Relief for the Poor

Since 1948, the formula for apportioning UN expenses has made an allowance for the low per capita incomes of many members. Based on the same principles of public finance that animate governments' progressive taxes, the low-income offset assumes that each dollar of income is far more necessary to someone living at subsistence level than it is to someone of considerable wealth. India and the Netherlands, for example, have roughly the same national income, but owing to a vast disparity in the number of people sharing that income—16 million in the case of the Netherlands, 982 million in the case of India—Dutch taxpayers might equitably be asked to pay more toward UN expenses than Indian taxpayers.

Governments implement this principle of progressivity in levying income taxes by setting rates that are low at the bottom brackets—the levels at which income is devoted to life's "necessities"—and that rise for each additional increment of income. For nearly five decades, the United Nations has made allowance for a state's low per capita income by discounting its share of world income by a percentage based on a global per capita income standard. For the three-year scale adopted at the end of 2000, the standard—the average per capita gross national product (GNP) of all Member States—was just under $4,800.

While relief for countries with average incomes below world per capita GNP is now generally accepted as fair, there is intense political dickering on how heavily this factor should be weighted. After all, when countries with per capita incomes less than the standard receive relief, the cost of their discount must be shifted to countries with per capita incomes above that amount.[10] The deepest discounts go to those whose per capita incomes are the furthest below the income standard. For India, the discount comes close to three-quarters off its share of world income; for Mexico, it is a bit less than a quarter. Taken together the discounts of all low-income countries are worth fully 8.36 percent of global income, which the current assessment scale shifts to the countries with per capita incomes above the global standard. China—by far the largest beneficiary of the low-income adjustment—and India alone save 3.42 percentage points between them.[11] There is no doubt the low-income discount accomplishes its intent. While the Canadian pays 4.5 cents per every $1,000 of income for UN expenses, the Indian pays 0.8 cents, the Egyptian 1.0 cent, the Mexican 3.0 cents, and the Bangladeshi a fifth of a cent.

The United States along with a number of other developed nations has urged the Committee on Contributions to consider adopting a weighting formula based on purchasing power parity (PPP), which would take into consideration the markedly lower cost of living in the developing world. This would recognize those countries' ability to finance their activities and maintain standards of living at levels effectively higher than what might be indicated by their per capita figure. This PPP methodology, by statistically increasing poor countries' imputed gross domestic product, has looked attractive to Washington because it would bring China's share of UN expenses, for example, several percentage points higher—reflecting coastal China's status among the world's top ten countries in terms of gross domestic product, rather than the poverty of its vast interior population. Developing countries have, however, resisted the PPP proposal, arguing that their lower domestic costs for labor and locally produced goods do not gain them more foreign exchange to pay hard currency dues to international organizations.

Relief is also afforded to countries struggling with a heavy burden of debt to foreign creditors. Initially considered on an ad hoc basis starting in 1969, the General Assembly insisted on a more methodical formula during the debt crisis of the 1980s. This is a far smaller benefit than the low per capita income discount; in total, it shifts three-quarters of a percentage point on the assessment scale from all debtors to industrialized countries. The largest beneficiaries are Mexico and Brazil, each of which shaves 0.06 percentage points off its assessment because of the debt offset; Indonesia and Russia, which are entitled to save 0.05 percentage points; and Argentina, saving 0.04.

Some of the tiniest and least-developed countries would, according to the UN formula, barely pay any assessment at all. However, the membership has consistently felt that all countries should pay some minimum amount as a condition of membership. Therefore, since the UN's founding, a "floor" has been set in the assessment scale, starting at 0.04 percent in 1946. On grounds of "equity," this floor has been reduced over the years to 0.001 percent of the budget by 1998—which for the year 2001 amounted to an assessment of $12,500.

Stabilizing Rates

Another point of issue in each assessment cycle has been the length of the base period used to insulate rates from single-year fluctuations in economic data. Income data had been calculated on averages of the prior three years until 1977, when the General Assembly became anxious to find a way of "mitigating extreme variations in assessments between two successive scales." By coincidence, this was precisely the period when the enormous surge in incomes of oil-producing states since 1974 was about to show up in the assessment scale. In order to avoid the "extreme variation" of a sudden jump in certain states' assessments, the Assembly switched to a seven-year average (1970–1977, inclusive), which succeeded in holding down the increase in oil producers' assessments. The Assembly extended the base period even further in 1981, adopting a ten-year average.

Several delegations pressed another device to slow the growth in assessments on fast-growing economies, called the "scheme of limits," which would have arbitrarily capped movement in rates from one assessment cycle to the next. Strenuous opposition by the Committee on Contributions dissuaded the Assembly from adopting the "scheme of limits" in 1977 and 1982, but its advocates finally prevailed in winning its incorporation into the assessment formula in 1985. By the time it was adopted, however, the formula had already caught up with the early beneficiaries of the oil price boom. Saudi Arabia's assessment, for example, had jumped more than fourteenfold from 0.06 percent in 1974 to 0.86 in 1984. Ironically, the scheme was adopted just as oil prices plunged dramatically, and the limits ended up slowing the rate at which the assessments of many oil producers fell. By 1995, Saudi Arabia's assessment was 0.80 percent of the total—even though its share of world income during the base period was 0.49 percent. The largest beneficiaries of the scheme of limits turned out, unintendedly, to be two of the leading industrialized countries: Japan and Italy.

These unexpected outcomes, plus the distress in the early 1990s experienced by many states abandoning a Communist economic system, where the scheme of limits prevented reductions in rates despite their industrial collapse and economic depression, created a powerful constituency for change in the 1990s. The scheme of limits was dismantled in two steps; the base period was pruned to a 7.5-year average in the scale adopted in 1997, and a combined 6- and 3-year average was used in the scale adopted in 2000.

The Ceiling

Many insist that the single greatest distortion of the principle of capacity to pay is the ceiling that has capped the U.S. contribution since the UN's founding, and yet it has also raised profound political issues of financial dependence. The United States fiercely resisted the first apportionment proposed by the UN's new Committee on Contributions in 1946, which called for the United States to bear 49.89 percent of the UN's $24 million budget on the ground that the United States enjoyed roughly half of world income at the time. Washington insisted that it should pay no more than a quarter of UN expenses, proposing a permanent ceiling of 25 percent as the maximum amount any Member State could be assessed for regular expenses. The Truman administration sent Senator Arthur H. Vandenberg of Michigan, the Republican leader on the Senate Foreign Relations Committee, to warn of the dangers of adopting the committee recommendation and to argue the U.S. position to the General Assembly:

> The few, in sheer self-defense, would probably insist upon special rights of audit and control which are at variance with the "sovereign equality" to which we are indispensably devoted. . . . We seek no dominion in the United Nations. We do not want it ourselves, and we would not grant it to others. It is not to "save money" for ourselves that we present this argument. It is to save the United Nations from an unwholesome fiscal climate in which our united and common judgments—our "sovereign equalities"—are not calculated to thrive.
>
> Neither we nor any other nation, in some other day, should be allowed a greater privilege in our councils than is measured by a maximum contribution of 25 percent per annum—far short of what, in common parlance, might be called "fiscal control."[12]

As the debate unfolded, the United States discovered what Vandenberg called "eloquent unanimity" among the UN's fifty other members: that the United States, the only major belligerent of World War II that emerged with its economic base intact, should shoulder half of UN costs, as the Committee on Contributions had proposed. After months of hard bargaining, a compromise was struck: the Assembly accepted the principle of a ceiling on the largest contributor's percentage rate, provisionally fixed at 39.89 percent, which the United States was assessed and paid. The difference between the near 50 percent share based on the formula and the rate finally approved—10 percentage points—was to be picked up in higher rates prorated among the other Member States. As war-ravaged economies recovered, that ceiling would be lowered further, with 33.33 percent as the interim target—a level finally reached in 1954—and 25 percent as the eventual final ceiling (see Table 9.1).

By the early 1970s, the U.S. share had gradually drifted down to 31.52 percent. In one swoop, however, it dropped to the 25 percent goal endorsed in 1946. The U.S. Congress—infuriated by the General Assembly's ouster in October 1971 of the U.S.-allied Chinese government in Taipei—decided in the 1972 appropriations cycle to slash the U.S. contribution unilaterally, and the Nixon administration, absorbed in big-power diplomacy and more impatient than any of its predecessors with the United Nations, made only muted objections. Congress voted to provide only enough funds to cover a 25 percent assessment. Fortunately for the United Nations, West German chancellor Willy Brandt's new *Ostpolitik* ("East policy") had opened the way to mutual recognition by the two states that had emerged from the postwar Allied occupation of Germany, and their respective superpower allies were now prepared to support the admission of both to the United Nations. Between them, Bonn and East Berlin would pick up 8.2 percent of UN expenses—which could be applied to reduction of the U.S. assessment and some other states' burdens as well. The two German states were duly admitted in 1973; Washington agreed to a halving of the minimum assessment on the tiniest and poorest states, from 0.04 to 0.02 percent, and the deal was done.

In the mid-1980s, the deliberate U.S. accumulation of massive arrears as a means to bend the United Nations to Washington's will on budget issues gave life to the warnings Arthur Vandenberg had issued forty years before about the dangers of excessive dependence on a single contributor. (Vandenberg was proved wrong, however, in his assertion that 25 percent would be too low a share to produce such an effect.) Sweden's prime minister at the time, Olaf Palme, proposed a radical reduction of the ceiling, to 10 percent, explicitly in order to make what Swedes called U.S. "blackmail" impossible. While some conservative circles in Washington began actively promoting the idea, convinced that the United Nations was too irrelevant to be worth influencing, Secretary of State George Shultz decisively rejected it as a foolish surrender of U.S. responsibility and of U.S. leverage. Most Member States also opposed it, for an obvious reason: they were not so committed to ensuring the UN's financial independence from Washington that they were willing to ante up an average 20 percent increase in their own assessments to pay for it. States preferred to concentrate on persuading the United States to pay its dues than to give the wealthy superpower a free ride.[13]

As explained previously, this debate flared with particular intensity in 2000 when the United States presented the congressional demand for a two-step reduction in the U.S. rate of assessment from 25 percent to 22 and then 20 percent, on which payment of $475 million in peacekeeping arrears was

Table 9.1 UN Assessment Rates for Selected Countries, 1946–2003

	Proposed 1946	Adopted 1946	1953	1964	1974	1984	1995	2000	2003
Brazil	1.20	1.94	1.45	1.03	0.77	1.39	1.62	1.47	2.39
Canada	3.10	3.35	3.30	3.12	3.18	3.08	3.07	2.73	2.56
China	2.75	6.30	5.62	4.57	5.50	0.88	0.72	1.00	1.53
Egypt	0.70	0.81	0.50	a	0.12	0.07	0.07	0.07	0.08
Ethiopia	0.07	0.08	0.10	0.05	0.02	0.01	0.01	0.01	0.004
France	5.50	6.30	5.75	5.94	5.86	6.51	6.32	6.55	6.47
Germany (Federal Republic)[b]	—	—	—	—	7.10[b]	8.54[b]	8.94	9.86	9.77
India	3.08[c]	3.35[c]	3.45	2.03	1.20	0.36	0.31	0.30	0.34
Italy	—	—	—	2.24	3.60	3.74	4.79	5.44	5.07
Japan	—	—	—	2.27	7.15	10.32	13.95	20.57	19.52
Mexico	0.54	0.66	0.70	0.74	0.86	0.88	0.78	1.00	1.09
Netherlands	1.40	1.47	1.25	1.01	1.24	1.78	1.58	1.63	1.74
Saudi Arabia	0.07	0.08	0.07	0.07	0.06	0.86	0.80	0.56	0.55
United Kingdom	10.50	11.98	10.38	7.58	5.31	4.67	5.27	5.09	5.54
United States	49.89	39.89	35.12	32.02	25.00	25.00	25.00	25.00	22.00
USSR/Russia	6.00	6.62	12.28	14.97	12.97	10.54	5.68[d]	1.08[d]	1.20[d]

Notes: a. In 1964, Egypt and Syria were federated in the United Arab Republic.

b. Until 1991, the Federal Republic of Germany represented only the western *länder*; Germany's eastern *länder* were represented by the German Democratic Republic (the Communist-ruled East Germany), which was assessed separately at a rate of 1.22 percent in 1974 and 1.39 percent in 1984.

c. Prorated, based on the allocation between India and Pakistan after partition in 1947. The rates proposed and adopted for the entire Dominion of India in 1946 were 3.73 and 4.09 percent respectively.

d. Figures for 1995 and after are for the Russian Federation only. To compare with figures for the Union of Soviet Socialist Republics, add 1.33 percent (the total of the other twelve former Soviet republics admitted to UN membership in 1991–1992) for 1995, 0.167 percent for 2000, and 0.027 percent for 2003.

conditioned. At the end of the year the General Assembly grudgingly set the ceiling at 22 percent for the next three-year period.[14]

Peacekeeping Assessments

In the early years of the United Nations, when peacekeeping was a rare occurrence, funds for peace activities were part of the regular budget. Subsequently, peacekeeping budgets were calculated separately from the regular budget and have been established on a mission-by-mission basis. Crises that trigger costly peacekeeping interventions, unlike the activities of the regular budget, are usually unforeseen. At times, as in the turbulent Congo operation of the early 1960s and the complex and numerous peacekeeping missions of the early 1990s, the costs to which they give rise can dwarf the UN's regular expenses. Poor Member States have long made the case that their bare-bones national budgets cannot absorb the shock of unplanned special assessments for peace-keeping missions, and insist that responsibility for financing emergency operations must inevitably fall primarily on the wealthier and more powerful countries. Indeed, in 1961, many newly independent countries promptly fell into delinquency on their rapidly spiraling peacekeeping bills. The Assembly voted to write down the peacekeeping assessments on smaller developing countries by 80 percent and on larger developing countries by 50 percent, expecting the resulting deficit to be covered by voluntary contributions. Two years later it switched to a 45 percent discount for all developing countries (defined as all states except Japan and specified Western and Soviet-bloc countries), again to be financed by voluntary contributions.

Year after year, the Assembly experimented with different discounts as it groped for a new model. Though unable to agree on an appropriate formula for the long term, in 1963 the Assembly specified the distinctive principles for establishing a special peacekeeping scale:

- The economically less developed countries have a relatively limited capacity to contribute toward peacekeeping operations involving heavy expenditures.
- Without prejudice to the principle of collective responsibility, every effort should be made to encourage voluntary contributions from Member States.
- The special responsibilities of the permanent members of the Security Council for the maintenance of peace and security should be borne in mind in connection with their contributions to the financing of peace and security operations.
- Where circumstances warrant, the General Assembly should give special consideration to the situation of any Member States that are vic-

tims of, and those that are otherwise involved in, the events or actions leading to a peacekeeping operation.

The scale remained subject to virtually annual tinkering even after the Congo operation ended. The issue seemed to become moot when the only remaining peacekeeping operation financed by a special assessment, that between Israel and Egypt, was withdrawn in 1967, precipitating a fateful Arab-Israeli war. But it returned in 1973, when the major powers on the Security Council decided to support a new UN peacekeeping force to separate Israeli forces from those of the Arab states that had fought a new war that October.

As the General Assembly grappled with apportioning the costs of the new operation, it settled on a formula consistent with the principles it had defined ten years before. Developing countries were divided into two classes: a group of least-developed countries, specified by name (mostly in Africa, but including such others as Afghanistan, Haiti, and Yemen), known as Category D, and all other developing countries, defined by not being included in the list of least-developed countries. The assessment on the Category D countries for the Arab-Israeli disengagement force would be only one-tenth of these countries' assessment for the regular UN budget. Thus Afghanistan, which in 1973 paid the then-minimum of 0.02 percent for the regular budget, would pay at a 0.002 percent rate for the peacekeeping mission. The assessment on all other developing countries (Category C) would be one-fifth of their regular assessment; for Mexico, then assessed at 0.86 percent, the peacekeeping rate would be 0.172 percent. The twenty-three developed countries (Category B) would pay the same rate for peacekeeping as for the regular budget. The discounts afforded to the many countries in Categories C and D were to be financed by the five permanent members of the Security Council—classified for this peacekeeping assessment scale as Category A—as a tangible expression of their "special responsibilities for the maintenance of peace and security." A total of 8.5 percentage points was shifted from the developing countries in Categories C and D to the five permanent members.

The United States and other Western countries, which were anxious to reestablish the peacekeeping force to guard against further outbreaks of fighting between Arabs and Israelis, reluctantly agreed to the formula, but only as an ad hoc measure. The resolution authorizing it described the scale as ad hoc, and delegates' speeches reiterated that it was simply a one-year expedient and most emphatically not a precedent for the future. But this ad hoc solution turned out to be durable. The United States did not contest its continuation in succeeding years, and when the next crisis exploded, requiring yet another peacekeeping mission—Israel's invasion of Lebanon in 1978—the Carter administration quickly accepted application of the same peacekeeping formula in order to get a mission on the ground, and Israeli forces out of Lebanon, as soon as possible. When peacekeeping missions were established in 1988 to monitor the Iran-Iraq cease-fire and preside over the South African withdrawal from Namibia and Cuban departure from Angola, the Reagan administration also accepted the now time-hallowed peacekeeping formula without protest.

It was the explosive growth of peacekeeping operations after the end of the Cold War that brought Washington's attention back to the peacekeeping assessment scale—aggravated by the shift in the assessments on the five permanent members. Since 1974, the changes in the regular assessment scale to benefit low-income countries had all but wiped out China's assessment, which fell from 5.50 percent in 1974 to 0.77 percent in 1994; this meant that China now paid virtually none of the Category A "premium," and that its old share was now being picked up by the remaining four. The fragmentation of the Soviet Union, and the subsequent collapse of the Russian economy, halved Moscow's share as well. London, Paris, and Washington were picking up the difference.

For the United States, picking up roughly two-fifths of an 8.5 percent redistribution from those considered poor was tolerable when total bills came to $30 million. When the United States was billed for nearly three-fifths of an almost 12-point redistribution on total bills edging up toward $1 billion, however, protests mounted in a capital obsessed with budget stringencies. Congressional leaders clamored for a cut.

One expedient proposed by the United States to cope with the unwelcome steep increase in peacekeeping assessments was reliance on voluntary contributions to finance new operations. When Boutros Boutros-Ghali, the UN's first Secretary-General from the African continent, called for a UN mission to deal with Somalia's disintegration in early 1992, the Bush administration drew the line: the United States would not approve any new UN mission unless it were funded by voluntary contributions, just as the UN-authorized war to expel Iraqi forces from Kuwait had been voluntarily funded. The prospect of a U.S. veto persuaded other members of the Security Council to agree to this arrangement as they authorized a small peacekeeping force. U.S. officials persuaded Pakistan to provide a troop contingent, but were markedly less successful in convincing their chosen funding "volunteer," Saudi Arabia—or any other country—to underwrite the cost. An understaffed, unfunded company of Pakistani soldiers soon found itself under siege between competing factions in Mogadishu, unable to restore order or protect food deliveries. Voluntary funding seemed not to work for a peacekeeping operation in a place where wealthier countries' direct interests were not apparently at stake.[15] Indeed, as Somalia's crisis deepened and its population faced mass starvation, President George H. W. Bush offered late in the year to dispatch a large U.S. military force to restore order and open secure food delivery routes. The U.S. military's "Restore Hope" intervention in Somalia, which cost the United States $1.5 billion, was succeeded by a large-scale UN peace operation funded by assessments.

If voluntary contributions would not provide reliable funding for UN peace operations, the burden of assessments could be avoided by delegating peacekeeping to regional organizations or to "coalitions of the willing," though in practice these faced the problem of finding a subset of countries both willing and able to provide not only the money but also the troops. Unfortunately, this formula would ultimately prove sustainable only in operations in the Balkans led by North Atlantic Treaty Organization (NATO) Member States. If the United States were to reduce what it viewed as a disproportionately burdensome share of UN peacekeeping costs, the United Nations would have to revise the peacekeeping scale of assessments.

As a candidate for president, Bill Clinton had proposed a reduction in the U.S. share of peacekeeping costs to 25 percent, and tied it to establishment of a UN rapid deployment force. After he took office, Congress legislated its claim to such a rate (minus the rapid deployment force) in the Foreign Relations Authorization Act for fiscal years 1994 and 1995, unilaterally capping the share of peacekeeping costs the United States would pay thereafter to 25 percent. Clinton signed the wide-ranging bill adopted by the Democratic-controlled 103rd Congress, but expressed for the record his objection to this and another withholding provision "because they could place the United States in violation of its international treaty obligations if reform is not achieved within the stated time."[16] A reduction in the U.S. peacekeeping assessment would become a major battleground between Washington and other Member States at the end of the decade.

In contrast to the bitter controversy over a reduction in the U.S. regular assessment, however, there was wide agreement that the peacekeeping scale had become seriously inequitable. States classified as "developing" in 1973 continued to claim entitlement to deep discounts a quarter century later, even though some had achieved high per capita incomes thanks to oil wealth, like Brunei and the United Arab Emirates (with 1998 per capita incomes of $18,038 and $16,666 respectively), or through rapid gains in economic product, such as Singapore at $31,139 (up from $8,722 in 1975). The other permanent members of the Council that had to share the cost of the deep peacekeeping discount for such high-income "developing" countries joined in pressing for reform based on ability to pay, and these states soon found themselves isolated and under pressure from not only Washington but also many developing countries to accept rationalization of their peacekeeping assessments.

When the General Assembly approved a new assessment scale for the regular budget at the end of 2000, it adopted an extraordinary companion resolution fixing a new scale for future peacekeeping assessments, to take effect in July 2001. Instead of an arbitrary classification of Member States into four categories, discounts would now be based on per capita income; the least-developed countries would still pay for peacekeeping at a rate that was just a tenth of their regular budget share (and thus, for Bangladesh, at 0.0001 percent), while countries with per capita incomes between roughly $500 and $9,600 were spread among six categories based on a sliding income scale. The handful of high-income countries that had, until 2000, enjoyed a large Category C discount adamantly refused to be classified as developed countries, for reasons of self-esteem, so a new Category C was created for Singapore, Qatar, Brunei, the United Arab Emirates, and Kuwait, allowing them still to claim to be part of the developing world with a nominal discount of 7.5 percent from their regular rate of assessment.[17]

A new peacekeeping assessment scale was established in 2000:

- Least-developed countries pay only 10 percent of regular budget share.
- Countries with per capita incomes of $500–$9,600 are categorized into six groups on a sliding scale.
- High-income developing countries pay the same rate as that of regular dues minus a discount of 7.5 percent.
- Developed countries pay the same rate as that of regular dues.
- The five permanent members of the Security Council pay the same rate as that of regular dues plus a surcharge, calculated on the reallocation of the remaining costs after the discounts to poorer countries have been made.

Voluntary Contributions

The United Nations does not live by assessments alone. Since the system's creation, assessed budgets have provided an administrative skeleton for UN agencies, while voluntary contributions have provided much of the flesh of program activities out in the field. Major states preferred to finance programs through voluntary contributions, especially programs in the economic and social fields, particularly when it seemed these would be temporary expenditures. The UN's first major undertaking was to provide relief for millions of displaced persons in Europe after the upheavals of World War II. By the time the UN Relief and Rehabilitation Agency was dissolved in 1947, it had spent $3.6 billion to care for war refugees awaiting repatriation or resettlement; the United States alone provided $2.8 billion. Inevitably, the prodigious U.S. generosity of the immediate postwar years would fade. While the United States continues to be the largest single government contributor of voluntary funds to most UN agencies, its support is now dwarfed by the aggregate of voluntary contributions from European Union governments, with Japan in some agencies close behind.

Donors have strong reasons for preferring to finance so much of the UN system's work through voluntary contributions. Most obviously, in doing so they avoid long-term budgetary commitments. This makes it easier for governments to retrench when politics demand stringency, and to revise their UN spending priorities as domestic political fancies change. By contrast, the pace at which a consensus on priorities can change in global bodies is glacial. Unlike assessed obligations, voluntary pledges are subject to normal appropriations scrutiny and revision by finance ministries and legislators back home. One result is that funding levels may vary widely from year to year. Voluntary contributions to the entire UN system, which totaled $7.1 billion in 1994 (slightly below their 1992 high), fell steadily over the next three years to $5.4 billion in 1997 before rising to $6.2 billion in 1999 (see Table 9.2).[18]

More important, voluntary financing gives donors far greater control over agency programs and spending than they enjoy over activities financed by assessments. Thus they have flexibility to respond quickly to changing assessments of program performance; if reports suggest a program is not tightly managed, or pursuing a different approach than the contributing government deems most desirable, it can cut off funding—which is what Britain and the Netherlands did with the UN Drug Control Programme in 2001 to signal their displeasure with its leadership. The twenty major donors may be a small minority in the General Assembly and have to compromise in pursuit of consensus, but on voluntary grants they have vast leverage to insist a project fulfill their expectations, or they won't fund it at all. Donor governments may set higher performance standards than would the UN membership at large; their primary interest is in results they can show their voters to sustain public support for providing assistance. Poorer countries, by contrast, have a second interest of equal priority: keeping the money flowing. Where they have strong political influence, as they do over assessed budgets, they often resist curtailment of spending on their countries (or on hiring their nationals), regardless of the programs' demonstrable impact.

Table 9.2   UN Voluntary Contributions, 1999 (in U.S.$ millions)

Trust Funds administered by United Nations Secretariat	181.8
United Nations Center for Human Settlements ("Habitat")	3.1
International Trade Center (UNCTAD/WTO)	10.8
United Nations Development Programme (UNDP)	694.3
United Nations Population Fund (UNFPA)	245.0
United Nations Environment Programme (UNEP)	43.7
United Nations High Commissioner for Refugees (UNHCR)	783.1
United Nations Children's Fund (UNICEF)	675.7
United Nations Refugee Works Agency (UNRWA)	227.1
United Nations University (UNU)	17.4
World Food Programme (WFP)	351.8

Source: United Nations, *Budgetary and Financial Situation of Organizations of the United Nations System,* Statistical Report of the Administrative Committee Coordination, UN Doc. A/55/525, October 26, 2000.

This does not mean that voluntary contributions give donors absolute control. In the early 1980s, when the U.S. right-to-life movement organized a fierce campaign against China's family-planning program for its reported reliance on abortion, it sought to deal a blow to Beijing by forcing the UN Population Fund (UNFPA) to suspend support for Chinese family-planning programs. On this issue, however, other donor countries and most developing countries were of one mind; and even after the United States cut off all its contributions to UNFPA, the agency's governing council refused to terminate its projects in China. Although some advocates of terminating U.S. funding believed they were punishing the agency, the more apparent effect was to reduce family-planning programs in many developing countries with burgeoning populations. Eight years later the Clinton administration resumed financing for UNFPA, though in Congress these contributions were still hotly contested.

Especially in the development area, some donor governments rely on UN agencies as the executing agency for what is, in reality, a bilateral aid grant arranged by officials of the donor and recipient governments. In other cases an agency will work with a developing country on a project design and then shop it among prospective donor governments until it finds a funder. In either case, the donor's earmarking will tie the agency to a specified purpose and recipient. Not surprisingly, agencies seek, wherever possible, the flexibility of "untied" grants that allow them to award project funding in accordance with their evaluation of need. This is as true of the independent specialized agencies, some of which rely heavily on voluntary contributions, as of the UN programs and funds overseen by the General Assembly (see Table 9.3).

Some major donor states, aware they can never have much influence if their limited voluntary contributions are allocated across the board, prefer to concentrate their donations strategically on one or two programs. This can allow these countries to become significant players in those programs, and perhaps to make a bid to nominate the program head. Thus did the Japanese, increasing their funding for the UN High Commissioner for Refugees, eventually claim the post for one of their nationals. Similarly, the Italians, by making massive contributions to the UN Drug Control Programme, won appointment of its executive director. The Nordic countries followed this strategy by focusing funding on the UN Development Programme (UNDP) and UNICEF, at least in part in the hope of wresting one of the top jobs from U.S. control.[19]

U.S. enthusiasm for contributing to UN program funds has waxed and waned. True, the United States often points to its large voluntary contributions to parts of the United Nations when it is criticized for not paying its regularly assessed dues to the Organization—although the U.S. share of total voluntary contributions is actually less than its share of assessments. Some Americans have been skeptical of the benefit, at least to the United States, of activities undertaken by international agencies. Bilateral aid programs are generally

Table 9.3   Contributions to UN Specialized Agencies, 1999 (in U.S.$ millions)

	Assessed	Voluntary
Food and Agriculture Organization (FAO)	320.4	123.5
International Atomic Energy Agency (IAEA)	210.8	84.5
International Civil Aviation Organization (ICAO)	47.4	35.5
International Labour Organization (ILO)	231.9	85.2
International Maritime Organization (IMO)	29.5	1.8
International Telecommunication Union (ITU)	85.1	57.7
United Nations Educational, Scientific, and Cultural Organization (UNESCO)	271.1	122.9
United Nations Industrial Development Organization (UNIDO)	64.8	42.1
Universal Postal Union (UPU)	21.4	2.6
World Health Organization (WHO)	418.8	256.4
World Intellectual Property Organization (WIPO)	12.3	0.1
World Meteorological Organization (WMO)	44.1	11.1

Source: United Nations, *Budgetary and Financial Situation of Organizations of the United Nations System,* Statistical Report of the Administrative Committee Coordination, UN Doc. A/55/525, October 26, 2000.

thought to tie their recipients more tightly to the donor, arguably advancing (when the United States is the donor) U.S. influence in the recipient society. Moreover, the United States can press tougher demands for potentially painful action by a recipient than can a UN agency, of which the recipient state is also a member. For example, the United States has pushed recipients of its anti-narcotics aid to undertake far more aggressive police action and military efforts against drug networks than has the UN Drug Control Programme. But there are many activities where bilateral programs are inappropriate and the multilateral framework indispensable, such as when implementing international environmental accords or assisting Palestinian refugees.

Nonstate Resources

In the aftermath of World War II, the leaders of what was then called the UN International Children's Emergency Fund (and what is still known as UNICEF) decided that the plight of children in lands ravaged by the war was so great, the resources available from governments to help them so limited, and the sympathy of the public at large in wealthier countries so strong, that they might succeed in raising funds directly from the public by well-crafted appeals. Indeed, the public responded for children, and national fundraising committees sprang up in dozens of countries to sell UNICEF holiday cards, collect spare change at international airports, and raise money from individuals through other ingenious devices. By century's end, nearly a fifth of UNICEF's revenues came from individuals' contributions.

Other agencies sought to imitate UNICEF's network, but with little success. Voluntary contributions from individuals require a compelling cause, favorable publicity in the media, and a clear and simple message. Without these preconditions, other UN programs simply could not build strong networks for raising small voluntary contributions from large numbers of individuals worldwide.

In 1997, however, a single individual, communications innovator and magnate Ted Turner, changed the landscape dramatically by announcing a $1 billion contribution to fund UN programs of demonstrable effectiveness for children's health, women's rights, and environmentally sustainable development, to be expended over a ten-year period through a new UN Foundation. The prospect of $100 million a year in new funding for specific projects in the field led the United Nations to create a special office to sift through the many applications from UN development agencies for the Turner foundation's support. A reasonably objective funding process was seen as a godsend by UN agencies that had been trying to shop around projects they believed had clear positive impact on poor societies but little attractiveness to Western aid administrators, whose priorities were shaped by bilateral or domestic political calculations. There had long been philanthropic support from U.S. foundations for scattered innovative programs proposed by some UN agencies, but this was the first foundation funding dedicated exclusively to the UN's projects in the field. At a time when many Western governments were slashing development aid—U.S. funding for development assistance plummeted from 0.21 percent of GNP in 1990 to 0.11 percent in 1999, and France's from 0.60 percent to 0.39 percent in that same period—the arrival of fresh resources from a private source was as welcome as it was unexpected. Other foundations dedicated to development assistance, like the new Gates Foundation, focused on health and learning programs, began to make funds available to discrete UN projects.

A clear sign of the UN development agencies' gradual evolution from the common enterprise and responsibility of public authorities to, in part, a charity in search of private funds, came with the creation of a UN fund to deal with HIV/AIDS in 2001. Secretary-General Kofi Annan won commitments from a number of major governments to the fund by the time of the General Assembly's special session on HIV/AIDS—but, quite remarkably, also drew pledges of contributions from some major multinational corporations, including Swiss insurer Winterthur and U.S. pharmaceutical maker Pfizer. The degree to which corporate and other private giving can become a reliable support for UN development funding was unclear as the twenty-first century began, and it occasioned much consternation in circles concerned about extension of private interests and corporate power. Nonetheless it represented a new development in UN finance.

Alternative Revenue Sources?

Of course, the United Nations and its agencies do not constitute a government. They have no power to levy taxes and no mechanism to collect them, and only the most enthusiastic advocate of global federalism can contemplate with any pleasure the creation of a worldwide tax-extraction machine. But it is not inconceivable that Member States might jointly decide to levy the same tax and dedicate it to their common programs. In 1978, the Carter administration suggested that the United States was prepared, in principle, to consider such automatic revenue alternatives, but its successors have signaled no interest in pursuing the idea.

In 1995, France's departing president, François Mitterrand, proposed to the UN Conference on Social Development in Copenhagen (called the "Social Summit") a revenue enhancer that actually has as its primary goal the strengthening of nations' monetary policy by calming the wild swings in currency markets. Echoing a proposal by retired Yale University professor James Tobin, Mitterrand argued that all governments have a deep interest in currency stability, but none by itself can control speculators who sense opportunities for quick profits in betting that a country with economic problems can be forced to devalue its currency. States should agree, declared Mitterrand, on a common tax on currency transactions.

The crucial element, Tobin noted in discussing the proposal in the 1994 *Human Development Report* of the UN Development Programme, is that "the tax would have to be worldwide, at the same rate in all markets. Otherwise it could be evaded by executing transactions in jurisdictions with no tax or lower tax."[20] He recalled J. Maynard Keynes's argument for a stock transaction tax—that it could "strengthen the weight of long-range fundamentals in stock-market pricing, as against speculators' guesses of the short-range behavior of other speculators. The same is true of the foreign exchange markets."[21] The plan's Achilles heel, however, lies in the requirement that *every* state ratify the convention establishing it. There may always be a Panama, a Cayman Islands, or a Switzerland ready to break ranks for parochial gain.

For both Mitterrand and Tobin, the rationale for the exchange tax is economic, not budgetary; the fact that such a tax would raise revenue is almost incidental. They vaguely suggest its proceeds could be applied to common international purposes, such as an IMF currency-stabilization fund to assist developing countries' economies. Based on Tobin's calculations, a 0.01 percent tax on spot transactions in foreign exchange, the level proposed by Mitterrand, could yield some $300 billion a year. Like any tax collected by states, it could remain with the governments that collect it, whether for national programs, for dedication to international assessments, or for distribution as tax relief to the citizenry. Alternatively, those governments could take a fixed share and forward a specified percentage to appropriate international organizations, like the IMF or the United Nations, for specified purposes; or the entire net amount, after deducting national administrative costs, could be forwarded to the international organization. As with any proposal for an automatic revenue stream, a major issue would arise over the politics of how an international organization would appropriate such special funds, by the same process as for its regular budget (in the UN's case, by vote of the General Assembly), or with concurrent approval by a special committee weighted in proportion to the share of revenue collected by each state.

Another potential revenue source suggested by some is the international trade in petroleum and hydrocarbons. This proposal would not require endorsement by all Member States; it would be effective simply if all the major oil exporters would agree to levy such a tax. Still, it would face a serious political problem: in a soft oil market, the exporting countries themselves might be forced to absorb the tax as they compete for buyers, and, as demonstrated by their resistance to tightening carbon emissions targets under the climate change convention, many of them are not prepared to cooperate on measures that might eventually result in lower demand for their major cash earner.

Another option sometimes suggested, specifically for payment of peacekeeping costs, is a surcharge on tickets for international air and sea travel. The usual justification for this plan, and the proposed earmarking for UN peace operations, rests on international passengers' supposed need for a secure and peaceful environment so their planes are not shot down. This is a tax that would be easy to administer, since most jurisdictions already impose similar levies. What would be harder to muster is the political will to tax average people to finance UN activities; these might come to see the United Nations as a tax-eating monster. Some citizen activists suggest a surcharge on the price of all arms sold in international markets.

A distinguished group of eminent persons charged with proposing a realizable program to strengthen financing for development—chaired by former Mexican president Ernesto Zedillo and including former U.S. treasury secretary Robert Rubin—recommended exploration of alternative revenue flows in 2001 to enhance development financing. Moreover, the Belgian government, in assuming the presidency of the European Union, vowed to put the "Tobin tax" concept on the front-burner of the EU agenda. But the opposition to any alternative revenue flow is likely to be formidable. When Secretary-General Boutros Boutros-Ghali even hinted at the idea in 1996, he was immediately assailed by the Clinton administration as severely as by its Republican foes in Congress. So deeply does this issue touch the nerves of those worried about state sovereignty and creeping world government that one of the conditions set by Congress in 1999 for payment of back arrears was that there be no *discussion* anywhere in the United Nations of possible international revenue authority. While a number of nongovernmental organizations submitting

briefs to the preparatory committee of the 2002 World Conference on Financing for Development proposed independent UN revenue streams, not a single
government even floated such an idea in its first several sessions.

Only the Seabed Authority, created by the UN Convention on the Law of
the Sea, which entered into force in late 1994, has authority today directly to
collect international revenues from deep seabed mining to finance its activities. In turn-of-the-century political circles, at least in the United States, one
may expect considerable resistance to any "new taxes," especially for a distant global organization like the United Nations.

Conclusion

Since its inception, the United Nations has grappled with the problem of
applying the principle of "capacity to pay" in determining levels of assessments for each of its Member States. Various formulas, offsets, and shelters
have been advanced over the years to redistribute the assessment burden from
states that felt that strict adherence to an income-based formula burdened
them too heavily. In the same spirit, the burden of assessment for peacekeeping has been figured differently from the regular budget, shifting some of the
burden toward those privileged permanent members of the Security Council
that bear greater power and responsibility within the United Nations for matters of peace. At the same time, there is an ongoing debate over how dependent the United Nations should be on its single largest contributor, and the disproportionate influence the United States has wielded through withholding
assessed funds has created painful dilemmas for other Member States.
Although nonstate resources, voluntary contributions, and international revenue sources all offer possible alternatives to assessments, for the foreseeable
future the United Nations will be dependent upon the contributions of Member States.

There remains an ongoing tension between the international legal obligation to pay assessed dues to the United Nations, embodied in its Charter, and
the preference of certain parties to view UN contributions as essentially a unilateral political decision. To a large extent, these struggles have determined
the roles the United Nations has been permitted to play, or not play, in world
affairs, as well as the resources available to it.

Notes

1. This was among the fourteen reservations demanded by Lodge, and resolutely
rejected by President Woodrow Wilson, aimed at disavowing obligations of the League
Covenant. Eighty years later, another chairman of the Senate Foreign Relations Committee affirmed his endorsement of the Lodge reservations in a speech to the UN Security Council and in legislation attaching conditions to partial payment of U.S. arrears
to the United Nations.

2. U.S. Letter, October 8, 1964, UN Document A/5739.

3. The 1965 resolution in effect relegated the controversial arrears to a comatose account, for which $73 million in assessments remains unpaid: France never contributed the $17 million it was assessed for the supposedly "unconstitutional" elements of the operation, and the Union of Soviet Socialist Republics dissolved with $39 million still outstanding in Congo assessments (though Moscow has been paying off other old Soviet arrears). While acquiescing in this resolution, U.S. representative Arthur Goldberg warned that if others could assert a right not to pay certain assessments with impunity from Article 19, the United States could do the same.

4. Washington had already destabilized the finances of most international organizations by a budget maneuver in 1981 motivated by domestic rather than international political concerns. To achieve the appearance of reducing federal spending in its first budget, the Reagan administration announced it would shift its payment of dues to the United Nations and other international agencies from February to October of the calendar year in which they were billed. This moved the payment from one federal budget cycle to the next, allowing the administration to claim a hefty, onetime foreign affairs "savings" when it omitted UN funding from its budget request for fiscal year 1982. The change wreaked havoc with international organization budgets, however, and left many strapped for cash by late summer each year. When Congress withheld funds later in the decade, the impact on the already weakened finances of UN agencies was disruptive. Most had obligated funds in accordance with the budget previously approved by the General Assembly, only to find late in the year that the U.S. share was not just late—but not going to materialize at all.

5. The major provisions of the agreement between the Clinton administration and its Senate foes on payment of UN arrears were settled in early 1997, but it took thirty months for the legislation to be enacted. During that period, while U.S. payment of current assessments was often delayed pending presidential "certification" that one or another administrative demand was being met, Congress did appropriate funds to pay the bulk of new assessments. Those assessments were, in any event, shrinking, as large UN peace operations in Bosnia and Haiti were phased down—but the fact that the United States was skating close to the level of delinquency at which it would lose its vote in the General Assembly was plainly a factor. Tellingly, when arrears would have triggered Article 19 vote forfeiture at the end of both 1998 and 1999, Congress quietly wrote into its omnibus budget resolutions language to waive its own certification requirements to allow payment of just enough to keep the United States below the Article 19 threshold. While hard-line UN opponents appeared to welcome a U.S.-UN confrontation over the UN "depriving" the United States of its vote, congressional leaders judged it politically inadvisable.

6. The arrears payment plan offered payment in three stages. In the first, $100 million would be paid to the United Nations for overdue assessments for selected peacekeeping budgets, upon presidential certification that the ideological "policy" conditions and a variety of administrative conditions, such as continued adherence to negative budget growth, had been met. In the second stage, $475 million would be paid on overdue assessments for various peacekeeping operations, allowing partial reimbursement to troop-contributing countries for contingents that had served years earlier in peace operations in Somalia, Haiti, the former Yugoslavia, and elsewhere, and the United States would also credit to itself the full $107 million in peacekeeping reimbursements it was awaiting from the UN for some of those same operations. The conditions for this second tranche, however, included the bitterly contested demand for reductions in the U.S. rate of assessment. In the third stage, $244 million would be paid to defray arrears accumulated at various specialized agencies, with only a small

portion covering arrears for the United Nations regular budget. Conditions added for this payment would require independent inspectors-general in specified specialized agencies, a further reduction in the U.S. rate of assessment for the regular budget to 20 percent (though this was ultimately made waivable), and either a General Assembly write-off of the remaining unpaid arrears or their formal repudiation by the U.S. Congress. Of the $1.3 billion in overdue assessments the United Nations awaited from the United States (for nearly all of which assessments the United States had voted), Washington would, under the arrears payment legislation, pay $712 million.

7. At the organization's creation, the formula for members' quotas was designed so that the U.S. quota would pay a third of the total, Britain would have roughly half the U.S. quota, and the Soviet Union and China would end up with the third and fourth highest quotas. As it happened, the Soviet government did not join.

8. Not only does each member gain a larger vote as its quota increases, but each of the five largest quota holders, as well as the two members with the largest net credit positions, is entitled to appoint one of the Fund's executive directors; the rest of the Fund's twenty-four directors are elected by the other members.

9. Perhaps the biggest challenge facing the Statistical Office over most of its first half century was the reconciliation of national income statistics from market economies, in which prices reflect economic values easily compared through convertible currencies, and the "material product" accounting of Communist economic planners, which excluded income generated by services not related to production of goods and in which prices were fixed administratively according to "social" measures of value rather than economic ones. Data from the Soviet Union and its allies often seemed arbitrary—just like the Soviet-decreed currency exchange rate for the ruble. Over time, UN statisticians devised a methodology for converting national income data from Communist countries that was, if not entirely satisfactory, at least economically defensible. In any event, for reasons of political prestige, the Soviets preferred a conversion rate that inflated their share of world economic product (and therefore their dues) in order to ensure they would be number two (after the United States).

10. The shift of this discount onto higher-income countries, compounded by the distorting impact of the ceiling, has created complaints about equity among the wealthy as well. Some delegations have at times suggested that the national income basis should be modified to ensure "horizontal" equity—that the ultimate assessment should result in a virtually identical cost per $1,000 of per capita income to taxpayers of all developed countries. As early as 1954, Canada proposed to place ceilings on what each country would pay as a fixed share of national income, rather than as a share of total contributions, as a guarantee of fairness. The Canadian scheme, offered then as a counterproposal to the U.S. petition for a reduced assessment, would effectively have capped Ottawa's contribution rather than Washington's; it was rejected. Five decades later, Canadians still complain that they are stuck with a higher bill than their neighbors to the south: Canada's regular UN assessment in 1993 cost Canadian taxpayers 5.48 cents per $1,000 of per capita income, in comparison to the 5.12 cents the U.S. assessment cost Americans. When the United States won a reduction in its rate in 2001, the gap widened. Ottawa's regular UN assessment now costs Canadians 4.5 cents per $1,000 of income, compared to the 3.2 cents that Washington's assessment costs Americans. The fact that the burden on both countries had declined during that period is largely the result both of "negative real growth" caps on United Nations budgets and of rising personal incomes.

11. In contrast, Russia has elected to waive all the low-income and debt discounts to which its current poverty would entitle it. Seeking continued recognition as a world power, it volunteered to pay at a rate of 1.20 percent—its share of world income—for

the 2001–2003 triennium, rather than the 0.65 percent rate the low-income and debt adjustments would have given it.

12. Arthur Vandenberg's statement to UN Fifth Committee, November 8, 1946, GA(I/2), Fifth Comt. p. 92.

13. Still, outside advocates have been touting the idea, ranging from hostile critics in the U.S. press to advocates of far-reaching UN reform, like former UN official Erskine Childers in his ambitious blueprint *Renewing the United Nations System* (written with Brian Urquhart). Childers insisted that "it is unwise that any member-state (it could be some other [than the United States] in the future) be responsible for so large a single segment of UN resources. A 10 or 12 percent ceiling is so important to the political health and stability of the world organization that it should be the starting premise of the assessment formula" (Uppsala: Dag Hammarskjöld Foundation, 1994), p. 154. Others object, however, that a further drop in the ceiling would unfairly transfer to citizens of smaller countries a financing burden that the wealthy United States (along with Japan, Germany, etc.) is perfectly capable of paying.

14. Most extraordinarily, to seal the deal the Clinton administration had to appeal to a nonstate party to intervene. Member States facing a stiff increase in their dues assessments as a result of the U.S. rate reduction finally balked at having to pay this unanticipated increase in assessments that would be levied just a month later, and they demanded that the United States cover those costs for the first year of the new scale. The administration had no hope of winning any postponement of the U.S. rate reduction from conservative senators, however, and turned to a wealthy individual, Ted Turner (who three years earlier had established and endowed the United Nations Foundation), to provide the U.S. government with the $34 million required to cover the 3 percent reduction in the U.S. share.

15. Even in Cyprus, where the North Atlantic alliance had a strong interest in a UN peacekeeping operation that kept the lid on conflict between alliance members Greece and Turkey, voluntary funding could not survive eventual donor fatigue, and the General Assembly agreed to cover $8.8 million of the operation's costs by assessment starting in 1993.

16. Public Papers of the Presidents, William J. Clinton, U.S. Government Printing Office, Washington, D.C., April 30, 1994; p. 809.

17. Thus, when the new scale was fully phased in, Singapore would pay a peacekeeping rate of 0.364 percent in 2003 (in relation to its regular rate of assessment of 0.393 percent), a substantial equalization compared to its 2000 peacekeeping rate of 0.036 percent.

18. The shifting fortunes of voluntary contributions may be traced in the reports of the United Nations Administrative and Coordinating Committee, available in such Secretariat documents as A/51/505, A/53/647, and A/55/525.

19. They were bitterly disappointed when Secretary-General Kofi Annan replaced the U.S. head of UNDP not with the Danish candidate the Nordics had proposed through the European Union, but a British official of the World Bank—also a European, certainly, but not exactly whom the Nordics had in mind. This occasioned fierce debate in Scandinavian policy circles as to whether the countries in the region needed to learn to play power politics the way the big states do, by withholding their large voluntary contributions in order to force the system to take their demands seriously.

20. James Tobin, "A Tax on International Currency Transactions," in *Human Development Report 1994* (New York: Oxford University Press, 1994), p. 70.

21. Ibid.

10

Informal Groups of Member States

Jochen Prantl and Jean E. Krasno

Shifting power relationships after the end of the Cold War and uneven adjustments to changing events reflect the international landscape as the world enters a new millennium. Adapting to this new environment, ad hoc coalitions of able and willing countries have emerged as a useful phenomenon in support of peaceful solutions to conflict in an age of uncertainty and changing contexts.

The United Nations, with its nearly universal membership, becomes a prism through which to view this transformation. In 1995, UN Secretary-General Boutros Boutros-Ghali explained in a speech:

> The increasing complexity of operations has led, on the political side, to the intensification of peacemaking efforts. Thus, a new concept, that of "Friends of the Secretary-General," "International Conferences," or "Contact Groups," means that, while the UN peacekeepers are on the ground, intense diplomatic efforts continue with many parties to a conflict in order to reach a political settlement.[1]

Groups of Friends of the Secretary-General may infer more direct ties to the UN than contact groups, but the dividing line between these is blurred in practice. While it is quite apparent that these groupings have taken over specific tasks in the field of management, resolution, and transition of conflicts—not only in those cases when UN peacekeepers are already on the ground—it is less obvious to what extent they influence governance in the Security Council, which still provides the framework for action. While informal groups have proliferated in the post–Cold War era, preceding cases can be found in the earliest days of UN crisis response. This chapter examines the emergence of informal ad hoc groupings in the UN context and their proliferation in the post–Cold War era.

The Janus-Faced Structure of the Security Council

The UN Security Council appears to operate in a Janus-faced manner, on one side appearing to be an open system while on the other side operating like a closed shop.[2] Informal ad hoc groups of states seem to play a part in that operating scheme as they must cope with and adapt to a two-faced Council and its governance structure.[3] The levels of analysis include the role of great powers in international organizations, the role and function of the Security Council according to the Charter, and the constitutional practice of the Council, elaborating on certain variants of the collective security scheme as envisioned in the Charter.

Since the end of the eighteenth century, it seemed to be a common pattern of great powers after the cessation of major wars to remodel the international order according to the lessons they had learned in order to prevent the outbreak of future conflicts.[4] The search for international order after World War II continued this tradition. However, it differed in one important aspect: while the Covenant of the League of Nations differentiated between just and unjust wars, the Charter of the UN tried to contain war via several provisions and, for the first time, outlawed war as a means of policy.[5]

The maintenance of international peace and security should be one of the primary functions of the UN in general and the Security Council in particular. Founded on the belief that aggression could be countered by the collective will of powerful states, the UN founding fathers perceived the Organization as the center of military action, or at least the center of its legitimacy. However, the functions allocated to the UN never implied that the Organization would have a monopoly on the use of force, and the veto was given to the five members of the former Grand Alliance (China, France, the United Kingdom, the United States, and the Soviet Union). The veto effectively blocked the UN from intervening, except by peaceful means under Chapter VI, and meant that the UN would only become involved in those conflicts where the five were not immediately affected—that is, in disputes between smaller states.[6]

Furthermore, it had been clear from the very beginning that the UN could work effectively only if the five victorious powers of World War II also were able and willing to cooperate in the future. Their solidarity has been, therefore, a precondition to the functioning of the Security Council. Writing his final report in 1945 on the UN Conference on International Organization in San Francisco, U.S. secretary of state Edward Stettinius said: "It was taken as axiomatic at Dumbarton Oaks, and continued to be the view of the Sponsoring Powers at San Francisco, that the cornerstone for world security is the unity of those nations which formed the core of the Grand Alliance against the Axis."[7] From this point of view, the conception rejuvenated the idea of the nineteenth-century great power concert.[8] Furthermore, it reflected President Franklin Roosevelt's vaguely defined concept of the four world policemen who should have the primary responsibility for maintaining and enforcing international peace and security.[9] Ideas for the conception of the Security Council had already been developed during World War II, whereby the overall approach appeared much more down-to-earth than the somewhat lofty model of the League of Nations. It emphasized the political responsibility of the great powers and their allocated function to maintain order.[10] It reflected the lessons learned from a misguided policy, as Edward Hallett Carr has observed in his analysis of international relations between 1919 and 1939: "Periods of crisis have been common in history. The characteristic feature of the twenty years between 1919 and 1939 was the abrupt descent from the visionary hopes of the first decade to the grim despair of the second, from a utopia which took little account of reality to a reality from which every element of utopia was rigorously excluded."[11]

One might conclude, consequently, that the fine-tuned balance between utopia and reality ought to be the defining moment for the future development of the UN Security Council. On the one hand, the Charter of the UN formulated high hopes "to save succeeding generations from the scourge of war."[12] On the other hand, it acknowledged the fact that if there should be any realistic chance to live up to those high expectations, the great powers had to be granted special privileges in order to keep engaged. In case of an institutional deadlock, the Charter offered, furthermore, the possibility of exit via the right of individual or collective defense to conduct conflict management outside the Organization: "Article 51 'turned the veto inside out' . . . by recognizing that a majority of powers cannot be prevented from cooperating to pursue *outside* an international organization a policy which the unanimity rule prevents them from pursuing *inside* the Organization."[13] This means, in essence, that building ad hoc coalitions of able and willing countries does not infringe on existing Charter provisions, but can be directly derived from them. However, Article 51 cannot be interpreted as a blank check to bypass the UN. It is not an invitation for unilateral action by single states, since there is a clear, although not clearly defined, reference that "a majority of powers" should have the right to conduct conflict management outside the Organization.

The key to understanding this provision lies less in the futile exploration of the question of how many states are needed to get this very majority, and more in the interpretation that a minority of one or two countries should not be able to stop a majority of like-minded states from taking action. Should members exert their right of individual or collective self-defense, however, the actions taken entail a clear time horizon: the Charter grants the possibility to act until the Security Council has agreed upon the measures to restore international peace and security.[14] The UN Security Council, therefore, shall come into play at the earliest possible stage.

The possibility of the veto was perceived as a kind of reinsurance, granting the great powers the possibility of an exit to preserve their vital national interests. Furthermore, the five victorious powers were granted the privilege of permanent membership on the Security Council, whereas the other (nonpermanent) members were to be elected for a term of two years, without being eligible for immediate reelection. The veto power in combination with the restrictions of Charter revision hermetically sealed the privileges of the great powers under the conditions of 1945.

However, it was not a new phenomenon to consider the allocation of special privileges and duties within a group of states characterized by an uneven power structure. It already existed in 1685, when the advocate Samuel Pufendorf observed in his opus *De Jure Naturae et Gentium Libri Octo:*

> Another consideration is that it would often involve great injustice in a system of confederates for the vote of a majority to bind the rest when there is a great difference in resources, and so one contributes more to the common safety than another. For despite the fact that those who contribute in proportion to their wealth appear to bear equal burdens, it may frequently happen that one man is readier to expose his own modest fortune to risk than another his, a large one. Thus supposing that one state of a system contributes more to the common defense than all the others together, it would be manifestly unjust for it to be possible for the rest to force such a state to undertake something that would devolve the chief burden upon it. But yet for the votes of each state to weigh in proportion to its contribution to the society would grant such a powerful state sovereignty over the rest.[15]

This fundamental problem of international relations has not significantly changed even three centuries later. UN membership is composed of a large group of states that have only limited capacities to contribute to the aims of the Charter. At the same time, there is a minority of states having more resources than those of the majority of other states taken together. Consequently, only a few members have the capacity for a credible projection of power. The former group generally refers to the principles of equality and sovereignty, the latter to the necessity of privileges given their exposed position, and the necessity of having an efficient organization. This clash of interests was already apparent during the San Francisco Conference in 1945. The structure of the Security Council reflects this circumstance by differentiating between permanent and nonpermanent members.

The thinking about how to model the international order after World War II led to an institution that mirrored a policy mix of elements of utopia and reality. The Security Council acts as the primary, though not exclusive, responsible body for the maintenance of international peace and security and acts on behalf of all UN Member States. Furthermore, it defines any threat to or breach of peace, deciding whether there is an act of aggression. It adopts resolutions that are legally binding for all members of the Organization, and even nonmembers can be affected to some extent. While the five permanent members of the Security Council possess the right of veto in all matters going beyond procedural questions, Article 51 of the Charter offers, via the right of collective or individual self-defense, a certain exit strategy to conduct conflict management outside the Organization. In addition, the right of the Security Council to adopt its own rules of procedure provides it with a flexible instrument to adapt the formula of its meetings according to changing circumstances, and it has done so in a limited number of cases.

The Possibility of Exit:
The UN Charter as Living Document

The system of collective security as agreed upon in San Francisco and embedded in the Charter of the UN faced a deep crisis immediately after its adoption.[16] The ambitious provisions of Chapter VII (Articles 43–48), which were to provide the UN with military contributions by Member States, were not implemented. The most obvious reason was the exacerbating antagonism between the United States and the Soviet Union, which already foreshadowed the defining nature of the Cold War. In the Security Council, this conflict of interests became visible through the increasing number of vetoes cast in formal meetings.[17]

While the Soviet Union, in the first ten years, used this privilege in seventy-five cases, and another twenty-six times in the second ten-year period, the United States did not use the veto at all through 1965 (see Table 10.1). Between 1966 and 1975, the United States used it twelve times, and from 1976 to 1985, in thirty-four cases. The year 1966 appears as watershed, since the recomposition of the Security Council, for example, the enlargement of its

Table 10.1   Use of the Veto in the UN Security Council, 1946–2000

	China	France	United Kingdom	United States	USSR/ Russia	Total
1946–1955	1	2	—	—	75	78
1956–1965	—	2	3	—	26	31
1966–1975	2	2	10	12	7	33
1976–1985	—	9	11	34	6	60
1986–1995	—	3	8	24	2	37
1996	—	—	—	—	—	—
1997	1	—	—	2	—	3
1998	—	—	—	—	—	—
1999	1	—	—	—	—	1
2000	—	—	—	—	—	—
Total	5	18	32	72	116	243

Sources: Sydney D. Bailey and Sam Daws, The Procedure of the UN Security Council, 3rd ed. (Oxford: Oxford University Press, 1998), p. 239; Global Policy Forum, New York, www.globalpolicy.org/security/data/vetotab.htm.

nonpermanent membership from six to ten seats, changed the institutional balance at the expense of Western powers. The action threshold was increased
from seven to nine votes, with the effect that, after 1966, 86 percent of all
vetoes were cast by the "Western P-3"—France, the United Kingdom and the
United States.[18] Even if these numbers suggest a paralysis of the Security
Council, closer scrutiny reveals a more accurate and complex picture. Even
for the so-called hot phase of the Cold War, complete blockage in the Council was not maintained. Sydney Bailey, Inis Claude, and Francis Delon point
to a considerable number of cases that support this argument.[19]

The classic linkage between the veto and incapacity of the Security
Council to act, therefore, has serious shortcomings in its explanatory power.
It is not only the veto that determines an active or passive role for the Council, but also other factors like political will or leadership by one single country or groups of states. Pointing reflexively to the veto as a monodimensional
explanation of the potential paralysis of the Security Council all too often
distracts from a broader understanding. This brings into question the truism
that Articles 43–48 could not be implemented due to Cold War antagonism.
It also reflects a deep-rooted reluctance of governments to become involved
in seemingly distant regions and risky military operations without reserving
the right to their explicit consent. The nonimplementation of central articles
in the Charter permitted an environment that led, according to Adam Roberts,
to three developments highlighting the inherent flexibility of the UN Charter. These variants of collective security include the tendency to use regional
alliances and military action in a multilateral framework; the authorization of
states to use military force on behalf of the UN; and the deployment of
peacekeeping operations under the authority of the UN.[20] Informal ad hoc
groupings of states are introduced here as a fourth variant of collective security, caused by, and evolving parallel to, the development of UN crisis
response.

Regional Alliances and Multilateral Action

The creation of regional alliances reflects the fact that states tend to use their
forces for military operations on a regional rather than global level.[21] The
development of nuclear weapons in the hands of a few states especially fos-
tered the trend toward the creation of regional alliances, which undermined
the far more ambitious system of global collective security. The emergence
of several regional alliances after 1945 was also accompanied by the tendency to use force in a multilateral framework rather than to intervene unilaterally. In addition, the pressure to legitimize state action increased significantly after World War II. The preference for multilateral action—or what
Ruth Wedgwood calls "technical multilateralism," employed to keep up the
appearance of collective action—gained currency.[22] When the United States
intervened in the Dominican Republic in 1965, it gained prior authorization

through a resolution adopted by the Organization of American States (OAS), thereby avoiding a Soviet veto in the UN Security Council. Furthermore, U.S. efforts were flanked by the deployment of an Inter-American Peace Force. Even the Soviet intervention in Czechoslovakia in 1968 was hidden as multilateral action of the Warsaw Pact, with participation of Bulgaria, the German Democratic Republic, Poland, and Hungary.[23] Also, the U.S. intervention in Grenada in October 1983 was based upon the platform of the rather inactive Organization of Eastern Caribbean States. These few examples, which could be pursued extensively, lead to the conclusion that the concept of collective security had become a screen behind which the great powers could hide their interests.

Regional alliances appear to be both a step toward and a step away from a system of collective security. Since 1945, there has not been a ripe moment in the international system for implementing such an ambitious scheme as global collective security. Consequently, arrangements of regional security should rather be seen as the best possible, though suboptimal, approach to the concept of collective security.[24] Regional alliances do remain suboptimal, since they have never been a substitute for the idea of a collective force under UN authority. However, this optimal solution of global collective security has always been out of reach. The structural conditions of the post–Cold War era have reinforced this trend toward regionalism in dealing with crisis situations that may endanger the maintenance of international peace and security. The reliance upon regional and subregional settings, including informal groups of states, constitutes a variant of collective security that "may cause sleepless nights for some international lawyers, but has often seemed to salve the concerns felt by other countries at the singular career of a country with formidable military power."[25]

Authorization of Military Force

The strongest variant of collective security has been UN authorization for others to use force. This shift of competence developed out of the circumstance that Member States could not agree upon the use of force during the Cold War era. The Korean War (1950–1953) marked the beginning of the subsequent practice to delegate the use of force to other states.[26] After the outbreak of the war on June 25, 1950, the Security Council determined there had been a breach of peace. It called for immediate cessation of hostilities and demanded the withdrawal of North Korean troops to the thirty-eighth parallel.[27] These far-reaching decisions were possible at this stage because the Soviet Union had conducted an "empty chair" policy at the time the crisis emerged: it had boycotted virtually all Council meetings in protest because the seat of China was still being held by the government in Taiwan instead of Communist Beijing. Consequently, the Security Council was able to authorize the United States to conduct a military operation under UN authority.[28] Due to this unusual activism of the Council, the Soviet Union terminated its boycott in August 1950 and vetoed all subsequent decisions of the Council.[29] Facing complete paralysis, U.S. secretary of state Dean Acheson submitted an action plan to the Western-dominated General Assembly, which was adopted on November 3, 1950, as the so-called Uniting for Peace resolution:

> If the Security Council, because of lack of unanimity of the permanent members, fails to exercise its primary responsibility for the maintenance of international peace and security in any case where there appears to be a threat to peace, breach of the peace, or act of aggression, the General Assembly shall consider the matter immediately with a view to making appropriate recommendations to Members for collective measures, including in the case of a breach of the peace or acts of aggression the use of armed force when necessary, to maintain or restore international peace and security. If not in session at the time, the General Assembly may meet in emergency special session within twenty-four hours of the request therefore. Such emergency special session may be called if requested by the Security Council on the vote of any seven members, or by a majority of the members of the United Nations.[30]

The General Assembly furthermore established a fourteen-member Peace Observation Commission,[31] which reports on potential threats to international peace and security, thereby entering into competition with the authority of the Security Council under Article 39 to "determine the existence of any threat to the peace, breach of the peace, or act of aggression." This "Uniting for Peace" procedure constituted a precedent case in the application of UN Charter provisions. The resolution significantly expanded the competence of the General Assembly, while restricting the provisions of Article 24, which had granted the primary responsibility for the maintenance of international peace and security to the Council. The resolution was a gate-opener, providing the General Assembly with the possibility of convening a special session and advising military measures on its own. This revaluation was limited, however, since the Assembly's vote did not imply a legally binding decision. The "Uniting for Peace" resolution pointed to the flexible, if not uncontested, mechanisms of the Charter that allowed the United Nations to take action even when the Security Council was blocked. Due to the contentious nature of the decision, this procedure has not been invoked very often.[32] One instance was during the Suez crisis in 1956, when the General Assembly adopted a resolution to send a ten-nation peacekeeping force to supervise the cessation of hostilities. Such agreement was possible since the interests of the two superpowers converged, acting against the veto of France and Britain, which were directly involved in the conflict. In consequence, this peacekeeping operation had been made possible by invoking the "Uniting for Peace" procedure, whereby the Soviet Union this time deliberately supported the decision taken by the General Assembly.

Peacekeeping Operations

The evolution of peacekeeping can be viewed as an ad hoc mechanism of the UN, customized out of practice. It also demonstrates another example of the flexibility of the UN Charter. Peacekeeping, as an instrument of the UN, is not explicitly mentioned in the Charter. Implicitly, it can be derived from Article 33,[33] which allows UN Member States, in the context of the pacific settlement of disputes, to use "other peaceful means of their own choice."[34] Other scholars define peacekeeping as a subsidiary organ established either by the General Assembly or the Security Council under Article 22 or Article 29 respectively.[35] Originally, UN peacekeeping forces fulfilled three distinct tasks.[36] First, the forces were expected to maintain impartiality between the conflicting parties. Second, and this remained valid up to the early 1990s, the consent of the parties to send UN peacekeeping forces was an absolute condition of every operation. Although this principle has been seriously tested in the post–Cold War era, it has not lost its importance. A third principle was to avoid the use of force. Early peacekeeping missions were allowed to use force only for purposes of self-defense. However, the Congo operation in the 1960s, as explained in Chapter 8, showed very quickly that UN peacekeeping tended to move within a gray zone between Chapters VI and VII of the UN Charter. After 1973, this restrictive interpretation changed with the deployment of interposition forces between the Egyptian and Israeli lines after the Yom Kippur War. In addition, the possibility to use force has been extended to those cases where parties hinder the ability of UN troops to fulfill their mandate.[37]

Furthermore, even between 1945 and 1989, peacekeeping had not been exclusively used in interstate conflicts. UN involvement in intrastate wars, which have become a normality since the end of the bipolar system, was already taking place in crises like those of the Congo (1960–1964) and Cyprus (since 1964).[38] In both cases, the Security Council decided to send interposition forces without being able to define clear-cut front lines or without an existing cease-fire between the parties concerned. All too often, the fundamental principles of peacekeeping, like impartiality, consent of the conflicting parties, and nonuse of force, have been put into question.

In sum, the evolution of UN peacekeeping constituted an innovative element in the collective use of force. Innovations like peacekeeping emerged within a complex international environment where the UN had to deal with crisis settings that challenged its constitutional framework. The consequence of this is that the UN has never been able to fulfill its functions as originally envisioned by its founders. In many cases, UN forces helped to stabilize the conflicts and, indeed, to keep the peace. On the other hand—and this has often been overlooked—the presence of peacekeeping forces often reduced the pressure to work toward long-term solutions of the conflicts. The tendency to freeze the status quo increased, while incentives for any long-term constructive management of the conflicts decreased.

The Emergence of Informal Ad Hoc Groupings of States

The Secretary-General, as the chief administrative officer of the United Nations, has always been exposed to the current international political climate in the performance of those functions entrusted to him by the principal organs of the UN according to Article 98 of the Charter. Exposure to political controversy becomes particularly apparent in his relationship to the Security Council, given its primary responsibility for the maintenance of international peace and security. Since the Council is a political body, resolutions reflect accordingly a precarious compromise of Member States, embodied in a diplomatic formula. In consequence, disagreement over the interpretation of resolutions adopted by the Council has been a common pattern. Securing compliance is very often left to the Secretariat, without any further guidance for the implementation of a given mandate. The Secretary-General is confronted with the perennial challenge not to antagonize the great powers in the execution of these delegated authorities, a matter of fact that applied especially, though by no means exclusively, to the Cold War period. He constantly must navigate between the Scylla of strictly limiting his role to those functions explicitly mentioned in the UN Charter and the Charybdis of overextending his responsibilities through a far-stretching interpretation of Charter provisions. Both extremes are detrimental to his office.

These structural conditions should be kept in mind when tracing the emergence of ad hoc groups of Member States, advising the Secretary-General on certain issues. These advisory committees became a common element during the term of Dag Hammarskjöld. Under his predecessor, Trygve Lie, the UN had been shaken by an increasingly divided Security Council, as the Korean War had made abundantly clear. Secretary-General Lie had supported the U.S. initiative to circumvent the paralyzed Security Council by referring the matter to the General Assembly, which brought him into open opposition with the Soviet Union. Once the Soviet delegation refused to recognize him as Secretary-General of the UN from February 1951 onward, having vetoed his renomination, Trygve Lie's room to maneuver became severely limited. He survived for three more years through a vote of the General Assembly to extend his term by that period. This had been almost a textbook example of the dangers the Secretary-General faced under Cold War conditions. Once he had lost his impartiality in the perception of key states, his office was doomed to remain politically paralyzed. Furthermore, the Secretariat had become a base for McCarthyite agitation over spying on subversive U.S. citizens who had allegedly infiltrated the Organization. However, not a single staff member was ever even charged with those accusations.[39] Although the General Assembly had voted to extend his term, Lie announced his resignation on November 10, 1952, as a consequence of these pressures.[40] In April 1953, when leaving office, the Secretary-General delivered a brief valedictory, hinting at the inherent potential of the Charter, yet to be explored: "The Charter is a flexible instrument, capable of adaptation and improvement, not merely by amendment but by interpretation and practice. I am convinced that the institutions of the United Nations system can be used by the Member States with far greater effect than in the past for the peace and progress of all those nations willing to cooperate."[41] Lie's successor, Hammarskjöld, would become a master of exploring yet uncharted territories of the UN Charter's constitutional practice, in this special sense becoming a "Machiavelli of Peace."[42]

The Advisory Committee on the Peaceful Uses of Atomic Energy

Hammarskjöld first became exposed to the instrument of an advisory committee in the context of preparing the Atoms for Peace Conference, to be held in Geneva from August 8 to August 20, 1955.[43] The conference responded to a number of proposals made by the Eisenhower administration to achieve arms control.[44] In his statement to the General Assembly on December 8, 1953, the U.S. president had come up with far-reaching proposals for establishing an international atomic energy agency under the aegis of the UN. In December 1954, the General Assembly accordingly adopted a resolution to hold an international technical conference under the auspices of the UN to explore possibilities of sharing technical information in the field of using nuclear energy for peaceful purposes.[45] Under the chairmanship of the Secretary-General, the Advisory Committee on the Peaceful Uses of Atomic Energy—composed of seven high-level scientists from Brazil, Canada, France, India, the Soviet Union, the United Kingdom, and the United States—prepared the program of the conference. The advisory committee held three series of meetings with the Secretary-General: January 17–28, 1955, at UN headquarters in New York; May 23–27 in Paris; and August 3–5 in Geneva.[46] After initial difficulties, especially reflecting Cold War tensions between the Soviet Union and the United States, the Secretary-General managed, as Brian Urquhart recalls, "to get rid of most of the political advisers on the delegations, after a certain amount of very plain speaking."[47] Thus, depoliticizing the composition of the committee resulted in a refocus of the discussion on scientific issues. The scientific members managed to tone down the political discourse.[48]

The Advisory Committee on the Peaceful Uses of Atomic Energy provided the platform for an almost "Habermas-like" discourse among equals beyond the political and ideological tensions of the Cold War. Hammarskjöld would establish similar committees as a means to assist the Secretary-General in the performance of his functions during crises at the Suez Canal, in Lebanon, and in the Congo.

The UN Emergency Force Advisory Committee

The idea of an advisory committee in the context of the Suez crisis in 1956, therefore, did not emerge out of the blue. The UN responded by setting up an international emergency force whose mandate developed out of the paralysis within the Security Council. Britain and France had subsequently vetoed two draft resolutions, introduced by the United States and resubmitted in an amended form by the Soviet Union. The blocked situation was overridden by the adoption of Security Council resolution 119, which had called an emergency special session of the General Assembly under the "Uniting for Peace" procedure.[49] Since this resolution referred to a procedural matter of the Council, it could be adopted over the objections of Britain and France by an affirmative vote of seven against two, with two abstentions (Australia and Belgium).

When the General Assembly decided upon the establishment of an interposition force, it asked the Secretary-General to set up the force and negotiate its deployment into Egypt. General Assembly resolution 998 requested Hammarskjöld to submit to the Assembly a plan within forty-eight hours for the establishment of an emergency force to secure and supervise the cessation of hostilities.[50] The UN Emergency Force (UNEF) derived its legitimacy, therefore, not by virtue of a Security Council mandate, but by a set of resolutions adopted by the General Assembly.

Hammarskjöld floated the idea of constituting an advisory committee in his second and final report on the plan for an emergency force.[51] The operation had to lay the foundation for something that had no explicit reference in the Charter, thereby constituting an entirely new concept of UN crisis response, which had to be planned from scratch. It was obvious that the Secretary-General was not able to present a full-fledged plan within the short period of two days, but rather guiding principles. Questions such as the regulations of the force or the policy of the force with regard to self-defense needed further deliberations. In his report, Hammarskjöld had already indicated that open matters should be dealt with by a small committee of the General Assembly. He stated, furthermore, that "this body might also serve as an advisory committee to the Secretary-General for questions relating to the operations."[52] General Assembly resolution 1001 formally constituted the UNEF Advisory Committee, originally composed of seven countries that were to provide troops to UNEF: Brazil, Canada, Ceylon, Colombia, India, Norway, and Pakistan; Yugoslavia would join later.

The committee held a total of forty-four meetings in the period between November 14, 1956, and December 31, 1959. After a long pause due to the smooth running of UNEF, the advisory committee was consulted again—for the last time—on May 18, 1967, under the chairmanship of then-Secretary-General U Thant, to advise him on the request of Egypt to withdraw UNEF. The records of the meeting were classified as confidential.

By consulting the committee, the Secretary-General had been able to secure continued feedback of his negotiations with the Egyptian government, without asking the entire General Assembly body for approval of his every step. For example, Hammarskjöld had negotiated with President Gamal Abdul

Nasser of Egypt three memoranda on the presence and functioning of UNEF. The low profile of the force, embodied in the restrictive definition of its functions—hardly the kind of takeover Britain and France had hoped for and advocated to their domestic audiences—posed a considerable embarrassment for the two permanent members of the Security Council. They asked the Secretary-General, therefore, not to publish the second and third memoranda in a report to the General Assembly containing those provisions.[53] Hammarskjöld had responded to their request in the affirmative, leaving the two memoranda out on the basis that he had delivered an oral report to the UN Advisory Committee, as the ad hoc executive committee of the General Assembly, "with a full account of the interpretations given."[54] Members of the advisory committee had actively participated in drafting the final wording of the Secretary-General's report to the General Assembly.[55] The Secretary-General used the small gathering as an effective tool to legitimize and sanction his quiet diplomacy, thereby circumventing potential criticism from the General Assembly, a large body consisting of eighty Member States at this time. Furthermore, by refraining from the publication of the two memoranda, he hoped to keep Britain and France, two permanent members of the Security Council he might need in the future to initiate Council action, in a cooperative mood. As Brian Urquhart recalls:

> It also allowed Hammarskjöld to say what he thought to a group of government representatives who would then explain things he could not say publicly. There was a very complicated arrangement, for example, about Sharm el Sheikh. . . . One of the points was that the Egyptians could not take over the coastal batteries again, and of course Fawzi,[56] representing a country which had just been invaded by three foreign armies, could not conceivably say publicly that a fourth group of foreigners would be sitting in one of the key strategic locations of Egypt. So Hammarskjöld simply said "Let me try it this way: I assume . . . that as long as UN troops are stationed in Sharm el Sheikh the Egyptians will find it unnecessary to be there," and Fawzi simply closed his eyes and nodded. Hammarskjöld could not possibly publish that, but he told the advisory committee and the advisory committee was a kind of guarantors' club.[57]

Member States serving on the committee therefore shared the considerable burden that the General Assembly's resolutions had put upon the shoulders of the Secretary-General, as Hammarskjöld pointed out at the fourth meeting on November 20, 1956: "There is one thing which is very pleasant from my point of view: that the mandate accepted in the resolution providing for this Committee is such that every responsibility in this whole Middle Eastern context that falls on me automatically falls on this Committee."[58] Even more, Hammarskjöld personally perceived the committee as a "cloud of angels"[59] over his head, granting leverage and feedback to the Secretary-General's efforts to implement the resolutions adopted by the General Assembly.

This burden-sharing function applied in particular to the early phase of setting up the UNEF operation, when the Secretary-General had the chief responsibility of "inventing" the first peacekeeping operation of the United Nations. Within the UNEF Advisory Committee, Lester Pearson of Canada especially expressed his concerns that if the UN should not be able to create this precedent successfully, "then police action by the United Nations in the future would be quite impossible."[60]

The episode around Nasser's request of a final withdrawal of UNEF in May 1967 shows the limited loyalty of Hammarskjöld's "cloud of angels," whose like-minded attitude lasted only as long as it did not interfere with their perceived national interests, and as long as the burden to share did not become too heavy. With the Six Day War already looming, the final decision to withdraw UNEF and the related responsibility fell on then-Secretary-General U Thant.

Nevertheless, the summary study of Secretary-General Hammarskjöld on the experience, derived from the establishment and operation of the force during the period of 1956–1958, referred to the UNEF Advisory Committee as a useful mechanism, which should be accepted as precedent for the future.[61] Based on the Secretary-General's experience with the UNEF Advisory Committee, one can draw the following conclusions:

1. Advisory committees were seen as most useful in complex crisis situations where the Secretary-General may have to secure compliance with extensive mandates entrusted to him either by the Security Council or the General Assembly. Support for the Secretary-General through these ad hoc arrangements may have an inward and an outward dimension. Inward-looking, the support of like-minded states decreases his vulnerability against criticism from the plenary of the General Assembly and the Security Council respectively. Outward-looking, informal ad hoc groupings may support the Secretary-General's efforts by bringing their influence to bear on the parties to a conflict.

2. While troop-contributing countries were the "natural candidates" to be represented on an advisory committee, this did not necessarily imply that all countries providing troops should be selected. The advisory committee had to reflect a trade-off between efficiency and inclusiveness.

3. Permanent members of the Security Council should, as a general rule, not be considered as members of an advisory committee. Such policy reflected the guidelines the Secretary-General had adopted regarding peacekeeping operations—that is, that the permanent five were not asked to provide troops to a mission. This aspect hints at the conclusion that advisory committees were perceived as a certain kind of counterbalance, strengthening the office of the Secretary-General against the General Assembly and the Security Council respectively.

The UNEF Advisory Committee showed clearly, at least in its early phase, the potential of informal ad hoc groupings of states. The fruitful combination of a Secretary-General willing and able to assume leadership, and a group of Member States comprising a small number of representatives and generally willing and able to assist the Secretary-General in his efforts, turned out to be a kind of model soon to be applied to other operations, such as those in Lebanon and the Congo.

The Congo Advisory Committee

The Congo Advisory Committee was set up amid serious tensions in the Security Council over the course of action during the Congo crisis in August 1960. Contrary to the Suez crisis, this time the Council had been able to give at least some international response to the crisis in the former Belgian Congo, which had erupted a few weeks after the country's independence on June 30, 1960. Invoking Article 99 of the Charter for the first time since the founding of the United Nations, the Secretary-General decided to bring the matter to the attention of the Security Council.

Securing compliance with a number of vague mandates emerging from the Council, including the responsibility if anything went wrong, was left to the Secretary-General. The Soviet delegation became increasingly uneasy with the Secretary-General's efforts to interpret the mandates adopted by the Council. The Soviet representative, Vasily V. Kuznetsov, even denied that the Secretary-General had a mandate to interpret Council resolutions.[62] The situation exacerbated after the assassination of Congo's Prime Minister Patrice Lumumba, culminating in the Soviet demand to dismiss Hammarskjöld. Even more, the Soviets no longer recognized him as an official of the United Nations, though the Soviet mission continued dealing with the Secretariat.[63] In response to the situation on the ground, the Security Council adopted resolution 161 on February 21, 1961, which considerably extended the framework for UN action on the ground, including the use of force in yet-to-be-clarified circumstances.[64] The resolution omitted any reference to the Secretary-General—the one who had to carry out the mandate—in order to gain Soviet abstention in that vote.

This overall setting hints at the different structural conditions under which the Congo Advisory Committee had to operate. While the UNEF Advisory Committee had advised the Secretary-General against the background of a blocked Security Council that was overridden by the General Assembly's "Uniting for Peace" resolution, on the Congo crisis, the Council proved unable to produce clear mandates to take charge of the crisis situation on the ground. Given the conflicting interests of the great powers, Council mandates tended to reflect a compromise on the basis of the lowest common denominator. Council members tended to pass the buck to the Secretary-General, imposing upon him the burden of interpreting the resolutions that had to be translated into action on the ground.

This may serve almost as a textbook example for the exposed stance the Secretary-General assumes when he has to implement resolutions serving as a fig leaf to hide the diverging positions of Council members. Hammarskjöld said accordingly in a statement before the Council: "Implementation obviously means interpretations in the first instance. . . . I have the right to expect guidance. That guidance could be given in many forms. But it should be obvious that if the Security Council says nothing I have no other choice than to follow my conviction."[65] In the Cold War context, convening a gathering of like-minded Member States, adding weight to the Secretary-General's position and thus serving as counterbalance to a divided Security Council, appeared therefore as the most promising strategy to share the burden (and the blame) growing out of the Secretary-General's responsibilities.

The Congo Advisory Committee seemed therefore to be the "natural solution" to increasing the leverage of the Secretary-General against the Security Council, by advising and backing up his actions in the execution of Security Council mandates. Hammarskjöld proposed "a parallel to the Advisory Committee established in the case of the UN Emergency Force," which responded to a similar request by the Soviet delegation to convene such a group.[66] While the proposal of the Soviet delegation obviously reflected the aim to gain greater control over the action of the Secretary-General, Hammarskjöld perceived the advisory committee at first instance as a means to decrease his vulnerability, increasing his room to maneuver in the Congo crisis. This problem of exposure and vulnerability has been, as noted earlier, a common pattern in the relationship between the Secretary-General and the Security Council. In this regard, the crisis in the Congo turned out to be a lens sharply focusing on the potential and limits of the office of the Secretary-General as a political organ of the UN.

In the perception of the Secretary-General, the Congo Advisory Committee should have been one of those various means at his disposal to assist him in dealing with this controversial political situation. However, the committee turned out to be a much larger and more unwieldy gathering than its predecessors, since it consisted of all eighteen countries contributing troops to the UN operation, meeting a total of seventy-five times in three years.[67] Looking at the size of the committee, Hammarskjöld disregarded one of his own lessons drawn out of the UNEF operation: "If the contributing States are numerous the size of the committee might become so large as to make it ineffective."[68] The verbatim records show that meetings tended to be lengthy, producing much more red tape than the UNEF Advisory Committee.[69] Furthermore, the atmosphere tended to be less informal, given the simultaneous English-French translations. The Secretariat had to distribute both an English and a French version of the verbatim records, which were classified—parallel to the UNEF Advisory Committee—as confidential. The closed meetings had been for the Secretary-General the "best means of consulting, getting advice and rallying support for the UN operation in Congo."[70]

However, such assessment has to be seen in the wider context of the difficult relationship between the Secretary-General and some permanent members of the Security Council, notably the Soviet Union. The account reflects the desperate position of the Secretary-General at this time rather than the validity of the committee as a means of supporting the Secretary-General in the interpretation of unclear mandates. Members on the Congo Advisory Committee were reluctant to commit themselves on controversial points. The Indian representative told Hammarskjöld during the second meeting quite bluntly that "so far as the mandate of the Security Council is concerned, it is for you to interpret it in the light of the discussions and resolutions of the Security Council, and that interpretation is really a matter between you and the Security Council."[71]

The basic split in the Council over what the UN could or should do in the Congo was merely mirrored within this group rather than discussed in a productive manner. The longer the crisis endured, the more members of the committee tended to leave all contentious issues and related decisions to Hammarskjöld, who had actually hoped to get some advice.[72] The frank exchange of views, which had been the special merit of the previous advisory committees, would no longer be possible if representatives, including the Secretary-General, did not want to run the danger of exposing themselves too much to the members of the Security Council. Furthermore, tension among committee members rose considerably.[73]

Nevertheless, the records show that Hammarskjöld saw a great potential in the advisory committees, not only as an instrument to advise the Secretary-General on the implementation or interpretation of resolutions, but also in terms of executive functions and in the longer-term implementation of resolutions or agreements. This requires a great deal of strategic coordination, which he would have liked to have seen delegated to those countries with a preexisting level of commitment. Hammarskjöld assessed quite clearly the burden that operations such as the one in the Congo put on the Secretariat, encroaching heavily on other tasks.[74]

The Western Contact Group on Namibia

The combination of efforts taken by a group of national governments and the UN, "working separately but within the framework of objectives defined by the UN Security Council,"[75] was the central feature of the development leading to the independence of Namibia on March 21, 1990. The conflict went far back, to 1946, when South Africa had refused to place South West Africa (later called Namibia) under a UN trusteeship. The UN finally had taken direct responsibility for the territory in October 1966, when the General

Assembly revoked South Africa's mandate, originally allotted under the League of Nations mandate system after World War I. It authorized the constitution of a council that had ultimate authority over the territory until Namibia gained its independence. However, South Africa continued to maintain its control over the territory. The legal dispute culminated in 1970, when the Security Council adopted a resolution that requested the International Court of Justice to give an advisory opinion on the question of the legal consequences of the continued presence of South Africa in Namibia.[76]

In February 1972, when the Council held a series of meetings away from headquarters in Addis Ababa, it adopted resolution 309,[77] which invited the Secretary-General, "in consultation and close cooperation with a group of the Security Council, composed of the representatives of Argentina, Somalia, and Yugoslavia, to initiate as soon as possible contacts will all parties concerned, with a view to establishing the necessary conditions so as to enable the people of Namibia . . . to exercise their right of self-determination and independence."[78] However, this gathering of like-minded states was not able to produce the critical mass of leverage needed to grant the Secretary-General additional weight in his negotiations with the government of South Africa. The Council therefore decided to discontinue further related efforts in December 1973.[79]

The situation somewhat changed when the United States became more focused on Namibia in the context of Secretary of State Henry Kissinger's two trips to the region in 1976. The high-level attention on the U.S. side certainly facilitated the adoption of resolution 385, which contained key principles for a negotiated settlement. First, the resolution required that free elections "under the supervision and control of the UN be held for the whole of Namibia as one political entity." Second, the UN should be enabled "to establish the necessary machinery within Namibia to supervise and control such elections, as well as to enable the people of Namibia to organize politically for the purpose of such elections." Third, it called upon South Africa to withdraw "its illegal administration maintained in Namibia and to transfer power to the people of Namibia with the assistance of the United Nations."[80]

The emergence of the Western Contact Group on Namibia coincided with the nonpermanent Council membership of Canada and the Federal Republic of Germany in 1977–1978. At this time, several General Assembly resolutions had been adopted under massive pressure of the Organization of African Unity (OAU), which criticized the attitude of Western countries toward apartheid in general, and their stance toward the situation in Namibia and Rhodesia in particular. From this perspective, the joint activities of the five Western members of the Council—Canada, France, West Germany, the United Kingdom, and the United States—therefore may be seen as an exit strategy to develop a constructive response to (and escape from) that pressure. The coincidence of five like-minded Western states serving on the Council opened the gate for a concerted approach.

In January 1977, West Germany had explored such a possibility in the Foreign Office among experts. Consultations with the U.S. State Department in late February had led to the conclusion that the United States had been working in a similar direction.[81] Furthermore, informal working-level contacts among the "Western five" on March 4 in New York had shown a high convergence of policy agendas, which resulted in a first consultation on the level of permanent representatives (including experts) on March 9, 1977. However, at that stage the U.S. mission was still waiting for the final decision of the White House to go ahead with this initiative. The next consultation took place a few days later, on March 16, at the Canadian mission, which may be seen as the first official meeting of the Western Contact Group on Namibia.[82] The group operated "*alongside* and *not in* the Security Council simply to avoid obstruction from the Soviets."[83] In addition, launching the initiative inside the Council might have resulted in a certain resistance by the African countries.[84]

The Western Contact Group on Namibia worked primarily at the level of high-ranking members of the five UN missions. On several key occasions, meetings took place at the foreign minister level along with their ambassadors in Pretoria, Lusaka, and other capitals.[85] In 1977–1978, when the contact group developed the negotiation strategy and later the proposal for a settlement of the Namibian situation, the group met daily in New York.[86] At the expert level, it consisted of Paul Lapointe of Canada, Albert Thabault of France, Hans-Joachim Vergau of West Germany, James Murray and Tom Richardson of the United Kingdom, and Donald McHenry of the United States. The group met alternately at the permanent mission of the United States, Canada, and the United Kingdom, and less often at the French and West German missions. Although the Western five did not have a rotating chairmanship, they always appointed a speaker to deliver statements to the public (the UN, the South Africans, the South West Africa People's Organization [SWAPO], the Frontline States, and of course the press) on behalf of the contact group. In 1977 it held four rounds of talks in South Africa, four in New York and Lusaka with SWAPO, and several rounds of talks with the heads of government of the Frontline States: Angola, Botswana, Mozambique, Tanzania, and Zambia, including two proximity talks at the foreign minister level in New York.[87]

The South African government had been forced to the negotiation table after the Western five had threatened "stern action," for example, the adoption of mandatory sanctions if the country did not comply. These negotiations prepared the ground for the settlement proposal that the contact group presented to the Council on April 10, 1978. The Council adopted the proposal in its resolution 431 on July 27, 1978, after having received acceptance by South Africa and SWAPO. The resolution also requested the Secretary-General first "to appoint a Special Representative for Namibia in order to ensure the early independence of Namibia through free elections under the supervision and control of the United Nations," and second "to submit at the earliest possible date a report containing his recommendations for the implementation of the proposal for a settlement of the Namibia situation in accordance with resolution 385 (1976)."[88] Secretary-General Kurt Waldheim and his Special Representative, Martti Ahtisaari, presented the implementation plan on August 29, 1978, based on the proposal of the Western Contact Group on Namibia. While SWAPO accepted the plan, South Africa rejected it on the grounds that the report of the Secretary-General significantly deviated from the Western proposal, especially with respect to the size of the UN military contingent.[89] Nevertheless, the Council adopted the plan, in its resolution 435, on September 29, 1978.

It would take another decade for resolution 435 to become fully implemented. Reasons for the South African resistance may be found in a complex mix of factors that had resulted in a loss of credible threat from the Western five.[90] First, the high-level meeting of the foreign ministers of the contact group with representatives of the South African government in Pretoria in October 1978 revealed that the Western countries would not deliver on the threat of stern action. Second, the change of governments in Britain, Canada, and France impacted on the degree of cooperation among the Western five. Third, the arrival of the Reagan administration in 1981 and the subsequent adoption of the so-called linkage policy, which established a linkage between the implementation of the settlement plan and the withdrawal of Cuban troops from the neighboring country of Angola, effectively granted South Africa a convenient lever for continued delay. And fourth, there seemed to persist a certain fear in South Africa that any settlement might have repercussions on the domestic situation—for example, increased pressure for internal reform. The multilateral approach of the contact group ended most visibly with France suspending its membership effective December 7, 1983. Although the French government still supported resolution 435, it strongly disapproved of the linkage policy. Consultations between the other members of the contact group shifted to the level of Africa experts, focusing on the continued engagement of the Frontline States with confidence-building measures. The United States had taken over the leadership, basically pushing its own agenda. The Cold War thaw facilitated the conclusion of bilateral and trilateral agreements among Angola, Cuba, and South Africa at UN headquarters in December 1988, which paved the way for the implementation of the settlement plan.[91]

The Western Contact Group on Namibia illustrates the possibility of a successful interaction between a coalition of like-minded states and the UN. Advisory committees have also shown that informal ad hoc groupings of states can assist the Secretary-General in his efforts to implement mandates given by the General Assembly or the Security Council. Study of the Western Contact Group on Namibia sheds light on a conflict where a direct UN involvement had proven ineffective. While the settlement proposal for the transition of Namibia to independence had been negotiated outside the UN, it was embedded inside the framework of objectives as outlined in Security Council resolution 385. Although the Secretary-General had not been directly involved,[92] the Western five kept the Secretariat fully informed throughout the negotiation process. Ambassadors of the contact group held regular meetings in the Secretary-General's office, briefing him and discussing the latest developments and pending initiatives. The UN Transition Assistance Group (UNTAG) secured the successful implementation of resolution 435, with the key element of ensuring "the early independence of Namibia through free and fair elections under the supervision and control of the United Nations."[93]

Although the shift in U.S. policy from 1981 onward effectively ended the multiparty mediation of the Western five, members of the contact group continued to play a role in the negotiations toward a settlement in Namibia. The resolution of the conflict, as former Secretary-General Javier Pérez de Cuéllar has argued, "stands as a model for the utilization of the disparate capacities of the Organization and of its members toward a commonly agreed goal."[94] At the same time, the case of Namibia is indicative of the sobering realities under which UN conflict resolution takes place. First, it demonstrates the systemic problems of the United Nations in the field of crisis management and how informal groups of states may alleviate crises. Second, it sheds light on the factors that define success or failure of informal groups of states. And third, it illustrates the potential and limits of engaging the United States in a cooperative framework such as the Western Contact Group on Namibia.

The Proliferation of Groups in the Postbipolar Era

Informal ad hoc groupings of states gained additional momentum with the breakdown of the bipolar system as the UN was asked to manage simultaneously more and more complex crises. The postbipolar era is characterized by a shift away from border conflicts between states to conditions of internal violence that often spill over into neighboring countries in the region, as witnessed in the former Yugoslavia and parts of Africa. These new scenarios involve a different mix of actors, ranging from regular armies to militias and armed civilians. They may include the collapse of state authority and an absence of governance, accompanied by the breakdown of law and order.

While the management of intrastate conflicts was the exception between 1945 and 1989, this practice became the norm in the 1990s and has continued into the twenty-first century. All but three of fifty-six registered, major armed conflicts in the period 1990–2000 were internal.[95] These conflicts may affect or are affected themselves by external factors such as the illicit trafficking of arms and natural resources, the cross-border transit of rebel and government forces, regional powers sending their own forces into the conflict, and the migration of refugees across borders. These transnational factors tend to sustain conflicts, with potentially destabilizing spillover effects on neighboring countries or the subregion. Most casualties occur on the civilian rather than the military side, with some sources assessing the ratio as nine to one.[96] All this means that the Secretary-General and even the Security Council need the help of Member States in managing this increased complexity.

Complex problems also require differentiated responses from the international community. For example, negotiated settlements that end complex crises are not only military arrangements to cease armed violence; they also include a variety of tasks. These address both military and civilian issues, such as the supervision of cease-fires, disarmament, demobilization of armed forces, integration of former combatants into civilian life, humanitarian relief, establishment and training of police forces, and the organization and supervision of elections. UN operations increasingly have had to combine peacekeeping with peacebuilding functions, reflecting the complex arrangements that ended armed conflicts.

The complexity of demands has been further amplified by the proliferation of UN operations in the field. To illustrate, the UN had established only thirteen peacekeeping operations in the forty years between 1948 and 1988. Yet in the short, seven-year period between 1988 and 1995, the Organization sent twenty-six operations into the field. By 2003, a total of fifty-seven peace operations had been deployed by the United Nations.

The number of Security Council meetings increased accordingly to cope with the new demands. Both formal meetings, which are open to all Member States, and informal consultations, which are closed sessions, grew in number. Until 2000, informal consultations clearly outweighed formal meetings, with the gap slowly closing given the increased number of public debates and open meetings of the Security Council at the end of the decade. While the Council held 55 formal meetings and 62 consultations in 1988, adopting 20 resolutions and 8 presidential statements, these numbers increased to 135 meetings and 251 consultations in 1995, with 66 resolutions and 63 statements (see Figures 10.1 and 10.2). Examination of the huge discrepancy between the number of formal (public) meetings and informal (closed) consultations of the Security Council sheds some light on demands for greater transparency and expansion of the Council. From 1991 onward, the number of informal consultations increased much faster than the number of formal meetings. The high point was reached in 1994, when the Security Council convened 165 formal meetings but closed the doors 273 times for informal consultations.

The increasing demands of the changing security environment have affected both the Security Council and the office of the Secretary-General. The Security Council responded by extending the scope of Article 39,[97] adopting far-reaching mandates to deal with the complexity of crisis situations. The Secretary-General had to oversee complex emergencies involving the complete spectrum of preventive diplomacy, peacekeeping, peace enforcement,

Figure 10.1   Formal Meetings and Informal Consultations of the UN Security Council, 1988–2000

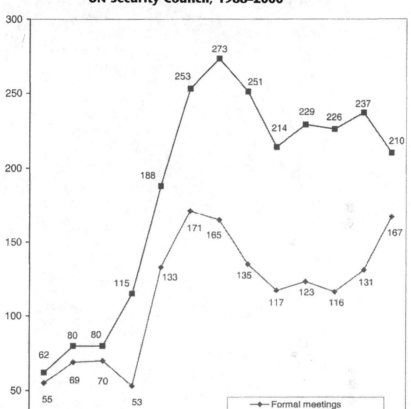

Source: Global Policy Forum, New York, www.globalpolicy.org/security/data/secmgtab.htm.

and peacebuilding, which he increasingly entrusted to special representatives acting on his behalf. Furthermore, the UN and its Member States continue to face hard choices regarding which conflicts to address. In 1996, then-Secretary-General Boutros-Ghali referred to this dilemma of selectivity: "Deciding when to act and when to refrain presents a profound ethical dilemma, but at present these choices are informed not by ethics but solely by power politics. The Secretary-General stands at the center of this quandary."[98] The situation has been exacerbated by the fact that the current formal composition of the

**Figure 10.2   Resolutions and Presidential Statements of the UN
Security Council, 1988–1999**

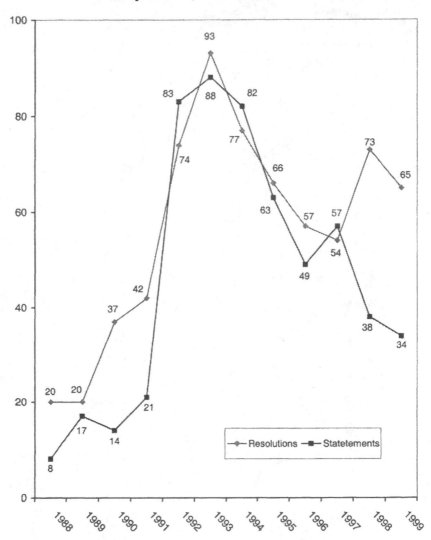

Source: Global Policy Forum, New York, www.globalpolicy.org/security/data/resolutn.htm.

permanent membership of the Council still mirrors the situation of 1945,
without taking into account the shifts in relative power among the actors of
the international system that have occurred since. The 1991 Gulf War had an
especially galvanizing effect on the reform debate because it revealed not only
the capability of the post–Cold War great power concert, epitomized in the

permanent membership of the Security Council, but also its incomplete structure.[99] It sharpened the perception of Member States that, under certain circumstances, such as removing Iraq from Kuwait, the Council had the capacity to impose order, although Chapter VII (Articles 43–48) was and has never been fully implemented. The motivation for reform grew only to some extent out of the newfound Council activism, but also out of the interest of many developing countries to conduct a kind of damage limitation. The far-reaching decisions taken by the Council to intervene in the "internal affairs" of states gave many countries a strong reminder that they could also be affected at some point in the future without having any significant influence on the decisionmaking process.[100]

In sum, informal ad hoc groupings of states proliferated out of the demands the UN faced on various levels. They offered a platform for increased cooperation, basically affecting the peacemaking efforts of the UN in three ways, as Secretary-General Boutros-Ghali outlined in 1995:

> First, it serves to impress upon the parties to a conflict that the international community is directly concerned with finding a solution to the conflict. Second, it provides a mechanism for conflict resolution that complements the efforts of the Secretary-General. Third, it provides one more channel for multilateral action by Member States. It serves to reinforce the principle that all are concerned in the work of the United Nations.[101]

Groups of Friends of the Secretary-General

In 1989, building on past experiences with ad hoc groups of Member States, the UN Secretariat created the Group of Friends of the Secretary-General on El Salvador. Since then, the concept of Groups of Friends has proliferated and mutated into a number of innovative responses to the ever-changing complex environment of international security affairs.

The Groups of Friends are made up of a small number of Member States, usually three to six members, whose representatives keep in close contact with the Secretary-General and support his efforts to find a peaceful solution to a specific crisis. Keeping the groups small is essential so that meetings can be called quickly and easily and so that a consensus can be maintained. A Group of Friends is formed around a specific issue, usually a country in crisis, for example, the Group of Friends of the Secretary-General on Haiti. The countries that form the group give the Secretary-General the leverage he needs to bring the parties to a conflict to the negotiating table and keep them engaged throughout the process. The formation and meeting structure is ad hoc and informal. Each group has come together under different circumstances and for different reasons, at times being called together directly by the Secretary-General and at other times through a self-selection process. Therefore, each group needs to be examined on a case-by-case basis. Nevertheless, there does seem to be a pattern to the phenomenon. In most instances, there is at least one member of the Security Council in the group, and in fact they may all be current serving members of the Council, forming a combination of permanent and nonpermanent members. This may vary, though, and members not on the Council may also be an important part of the group.

Creation of the First Group of Friends

In December 1989, Secretary-General Javier Pérez de Cuéllar began the process to establish the Group of Friends on El Salvador, the first such group, as a way of support for the Secretary-General's role in using his good offices. The concept was specifically conceived by Alvaro de Soto with the help of Francesc Vendrell and supported by the Secretary-General. It was understood to be a tool specifically at the service of the Secretary-General in his efforts on the issue at hand. Thus it was intended from the onset that any action would be conducted only at the request, or under the auspices, of the Secretary-General.

The idea to form a group of like-minded states supportive of the Secretary-General's effort was created to work out a negotiated political solution to the conflict in El Salvador through the support of governments that were not allied to either party to the conflict or that had no stake in its outcome. The term "Group of Friends of the Secretary-General" evolved later. At that time the UN, while it had been involved in Central America and particularly in Nicaragua, was not yet involved in El Salvador.

In 1989, Salvadoran president Alfredo Cristiani, elected to office in spring 1989, contacted the Secretary-General to ask his assistance. At about the same time, the rebel group Farabundo Martí National Liberation Front (FMLN) contacted Alvaro de Soto, through Rubén Zamora. Because FMLN members were unable to get U.S. visas during that era, it was decided to arrange a secret meeting between the leaders of the FMLN and de Soto in Canada on December 6. The timing was important because there was a meeting of the Central American presidents planned for December 8, at which they hoped to have the presidents announce the new role of the UN. The result of contacts with the two sides, which was formalized at the Central American meeting two days later, was that the UN would take up the role as intermediary, utilizing the good offices of the Secretary-General to get the talks going.

The Secretary-General and Alvaro de Soto knew that they would need the leverage that could only be provided by countries willing to take on the issue. They were searching for a way to create a group of countries that would act as a kind of support for the Secretary-General. It was vital for the success of the negotiations between the parties to ensure that the impartiality of the Secretary-General was not compromised and to counterbalance attempts at manipulation of the Secretary-General's efforts by one or another member of the Security Council acting as an ally for only one of the parties to the conflict, for example, the United States in supporting the Salvadoran government. Loss of impartiality would lead to the defection of one or both of the parties from the negotiations.

While U.S. support of the Salvadoran government was essentially bilateral, U.S. views were well known and compromised the impartiality of the Security Council. The United States did apparently complain that some members of the Secretariat, primarily de Soto, were pro-FMLN, and the Secretary-General had to discuss this with the U.S. president at the time.[102] In fact, if the Secretary-General needed protection from pressure, it was more directly from the United States rather than from the entire Security Council.

It was thought by de Soto at the time that the Secretary-General might borrow a device that is frequently used in intergovernmental bodies, which is the notion of "friends of the chairman" or "friends of the president." Frequently, when there is a standoff on an issue, and it is clear that a small negotiating forum is needed in order to achieve results, the chairman might simply gather a group of friends. There is no commitment placed on any participant. However, the chairman will choose the members properly so that he will have inside the room all those whom he feels need to be a party to any deal that might be struck. The chairman retains a certain deniability to the extent that he can always say that he was just meeting with a "group of friends." One can imagine many occasions where agreements that could not have been achieved in a formally constituted group, or in a large gathering such as the full membership of the General Assembly, can emerge from such a format.

On El Salvador, Secretary-General Pérez de Cuéllar and his staff formed a three-level diplomatic strategy. One level included the parties to the conflict, the government and the FMLN; the second was a group of very interested states, namely the United States, the Soviet Union, and Cuba; and the third comprised countries that were not directly interested but that wanted to support peace in the region and that could strengthen the position of the Secretary-General, the "Group of Friends." The original members of the Group of Friends were Colombia, Mexico, Venezuela, and Spain.

When the Central American presidents met on December 8, 1989, at the summit meeting in Costa Rica, they requested that the Secretary-General help them obtain the cooperation of countries outside Central America whose assistance in the process was necessary to make it work. Simultaneously, the Secretary-General was requested by the parties to offer his good offices in mediating the conflict. With these requests in hand, the United Nations had the authority it needed to move ahead.

The four countries that composed the group were already committed to finding a peaceful solution to the conflict and had openly expressed a commitment to removing the conflict from the entanglements of the East-West rivalry. The United States viewed the rebels as a Communist threat and a vehicle for Soviet influence in the Western Hemisphere. And in truth, the rebels

UN Photo 179073

Signing of the El Salvador peace accord, December 31, 1991. Seated at center is Secretary-General Pérez de Cuéllar and standing directly behind are his four Friends; from left to right, UN Ambassadors Juan Luis Yañez (Spain), Jorge Montaño (Mexico), Diego Arria (Venezuela), and Fernando Cepeda (Colombia).

had been receiving Cuban and Soviet support. But the Friends believed that the conflict grew out of poverty rather than ideological differences and wanted to prevent it from becoming a large-scale regional war with continued escalation of weapons pouring in from both superpowers.

Each of the countries played an important role both in maintaining the consensus of the group and in offering something unique to the process. Mexico had provided the FMLN with political asylum and therefore was able to offer a safe venue for meetings between the parties. Colombia, faced with internal conflicts of its own, was concerned to see that a peaceful solution would be achieved. In addition, Colombia was serving on the Security Council at the time, making it instrumental in ensuring that the Secretary-General was given the mandate by the Council to use his good offices. Venezuela's president was highly engaged personally in the process and would contact the guerrilla leaders, summon them to Caracas, and talk directly to them. He would also telephone the president of El Salvador. Spain was also a key player due to President Felipe González's influential activism in the region.

Mexico and Venezuela claim that their support was considered unconditional. Both countries had such close ties with El Salvador that they seemed to have a kind of authority, perhaps even a moral authority, without having to express it overtly. For example, both Mexico and Venezuela, oil-producing countries, had long-standing agreements with all the Central American and Caribbean countries on the sale of oil beginning in the mid-1970s, called the San José Program. Venezuela would sell oil to El Salvador, for example, at current market prices, but then the Venezuelan Investment Fund, a publicly owned facility, would open a credit account with El Salvador equivalent to 30 percent of its oil bill. These funds could then be used for development projects. The plan would last for fourteen years, with a seven-year grace period and seven more years to pay it off at very low interest rates. Mexico has a similar program, also called the San José Program. But the two countries never used this program explicitly as a negotiating tool during their intermediation as members of the Group of Friends, or at any other time during the peace process.[103]

The Purpose and Function of a Group of Friends

The goal of the Group of Friends process is to use more than one country to exert pressure and present a common view that represents the international community as a whole. On his own, the Secretary-General, as the head administrator of the UN, cannot pressure state parties to act. His abilities are extremely limited without the backing of key Member States to exert pressure. The Group of Friends offers the Secretary-General some "comfort space" in which to take action, with the backing of key members to keep a peace process on track and to harness rival would-be mediators to work in the same direction rather than at cross-purposes. It can prove extremely difficult to find a solution to a conflict if a number of actors are trying to carry on separate mediation efforts simultaneously with the parties involved. A Group of Friends can coordinate those efforts into one ongoing process.

The group can be used during the negotiation process prior to reaching a formal agreement, or the Friends might be used to aid in the implementation of an agreement after the parties have found some common ground but are dragging their heals. A Friend can invite one or more of the parties to its capital for a round of serious talks to probe for solutions. In the Salvadoran case, both Mexico and Venezuela as Friends invited the parties to their countries to meet and carry on negotiations. In this sense, a head of government can facil-

itate negotiations by supplying a venue for dialogue and can deliver or withhold rewards in a way that the Secretary-General cannot.

The language in a peace agreement can often be very general and may
need further clarification when it comes time to implement the provisions of
an accord. It will also need to be translated into practice in a way that is faithful to the spirit of the agreement and acceptable to the parties. This requires a
continued process of negotiation with the help of the Secretary-General and
the Friends, who keep in contact with the parties, ensure that implementation
is staying on course, and prevent the diplomatic process from breaking down.
The agreement on El Salvador called for the military forces of the government
and the FMLN to withdraw to confined areas, government forces to their gar-
risons and the FMLN to camps. However, the agreement did not contain a
map specifying the location of the camps. Some of the camps ended up in
areas where there was not enough available drinking water or in areas that
were subject to flooding. UN agencies had to coordinate efforts to alleviate
these problems and were aided by donor support through the Friends and others Member States. Failure to establish adequate camps for the FMLN already
had slowed the process and could have derailed it altogether.

There is often a key leader in the group, one who can apply leverage and
pressure and get an intransigent party to see the "wisdom" of complying with
the terms of the agreement. A certain amount of carrot-and-stick diplomacy
can be carried out by a Member State that the Secretary-General would be
unable to undertake. In the case of El Salvador, the Mexican government,
through its Permanent Representative to the United Nations, Ambassador
Jorge Montaño, the president of Venezuela, Carlos Andrés Pérez, and
Venezuela's ambassador to the United Nations, Diego Arria, were personally
engaged in the process.

The United States, which became a Friend in what was referred to as the
"Four Plus One," provided funds for judicial reform and training for the new
national police. Also, in the agreement it was stated that a land distribution
plan had to be implemented, and FMLN forces were threatening not to turn in
their weapons until the land distribution plan was under way.[104] To support
this part of the agreement, the United States donated funds to the lending
institutions in El Salvador in order to provide loans to those eligible to pur-
chase small plots of land. Spain provided a large police contingent along with
financial and technical support for the new national police. Mexico,
Venezuela, and Colombia also provided police contingents.[105]

It is extremely important, if the mediation is to work, that the group and
all its members are perceived by the parties to be impartial. If a Friend is seen
to be taking sides, then the process is likely to break down. Without impartiality, the parties may lose confidence that the negotiations can serve them
fairly. They may decide that they can do better by returning to the fighting to
achieve what they want. It can be a delicate balancing act, and outsiders may

see the Group of Friends as having a stake in the outcome. However, the key is the perceptions of the parties and the careful orchestration that takes place behind the scenes by the Secretary-General and his staff to ensure that impartiality is maintained during any interaction with both sides.

In addition to keeping the process on track and presenting a common policy on the issue, the group takes on a number of other functions. Friends meet and prepare language for resolutions that are being considered by the Security Council or in the General Assembly. Then they become a vehicle to deliver and support the resolution, using their weight to persuade other Member States to come on board. Because they are focused on the day-to-day events surrounding the process, they are generally considered to be the best-informed and most engaged members. Their view is generally accepted by other Member States, which may not be following the issue as closely. By not taking sides, the Friends are only interested in restoring peace so that relations in the region can be normalized. Their involvement in the process, as explained above, will only be productive as long as the parties are willing to accept their role as intermediaries. Through these activities, the Group of Friends provides another "channel for multilateral action by Member States"[106] ancillary to the more formal UN bodies.

In their capacity as concerned Member States, the Group of Friends can fill another very important role. The Secretary-General touched on this additional function in a speech in May 1995:

> The complexity of peace-keeping operations of the second generation is such, that, in recent years, we have been confronted with a new type of problem: how to terminate a mission. Typically, two possibilities should be considered. First, when, as in Cambodia, a mission has fulfilled its mandate, and the country is at peace, the issue of terminating the mission arises. Some governments, understandably, are reluctant to have the mission continue at full strength. But a continued international presence is necessary to complete peace-building, to ensure that the country does not slide back into conflict. . . .
> The second possibility is that the mission has not fulfilled its mandate.
> . . .
> Thus, in Somalia, a group of nations, among them the United States, the United Kingdom and Italy helped the pullout of UN troops.[107]

When peacekeeping troops have left the country and the UN is no longer involved in a major way, the Group of Friends can offer the Secretary-General and the UN a means of preventing conflict from erupting again by continuing to mediate disputes and offering incentives to the parties to continue to manage the peace. The Group of Friends on El Salvador continued to meet for several years and offer their assistance to the Secretary-General as needed. A subsequent Group of Friends on Guatemala, which emerged out of the Group of Friends on El Salvador, also continued to meet long after the peace process had formally ended.

The Friends of the Secretary-General on the question of Haiti have also continued to offer support. A letter signed by these Friends, including Ambassadors Emilio Cárdenas (Argentina), Robert R. Fowler (Canada), Jean Bernard Merimée (France), Enrique Tejera-Paris (Venezuela), and Madeleine Albright (the United States), which was circulated as an official document of the United Nations on April 17, 1995, underlined the signers' "firm support for President Jean Bertrand Aristide and the Government of Haiti" and "the importance of immediate and sustained international assistance in supporting the Haitian people through international financial institutions and bilateral and multilateral programmes." The letter also stated that "the Friends join the Secretary-General's call of March 23 for Member States to contribute to the creation of an adequate police force in Haiti and to the international police monitoring programme."[108] This sustained support offers the United Nations a low-cost yet ongoing mechanism carried out by a group of members who are sincerely concerned with the maintenance of peace in the country in question.

Countries That Have Formed Groups of Friends

El Salvador (begun in December 1989): Colombia, Mexico, Spain, Venezuela, and behind the scenes, the United States, referred to as the "Four Plus One."

Haiti (begun in approximately January 1993): Canada, France, the United States, and Venezuela, later joined by Argentina and again by Chile as these countries replaced each other on the Security Council.

Western Sahara (begun in approximately April 1993): France, Spain, the United Kingdom, the United States, and later Djibouti, Cape Verde, and Venezuela.

Georgia (begun in approximately December 1993): A self-constituted group referred to as the "Friends of Georgia" rather than the "Friends of the Secretary-General," including France, Germany, Russia, the United Kingdom, and the United States.

Guatemala (begun in approximately January 1994): A self-constituted group referred to as the "Friends of the Guatemalan Peace Process" (to act as Friends of the Secretary-General is only part of their activity), including Colombia, Mexico, Norway, Spain, the United States, and Venezuela.

Suriname (begun in 1994): Brazil, the Netherlands, the United States, and Venezuela.

Afghanistan (begun in 1994): Called the "Friends Group on Afghanistan," a self-constituted group including Iran, Pakistan, Russia, Saudi Arabia, and the United States. This grouping did not work, and another group was formed, called the "Six Plus Two," consisting of China, Iran, Pakistan, Tajikistan, Turkmenistan, and

Uzbekistan, plus Russia and the United States. Other groups on Afghanistan include the "Group of 21" and the "Afghanistan Support Group," formed in 1996 of the primary donor countries to Afghanistan.

Tajikistan (begun in approximately May 1995): Afghanistan, Iran, Kazakhstan, Turkey, Turkmenistan, the United States, and Uzbekistan.

"Friends of Rapid Reaction" (begun in September 1995): Canada and the Netherlands, plus twenty-two other countries.

Central African Republic (begun in 1998): Called the "Friends of the Central African Republic," including Canada, Côte d'Ivoire, France, Gabon, Kenya, Senegal, Togo, and the United States.

Guinea-Bissau (begun in 1999): Called the "Friends of Guinea-Bissau," coordinated by Gambia, including Brazil, Canada, France, Germany, Guinea, Italy, the Netherlands, Nigeria, Portugal, Senegal, Sweden, Togo, and the United States.

East Timor (begun in 1999): Called the "Core Group on East Timor" and gathered outside the UN framework, including Australia, Austria, Brazil, Japan, New Zealand, the United Kingdom, the United States, and the World Bank.

Kosovo (begun in 1999): Called the "Group of Friends of Kosovo," including eighteen countries and three international organizations: Austria, Belgium, Canada, China, Denmark, Finland, France, Germany, Greece, Italy, Japan, the Netherlands, Russia, Spain, Sweden, Turkey, the United Kingdom, and the United States; the Organization for Security and Cooperation in Europe, the European Union, and the Organization of Islamic Conferences (which has 56 Islamic state members).

Ethiopia and Eritrea (begun in 2000): called the "Friends of Eritrea and Ethiopia," coordinated by the Netherlands, including Algeria, Canada, Denmark, India, Ireland, Germany, Italy, Jordan, Kenya, the Netherlands, Norway, France, the United States and DPKO (Department of Peacekeeping Operations).

It is interesting to note the approximate three-year gap in constituting Friends groups between 1995–1996 and 1999 (with the only exception being the Friends of the Central African Republic, established in 1998), which resumed with the formation of groups on Guinea-Bissau, East Timor, and Kosovo. This reflects a disappointment with the process during those years, as many conflicts remained unresolved. Growing disillusionment with the capabilities of the UN as a peacekeeping organization led to a slowdown in related activities between 1996 and 1998, when peacekeeping expenditures dropped significantly, from $3.36 billion in 1995 to $1 billion in fiscal year 1998–1999 (see

Figure 10.3). Yet the number of Council meetings remained high, with, for example, 116 formal meetings and 226 consultations in 1998. In 1999–2000, the pendulum swung back and the Council adopted another four operations, causing peacekeeping expenditures to rise again to $1.7 billion.[109] The proliferation of informal ad hoc groupings of states, especially between 1991 and

Figure 10.3   Costs of UN Peacekeeping Forces, 1991–2001 (in U.S.$ millions)

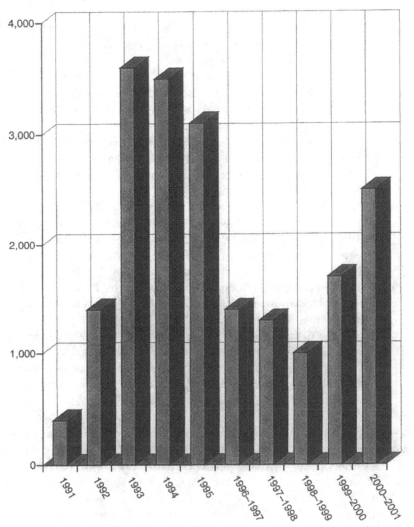

Source: United Nations Department of Peacekeeping Operations, www.un.org/depts/dpko/pub/pdf/7.pdf.

Note: Data for 2000–2001 are estimated.

1994 and again from 1999 onward, appears to coincide with these developments. The crises of East Timor and Kosovo apparently reinvigorated the need to go back to a means of support that had worked in the past and that could play a role in keeping peace processes on track.

A Group of Friends forms most easily when a similar mechanism has already been in existence. For example, the Group of Friends on El Salvador evolved largely out of the Contadora Process and the countries that had supported that effort (adding Spain but not including Panama). However, becoming a member of a Group of Friends gives these countries a specific role to play within the larger UN system, provides a support mechanism for the Secretary-General, and offers stability to the group, which membership, as such, provides. It is important that the members are like-minded and have the political will to stay with the issue. Maintaining a like-minded or common approach is essential so that the Friends act according to the same principles when applying pressure to the parties. It would be counter to the process if each "Friend" were putting pressure on the parties to behave in a different manner. A Group of Friends most likely cannot form if the members are too far apart on the issues, for example, the Contact Group on the Former Yugoslavia was not a Friends group because the members had different views on the outcome of the conflict (the United States siding with the Bosnian government and Russia siding with the Serbs).

How Does a Group of Friends Function?

The way a Group of Friends functions takes on a triangular dimension with the following pivotal apexes of activity: New York, the field (in the country in question), and the capitals of the members of the group. The Friends are constituted in New York but usually have a counterpart in the field. There seems to be a flow of activity among the ambassadors of the group who are in the country where the operation is taking place, back to their capitals, and also to and from the ambassadors and the Secretary-General in New York.

The group itself does not always have to meet physically. Contact may take place by phone or one-on-one between the members or with the Secretary-General. Sometimes, they may want to meet but cannot. They may work better by not coming together. Members of the group may not want to be seen working with another member for reasons outside the particular issue of focus due to political sensitivities. However, for some groups, meeting as a whole is essential in order to develop and maintain a consensus. These meetings generally take place in New York among the Member State ambassadors to the United Nations and the Secretary-General. Meetings are primarily held in New York when consensus needs to be developed within the Security Council on the drafting of a resolution or the formulation of policy. New York also becomes the venue for meeting individually with the parties to the dispute.

Meetings in the field tend to take place after an agreement has been reached between the parties to the conflict and implementation is under way. These discussions are held with the Special Representative of the Secretary-General and the ambassadors to the country in question from the members of the Group of Friends. Hence the group can actually be active in many places. If the Secretary-General is traveling, and the need arises, he may call a meeting of the Group of Friends by meeting with their ambassadors in whatever country he might be visiting, a very useful aspect of this particular mechanism. The Secretary-General, on a visit to France, convened a meeting with the Group of Friends of the Secretary-General on Haiti, for example, and met in Paris with a representative of the French government and the other ambassadors to France from the group.

Policy decisions, however, are made in the capitals of each of the Member States involved, and the ambassadors report information back to their own capitals. Ideas can come from any side of the triangle, but decisions generally are made by the governments. An ambassador from a small country may have more leeway to make policy decisions on his or her own. However, the ambassadors from the larger countries will receive directions from, or at least confer with, their government back home. The ambassadors are appointed by and serve their governments and must take their direction from government leaders. So the link to the capitals is essential, particularly when governments may be asked to apply leverage and then must be able to deliver on any promises made to the parties. In El Salvador, Spain contributed resources to the camps when demobilization of the military factions was in jeopardy. This information was transmitted from the field to Madrid, and funding was made available to get the demobilization process back on track.[110]

Problems arising in the field could be conveyed by the Special Representative to the local ambassadors, who in turn might contact their capitals. Simultaneously, the Special Representative could be in contact with the Secretary-General in New York, who could call an emergency meeting of the group, could meet with them individually (which has often been the case), or could reach them by phone. New York can be a useful venue because all the members are in close proximity and can meet with the Secretary-General very quickly and easily. Also, New York has the advantage of allowing discussions to take place invisibly. Diplomats are often reluctant to make a symbolic statement by traveling to another country for a meeting.

The UN Secretariat can also play a key role in this mechanism by providing background information and supporting the work of the special political adviser to the special envoy or representative of the Secretary-General on the country in question. These political advisers come from within the office of the Secretary-General or from the Department of Political Affairs, serving at the regional division (or desk) for the country in question. The special adviser reports directly to the envoy or representative of the Secretary-General and not to an undersecretary. A special political adviser may have language and diplomatic skills that enhance the negotiating process and may travel for the Secretary-General, or his envoy or representative, when needed. For example, Alvaro de Soto of the Secretariat played a very important role in assisting the successive Special Representatives to El Salvador (Iqbal Riza, Augusto Ramirez-Ocampo, and Enrique ter Horst)[111] and provided an important continuity to the process when these representatives replaced one another. On Haiti, Francesc Vendrell played a significant role in assisting Special Envoy Dante Caputo, who was also assisted by Nicole Lannegrace of the UN Department of Political Affairs. Lannegrace continued on to assist the Special Representative to Haiti, Lakhdar Brahimi, when Caputo resigned.

Under What Circumstances Is a Group of Friends Formed or Not Formed?

In order to form a group, certain conditions are needed. First, it is necessary to have credible players, those in the region who don't have a national stake in the outcome that serves one party over the other, or a tainted history in the region that cannot be overcome. It is helpful to have one or two credible players outside the region who have the capacity to apply pressure through power or by offering resources, for example, the U.S. loans to El Salvador for land reform and Spain's significant contribution to military and police observers in El Salvador. Second, it is important that a Friends group comprise countries that have enough political will to take on the issue and stay with it through various crises, while maintaining a consensus with one another and the Secretary-General. Third, there must be a legitimate contact inside the target country to deal with on a consistent basis and to provide consent. In Somalia, there was no government to deal with, and in Burundi the government told the United Nations to stay out.

There are various reasons for which a Group of Friends will not come together. First, a group will not form if there are no countries that can trust one another or that can reach consensus on a common policy. For example, countries that might be interested in being engaged on the issue must not be looking for a particular outcome to the conflict that might favor one side or the other or serve their own interests rather than the interest of peace—problems that arose with the contact group in Bosnia. Second, a group won't form if the crisis comes at a time when the key members are already overloaded or feel that they should not get involved in a hostile situation, for example, the crisis in Burundi. Third, a group won't form if there is no one in the country under crisis to deal with and Member States are not prepared to mount the necessary means to deal with the situation by force without invitation.

It was difficult to rally support in Rwanda to stop the genocide because countries were hesitant to get involved in the midst of hostilities. The Security Council had been unable to take speedy action. France was the only nation willing to deploy troops to Rwanda during the crisis, and even though it had a history of interests in the region, there was no one else willing to intervene and no capacity to form a group. As with France in Rwanda or Nigeria's involvement in Liberia, a country with an interest in the region may be especially willing to intervene. While such a country may provide the needed assistance in a crisis, the international community needs to be careful that the interested intervener is not pursuing its own hegemonic goals at the cost of the country in crisis. The trade-offs here are complex.

If a group cannot come together to apply common pressure on a specific issue, the Secretary-General will try to keep an informative process going and the dialogue alive by continuing to meet with key ambassadors to the United Nations and by keeping in close contact with UN agencies to encourage preventive action.

Skepticism at the United Nations

While ad hoc groups can be, and have been, very useful tools, they have not always worked, particularly when members of the group are unable to maintain a consensus or separate their own interests from the peace process. The Friends of Tajikistan is a case in point: one of the Friends, Afghanistan, had been deeply embroiled in a war of its own and is still unstable.

The concept of Groups of Friends has been viewed as highly undemocratic by a few members of the UN, particularly in the mid-1990s.[112] At that time, the Friends of El Salvador and the group on Haiti were both active. In addition, during that period, Groups of Friends formed on Western Sahara, Georgia, and Guatemala. These skeptical members, who were serving on the Security Council at the time, felt that the whole Security Council should be involved in the work of the Group of Friends, not just an elite few. They were angry that the groups met privately and refused to discuss with the other members of the Security Council what they were doing. A few Council members who were not in the Group of Friends resented that drafts of resolutions were presented to the Council as a finished product. They felt that what the groups were doing, in fact, was the role of the entire Security Council, which is the institution within the United Nations designated to handle these kinds of issues. They particularly resented that, after the end of the Cold War, just at the time when the Security Council was finally capable of taking action, these other elite groups were usurping that right and marginalizing the work of the legally constituted bodies. Their concern rose as the number of the Friends groups began to grow. These members requested that the work of the Friends be made more open and available to the entire Council. These requests later led to greater communication between the groups and the Security Council, and many of those members who were highly critical of Friends groups have since expressed their belief that the process is evolving in a positive direction and becoming more open and democratic.[113]

UN members recognize that it is useful to have a clearinghouse for mediation. They also recognize that countries that have leverage can play a useful role from time to time through "heavy arm-twisting" when parties to a conflict have become intransigent. But there was a concern that these Groups of Friends were not acting in a manner that was accountable to the Security Council or the General Assembly and were bypassing these institutions.[114] The negative reaction to the formation of Groups of Friends as elitist will have to be reckoned with by the Secretary-General if the groups are to function in a positive way within the larger context of the UN. This can be done through greater communication with the Security Council and/or the General Assembly. While it is fair to ask Friends groups to be in communication with the Security Council, efforts to curtail the use of Friends under accusations of elitism are counterproductive to the goals of the UN, namely international peace and security.

The Friends of Rapid Reaction

While most ad hoc groups focus on a country in crisis, the mechanism has also been adopted to apply leverage on a particular issue, for example, developing a rapid reaction UN capability. In various reports, the Secretary-General had asked Member States to explore the possibility of developing a rapid reaction or rapid deployment capability, particularly in the aftermath of the tragedy in Rwanda. The Friends of Rapid Reaction was formed during the period of the general debate of the General Assembly in fall 1995, the fiftieth anniversary of the United Nations. The Canadian government, whose General Romeo Dallaire had been the UN force commander in Rwanda during the crisis,[115] had released a report in September 1995 on developing a rapid reaction capability for the United Nations. Produced with the support of the Canadian government, it stimulated the formation of a group of like-minded countries that developed a consensus based on many of the concepts in the report. The cochairs of the Friends of Rapid Reaction were Canada and the Netherlands. The group had an additional twenty-two members, including all the Nordic countries, and representation from the Group of 77 as well as other supporting Member States.

The rapid reaction group purposefully did not include any of the permanent five. Politically, it was considered by the cochairs to be better if the United States and other permanent members were not seen to dominate the process. Also, because the United States had been delinquent in paying its assessments during that period, many countries did not want to join any group of which it was a member. For a time, there appeared to be widespread anger at the United States for withholding its payments, leaving the UN in the worst financial crisis of its fifty-year history. The group kept in communication with the five permanent members, however, essentially through the Military Staff Committee, which continues to meet, albeit only at the colonel level. The group also consulted regularly with the UN Secretariat in the Department of Peacekeeping Operations (DPKO).

The Friends of Rapid Reaction represented an expansion and evolution of the Friends concept.[116] While earlier groups were centered around a crisis in a country or region, this Friends group was focused on an operational reform of the UN. Its mandate was significantly different and its role was therefore changed from that of the small, tight groups that meet in confidence and carry out sensitive diplomatic negotiations. This group was much larger, having twenty-four members instead of the usual three to six. The purpose here was to develop a broad consensus and to build the means to launch the project.

The consensus of the group seemed to be fairly broad, basically that (1) the UN should have a rapid reaction capability; (2) the Member States would loan officers to establish and maintain an operational-level headquarters located in New York, which would be responsible for planning and for advance preparations; (3) the UN, when needed, would be able to assemble from Member States a multifunctional force of up to 5,000 military and civilian personnel and rapidly deploy it under the control of the operational-level headquarters; and (4) forces would be provided through the standby arrangements that have already been established with most UN countries, which state what troops and equipment can be made available to the United Nations as needed on a case-by-case basis.

Members of the Friends of Rapid Reaction had good representation from various regions of the world that were in agreement, including Latin America, Africa, and Asia, as well as Europe.[117] They also worked with DPKO. The advantage to DPKO is that this operational headquarters could be deployed immediately and intact into the field. Then DPKO would not suddenly be required to shop around for military officers to send on a mission. DPKO would also not have to give up its own staff to go into the field and could continue its role of arranging the logistics for deployment and liaising with the Secretary-General and the Member States through the UN base in New York. DPKO now has a staff of about 600, only some of whom are military officers. The rest are support and planning staff. Now with some fifteen UN operations in the field, DPKO cannot afford to lose officers to a sudden crisis situation.

There was a great deal of optimism about the implementation of the rapid reaction plan in the beginning, but momentum waned when some Member States from the developing world feared that the force would be used most often in the Third World and might violate the sovereign rights of the country involved. There was also some backlash against the formation of the Friends group because a few troop-contributing countries, which had not been invited to join the group, were angry about their exclusion. The Friends thought that they would have the headquarters up and running in about two years, but this was slowed by differences within the General Assembly.[118] The Member States had planned to cover all the costs, with none to the United Nations.

This could be an advantage at a time when the United Nations is under budgetary stress.

By 2002, consensus on creating a rapid reaction headquarters had accumulated and a sufficient critical mass had come together to overcome the previous obstacles, due to the continued work of the Friends to build support. Sensitivities on issues of sovereignty by some members of the nonaligned movement were counterproductive to the needs of other countries, particularly in Africa, that were often in need of rapid deployment on humanitarian grounds. Now, many in the nonaligned movement are supportive of the rapid reaction movement, understanding that if the UN does not have this capacity, then countries in the North will step in to fill the vacuum. If the UN is involved, then troop-contributing countries from around the world will participate and the equipment that can be provided by Northern countries will be utilized by all the members. The first steps have been taken to create an operational headquarters for rapid deployment in New York, with equipment storage and logistical support in Brindisi, Italy. At the same time, the Danish had been creating what is called the Standby High Readiness Brigade (SHIRBRIG), an international force trained to work in cooperation with the Canadian-Dutch plan for the operational headquarters.[119] The first test of this deployment mechanism has been the recent deployment of SHIRBRIG to Ethiopia-Eritrea. The problem with SHIRBRIG as a concept is, now that it is deployed in Ethiopia-Eritrea, it is unavailable for rapid deployment elsewhere. Nevertheless, the Friends group was instrumental in building support for this new mechanism and demonstrates that these kinds of groupings of Member States can be used in response to issues other than country-specific crises.

Conclusion

The formation of ad hoc groupings of states has become a useful tool to move a process forward in resolving an intransigent problem and to provide advice or support to the Secretary-General. It offers the Secretary-General and the United Nations a mechanism for taking action to resolve an issue through the support of a group of like-minded Member States in a way that would otherwise be more difficult for the Secretary-General to do without the backing of Member States that can offer both legitimacy and leverage. Ad hoc groups can help keep the process on track, channel mediation through one consistent source, formulate policy, and apply pressure on the parties to a conflict to cooperate in implementing an agreement. The groups offer the UN and Secretary-General a clearinghouse to coordinate different channels of mediation, a sounding board to try out different ideas, and a basis of consensus to cushion the Secretary-General when tough decisions have to be made.

At a time when the Security Council is seized with numerous global issues, an ad hoc group of Member States, along with the Secretary-General, can specialize on a specific issue and carry out the needed information-gathering and policy preparation for the rest of the members, forming a kind of expert committee. One of the advantages of the mechanism is its versatility. Ambassadors anywhere in the world, as representatives of the members of a group, can meet when needed to keep the process going. The personalities of these actors are important. Active leadership can keep the process on track, but a player who tries to take over the action and take initiatives outside the consensus of the group can spoil the efforts to achieve a peaceful solution.

As seen with the Friends of Rapid Reaction, this tool can also be used to support the implementation of a new concept or structural reform and is not limited to dealing with a country or region in crisis. It gives the members of the UN, whether on the Security Council or not, a greater role in the functions of the Organization. Where there is sufficient will by the group, it can stay with an issue and maintain an ongoing presence after the UN has officially ended its mission. There are times, as discussed above, when a group cannot be formed, and there may be times when a group will not be effective.

Also, it is important to take into account the negative reaction by some members to the formation of what they may see as elite groups that operate outside the legitimate bodies of the UN without some kind of accountability. The negative reaction may fade, however, if those members themselves become involved in such "elitist grouping."[120] Guidance by an impartial Secretary-General is very important, so that self-selected Member States do not band together to push a solution that serves their interests and ignores the interests of the parties involved. Objections notwithstanding, this innovative mechanism continues to grow and evolve. Adjustments can be made, as they already have been, to make ad hoc groups more effective and more acceptable to the other members of the Security Council and the United Nations as a whole. Ad hoc groups of Member States have clearly emerged as another useful tool for the Secretary-General as he seeks to resolve conflicts, prevent parties from returning to violence, and promote international peace and security.

Notes

1. UN Doc. SG/SM/5624, press release, May 1, 1995.

2. Janus appears in Roman mythology as a two-faced deity, with each face looking in opposite directions. He was usually associated with vigilance and new beginnings, because he could look backward and forward at the same time. The doors of his temple were open during times of war and closed in times of peace.

3. For a more detailed discussion of Security Council decisionmaking, see Sydney D. Bailey and Sam Daws, *The Procedure of the UN Security Council*, 3rd ed. (Oxford: Oxford University Press, 1998).

4. See Francis Harry Hinsley, "Peace and War in Modern Times," in Raimo Väyrynen, ed., *The Quest for Peace: Transcending Collective Violence and War Among Societies, Cultures, and States* (London: Sage, 1987), p. 65.

5. The right of individual and collective defense as later embodied in Article 51 remained unaffected. Ibid., p. 67.

6. See Francis Harry Hinsley, *Power and the Pursuit of Peace: Theory and Practice in the History of Relations Between States* (Cambridge: Cambridge University Press, 1963), p. 340.

7. Quoted in James S. Sutterlin, "The Past as Prologue," in Bruce Russett, ed., *The Once and Future Security Council* (New York: St. Martin's Press, 1997), p. 3.

8. See Herbert George Nicholas, *The United Nations as a Political Institution,* 5th ed. (London: Oxford University Press, 1975), p. 19.

9. See Georg Schild, *Bretton Woods and Dumbarton Oaks: American Economic and Political Post-War Planning in the Summer of 1944* (Basingstoke, Hampshire, UK: Macmillan, 1995), p. 22; and Townsend Hoopes and Douglas Brinkley, *FDR and the Creation of the U.N.* (New Haven, Conn.: Yale University Press, 1997), pp. 43–54.

10. See Jürgen Heideking, "Völkerbund und Vereinte Nationen in der internationalen Politik," *Aus Politik und Zeitgeschichte* 36, no. 33 (September 1983): 6.

11. Edward Hallett Carr, *The Twenty Years' Crisis 1919–1939: An Introduction to the Study of International Relations,* 2nd ed. (London: Macmillan, 1961), p. 224.

12. See the preamble to the UN Charter.

13. Martin Wight, *Power Politics* (London: Leicester University Press, 1978), p. 218, emphasis added.

14. See Bruno Simma, *The Charter of the United Nations: A Commentary* (Oxford: Oxford University Press, 1994), pp. 661–678.

15. Samuel Pufendorf, *De Jure Naturae et Gentium Libri Octo,* vol. 2, translation of the 1688 edition by C. H. Oldfather and W. Λ. Oldfather, *The Classics of International Law,* no. 17 (1934): 1051, quoted in Bardo Fassbender, *UN Security Council and the Right of Veto: A Constitutional Perspective* (The Hague: Kluwer Law International, 1998), p. 17.

16. See Fernand van Langenhove, *La crise du système de sécurité collective des Nations Unies, 1946–1957* (The Hague: M. Nijhoff, 1958).

17. Bailey and Daws, *Procedure of the UN Security Council,* p. 239.

18. Ibid., p. 228.

19. See Sydney D. Bailey, *Voting in the Security Council* (Bloomington: Indiana University Press, 1969); Inis L. Claude Jr., *Swords Into Plowshares: The Problems and Progress of International Organization,* 3rd ed. (New York: Random House, 1964), p. 140.

20. Adam Roberts, "The United Nations: Variants of Collective Security," in Ngaire Woods, ed., *Explaining International Relations Since 1945* (Oxford: Oxford University Press, 1996), pp. 309–336.

21. Ibid., p. 319.

22. Ruth Wedgwood, "Unilateral Action in a Multilateral World," in Stewart Patrick and Shepard Forman, eds., *Multilateralism and U.S. Foreign Policy: Ambivalent Engagement* (Boulder: Lynne Rienner, 2002), p. 178.

23. Roberts, "The United Nations," p. 319.

24. Ibid., p. 322.

25. Wedgwood, "Unilateral Action in a Multilateral World," p. 185.

26. See Richard Hiscocks, *The Security Council: A Study in Adolescence* (New York: Free Press, 1973), pp. 163–164.

27. Ibid.

28. UN Doc. S/84, July 7, 1950.

29. Hiscocks, *Security Council,* p. 166.

30. The title of this resolution stems from its introductory call: "Uniting for Peace
. . ." The resolution was adopted by the General Assembly with fifty-two votes in
favor, five against, and two abstentions. UN Doc. A/RES/377, November 3, 1950,
operative para. 1.

31. The fourteen members were China, Colombia, Czechoslovakia, France, India,
Iraq, Israel, New Zealand, Pakistan, the Soviet Union, Sweden, the United Kingdom,
the United States, and Uruguay. See ibid., operative para. 3.

32. Ten emergency special sessions have been convened so far. See www.un.org/
ga/documents/liemsps.htm.

33. Roberts, "The United Nations," p. 327.

34. Measures for the pacific settlement of disputes include negotiation, inquiry,
mediation, conciliation, arbitration, judicial settlement, resort to regional agencies of
arrangements, and other peaceful means. See Simma, Charter of the United Nations,
pp. 505–514.

35. See ibid., pp. 565–603.

36. Roberts, "The United Nations," p. 327.

37. Marrack Goulding, "The Evolution of United Nations Peacekeeping," International Affairs 69, no. 3 (July 1993): 455.

38. See Anthony Parsons, From Cold War to Hot Peace: UN Interventions
1947–1995 (London: Penguin, 1995), pp. 77–93, 167–182.

39. Nicholas, United Nations as a Political Institution, p. 56.

40. See UN Doc. A/2253, November 10, 1956.

41. Andrew W. Cordier and Wilder Foote, eds., Public Papers of the Secretaries-
General of the United Nations, vol. 1, Trygve Lie (New York: Columbia University
Press, 1969), p. 513.

42. Thomas L. Hughes, "On the Causes of Our Discontents," Foreign Affairs 47,
no. 4 (1969): 660.

43. See UN Doc. A/2967, September 14, 1955, para. 3.

44. In January 1953, Dwight D. Eisenhower had taken office as president of the
United States.

45. See UN Doc. A/RES/230, December 4, 1954.

46. The committee consisted of Nobel Prize winners Sir John Cockcroft of the
United Kingdom and I. I. Rabi of the United States. Further representatives were
Soviet Academy member D. V. Skobeltzin; Homi Bhabba of India and W. B. Lewis of
Canada, both heads of their countries' atomic energy programs; Bertrand Goldschmidt
of France; and J. Costa Ribeiro of Brazil. See UN Doc. A/2967, September 14, 1955,
para. 3; UN oral history interview with Brian Urquhart, October 15, 1984; and Brian
Urquhart, Hammarskjöld (New York: Harper and Row, 1972), p. 83.

47. Interview with Urquhart.

48. Ibid.

49. UN Doc. A/RES/119, October 31, 1956.

50. UN Doc. A/RES/998 (ES-I), November 4, 1956.

51. UN Doc. A/3302, November 6, 1956.

52. UN Doc. A/3302, November 6, 1956, para. 18.

53. Urquhart, Hammarskjöld, p. 192.

54. UN Doc. A/3375, November 20, 1956, para. 2.

55. See Papers of the Secretaries-General, UNEF Advisory Committee, Verbatim
Records, fourth meeting, November 20, 1956.

56. Mahmoud Fawzi was foreign minister of Egypt from 1952 to 1964.

57. Interview with Urquhart.

58. *Papers of the Secretaries-General, UNEF Advisory Committee, Verbatim Records,* fourth meeting, November 20, 1956.

59. Telephone interview with Brian Urquhart, February 7, 2001.

60. *Papers of the Secretaries-General, UNEF Advisory Committee, Verbatim Records,* first meeting, November 14, 1956.

61. UN Doc. A/3943, October 9, 1958, para. 181.

62. See *Repertoire of the Practice of the Security Council: Supplement 1959– 1963* (New York: United Nations, 1965), p. 105.

63. Urquhart, *Hammarskjöld,* p. 506.

64. See UN Doc. S/4741, February 21, 1961, operative para. A-1.

65. See *Repertoire of the Practice of the Security Council,* pp. 105–106.

66. See ibid., pp. 117–118.

67. See *Papers of the Secretaries-General, Congo Advisory Committee, Verbatim Records,* 1960–1963.

68. UN Doc. A/3943, October 9, 1958, para. 181.

69. Committee meetings often lasted three to four hours. Verbatim records used to be bulky documents of 70 to 100 pages.

70. Urquhart, *Hammarskjöld,* p. 437.

71. *Papers of the Secretaries-General, Congo Advisory Committee, Verbatim Records,* second meeting, August 26, 1960.

72. This became especially obvious after Lumumba's assassination. See *Papers of the Secretaries-General, Congo Advisory Committee, Verbatim Records,* twenty-third meeting, February 21, 1961.

73. See *Papers of the Secretaries-General, Congo Advisory Committee, Verbatim Records,* thirty-fifth meeting, March 13, 1961. The Indian representative even threatened that the Advisory Committee would have to be closed down if the criticism among its members continued.

74. *Papers of the Secretaries-General, Congo Advisory Committee, Verbatim Records,* twenty-third meeting, February 21, 1961.

75. Javier Pérez de Cuéllar, *Pilgrimage for Peace: A Secretary-General's Memoir* (New York: St. Martin's Press, 1997), p. 320.

76. See UN Doc. S/RES/284, July 29, 1970, adopted by twelve votes in favor, none against, with Poland, the Soviet Union, and the United Kingdom abstaining.

77. I thank Barbara Blenman, Security Council Affairs Division, UN Secretariat, for bringing this aspect to my attention. Interview with Barbara Blenman, New York, December 11, 2000.

78. UN Doc. S/RES/309, February 9, 1972, operative para. 1.

79. See UN Doc. S/RES/342, December 11, 1973, operative para. 2.

80. See UN Doc. S/RES/385, January 30, 1976, operative paras. 7–8, 10.

81. See Hans-Joachim Vergau, "Genscher und das südliche Afrika," in Hans-Dieter Lucas, ed., *Genscher, Deutschland und Europa* (Baden-Baden: Nomos, 2002).

82. Ibid.

83. Donald McHenry, "The Contact Group and Initial Negotiations (1978– 1981)," in Heribert Weil and Mathew Braham, eds., *The Namibian Peace Process: Implications and Lessons for the Future* (Freiburg: Arnold Bergstraesser Institut, 1994), p. 13, emphasis added.

84. Ibid.

85. Margaret P. Karns, "Ad Hoc Multilateral Diplomacy: The United States, the Contact Group, and Namibia," *International Organization* 41, no. 1 (Winter 1987): 101.

86. Ibid.

87. Hans-Joachim Vergau, "Namibia-Kontaktgruppe: Katalysator des Interesse-nausgleichs," *Vereinte Nationen* 50, no. 2 (2002): 48–49.

88. UN Doc. S/RES/431, July 27, 1978, operative paras. 1–2.

89. See UN Doc. S/12853, September 20, 1978.

90. McHenry, "Contact Group and Initial Negotiations," p. 17.

91. See the bilateral agreement between Cuba and Angola and the tripartite agreement among Angola, Cuba, and South Africa, signed on December 22, 1988, reprinted in Chester A. Crocker, *High Noon in Southern Africa: Making Peace in a Rough Neighborhood* (New York: W. W. Norton, 1992), pp. 506–511.

92. Martti Ahtisaari, the Special Representative of the Secretary-General, attended many meetings of the contact group, which meant, in effect, an involvement of the United Nations through the back door.

93. UN Doc. S/RES/435, September 29, 1978, operative para. 3.

94. Pérez de Cuéllar, *Pilgrimage for Peace,* p. 321.

95. These conflicts included Iraq-Kuwait, India-Pakistan, and Eritrea-Ethiopia. See *SIPRI Yearbook 2001: Armaments, Disarmament, and International Security* (Oxford: Oxford University Press, 2001).

96. See Carnegie Commission on Preventing Deadly Conflict, *Preventing Deadly Conflict* (New York: Carnegie Corporation of New York, December 1997), p. xvii.

97. See Helmut Freudenschuß, "Article 39 of the UN Charter Revisited: Threats to Peace and Recent Practice of the UN Security Council," *Austrian Journal of International Law* 46, no. 1 (1993): 1–39.

98. Boutros Boutros-Ghali, "Global Leadership After the Cold War," *Foreign Affairs* 75, no. 2 (1996): 93–94.

99. See Parsons, *From Cold War to Hot Peace,* pp. 55–73; and Cameron R. Hume, *The United Nations, Iran, and Iraq: How Peacemaking Changed* (Bloomington: Indiana University Press, 1994).

100. Bailey and Daws, *Procedure of the UN Security Council,* p. 384.

101. UN Doc. SG/SM/5624.

102. This information was gathered from an interview with a former political adviser to Secretary-General Javier Pérez de Cuéllar.

103. This fact was maintained in interviews with Ambassadors Manuel Tello and Gustavo Albin of Mexico, Ambassador Diego Arria of Venezuela, and Beatrice Rangel, vice president and senior adviser to the Cisneros Group of Companies.

104. On September 30, 1992, the FMLN informed the United Nations that, in order to maintain the link in the original timetable between the key undertakings of the two parties, it would suspend demobilization of its forces until new dates had been set for the start of the transfer of land and other aspects of the agreement that had fallen behind schedule. See http://ralph.gmu.edu/cfpa/peace/html.onusal, p. 4.

105. Information gathered from an additional interview with a member of the UN Secretariat closely associated with the mission in El Salvador; interview at the United Nations, October 2, 1996.

106. UN Doc. SG/SM/5624.

107. Ibid.

108. UN Doc. S/1995/306, April 17, 1995.

109. Data as provided by the website of the United Nations Department of Peace-keeping Operations. See www.un.org/depts/dpko/dpko/co_mission/co_miss.htm; www.un.org/depts/dpko/dpko/cu_mission/body.htm; www.un.org/depts/dpko/dpko/pub/pdf/1.pdf; and www.un.org/depts/dpko/dpko/pub/pdf/7.pdf. Commencing July 1,

1996, the peacekeeping budget cycle changed from January 1 to December 31 of the same year to July 1 to June 30 of the following year.

110. See http://ralph@gmu.edu/cfpa/peace/html.onusal.

111. Ibid.

112. This information was gathered from an interview with a representative of one of the Member States on May 7, 1996.

113. Ibid.

114. Ibid.

115. By resolution 872 (1993) the Security Council established the UN Assistance Mission in Rwanda (UNAMIR). It was composed of 2,459 military personnel and 60 civilian police observers.

116. Later the name "Friends of Rapid Reaction" was changed to "Friends of Rapid Deployment," or FORD.

117. Barbara Crossette, "UN Ready to Establish a Military Crisis Team," *International Herald Tribune,* July 22, 1996; and Crossette, "At the United Nations: A Proposal to Speed Aid During Crisis," *New York Times,* July 21, 1996, sec. 1, p. 9. The representatives to the meetings are generally the military attachés to the missions.

118. This information was gathered through an interview on April 9, 1996, with a member of a mission to the United Nations who supports the rapid reaction project.

119. Deployment of SHIRBRIG is still subject to parliamentary approval on a case-by-case basis and is therefore not under the control of the United Nations for immediate deployment. For more information, see www.shirbrig.dk.

120. For example, the Group of Friends of the Secretary-General on Haiti faced negative reactions by one Member State that criticized the "undemocratic nature" of the ad hoc grouping. Notably, the same member readily participated in the Core Group on East Timor, another informal gathering constituted a few years later.

11

Reforming the United Nations: Lessons from a History in Progress

Edward C. Luck

The never-ending quest for reform, for improving the functioning of the United Nations, has been an integral part of the life of the world body since its earliest days. Indeed, one of the more controversial issues at the UN founding conference in San Francisco during spring 1945 was how the process of amending its Charter should be structured and when a general review conference of its provisions should be called.[1] Those delegations unhappy with some of the compromises reached in San Francisco, especially concerning the inequities of the veto power granted the "big five" permanent members (P-5) of the Security Council, wanted to schedule a general review relatively soon and to make the hurdles to amendment relatively low. The Soviet Union and, to a lesser extent, the other "big five" powers, on the other hand, naturally preferred to keep the barriers to Charter change relatively high.

On a more operational level, the UN had barely passed its second birthday before members of the U.S. Congress started to call for sweeping reforms of UN finance and administration. In October 1947 the Senate Expenditures Committee launched a study that found serious problems of overlap, duplication of effort, weak coordination, proliferating mandates and programs, and overly generous compensation of staff within the infant but rapidly growing UN system.[2] Similar complaints have been voiced countless times since.

Through the years, scores of independent commissions, governmental studies, and scholars have put forward literally hundreds of proposals aimed at making the world body work better, decide more fairly, modify its mandate, or operate more efficiently. Not to be left behind by the reform bandwagon, successive Secretaries-General and units of the Secretariat have engaged in frequent, if episodic, bouts of self-examination and self-criticism, offering their own reform agendas.

What explains this apparently irresistible impulse for reforming the United Nations? Six factors suggest themselves:

359

A view of the Secretariat building at United Nations headquarters, New York. The Secretariat has undergone several rounds of reform at the UN.

1. Public institutions depend on recurring processes of criticism, reassessment, change, and renewal to retain their relevance and vitality. Reform is a sign of institutional health and dynamism, not a penalty for bad behavior.

2. Highly complex, decentralized, and multifaceted institutions, like the UN system, offer more targets for criticism and more opportunities for change. The temptation to tinker with the United Nations is only magnified by its high visibility, symbolic aura, and broad agenda.

3. The diversity of UN membership and the ambitious nature of its mandates make it highly likely that some constituencies will be seriously disappointed with its power-sharing arrangements and/or its accomplishments at any point in time. Persistent disappointment or feelings of disenfranchisement have often led to calls for reform.

4. As the world changes, so do the politics of the UN and the priorities of its Member States. In looking to the UN to fulfill new mandates that exceed its capacities, influential nongovernmental organizations (NGOs) often look to structural innovations or to the creation of new bodies to close the gap between expectations and capabilities. In both cases, proposals for reform usually follow.

5. Critics keep calling for reform in part because the United Nations has been so slow in delivering it. As the major powers hoped in San Francisco, formal institutional and structural reforms have proven hard to achieve in the UN system. The concerns about UN management and finance voiced by Congress in the late 1940s, moreover, were echoed a half-century later in the late 1990s.

6. The universality of the UN has fueled a dual pattern on the intergovernmental level: frequent calls for change by one Member State or group, followed by blocking moves by others with divergent interests or perspectives. At times, it seems as if every Member State is in favor of some sort of reform, but their individual notions of what this should entail differ so markedly as to make consensus on the direction reform should take hard to achieve.

These dynamics ensure almost continuous attention to the reform agenda, but much slower progress on the intergovernmental than Secretariat plane.

If gauged by the sheer quantity of deliberations, debates, studies, and resolutions devoted to it, reform has become one of the enduring pastimes and primary products of the UN system. For example, during the last broad-based reform drive, from 1995 to 1997, the General Assembly was consumed with no less than five working groups on different aspects of reform, its president was engrossed in developing his own reform package, the Security Council reviewed its working methods, the Economic and Social Council (ECOSOC) adopted new procedures for relating to NGOs, and the new Secretary-General offered a comprehensive, if generally modest, plan for Secretariat reform. Before the dust had settled from these battles, the U.S.-led drive to have the

Member State assessment scales revised took center stage in the Assembly from 1998 to 2000. And in September 2002, a reform study led by the Deputy Secretary-General called for aligning activities with the priorities voiced in the Millennium Declaration, trimming reporting, improving coordination, streamlining the budgeting process, and improving human resource management.

The hardest reforms to achieve, of course, are those entailing amendments to the UN Charter. As noted above, after a good deal of divisive debate, the big five managed at San Francisco to set the political bar quite high for any modifications of the Charter. Contending that their unity was key to making the new body more successful at securing the peace than its predecessor, the League of Nations, the five insisted on their having individual vetoes over amendments to the Charter. As a result, Article 108 stipulates:

> Amendments to the present Charter shall come into force for all Members of the United Nations when they have been adopted by a vote of two thirds of the members of the General Assembly and ratified in accordance with their respective constitutional processes by two thirds of the Members of the United Nations, including all the permanent members of the Security Council.

Some of the other delegations not only objected to the inequity of these provisions but also fretted that those Member States in the minority opposing a particular amendment were given no recourse. Unlike the League Covenant, the Charter offers no mechanism for a dissatisfied member to withdraw from the UN—a practice that had disabled the League in the years preceding World War II. As a gesture toward these concerns, Article 109 offers the possibility of convening a general conference to review the Charter. While a number of delegations at San Francisco expected this to take place within the Organization's first decade, the polarization of the membership during the Cold War years made this look like an unpromising course.[3]

As discussed in the next section, the Charter has been amended only three times in over half a century. The Security Council has been enlarged once and the Economic and Social Council twice. The last of these moves took place almost three decades ago. So, while much of the public debate on reform continues to focus on possible Charter amendments, such as further expanding and diversifying the composition of the Security Council, in practice this has proved to be difficult to accomplish.

Much of the action, instead, has occurred below this level and often with little publicity. The rules of procedure for the Security Council, the General Assembly, and ECOSOC have repeatedly been modified, as have their rosters of subsidiary bodies.[4] The latter, naturally, have been more prone to expansion to meet new priorities than to contraction as old mandates fade. The relationships among UN bodies have provided material for successive waves of reform aimed at greater coordination, coherence, or even unity of purpose among the UN's many and disparate pieces. The activities of one principal organ, the Trusteeship Council, were suspended when the task of eliminating it from the Charter appeared too ambitious.[5] Financial, administrative, and personnel matters have been the target of so many reform and retrenchment campaigns through the years that some wags in the Secretariat have suggested that the most useful reform would be to declare a moratorium on introspection and reform so that the UN's workers could get back to their assigned tasks. More serious, the dizzying diversity of initiatives and proposals labeled "reform" has led to some reflective inquiries about the proper meaning of the term.[6]

In theory, it would be analytically cleaner to adopt a relatively narrow and rigorous definition, such as the following: reform is the purposeful act of modifying the structure, composition, decisionmaking procedures, working methods, funding, or staffing of an institution in order to enhance its efficiency and/or effectiveness in advancing its core goals and principles. In terms of the UN, this would encompass those steps intended to make the Organization more efficient, more effective, and/or more capable of fulfilling the purposes laid out in Article 1 of its Charter, consistent with the principles expressed in Article 2.

In practice, however, many other endeavors have also been called "reform" by one party or another in the world body. In this field, as in others, the seemingly irresistible impulse at the UN to expand the definition and scope of basic terms until they begin to lose their meaning, as well as their analytical value, is much in evidence. Reform has taken on so many guises through the years as to be almost unrecognizable. When there appears to be political momentum behind a reform exercise, various delegations are quick to repackage some of their favorite perennial hobbyhorses as innovative reform measures. Few Member States, for example, are reticent about claiming that measures to reduce their assessments or to increase their voice in the Organization qualify as essential reforms that would make the United Nations both more effective and more equitable. Seen in that context, of course, what looks like reform to one national delegation may appear regressive to others. At other points, when the term "reform" has taken on negative connotations, there has been a reticence to label reform measures by their real name. It was telling, for example, that during the intergovernmental deliberations of the late 1990s none of the five reform working groups established in the General Assembly had the term included in their elongated and carefully negotiated titles.[7] Clearly the notion of reform is more popular with larger and richer delegations than with others these days.

Another unsettled question—whether reform should encompass changes in what the UN does, for example, in its mandates and priorities, or only modifications in its administration, budgeting, financing, structure, and decisionmaking methods—also directly affects the scope of the concept. Judging from the titles and mandates of the five reform working groups in the General Assembly referred to above, it would seem that some believe that adjustments in programmatic substance should be included, as well as steps related to structure and procedures. In addition to the more traditional areas of Security Council, financial, and management reform, there were also working groups on an agenda for peace and an agenda for development that ranged over most of the UN's extensive substantive interests. Reform was not treated as an abstract phenomenon, but rather as one of the potential tools for strengthening the Organization's capacities for dealing with specific issue areas.[8] Given this context, it is understandable why the United Nations has not sought to develop a single definition of reform that would be acceptable to all or most of the Member States. Such an undertaking might well prove as frustrating, controversial, and time-consuming as the decades-long attempts to negotiate universal definitions for terms such as "aggression" or "terrorism."

The first step toward understanding the twisting course of UN reform efforts through the years and the confusing maze of reform proposals that have been put forward is to bear in mind the fundamentally political nature of the United Nations. Within the UN context, even seemingly routine matters of administration, personnel, and finance have a way of assuming a political character, should one group of Member States or another come to perceive potential slights to their interests, stature, or priorities. To put it crudely, much of the reform debate, at its basest level, is a struggle over political turf, over who is perceived to gain or lose influence within the Organization if the proposed changes are enacted or implemented. One of the most frequently voiced questions in UN corridors during the late 1990s reform exercise was: "Reform for what purpose?" To gain support, the answers needed to be on two levels: substantive and political. Even if the goal of a particular proposal was to enhance efficiency, to some it mattered a good deal in which priority areas these efficiencies were to be carried out, who headed those programs, and whether the balance of attention and resources vis-à-vis other priorities would be affected. In short, much of the reform debate has been about three things: who makes decisions, who implements them, and who pays. If these political questions are settled, then international cooperation on moving the reform agenda will most assuredly flourish.

Who Decides? Reforming the UN's Intergovernmental Organs

For the UN's first three decades, reform of its intergovernmental bodies was largely a question of numbers. How large should ECOSOC and the Security Council be to represent properly the UN's rapidly growing membership?[9] What should the balance be between different geographical or ideological groups of states? In other words, who decides? For the past two-plus decades, however, the emphasis has shifted. While debates about numbers and names have continued without agreement, the action in terms of reform progress has moved to matters of working methods and of relations with other organs and with civil society. The key "Who decides?" questions have become: "How are decisions reached, including whether there should be limitations on the use of the veto in the Security Council?" and "Who is consulted along the way, even if the formal composition of these bodies has not changed?"

During the 1950s and 1960s, one of the UN's cardinal achievements was to serve as midwife to the decolonization process. With the resulting influx of newly independent Member States, the ranks of UN members swelled from 51 in 1945 to 114 in 1963 (compared to 191 in 2003). Though only three African and three Asian countries were among the founders at San Francisco, by the early 1960s more than half of the Member States came from those two regions.[10] In 1956, after 20 new Member States were admitted to the UN over the two previous years, the calls for enlarging the two Councils came into the open. The original "gentlemen's agreement" on the geographical distribution of nonpermanent seats in the Security Council could no longer hold, since Latin America and Europe increasingly appeared to be "overrepresented" and the new majority "underrepresented." Unresolved squabbles over the six nonpermanent seats led to the constitutionally questionable practice of dividing a two-year term between countries from different regions. At one point, the Soviet Union favored redistributing the existing six nonpermanent seats, a step that would not have required Charter amendment. But this would have entailed a major sacrifice on the part of the West-leaning nations of Latin America and Europe, something Washington opposed.

The expansion of ECOSOC, in contrast, appeared to be a simpler and less consequential step. One-third of its eighteen members were elected each year for three-year terms, with each member having a single vote and equal rights. Not only were there no permanent members or vetoes in ECOSOC, but its mandate avoided core security issues, its primary task was coordination not policy, and its decisions were only recommendations, with none of the binding character of Security Council decisions under Chapter VII.[11] So as early as 1956, U.S. representatives acknowledged that both Councils should eventually be enlarged and suggested that the initial focus be on ECOSOC expansion.[12]

The developing countries, on the other hand, were especially keen on having a louder voice in the Security Council, which had become increasingly active in dispute resolution and peacekeeping efforts in the developing world. Some complained that their second-class status in the world body seemed to mirror the colonial status that they had recently struggled to overcome. For example, the heads of state of the members of the new Organization of African Unity (OAU), at their founding meeting in 1963, made this the topic of their very first joint summit resolution. In this context, and given their competition for influence in what was then known as the "Third World," neither Washington nor Moscow wanted to be the first to oppose openly the growing campaign for enlargement, whatever their actual misgivings.[13]

The expansion debate came to a head at the eighteenth General Assembly session in fall 1963.[14] Despite the building momentum, there was no consensus during the Assembly debate on either the need for an immediate expansion or the dimensions and voting rules of the enlarged bodies. On the final day of the session, none of the P-5—all of whose ratifications would be needed for formal amendment—voted in favor of the resolution to expand ECOSOC, and only China, of the five, voted for the resolution to expand the Security Council. During the debates preceding the votes, all P-5 members had called, in one form or another, for more time and further consultation before action was taken.

Nevertheless, on December 17, 1963, the General Assembly passed resolutions 1990 (XVIII) and 1991 (XVIII), the latter for the first time calling for amendments to the UN Charter. The first resolution, which passed 111 votes to none, enlarged the General Assembly's gate-keeping General Committee to permit fuller representation of the new African and Asian members. The second resolution was divided into two parts, each subject to its own roll call vote. Part A, to expand the Security Council from eleven to fifteen members, to increase the majority required from seven to nine, and to specify the geographical distribution of the ten nonpermanent members, was adopted by a vote of 97 to 11, with 4 abstentions. Those opposed included France and the Soviet bloc, while the United States and the UK were among those abstaining. Part B, which passed 96 to 11, with 4 abstentions, enlarged ECOSOC from eighteen to twenty-seven members and indicated the geographical breakdown of the nine new members. The only difference in the voting pattern was that the Republic of China shifted from an affirmative vote in Part A to an abstention on Part B, dealing with ECOSOC, a body on which it had been denied a seat in recent years. Adding a note of urgency, both parts called on the Member States to ratify the amendments by September 1, 1965, less than two years away.

Following the Assembly vote, the expansion bandwagon inexorably gathered momentum. Of the P-5, the Soviet Union was the first to reverse course and to ratify the amendments (followed, of course, by the rest of the Soviet bloc). By the time the U.S. Senate Foreign Relations Committee held hearings on this question in late April 1965, the United Kingdom had also announced its intention to ratify the alterations in the Charter, and 65 of the required 76 Member State ratifications had already been completed. When the Senate gave its consent to ratification in June, France had added its intention to ratify, and 71 of the 76 required ratifications were in hand. Though none of the permanent members had voted for both amendments in the General Assembly, within nineteen months all had overcome their reservations and ratified them.

The reasons for this remarkable about-face could be instructive for future efforts to amend the Charter. In theory, because of the need to attain ratification by all P-5 members, the amendment process is ultimately subject to a veto by any of them, including a pocket veto in which one or more of them simply fail to act. In practice, however, this step can be invoked only after at least a two-thirds majority of the Member States have expressed support for the amendment through their votes in the Assembly and possibly through their national ratification processes. So, in terms of the politics of the UN, the costs of vetoing a proposed Charter amendment can be quite high, and this has never been done once an amendment has cleared the Assembly. The political costs are disproportionately high, of course, if one permanent member has to cast a lonely veto, so there is a premium on cooperation among the five.

Cold War politics and the lack of coordination among the five were not the only explanations for this historic reversal. The UN's precarious financial position also contributed. In the early 1960s, the United Nations was in the midst of a severe financial and constitutional crisis, brought on by the refusals of the Soviet Union, France, and some developing countries to pay their assessments for the UN's first two large-scale peacekeeping operations, in the Congo and the Middle East, despite the decision of the International Court of Justice that they were required to do so. Washington and most Western capitals were very concerned with rallying the support of developing countries on these questions. The Article 19 crisis reached its boiling point in 1964, when the Soviet Union threatened to quit the UN, the United States pushed to have Moscow denied its vote in the General Assembly under Article 19 of the Charter for its accumulated arrears, and as a result, voting was suspended in the Assembly session that fall.[15] For those capitals concerned about preserving the fiscal and political integrity of the UN—and in those days Washington was in the front ranks—this was no time to veto reforms sought so fervently by the developing-country majority.

Then, as now, the dominant argument for expansion of both Councils was equity, not performance in fulfilling their august missions. In their statements before the Senate Foreign Relations Committee on this matter, none of the Johnson administration witnesses raised cautions about whether the expanded Councils would be better equipped to carry out their missions effectively, or whether due regard would be paid to the first Charter qualification for Security Council membership: the Member State's contribution to the maintenance of international peace and security.[16] Nor, in turn, did any of the committee members ask such pointed questions about the effects of the amendments during the public hearings, which ranged over a wide spectrum of UN and foreign policy matters. On the floor of the House, several representatives spoke in favor of the amendments and none raised these issues.[17] Prior to giving its consent to ratification virtually without dissent, by a 71–0 vote, the Senate held a perfunctory debate on the floor.[18] Only Strom Thurmond, the conservative Republican from South Carolina, spoke against the measure.[19] So, with ringing words of endorsement from the Johnson administration and a unanimous vote by the Senate, the United States acceded to the proposition that bigger is better in terms of UN fora.

A scant six years later, with this precedent firmly in place, the United States put forward a package of ECOSOC reform measures that included a substantial enlargement.[20] Many developing countries wanted to go further and faster, proposing a doubling of the size of ECOSOC, from twenty-seven to fifty-four members. In opposing this step, the French representative complained that the General Assembly had not "devoted as much time to this problem as it did 10 years ago, the last time the membership of the Economic and Social Council was enlarged."[21] Arguing that the Council's "authority is not necessarily a function of the size of its membership and the distribution of seats among regions," he suggested that already "the number of seats is too large."[22] Along similar lines, the Soviet delegate stressed that "the belief that the work of the Council can be improved solely through enlargement and through corresponding changes in the United Nations Charter is unfounded."[23] The United States, however, had accepted the principle of proportional growth in ECOSOC to parallel the proliferation of UN members, which reached 135—well beyond State Department predictions—by the end of 1973, the year the second expansion of ECOSOC came into force.[24] When the question of doubling the membership of ECOSOC came to a head in 1971, first in ECOSOC and then in the General Assembly, on both occasions the United States was the only P-5 member to vote in favor.[25] In terms of ratification, however, the United States was the last of the P-5 (including China) to complete the process, with the others deciding once again not to resist the international political tide. With the deposit of the U.S. ratification on September 24, 1973, this second expansion of ECOSOC, the last Charter amendment to be accomplished, came into force.

Calls for ECOSOC reform, of course, hardly subsided with this second increment to its membership. Indeed, many Member States went along with the two expansion steps on the assumption that they would be followed by measures to enhance ECOSOC's working methods, to bolster its capacity to coordinate systemwide programs, and to rationalize its structure.[26] By the early 1970s, it had become increasingly apparent that the UN system was failing to fulfill the expectations of Member States—from the North as well as the South—in the realm of economic and social development, despite the fact that some four-fifths of its outlays then went to such programs.[27] A group of high-level experts, appointed by the Secretary-General under a mandate from the General Assembly, concluded in 1975 that the revitalization of ECOSOC would be one of the keys to more effective global policymaking.[28] Their report urged ECOSOC to adopt a biennial calendar, with a series of short subject-oriented sessions, a one-week ministerial session, and annual reviews of program budgets, medium-term plans, and operational activities. It stressed the utility of the Council establishing small negotiating groups to facilitate the search for common ground on key economic issues, as well as initiating consultations at an early stage with the most affected states on each issue. In addition, the report identified steps to raise the level of participation in ECOSOC sessions and called on the Council to assume the responsibilities of many of its subsidiary bodies.

A number of UN-sponsored and independent studies have proposed even more sweeping reorganizations of ECOSOC.[29] Some would enlarge it further, while others would eliminate it altogether or divide it in two. Several have advocated the creation of a smaller executive body to set priorities and negotiate key issues, and most urge that the specialized agencies be made more subservient to the Council. Some of the more modest reform proposals have been realized—the institution of a high-level segment, shorter sessions, a somewhat more theme-oriented agenda, and greater use of panels of independent experts on selected issues—but there has been no agreement among the Member States on a more fundamental restructuring. One area where ECOSOC has been somewhat more innovative, however, is in recasting and clarifying the rules for the engagement of NGOs in the work of the UN.[30] In this respect, ECOSOC reform progress compares favorably to that of the General Assembly, which has resisted the adoption of new rules for NGO access.

In retrospect, however, the effects of ECOSOC expansion appear to have been mixed at best. As some developing countries have gained a stronger sense of ownership of the Council, developed countries on the whole have been more prone to question its relevance and effectiveness.[31] In part because of its unwieldy size—too big for serious negotiation and too small to represent the membership as a whole—ECOSOC has been the target of repeated reform campaigns during the 1970s, 1980s, and 1990s. It is not evident, moreover, that ECOSOC has found it any easier to coordinate the disparate and decentralized pieces of the UN system as it has itself grown larger and more diverse. After all, ECOSOC's powers have not expanded appreciably, its decisions remain only recommendations, it is still subservient to the Assembly on political questions, and the specialized agencies and the Bretton Woods institutions (the World Bank and the International Monetary Fund [IMF]), as always, have their own political and financial constituencies, charters, and governing bodies. For these and similar constitutional reasons, the enlargement of ECOSOC has been irrelevant to addressing that body's core weaknesses.

Though they were linked in the package of Charter amendments that came into force in 1965, the efforts to reform ECOSOC and the Security Council have followed quite distinct paths since then. The Security Council, for instance, has not undergone a second tranche of expansion. Yet the pressures for enlarging the Security Council, at least judging by the public expressions of Member State policies, have been far greater than has been the case for ECOSOC. But then, of course, so too has been the resistance to tinkering with a body charged with such awesome security responsibilities. The mixed results of ECOSOC expansion are often cited as reasons not to enlarge the Council. The end of the Cold War, moreover, has had a far more profound effect on the debate over changes in the Security Council than in ECOSOC. On the one hand, the Council was rejuvenated as East-West divisions began to fade and the scope of its possible actions grew dramatically. Its newfound activism led some to declare that there had been nothing wrong with its structure and working methods, only a lack of political will, and that if there was nothing amiss in its performance, then there was no need to fix it. On the other hand, once the Council was freed of its Cold War shackles, it appeared to become, more than ever, the most dynamic and consequential piece of the system. The attractiveness of becoming a member rose, as did the stigma of being excluded from this inequitable and, some said, anachronistic club. In the consensus-driven atmosphere of this new era, moreover, the casting of vetoes came to appear decidedly out of step with the tenor of the times.

In 1993 the General Assembly convened the "Open-Ended Working Group on the Question of Equitable Representation and Increase in the Membership of the Security Council and Other Matters Related to the Security Council," a body whose very title embodied the complexities, uncertainties, and general awkwardness of its mandate. It divided its task into two clusters: one on membership, including expansion, the veto, and voting; the second on enhancing transparency through improved working methods and decision-making processes. While the first cluster has attracted far more public attention and Member State rhetoric, the second has spurred the greater progress.[32] By 2003 the 191 members of the General Assembly had not been able to come close to agreement on any Council reform package. But their high-profile debate has encouraged the Security Council to take a number of parallel steps on the second cluster, working methods.

As the pace and profile of Security Council activities rose during the 1990s, a series of modifications in its working methods were adopted.[33] Among these were the following:

- Under the Arria formula, a member of the Council invites the others to meet with one or more independent experts for a candid exchange of views on a pressing issue before the Council. This innovative practice, which permits more direct input from civil society and encourages Council members to reflect on the complexities of the choices facing them, has proven quite popular, as have more formal meetings with agency heads and others with knowledge of developments in the field.
- The Council has also participated in a number of retreats, away from headquarters, with the Secretary-General, other UN officials, and sometimes leading independent experts.

- Council members have undertaken a number of missions to visit areas where developments are of particular interest or concern to the Council. This has allowed much more extensive contact with government officials, NGOs, and UN personnel on the ground in regions of crisis.
- The Council has met a number of times over the past decade at either the foreign minister or summit level.
- To assist transparency and accountability, it has become common practice for the president of the Council to brief nonmembers, and often the press, on the results of informal (private) consultations.
- Tentative forecasts and the provisional agendas for the Council's upcoming work are now provided regularly to nonmembers, as are provisional draft resolutions.
- Consultations among Security Council members and troop contributors, along with key Secretariat officials, are now held on a more regular basis.

While acknowledging the progress that has been made on the second cluster, most Member States contend that it has not gone nearly far enough. The ten nonpermanent members of the Security Council called for the institutionalization of the steps that had been taken, for taking several of them further, and for more public meetings and fewer informal consultations.[34] It is questionable, however, whether all of the transparency and reporting measures called for would result in a more efficient or effective Security Council. The bulk of the negotiations among the members are bound to be carried out in private, and the public sessions of the Council have become opportunities largely for restating official positions and for public rationalizations. Even nonmembers of the Council frequently complain of the number and repetitiveness of the speeches given in the formal, public sessions. While it would aid accountability to require states to explain why they cast each veto, and the Council could be more forthcoming in its reports to the General Assembly, excessively detailed or frequent reporting could make it that much harder for an already overburdened Council to devote sufficient time and attention to its wide-ranging substantive work.

The first cluster has proven more problematic. Most distinct, the volume of complaints about the veto privilege of the P-5, a point of contention since the founding conference in San Francisco, seemed to rise precipitously during the 1990s.[35] Most of the other 186 Member States, as well as numerous scholars and blue ribbon commissions, have criticized the veto provision for being inequitable, undemocratic, and debilitating to the capacity of the Council to fulfill its core responsibility for the maintenance of international peace and security. Others, however, have stressed that the principle of unanimity among the major powers was central to the conception of the UN, and that principle has permitted it not only to survive the tensions of the Cold War, but also to play a role in helping to resolve them.

The veto controversy has complicated progress on the array of first-cluster issues in several ways:

- Since Article 108 gives the permanent members a veto over Charter amendments, they can trump any efforts to weaken formally their veto power.
- Those seeking to expand the number and geographical spread of the permanent members face a dilemma: Should additional permanent members, in the name of equity, be given the very veto power that critics claim is so debilitating to the work of the Council? Wouldn't a Council with eight or ten permanent members be even more restricted in terms of where it could act, and wouldn't the common denominator for Council action be even lower in most cases?[36]
- Alternative formulas for coping with the veto dilemma raise additional concerns. A number of delegations criticized the proposal by Ismail Razali, when he was president of the General Assembly in 1997, to add five permanent members without veto power because they said it would add a third layer to the Council hierarchy.[37] Asking the current permanent members to exercise greater restraint in their use of the veto, for example, by restricting it to matters under Chapter VII of the Charter, offers no guarantees and sets a precedent of calling on selected Member States to relinquish rights given them under the Charter.[38]
- Divisive questions about which states should have the veto have exacerbated splits within each region about which local states should be on the Council, especially since most security threats come from within one's own region, not from afar. Moreover, there is no provision in the Charter suggesting that one Member State may or should represent the interests and positions of others, neighbors or not.

So, while the General Assembly working group has made progress on narrowing differences over the size of a reformed Council, there has been little agreement either about names or about vetoes.

In sum, though it has now been almost thirty years since the Assembly last voted to amend the Charter, there seems to be little prospect of further amendments anytime soon. In retrospect, the three Charter amendments did make participation in the Security Council and ECOSOC accessible to more Member States, more of the time. They made some accommodation, if not full places, at the decisionmaking table for the scores of new members. They demonstrated a degree of flexibility, for example, some willingness to adapt to changing circumstances. But clearly they did not address the root shortcomings of either body, nor quench the public's thirst for stronger tools and machinery for dealing with the world's persistent security, economic, and social problems. Indeed, the fact that the only Charter revisions that have proven capable of sparking wide support among the members have been those to increase the size of limited membership bodies has also served to fuel skepticism about whether Charter reform is the best route to a stronger and more effective United Nations.

Who Implements? Coordination and Management

Though lacking the high drama of the debates over who decides, the question of implementation—how the mandates agreed upon by the intergovernmental bodies are to be carried out—has generated sustained attention since the UN's infancy. At its opening session in London, Arthur H. Vandenberg, the influential Republican senator who led the administrative and financial committee in both San Francisco and London, warned his colleagues against mistaking "pomp for power" and letting their aspirations for the United Nations "outrun its resources."[39] The next year, in November 1946, he wrote to Secretary of State James Byrnes that the specialized agencies "are being created entirely too rapidly and too ambitiously."[40] The following year, as noted above, the U.S. Senate initiated its first critical review of UN management and administration. The problems identified—overlap, duplication, coordination, proliferation of papers and mandates, and staff competence and compensation—have formed the core of the reform agenda ever since, in part because such challenges are common in, perhaps endemic to, complex multilateral organizations.

International bodies may properly be assessed first and foremost by what they stand for and seek to accomplish, the things determined by their constitutions and principal intergovernmental decisionmaking bodies. Yet over time, the most stinging rebukes are often about their failure to perform, about the gaps between their high purposes and meager capacities to carry them out. It has been to this second set of challenges, to narrowing the implementation gap, that most of the UN's internal reform efforts have been devoted.

From early on, two characteristics of the UN system underlined the value of developing effective practices and/or mechanisms for coordination: one was the interdisciplinary and multisectoral nature of many of the key issues on the international agenda, and the other was the complex and horizontally segmented mix of agencies, funds, and programs that composed the "system." The whole, it seemed, often acted as less than the sum of its parts. The Charter, in Articles 57 and 63, called on ECOSOC to "enter into agreements" with the various specialized agencies, several of which predated the world body, so as to bring them "into relationship with the United Nations." ECOSOC was asked to coordinate their activities "through consultations and recommendations," while Article 64 gave ECOSOC permission to seek reports from the agencies. Nowhere in the Charter, however, is there any suggestion that ECOSOC would have any binding power over them.

In practice, of course, a number of the agencies had their own boards, bylaws, mandates, and funding sources, giving them every reason to maintain a substantial degree of independence from the General Assembly, which lacked budgetary authority over them (Article 17[3] of the Charter). Since the major donor countries were members of most of these agencies, they could, if they worked together, enforce substantial discipline and coherence on the pieces of the system. But this would have required a degree of coordination among national ministries and within capitals that was only occasionally achieved. According to the 1948 Senate review, "a considerable portion of the problem of coordination seems to be due to the failure of national governments to achieve coordination in their own policy formulation. As a result, various departments of government often tend toward an autonomous handling of relationships with specific international organizations."[41] Within the UN system, the senators found that weaknesses in program coordination were compounded by an inability to set and maintain clear priorities:

> The United Nations and the specialized agencies have limited budgets and limited staffs with which to perform their various functions. It therefore becomes necessary that some sort of fairly rigid priority system be established with respect to the projects undertaken if the maximum use is to be made of the funds available. There appears to be a tendency on the part of the agencies concerned to undertake far more than they can hope to accomplish, and very often without proper regard for the importance of the work undertaken. . . . The result is that funds are spread very thin and very little is accomplished generally.
>
> Whenever a particular project appears important at the moment, a new commission or committee is appointed to look into the matter. This ultimately results in a proliferation of bodies, attempting to accomplish a great deal of work, much of which constitutes duplication of effort already being made and some of which overlaps other projects.[42]

Of course, the Member States, with their disparate interests and priorities, have been as much or more to blame as the Secretariat for the proliferation of mandates and the mismatch between ambitions and resources, problems that continue to plague the world body. To be fair, however, at times the various agencies and programs have managed to pull together to respond to emergencies and special opportunities with a sense of common purpose. When the goal is clearly articulated by the Secretary-General and the Member States pull together, so do the programs and agencies. On the whole, though, the highly decentralized nature of the system and its resistance to integrative reforms have tended to fuel perceptions of institutional disarray and fragmentation.

No one has more pungently described the malady or more painstakingly detailed possible remedies than Sir Robert Jackson, a former high-ranking international civil servant from Australia who had been tapped in 1968 by the United Nations Development Programme (UNDP) to carry out a "study of the capacity of the United Nations system to carry out an expanded development program."[43] Unlike the more pessimistic premises of recent reforms, which have been identified with cost and post retrenchments, this assessment was undertaken at a time of rapid growth in development funding through multilateral channels. The challenge was not whether the world body could do more with less, but whether the UN could handle another doubling of its development programs in the course of a few years time.

Sir Robert and his small team of researchers produced a report of almost 600 pages, laying out a detailed plan for restructuring the way the UN goes about assisting the development process. Yet it was a few unvarnished comments in the report's foreword about the shortcomings of the existing arrangements that gained the study almost instantaneous notoriety around the world. Sir Robert noted that he had been left with two strong impressions: one positive, one negative. On the plus side, he was "convinced that technical co-operation and pre-investment are one of the most effective ways of assisting the developing countries in achieving economic and social progress. I believe the United Nations, despite its present limitations, has demonstrated conclusively that it is the ideal instrument for the job."[44] There was, according to Sir Robert, "an unprecedented opportunity to revitalize the United Nations development system." Yet he doubted that the governments of the world could grasp this chance given "the great inertia of this elaborate administrative structure which no one, it seems, can change. Yet change is now imperative."

The UN development "machine," in Sir Robert's view, had evolved into "probably the most complex organization in the world." He pointed out that "about thirty separate governing bodies" tried to exercise control over different pieces of the administrative machine, yet "at the headquarters level, there is no real 'Headpiece'—no central coordinating organization—which could exercise effective control." He luridly described the "administrative tentacles" that ran down to a vast complex of regional, subregional, and field offices in over ninety developing countries. Governments could not control the process, and "the machine is incapable of intelligently controlling itself." As a result, "unmanageable in the strictest sense of the word," the machine "is becoming slower and more unwieldy, like some prehistoric monster." While praising the largely good work of UNDP, he concluded that management lapses and structural shortcomings had permitted about 20 percent of the programs to qualify as "deadwood," or "nonessential projects."

He had surmised, moreover, that his preferred solution was not politically feasible: "In theory, complete control of the machine would require the consolidation of all of the component parts—the United Nations and the Specialized Agencies—into a single organization, which is not within the realms of possibility." Movement in this direction, even restructuring UNDP into "a strong central coordinating organization," would be resisted, he feared, by UN officials, by agencies that had "become the equivalent of principalities," and by those national ministries that tend to take positions in UN agencies that conflict with their "government's policies toward the UN system as a whole."

An alternative way to reform the machine without amending the Charter, in his view, "would be to centralize the budgets of all of the Specialized Agencies—and bring them under effective coordinated control in ECOSOC. Then you really would see opposition to change! That battle was fought out when I was at Lake Success in the early days and the supporters of the sectoral approach won the day." Moreover, the UN system had become "a disproportionately old and bureaucratic organization," plagued with a pervasive sense of "negativism." Based on his consultations, Sir Robert had concluded that "the UN system has more than its fair share of 'experts' in the art of describing how things cannot be done."

For all of his doubts, Sir Robert saw some rays of light ahead. He urged his readers to reflect on how much the developing countries had already achieved, on the advances of science and technology, on the growing interdependence of nations, on the principles the General Assembly had articulated for relations between the UN and the Third World, and on the complementary roles that had been carved out for UNDP and the specialized agencies. With greater funds and top-flight managerial talent, he argued, a great deal could be accomplished given these favorable conditions. "The sheer force of political circumstances," he concluded, "will compel governments to act sooner or later."

The study emphasized the importance of clarifying and defining the respective roles of the various pieces of the system. "The World Bank Group should be the chief arm of the UN system in the field of capital investment, while UNDP should perform the same function for basic technical co-operation and pre-investment." UNDP should serve "as the hub of the UN development system," coordinating the efforts of the specialized agencies and other UN operational programs at the country level through UNDP resident representatives; at headquarters through a new program policy staff, four regional bureaus, and a technical advisory panel; and at the highest interagency level through the replacement of the Inter-Agency Consultative Board (IACB) with a more powerful Policy Coordination Committee. The specialized agencies would serve both as executing agents for projects contracted with UNDP and as technical advisers in their respective fields of expertise, but "UNDP would assume full responsibility for all development activities carried out under its aegis, and with its funds, irrespective of which agency or other institution executed a particular programme or project on its behalf."[45] Therefore, the agencies would have to be accountable to the administrator of the UNDP for these projects, just as he would be accountable to governments and to the UNDP Governing Council.

Following the suggested reorganization of UNDP, the study urged consideration of the merger of the governing bodies of the World Food Programme

(WFP), the UN Children's Fund (UNICEF), and UNDP. Calling for a decentralization of line authority within UNDP, the report recommended a strengthening of the role of the resident representatives, an enhancement of the authority of the administrator, and a focus on policymaking by the Governing Council. To facilitate a more decentralized apparatus, the report also stressed the need to upgrade the quality of the Secretariat, especially the resident representatives, and to improve communications throughout the system.[46]

While much of Sir Robert's plan depended on establishing this more integrated organizational structure, in many ways the operational heart of his vision centered on the institution of country-based programming and a "UN Development Cooperation Cycle."[47] The latter would consist of five phases: country program and annual review; formulation and appraisal of projects; implementation; evaluation; and follow-up. The country program would be prepared by the recipient government and the UNDP resident representative, hopefully with the participation of the agencies and in association with the World Bank, and then submitted to the UNDP Governing Council for approval. This process would provide each developing country with "a comprehensive view of the total cooperation it might expect from the UN development system during the whole period of its national development plan." For developed countries, it would provide an overview of the use of resources, facilitate forward planning, and permit bilateral and multilateral programs to be harmonized country by country.

Much of the thrust of Jackson's vision has been implemented, some at that point and some over time. But the core dilemmas that he identified have not disappeared. In particular, though his proposed combination of central authority and country-based programming has its attractions, it does not eliminate the possibility of disputes between the priorities of field-level and headquarters-level decisionmaking. This tension between centralization and decentralization has plagued UN reform efforts from the Organization's early days.[48]

Because the Secretary-General lacks the power either of the purse or of appointment in dealing with the specialized agencies and the Bretton Woods institutions, he must rely on persuasion, personality, and indirect appeals to publics and Member States to give a sense of direction and coherence to the system as a whole.[49] Some Secretaries-General, and Kofi Annan has set an especially good example, are better at pulling the disparate pieces of the system together than others have been. More fundamentally, the capacity of the Member States to set and hold priorities has been markedly episodic. Divisions or indifference among the Member States, in turn, provide ample opportunities for agency heads to engage in splitting tactics or to pursue independent agendas. As a 1987 blue ribbon commission convened by the United Nations Association of the United States of America (UNA-USA) put it, the system's potential for interdisciplinary analysis and integrated implementation efforts has been hampered by the fact that "there is no center at the center of the U.N. system."[50]

The next wave of social and economic restructuring, undertaken between 1974 and 1977, unfolded in a much less propitious political context than had Jackson's capacity study a few years before.[51] The early 1970s saw growing strains between developed and developing countries on a host of economic, energy, trade, and financial questions of a bilateral, regional, and global nature. While solutions to problems of the magnitude of the oil crisis far transcended the bounds of the UN system, the world body, with its broad-based membership, became the favorite forum for the countries of the South to raise their concerns about the equity of the existing economic and political system. Through their numbers in the one-nation, one-vote General Assembly, the developing countries sought to codify a series of principles, targets, and procedures that would define a new set of global economic relationships. In this larger political context, the question of UN reform took on a more intense and divisive meaning in terms of the control, direction, and priorities of UN bodies. Amid calls by the developing countries for a new international economic order (NIEO), in 1974 the General Assembly (resolution 3343 [XXIX]) asked the Secretary-General to appoint a group of experts to prepare "a study containing proposals on structural changes within the UN system so as to make it fully capable of dealing with problems of international economic co-operation in a comprehensive manner." With Professor Richard N. Gardner of Columbia University as its rapporteur, the group of experts reached a consensus on a broad-ranging report in only four months of deliberations during the first half of 1975.

The experts' report acknowledged that "no amount of restructuring can replace the political will of Member States to discharge their obligations under Article 56 of the Charter."[52] It stressed that the group viewed efficiencies and financial economies at best as secondary factors in its deliberations, though they expected that some of their recommendations could lead to staff reductions and budgetary savings. Of higher priority to the group was the need to bring much greater coherence to the planning, programming, and budgetary processes of the UN system. According to the report, at that point, of the almost $1.5 billion expended annually by the system, less than one-quarter was covered by the regular budget, one-quarter by fifteen largely autonomous specialized agencies, one-quarter by UNDP, and one-quarter by voluntary contributions. Recognizing that this arrangement made policy direction and priority-setting that much more problematic, the experts called for a series of steps to make the budgetary and programmatic reporting of the various pieces of the system at least sufficiently compatible to permit the possibility of cross-sectoral planning and monitoring.

The proposed innovation that attracted the most attention was for the creation of the post of director-general for development and international economic cooperation, to be placed above agency heads and undersecretaries-general, as the second highest official in the world body. The director-general would be supported by two deputy directors-general, one for research and policy and the other to head a new United Nations development authority. While the director-general could not exercise authority over the relatively autonomous specialized agencies, he or she would be in charge of interagency coordination and operational activities and would chair a new interagency advisory committee on economic cooperation and development. It was suggested that the post be occupied by "a national of a developing country at least during those years when the post of Secretary-General is occupied by a developed country."[53]

The report also advocated the consolidation of all of the funds for technical assistance and preinvestment activities—except for those of UNICEF—into a new UN development authority. In a politically charged recommendation on a matter of high priority to the capitals of both developed and developing countries, the group urged that the weighted voting systems in the IMF and World Bank be revised "to reflect the new balance of economic power and the legitimate interest of developing countries in a greater voice in the operation" of those institutions.[54] The report did not specify how this should be done, and in any case the General Assembly has no authority over the Bretton Woods institutions and the specialized agencies.

Though the experts from around the world had managed to reach a consensus on a shared vision in short order, the same could not be said either of the Member States or of the heads of the various parts of the UN system. Though welcoming some aspects of the report, the West cautioned against any changes that might worsen the unstable North-South political dynamic of the time or weaken its control of the Bretton Woods institutions. The East opposed steps that would entail Charter amendment or additional costs. The Group of 77 (G-77) lacked a coherent view, other than placing a higher priority on the achievement of the NIEO and on expanding the authority of the General Assembly than on restructuring the system. Wary of the implications of greater institutional integration, the G-77 preferred to stress the need for a third expansion of ECOSOC.[55]

Finally, on December 20, 1977, more than three years after the economic and social restructuring exercise was launched with the mandating of the group of experts, the General Assembly, without vote, endorsed a substantially weakened version of the group's proposals (resolution 32/197). The parallels also included measures to rationalize the work of the Second and Third Committees, to biennialize the agenda of ECOSOC, to institute shorter and more frequent subject-oriented sessions of ECOSOC over the course of the year, to hold periodic sessions of the Council at the ministerial level, and to have the Council "assume to the maximum extent possible direct responsibility for performing the functions of its subsidiary bodies." Lost, however, was the experts' core notion of small negotiating groups in both bodies on key economic issues. Instead, the Assembly predictably called for the consideration of ways to enable all Member States to participate in the work of the Council and to make "the Council fully representative." The idea of facilitating agreement through the convening of smaller groups of states on an ad hoc basis, for all of its appeal to logic, simply cut across the grain of the current political dynamics at a time of continuing North-South struggles over an array of macroeconomic issues.

Though the post of director-general survived the negotiating process, it was stripped of the authority and support structures that would have allowed it to be a powerful new locus for policy coordination and advocacy within the system. The two new deputy director-general posts were not established, none of the existing undersecretary-general posts were eliminated, the funds were not consolidated into a UN development authority, and their governing boards were not merged. The resolution called for greater uniformity in financial and administrative procedures and extolled UNDP's country-based programming process, but essentially the director-general was superimposed on the existing highly decentralized structure, without the authority to reshape or redirect it. Kenneth Dadzie, the Ghanian chairman of the Ad Hoc Committee, was appointed to be the first director-general. Though widely liked, he had little real power and was never fully accepted by the Secretary-General.

Over the years, the post came to be seen at best as marginally useful at moving these issues within the Secretariat, and at worst as a high-level appendage with little influence. Fourteen years later, in a sweeping gesture of unilaterally imposed reform, incoming Secretary-General Boutros Boutros-Ghali unceremoniously included the position of director-general as one of a list of eighteen high-level posts he was abolishing "to redress the fragmentation which existed in the Secretariat" and "to consolidate and streamline the Organization's activities into well-defined functional categories."[56]

Nevertheless, below the intergovernmental level, the efforts to bolster the system's capacity for coherent implementation of mandates have continued. The Joint Inspection Unit (JIU) has undertaken a number of assessments of how these efforts have been faring or might be enhanced. For example, a 1999 JIU report reviewed the history of steps to strengthen the Administrative Committee on Coordination (ACC), and called for further modifications, including of its name.[57] Established by ECOSOC in 1946 (resolution 13 [III]), the ACC was the only forum that convened the executive heads of all of the Organizations of the UN system, under the chairmanship of the Secretary-General, to focus on questions of coordination and crosscutting policy issues. While its effectiveness had varied with the personalities involved, its agenda had become increasingly substantive in recent years. In 2000 the name of the ACC was changed to the Chief Executives Board (CEB) and the responsibilities for coordination were divided into a High-Level Committee on Management (HCLM) and a High-Level Committee on Programmes (HLCP).

Achieving greater unity of purpose was a central theme of Secretary-General Kofi Annan's 1997 reform plan. Earlier that year, he organized four sectoral executive committees to bring together all relevant departments, funds, and programs under the headings of peace and security, the UN Development Group, humanitarian affairs, and economic and social issues.[58] He established a senior management group to act as a sort of cabinet on management issues, and a strategic planning unit to identify and assess crosscutting issues and trends. He also asked the General Assembly to establish the post of Deputy Secretary-General to address, among other things, questions that "cross functional sectors and Secretariat units."[59] While seeking to improve communication and the sense of common purpose at headquarters level, the Secretary-General also recognized the value in delegating authority and initiatives to the country level for operational development and humanitarian programs. In this regard, he called for "decentralization of decision-making at the country level and consolidation of the UN's presence under 'one flag.'"[60] Consolidations were undertaken to create a single Department of Economic and Social Affairs and a unified office to combat crime, drugs, and terrorism in Vienna.

While these steps have modified in significant ways the internal workings of the United Nations, they have had relatively little impact either on the way intergovernmental decisions are made or on the way others perceive the world body. As Kofi Annan has often pointed out, reform is a process, not an event. In closing his reform report, he captured these points nicely:

> In an organization as large and complex as the United Nations, reform necessarily consists not of one or two simple actions but a multitude of tasks that amount to a major agenda that must be pursued over time. But the world will not measure the reform process by the number of items on the agenda—by how many more or fewer activities are undertaken, or how many committees are formed or disbanded. The Organization will be judged, rightly, by the impact all these efforts have on the poor, the hungry, the sick and the threatened—the peoples of the world whom the United Nations exists to serve.[61]

Who Pays? Assessments, Finance, and Budgeting

Chapter 9, by Jeffrey Laurenti, very thoroughly covers the evolution of who pays and how much. However, a few additional comments are useful here to describe some of the reforms that developed as a consequence of the political wrangling over budgetary questions. The UN Charter is quite explicit about who decides on other matters; however, when it comes to revenues and outlays, the Charter has relatively little to say, leaving these core matters to be determined by the Member States over time. According to Article 17:

1. The General Assembly should consider and approve the budget of the Organization.
2. The expenses of the Organization shall be borne by the Members as apportioned by the General Assembly.

Article 18(2) lists "budgeting questions" as among those "important questions" requiring "a two-thirds majority of the members present and voting." The skeletal nature of these provisions did not reflect a downplaying of the potential importance of these issues at the San Francisco founding conference or the preparatory meetings that led up to it. Rather, it was widely believed that open debates on finance and burden sharing would become so contentious and divisive as to threaten the sense of unity and common purpose the founding members were seeking to achieve.[62] Recognizing how acutely political questions of outlays and assessments would be, moreover, the founders of the world body felt it best to let the answers be adjusted periodically according to the ebb and flow of political power and economic means among the Member States over time. Thus, in seeking to postpone or finesse the issue, they ensured that finance would be a hardy perennial on the reform agenda for years to come.

No doubt, the most highly charged issue has been the assessment scale, which determines the relative burden borne by each member for financing the UN's regular budget and, since the late 1950s, its peacekeeping operations.[63] Other than assigning the task of apportionment to the Assembly, the Charter provides neither a mechanism nor a set of principles by which this determination should be made. These tasks were assigned in 1945 to an expert committee on contributions, which encountered politically turbulent seas when it sought to lay down both a set of criteria and its initial recommendations for the percentage assessments for each Member State.[64]

As discussed in Chapter 9, the capacity to pay has been the underlying principle for assessing states. Yet as more and more developing nations with very low capacities to pay joined the UN, placing more demands on the Organization, the United States began to complain. As Jeane Kirkpatrick testified before the Senate Committee on Governmental Affairs in May 1985, soon after she stepped down from the post of UN Permanent Representative: "The countries who pay the bills do not have the votes, and the countries who have the votes do not pay the bill. . . . The countries which contribute more than 85 percent of the U.N. budget regularly vote against that budget, but are unable to prevent its increases because the countries who pay less than 10 percent of the U.N. budget have the votes."[65]

Likewise, Alan Keyes, the assistant secretary of state for international organization affairs, complained at a House hearing about the "fundamental disequilibrium between the size of contributions by certain Member States and their influence on the U.N. budgetary process." In his view, "a majority of U.N. members contribute little to the budget, and therefore have no incentive to take a positive interest in making serious and responsible budget decisions."[66]

Fair or not, these arguments found a ready audience in Congress. Finding that the UN and its specialized agencies "have not paid sufficient attention in the development of their budgets to the views of the member governments who are major financial contributors," in August 1985 Congress passed the Kassebaum-Solomon Amendment as part of the Foreign Relations Authorization Act for fiscal years 1986 and 1987.[67] It precluded for fiscal year 1987 and beyond payment of assessed contributions of over 20 percent to the UN or any of its specialized agencies—which meant the withholding of 20 percent of the U.S. contribution—until they adopted weighted voting on budgetary matters "proportionate to the contribution of each such member state." In seeking to assert greater control by the major contributors over spending, Republican senator Nancy Kassebaum insisted that her aim was to strengthen, not weaken, the world body.[68] Putting their intent more bluntly, her cosponsor, the veteran Republican representative Gerald Solomon of New York, later remarked that "the way to get the attention of a mule is to hit him in the head with a 2x4. The way to get the attention of the United Nations was to pass the Kassebaum-Solomon amendment."[69]

The worsening financial crisis and the growing U.S. withholdings gave the UN's fortieth General Assembly session a markedly somber cast. After weeks of sharp debate, much of it directed toward U.S. withholding tactics, the Assembly agreed to establish a group of eighteen experts, though with a limited mandate, as most developing countries preferred. The group's purpose was to

- conduct a thorough review of the administrative and financial matters of the United Nations, with a view to identifying measures for further improving the efficiency of its administrative and financial functioning, which would contribute to strengthening its effectiveness in dealing with political, economic, and social issues; and
- submit to the General Assembly, before the opening of its forty-first session, a report containing the observations and recommendations of the Group.[70]

The experts were to stick to questions of efficiency and to avoid political matters, such as the relative priority of security and economic/social questions in the work of the UN.[71]

Meanwhile, Secretary-General Pérez de Cuéllar and his top managers had been undertaking a review of possible personnel and spending cuts in parallel to the deliberations of the Group of 18. In January and March of 1986, the Secretary-General announced two series of economy measures, such as reductions in travel, consultants, overtime, recruitment, promotions, benefits, and maintenance. While not eliminating any mandated posts or activities, these initial steps produced an estimated $30 million in savings.[72] Department heads were asked to identify how an additional 10 percent reduction in outlays could be achieved, if required. Deeper cuts and more far-reaching reforms, however, would require action by the Member States, since they are responsible for setting program mandates and priorities. So the Secretary-General asked the General Assembly to resume its fortieth session in late April 1986 to consider further economies to ease the worsening financial crisis. In the end, the Assembly, despite the considerable reluctance of many developing countries, adopted the Secretary-General's interim package of austerity measures with the caveat that "no project or programme for which there was a legislative mandate would be eliminated if adequate financial resources were available."[73]

The Group of 18 had only six months to try to forge a consensus on matters on which the Member States were deeply divided. It soon became painfully obvious that there was little chance of the group reaching agreement on a proposal for a new scale of assessments, something the Secretary-General had urged them to examine.[74] Reportedly, the U.S. expert in the group rebuffed suggestions by some of the other members that the possibility of lowering the U.S. assessment rate, as had been proposed by Olof Palme and others, be considered in their deliberations.[75] Likewise, questions relating to the elimination of marginal intergovernmental bodies, to a restructuring of the UN's programs, or to recasting priorities among activities and budget line items also proved too divisive to be tackled. The group's report acknowledged problems of duplication and insufficient coordination of agendas and programs, but stated that the group did not have time to undertake an in-depth review, which "should be entrusted to an intergovernmental body."[76] The group likewise called for a streamlining of the machinery for interagency coordination, but failed to specify how this should be done (recommendations 9–13). It urged reductions in the number and duration of conferences, and in documentation, travel costs, and conference facilities (recommendations 1–7, 38). To improve the monitoring, evaluation, and inspection of UN activities, the group recommended an upgrading of the Joint Inspection Unit, a broadening of its mandate, and closer coordination and a clearer division of labor between the JIU and external auditors (recommendations 63–67).

As seems perennially to be the case with intergovernmental bodies, the one target the Member States can readily agree to criticize is the Secretariat.[77] In this respect, the group's report was both specific and far-reaching. Noting that the number of posts funded through the UN regular budget had grown more than sevenfold in forty years, from 1,546 in 1946 to 11,423 in 1986, the report devoted two full chapters to Secretariat-related questions. Of greater concern to coherent management than these aggregate numbers was that the structure was "both too top-heavy and too complex," with twenty-eight posts at the Under-Secretary-General level and twenty-nine posts at the Assistant Secretary-General level under the regular budget, plus an additional seven and twenty-three, respectively, financed through extrabudgetary sources.[78] The experts thus called for a 15 percent reduction in the overall number of regular budget posts and a deeper 25 percent cut in Under-Secretary-General and Assistant Secretary-General regular budget posts, both to be achieved within a three-year period (recommendation 15). They also proposed a consolidation of the political departments, a review of those devoted to economic and social affairs, a streamlining of administration, and a review of public information activities, though these recommendations were mostly expressed in general terms (recommendations 16–40).

While the Group of 18 report, which included a consensus-based decisionmaking process, was generally well-received, many delegations were wary of institutionalizing a U.S. financial veto over the UN's budget and programs, which would be the result of the consensus requirement. Delegations did not want to appear to buckle in the face of U.S. financial and political pressure. The developing countries, in particular, seemed far less concerned about Secretariat retrenchment than about how their own voice and influence in the United Nations might be affected by modification in the procedures for intergovernmental decisionmaking. The one-nation, one-vote rule mattered to them in terms of both principle and national interest. This sensitivity was especially apparent in the question of budgeting, the one area in which the Charter permits the Assembly to make binding decisions on its own accord.

Yet on December 19, 1986, a weary Assembly approved by consensus resolution 41/213, calling for implementation of the agreed upon proposals of the Group of 18 and of a new consensus-based planning, programming, and budgeting process. Three factors helped to turn the tide. First, throughout the fall, the financial straits of the UN had grown more desperate. According to UN officials, the Organization, which opened 1986 with a $240 million deficit, had since depleted its contingency funds and exhausted ways of shifting funds among different accounts, leaving it increasingly vulnerable to financial pressures imposed by Member State withholdings.[79] At the end of October, the Secretary-General terminated ten top officials, while maintaining the cuts and freezes announced earlier in the year. There was growing talk of "payless paydays" if the United States—and other countries—did not make substantial additional payments before year's end.[80] Second, top U.S. officials and legislators began to make a positive linkage between UN reform and congressional restraint, contending that together they could produce a more effective and sounder world body.[81] The U.S. administration lobbied key capitals in the developing world on the value of consensus-based decisionmaking, including sending an envoy with this message from Washington to selected capitals in Africa in early December—seen as the key to moving the process in New York.[82] Third, in New York, the president of the General Assembly, Humayun Rasheed Choudhury of Bangladesh, helped shape a diplomatically worded description of the new budget process that would be relatively inoffensive to all parties.

Despite Choudhury's reassuring language, many delegations wanted an opinion from the UN Legal Counsel that these provisions would not undermine Article 18 of the Charter, which stipulates that "each member of the General Assembly shall have one vote" and that "important questions," including budgetary ones, require a two-thirds majority. The Counsel's opinion, included as Annex II of the resolution, found that "these draft proposals read separately or together do not in any way prejudice the provisions of Article 18 of the Charter of the United Nations or of the relevant rules of procedure of the General Assembly giving effect to that Article."[83]

With all of the horse-trading, however, opinions were divided about whether the multilateral negotiations had produced a mouse or something of historic proportions. Maurice Bertrand, a member of the group and a former JIU inspector, was skeptical. In his view, the resolution "defined the process of decision-making regarding the size and content of the programme budget so obscurely that everyone could declare himself satisfied but nothing was really settled."[84] As U.S. Permanent Representative Vernon Walters acknowledged, "we got most of what we wanted and so did nearly everyone else."[85] But he also claimed that "what has been done here is something really historic. We have gotten the things that the United States intended."[86] Based on these results, he said that he would urge Congress to repeal the Kassebaum-Solomon Amendment and to appropriate the full U.S.-assessed contribution to the world body. Yet critics could argue that very little had changed, given the option to resort to voting if consensus fails. On the other hand, while the new process fell well short of weighted voting, the emphasis had shifted toward the presumption that consensus was the preferred way to determine the size and shape of the budget. The new system, however, offered no guarantees. Small contributors, as well as large ones, could conceivably prevent the attainment of a consensus in the Committee for Programme and Coordination (CPC). While traditionally the P-5 had regularly been elected to the CPC, there was no formal rule requiring that the United States or any of the others be seated.[87] Even if the CPC reached a consensus, the Assembly retained its prerogative to accept, modify, or reject those recommendations.

As President Choudhury asserted, the new mechanism would depend on a tacit agreement between the big contributors and the developing countries, as well as on Congress's willingness to provide sustained financial support.[88] In the State Department's view, the new system would change relationships and assumptions among the Member States:

> This process has the effect of reducing the ability of the numerical majority to dictate decisions about the size and use of UN resources. If the resort to majority power cannot simply be assumed, real compromise becomes essential. Trade-offs must be achieved between minority and majority viewpoints, involving the exchange and modification of tangible interests. That is why the reform program budget decision-making process is so significant.[89]

More bluntly, Assistant Secretary of State Alan Keyes cautioned that the United States would consider further funding cuts down the road if the CPC failed to maintain a consensus. The hesitant steps toward implementing the 1986 reforms were monitored closely by Congress and the Reagan administration. The week after the General Assembly in 1987 decided to expand the CPC membership from twenty-one to thirty-four, Congress enacted legislation placing new conditions on U.S. payments to the UN, this time geared to the implementation of the provisions of resolution 41/213.[90] Though a range of assessments could be heard in Washington about the degree of progress being made in carrying out these provisions, over the course of 1988 the Reagan administration seemed to gain greater confidence that UN reform, on balance, was moving forward. The Secretary-General had not yet reached the 15 percent personnel cut targeted for the end of 1989, but he appeared to be closing in on that goal.[91] The 1988–1989 budget estimates were revised modestly upward, but with the United States joining the consensus because the additional outlays related to UN peacekeeping operations in Afghanistan and the Western Sahara, which the United States strongly supported. These add-ons were termed by the U.S. delegation as ones that were "critically important" or would "strengthen the Organization," unlike ones in earlier years that "were marginally useful, and, in some cases, politically divisive." Though the 41/213 procedures had not yet been fully operationalized, the United States was pleased with the way the 1990–1991 budget outline had been developed and, again, joined in the consensus approval of it.

More fundamentally, the larger political context within which relations with the UN had been viewed was changing in important ways. The Soviet Union had agreed to withdraw its forces from Afghanistan, and Mikhail Gorbachev was bringing "new thinking" to Soviet domestic and foreign policy. The prospects and utility of UN peacekeeping operations were rising in Washington's strategic calculations. In the U.S. presidential election campaign, both candidates pledged to repay U.S. arrears to the world body. On the eve of the president's final speech to the General Assembly, the White House announced its decision to authorize the release of outstanding 1988 dues and to develop a multiyear plan to pay back the accumulated arrears.[92]

These years of crisis in U.S.-UN relations produced a number of intriguing ironies and lessons for the process of UN reform and renewal. Most striking was the metamorphosis in Reagan administration attitudes toward, and perceptions of, the UN. The question of reform played a major role in this transformation, at first seeming to confirm the widely held assumption that the Organization would never change and later, after resolution 41/213, fueling a sense that the world body had been somehow transformed into a far more effective and promising vehicle. Positive developments in the larger political atmosphere mattered a great deal in the end, boosting both reform and U.S.-UN relations. By the latter stages of the second Reagan term, U.S. officials seemed inclined to see the reform glass as half full, when earlier it appeared at best as half empty. The ultimate irony was that the Reagan team had left office and the United States was committed to full funding and to repaying the arrears *before* the supposedly pivotal consensus-based budgeting mechanism was fully realized in December 1989.[93] Ultimately, it required carrots, as well as sticks, to accomplish durable fiscal reform.

As Laurenti describes in Chapter 9, the progress of the 1980s hardly satiated the financial reform agenda and the debate was rekindled in the 1990s. Indeed, it took the terrorist attacks on the United States of September 11, 2001, and mounting pressure from the Bush administration for the House finally to vote to pay the arrears to the UN body (and for the Senate to confirm John Negroponte as the U.S. Permanent Representative to the UN, after some nine months of waiting). To those hoping for a promising new chapter in U.S. relations with the United Nations or an end to the squabbles over dues and assessments, these developments could not offer much encouragement.

Conclusion

As this historical review makes abundantly clear, the process of institutional change at the UN works in subtle, complex, and uneven ways. The dual phenomena of reform and adaptation have not been widely studied and are not well understood.[94] Some of the following lessons, drawn from this review, are consistent with prevalent assumptions, but others seem counterintuitive.

1. Reform does *not* come easily to the UN system. The Secretary-General has little leverage, the system is diffuse, and the Member States are rarely united behind specific reform goals. Any number of reform initiatives have fizzled because the sponsors lacked the time, patience, political capital, or commitment to see the process through to the end.

2. On the other hand, the process of reform is a constant. Big waves of high-visibility initiatives may only come every five to seven years, but less publicized and less contentious tinkering closer to the surface never seems to cease. In the UN, as the premier multilateral political entity, a premium is put

on consultative processes. At times, process seems more important than results, while at other times process *is* the desired result.

3. Those unaware of the history of reform may indeed be condemned to repeat it. Since conditions change, it may make sense to test the waters again from time to time with proposals that have been tried before. But a lot of time and aggravation can be saved by learning the history first, especially because the UN is such a precedent-dependent institution. Delegations that are uncertain or reluctant to press forward on a particular initiative can be counted on to recite their version of the history of past efforts and steps on that subject.

4. The key to UN reform, in that sense, may lie less in trying to be innovative than in understanding why past initiatives have failed and how the strategies and tactics for achieving them could be improved. Scholars and commissions thus might utilize their time more productively in thinking through how to advance existing proposals than in developing new ones that have little chance of implementation.

5. More study is needed of how scholars and commissions have helped to shape the UN reform process.[95] In a few of the cases addressed here, such as the Jackson capacity study, the Group of 18, the Razali plan, and Kofi Annan's July 1997 package, there have been direct, creative, and productive interactions between idea producers from civil society and the official reform processes. In each case, of course, the independent voice is sought by those actors who believe that this expert input will help to bolster their case for or against a particular step. In turn, the perspectives, values, and positions of official actors may well have been shaped to some extent by what scholars and blue ribbon commissions had been saying and/or writing. At the same time, however, it is striking how often the reform debates have proceeded with only modest or marginal input from civil society, which is readily excluded from these processes and which tends to gravitate to less technical and tedious topics. Though they took place at the height of the clamor for greater NGO access to UN proceedings, the five General Assembly working groups established during the mid-1990s largely operated behind closed doors and interacted regularly with only a handful of enterprising NGO representatives.

6. When it comes to moving an agenda for reform in the UN, it is not always clear where power dwells (or who, if anyone, is in charge). In the 1960s, none of the P-5 voted for the expansion of both ECOSOC and the Security Council, yet all eventually found it easier to go along with the tide for expansion. In the 1990s, by contrast, their mere ambivalence helped to foster doubts and divisions among the rest of the membership regarding enlarging the Security Council. Through dues withholding, the United States has been able to achieve some of its financial goals, but has less to show in terms of structural, institutional, or programmatic change. And to the extent that financial leverage matters, the United States has worked hard to ensure that it has less and less of this dwindling asset at the UN. Some Secretaries-

General, moreover, have been far more adept than others at playing their modest reform cards.

7. Change happens even if reform doesn't. The UN is highly adaptable to changing world conditions. Sometimes formal reform follows (it never leads). When reform fails to keep pace with changing needs or conditions, entrepreneurial UN officials, Member States, and civil society representatives are all adept at circumventing the rules and procedures to get things done. Given the often glacial pace of institutional reform, it is not surprising that through the years more and more funding and programmatic initiatives have avoided the regular budget and scrutiny by the Assembly, finding voluntary and ad hoc routes instead.

8. The course of reform tends to be decidedly unpredictable. Rarely does a reform wave end up where its initiators expected. Sometimes the detour takes place at the negotiating stage, sometimes during implementation. Given the number and diversity of players in the UN community, as well as the episodic nature of the engagement of national leaders in these matters, it is very difficult to map the political course reform initiatives are likely to take. They invite free-riding, empty gestures, and a playing to domestic audiences along the way.

9. As this review has demonstrated, the temptation to mistake modest and short-term adjustments for epochal change has proven irresistible time and again. Unfortunately, such repeated overselling of reform accomplishments has tended to undermine support for reform in two ways: it has led to overly high expectations and resulting disillusionment with the whole enterprise; and it has too often made the best the enemy of the good, encouraging flashy proposals that squeeze out sound but incremental ones.

Where do these lessons leave us in terms of future prospects? If the energies of the reform drive of the late 1990s—the most comprehensive and inclusive yet undertaken—have largely subsided, where will the enthusiasms and agendas come from for the next round? And what dangers lie ahead?

In terms of historical lessons, perhaps the most important is also the most obvious: UN reform has an unusually full and rich history. The impulse to improve the workings of the world body has been present since San Francisco. It ebbs and flows, of course, but it keeps coming back. The tensions, divisions, and distasteful compromises of the last reform drive have left delegations, officials, specialists, and even private foundations with a mighty antireform hangover. In UN circles, congressional withholdings have given reform a bad name. But a lot of parties have also been left with a sense of incomplete agendas and unfulfilled ambitions. Very few delegations, in particular, got what they wanted out of the last reform campaign.

As this chapter documents, the pace of UN reform has become markedly skewed. There have been repeated incremental refinements to the UN's response to the question, "Who implements?" The 2002 Secretariat-led reform may have added another step or two. Likewise, the struggle over "Who pays?" never ends. The most disgruntled party, the United States, has been forcing its will on the rest and getting results. Others are deeply resentful of its tactics, but can live with the results. There has been no new answer, however, to the core question of "Who decides?" for the past three decades. The ongoing debate about Security Council reform, in particular, increasingly revolves around complaints about the inequity of the current system.

The rhetoric of injustice and inequity sounds a lot like that of the early 1960s, the last and only time the Security Council was enlarged. But should the same tactics be employed this time around? In the 1960s, the developing countries in essence used their overwhelming numbers in the Assembly to compel the permanent members to accept expansion of the Security Council and ECOSOC as a virtual fait accompli. The rapid growth of UN membership gave them a strong rationale and the Cold War gave them political leverage. Today, their case is weaker and the political situation is more dynamic and possibly more volatile. Unlike the 1960s, today all the permanent members agree that some expansion of nonpermanent membership on the Security Council is justified, as well as some increase in permanent membership, though not necessarily with the veto power. Moreover, there is little evidence that the developing countries could present a united front behind a single formula for expansion at this point, particularly when the matters of permanent membership and the veto are included.

The Razali plan recognized that deciding on the size and shape of the Council and on the countries that would be new permanent members are two quite different challenges. It therefore proposed that they be handled in stages. First, the Member States would need to decide on the aggregate size of the Council and on the number and regions of the new permanent members, as well as on the sensitive question of who would or would not have the veto. The next step, once these matters are settled, would be to give the Member States a specified period of time to come up with the country names to fill in the blanks. Presumably this would be decided regionally, initially, and then approved by the whole Assembly, though there are a number of ways this could be done. Tellingly, the primary opposition to the Razali plan, centered around the so-called coffee club, came from middle powers that felt that they would be somewhat disenfranchised under a plan that would elevate certain large developing countries to permanent member status without reducing the current number of permanent members. The P-5, in other words, may pose one set of obstacles to Security Council reform, but an equally difficult hurdle—so far an insurmountable one—derives from profound differences both within regions and within the ranks of the 186 Member States that are not permanent members. So there is every reason to expect that the skewed character of UN reform progress will remain for the foreseeable future.

The question of "Who decides?" raises a related dilemma: Should the goal of UN reform be to make its decisionmaking processes more reflective of the membership as a whole or more in line with the prevailing balance of power and capacity outside of its halls? Clearly, most Member States, in calling for democratization, equity, and transparency, have the former in mind. The founders, as noted earlier, recognized this dilemma and sought, in the creation of an Assembly and a Council, to have it both ways. Today, however, the question is more pointed because of the growing imbalance of power in the real world outside. The United States has not only built an unrivaled power position, including importantly in the projection of military force, but has also shown a growing willingness to go it alone on a number of issues of great concern to the rest of the membership. The latter, in turn, have begun to see multilateral organization as a way of discouraging or even countering the unilateral instincts of the United States. It is frequently said, as well, that the UN is an organization for smaller countries and should be restructured to reflect this. So the bulk of reform proposals put forward by Member States— and often by NGOs as well—would have the intentional or unintentional effect of trying to reduce U.S. influence in the United Nations. The United States, for its part, as seen in the struggle over the assessment scale, would like to have its cake and eat it too: to scale back its financial commitment, while gaining a role in decisionmaking in the UN more reflective of its power position outside. The competition between these opposing and largely incompatible visions of reform is likely to define the terms of the reform struggle even more in the coming years than it did in the turbulent 1990s. The question of U.S. power and influence within the world body, it seems, will become the subtext for much of the debate about what kind of a UN the world will need in the future: one that constrains or multiplies U.S. power?

People, however, will also matter. Kofi Annan, perhaps because of his thirty-plus years in the Secretariat, has been more attentive to reform issues than his predecessors. As chronicled above, he has taken a number of steps to improve the inner workings of the central UN and its relations with other multilateral institutions. Not insignificantly, he has been perceived in Washington as a major force for management reform. While the actual accomplishments of recent reforms have been less revolutionary than boosters would suggest, the overall record has been relatively consistent and positive under Annan's tenure. Now that he is well into his second term, however, the question of how this momentum can best be ensured under his successor—whoever he or she may be—needs to be addressed. Potential candidates for the post may be reluctant to run on a reform platform (except in Washington and a few other major donor capitals, of course), given the hangover from the last big round of reforms and worries others have of U.S. dominance. In terms of the "Who implements?" issues, the only ones over which the Secretary-General can exercise decisive influence, the possibility of slippage is always present. So too are pressures to create new posts and increase spending, especially after so many years of relative austerity. The next Secretary-General will have big shoes to fill, since it is never easy to succeed a popular leader. The political dilemmas noted above, moreover, suggest that the dual tasks of political management and institutional management will be merged in a most challenging way. But after all, in the United Nations, reform has always been about politics. This is what its history teaches us.

Notes

1. Ruth B. Russell, *A History of the United Nations Charter: The Role of the United States 1940–45* (Washington, D.C.: Brookings Institution, 1958), pp. 742–749.

2. Senate Committee on Expenditures in the Executive Departments, *United States Relations with International Organizations,* 80th Congress, 2nd sess., 1948, Senate Report 1757, pp. 11–19.

3. For ideas for a 1995 review conference, see Francis O. Wilcox and Carl M. Marcy, *Proposals for Changes in the United Nations* (Washington, D.C.: Brookings Institution, 1955).

4. Sidney D. Bailey and Sam Daws, *The Procedure of the UN Security Council,* 3rd ed. (Oxford: Oxford University Press, 1998).

5. See A/49/1, para. 46, and A/50/1, para. 69. For a proposal to revive and reorient the Trusteeship Council, see Kofi Annan, Report of the Secretary-General, *Renewing the United Nations: A Programme for Reform,* A/51/950, July 17, 1997, paras. 84–85, 282; Note by the Secretary-General, *United Nations Reform: Measures and Proposals: A New Concept of Trusteeship,* A/52/849, March 31, 1998; and Report of the Secretary-General, *United Nations Reform: Measures and Proposals, Environment and Human Settlements,* A/53/463, October 6, 1998, para. 61 and recommendation 24(b).

6. For example, see W. Andy Knight, *A Changing United Nations: Multilateral Evolution and the Quest for Global Governance* (New York: Palgrave, 2000), pp. 41–50.

7. The five groups included the Open-Ended Working Group on the Question of Equitable Representation and Increase in Membership of the Security Council and Other Matters Related to the Security Council; the Ad Hoc Open-Ended Working Group of the General Assembly on an Agenda for Development; and the High-Level Open-Ended Working Group on the Strengthening of the United Nations System.

8. See, for example, the so-called Brahimi Report, on UN peace operations, A/55/305, August 21, 2000.

9. Of the UN's four principal intergovernmental organs, this review focuses on the two that have been the targets of the most reform attention: the Economic and Social Council and the Security Council. For the results of the latest drive to improve the General Assembly's performance, achieved by the Strengthening Working Group in 1997, see *Report of the Open-Ended High-Level Working Group on the Strengthening of the United Nations System,* A/51/24, July 18, 1997.

10. This count of founding members deletes Australia, New Zealand, and several countries of the Middle East.

11. One of the few studies of ECOSOC was by Walter R. Sharp, *The United Nations Economic and Social Council* (New York: Columbia University Press, 1969).

12. Report by the President to the Congress for the Year 1963, *U.S. Participation in the U.N.*, Department of State (Washington, D.C.: U.S. Government Printing Office, 1964), pp. 143–161.

13. Nikolai Fedorenko, the Soviet Permanent Representative to the United Nations, to the Special Political Committee on December 10, 1963, A/SPC/96, pp. 1–9.

14. See A/PV.1285, December 17, 1963, pp. 6–17; A/5487, September 4, 1963, pp. 1–4; and A/5502, July 16, 1962–July 15, 1963, pp. 95–96.

15. Edward C. Luck, *Mixed Messages: American Politics and International Organization, 1919–1999* (Washington, D.C.: Brookings Institution Press, 1999), pp. 233–238.

16. But see U.S. Senate Committee on Foreign Relations, *Hearings on United Nations Charter Amendments*, 89th Congress, 1st sess., 1965 (Washington, D.C.: U.S. Government Printing Office, 1965), no. 89-51678-1, p. 22.

17. U.S. House of Representatives, *Congressional Record*, 89th Congress, 1st sess., 1965, vol. 111, pt. 7 (Washington, D.C.: U.S. Government Printing Office, 1965), pp. 8713–8716.

18. U.S. Senate, *Congressional Record*, 89th Congress, 1st sess., 1965, vol. 111, pt. 9 (Washington, D.C.: U.S. Government Printing Office, 1965), pp. 12547–12559.

19. Ibid., pp. 12548–12549.

20. Report by the President to the Congress for the Year 1971, *U.S. Participation in the U.N.* (Washington, D.C.: U.S. Government Printing Office, 1972), pp. 134–136.

21. A/PV.2026, p. 1.

22. Ibid., pp. 1–2.

23. Ibid., p. 3.

24. Statement of Martin F. Herz, acting assistant secretary of state, Bureau of International Organization Affairs, to the Senate Foreign Relations Committee, July 24, 1973, reproduced as an appendix in the committee's report, *Amendment to Article 61 of the Charter of the United Nations*, July 26, 1973, 93rd Congress, 1st sess., Executive Report no. 93-9, pp. 2–4.

25. See *Report of the Economic and Social Council on the Work of Its Fiftieth and Fifty-first Sessions, General Assembly, Official Records: Twenty-sixth Session, Supplement no. 3* (A/8403), pp. 9–13. See also A/PV. 2026, p. 2. China was not a member of ECOSOC and was absent for the Assembly vote.

26. Ronald I. Meltzer, "Restructuring the United Nations System: Institutional Reform Efforts in the Context of North-South Relations," *International Organization* 32, no. 4 (Autumn 1978): 993–1018.

27. Report of the Group of Experts on the Structure of the United Nations System, *A New United Nations Structure for Global Economic Co-operation*, E/AC.62.9 (New York: United Nations, 1975), p. 1.

28. Ibid., pp. 13–19.

29. Sir Robert G. A. Jackson, *A Study of the Capacity of the United Nations Development System*, vols. 1–2, DP/5 (Geneva: United Nations, 1969); Peter J. Fromuth, ed., *A Successor Vision: The United Nations of Tomorrow* (New York: United Nations Association of the United States of America, 1988); Independent Working Group on the Future of the United Nations, *The United Nations in Its Second Half-Century: The Report of the Independent Working Group on the Future of the United Nations* (New York: Yale University/Ford Foundation, 1995); Commission on Global Governance, *Our Global Neighborhood* (New York: Oxford University Press, 1995); South Centre, *For a Strong and Democratic United Nations: A South Perspective of*

UN Reform (Geneva: South Centre, 1996); and South Centre, *The Economic Role of the United Nations* (Dar-es-Salaam and Geneva: South Centre, 1992).

30. ECOSOC, resolution 1996/31, July 25, 1996. Also see the NGLS Roundup of November 1996, available at www.globalpolicy.org/ngos/docs96/review.htm.

31. Maurice Bertrand, *Some Reflections on Reform of the United Nations,* Joint Inspection Unit, JIU/REP/85/9 (Geneva: United Nations, 1985), p. 59.

32. See GA/9945, November 1, 2001; GA/9692 and GA/9693, December 20, 1999; and A/[49-55]/47 (1994 to 2000).

33. See Note by the President of the Security Council, S/2002/603 and A/AC/247/1996/CRP.4.

34. Memorandum by the Elected Members on Transparency in the Security Council, December 22, 1997, www.globalpolicy.org/security/docs/memo1297.htm.

35. Russell, *History of the United Nations Charter,* pp. 713–749.

36. As the Commission on Global Governance phrased it, "to add more permanent members and give them a veto would be regression, not reform." *Our Global Neighborhood* (New York: Oxford University Press, 1995), p. 239.

37. The Razali plan can be found at www.globalpolicy.org/security/reform/raz-497.htm.

38. Razali called for such restraint, as did the Independent Working Group on the Future of the United Nations in *The United Nations in Its Second Half-Century,* p. 16.

39. Arthur H. Vandenberg Jr., ed., *The Private Papers of Senator Vandenberg* (Boston: Houghton Mifflin, 1952), pp. 238–239.

40. U.S. Department of State, *Foreign Relations of the United States, 1946,* vol. 1, *General: The United Nations* (Washington, D.C.: U.S. Government Printing Office, 1972), p. 494.

41. Senate Committee on Expenditures, *United States Relations,* pp. 16–18.

42. Ibid., pp. 17–18.

43. UNDP, *Progress Report by the Administrator to the Governing Council,* May 9, 1968, DP/L.79, p. 2.

44. Jackson, *Capacity Study,* vol. 1, pp. ii–x, 10, 21, 34–36, 49.

45. Ibid., vol. 2, pp. 302, 329, 335–337.

46. Ibid.; see vol. 2, chaps. 8 (pp. 339–372) and 6 (pp. 215–278) respectively.

47. Ibid., vol. 1, pp. 25–29.

48. Johan Kaufmann, "The Capacity of the United Nations Development Program: The Jackson Report," *International Organization* 25, no. 1 (Winter 1971): 946.

49. This was lamented in the 1948 Senate report. Senate Committee on Expenditures, *United States Relations,* p. 18.

50. Fromuth, *Successor Vision,* p. xx.

51. Rosemary Righter, *Utopia Lost: The United Nations and World Order* (New York: Twentieth Century Fund, 1995), pp. 155–184.

52. Report of the Group of Experts on the Structure of the United Nations System, *New United Nations Structure,* p. 1.

53. Ibid., p. 23.

54. Ibid., pp. 56–57.

55. *Contributions by the Executive Heads of the Organization of the United Nations System,* A/AC.179/16, October 20, 1977, and *Note by the Secretary-General,* A/AC.179/6, April 15, 1976.

56. A/46/882, February 21, 1992, and A/C.5/47/2, June 2, 1993. Ironically, by that point the last few incumbents of the post of director-general had been French nationals, so the goal of making this a high-level post for developing-country nationals was not being served in any case.

57. E/1999/L. 61, December 15, 1999.

58. For a listing of these units, see Annan, *Renewing the United Nations*, p. 31.

59. Ibid., p. 17, para. 38.

60. Ibid., p. 6, plus p. 20, paras. 49–51. For the rationale and workings of the new UN Development Group and other aspects of development cooperation, see pp. 49–56, paras. 146–169 and actions 9–11.

61. Ibid., p. 90, para. 283.

62. J. David Singer, *Financing International Organization: The United Nations Budget Process* (The Hague: M. Nijhoff, 1961), pp. 122–123; and Russell, *History of the United Nations Charter*, pp. 62–63.

63. While voluntary payments for particular agencies, programs, or trust funds have grown very substantially over time, they have not proven nearly so controversial as assessments either in UN fora or in capitals.

64. For a more detailed account of these early debates, see Singer, *Financing International Organization*, pp. 122–146.

65. *U.S. Financial and Political Involvement in the United Nations*, 99th Congress, 1st sess., 1985 (Washington, D.C.: U.S. Government Printing Office, 1985), p. 6.

66. Committee on Foreign Affairs, *Impact of Gramm-Rudman-Hollings on U.S. Contributions to International Organizations*, 99th Congress, 2nd session, 1986 (Washington, D.C.: U.S. Government Printing Office, 1986), no. 86-H381-79, p. 7.

67. Section 143 of Public Law 99-93 (H.R. 2068), August 16, 1985.

68. See U.S. Congress, *Congressional Record*, 99th Congress, 1st sess., 1985, vol. 131, pt. 11 (Washington, D.C.: U.S. Government Printing Office, 1985), pp. 14937–14940. Also see U.S. House or Representatives, *Congressional Record*, May 8, 1985, 99th Congress, 1st sess., vol. 131, pt. 8 (Washington, D.C.: U.S. Government Printing Office, 1985), pp. 11096–11098.

69. House Subcommittee on Human Rights and International Organizations and Subcommittee on International Operations, Committee on Foreign Affairs, *Recent Developments in the United Nations System*, 100th Congress, 2nd sess., 1988 (Washington, D.C.: U.S. Government Printing Office, 1988), no. 88-H381-61, p. 66.

70. Subparagraphs 2(a)–2(b) of resolution 40/237, December 18, 1985.

71. See A/40/PV.121, pp. 7–8, 16, 27, 41.

72. See Tapio Kanninen, *Leadership and Reform: The Secretary-General and the UN Financial Crisis of the Late 1980s* (The Hague: Kluwer Law International, 1995), pp. 44–45; and A/40/1102, pp. 5–8, paras. 15–31.

73. Subparagraph (c) of resolution 40/572, and A/40/1102 and its addenda.

74. Tapio Kanninen, *Leadership and Reform*, p. 51. The Secretary-General called for a reduction in the U.S. assessment to 15 or 20 percent and for the five permanent members to pay "more or less the same amount." Elaine Sciolino, "U.N. Chief Suggests U.S. Contribution Be Cut," *New York Times*, April 29, 1986.

75. Kanninen, *Leadership*, p. 73.

76. *Report of the High-Level Intergovernmental Experts to Review the Efficiency of the Administrative and Financial Functioning of the United Nations*, A/41/49, p. 4, para. 19. Also see p. 7, para. 22, and recommendation 8, pp. 7–8.

77. Maurice Bertrand, *The Third Generation World Organization* (Dordrecht, Netherlands: M. Nijhoff, 1989), p. 111.

78. A/41/49, pp. 1, 10.

79. Michael J. Berlin, "U.N. Adopts Agreement to Trim Costs; Weighted Voting, Staff Cuts Approved," *Washington Post*, December 20, 1986.

80. Don Shannon, "State Department to Lobby Congress for U.N. Budget," *Los Angeles Times*, September 15, 1986; and James F. Clarity, Milt Freudenheim, and Katherine Roberts, "U.N.'s Bloated Bottom Line," *New York Times*, August 24, 1986.

81. See Alan L. Keyes, "Why Imperil U.N. Reform?" *New York Times*, September 25, 1986; José S. Sorzano, "The Congress Is Not 'Bashing' the UN," *Christian Science Monitor*, August 19, 1986; and Dante B. Fascell, "Enough U.N.-Bashing," *New York Times*, September 19, 1986.

82. The United States circulated a UNA-USA report that proposed a similar consensus-based budgeting mechanism and that was signed by four African leaders, a Latin American foreign minister, and Senator Kassebaum, among others. See United Nations Management and Decision-Making Project, *U.N. Leadership: The Roles of the Secretary-General and the Member States* (New York: UNA-USA, December 1986).

83. A/41/PV.102, pp. 7–8.

84. Bertrand, *Third Generation*, p. 115.

85. Quoted in Elaine Sciolino, "U.N. Assembly Favors Plan to Alter the Budget Process," *New York Times*, December 20, 1986.

86. "Walters Says U.S. Should Restore U.N. Dues," *New York Times*, December 21, 1986.

87. The CPC was established by ECOSOC as a subsidiary body by resolution 920 (XXXIV) of 1962. Also see ECOSOC resolutions 1171 (XLI) of 1966, and 2008 (LX) of 1976. It serves as the principal subsidiary body of both ECOSOC and the General Assembly for planning, programming, and coordination. Its members are nominated by the Council and elected by the Assembly for three-year terms, according to a formula for equitable geographical distribution.

88. Berlin, "U.N. Adopts Agreement."

89. *United States Participation in the UN* (Washington, D.C.: U.S. Government Printing Office, 1986), p. 306.

90. Public Law 100-204, sec. 143, December 22, 1987, Foreign Relations Authorization Act, fiscal rears 1988 and 1989. In essence, Congress—a full year after the passage of 41/213—decided to ease one condition but to add two new ones before the United Nations could receive full funding.

91. Report by the President to the Congress for the Year 1988, *United States Participation in the UN* (Washington, D.C.: U.S. Government Printing Office, 1989), pp. 305–306, 309, 310.

92. Elaine Sciolino, "Reagan, in Switch, Says U.S. Will Pay Some Old U.N. Dues," *New York Times*, September 14, 1988; and Lou Cannon, "U.S. to Pay Dues, Debt to U.N.; White House Offers Olive Branch, Praise for Fiscal Reforms," *Washington Post*, September 14, 1988.

93. See U.S. statement, A/44/PV.84, pp. 17–21.

94. But see Knight, *Changing United Nations*, and Kanninen, *Leadership and Reform*.

95. Edward C. Luck, "Blue Ribbon Power: Independent Commissions and UN Reform," *International Studies Perspectives*, no. 1 (2000); 89–104.

Acronyms

ACABQ	Advisory Committee on Administrative and Budgetary Questions
ACC	Administrative Committee on Coordination
ACUNS	Academic Council on the United Nations System
AIDS	acquired immunodeficiency syndrome
AU	African Union (formerly OAU)
BWC	Biological Weapons Convention
CCD	Conference of the Committee on Disarmament
CEB	Chief Executives Board
CIVPOL	civilian police
CNN	Cable News Network
COPAZ	National Commission for the Consolidation of Peace
CPC	Committee for Programme and Coordination
CSD	Commission for Sustainable Development
CTBT	Comprehensive Nuclear Test Ban Treaty
CWC	Chemical Weapons Convention
DDR	demobilization, disarmament, and reintegration
DOMREP	United Nations Mission in the Dominican Republic
DPA	Department of Political Affairs
DPI	Department of Public Information
DPKO	Department of Peacekeeping Operations
EAD	Electoral Assistance Division
EAS	Electoral Assistance Secretariat
EAU	Electoral Assistance Unit
ECLAC	Economic Commission for Latin America and the Caribbean
ECOSOC	Economic and Social Council
ECOWAS	Economic Organization of West African States
ENDC	Eighteen-Nation Committee on Disarmament
ETONU-MEX	Technical Assistance Team in Mexico

EU	European Union
FALD	Field Administration and Logistics Division
FAO	Food and Agriculture Organization
FEI	Federal Electorate Institute
FMLN	Farabundo Martí National Liberation Front
G8	Group of Eight
G-77	Group of 77
GATT	General Agreement on Tariffs and Trade
GEF	Global Environmental Facility
GNP	gross national product
Habitat	United Nations Center for Human Settlements
HCLM	High-Level Committee on Management
HIV	human immunodeficiency virus
HLCP	High-Level Committee on Programmes
IACB	Inter-Agency Consultative Board
IAEA	International Atomic Energy Agency
IBRD	International Bank for Reconstruction and Development
ICAO	International Civil Aviation Organization
ICC	International Criminal Court
ICJ	International Court of Justice
ICRC	International Committee of the Red Cross
ICTR	International Criminal Tribunal for Rwanda
ICTY	International Criminal Tribunal for the Former Yugoslavia
IDA	International Development Association
IDP	internally displaced person
IFAD	International Fund for Agricultural Development
IFC	International Finance Corporation
IFES	International Foundation for Election Systems
ILC	International Law Commission
ILO	International Labour Organization
IMF	International Monetary Fund
IMO	International Maritime Organization
INSTRAW	International Research and Training Institute for the Advancement of Women
IPEC	International Programme on the Elimination of Child Labour
IRO	International Refugee Organization
ITMF	Integrated Missions Task Force
ITU	International Telecommunications Union
JIOG	Joint International Observer Group
JIU	Joint Inspection Unit
MAD	mutual assured destruction
MINUCI	United Nations Mission in Côte d'Ivoire

MINUGUA	United Nations Verification Mission in Guatemala
MINURCA	United Nations Mission in the Central African Republic
MINURSO	United Nations Mission for the Referendum in Western Sahara
MIPONUH	United Nations Civilian Police Mission in Haiti
MONUA	United Nations Observer Mission in Angola
MONUC	United Nations Organization Mission in the Democratic Republic of Congo
MP	member of parliament
MPR	Indonesian People's Assembly
NAM	needs assessment mission
NATO	North Atlantic Treaty Organization
NDI	National Democratic Institute
NECBAT	Netherlands and Canadian Battalion
NGO	nongovernmental organization
NIEO	new international economic order
OAS	Organization of American States
OAU	Organization of African Unity
OCHA	Office for the Coordination of Humanitarian Affairs
OECD	Organization for Economic Cooperation and Development
OHCHR	Office of the High Commissioner for Human Rights
OLA	Office of Legal Affairs
ONUC	United Nations Operation in the Congo
ONUCA	United Nations Observer Group in Central America
ONUMOZ	United Nations Operation in Mozambique
ONUSAL	United Nations Observer Mission in El Salvador
OPCW	Organization for the Prohibition of Chemical Weapons
OSCE	Organization for Security and Cooperation in Europe
OSS	Office of Strategic Services
P-5	permanent five
PDK	Party of Democratic Kampuchea
PGA	Parliamentarians for Global Action
PLO	Palestine Liberation Organization
PPP	purchasing power parity
Renamo	Mozambique National Resistance
RUF	Revolutionary United Front
SHIRBRIG	Standby High Readiness Brigade
SWAPO	South West Africa People's Organization
TRC	Truth and Reconciliation Commission
UDHR	Universal Declaration of Human Rights
UK	United Kingdom
UN	United Nations
UNA-USA	United Nations Association of the United States of America

UNAIDS	Joint United Nations Programme on HIV/AIDS
UNAMA	United Nations Assistance Mission in Afghanistan
UNAMIC	United Nations Advance Mission in Cambodia
UNAMIR	United Nations Assistance Mission in Rwanda
UNAMSIL	United Nations Mission in Sierra Leone
UNASOG	United Nations Aouzou Strip Observer Group
UNAVEM	United Nations Angola Verification Mission
UNCC	United Nations Compensation Commission
UNCITRAL	United Nations Commission on International Trade Law
UNCRO	United Nations Confidence Restoration Operation in Croatia
UNCTAD	United Nations Conference on Trade and Development
UNDAF	UNDP Assistance Framework
UNDCP	United Nations Drug Control Programme
UNDOF	United Nations Disengagement Observer Force
UNDP	United Nations Development Programme
UNEF	United Nations Emergency Force
UNEP	United Nations Environment Programme
UNESCO	United Nations Educational, Scientific, and Cultural Organization
UNFEOM	United Nations Fijian Electoral Observation Mission
UNFICYP	United Nations Peacekeeping Force in Cyprus
UNFPA	United Nations Population Fund
UNGOMAP	United Nations Good Offices Mission in Afghanistan and Pakistan
UNHCHR	United Nations High Commissioner for Human Rights
UNHCR	United Nations High Commissioner for Refugees
UNICEF	United Nations Children's Fund (formerly United Nations International Children's Emergency Fund)
UNIDIR	United Nations Institute for Disarmament Research
UNIDO	United Nations Industrial Development Organization
UNIFEM	United Nations Development Fund for Women
UNIFIL	United Nations Interim Force in Lebanon
UNIIMOG	United Nations Iran-Iraq Military Observer Group
UNIKOM	United Nations Iraq-Kuwait Observation Mission
UNIPOM	United Nations India-Pakistan Observation Mission
UNITA	Union for the Total Independence of Angola
UNITAF	Unified Task Force
UNITAR	United Nations Institute for Training and Research
UNMEE	United Nations Mission in Ethiopia and Eritrea
UNMIBH	United Nations Mission in Bosnia and Herzegovina
UNMIH	United Nations Mission in Haiti, 1993–1996
UNMIK	United Nations Mission in Kosovo

UNMIL	United Nations Mission in Liberia
UNMISET	United Nations Mission of Support in East Timor
UNMOGIP	United Nations Military Observer Group in India and Pakistan
UNMOP	United Nations Mission of Observers in Prevlaka
UNMOT	United Nations Mission of Observers in Tajikistan
UNOGIL	United Nations Observation Group in Lebanon
UNOMIG	United Nations Observer Mission in Georgia
UNOMIL	United Nations Observer Mission in Liberia
UNOMSIL	United Nations Observer Mission in Sierra Leone
UNOMUR	United Nations Observer Mission in Uganda-Rwanda
UNOSOM	United Nations Operation in Somalia
UNPREDEP	United Nations Preventive Deployment Force
UNPROFOR	United Nations Protection Force
UNRISD	United Nations Research Institute for Social Development
UNRRA	United Nations Relief and Rehabilitation Administration
UNRWA	United Nations Relief and Works Agency for Palestine Refugees
UNSCOB	United Nations Special Committee on the Balkans
UNSF	United Nations Security Force in West New Guinea
UNSMIH	United Nations Support Mission in Haiti
UNSTRAW	United Nations Research and Training Institute for the Advancement of Women
UNTAC	United Nations Transitional Authority in Cambodia
UNTAES	United Nations Transitional Administration for Eastern Slavonia, Baranja, and Western Sirmium
UNTAET	United Nations Transitional Administration in East Timor
UNTAG	United Nations Transition Assistance Group
UNTMIH	United Nations Transition Mission in Haiti
UNTSO	United Nations Truce Supervision Organization
UNU	United Nations University
UNYOM	United Nations Yemen Observation Mission
UPU	Universal Postal Union
WFP	World Food Programme
WHO	World Health Organization
WIPO	World Intellectual Property Organization
WMO	World Meteorological Organization
WTO	World Trade Organization

Selected Bibliography

Books and Reports

Alger, Chadwick F., ed. *The Future of the United Nations System: Potential for the Twenty-First Century.* Tokyo: United Nations University Press, 1998.

Alger, Chadwick F., Gene M. Lyons, and John E. Trent, eds. *The United Nations System: The Politics of Member States.* Tokyo: United Nations University Press, 1995.

Annan, Kofi. *Strengthening of the United Nations: An Agenda for Further Change.* Report of the Secretary General. UN Doc. A/57/387, September 9, 2002.

Annual Report of the Secretary General on the Work of the Organization. New York: United Nations, 1946—. Issued each fall prior to the regular session of the General Assembly.

Bailey, Sidney D., and Sam Daws. *The Procedure of the UN Security Council.* 3rd ed. Oxford: Oxford University Press, 1998.

Basic Facts About the United Nations. New York: United Nations Department of Public Information, 2000.

Blue Helmets: A Review of United Nations Peace-Keeping. 3rd ed. New York: United Nations, 1996.

Boutros-Ghali, Boutros. *An Agenda for Development.* New York: United Nations, 1995.

———. *An Agenda for Peace.* New York: United Nations, 1992.

———. *Unvanquished: A U.S.-U.N. Saga.* New York: Random House, 1999.

Brahimi, Lakhdar. *Report of the Panel on United Nations Peace Operations.* Brahimi Report. UN Doc. A/55/305, August 21, 2000.

Bull, Hedley. *The Anarchical Society: A Study of Order in World Politics.* New York: Columbia University Press, 1977.

Chasek, Pamela S., ed. *The Global Environment in the Twenty-First Century: Prospects for International Cooperation.* Tokyo: United Nations University Press, 2000.

Clark, Roger S. *The United Nations Crime Prevention and Criminal Justice Program: Formation of Standards and Efforts at Their Implementation.* Philadelphia: University of Pennsylvania Press, 1994.

Claude, Inis L., Jr. *Swords Into Plowshares: The Problems and Progress of International Organization.* 4th ed. New York: Random House, 1984.

Commission on Global Governance. *Our Global Neighborhood.* New York: Oxford University Press, 1995.

Danieli, Yael, ed. *Sharing the Front Line and the Back Hills: Peacekeepers, Humanitarian Aid Workers, and the Media in the Midst of Crisis.* Amityville, N.Y.: Baywood, 2001.

Danieli, Yael, Elsa Stamatopolou, and Clarence J. Dias, eds. *The Universal Declaration of Human Rights: Fifty Years and Beyond.* Amityville, N.Y.: Baywood, 1999.

Drinan, Robert F. *The Mobilization of Shame: A World View of Human Rights.* New Haven, Conn.: Yale University Press, 2001.

Durch, William J., ed. *UN Peacekeeping, American Policy, and the Uncivil Wars of the 1990s.* New York: St. Martin's Press, 1996.

Eichelberger, Clark M. *UN: The First Twenty Years.* New York: Harper and Row, 1965.

Emmerij, Louis, Richard Jolly, and Thomas G. Weiss. *Ahead of the Curve.* United Nations Intellectual History Project, vol. 1. Bloomington: Indiana University Press, 2001.

Epstein, William. *The United Nations and Nuclear Disarmament: Achievements in the Way to a Nuclear-Free World.* New York: United Nations, 1997.

Fasulo, Linda M. *Representing America: Experiences of U.S. Diplomats at the U.N.* New York: Praeger, 1984.

Forsythe, David P. *Human Rights in International Relations.* New York: Cambridge University Press, 2000.

Franck, Thomas M., ed. *Delegating State Powers: The Effect of Treaty Regimes on Democracy and Sovereignty.* Ardsley, N.Y.: Transnational, 2000.

Friedman, Thomas. *The Lexus and the Olive Tree: Understanding Globalization.* Rev. ed. New York: Farrar, Straus, and Giroux, 2000.

Glenn, Jerome C., and Theodore J. Gordon. *2001: State of the Future.* Millennium Project. Washington, D.C.: American Council for the United Nations University. Also available on CD-ROM.

A Global Agenda: Issues Before the Fifty-sixth General Assembly of the United Nations. New York: United Nations Association of the United States of America, 2001. Annual publication.

Global Economic Prospects 2002: Making Trade Work for the World's Poor. Washington, D.C.: World Bank, 2001.

Hannum, Hurst, ed. *Guide to International Human Rights Practice.* Ardsley, N.Y.: Transnational, 1999.

Holtze, James. *Divided It Stands: Can the United Nations Work?* Atlanta: Turner, 1995.

Human Development Report 2001: Making New Technologies Work for Human Development. New York: Oxford University Press and the United Nations Development Programme, 2001. Annual publication.

Human Rights Watch World Report 2001. New York: Human Rights Watch, 2001.

Ignatieff, Michael. *Human Rights as Politics and Idolatry.* Princeton: Princeton University Press, 2003.

International Instruments Related to the Prevention and Suppression of International Terrorism. New York: United Nations Office of Legal Affairs, 2001.

Joyner, Christopher C. *The United Nations and International Law.* Cambridge: Cambridge University Press, 1997.

Krasno, Jean, Don Daniel, and Bradd Hayes, eds. *Leveraging for Success in United Nations Peace Operations.* Westport, Conn.: Praeger, 2003.

Luck, Edward C. *Mixed Messages: American Politics and International Organization.* Washington, D.C.: Brookings Institution, 1999.

Meisler, Stanley. *United Nations: The First Fifty Years*. New York: Atlantic Monthly Press, 1995.

Meron, Theodor. *Human Rights and Humanitarian Norms as Customary Law*. Oxford: Clarendon Press, 1989.

Oakley, Robert B., Michael J. Dziedzic, and Eliot M. Goldberg, eds. *Policing the New World Disorder: Peace Operations and Public Security*. Washington, D.C.: National Defense University Press, 1998.

Pérez de Cuéllar, Javier. *Pilgrimage for Peace*. New York: St. Martin's Press, 1997.

Pillar, Paul R. *Terrorism and U.S. Foreign Policy*. Washington, D.C.: Brookings Institution, 2001.

Powers, Samantha. *A Problem from Hell: America and the Age of Genocide*. New York: Basic Books, 2002.

Ratner, Steven R. *The New UN Peacekeeping: Building Peace in Lands of Conflict After the Cold War*. New York: St. Martin's Press, 1996.

Rotfield, Adam D., et al. *Arms Control and Disarmament: A New Conceptual Approach*. New York: United Nations Department for Disarmament Affairs, 2000.

Ruggie, John G., ed. *Multilateralism Matters*. New York: Columbia University Press, 1993.

Russell, Ruth B. *A History of the United Nations Charter: The Role of the United States, 1940–45*. Washington, D.C.: Brookings Institution, 1958.

Schechter, Michael G., ed. *United Nations–Sponsored World Conferences*. Tokyo: United Nations University Press, 2001.

Sewall, Sarah B., and Carl Kaysen, eds. *The United States and the International Criminal Court*. Lanham, Md.: Rowman and Littlefield, 2000.

Simmons, P. J., and Chantal de Jonge Oudraat, eds. *Managing Global Issues: Lessons Learned*. Washington, D.C.: Carnegie Endowment for International Peace, 2001.

Spector, Leonard, and Jacqueline Smith. *Nuclear Ambitions: The Spread of Nuclear Weapons, 1989–90*. Boulder: Westview Press, 1990.

Steiner, Henry J., and Philip Alston. *International Human Rights in Context, Law, Politics, Morals*. 2nd ed. New York: Oxford University Press, 2000.

Sutterlin, James S. *The United Nations and the Maintenance of International Security: A Challenge to Be Met*. 2nd ed. Westport, Conn.: Praeger, 2003.

Thomas, Daniel C. *The Helsinki Effect: International Norms, Human Rights, and the Demise of Communism*. Princeton: Princeton University Press, 2001.

Thomas, Ward. *The Ethics of Destruction: Norms and Force in International Relations*. Ithaca: Cornell University Press, 2001.

The UN at Fifty: Statements by World Leaders, New York, 22–24 October, 1995. New York: United Nations, 1996.

Waldheim, Kurt. *Building the Future Order: The Search for Peace in the Interdependent World*. New York: Free Press, 1980.

We the Peoples: The Role of the United Nations in the Twenty-First Century. New York: United Nations Department of Public Information, 2000.

Weiss, Thomas G., and Leon Gordenker, eds. *NGOs, the UN, and Global Governance*. Boulder: Lynne Rienner, 1996.

Journals

American Journal of International Law. Published by the American Society of International Law.

Foreign Affairs. Published by the Council on Foreign Relations.
Foreign Policy. Published by the Carnegie Endowment for International Peace.
Global Governance: A Review of Multilateralism and International Organizations. Published by Lynne Rienner in cooperation with the Academic Council on the United Nations System and the United Nations University.

UN System Websites

Food and Agriculture Organization (FAO): www.fao.org.
International Atomic Energy Agency (IAEA): www.iaea.org.
International Civil Aviation Organization (ICAO): www.icao.int.
International Fund for Agricultural Development (IFAD): www.ifad.org.
International Labour Organization (ILO): www.ilo.org.
International Maritime Organization (IMO): www.imo.org.
International Monetary Fund (IMF): www.imf.int.
International Telecommunications Union (ITU): www.itu.int.
Joint United Nations Program on HIV/AIDS: www.unaids.org.
United Nations: www.un.org, www.unsyst.org.
United Nations Children's Fund (UNICEF): www.unicef.org.
United Nations Development Programme (UNDP): www.undp.org.
United Nations Drug Control Programme (UNDCP): www.undcp.org.
United Nations Educational, Scientific, and Cultural Organization (UNESCO): www.unesco.org.
United Nations Environment Programme (UNEP): www.unep.org.
United Nations High Commissioner for Human Rights (UNHCHR): www.unhchr.ch.
United Nations High Commissioner for Refugees (UNHCR): www.unhcr.ch.
United Nations Industrial Development Organization (UNIDO): www.unido.org.
United Nations Population Fund (UNFPA): www.unfpa.org.
United Nations University (UNU): www.unu.edu.
Universal Postal Union (UPU): www.upu.int.
World Bank: www.worldbank.org.
World Food Programme (WFP): www.wfp.org.
World Health Organization (WHO): www.who.int.
World Intellectual Property Organization (WIPO): www.wipo.int.
World Meteorological Organization (WMO): www.wmo.ch.

The Contributors

Derek Boothby joined the United Nations in 1978 and served in the UN Department for Disarmament Affairs from 1980 to 1991. In 1990 he was the Deputy Secretary-General of the Review Conference of the Nuclear Nonproliferation Treaty. In March 1991 he helped to organize UN weapons inspections in Iraq. In 1993 he became director of the Europe Division in the UN Department of Political Affairs. Since 1998 he has worked independently as a consultant on international political and security affairs.

Jacques Fomerand studied law and graduated in political science at the University of Aix-en-Provence, France, and earned a Ph.D. in political science at the City University of New York. He joined the UN Secretariat in 1977, serving in the office of the Under-Secretary-General of the Department of Economic and Social Affairs. From 1992 to June 2003, when he retired from UN service, he was director of the United Nations University Office in North America. Dr. Fomerand is currently completing his book *Dictionary of the United Nations*.

Jean E. Krasno has a B.F.A. from the University of Illinois, where she graduated summa cum laude, an M.A. from Stanford University, and a Ph.D. from the City University of New York in international politics. She joined Yale University in June 1995 with an appointment in the Department of Political Science associated with United Nations studies and is currently a fellow in international security studies at Yale. She was executive director of the Academic Council on the United Nations System (ACUNS) from July 1998 to June 2003. Her publications include *The United Nations and Iraq: Defanging the Viper* (coauthored with James Sutterlin), and *Leveraging for Success in United Nations Peace Operations* (coedited with Don Daniel and Bradd Hayes).

Jeffrey Laurenti is senior adviser to the United Nations Foundation. Until 2003, he had directed the policy studies program at the United Nations Association of the United States of America (UNA-USA), on whose board of directors he now sits. He is author of numerous monographs, articles, and papers on a wide range of issues in their UN dimension. Laurenti came to the UN arena after service as executive director of the New Jersey Senate, senior issues adviser in the Mondale presidential campaign, and candidate for the U.S. House of Representatives from New Jersey. He earned his B.A. degree at Harvard College, magna cum laude, and an M.A. in public affairs at Princeton University's Woodrow Wilson School.

Edward C. Luck is professor of practice in international and public affairs and director of the Center on International Organization in the School of International and Public Affairs (SIPA) at Columbia University. From 1995 to 1997 he played a key role in the UN reform process as a senior consultant to the Department of Administration and Management of the United Nations and as staff director of the General Assembly's Open-Ended High-Level Working Group on the Strengthening of the United Nations System. From 1984 to 1994, Dr. Luck served as president and chief executive officer of the United Nations Association of the United States of America (UNA-USA). He holds a B.A. from Dartmouth College and an M.A. and Ph.D. from Columbia University. His most recent publication is *Mixed Messages: American Politics and International Organization 1919–1999.*

Robin Ludwig holds an M.A. in international affairs from Columbia University and a Ph.D. in political science from the University of Michigan. She is a senior political affairs officer in the Department of Political Affairs, UN Secretariat. Since the establishment of the Electoral Assistance Division in 1992, she has participated in providing UN support and assistance for democratic elections in countries worldwide. Dr. Ludwig has worked with the UN for twenty-five years and has held several political affairs posts, including acting director of the Americas Division, executive assistant to the Deputy Secretary-General, and chief of the Peace Studies Unit.

Charles Norchi has a B.A. from Harvard University, a J.D. from Case Western Reserve Law School, and an LL.M. and J.S.D. from Yale Law School. He is a professor of history at Sarah Lawrence College, where he teaches international human rights and international law. He was founding director of the Washington, D.C.–based War Crimes Project of the Committee for a Free Afghanistan, has served as executive director of the International League for Human Rights in New York, and is a director of the Policy Sciences Center at Yale Law School. He has worked extensively in Afghanistan and South Asia. Norchi has written articles for the *New York Times,* the *Harvard Law Review, Crosslines,* and the *Yale Journal of World Affairs,* and was a contributor to *The Pivotal States: A New Framework for U.S. Policy in the Developing World.*

Jochen Prantl is a Ph.D. candidate in international relations at St. Antony's College, University of Oxford, where he is writing his doctoral thesis on informal groups of states within the UN. In 2000–2001 he was visiting fellow in United Nations studies at Yale University. In 1995–1996 he was a member of the Delegation of the European Commission to the United Nations in New York. He is a graduate of the University of Bonn, with degrees in political science, Spanish, and the history of art. His recent publications include "Security and Stability in Northern Europe: A Threat Assessment" and "The Brahimi Report: Overcoming the North-South Divide."

Joe Sills received his B.A., magna cum laude, from Vanderbilt University and his M.A. in Arab area studies from the American University of Beirut, in Lebanon. He joined the UN in July 1981, following eight years as vice president of the United Nations Association of the United States of America (UNA-USA). For six years he was associate spokesman for Secretary-General Javier Pérez de Cuéllar, after which he became director of the Communications and Project Management Division of the Department of Public Information. For over three years Sills was spokesman for UN Secretary-General Boutros Boutros-Ghali. After his retirement in 1998, he has remained active in UN-related matters, serving as a consultant to the UN Compensation Commission, the American Council for the UN University, the UN Foundation, and the International Labour Organization.

Index

Abe, Nobuyasu, 223(n26)
ACE project (Administration and Cost of Elections), 132
Acheson, Dean, 318
Ad hoc groups, 311, 320; Congo Advisory Committee, 325–327; functions and characteristics of, 324–325; Groups of Friends, 335–339; peaceful uses for atomic energy, 321; PKOs as, 319; post–Cold War growth of, 331–335; SC's open system, closed shop dichotomy, 312–315; UN Emergency Force, 321–325; Western Contact Group on Namibia, 327–331
Ad hoc tribunals, 52–53
Adjustment with a Human Face, 178
Administrative Committee on Coordination (ACC), 380–381
Administrative issues, 5
Administrative reform, 363–364
Advisors, human rights, 94
Advisory Committee on Administrative and Budgetary Questions (ACABQ), 274–275
Advisory Committee on the Peaceful Uses of Atomic Energy, 321
Advisory committees. *See* Ad hoc groups
Advocacy groups, 67–68
Afghan Independent Human Rights Commission, 103–104
Afghanistan, 101–104; Group of Friends, 342; humanitarian aid, 184; human rights abuses, 114(n28); PKO assessment, 296; request for electoral assistance, 133(table); Soviet occupation, 198; Tajikistan Friends Group, 348; U.S. support of PKO, 387
African Nuclear-Weapon-Free Zone Treaty, 203
African states: Cold War tensions affecting, 242–243; after decolonization, 116–117; SC seat distribution, 365; UN budgeting for, 275. *See also individual countries*
Agenda for Development, An, 55
Agenda for Peace, An, 54–55
Aggression, crimes of, 98
Agreement on Provisional Arrangements in Afghanistan Pending the Re-establishment of Permanent Government Institutions, 102–103
Agreements on a Comprehensive Political Settlement of the Cambodia Conflict (Paris Agreements), 124–125
Agriculture. *See* Food production
Ahtisaari, Martti, 122, 330, 356(n92)
AIDS. *See* HIV/AIDS
Air travel tax, 305
Ajello, Aldo, 124
Akashi, Yasushi, 125–126
Albania: disarmament, 215; request for electoral assistance, 133(table); UNSCOB peacekeeping, 228
Albright, Madeleine, 342
Algeria: request for electoral assistance, 133(table)

Al-Qaida, 102, 208
Angola: Cuban withdrawal from, 122,
    244, 330; elections and electoral
    assistance, 118(fig.), 123,
    134(table); peace accords, 115;
    socialist government, 243
Annan, Kofi, 7, 389; addressing
    globalization, 71; addressing UN
    reform, 392; HIV/AIDS funding,
    303; institutional analysis, 377;
    institutional reform, 381; Nobel
    Peace Prize, 56; setting UN
    priorities, 55
Antarctic Treaty (1959), 196, 203
Anthrax, 207
Anti-Ballistic Missile Treaty, 202
Antipersonnel landmines. See
    Landmines
Apartheid, 96
Application of human rights, 105
Arab countries, 34, 37–38, 280
Arbitration, 4
Arbitration and Mediation Center, 58
Argentina, 27, 30–33; assessment
    obligation, 291; disarmament, 200;
    Group of Friends, 342; request for
    electoral assistance, 134(table)
Aristide, Jean Bertrand, 342
Armenia: request for electoral
    assistance, 134(table); WTO
    membership, 15
Arms race, 195–196
Arms regulation, post-war progress on,
    193
Arms trade: intrastate conflict
    influencing, 331; post–Cold War
    surge in intrastate conflict,
    211–213; UN Register of
    Conventional Arms, 211
Arrears. See Assessment
Arria, Diego, 338(fig.), 340
Arria formula, 370
Arsanjani, Mahnoush, 97
Arsenis, Gerasimos, 178
Article 19, 276–277, 279, 284–285,
    307(n5)
Article 99, 234
Asia: Cold War tensions affecting, 242;
    SC seat distribution, 365; UN
    budgeting for, 275
Asian financial crisis, 70

Assembly, right to, 109
Assessment, 278–279; capacity to pay,
    287–289; ceiling capping, 292–295;
    ceiling for, 295, 309(nn 13,14);
    controversy over, 396(n63); dues
    withholding for Congo PKO, 279,
    307(n3); low income offset,
    289–291, 308(nn 10, 11); as
    obligation, 276–277; P-5
    contribution, 396(n74); P-5
    obligations, 308(n7); partial
    payment of arrears, 284, 307(n5);
    for PKO, 295–299; Reagan
    administration affecting U.S.
    payment, 307(n4); for selected
    countries, 294(table); Soviet
    withholding, 278–279; stabilizing
    rates, 291–292; U.S. dispute over
    scale, 307(n6); U.S. negotiating
    payment of arrears, 284–287,
    307(nn 4, 5, 6); U.S. withholding,
    279–284, 306(n1), 307(n3)
Assessment scale, 382–388
Asylum, 109
Atomic energy, peaceful uses of, 321
Atomic Energy Commission (AEC),
    195, 354(n46)
Atomic weapons. See Nuclear weapons
Atoms for Peace Conference, 321
Australia: Bruce Committee, 164, 166;
    Suez crisis voting, 322; veto
    provision, 38
Aviation, civil, 57, 236, 302(table)
Ayala Lasso, José, 91
Azerbaijan: request for electoral
    assistance, 135(table)

Bangkok Treaty (1997), 203
Bangladesh: assessment obligation, 290;
    request for electoral assistance,
    135(table)
Barcelona Traction case, 97
Baruch Plan, 195
Baseline human goals, 67
Basic Facts, 74(n30)
Belgium, 21; Congo's independence,
    232–233; Rwanda PKO, 253; Suez
    crisis voting, 322
Benin: request for electoral assistance,
    136(table)
Ben Omar, Driss, 235
Berlin Wall, 242, 244, 248

Bermuda, 6
Bertrand, Maurice, 386
Betancur, Belisario, 250
Bhabba, Homi, 354(n46)
Big three agencies, 59–60
Bilateral aid, 184
Bilateral diplomacy, 21
Biodiversity, 64
Biological weapons, 197, 207–209
Biological Weapons Convention (BWC), 208–209
Biological Weapons Treaty (1972), 197
Black September, 240
Bloom, Sol, 41(fig.)
Blue helmets, 230–231
Bogomolov, Alexandre, 82
Bolivia: request for electoral assistance, 136(table)
Bolton, John R., 208
Bonn Agreement, 102–103
Booby traps, 215
Border disputes, 10
Bosnia, 182, 247–248, 251, 254–255, 347
Botha, P. W., 244
Boutros-Ghali, Boutros, 7; ad hoc coalitions, 311; on ad hoc groupings of states, 335; alternative revenue sources, 305; election of, 13; El Salvador mediation, 248; institutional reform, 380; micro-disarmament proposal, 211; observations on world conferences, 68; prioritizing PKOs, 333; strengthening peacemaking, 54–55; U.S. hostility toward, 55; Vienna Declaration, 88–89
Brahimi, Lakhdar, 347
Brahimi Report, 255
Brazil: assessment obligation, 291, 294(table); disarmament, 200; Group of Friends, 342; New Agenda Coalition, 202; request for electoral assistance, 136(table); UN Emergency Force troops, 322
Bretton Woods Institutions: addressing North-South equity gap, 379; ECOSOC and development programs, 167; ECOSOC reform, 369; functions of, 58; funding for, 271; North-South controversy over

development authority, 168–169. See also International Monetary Fund; World Bank
Britain, 318; assessment obligation, 308(n7); chemical weapons, 207; Dumbarton Oaks and Yalta, 26–30; nomination of the Secretary-General, 38; Suez crisis, 322–323; trusteeship and independence, 35–36; veto provision, 38. See also United Kingdom
Brody, Reed, 75(n41)
Bruer, Rolf, 71
Brunei: PKO assessment, 298–299
Bruntland, Gro Harlem, 47
Budget affairs: budgetmaking process, 273–276; centralizing agency budget under ECOSOC, 376; financial reform, 363–364; GA committees, 5; peacekeeping operations expenditures, 343–345, 344(fig.); responsibility for, 44(n28); revenues and outlay, 381–388; SC and ECOSOC expansion, 367; UN Organizations' annual budget and revenues, 271–272; U.S. opposition to budget increase, 281–283; voting practice, 17(n5). See also Assessment; Funding
Buergenthal, Thomas, 250
Bulgaria, 115, 228
Bully pulpit, Secretary-General position as, 7, 55
Bunche, Ralph, 25–26, 230, 232–234
Burden-sharing, 382–388
Burkina Faso: request for electoral assistance, 136(table)
Burundi: request for electoral assistance, 136(table)
Bush, George H. W., 244–245
Bush, George W., administration, 213, 388
BWI. See Bretton Woods Institutions
Byelorussia, 28, 33, 135(table)
Byrnes, James, 373

Cadogan, Alexander, 26–27, 29–30
Cambodia: electoral assistance, 129, 136–137(table); land mine disarmament, 214(fig.); mediated solution for conflict, 244, 246;

peace accords, 115; terminating a
PKO, 341; Vietnam conflict, 243
Cameroon, 137(table), 215
Camp David Accords, 232
Canada: assessment obligation, 288,
290, 294(table), 308(n10); Group of
Friends, 342; Namibia action,
328–329; Ottawa Convention, 213;
rapid reaction capability, 349; Suez
crisis, 230; UN Emergency Force
troops, 322
Capacity building, 179–181
Cape Verde, 137(table), 342
Caputo, Dante, 347
Cárdenas, Emilio, 342
Carr, Edward Hallett, 313
Carter administration, 280–281,
296–297, 304
Cassin, Rene, 81
Center for Human Rights, 119
Central authority, lack of, 375–378
Cepeda, Fernando, 338(fig.)
Ceylon: UN Emergency Force troops,
322
Chad: request for electoral assistance,
138(table)
Chain of events theory, 37, 45(n39)
Chamber, of the ICJ, 10
Chamoun, Camille, 240
Chapultepec conference, 30–31, 36, 40
Charter: amendment reform, 362–363;
budget reform, 386; Chapultepec
conference, 30–31; Commission on
Human Rights, 92–95; commitment
to peace and security, 193–194;
Congo crisis, 234; Dumbarton Oaks
and Yalta outlines, 26–30; financing
provisions, 273; GA's ability to act
without SC consent, 318; human
rights, 61–62, 79–81; importance of
interpretation and practice,
320–321; membership issues,
32–33; outlawing war, 312–313,
353(n5); Pacific Settlement of
Disputes, 4; peace and security
through development, 163;
peacekeeping operations, 225–226,
319; reform attempts, 359;
revenues and outlay, 381; San
Francisco conference, 31–32; SC
authority, 51; SC voting practice,

12; Secretary-General's mandate,
6–7; signing and implementation
of, 40–43, 44(n5); standards and
norms, 48–49; "Uniting for Peace"
resolution, 278; U.S. goals for
drafting, 23; veto provision, 45(nn
45, 47). See also San Francisco
conference
Chechnya, 183
Chemical weapons, 198, 205–209
Chemical Weapons Convention (CWC),
206–207, 218
Chiapas: request for electoral assistance,
150(table)
Chief Executives Board (CEB, formerly
Administrative Committee on
Coordination), 380–381
Childers, Erskine, 309(n13)
Children: child labor treaties, 59–60,
74(n30); PKO human rights
mandate, 100–101; UDHR on
women and children, 111; UNICEF
and UNDP, 14, 66–67; Vienna
Declaration provisions, 87–88. See
also UNICEF
Chile, 243, 342
China: assessment obligation, 290,
294(table), 308(n7); Charter
signing, 44(n5); chemical weapons,
206; Communist control of,
242–243; Communist regime as
representative of, 280;
Comprehensive Test Ban Treaty,
205; Conference on Disarmament,
220; conventional weapons
spending, 210; Dumbarton Oaks
and Yalta, 26; electoral process and
assistance, 117, 119; employee
kickbacks, 281; Group of Friends,
342–343; humanitarian
intervention, 183; nuclear weapons
capability, 200–201; SC and
ECOSOC expansion, 366; Soviet
protest over Taiwan's
representation, 317; use of the veto
in the Security Council, 315(table) ;
U.S. leveraging voluntary
contributions against, 301; WTO
membership, 15
Choudhoury, Humayun Rasheed,
386–387

Churchill, Winston, 27–30
Civil aviation, 57, 236, 302(table)
Civil conflicts, 182–183, 232–239, 319, 331–332. *See also* Congo; El Salvador; Sierra Leone
Civilian police, 250
Civilizations, clash of, 105–106
Civil rights, 95
Civil society, 67–68; civilian nuclear program, 60–61; coordination and collaboration with the UN, 174; development partnerships, 180; ECOSOC as voice of, 7–8; intrastate conflict influencing, 332; OHCHR, 90; UN, business, and civil society in development, 185–186. *See also* Nongovernmental organizations
Climate, 58, 64
Clinton, Bill, 205, 252, 298
Clinton administration, 213, 284, 307(n5), 309(n14)
CNN factor, 247
Coalition for the International Criminal Court, 68
Cockroft, John, 354(n46)
Codex Alimentarius, 60
Coherence, UN's lack of, 178
Cold War: Charter's use of force provision, 39–40; conventional weapons use, 209–210; decline and disintegration of the Soviet system, 243–245; East-West confrontations over development, 169–170; electoral assistance following Soviet collapse, 115–116; P-5 use of the veto in the Security Council, 315(table); post–Cold War surge in intrastate conflict, 211–213; SC's inability to regulate armaments during, 194–197; spread and containment of Communism, 242–243; superpower hostility over Congo PKO, 278–279. *See also* U.S.-Soviet relations
Collective defense, 313, 353(n5); collective force versus collective security, 45(n47); regional alliances and multilateral action, 316–317; UN authorization of military force, 317–318

Collective security: Charter flexibility, 315–316; versus collective force, 45(n47)
Colombia, 38, 138(table), 322, 336–338, 342
Colonialism. *See* Decolonization; Trusteeship
Commemorative days, weeks, years, and decades, 174–175
Commission for Conventional Armaments, 195, 209
Commission for Sustainable Development (CSD), 164
Commission on Human Rights (CHR), 81, 92–95
Committee Against Torture, 95–96
Committee for Programme and Coordination (CPC), 386–387, 397(n87)
Committee on Contributions, 292
Committee on Economic, Social, and Cultural Rights, 95
Committee on Human Rights, 95
Committee on the Elimination of Discrimination Against Women, 95–96
Committee on the Elimination of Racial Discrimination, 95
Committee on the Rights of the Child, 95
Committees of the General Assembly, 5–6
Common Country Assessment, 180
Commonwealth, 120, 162(n2)
Communications industry, 21, 57
Communism, 242–243
Comoros: request for electoral assistance, 138–139(table)
Compensation tribunals, 53
Competency of UN institutions, 33, 39
Complementarity, principle of, 97–98
Comprehensive Test Ban Treaty (CTBT), 202, 204–205, 218
Concert of Europe, 21–22
Conference, diplomacy by: bilateral diplomacy, 21; Dumbarton Oaks and Yalta, 25–30. *See also* World conferences
Conference of the Committee on Disarmament (CCD), 196, 219–220

Conference on Disarmament, 202, 219–220

Conflict prevention and resolution, 4, 12; Charter provisions setting norms, 48–49; clash of civilizations, 105–106; El Salvador mediation, 248–251; post–Cold War mediation in socialist states, 244–245. *See also* Groups of Friends; Peacekeeping operations

Congo, Democratic Republic of (formerly Zaire), 140–141(table), 183

Congo Advisory Committee, 325–327

Congo crisis: call for Hammarskjöld's resignation, 55; end of budget consensus, 277; humanitarian aid, 184; peacekeeping operation, 232–239, 277–279; PKO as alternative to force, 319; request for electoral assistance, 139(table)

Congress, U.S.: alternative revenue sources, 305; assessment arrears, 284–285, 307(n5); call for UN reform, 359; capping assessment, 293; capping PKO contribution, 283–284; Charter ratification, 42; Kassebaum-Solomon Amendment, 383; Senate Expenditures Committee, 359; Senate Foreign Relations Committee, 285, 366–368; U.S. membership in the UN, 24; veto provision, 38

Congress of Vienna, 21

Connally, Tom, 24–25, 38, 41(fig.), 45(n45)

Consensus (unanimity) practice, 11–12, 347; budget establishment, 17(n5); budgetmaking, 276; disarmament agreement, 198

Constitution, Afghanistan's, 103–104

Consultations (closed meetings), 52, 333(fig.)

Consultative status, 186

Contadora Process, 345

Convention Against Torture and Other Cruel, Inhuman, or Degrading Treatment or Punishment, 95–96

Conventional disarmament, 209

Conventional weapons, 195, 198, 209–216

Convention for the Suppression of Terrorist Bombing (1997), 69

Convention for the Suppression of the Financing of Terrorism (1999), 69

Convention on Certain Conventional Weapons, 215

Convention on the Elimination of All Forms of Discrimination Against Women, 95

Convention on the Prevention and Punishment of the Crime of Genocide, 97–98

Convention on the Prohibition of the Development and Stockpiling of Bacteriological (Biological) and Toxin Weapons and on Their Destruction (1972), 197, 206–208

Convention on the Rights of the Child, 87–88, 95

Coordination and support of elections, 128–130

Copenhagen summit, 174

Copyrights, 58

Corporate sector involvement in UN processes, 187–188, 303

Côte d'Ivoire: request for electoral assistance, 140(table)

Council of Europe, 30

Counter-Terrorism Committee, 69

Crane, David, 258

Crime prevention, 63–64, 171, 381

Crimes against humanity, 97–100

Criminal justice, 63–64

Cristiani, Alfredo, 244, 336

Crocker, Chester, 244

Cross-border activities, 57–58, 173

CTBT. *See* Comprehensive Test Ban Treaty

Cuba, 38, 119; budgeting for development, 275; Nonproliferation Treaty, 201; supporting rebel groups, 243; withdrawal from Angola, 122, 330

Cultural issues: GA committees, 5; global and local norms, 47–48; human rights promotion and application, 104–106; Universal Declaration of Human Rights, 83

Cyprus, 239–242, 250, 279, 309(n15)

Czechoslovakia, 115, 317

Dadzie, Kenneth, 380

Dallaire, Romeo, 253, 349
Danzig, Germany, 227
Days, commemorative, 174–175
Dayton Accords (1995), 255
Debt burden and repayment, 13, 173, 290–291
Decades, commemorative, 174–175
Decisionmaking process, 364–373
Declaration on Decolonization (1960), 6
Declaration on the Rights of Disabled Persons (1975), 54
Declarations of the General Assembly, 53
Decolonization, 6; Congo PKO, 278; developing countries' push for development programs, 169–171; elections and, 116–117; Namibia, 121–122; obsolescence of Trusteeship Council, 43; post-war progress, 193; trusteeship issues, 28–29; UN role in, 365
De Jure Naturae et Gentium Libri Octo (Pufendorf), 314
de Klerk, F. W., 244
Del Ponte, Carla, 99
Demobilization, disarmament, and reintegration, 216–217, 251, 257
Democracy, Vienna Declaration on, 87
Democratic Republic of Timor-Leste, 128
Democratization: electoral process and, 132–133; following Soviet collapse, 116
Demographic Yearbook, 176
Demonstrations: anti-nuclear, 199; anti-trade, 15–16
Denmark: arms race study, 209; SHIRBRIG, 351
Department for Disarmament Affairs, 220–221
Department of Humanitarian Affairs, 183
Department of Peacekeeping Operations (DPKO), 6, 100, 255–256, 350
Department of Political Affairs (DPA), 6, 100, 115, 119, 220, 245
Department of Public Information (DPI), 6
Desertification, 65, 171
de Soto, Alvaro, 248, 336–337, 347
Detention, 94, 109

Developing countries: assessment scale, 382–384; call for global economic reform, 378–379; challenging U.S. dominance in the GA, 279–281; ECOSOC membership, 8; enlargement of ECOSOC and the SC, 365–366; environmental conferences, 65; failure to pay PKO assessments, 367; low income offset for assessment, 289–291, 308(nn 10, 11; North-South tensions over UN role in, 168–171; PKO assessment, 296, 298; post–Cold War UN responsibilities, 245; special agencies and, 57–59; UN budgetmaking, 275–276; UN Register of Conventional Arms, 211
Development, economic, 173; alternative funding sources for, 305; analysis of expanded programs, 375–380; as basic human right, 100–101; capacity development and the creation of UNDP, 179–181; Charter mandate, 163; disaster relief, 182; economic leadership, 178–179; El Salvador negotiations, 339; FAO function, 59; globalization and, 71; as heart of UN Organizations, 188; NGO role, 186; norms and standards, 166–167; North-South tensions over UN role in, 168–171; policy analysis and studies, 175–177; Secretariat reorganization, 61; as source of humanitarian relief funding, 184–185; sustainable development, 58–59, 66, 168–169, 172–173; UN Development Decade, 175; Vienna Declaration, 87; World Bank, 13–14; world conferences, 171–174. See also UN Development Programme
Dhanapala, Jayantha, 217, 223(n26)
Diplomacy: bilateral, 21; Groups of Friends, 336–339; NGO involvement, 173–174, 187; pacific settlement of disputes, 4; Secretariat's role in, 6
Director general for ECOSOC, 395(n56)
Disabled persons, 54, 215
Disappearance, 94

Disarmament: biological weapons, 207–209; chemical weapons, 205–207; Cold War arms race, 194–197; constant struggles for, 221–222; conventional weapons, 209–215; demobilization, disarmament, and reintegration, 216–217, 251, 257; Department for Disarmament Affairs, 220–221; GA special sessions, 197–199; inhumane weapons, 215–216; landmines, 213; NGOs and public interest, 217–218; Nonproliferation Treaty, 201–202; nuclear free zones, 203–204; nuclear test bans, 204–205; nuclear weapons, 195–196; peacebuilding and peacekeeping, 216–217; post-war progress, 193; practical measures, 213, 215; security assurances, 202–203; UN machinery for, 218–219; world conferences, 172. *See also* Demobilization, disarmament, and reintegration

Disarmament Commission, 195, 219

Disarmament Times, 218

Disaster relief, 164; institutional capacity, 181–185; mountain development, 174–175; UNICEF, 14

Discrimination, 74(n30), 95, 109, 172

Disease: HIV/AIDS, 14, 60, 174, 176, 303; immunization programs, 164; nineteenth-century increase in trade and migration, 21; Rwanda's refugees, 253; UNICEF's goals in health care, 67; WHO services, 14–15

Displaced persons, 15, 100–101

Dispute resolution, Charter setting norms for, 48–49

Dominican Republic, 141(table), 316–317

DPKO. *See* Department of Peacekeeping Operations

Drug trafficking, world conferences on, 172

Dues. *See* Assessment

Dumbarton Oaks, 25–30, 36, 40

Durban conference, 65, 75(n41)

Early warning, 177

Eastern Slavonia (Croatia), 141(table), 256

East Timor, 6, 52, 126–128, 131, 141(table), 345, 357(n121)

East-West tensions, 115

E-commerce, 57

Economic affairs: development reform, 374–380; Dumbarton Oaks provisions, 27; economic pressure for human rights compliance, 105; ECOSOC's role and organization, 167; flagship reports, 177; GA committees, 5; North-South divide over UN role in, 168–171; Secretariat reorganization, 61. *See also* Assessment; Bretton Woods Institutions; Budget; Funding

Economic and Social Council (ECOSOC), 81; annual budget, 271; Bruce Committee report, 166; centralizing agency budget under, 376; Charter amendment reform, 362–363; Charter provisions for NGO cooperation, 186; Charter's stipulations for, 373; Commission on Human Rights, 92–95; Committee for Programme and Coordination, 397(n87); director general, 395(n56); Dumbarton Oaks Charter outline, 26; early innovation and current lack of leadership, 178–179; enlargement, 42–43, 169; expansion and reform, 365–370, 389–390; functions and bodies of, 7–8; policy analysis and studies, 175–177; reform packages, 361; UNDP programs, 181; Yalta provisions for, 29–30

Economic Commission for Latin America, 169

Economic Commission for Latin America and the Caribbean (ECLAC), 178

ECOSOC. *See* Economic and Social Council

Ecuador: request for electoral assistance, 141(table)

Eden, Anthony, 28–29

Education: human rights education, 90–91; individual's right to, 112;

reintegration in Sierra Leone, 257–258; UNESCO, 59; Universal Declaration of Human Rights, 83; world conferences, 172

Egypt: Arab-Israeli war, 296; assessment obligation, 290, 294(table); chemical weapons, 206; Communist presence, 243; independent status of, 116; New Agenda Coalition, 202; peacekeeping operations, 228. See also Suez crisis

Eighteen-Nation Committee on Disarmament (ENDC), 196, 219–220

Eisenhower, Dwight D., 354(n44)

Eisenhower administration, 321

Election commission, 132

Elections: Cambodia, 124–126; coordination and support, 128–130; electoral assistance procedure, 119–120; following decolonization, 116–117; future trends, 131–133; GA debate on electoral assistance, 117; Namibia, 328; observers, 130–131; organization and conduct, 124–128; Sierra Leone, 258–259; supervision of, 120–122; technical assistance, 131; verification, 122–124; voter turnout, 127

Elections Canada, 132

Electoral assistance, 115–118

Electoral Assistance Division (EAD), 119–120, 131

Electoral Assistance Secretariat (EAS), 128–129

Electoral Assistance Unit (EAU), 115, 118–119, 128–129

Electoral Commission, 124

Electoral Tribunal, 124

Eloquent unanimity, 292

El Salvador, 356(n104); child labor treaties, 60; Cold War tensions affecting, 243; disarmament, 216; election verification, 123; Groups of Friends, 336, 339–340, 346–348; mediation process, 248–251; peace accords, 115; possibility of a mediated solution, 245–246; request for electoral assistance, 142(table)

Emergency force, 321–325

Emergency relief. See Disaster relief

Employment issues, 173

Energy sources, 171

Enlargement of SC and ECOSOC, 42–43, 365–368, 389–390

Environmental disasters, 53

Environmental issues: marine pollution, 57; Stockholm Conference, 64–65; UNDP's focus on, 180; world conferences, 172–173

Equatorial Guinea: request for electoral assistance, 142–143(table)

Equity as expansion issue, 367

Eritrea, 143(table), 184, 351

Ermacora, Felix, 101–102

Estonia: request for electoral assistance, 143(table)

Ethiopia, 22, 351; assessment obligation, 294(table); Communist presence, 243; independent status of, 116; request for electoral assistance, 143(table)

Ethnicity, 65, 104

ETONU-MEX. See Technical Assistance Team in Mexico

European Union, 120, 275–276, 365

Evatt, Herbert, 38

Exchange tax, 304–305

Excimer lasers, 209, 222(n13)

Expanded Program of Technical Assistance, 170

Expression, freedom of, 109

Extremism, 105

Fair trial provision, 98

Falkland/Malvinas Islands, 6

Family and marriage, right to, 109

FAO. See Food and Agriculture Organization

Farabundo Martí National Liberation Front (FMLN), 248–251, 336–337, 340, 356(n104)

Fawzi, Mahmoud, 323, 354(n56)

Federation of International Institutions, 185

Feshbach, Murray, 244

Field Administration and Logistics Division (FALD), 127

1503 Procedure, 93–94

Fifth Committee, 275, 285

Figueredo, Reinaldo, 250
Fiji: request for electoral assistance, 143(table)
Finance. *See* Bretton Woods Institutions; Budget; Funding
Finkelstein, Lawrence, 34–35, 37–38
First Committee, 219
Flag, UN, 19, 20(fig.), 31–32
Flagship reports, 177–179
Focal Points, 117–118
Food and Agriculture Organization (FAO), 59; annual budget, 272; voluntary contributions, 302(table)
Food production, 58; Codex Alimentarius, 60; FAO functions, 59; world conferences, 171–172
Foreign Relations Authorization Act, 298
Four Plus One, 340, 342
Fourth World Conference on Women, 65
Fowler, Robert R., 342
Framework Convention on Global Climate Change (1992), 64
France, 318; assessment, 287–288, 294(table); Comprehensive Test Ban Treaty, 205; Conference on Disarmament, 220; conventional weapons spending, 210; dues withholding for Congo PKO, 307(n3); ECOSOC expansion and reform, 368; failure to pay PKO assessments, 367; Group of Friends, 342; initial organizational meetings, 23; negotiating U.S. arrears payment, 285–286; nomination of the Secretary-General, 38; nuclear weapons capability, 200; Rwanda PKO, 253, 347–348; SC and ECOSOC expansion, 366; Soviet position on Congo, 278; Suez crisis, 229–230, 322–323; trusteeship of Syria and Lebanon, 34; use of the veto in the Security Council, 315(table); Western Contact Group on Namibia, 330
Fraud, election, 130
Free City (Danzig), 227
Friends groups. *See* Groups of Friends
Fuel-air explosives, 209
Fuentes, Elena, 251

Functionalism, 171
Funding: alternative sources for, 304–306; assessment as obligation, 276–277; assessment scale, 382–388; Bretton Woods Institutions, 13–14; for cooperative human rights activities, 90; electoral assistance, 123; funding development programs, 168; humanitarian relief, 183; lending institutions, 58; nonstate resources, 302–303; PKOs, 239–240, 295–299; political commitment of Member States, 272–273; Rapid Reaction Force, 350–351; voluntary contribution to program activities, 299–302. *See also* Assessment
Funds, 13–17
Furtado, Celso, 178

GA. *See* General Assembly
Gabon: request for electoral assistance, 143(table)
Gambia: request for electoral assistance, 144(table)
Garcia Robles, Alfonso, 30, 33
Gates Foundation, 303
Gay and lesbian groups, 284
Gender. *See* Women
General Agreement on Tariffs and Trade (GATT), 15
General Assembly (GA): annual budget, 271; appointment of the High Commissioner for Human Rights, 89; assessment scale, 288–289; budget, 44(n28), 273–275; Charter amendment reform, 362–363; chemical weapons report, 207–208; competency debate, 29, 33; Comprehensive Test Ban Treaty, 204–205; creation of the AEC, 195; crimes of aggression, 98; Department for Disarmament Affairs, 220–221; and developing countries, 279–281, 378–379; disarmament, 194–199, 219; disaster relief, 182; Dumbarton Oaks provision for, 26; ECOSOC's role and organization for economic and social affairs, 166–167; election of the Secretary-General, 12–13, 38; election supervision,

121–122; electoral assistance, 115, 117; expansion of SC and ECOSOC, 366; first opening session, 42; functions and committees, 5–6, 53–54; human rights, 81; norms and standards for development, 166–167; reform packages, 361; small arms trade study, 212; South Africa and Namibia, 327–328; Suez crisis, 323–324; UN Emergency force, 322; "Uniting for Peace" resolution, 178, 318; Universal Declaration of Human Rights, 62; voting practices, 12, 17(n5); world conferences, 172

Genetically modified organisms, 64

Geneva Conventions on the Law of the Sea (1958), 50, 171, 206, 281, 284

Geneva Protocol (1925), 215

Genocide, 19–20, 97–98, 100, 182–183, 253

Georgia: Group of Friends, 342, 348; request for electoral assistance, 144(table)

Germany, 242; assessment, 287–288, 293, 294(table); conventional weapons spending, 210; distribution of military and economic power, 5; East German independence, 115; Group of Friends, 342; League of Nations membership, 22; League of Nations PKOs, 227; Namibia action, 328–329; UN membership, 280; Western Contact Group on Namibia, 328

Ghana: Congo crisis and, 236; request for electoral assistance, 144(table)

Gilbert, Prentiss, 22

Global Compact (2000), 71–73, 187–188

Global conferences. See World conferences

Global conflict, 4

Global dialogue, 5

Global Environmental Facility (GEF), 163–164

Globalization, 70–73, 177–178

Global policy networks, 68

Global security, 65

Global warming, 64

Goals, institutional, 373–374

Golan Heights, 239

Goldberg, Arthur, 307(n3)

Goldschmidt, Bertrand, 354(n46)

González, Felipe, 339

Gorbachev, Mikhail, 244

Governance: Afghanistan's draft constitution, 103–104; decolonization and, 6; individual rights, 111; NGO role, 186; North-South controversy over development authority, 168–169; Soviet collapse and governance alternatives, 115–116; Trusteeship Council's functions, 8; UNDP's focus on, 180

Great power concert, 312

Great powers, 21; human rights, 40; post-conflict molding of the international order, 312–314

Greece, 21; curbing Communist influence, 242; Cyprus mission, 239; early UN PKOs, 228

Greenstock, Jeremy, 70

Gromyko, Andrei, 26–27, 30

Gromyko Plan, 195

Group of Eight (G8), 168

Group of 18 (G-18), 384–385, 389

Group of 77 (G-77), 275–276, 379

Groups of Friends, 311, 335–339; conditions for forming, 347–348; criticism from within the UN, 348–349; El Salvador group, 336–339; Friends of Rapid Reaction, 349–351; process of, 345–347; purpose and function, 339–342

Guatemala: disarmament, 215; Group of Friends, 342, 348; request for electoral assistance, 144(table); terminating a PKO, 341

Guinea: request for electoral assistance, 144–145(table)

Guinea-Bissau: request for electoral assistance, 145(table)

Gulf War, 206, 334–335

Gusmão, Jose Alexandre Xanana, 128

Guyana: request for electoral assistance, 145–146(table)

Habibie, B. J., 126

Habitat, 166, 178, 300(table)

Hague Conferences (1899, 1907), 21, 63

Haiti, 179, 183; Group of Friends, 342, 347–348, 357(n121); request for electoral assistance, 146(table)

Hammarskjöld, Dag, 7, 55, 221; advisory committees, 320; Congo crisis, 232–237; insistence on impartiality, 252–253; Soviet call for dismissal, 325; Suez crisis, 229–232, 277–278, 322–323

Harriman, Averell, 37

Health issues, 171; Codex Alimentarius, 60; medical treatment, 165(fig.); nineteenth-century spread of disease, 21; UNAIDS, 60; UNICEF services and goals, 14, 67; WHO services, 14–15, 59

Helms, Jesse, 280–281, 285, 286(fig.)

Hezbollah, 241

Higgins, Rosalyn, 10

High seas, 203

Hingha Norman, Sam, 258

Hiroshima bombing, 39–40, 193

Hiss, Alger: on Charter signing, 40, 42; San Francisco Conference, 22, 25–30; on use of force provision, 39–40

HIV/AIDS, 14, 60, 174, 176, 303

Hodgson, William, 82

Holbrooke, Richard, 285, 286(fig.)

Holocaust, 61

Honduras: request for electoral assistance, 146(table)

Hostage situations, 257

Hull, Cordell, 23–28

Human Development Report (UNDP), 14, 177, 304

Human dignity, 79–80, 83, 107, 114(n36)

Humanitarian affairs, 215–216

Humanitarian assistance: Bosnia, 255; GA committees, 5; institutional capacity, 181–185; the "other" United Nations, 166; Secretariat reorganization, 61; World Bank as conflicting organization, 13–14. *See also* Economic and Social Council

Human resource development, 180

Human rights: application, 105; challenges of promotion, 104–105; commission, 40; Commission on Human Rights, 92–95; democratic change and electoral assistance, 116; development and, 164; El Salvador mediation, 249–251; global norm setting, 61–63; human dignity, 79–80, 107; ICJ, 96–100; International Labour Organization treaties, 59–60; international law, 50; norm termination, 106; Office of the High Commissioner on Refugees, 89–91; peacekeeping and, 100–101; San Francisco provision, 40, 49; Security Council function, 85–86; specialized agencies, 86; treatment of prisoners, 63–64; treaty bodies, 95–96; Universal Declaration of Human Rights, 81–85, 107–112; war-torn countries, 101–104; world conferences, 86–89, 171

Human Rights Day, 62

Human rights violations, 93–94, 99–100; Afghanistan, 102–103, 114(n28); norm termination, 106; Sierra Leone, 258

Human security, 3–4

Human settlements, 172

Humphrey, John, 82

Hungary: request for electoral assistance, 146(table)

Huntington, Samuel P., 105

Hutu tribe, 253

Hydroacoustic stations, 204, 222(n4)

ILO Convention on the Worst Forms of Child Labour (1999), 59

ILO World Employment Conference, 173

IMF. *See* International Monetary Fund

Immunization programs, 164

Incendiary weapons, 215

Income gap, 14; globalization and, 70–71; loss of innovation to address, 178; world conference on, 173

Independence: Congo, 232–233; after decolonization, 116–117; East Timor, 127–128; Namibia, 115, 121–122; obsolescence of

Trusteeship Council, 43; post-war
    progress, 193; Soviet republics,   •
    115; trusteeship issues and Charter
    wording, 35–36
Independent Electoral Commission, 127
Independent Human Rights
    Commission, 103
India, 28; assessment obligation,
    288–290, 294(table);
    Comprehensive Test Ban Treaty,
    205; electoral assistance debate,
    117; globalization, 70;
    Nonproliferation Treaty, 201;
    nuclear weapons capability, 201;
    UN Emergency Force troops, 322;
    UN peacekeeping, 228
Indigenous people, Vienna Declaration
    provisions for, 87–88
Indiscriminate weapons, 215–216
Individual defense, 313
Individual rights, 83
Indonesia, 52; assessment obligation,
    291; electoral assistance, 126–128,
    130, 147(table); globalization, 70
Indonesian People's Assembly (MPR),
    126
Industrial property, 58
Infant health, 67
Infrasound stations, 204
Infrastructure building and restoration,
    180
Inhumane weapons, 215–216
Institution building, 180
Integrated Missions Task Force (ITMF),
    100
Intellectual property rights, 58
Inter-Agency Consultative Board
    (IACB), 376
Inter-American Conference on the
    Problems of Peace and War. See
    Chapultepec conference
Inter-American Peace Force, 317
Intergovernmental agreements, 57
Intergovernmental Panel on Climate
    Change, 64
Intergovernmental processes, 177–178
International Atomic Energy Agency
    (IAEA), 56, 60–61; Argentina-
    Brazil disarmament agreement,
    200; Basic Facts, 74(n30); NPT

implementation, 201; voluntary
    contributions, 302(table)
International Bank for Reconstruction
    and Development (IBRD). See
    World Bank
International Bill of Human Rights, 81
International Campaign to Ban
    Landmines, 218
International Civil Aviation Organization
    (ICAO), 57, 236, 302(table)
International Convention on the
    Elimination of All Forms of Racial
    Discrimination, 95–96
International Court of Justice (ICJ):
    Dumbarton Oaks provision for, 26;
    functions of, 9–10; human rights,
    96–100; setting global norms, 49;
    South African control of Namibia,
    328; Soviet attempt to block Congo
    PKO, 278; state sovereignty over
    the individual, 86; voting practice,
    13
International Covenant on Civil and
    Political Rights, 81, 95–96
International Covenant on Economic,
    Social, and Cultural Rights, 81, 95
International Criminal Court (ICC), 6,
    50, 52–53, 68, 97–98
International Criminal Tribunal for
    Rwanda (ICTR), 52, 100
International Criminal Tribunal for the
    Former Yugoslavia (ICTY), 52, 99
International Decade of the World's
    Indigenous Peoples, 88
International Development Agency
    (IDA), 13, 163, 167, 170
International Finance Corporation (IFC),
    163, 167, 170
International Foundation for Election
    Systems (IFES), 129, 132
International Fund for Agricultural
    Development (IFAD), 58, 163
International IDEA, 132
International Labour Organization
    (ILO), 59–60; Fundamental
    Principles for Rights at Work, 71;
    NGO participation, 186; policy
    analysis, 177; voluntary
    contributions, 302(table)
International law: development and
    codification of, 49–50; UDHR as,

84–85; U.S. assessment
withholding, 282–283
International Law Commission (ILC), 6,
50
International Maritime Organization
(IMO), 57, 302(table)
International Monetary Fund (IMF), 13,
287–288. *See also* Bretton Woods
Institutions
International Physicians for the
Prevention of Nuclear War, 218
International Programme on the
Elimination of Child Labour
(IPEC), 59
International Refugee Organization
(IRO), 181
International regimes, 48
International Research and Training
Institute for the Advancement of
Women (INSTRAW), 167
International Telecommunications Union
(ITU), 57, 302(table)
International Telegraphic Union, 21
International Trade Center
(UNCTAD/WTO), 300(table)
International Trade Statistics Yearbook,
176
Internet regulation, 58, 68
Intervention, military. *See* Military force
Intrastate conflict. *See* Civil conflicts
Iran, 198, 208
Iran-Iraq War, 206
Iraq, 52–53, 208, 246, 283, 335
Ireland: New Agenda Coalition, 202
Israel, 280–281; Arab-Israeli war, 296;
Comprehensive Test Ban Treaty,
205; Durban conference walkout,
75(n41); Nonproliferation Treaty,
201; nuclear weapons capability,
200; peacekeeping operations, 228;
PLO attacks from Lebanon, 241;
Yom Kippur War, 319. *See also*
Suez crisis
Italy: assessment, 287, 291, 294(table);
League of Nations membership, 22;
voluntary contributions, 301

Jackson, Robert, 374–377
Jamaica: request for electoral assistance,
147(table)
Janus, 312, 352(n2)

Japan: assessment obligation, 288, 291,
294(table); chemical weapons, 206;
distribution of military and
economic power, 5; Dumbarton
Oaks and Yalta, 26; League of
Nations membership, 22;
trusteeship and, 35; UN voluntary
contributions, 301; zero-growth
budgets, 276
Jayawardina, Lal, 178
Jebb, Gladwyn, 29–30
Johannesburg conference, 172–174, 187
Joint Inspection Unit (JIU), 380, 384
Joint International Observer Group
(JIOG), 129
Jolly, Richard, 67
Jordan, 52; eviction of the PLO, 240;
peacekeeping operations, 228;
request for electoral assistance,
147(table)
Judicial issues. *See* International Court
of Justice
Just and lasting peace, 40

Kaldor, Nicolas, 178
Kalecki, Michal, 178
Kampuchea, 126
Kasavubu, Joseph, 233, 236
Kashmir, 273, 277
Kassebaum, Nancy, 383, 397(n82)
Kassebaum-Solomon Amendment
(1985), 383, 386
Kennan, George, 242
Kenya: electoral assistance, 130,
147(table)
Keyes, Alan, 383, 387
Keynes, John Maynard, 304
Khadduri, Majid, 37
Khrushchev, Nikita, 238
Kirk, Grayson, 25
Kirkpatrick, Jeanne, 382–388
Kissinger, Henry, 328
Koo, V. K. Wellington, 26
Korea, 55, 119, 229, 317–318, 320
Kosovo, 183, 345; PKO's human rights
mandate, 100; request for electoral
assistance, 147(table)
Kurdish refugees, 182
Kuwait, 53, 283, 335; PKO assessment,
298–299
Kuznetsov, Vasily V., 325

Kyoto Protocol (1997), 64–66
Kyrgyzstan: request for electoral
    assistance, 147(table)

Labor issues, 59–60, 74(n30), 111
Landmines, 211–213, 214(fig.), 215,
    218, 223(n23)
Landmine treaty, 65–66
Lannegrace, Nicole, 347
Lao People's Democratic Republic, 119
Lapointe, Paul, 329
Latin American member states:
    Argentina's membership, 32–33;
    Bush's foreign policy, 245;
    Chapultepec conference, 30–31, 36,
    40; Cold War tensions affecting,
    242; Communist-influenced
    governments, 243; human rights,
    40; League of Nations PKOs, 227;
    North-South controversy over
    development authority, 168–169;
    SC seat distribution, 365; veto
    provision, 38. See also individual
    countries
Latvia: request for electoral assistance,
    148(table)
Law of the Sea, 50, 171, 206, 281, 284
Leadership, 178–179, 188–189
League Assembly, 22
League Council, 22, 226
League Covenant, 362
League of Nations: assessment
    obligation and, 277; creation of,
    21–23, 63; four powers' attitude
    toward, 26; just and unjust wars,
    312–313; NGO involvement, 185;
    origins of UN peacekeeping,
    226–228; Secretary-General's role,
    54; South African control of
    Namibia, 328; structures and
    activities, 164, 166; termination of,
    44(n29); trusteeship issues, 34
Lebanon, 34, 239–242
Legal issues: development and
    codification of international law,
    49–50; GA committees, 5. See also
    International Court of Justice;
    International Criminal Court
Lending institutions. See International
    Fund for Agricultural Development;

International Monetary Fund;
    World Bank
Lesotho: electoral assistance, 129,
    148(table)
Lewis, Arthur, 178
Lewis, W. B., 354(n46)
Liberia, 348; independent status of, 116;
    request for electoral assistance,
    148(table); support of Sierra
    Leone's insurgency, 257
Lie, Trygve, 7, 55, 320–321
Light weapons, 211–213
Linkage policy, 330
Literacy programs, 164
Lithuania, 28
Living standards, 111
Lodge, Henry Cabot, 277, 306(n1)
Logo, UN, 19, 20(fig.), 31–32
Lomé Accords, 258
Loya Jirgah (Afghanistan), 103–104
Lumumba, Patrice, 233, 236, 238, 325
Lundquist, Oliver, 31–32

Macedonia: request for electoral
    assistance, 161(table)
Madagascar: request for electoral
    assistance, 149(table)
Majority voting, 11
Major powers, determining identity of,
    43
Major power veto. See Veto
Malawi: electoral assistance, 128–129,
    149(table)
Mali: electoral assistance, 129,
    149–150(table)
Malik, Charles, 81
Malinowski, W. R., 178
Malta Conference, 29
Manchuria, 22
Manley, John, 75(n41)
Maritime regulations, 57
Martin, Ian, 127
Mauritania: request for electoral
    assistance, 150(table)
Mauritius: request for electoral
    assistance, 150(table)
McHenry, Donald, 329
McLaughlin, Donald, 31–32
Media, news, 247
Mediation: Arbitration and Mediation
    Center, 58; El Salvador, 248–251;

Groups of Friends as mediators, 340; Mozambique, 246

Membership issues: Argentina, the Ukraine, Byelorussia, 32–33; Dumbarton Oaks and Yalta debates, 26–29; enlargement, 42–43; PKO participation, 51–52

Member States: budgetmaking process, 273–276; defining reform, 363–364; independent statehood, 116; privileges of permanent and non-permanent members, 314–315; requests for electoral assistance, 133–162(tables); SC expansion and reform, 370–371; withdrawal from the UN, 362. *See also* Assessment

Mermée, Jean Bernard, 342

Mexico: assessment obligation, 290–291, 294(table); electoral assistance, 130, 150(table); Group of Friends, 336–340, 342; humanitarian intervention, 183; New Agenda Coalition, 202; PKO assessment, 296

Micro-disarmament proposal, 211

Middle East, 228

Military force, 4; Hammarskjöld's bully pulpit approach to intervention, 55; in a multilateral framework, 316–317; PKO as alternative to, 319; pressure for human rights compliance, 105; rapid reaction capability, 349–351; SC control of, 4–5; SC mandate, 51; against terrorist activity, 69; UN authorization of, 317–318; use of force provision, 39–40. *See also* Peacekeeping operations

Military spending: conventional weapons, 209–210; disarmament, 197; Soviet collapse attributed to, 244; United States, 226

Military Staff Committee, 194, 349–350

Millennium Declaration (2000), 3, 43, 362

Millennium Summit, 174

Ministerial Conference, 15–16

Mitterrand, François, 304

Mojaddedi, Sibghatullah, 104

Moldova, Republic of: request for electoral assistance, 154–155(table)

Molotov, Vyacheslav, 28–29, 33, 37

Montaño, Jorge, 338(fig.), 340

Monterrey conference, 174

Montreal Protocol (1987), 64

Mosak, Jacob, 178

Moscow Declaration (1943), 23

Mountain communities, 174–175

Mozambique: disarmament, 216; election verification, 123; electoral assistance, 117, 151(table); peace accords, 115; possibility of a mediated solution, 246; socialist government, 243

Mselle, Conrad, 274

Mujahidin (Afghan resistance movement), 101

Multilateral action, 316–317

Multilateral aid, 184

Multilateral treaties, 11, 21; Chemical Weapons Convention, 206–207; creation of the UN, 23–25; development and codification of international law, 49–50; nuclear weapons, 196–197

Murray, James, 329

Mutual assured destruction (MAD), 197

Myrdal, Gunnar, 178

Nagasaki bombing, 193

Namibia, 10; assessment withholding in support of, 281; elections, 117, 119, 121, 151(table); ICJ advisory opinion on South Africa occupation, 96; possibility of a mediated solution, 246; Western Contact Group on Namibia, 327–331

Napalm, 215

Napoleonic Wars, 21

Nasser, Gamal Abdul, 229, 232, 322–323

Nationality, 109

National missile defense, 220

NATO, 194, 298

Natural disasters, 172, 182. *See also* Disaster relief

Nazi Germany, 40

Needs assessment mission (NAM), 119–120

Negotiated settlements, 332, 336–339; Arbitration and Mediation Center, 58; El Salvador, 248–251; Groups

of Friends as mediators, 340;
Mozambique, 246
Negroponte, John, 388
Nepal: child labor treaties, 60; electoral
assistance, 129, 151(table)
Netherlands: assessment obligation, 289,
294(table); Group of Friends, 342;
inadequacy of Bosnia response,
255; Rapid Reaction, 349;
voluntary contributions, 300
Netherlands Antilles: request for
electoral assistance, 151(table)
Networks, 57
Networks of concern, 173
New Agenda Coalition, 202
New Zealand: New Agenda Coalition,
202; nuclear weapons free zones,
203
NGOs. See Nongovernmental
organizations
Nicaragua: election verification, 123;
electoral assistance, 117,
151–152(table); peace accords, 115
Niger: electoral assistance, 129,
152–153(table)
Nigeria, 129, 153(table), 348
Nixon administration, 293
Nobel Peace Prize, 14, 56, 218,
223(n23), 232
No-first-use policy, 201
Nongovernmental organizations
(NGOs): Charter provision for
NGO collaboration, 185–188;
Comprehensive Test Ban Treaty,
204–205; consultative status with
ECOSOC, 167; disabled persons
capacities, 54; disarmament issues,
217–218; disaster relief for
refugees, 181–182; ECOSOC
restructuring of, 369; functions of,
7; GA special session on
disarmament, 198–199; global
norm setting, 67–68; human rights,
80, 88, 90, 92; Ottawa Convention,
213, 223(n23); reform and, 361;
response to Global Compact,
187–188; Sierra Leone's
reintegration, 257–258; U.S.
assessment withholding because of,
283–284; world conferences,
173–174

Non-nuclear weapons states, 201–202
Nonproliferation Treaty (NPT), 61, 196,
201–203, 217
Norms, global: Boutros-Ghali's
observation on, 68; Charter
provision, 48 49; crime prevention
and criminal justice, 63–64;
disarmament, 221–222; global and
local norms, 47–48; globalization,
70–72; human rights, 61–63, 105;
international law, 49–50; NGOs'
role in setting, 67–68; SC role in
furthering, 51–53; Secretary-
General's role in forming, 54–56;
specialized agencies and, 56–61;
Stockholm Conference on
environmental issues, 64–65;
terrorism, 69–70; UNICEF's
implementation, 66–67; world
conference role in building, 65–66
Norm termination, 106
North Korea: biological weapons, 208
North-South divide: development
programs' roles and goals,
168–171; economic and political
reform to increase equity, 378–379;
global conference policy setting,
response, and funding, 172–173;
response to Global Compact,
187–188
Norway, 14; Group of Friends, 342; UN
Emergency Force troops, 322
Nuclear energy, peaceful uses for, 321
Nuclear free zones, 203–204
Nuclear regulation, 60–61
Nuclear terrorism, 69
Nuclear weapons, 39–40; creation of
regional alliances, 316; creation of
the AEC, 195; GA special sessions
on disarmament, 197–199;
Nonproliferation Treaty, 201–202;
nuclear free zones, 203–204;
nuclear test bans, 204–205;
Pakistan's tests of, 201; post–Cold
War capability, 199–201; security
assurances, 202–203; testing,
201–202, 204–205, 218; World War
II programs, 193–194
Nutrition, 14, 58. See also Food
production

Observers, election, 128–132

October 24 (UN Day), 42
Office of Legal Affairs (OLA), 6
Office of the Coordinator of
    Humanitarian Affairs (OCHA),
    183, 185
Office of the High Commissioner for
    Human Rights (OHCHR), 89–91,
    95; ICC and, 98; PKO's human
    rights mandate, 100; promotion of
    human rights standards, 104–105
Oil industry, 339
Oil tax, 305
Open-Ended Working Group on the
    Question of Equitable
    Representation and Increase in the
    Membership of the Security
    Council and Other Matters Related
    to the Security Council, 370
Operation Litani, 241
Operation Turquoise, 253
Organization and conducting of
    elections, 120–121, 124–128
Organization for African Unity (OAU),
    365–368
Organization for Economic Cooperation
    and Development (OECD), 168
Organization for Security and
    Cooperation in Europe (OSCE),
    287
Organization for the Prohibition of
    Chemical Weapons (OPCW), 207
Organization of American States (OAS),
    30, 251, 287, 317
Organized crime, 64
Ortega, Daniel, 243
Ortega, Humberto, 243
Ostpolitik, 293
"Other" United Nations, 166, 189(11)
Ottawa Convention (1997), 65–66, 213,
    223(n23)
Outer Space Treaty (1967), 54, 196

Pacific settlement, 354(n34)
Pacific Settlement of Disputes, 4
Padillo Nervo, Luis, 30
Pakistan: Comprehensive Test Ban
    Treaty, 205; electoral assistance,
    153(table); Group of Friends, 342;
    Nonproliferation Treaty, 201;
    nuclear weapons tests, 201;
    Somalis losses, 252; UN

Emergency Force troops, 322; UN
    peacekeeping, 228
Palau, 8
Palermo Convention, 64
Palestine, 273; electoral assistance,
    154(table); funding PKO for, 277
Palestine Liberation Organization
    (PLO), 240–241, 281
Palme, Olaf, 293, 384–385
Panama: electoral assistance, 154(table)
Pan-American Union, 30
Paraguay: electoral assistance,
    154(table)
Paris Agreements, 124–125
Parliamentarians for Global Action
    (PGA), 67
Parra Perez, C., 30
Partial Test-Ban Treaty (1963), 196, 204
Pasvolsky, Leo, 25, 44(n10), 45(n39)
Pavlov, Alexei, 82
Peace accords, 115
Peace and security, 312–313, 381;
    Charter mandate for, 193–194;
    development as path to, 163;
    Secretariat reorganization, 61. See
    also Security Council
Peaceful Nuclear Explosions Treaty
    (1976), 204
Peacekeeping operations (PKOs): as ad
    hoc alliance, 319; annual budget,
    272; assessments for, 295–299;
    assessment withholding for Congo,
    307(n3); as collective security
    measure, 316; Congo, 232–239,
    277–279, 325–327; creation of,
    229–232; Cyprus and Lebanon,
    239–242, 279; disarmament,
    demobilization, and reintegration,
    216–217; diverting PKO funds to
    humanitarian aid, 184–185; early
    UN years, 227–228; election
    verification, 123–124; electoral
    assistance in Cambodia, 124–126;
    electoral assistance in East Timor,
    126–128; expenditures for, 343–345;
    failures, 251–255; financing, 382;
    Hammarskjöld's position on, 55;
    human rights and, 100–101; League
    of Nations period, 226–228;
    Member States' failure to pay for,
    367; need for Member States
    participation and contribution,

253–254; original budget for, 277; origins of, 225–226; past and present operations, 260–267; post–Cold War, 246–248, 332–335; provisions for participation in, 51–52; recent advances, 255–259; successes, 248–251; Suez crisis, 229–232, 321–325; terminating an operation, 341; "the other UN," 166, 189(n1); underfunding through U.S. assessment withholding, 283–284; U.S. dispute over payment for, 284–285, 307(n6); U.S. funding, 387

Peace-loving nations, 26–27
Peace Observation Commission, 318
Pearson, Lester Bowles, 230–232, 324
Pelindaba Treaty, 203
Peng Chun Chang, 81
Pérez, Carlos Andrés, 340
Pérez de Cuéllar, Javier, 7, 331, 338(fig.), 384; El Salvador mediation, 248; Groups of Friends, 336–337
Perez Guerrero, Manuel, 30–31
Permanent Court of International Justice, 21
Permanent Five (P-5): assessment contribution, 396(n74); Charter amendment reform, 362–363; Committee for Programme and Coordination seats, 386–387; Rapid Reaction, 349; Razali Plan, 372; SC and ECOSOC expansion, 366; SC authority over, 51; SC voting procedures, 11–12; uneven power structure and special privileges of, 312–315; veto provision debates, 36–38, 45(n47). *See also* China; France; Soviet Union; United Kingdom; United States
Personnel reform, 363–364
Peru: request for electoral assistance, 154(table)
Petroleum trade as alternative revenue source, 305
P-5. *See* Permanent Five
Philippine Islands: request for electoral assistance, 154(table); trusteeship and independence, 35–36
Point Four proposals, 170

Poison gas, 215
Poland, 28, 33, 40, 45(n53), 115, 227–228
Policemen, great powers as, 312–313
Policy analysis and studies, 175–177
Policy Coordination Committee, 376
Policy dialogues, 187
Polio, 67
Political issues: assessment scale, 288, 290; Charter reform, 364; developing countries' call for global economic reform, 378–379; GA committees, 5–6; politics of humanitarian aid, 184–185; "Uniting for Peace" resolution, 229, 278–279, 318, 322, 325; U.S. nonpayment of assessment, 279–284; vetoing Charter amendment reform, 367
Ponce, Réne Emilio, 251
Population, world conference on, 171, 173
Postal systems, 57–58
Post-conflict states: promotion of human rights standards, 104–105
Poverty: eradication proclamations, 175–176; globalization, 70–71; UNDP's focus on, 180; world conference on, 173
Power of the purse, 273
Practical disarmament measures, 213, 215
Prebisch, Raul, 178
Prem Chand, Dewan, 237
Privacy, 83
Private sector involvement in UN processes, 187–188
Programs, 13–17
Promotion of human rights standards, 104–105
Property rights, 109
Protocol for the Prohibition of the Use in War of Asphyxiating, Poisonous, or Other Gases, and of Bacteriological Methods of Warfare, 205–206
Public interest, 217–218
Pufendorf, Samuel, 314
Purchasing power parity (PPP), 290

Rabi, I. I., 354(n46)
Racism, 65, 172

Radiation protection, 60–61
Radionuclide, 204, 222(n4)
Ramirez-Ocampo, Augusto, 347
Rape, 99
Rapid deployment force, 298
Rapid Reaction, 349–351
Rarotonga, Treaty of (1986), 203
Razali, Ismail, 372
Razali plan, 372, 389, 391
Reagan, Ronald, 245, 283
Reagan administration, 281, 307(n4), 330, 387
Red Cross organization, 181–182, 185, 213
Referendum Commission, 128–129
Reform: assessment scale and fiscal outlay, 382–388; budget cuts, 384–385; characteristics of UN reform, 388–390; core issues of the reform agenda, 373; decisionmaking process of, 364–373; defining, 359–364; development programs, 375–380; ECOSOC, 364–370; Security Council, 369–373
Refugees, 15, 65; humanitarian relief funding, 185; intrastate conflict influencing migration, 331; Lebanese, 240; from Somalia, 253; World War II disaster relief, 181. See also UN High Commissioner for Refugees
Regimes, international, 48
Regional organizations: collective security and multilateral action, 316–317; competency of, 33; development organizations, 167; election administration, 132; electoral assistance procedures, 120–121; Latin American countries, 30–31; nuclear weapons free zones, 203; Organization for Security and Cooperation in Europe, 287
Regional security council, 29–30
Regulations and standards, 58–59
Reintegration. See Demobilization, disarmament, and reintegration
Religion, 83, 102, 104, 109
Renamo. See Resistencia Nacional Mocambicana

Renewing the United Nations System (Childers and Urquhart), 309(n13)
Research, 58–59
Resistencia Nacional Mocambicana (Renamo), 123
Resolution 161, 325
Resolution 260, 97
Resolution 309, 328
Resolution 385, 328, 331
Resolution 435, 121, 330
Resolution 688, 182
Resolution 827, 99
Resolution 1296, 186
Resolution 1368, 69
Resolution 1373, 69
Resolution 41/213, 386–387
Resolution 52/12, 220
Resolution 35/142 B, 210
Resolution 1514 (XV), 6
Resolution A/46/130, 119
Resolution A/46/137, 117
Resolution A/48/141, 89
Resolutions, General Assembly, 53–54, 117–119
Resolutions, Security Council, 334(fig.)
Resource access: Congo, 234; environmental conference, 64–65; intrastate conflict influencing, 331; poverty reduction, 176
Respect for the Principles of National Sovereignty and Noninterference in the Internal Affairs of States in Their Electoral Processes (Resolution A/46/130), 119
Revenue. See Assessment
Review and Extension Conference of the Parties to the Treaty on the Nonproliferation of Nuclear Weapons, 217
Revolutionary United Front (RUF), 257–259
Rhodesia, 328
Richardson, Tom, 329
Rio Earth Summit, 67, 173, 186–187
Rio Principles, 71–72
Riza, Iqbal, 347
Robinson, Mary, 79, 91–92
Rockefeller, Nelson, 32
Romania, 115, 155(table)
Rome Statute (1998), 97–99
Romulo, Carlos, 35, 43
Roosèvelt, Eleanor, 40, 81

Roosevelt, Franklin, 23–28, 31, 35, 312–313
Roschin, Alexei, 23, 27, 33, 39
Rubin, Robert, 305
Russian Federation: arms reduction, 201; assessment, 287, 291, 294(table), 308(n11); chemical weapons destruction, 207; Comprehensive Test Ban Treaty, 205; Conference on Disarmament, 220; Group of Friends, 342; request for electoral assistance, 155(table); use of the veto in the Security Council, 315(table); WTO status, 15
Rwanda, 52, 100, 357(n115); genocide, 347–348; humanitarian assistance, 182–183; need for rapid reaction, 349; request for electoral assistance, 155(table); as UN failure, 251, 253–254

Safe areas, 255
Safeguards, nuclear, 60 61
Salvadoran Group of Friends, 336–337
Sanctions, 4, 61–62; circumventing, 52; Italy's invasion of Ethiopia, 22–23; South Africa's occupation of Namibia, 329
San Francisco conference, 31–32; Charter provision for NGO collaboration, 185–188; Charter signing, 40–43; competency of the General Assembly, 33; human rights, 40; membership debates, 32–33; Secretary-General's role, 38–39; self-defense, 36; themes and debates, 32–40; trusteeship, 34–36; use of force provision, 39–40; veto provision debates, 36–38
San José Program, 339
Sankoh, Foday, 258
Santa Cruz, Hernan, 81–82
São Tomé and Principe: request for electoral assistance, 156(table)
Saudi Arabia, 31, 291, 294(table), 342
SC. See Security Council
Schachter, Oscar, 84–85
Scheme of limits, 291–292
Schultz, George, 293

Seabed Arms Control Treaty (1971), 54, 197, 203, 306
Seattle meeting, 15–16
Second Disarmament Decade, 198
Second UN Conference on Human Settlements, 65
Secretariat, 360(fig.); budget, 271, 274; Dumbarton Oaks provision for, 26; evolution of the bureaucracy, 42; functions and departments of, 6–7; Groups of Friends, 346–347; human rights issues, 61. See also Secretary-General
Secretary-General: appointment of the High Commissioner for Human Rights, 89; budget cuts, 387; chemical weapons report, 207–208; Congo Advisory Committee, 325–327; economic measures, 384–385; election of, 12–13; electoral assistance, 119; functions and characteristics of advisory committees, 324–325; functions and departments of, 3, 6; Global Compact, 187–188; Groups of Friends, 335–339; humanitarian relief, 185; leadership role, 189; political nature of actions, 320–321; post–Cold War increase in PKO demand, 332–335; reform, 361, 392–393; San Francisco Conference provision for role of, 38–39; small arms trade study, 212; Suez Crisis, 231, 323–324; UN Register of Conventional Arms, 210–211. See also Groups of Friends; Secretariat; individual Secretaries General
Security. See Military force
Security assurances, 202–203
Security Council (SC): annual budget, 271; anti-terrorism measures, 69; arms regulations attempts during the Cold War, 194–197; budget cuts, 385; Charter amendment reform, 362–363; competency of the Secretary-General, 39; Congo Advisory Committee, 325–327; Congo crisis, 234–235; Dumbarton Oaks provision for, 26; election of the Secretary-General, 12–13, 38; election supervision, 121–122;

evolution of, 42; expansion and reform, 365–373; formal meetings and informal consultations, 333(fig.); functions of, 3–5; furthering global norms, 51–53; GA competency, 33; human rights, 85–86; Korean War, 317–318; lack of power over finances and BWI, 377; NGO participation in SC meetings, 186; open system, closed shop dichotomy, 312–315; permanent members, 4; political nature of actions and resolutions, 320; post–Cold War increase in PKOs, 332–335; reform packages, 361; resolutions and presidential statements, 334(fig.); security assurances, 202–203; South Africa's presence in Namibia, 121–122; Suez crisis, 229; veto provision, 74(n15); voting procedures, 11–12. See also Peacekeeping operations; Veto

Seismic stations, 204

Self-defense, 36, 319, 353(n5)

Self-determination, 36

Senegal: request for electoral assistance, 156(table)

September 11, 2001, terrorist attacks, 69, 102

Seychelles: request for electoral assistance, 156(table)

Shipping, 57

SHIRBRIG. See Standby High Readiness Brigade

Siad Barre, Mohamed, 243, 246

Sierra Leone, 14; disarmament, 216–217; humanitarian aid, 184; PKO's human rights mandate, 100; request for electoral assistance, 157(table); as UN PKO success, 256–259; WTO membership, 15

Singapore, 309(n17)

Singer, Hans, 178

Singh, Manmihan, 178

Six Day War, 232

Six Plus Two group, 342–343

Skobeltzin, D. V., 354(n46)

Slavery, 83, 108

Small arms, 211–213

Social affairs: development reform, 374–380; Dumbarton Oaks provisions, 27; ECOSOC's role and organization, 167; GA committees, 5; North-South divide over UN role in, 168–171; Secretariat reorganization, 61. See also Economic and Social Council

Socialism, demise of, 115–116

Social security, 111

Social Summit (1995), 67, 304

Societal norms. See Norms, global

Solomon, Gerald, 383

Solomon Islands: request for electoral assistance, 157(table)

Somalia, 247–248; East-West tensions, 243; Group of Friends, 347; humanitarian assistance, 182; PKO funding, 297; power vacuum, 246–248; terminating a PKO, 341; as UN failure, 251–253

Somoza Debayle, Anastasio, 243

South Africa: assessment withholding in support of Namibia, 281; election supervision, 121–122; electoral assistance, 129, 157(table); ICJ advisory opinion on Namibia, 96; independent status of, 116; New Agenda Coalition, 202; nuclear weapons program, 200; Western Contact Group on Namibia, 327–331

South Pacific Nuclear Free Zone Treaty (1986), 203

South West Africa People's Organization (SWAPO), 122, 281, 329–330

Sovereignty, 3; assessment obligation and, 277; electoral assistance and, 117–119; humanitarian intervention, 183–184; India's UN membership, 28; international human rights and, 85–86; rapid reaction force, 351; uneven power structure and special privileges within a group, 314

Soviet Union: Afghanistan occupation, 101–102; assessment obligation, 294(table), 308(n7); circumventing SC voting procedures, 12; Congo crisis, 237–238, 325–327; conventional weapons spending,

210; Czech intervention as multilateral action, 317; decline and collapse of, 244; disintegration of, 115; dissatisfaction with Congo policy, 278; dues withholding for Congo PKO, 307(n3); Dumbarton Oaks and Yalta, 26–30; ECOSOC expansion and reform, 368; El Salvador conflict, 337–338; employee kickbacks, 281; failure to pay PKO assessments, 367; Group of Friends, 345; Korean War, 317–318, 320; London Poles, 45(n53); membership of Argentina, the Ukraine, and Byelorussia, 33; nomination of the Secretary-General, 38; nuclear weapons stance, 195; post–Cold War nuclear capability, 200; response to Suez crisis, 229; SC and ECOSOC expansion, 365–368; security assurances, 202–203; Suez crisis, 322; UN reform, 387; UNSCOB peacekeeping, 228; use of force provision, 39–40; veto provision debate, 37; zero-growth budgets, 282. *See also* U.S.-Soviet relations

Spain, 336–337, 340, 346–347
Special Court for Sierra Leone, 258
Special Fund, 163, 170, 179
Specialized agencies, 13–17, 56–61, 272, 302(table)
Special Rapporteurs, 87–88, 94, 101–102
Special Representatives: Cambodia, 125; election supervision, 121–123; Groups of Friends, 346; for Namibia, 329–330
Special sessions, 220–221, 318, 354(n32)
Sri Lanka: request for electoral assistance, 157(table)
Stalin, Josef, 27–30, 33, 37
Standard Rules on the Equalization of Opportunities for Persons with Disabilities (1993), 54
Standards. *See* Norms, global
Standards and regulations, 57–58
Standby High Readiness Brigade (SHIRBRIG), 351, 357(n120)
Stassen, Harold, 24–25, 35–37

State, sovereign: as basis for UN organization, 20–21; human rights responsibilities, 62; individual rights as granted by, 83–84
Statistical Yearbook, 175–176
Stettinius, Edward, 25–30, 40, 41(fig.), 312
Stettinius blue, 32
Stockholm Conference, 64–65, 67
St. Petersburg Declaration (1868), 215
Subcommission on the Promotion and Protection of Human Rights, 92
Subsidies, 172–173
Sudan: biological weapons, 208; request for electoral assistance, 157(table)
Suez crisis, 12, 228–232, 318, 321–323
Supervision, electoral, 120–122
Suriname Group of Friends, 342
Sustainable development, 58–59, 66, 168–169, 172–173
Swaziland: request for electoral assistance, 158(table)
Sweden: New Agenda Coalition, 202
Syria, 34, 208, 240

Taiwan: Communist control of China, 242–243; Soviet protest over representation, 317; WTO membership, 15
Tajikistan, 158(table), 342–343, 348
Taliban, 102
Tanzania: child labor treaties, 60; elections, 119, 129, 159–160(table)
Taylor, Charles, 257–258
Technical assistance programs, 131–133, 179
Technical Assistance Team in Mexico (ETONU-MEX), 130
Technical multilateralism, 316
Tejera-Paris, Enrique, 342
Telecommunications, 57
Ten Nation Committee on Disarmament, 195–196
ter Horst, Enrique, 347
Territorial disputes, 10, 21, 35
Territorial integrity, 85
Terrorism: biological weapons, 208; chemical weapons, 206; PLO as terrorist organization, 281; setting global norms and standards, 69–70; U.S. payment of arrears, 388

Testing, weapons: India and Pakistan, 201, 205; test bans, 202, 204–205, 218
Thabault, Albert, 329
Thematic hearings, 258
Third Committee, 119, 166
Third World. *See* Developing countries
Thirty Years War, 63
Threshold Test Ban Treaty (1976), 204
Thurmond, Strom, 367–368
Time-bound programs, 60
Tlatelolco, Treaty of (1967), 196, 203
Tobin, James, 304
Togo: request for electoral assistance, 158(table)
Torture, 83, 94–95, 99, 108
Trade issues, 171–172. *See also* World Trade Organization
Trade law, 50
Transitional governments, 58–59, 127–128
Transition justice, 98
Transparency, 370–371
Treaties, 53–54, 95–96. *See also* *individual treaties*
Treaty Banning Nuclear Weapon Tests in the Atmosphere, in Outer Space, and Under Water (1963), 196, 204
Treaty for the Prohibition of Nuclear Weapons in Latin America (1967), 196
Treaty norms, 48
Treaty on Principles Governing the Activities of States in the Exploration and Use of Outer Space, Including the Moon and Other Celestial Bodies (1967), 54, 196
Treaty on the Limitations of Underground Nuclear Weapon Tests (1976), 204
Treaty on the Nonproliferation of Nuclear Weapons (1968), 54, 196
Treaty on the Prohibition of the Emplacement of Nuclear Weapons and Other Weapons of Mass Destruction on the Sea-Bed and the Ocean Floor and in the Subsoil Thereof (1971), 54, 197, 203, 306
Treaty on the Southeast Asia Nuclear-Weapon-Free Zone (1997), 203

Trial, right to, 109
Truman, Harry, 31, 33, 37, 40–42, 41(fig.), 170
Trusteeship, 28–29, 34–36; Dumbarton Oaks provision for, 26; Namibia, 327–328
Trusteeship Council, 8, 43, 363
Truth and Reconciliation Commission (TRC), 258
Tshombe, Moise, 236–237
Tueni, Ghassan, 240–241
Turkey, 21, 239
Turkmenistan: Group of Friends, 342–343
Turner, Ted, 303
Tutsi genocide, 182–183, 253
1235 Procedure, 93–94
20/20 Initiative, 174

UDHR. *See* Universal Declaration of Human Rights
Uganda, 158–159(table), 253
Ukraine, 28, 33, 159(table)
UN Angola Verification Mission (UNAVEM), 239
Unanimity clause, 36–37
UN Assistance Mission in Rwanda (UNAMIR), 357(n115)
UN Association of the United States of America (UN-USA), 377–378, 397(n82)
UN Center for Human Rights, 89
UN Center for Human Settlements (Habitat). *See* Habitat
UN Children's Fund (UNICEF), 14, 66–67, 163; annual budget, 271; Congo crisis, 236; development policy, 166; development reform plan, 377; flagship report, 178; medical treatment, 165(fig.); nonstate funding, 302–303; voluntary contributions, 300(table), 301
UN Compensation Commission (UNCC), 53
UN Conference on Environment and Development, 65
UN Conference on Social Development, 304
UN Conference on the Illicit Trade in Small Arms and Light Weapons in All Its Aspects, 212

UN Conference on Trade and Development (UNCTAD), 163, 166, 178
UN Convention Against Transnational Organized Crime, 64
UN Convention on Biodiversity (1992), 64
UN Decade for Human Rights Education, 90–91
UN Decade of Disabled Persons, 54
UN Department for Disarmament Affairs, 211
UN Department of Management, 274
UN Development Cooperation Cycle, 377
UN Development Programme (UNDP), 14, 60, 163; creation of, 179–181; development functions, 166; electoral assistance, 124, 132; flagship reports, 177; need for restructuring, 374–377; 20/20 Initiative, 174; UN voluntary contributions, 300(table)
UN Disengagement Observer Force (UNDOF), 239
UNDP Assistance Framework (UNDAF), 181
UN Drug Control Programme (UNDCP), 60, 300–302
UN Educational, Scientific, and Cultural Organization (UNESCO), 59–60, 285, 302(table)
UN Emergency Force (UNEF), 231–232, 239, 321–325
UN Emergency Force Advisory Committee, 321–325
UN Environment Programme (UNEP), 64; development policy, 166; loss of leadership, 178; UN voluntary contributions, 300(table)
UNESCO. See UN Educational, Scientific, and Cultural Organization
UN Fund for Population Activities (UNFPA), 166
UNHCR. See UN High Commissioner for Refugees
UN High Commissioner for Refugees (UNHCR), 15, 301; Afghanistan, 101; annual budget, 271; development policy, 166; history of

disaster relief, 181; UN voluntary contributions, 300(table)
UNICEF. See UN Children's Fund
UNIDO. See UN Industrial Development Organization
Unified Task Force (UNITAF), 252
UN Industrial Development Organization (UNIDO), 58–59, 302(table)
UN Institute for Disarmament Research (UNIDIR), 167
UN Institute for Training and Research (UNITAR), 167
UN institutions. See Economic and Social Council; General Assembly; International Court of Justice; Secretariat; Security Council; Trusteeship Council
UN Interim Force in Lebanon (UNIFIL), 240–242
Union of Soviet Socialist Republics (USSR). See Soviet Union
United Arab Emirates: PKO assessment, 298–299
United Kingdom: assessment, 287, 294(table); Comprehensive Test Ban Treaty, 205; conventional weapons spending, 210; Groups of Friends, 342; Lebanon PKO, 240; nuclear weapons capability, 200; SC and ECOSOC expansion, 366; security assurances, 202–203; Suez crisis, 229–230; use of the veto in the Security Council, 315(table); voluntary contributions, 300. See also Britain
United Nations Day, 42
United Nations University (UNU), 167, 300(table)
United States: assessment obligation, 277, 287, 292–293, 294(table), 308(n7); assessment scale proposal, 290; assessment scale reform, 384–388; assessment withholding, 279–284, 307(nn 3, 4, 6); atomic energy for peaceful uses, 321; biological weapons, 208; blocking Boutros-Ghali's reelection, 55–56; call for UN reform, 359; Charter ratification, 42; chemical weapons, 206; Comprehensive Test Ban

Treaty, 205; Conference on Disarmament, 220; conventional weapons spending, 210; creation of League of Nations, 22; creation of UN organization, 23–24; Dominican Republic intervention as multilateral action, 316–317; dues withholding for Congo PKO, 307(n3); Dumbarton Oaks and Yalta, 25–26; Durban conference walkout, 75(n41); ECOSOC expansion and reform, 367–368; El Salvador conflict, 337–338; failure to sign Ottawa Convention, 213; GA resolutions on electoral assistance, 117–118; Group of Friends, 342, 345, 347; human rights provision, 40; humanitarian aid, 184; Korean War, 317–318, 320; Lebanon PKO, 240–241; membership of Argentina, the Ukraine, and Byelorussa, 33; negotiating payment of arrears, 284–287; NGOs at San Francisco Conference, 185–186; nomination of the Secretary-General, 38; North-South divide over development programs, 170–171; nuclear weapons programs, 194–196; outside forces negotiating arrears payment, 295, 309(n14); PKO assessment, 51–52, 296–297; post–Cold War nuclear capability, 200; pressure for zero budget growth, 275–276, 281–283; reform of Member State assessment, 361–362; Rome Statute, 98–99; Rwanda PKO, 253; SC and ECOSOC expansion, 366; security assurances, 202–203; Somalia operation, 252; South African control over Namibia, 328; trusteeship debate, 34–35; use of force provision, 39; veto provision, 12, 36–38, 315(table); World War II relief funding, 299. *See also* U.S.-Soviet relations
"Uniting for Peace" resolution, 12, 178, 229, 278, 318, 322, 325, 354(n30)

Universal Declaration of Human Rights (UDHR), 40, 53–54, 62, 71, 81–87, 103–112
Universal membership, 32–33
Universal Postal Union (UPU), 21, 57–58, 302(table)
UN Military Staff Committee, 27
UN Mission in Mozambique (ONUMOZ), 123–124
UN Mission in Sierra Leone (UNAMSIL), 216–217, 257–259
UN Observation Group in Lebanon (UNOGIL), 240
UN Observer Group in Central America (ONUCA), 251
UN Observer Mission in El Salvador (ONUSAL), 248
UN Office for Drug Control and Crime Prevention, 70
UN Operation in Mozambique (ONUMOZ), 250–251
UN Operation in Somalia (UNOSOM), 251–252
UN Operation in the Congo (ONUC), 234
UN Population Fund (UNFPA), 60, 301
UN Programme on HIV/AIDS (UNAIDS), 60
UN Protection Force (UNPROFOR), 254–255
UN Register of Conventional Arms, 210–211
UN Relief and Rehabilitation Administration (UNRRA), 181, 299
UN Relief and Works Agency (UNRWA), 300(table)
UN Special Committee on the Balkans (UNSCOB), 228–229
UN Statistical Office, 288–289, 308
UN system Staff College, 167
UN Transitional Administration in Cambodia (UNTAC), 124–126
UN Transitional Administration in East Timor (UNTAET), 127–128
UN Transition Assistance Group (UNTAG), 121–122, 239, 331
UN Truce Supervision Organization (UNTSO), 228, 231, 246
UNU. *See* United Nations University
UN Verification Mission in Angola (UNAVEM), 123–124

Upper Silesia, 227
Urquhart, Brian, 229–230, 232, 234–235
Urquidi, Victor, 178
U.S. Bill of Rights, 61
U.S. Congressional Research Service, 211
Use of force provision, 194
U.S.-Soviet relations: Cold War hostilities impairing SC function, 315; Cold War hostilities over development, 170; containment of Communism, 242–243; failure to anticipate Soviet collapse, 244; onset of the Cold War and the arms race, 194–197; Soviet withholding of assessment, 278–279; U.S.-Soviet hostility and arms production, 198
USSR. See Soviet Union
U.S. Virgin Islands, 6
U Thant, 7, 55, 237, 322, 324
Uzbekistan: Group of Friends, 343; request for electoral assistance, 160(table)

Vandenberg, Arthur, 24–25, 33, 37, 41(fig.), 292, 373
Vendrell, Francesc, 347
Venezuela: Group of Friends, 336–338, 342; request for electoral assistance, 160(table)
Venezuelan Investment Fund, 339
Vergau, Hans-Joachim, 329
Verification: Biological Weapons Convention, 208; Biological Weapons Treaty, 197; Chemical Weapons Convention, 207; Comprehensive Test Ban Treaty, 205; electoral, 120–124
Versailles, Treaty of (1919), 59, 226–227
Veto, 74(n15); budgetmaking, 276; Charter amendment reform, 362, 367; circumventing regional alliances and multilateral action, 316–317; circumventing SC through "Uniting for Peace" resolution, 318; collective security versus collective force, 45(n47); Connally's support for, 45(n45); Dumbarton Oaks and Yalta debate

over, 27; individual and collective defense, 313–314; nomination of the Secretary-General, 38; P-5 use of the veto in the Security Council, 315(table); preventing intervention, 312; San Francisco conference debates over, 36–38; SC authority, 51; SC expansion and reform, 370–372; SC voting procedures, 12; Soviet leverage of Argentina membership, 33; Yalta debate, 29
Vieira de Mello, Sergio, 91, 94–95, 127
Vienna Convention for the Protection of the Ozone Layer (1985), 64
Vienna Declaration (1993), 87–89
Vietnam, 119, 206, 242–243, 280
Vigier, Henri, 228
Voltaire, 43
Voluntary contributions, 279, 282–283, 297–302, 309(n15), 396(n63)
Voter turnout, 127
Voting procedures, UN: assessment scale, 308(n8), 382–383, 386; Bretton Woods Institutions, 379; Charter amendment reform, 362; consensus, 17(n5); Dumbarton Oaks provisions for SC voting, 26–27; League of Nations, 22; SC expansion and reform, 370–371; UN system, 10–13; U.S. opposition to budgetary process, 282. See also Elections

Waldheim, Kurt, 7, 330
Walters, Vernon, 386
War: crimes against humanity, 97–100; four major powers as hedge against, 24; League of Nations stance on, 22–23; war crimes, 97–98
Warsaw Treaty Organization, 194
Washington Consensus, 170–171
Water access, 171
Wealth as human value, 83
Weapons, conventional, 195, 198, 209–216
Weapons of mass destruction (WMD): biological weapons, 197, 207–209; chemical weapons, 198, 205–207; inspections, 60–61;

Nonproliferation Treaty, 201–202; nuclear free zones, 203–204; nuclear test bans, 204–205; nuclear weapons, 199–201; security assurances, 202–203; testing, 201–202, 204–205, 218
Weather, 58
Webster, Charles, 38
Weeks, commemorative, 174–175
Western Contact Group on Namibia, 327–331
Western P-3. *See* France; United Kingdom; United States
Western Sahara, 6, 10, 160(table), 342, 348, 387
Westphalia, Treaty of (1648), 21, 63
We the Peoples: The Role of the United Nations in the Twenty-First Century, 55
WHO. *See* World Health Organization
Williams, Jodie, 223(n23)
Wilson, Geoffrey, 82
Wilson, Woodrow, 22, 306(n1)
WIPO. *See* World Intellectual Property Organization
Women, 98; human rights, 40; PKOs' human rights mandate, 100–101; rights under Afghanistan's draft constitution, 104; under the Taliban, 102; treaties protecting, 95; UDHR on women and children, 111; UNDP's focus on gender issues, 180; UNICEF services for, 14; Vienna Declaration provisions, 87–88; world conferences, 171
Work, right to, 111
Work force, 59–60, 171, 176
Working Capital Fund, 182
Working Group on Situations, 93
World AIDS Day, 60
World Bank, 13; development reform plan, 376–377; reintegration in Sierra Leone, 258; UNAIDS sponsorship, 60. *See also* Bretton Woods Institutions
World Conference on Education for All, 65
World Conference on Human Rights, 65, 87

World Conference on Population and Development, 65
World conferences, 63–68, 86–89, 171–174, 180, 186
World Congress of International Association, 185
World Court. *See* International Court of Justice
World Economic and Social Survey, 177, 179
World Economic Forum, 187
World Food Programme (WFP), 163, 166, 300(table), 376–377
World Food Summit, 65
World Health Organization (WHO), 14–15, 59; Codex Alimentarius, 60; Congo crisis, 236; immunization programs, 164; policy analysis, 176; Rwanda's refugees, 253; voluntary contributions, 302(table)
World Intellectual Property Organization (WIPO), 58, 302(table)
World Meteorological Organization (WMO), 58, 272, 302(table)
World Summit for Children (1990), 65–66
World Summit for Social Development, 65
World Summit on Sustainable Development, 66
World Trade Organization (WTO), 15, 167
World War I, 22, 226
World War II, 19–20, 23–25; biological weapons, 207; chemical weapons, 206; disaster relief, 181; human rights norms as outgrowth of, 61; nuclear weapons programs, 193–194; relief funding, 299; trusteeship and, 35
WTO. *See* World Trade Organization

Yalta Conference, 27–30, 36
Yañez, Juan Luis, 338(fig.)
Years, commemorative, 174–175
Yemen: chemical weapons, 206; request for electoral assistance, 160(table)
Yom Kippur War, 232, 319
Yugoslavia, 52, 99, 228, 247–248, 254–255, 322

Zaire, 161(table), 183
Zambia: request for electoral assistance, 161(table)
Zamora, Rubén, 336
Zedillo, Ernesto, 305
Zero budget growth, 275–276, 281–282
Zimbabwe: electoral processes and assistance, 119, 161(table)

About the Book

Despite the high visibility of the United Nations in various peacekeeping operations, the enormous role that it plays in the global arena goes largely unnoticed. This new book focuses on that larger role, bringing to life the evolutionary process of multilateral interaction that is the foundation of the organization, the sometimes heated politics behind its operations, and the key personalities who have shaped it.

The authors move from the creation of the UN to the present debates about reform. Their discussion of UN activities—in the areas of human rights, elections, development, disarmament, and peacekeeping—as well as procedures offers an accessible introduction to a complex, critical subject.

Jean E. Krasno is associate research scholar and lecturer in political science at Yale University, where she is also deputy director of the Yale United Nations Oral History Project. She is coauthor of *The United Nations and Iraq: Defanging the Viper* and coeditor of *Leveraging for Success in United Nations Peace Operations*.